P9-DGP-499

DANGEROUS
CAPABILITIES

DANGEROUS CAPABILITIES

PAUL NITZE
AND THE COLD WAR

David Callahan

An Edward Burlingame Book
An Imprint of HarperCollins*Publishers*

DANGEROUS CAPABILITIES. Copyright © 1990 by David Callahan. All rights reserved. Printed in the United States of America. No part of this book may be used or reproduced in any manner whatsoever without written permission except in the case of brief quotations embodied in critical articles and reviews. For information address HarperCollins Publishers, 10 East 53rd Street, New York, NY 10022.

FIRST EDITION

Designed by Ruth Kolbert

Maps by Paul J. Pugliese

Library of Congress Cataloging-in-Publication Data
Callahan, David, 1965–
    Dangerous capabilities: Paul Nitze and the cold war / David Callahan.
      p. cm.
    Includes bibliographical references
    ISBN 0-06-016266-X
    1. United States—Foreign relations—1945– 2. United States—
National security. 3. Cold War. 4. Nitze, Paul H. 5. Anti-
communist movements—United States—History—20th century.
I. Title.
E743.C233 1990   89-46520
327.73—dc20

---

90 91 92 93 94 CC/RRD 10 9 8 7 6 5 4 3 2 1

For My Parents

CONTENTS

Maps   ix

Prologue   Dawn   1

PART I
THE PURSUIT OF INFLUENCE

Chapter 1   Hotchkiss, Harvard, Wall Street   11
Chapter 2   Rubble and Ruin   33
Chapter 3   A Weapon So Powerful   62
Chapter 4   The Threat Assessed   92
Chapter 5   The Best Job in the World   124
Chapter 6   The Outer Darkness   153

PART II
IMPLEMENTING AN IDEOLOGY

Chapter 7   To the Pentagon   181
Chapter 8   Bluffing at the Brink   209
Chapter 9   Khrushchev's Gamble   232
Chapter 10   A Game Called Arms Control   251
Chapter 11   His Own Ship   270
Chapter 12   Debacle in Southeast Asia   288

PART III
A NEW ARENA

Chapter 13   A Unique Endeavor   319
Chapter 14   Disillusionment   350
Chapter 15   The Committee   370
Chapter 16   A Poisonous Fellow   396

PART IV
THE LAST CRUSADE

Chapter 17   Back to Geneva   415
Chapter 18   Heretic at State   445
Chapter 19   Reykjavik and Beyond   470

Epilogue   Dusk   493

Acknowledgments   505

Sources   509

Interviews by the Author   513

Notes   515

Index   553

Picture Credits   572

Illustrations follow page 208

MAPS

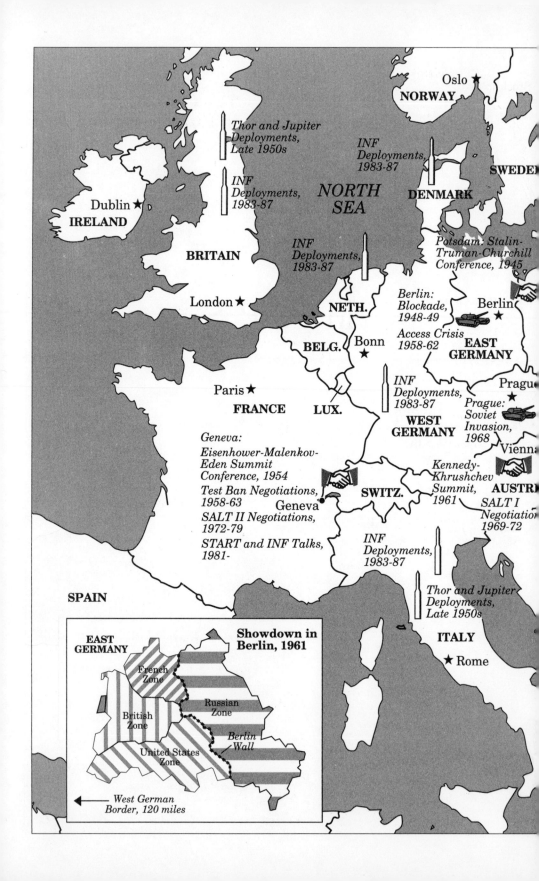

Oslo ★
NORWAY

*Thor and Jupiter
Deployments,
Late 1950s*

*INF
Deployments,
1983-87*

SWEDEN

*INF
Deployments,
1983-87*

**NORTH
SEA**

DENMARK

Dublin ★
IRELAND

*INF
Deployments,
1983-87*

BRITAIN

*Potsdam: Stalin-
Truman-Churchill
Conference, 1945*

London ★

NETH.

*INF
Deployments,
1983-87*

*Berlin:
Blockade,
1948-49*

Berlin
★

*Access Crisis
1958-62*

**EAST
GERMANY**

BELG.

Bonn
★

Paris ★
FRANCE

LUX.

*INF
Deployments,
1983-87*

**WEST
GERMANY**

Pragu

*Prague:
Soviet
Invasion,
1968*

*Geneva:
Eisenhower-Malenkov-
Eden Summit
Conference, 1954*

*Test Ban Negotiations,
1958-63*

Geneva

SWITZ.

*Kennedy-
Khrushchev
Summit,
1961*

Vienn

AUSTR

*SALT I
Negotiatio
1969-72*

*SALT II Negotiations,
1972-79*

*START and INF Talks,
1981-*

*INF
Deployments,
1983-87*

*Thor and Jupiter
Deployments,
Late 1950s*

SPAIN

ITALY

★ Rome

**EAST
GERMANY**

French
Zone

**Showdown in
Berlin, 1961**

British
Zone

Russian
Zone

*Berlin
Wall*

United States
Zone

← *West German
Border, 120 miles*

The Cold War in Europe

Peking: Communist Forces
Declare Government,
October 1, 1949

Shanghai

•Wuhan

•Chungking

C H I N A

Taipei

TAIWAN

Fall of
Dien Bien
Phu, 1954

Hong Kong

Dien Bien Phu   Hanoi

BURMA

LAOS   NORTH
VIETNAM

Huk Rebellion, 1954; Rise of
New People's Army, 1980s

Rise of
Pathet
Lao, 1950s

Tonkin
Gulf
Incident,
August 4,
1964

Vientiane

Siege of Khe Sanh,
1967-68

SOUTH
CHINA
SEA

Manila

Hue

THAILAND

Ho Chi
Minh Trail

Hue: Tet
Offensive,
1968

Bangkok

CAMBODIA   Pleiku

Invasion of
Cambodia,
May 1970

Pleiku: Vietcong
Mortar Attack,
February 7, 1965

Phnom Penh

Saigon: Tet
Offensive,
1968

Triumph of
Khmer Rouge,
1970-1975

Saigon

SOUTH
VIETNAM

0   400 miles

Communist
Insurgency,
1948-1960

M A L A Y S I A

Singapore

I N D O N E S I A

The Cold War in Asia

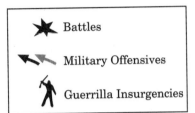

★	Battles
←	Military Offensives
🧍	Guerrilla Insurgencies

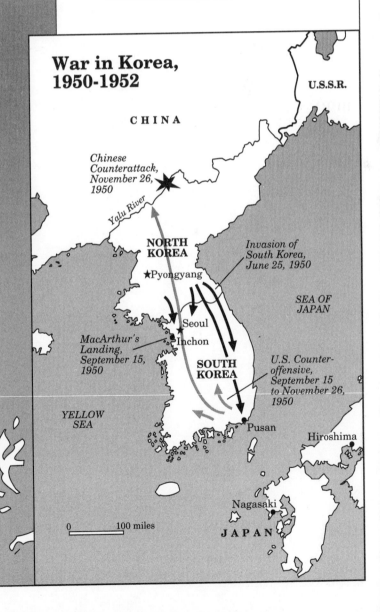

PACIFIC
OCEAN

War in Korea, 1950-1952

U.S.S.R.

CHINA

Chinese
Counterattack,
November 26,
1950

Yalu River

PHILIPPINES

NORTH
KOREA

★Pyongyang

Invasion of
South Korea,
June 25, 1950

SEA OF
JAPAN

Seoul

Inchon

MacArthur's
Landing,
September 15,
1950

SOUTH
KOREA

U.S. Counter-
offensive,
September 15
to November 26,
1950

YELLOW
SEA

Pusan

Hiroshima

0   100 miles

Nagasaki

JAPAN

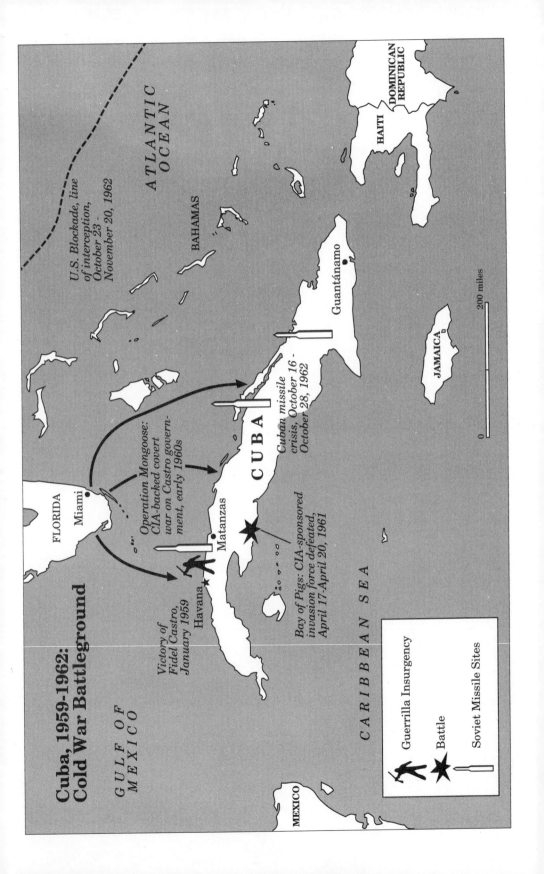

Cuba, 1959-1962: Cold War Battleground

GULF OF MEXICO

FLORIDA

Miami

ATLANTIC OCEAN

U.S. Blockade, line of interception, October 23 - November 20, 1962

BAHAMAS

Operation Mongoose: CIA-backed covert war on Castro government, early 1960s

Guantánamo

C U B A

Cuban missile crisis, October 16 - October 28, 1962

Matanzas

Victory of Fidel Castro, January 1959

Havana

Bay of Pigs: CIA-sponsored invasion force defeated, April 17-April 20, 1961

MEXICO

HAITI

DOMINICAN REPUBLIC

JAMAICA

200 miles

0

CARIBBEAN SEA

Guerrilla Insurgency

Battle

Soviet Missile Sites

DANGEROUS CAPABILITIES

Dawn

ONCE THE BLACK TILED ROOFS OF HIROSHIMA stretched block after block, each sitting atop a tidy wooden home. Now there was only rubble. An aide Nitze sent to the city to requisition housing reported there was none to be found. Of the roughly seventy-six thousand buildings in Hiroshima, only seven thousand had come through the atomic bombing unscathed, and there was no lodging for the large team of experts from the United States Strategic Bombing Survey who would study the ruins for over two months. Instead, the Americans resided on two destroyers. But because Hiroshima's harbor had been heavily mined by the U.S. Air Force, the ships couldn't be anchored outside the city, and were moored near the town of Hirowan. Every morning the research teams had to ride through the chilly autumn waters on landing craft, clamber onto the docks, and then drive forty miles to Hiroshima.

As vice-chairman of the survey, Paul Nitze stayed in comfortable quarters in Tokyo's Imperial Hotel and worked in spacious offices overlooking the well-manicured grounds of the Imperial Palace. But on his trip to the regional headquarters in Hiroshima, Nitze tasted life on the cramped destroyers and saw firsthand what one B-29 bomber carrying a single atomic bomb had done to Japan's seventh largest city.

From a distance, driving toward Hiroshima, the damage didn't look that bad. In Germany Nitze had seen areas far on the outskirts of target cities smashed by loads of misdirected bombs. It was different here. Within four miles of the city's center there were only a few stripped roofs and shattered windows. Driving closer there was more of the same kind of damage; it looked as though a tropical storm had passed through, but still no rubble. Even within two miles of the center, Hiroshima's crowded suburbs were relatively intact.

And then suddenly, just a bit further, there came into view a wasteland, a vast plain of destruction stretching as far as one could see. A few battered concrete buildings still stood, and burnt trees and telephone poles poked up from the rubble. But for the most part the obliteration of the city's center was total.

From his experts who were conducting interviews with survivors and studying the damage, Nitze learned how Hiroshima had died. It was a story of nearly unimaginable horror. The atomic bomb—christened "little boy"—had detonated without warning at 8:15 on the warm and calm summer morning of August 6, 1945. When the tremendous flash of blue-white light lit up the sky, the streets of Hiroshima were bustling with people on their way to work and schoolyards were filled with assemblies of children. Thousands died instantly from the searing heat wave and powerful blast that thundered out from ground zero. Tens of thousands more died as radioactive black rain poured down on the city for the next eight hours. Over 130,000 Japanese lost their lives in the atomic attack on Hiroshima.

To many, the destruction of Hiroshima—and the similar fate that befell Nagasaki three days later—instantly transformed the nature of warfare, ushering in an age in which military technology had the power to destroy all humankind. Because of this new reality, it was widely thought that war as the world once knew it would become obsolete, its rules nullified by an absolute weapon whose use would be suicidal.

Paul Nitze learned a different lesson in Japan. Inspecting the wastelands of Hiroshima and Nagasaki, he saw much the same thing he had seen when the Strategic Bombing Survey visited the lunar landscapes that had once been the great cities of Germany. The fact that a sole bomber carrying a single weapon had done such damage was impressive, but it did not seem revolutionary. Touring Nagasaki, Nitze was told that the city's railroads were back in operation within two days of the attack. He also saw crude tunnels that had sheltered four hundred Japanese when the bomb exploded. Unlike tens of thousands of people elsewhere in the city, those in the shelters had survived.

Although cities could be destroyed more easily in an atomic war, Nitze came to believe that a determined nation could protect much of its population and industry. It could disperse its factories, shelter its people, and build better air defenses and early warning facilities to stop incoming bombers.

The lesson Nitze learned from Hiroshima and Nagasaki, then, was not that war would become obsolete, but that it would become more dangerous and complex. In preatomic warfare a surprise attack might be a devastating setback, but now it could be far worse. In the atomic age there had to be constant vigilance. The day was over when the United States could rely on the great oceans to buffer it from aggression, and in the months following the end of World War II, Nitze argued that it would have to prepare ceaselessly for aggression by having a large standing army, spending huge amounts of money to maintain technological superiority over potential enemies, and never pursuing a policy of appeasement.

In calling for a heavily armed America, what Paul Nitze hoped for was a postwar era of order and stability. This longing was rooted in the experience of coming of age in the turbulence of the early twentieth century.

As a boy, Nitze was traveling with his parents in Europe when World War I broke out. As a young man, he was working on Wall Street when the stock market crashed. Like many of his generation, his political philosophy was shaped by fear of cataclysmic events. He believed that what had happened during the late 1930s and early 1940s could happen again. Having watched Hitler conquer Europe with ease, it was not hard for him to imagine Russia's Red Army making a dash for the English Channel. And what the Japanese had done at Pearl Harbor was nothing compared to the damage a fleet of modern bombers carrying atomic weapons could do in a surprise attack.

Through most of the postwar period, Paul Nitze would crusade to insure that the United States and the west would never again be caught unprepared and vulnerable to the military designs of a totalitarian power. The crusade started directly after the war and it waxed and waned in intensity for forty-five years. At times it would take Paul Nitze to the pinnacle of Washington's foreign policy world; at times it would relegate him to the role of bitter dissident. To some, Paul Nitze the

crusader would become a hero and living legend, a man of great pre-
science and insight. To others Paul Nitze the crusader seemed a zealot
shackled to a pessimistic cold war ideology, a narrow-minded dogmatist
who did not understand the Soviet Union and whose technocratic
mind set produced an obsession with military force.

And what made Paul Nitze so difficult a man to judge was that his
crusade for western security took two different forms.

During periods of the postwar era when he believed the west to be
weak, the crusade was militant in nature and belligerent in tone. Its
underlying premise was that the west was perilously vulnerable to a
surprise attack by the Soviet Union. Its guiding logic was a total distrust
of Moscow's intentions, and a belief that the Kremlin would exploit
every opportunity to damage the United States. Its chief recommendation, always, was a call for massive increases in defense spending.

But beginning in the 1960s, Nitze's crusade to enhance western
security changed. For all of his support of a greater American military
effort, he came to see that weapons technology could escape the control
of human beings. He saw that an arms competition with no limits could
yield an unpredictable world in which neither superpower would be
safe. To make the delicate balance of terror less precarious, Nitze
believed that the United States should negotiate with the Soviet Union
on nuclear arms.

For the last twenty years of his career, from the late 1960s to the
end of the Reagan presidency in the late 1980s, Nitze worked to reduce
the nuclear arsenals of the United States and the Soviet Union. It was
an effort filled with bureaucratic battles, personal setbacks, and, at
times, deep disillusionment. Also, Nitze's quest for arms control often
came into direct conflict with his agenda for vigilance, pulling him in
opposite directions and leaving friends and colleagues confused about
where he stood.

Consequently, Nitze's critics have attacked him from all sides.
When he pressed for military buildups, his critics came from the left.
Soviet experts charged that he distorted and overstated the threat of
Russian aggression, that he didn't appreciate the cautious nature of
the Kremlin leadership. Economists attacked his belief that higher
defense spending was compatible with American prosperity. They
countered his calls for massive defense budgets with predictions of
industrial decline. Strategists and diplomats ridiculed Nitze's scenarios for surprise attacks and "limited" nuclear war. To them, Paul
Nitze personified the Dr. Strangelove mentality that helped fuel an
endless arms race.

When Nitze's crusade was for arms control, it was the right that attacked him. These critics saw Nitze as an incurable problem solver who pursued arms control as an end in itself and neglected the broader context of the Cold War. They saw him as a former hawk turned dangerous dove, an arms controller out of control. During the Reagan era, when an aging Nitze fought tenaciously for treaties in intermediate- and long-range nuclear weapons, conservatives charged that it was partly ego that energized his tireless crusade. Some suspected that in his quest for a personal triumph to crown his long career, Paul Nitze had forgotten his principles.

Over the years, the attacks from the right were most damaging. They began in the 1950s, when he was closely associated with Secretary of State Dean Acheson. More than anyone else in Washington, the American right hated Acheson. It hated him for his Ivy League elitism, his haughty demeanor, and his aristocratic mustache. It hated him for the eastern establishment, internationalist perspective he represented. And because the right hated Acheson, it hated his most brilliant protégé, Paul Nitze. In 1953 this hatred cost Nitze a job in the Pentagon under President Eisenhower. A decade later right-wing senators almost denied him the post of navy secretary. Even in 1974, more than two decades after Dean Acheson had left government, Senator Barry Goldwater blocked Nitze's appointment to be an assistant secretary of defense, charging that he wanted to bring about the unilateral disarmament of the United States.

Despite occasional setbacks Nitze's time in Washington was a charmed journey through one of the most daunting bureaucratic mine fields in the world. He arrived in the capital on a June day in 1940, when Washington was still a sleepy southern city. The 33-year-old Nitze brought with him a wardrobe of expensive suits and the mind set of a Wall Street banker. A lean and compact man, standing five feet nine inches, with blue eyes and a silver tint already creeping into his full head of hair, he was attractive but hardly formidable in appearance. And if his appearance would not command attention, neither would his manner guarantee success. Focused and serious, Nitze seemed aggressive in a town known for its relaxed style. A product of well-to-do academic parents and the genteel refinement of Hotchkiss and Harvard, Nitze's voice was soft and aristocratic. He avoided rhetorical flourishes and his conversation often seemed stiff and intellectual.

In Washington the path to power often began with a surrender to the city's bureaucratic barons. But this was not something that came easily to Nitze either. Although he was a loyal member of the clubby group of eastern establishment bankers and lawyers who shaped America's postwar policy, Nitze's rise to influence would not be marked by shady deals and the abandonment of principle. Instead, his impact on world affairs would come from persistence. In the day-to-day work of government, Nitze would inevitably be the man who knew the most about the subject under discussion, who was always scribbling notes and identifying the central questions for debate. With his persistence and a creative, restless mind, Nitze became, again and again, a major influence in shaping America's foreign policy agenda at the highest levels of government.

Serving under six presidents from Roosevelt to Reagan, Nitze held over a dozen different government posts. In almost every one of these he had an impact on government policy, playing a critical role in such seminal episodes in postwar history as the Marshall Plan, the H-bomb debate, the Korean war, the Berlin and Cuban missile crises, the Vietnam war, SALT, and the arms control negotiations of the Reagan years. In a city where people rarely wield influence for more than two decades—and often for less than one presidential term—Paul Nitze was a key player from the dawn of the nuclear age to the final days of the Cold War.

How he did this, how Nitze remained so effective for so long, is a tale of exhausting bureaucratic battles waged in an atmosphere of intense secrecy. It is a tale of how Nitze positioned himself on the winning side of historical events, of how he became an indispensable ally to the most powerful people in Washington—or their most indefatigable opponent.

But more than anything, Paul Nitze's odyssey in the postwar era is the tale of the greatest ideological conflict in modern history. During the early days of Cold War, when Europe lay in ruins and powerful new weapons were coming into the American and Russian arsenals, Nitze was one of the Truman administration's leading strategic thinkers. In the turbulent Kennedy era, when nuclear war seemed all too possible, Nitze played a key role in managing the crises in Berlin and Cuba. And when the Cold War was channeled into the arena of arms control—a game of steely nerves and high stakes—Paul Nitze became one of the government's most knowledgeable and experienced negotiators.

More than any of his contemporaries, he personified the American approach to the Cold War. His intentions were good, but his moral righteousness often blinded him to the excesses of American power and the contradictions of U.S. foreign policy. His competence was unquestioned, but his emphasis on quantitative analysis and technocratic solutions led to a narrow view of national security and a fixation with military force. For Nitze, also, change came slowly. Even when the chief tenets of cold war thinking had been discredited in Vietnam and the dogma of nuclear supremacy seemed archaic, Nitze remained a believer—a faith mirrored in the national security establishment as a whole.

And even when the costs of waging the Cold War climbed ever higher, Nitze never swayed from his commitment to vast defense budgets. At the beginning of the superpower struggle, in the late 1940s, the United States was the world's dominant economic power. By the 1980s, after decades of following the advice of Nitze and like-minded officials to spend more on defense—while reducing funds for investment in infrastructure and industrial research—the United States had lost that dominance. The nation may have prevailed over the Soviet Union, but in doing so it had neglected other elements of national strategy so vital to its long-term security and prosperity.

With the Cold War waning and Mikhail Gorbachev spearheading a revolution in the Soviet Union, the passion of the East–West rivalry has finally cooled. But why this passion was so great for so long, why trillions of dollars and rubles were spent on arms, and why so many died in superpower proxy wars, are questions intimately linked to the life of Paul Nitze. To understand this life is to begin to understand the Cold War.

PART I

THE PURSUIT OF INFLUENCE

CHAPTER 1

Hotchkiss, Harvard, Wall Street

A T 2:05 A.M. on a cool summer night in late July 1916, a terrifying blast rocked the munitions depot on Black Tom Island in New York Harbor. The explosion shook nearby bridges and blew out the windows of cars crossing their spans. Houses rattled in places as far off as Camden and Philadelphia. In Manhattan police were called out to restore order and prevent looting. Panicked party-goers in tuxedos and evening gowns poured onto the streets to see what was happening. Although the United States remained officially neutral in the war raging in Europe, and there was no evidence linking foreign agents to the explosion, German sabotage was suspected.

By 1916 life for German-Americans was growing uncomfortable. Stimulated by a steady flow of anti-German propaganda, there flourished a seething hatred for the rapacious "huns" and their diabolic master Kaiser Wilhelm. Almost every week the newspapers carried stories of German spies and vigilante attacks on German sympathizers. In one western town a man was dragged out of a bar and hanged after he toasted the kaiser.

For Paul Nitze, not yet 10 years old, the war was making life hard. On the streets he and his sister Elizabeth were sometimes mocked and bullied by other children. Questions of patriotism and loyalty—so long taken for granted—were now more awkward.

Years after he had risen to power, Paul Nitze explained himself to a younger man: "What you should know is that I am German. I am all German. I am proud to be German. There is nothing non-German about me."

Nitze's grandfather immigrated to the United States from Germany after the Civil War. He settled in Baltimore and became a successful banker. Eschewing the world of high finance, his eldest son, William Nitze, chose to go into academia. Entering Johns Hopkins University in his mid teens, he distinguished himself as a prodigy, graduating with high honors at the age of 18. He went on to Columbia, where he earned a doctorate in Romance languages, with a specialty in philology, by the age of 23. Along the way, Nitze married a dark and intense woman from Baltimore named Anina Hilken. She was also of German descent.

In 1903 Nitze was invited to become an associate professor of Romance languages at Amherst College in Massachusetts. Moving into a comfortable brick apartment overlooking the grassy common, William and Anina settled into the leisurely pace of a New England country town. By this time they had a daughter Elizabeth, and William was already making a name for himself as a prolific scholar.

On January 16, 1907, Anina gave birth to a son, Paul Henry. From the beginning little Paul was given lavish attention. He was, he recalled, "the oldest son of the oldest son of the oldest son of oldest son of the Nitze family going back to the seventeenth century." He was also a particularly bright and attractive child. Almost as soon as he could speak, Paul's parents pushed him to think and explore. He and his sister were continually quizzed at the dinner table. The questions could be remarkably difficult and flimsy answers were not acceptable. "I always felt that I was asked to make up my mind as an adult on adult issues," Nitze recalled.[1]

In 1908 William Nitze's career took an exciting turn when he was asked to chair the department of Romance languages at the University of Chicago. In contrast to staid Amherst, where the spectacular fall foliage was the year's most exciting event, Chicago was aswirl with all the excitement of early twentieth-century America. William cultivated a wide group of friends who enthusiastically pursued studies esoteric even among academics, and Anina became a popular figure in more glamorous social circles. A flapper of sorts, she smoked cigarettes in public and stirred up controversy with her offbeat opinions. Once she mortgaged the house to provide bail for one of Clarence Darrow's left-wing clients. Her taste in art and music was varied and unusual.

Anina's passion for her children was immense. With William busy cranking out articles and books on such subjects as "Glastonbury and the Holy Grail," Anina devoted enormous energy to Elizabeth and Paul. Nitze recalled later that his mother "loved me beyond any normal maternal love. It became overwhelming." With her incredible vibrance, strong views, and thinly veiled contempt for convention, Anina taught her son to look slightly askance at his surroundings and to challenge the common wisdom. She was, Nitze said, "by far the greatest influence in my life."

As a young boy, Paul was sent to an experimental elementary school run by the university's School of Education. In contrast to the rigid educational practices of the day, the school encouraged its students to explore a wide range of activities as well as more traditional topics of study. During this time Paul developed an avid interest in Greek civilization.

Money was never a problem for the Nitze family. William's wealthy father made sure that his son could ponder Romance languages in comfort with ample resources for travel. Every summer the Nitzes would head for Europe. During the summer of 1914, when Paul was 7 years old, the family was traveling through Austria and Germany. They were in Munich when England declared war on Germany and Nitze would never forget watching German soldiers march through the streets on the way to the front, flowers stuck in their rifle barrels. Through August, as war enveloped the continent, the family was trapped in Germany. Finally, William got the family on a Dutch steamer back to the United States.

At the University of Chicago High School, the young Nitze did well. It was an interesting school, with a mix of students that included the children of rich Jewish businessmen and the stiffer offspring of Protestant academics. One boy Nitze shared a desk with was Richard Loeb, who later, with a friend named Nathan Leopold, would commit an infamous murder.

To get to school every morning, Nitze had to traverse a mean neighborhood where he was terrorized by a gang run by three sons of a local tailor. Primly dressed in a suit and tie, Nitze was an easy target for bullying. To protect himself, he joined an Italian street gang a few blocks away. With this new balance of power in place, life became a bit easier.

By the age of 15 Nitze had finished high school. He had assumed that he would attend the University of Chicago, but William Nitze vetoed the idea. He suggested that Nitze attend Hotchkiss, a preparatory school in northwestern Connecticut, and then go on from there to an Ivy League school. Nitze agreed.

With its rolling hills and isolated setting, Hotchkiss was serene and beautiful, but lacked the excitement of Chicago. To find fun, one had to invent it, and Nitze did so by breaking rules. Caught for a number of infractions, he was "sequestered," a disciplinary practice the school had invented to replace expulsion. It entailed being confined to the dormitory, being banned from sports, and having to do a three-mile run every day. Nitze's mocking response to the punishment was to form the "Sequestrian Club" and to order watch-chain pendants emblazoned with the name of the club and the figure of a man running inside a triangle. When the headmaster found out about Nitze's stunt, he was furious, but because sequestering was the highest punishment available in the school, he could do nothing more than deliver a stern lecture to Nitze.

By his own admission, Nitze didn't do much work at Hotchkiss. "The main thing on my mind was my peers and having fun with them and getting along with them," he said later. Studies came second. His lackluster academic performance fueled an already growing feeling on the part of his father than young Paul wasn't amounting to much and that he was becoming a playboy rather than a scholar. For years William Nitze had noticed that his daughter Elizabeth was the more thoughtful of the children, the one who always seemed to have a book in her hand. Now, as Paul frittered away his time at Hotchkiss, Professor Nitze's disappointment with his only son grew greater.

During his senior year at Hotchkiss Nitze found himself unbearably restless. He wanted to see more of the world, to have things happen in his life, to go on adventures. "I finally got the feeling that all this life that I had been part of in Chicago and Hotchkiss was in a way artificial and separated from the real world, and that what I really wanted to do was to get away from all this and dive into the real world," he said. Feeding this desire were the novels of Joseph Conrad. Read in the sterile atmosphere of boarding school conformity, the exotic exploits of Conrad's characters fired Nitze's imagination. With only months to go before graduation, he decided to run away to sea. Visiting Baltimore, Paul confided his plan to his grandfather, the white-haired patriarch of the Nitze family and a man Paul admired immensely. The old man sympathized with his grandson's desire to see the world, but convinced him that finishing school first would make a good deal of sense. He then arranged to have Paul ship aboard a German ship, the SS *Lutzo*, over the summer.

The *Lutzo* called at Halifax, Cobh, and then Hamburg. Nitze served as an apprentice in the engine room.

Deep in the rumbling bowels of the ship, he came to see that the life of a seaman was not the glamorous string of adventures portrayed in Conrad's novels. Still, the experience did allow him to see beyond the stilted and narrow reality of the prep school student. The commanding officer of the engine room was a colorful man named Otto Knocke, and during the long days he regaled his young charge with stories about being a prisoner of war in World War I and almost being executed by the French on two occasions. He talked about Germany before the war, and the economic ravages that followed it. "He took me in hand and taught me not only about the ship's engines, but also about the world," Nitze recalled.[2] In Hamburg Nitze saw firsthand the runaway inflation that Knocke had talked about.

Enrolling at Harvard in the fall of 1924, Nitze began to learn more about a slice of reality he could appreciate: partying: "In those days grades didn't count," he said later. "Harvard was more like a European university. You just tried to absorb wisdom. We all drank too much, had girls, and a rich, glorious life." Prohibition may have been the law of the land, but the spirits flowed freely in Cambridge. With the strictures of preparatory school rules no longer holding him back, Nitze plunged zestfully into the drunken action. His grades plummeted. At one point he skipped his final exam in an economics course to attend a party in Newport. He received a zero in the course.

Among the more staid members of his class, Nitze made almost no impression during his Harvard years. "He wasn't terribly widely known," recalled John Chase, the class president. "We weren't on the same wavelength in our interests." While Chase and the other top figures on campus were three-letter men, Nitze avoided the major sports, with the exception of a short and inglorious stint on the Harvard freshman football squad. "He was not an athlete," said Chase. Nor was Nitze deeply involved in campus politics or the school paper. He had plenty of friends, but they tended to be men like Charles Bohlen, his suave and hard-drinking clubmate from the Porcellian.

Located above a clothing store across Massachusetts Avenue from Harvard Yard, the Porcellian clubhouse was the scene of wild debauchery. Its members were not chosen for academic achievement or athletic performance. "The club prided itself on not being based on merit in any way," Nitze recalled. Wit and charm and a sense of adventure were the qualities members valued. So was the ability to hold one's alcohol. The clubhouse featured no billiards or card tables or similar distractions; the chief pastime was drinking. Club members participated in a ritual known as "The Day of the Book." It started upon awakening with shots of gin, moved on to champagne at breakfast, and then a martini every hour for the rest of the day. After dinner a switch was made to scotch. The goal was to still be standing at midnight.[3]

During his senior year at Harvard Nitze was plagued by recurring hepatitis. A long canoe trip undertaken on a drunken dare made his health worse. He was hospitalized and barely survived. By the spring of 1928, however, he had gotten himself together to the point that he was able to graduate cum laude. His major was economics, and with the exception of the course he flunked, Nitze did well in the subject. It appealed to him, he recalled, because it seemed to him to be "someplace where I can have some bearing upon the levers of influence." More so than other subjects, economics seemed grounded in the real world. "It has a bearing on how people behave and why," Nitze said.

Casting about for what to do next, Nitze was sure of one thing: He did not want to be an academic. His father was a scholar of great repute by this time, one of the country's leading philologists. Nitze had grown up among intellectuals. He had respect for their knowledge and for their disciplined mastery of arcane material, but he wondered what contribution his father and his colleagues were making to the world's welfare. What purpose was served by a debate over French phonetics? Whose life was changed by William Nitze's book, *Lancelot and Guinevere?* "The thing that I couldn't get over," Nitze said later, "was that here was a group that I thought was the most admirable group of men one could imagine, and they were having no impact upon the things that were going on in the world that seemed to me to be the most tragic and important."

After Harvard, Nitze sought to "get into the world of practical affairs as rapidly as possible." In the late 1920s, when the most important men in the United States were those who made the most money, this meant going into business. Nitze became a cost accountant at a factory in Philadelphia run by his brother-in-law's company, the Container Corporation of America. The plant was located in the worst section of Philadelphia and the work, interesting at first, soon became monotonous and distasteful. After a short time Nitze was transferred to another of the company's factories, this one in Bridgeport, Connecticut.

A company official promised him a bright future if he stayed long enough, but after six months Nitze recalled, "I'd gotten to the point where I felt I knew all that I wanted to know about accounting. I decided to I wanted to do something else."

With a bull market raging on Wall Street, investment banking seemed to be the most glamorous career in the private sector. Applying for a job with the Chicago investment firm that handled his father's finances, Bacon, Whipple & Company, Nitze received an interesting offer. Bacon, Whipple wanted to know whether to invest money in Germany. The newspapers gave them scant sense of what was happening in the Weimar Republic, and their contacts in Europe couldn't tell them much more. What the firm wanted was someone to investigate the situation firsthand, and since Nitze knew German and was familiar with Germany, the firm thought he might be the person for that job. Bacon, Whipple offered to pay his transportation over and back. It would give him no salary, but would compensate him if it was satisfied with the report. With money from his father and a trust fund, Nitze was able to accept the offer.

To assess the economic situation in Germany, Nitze would have to talk to top bankers and financiers. This required letters of introduction. On the recommendation of a friend's mother, Nitze went to see Clarence Dillon, head of the Wall Street firm Dillon, Read and Company. Ushered into Dillon's plush private dining room forty stories above New York's streets, Nitze hurriedly explained his trip and asked for the letters.

Dillon was confused by Nitze's opening. Before him was a young man who was immaculately dressed and reasonably articulate, but whose young face indicated that he could be hardly over 20. And he was saying that he planned to go to Germany and meet with top financial leaders in order to write a report on the German investment climate. Was this some kind of a joke?

What do you want to do with your life? Dillon asked. Nitze replied that he wanted to be an investment banker. Dillon then asked what part of the investment banking business Nitze wanted to be in. Not expecting to be quizzed on his career goals, Nitze stammered that he was interesting in being an investment banker who dealt with broader questions of investment policy, the big picture.

Dillon scoffed at the notion. Pointing to a paper on his desk, he explained that he was going over an advertisement for a bond issue that Dillon, Read was going to offer to the public. The advertisement had been gone over by the company's experts and accountants, but he, the president, was going over it himself to make sure there were no errors. The only way you can deal with policy, Dillon lectured, is to be a master of detail. If you can master the details, then you can aspire to deal with the broader issues. But the details must come first.

In full stride now, Dillon turned to the proposed trip to Germany. He asked Nitze how old he was and Nitze told him his age. What made him think that he could understand what was happening in Germany at the age of 22? Dillon demanded. And suppose Nitze did write a good report. Why would anybody pay any attention to it? Did Nitze really think that anybody was going to invest money in Germany based on a report written by a 22-year-old?

"He tore me apart," Nitze said later, chuckling.

His tirade finished, Dillon told Nitze he should go to a small firm he knew of in Milwaukee to learn the details of commercial banking. Then Nitze could consider getting into investment banking. But Dillon did grudgingly consent to play along with Nitze's little fantasy and write the letters of introduction.

Arriving in Paris in the spring of 1929, Nitze ran into some friends and decided to stay a while. With money and time to spare, there were few more enchanting places he could have chosen to visit. The cultural center of the world in the spring of 1929, its population of artists and writers, including expatriate Americans, was at an all-time high. As leaves budded on the trees and the flowers bloomed, the sidewalk cafés along its boulevards filled with thousands of intense and sophisticated young people. At night swank clubs were packed into the morning hours.

Through his friend Pat Morgan, Nitze met Ernest Hemingway, James Joyce, and other Paris luminaries. His brief stopover turned into a three-month party and one of the most stimulating experiences of his life. "Those were glorious days in the spring of '29," Nitze said later, "just a marvelous time."

As the summer heat descended on Paris, Nitze headed for Germany. With Dillon's letters of introduction and his passable German, he was able to set up meetings with bankers and leaders of industry and labor.

Their assessment of Germany was mixed. On the surface Germany appeared stable. Following his trip on the SS *Lutzo* in 1924, Nitze had encountered a country in the grip of uncontrollable inflation. But with the election of Paul von Hindenburg in 1925 and the stabilization of the currency, Germany had begun a remarkable economic recovery. By 1929 it appeared to be headed for a period of prosperity.

A closer look at Germany's economy revealed danger signs. Germany's growth was heavily dependent on foreign loans and its own economic resources were stretched thin, Nitze was told. If the foreign money kept flowing in and growth continued, the economy would remain stable. But if the growth stopped, if the loans dried up, the delicate structure of Germany's new prosperity would collapse. In a worldwide recession, Nitze believed, "the foreign bankers would cease to give credit to the Germans and there would be a contraction beyond belief."

And the threat of a recession was not the only problem facing the Weimar Republic. The political scene was dangerously combustible as well. An American newspaperman told Nitze of a charismatic leader named Adolf Hitler whose Nazi party was growing rapidly stronger. It was obvious that Hindenburg, at the age of 82, would not dominate the political scene much longer, and the very existence of the Weimar Republic was in question. An institution closely linked in the minds of most Germans to the hated Versailles treaty and to the economic hardships of the 1920s, the Weimar Republic was hardly revered. "My impression was that the political scene in Germany was one that couldn't possibly be sustained," Nitze recalled.

Feeding political discord was social decay. Nitze could see it most graphically in Berlin. While Paris had been cultured and sophisticated, Berlin was the raciest city in Europe. All over town, lasciviousness flourished. Nightclubs, the stage, and the screen featured nude performers in all states of wild abandon. Prostitutes paraded the streets in the thousands. Hordes of revelers showed up at transvestite balls. The use of cocaine and morphine was widespread. The scene had the feel of a final, reckless party aboard a doomed ocean liner.

Returning to Paris, Nitze moved in with a group of friends and began writing a highly pessimistic report. While there appeared to be a lucrative opportunity to invest in companies doing business in Germany, Nitze judged the risks to be too high. He argued that "the whole thing could tumble down like a house of cards in any kind of recession and that you ought to have your head examined if you invested any money in Germany." When he was finished, he joined his Parisian friends for a bike tour through Holland and then headed back to the United States.

On his way to Chicago, Nitze stopped by to see Clarence Dillon again and gave him a copy of the report. Reading it over, Dillon was impressed. He was impressed by the analysis of Germany and he was impressed by the gutsy 22-year-old who had scoffed at his advice six months earlier and had done what he had set out to do. Interested in getting acquainted with this unusual young man, Dillon invited Nitze out to his New Jersey mansion for the weekend.

"We went in style," Nitze said later. In Dillon's Rolls-Royce they drove on the marginal roads that traversed the swamp of east New Jersey and then on through the slums of Newark. As they drove, Dillon talked.

It was September 1929. Never had the United States been wealthier. Never had the riches of investment banking been so plentiful. For years the stock market had soared ever higher. Fortunes were made in a matter of months. And with these fortunes were built grand country retreats and apartments on New York's upper East Side. For America's financiers it was a time of excess and arrogance, a time when it seemed that nothing stood in the way of unlimited prosperity.

Dillon himself had done remarkably well—as Nitze could see from his comfortable seat in the Rolls-Royce. The son of a prosperous Polish Jew who owned a general store and tracts of land in Paris, Texas, Dillon was a Harvard graduate and a man of extraordinary intellect. In the years following Harvard his life had taken a series of bizarre twists. Dillon's father died, leaving him with the land in Texas. Not interested in living in Texas, Dillon quickly sold the land. Later, oil was found on the property, and for years Dillon was haunted by the thought of the vast wealth that had slipped through his hands.

With the money from the sale, Dillon bought a machine tool company in Milwaukee. The business went poorly. One day he was standing on a train platform in suburban Milwaukee when an express train came through and hit a dog at a grade crossing. The bloody carcass of the dog flew up and knocked Dillon to the ground, cracking his skull. To force a change in the law on grade crossing—a passionately contested issue of that day—Dillon sued the railroad and won a large settlement.

Told by his doctors that he would have to spend a year resting, Dillon went to Paris, France, where he learned the art of French cuisine. There, he happened to meet a Wall Street investor named Bill Phillips who worked at the firm of William A. Read and Company. Phillips suggested that Dillon abandon the expatriate life for a job with the firm. With his wife and infant child Douglas in tow, Dillon moved to New York. Over the next few years his great ability insured that he moved steadily up through the ranks of the company. Over time he amassed considerable wealth, and when Read died at the end of World War I, Dillon became the chief stockholder and took over the company. Dillon built a great mansion in New Jersey, and on the grounds he erected statues of his two heroes: David, the slayer of Goliath, and Napoleon.

The 1920s had been good to Clarence Dillon. But now, he told Nitze, bad times were looming ahead. In recent months there had been a slight falloff in the stock market after which it had rebounded and surged to new heights. Nitze asked Dillon whether this presaged a recession.

Dillon thought for a while and replied that it meant the end of an era.

What did that mean? Nitze asked.

Dillon explained that throughout history different elites had controlled society. Religious leaders, military men, and government bureaucrats had each been dominant at one time or another. Men of money, said Dillon, were in control now. Since the Civil War, the power brokers of Wall Street had been more influential than the men in Washington. But this wouldn't last, Dillon said. The coming recession would be serious and it would herald the end of Wall Street's dominance. "Everything will change," he concluded.

Nitze was taken aback by Dillon's dire assessment of the future. "He not only had a sense that the crash was coming, but that this was going to be much more serious than most people realized."

What was Dillon planning to do about the coming disaster? Nitze asked.

Dillon replied that he had already done something. He'd made plans to lay off almost the entire staff of Dillon, Read—almost 4,000 employees—and retain a staff of only 50, making it a wholesale business.

Nitze reflected that he had little chance of getting a job at Dillon, Read, but before the weekend was out, Dillon said that he thought Nitze's views were different and he valued such views. Nearly everybody in the late 1920s was saying to invest in Germany, Nitze recalled. "Nobody else had done the simple analysis of the economic and political scene." Dillon was impressed by that.

Shortly after returning to Chicago, Nitze got a telegram from Dillon offering him a job. At the age of 22 Paul Nitze became Clarence Dillon's "fifty-first man."

On a day in early October 1929 Nitze donned his best business suit and made his way to the offices of Dillon, Read, at 28 Nassau Street. He was assigned a desk in a hall next to the toilet and given a secretary who was so attractive she made him tremble. Nitze's career as an investment banker had finally begun.

A few weeks later the stock market crashed.

At Dillon, Read, Nitze scrambled to make himself useful amid the chaos of Black Thursday. Dillon called him into his office and told him to sell 2,000 shares of a company's stock. The problem was that Nitze had never sold any stock and he didn't know what to do. Finally, he got hold of a brokerage firm and began to sell the stock in fifty-share blocks. Within hours the price of the stock had fallen. Nitze went back to Dillon's office and meekly asked what he should do. "I told you to sell it, sell it," Dillon bellowed. By the end of the day the stock was worth half of what it had been that morning.

The financial panic that swept Wall Street and the western world following the crash was apocalyptic in scope and effect. Within four years there would be sixteen million unemployed Americans and the U.S. Gross National Product would fall from $103 billion to $55 billion. The immediate impact on Wall Street was massive layoffs. Whole firms were dismantled almost overnight as financiers scurried to stem their losses. Entire fortunes disappeared in a matter of hours. At Dillon, Read the impact was less dramatic. Nitze may have been "the last man hired on Wall Street," but he would not be the first fired. Dillon's plan of becoming a wholesale firm worked, and his small staff remained intact.

Nitze's luck was stunning. Even as the depression worsened in the years to come, worsened to the point that former executives stood among groups of men hoping to get a day's manual labor and the wheels of industry were frozen in place, Paul Nitze had a job. And it was not an ordinary job. Almost immediately, Nitze became one of Clarence Dillon's favorites. Dillon made Nitze his personal assistant and tutored him in the intricacies of investment banking, always emphasizing the importance of details. It was the kind of job that Nitze had dreamed about, and the brilliant financier who made it possible became his first mentor.

Nitze's preferential treatment quickly earned him the enmity of the partners at Dillon, Read. At times it seemed that Dillon encouraged that enmity. When a partner came to Dillon (or the "Baron" as he liked to be called) with a deal, Dillon often asked Nitze to check it out. "Oh boy, they really loathed me," Nitze recalled. "As far as the partners were concerned I was the most objectionable little whippersnapper they ever saw."

The best aspect of Nitze's new job was that Dillon let him do his own deals. Nitze accepted the challenge with zeal, reveling in the excitement of finally making big things happen by himself. For over a year Dillon let Nitze do almost any deal he wanted. At first, all went well. Then Nitze became reckless and attempted to orchestrate the takeover of a company by buying the majority of its stock. It was a deal that Nitze thought would make him famous as "the boy wonder of Wall Street." Instead, the firm lost over a million dollars. Dillon was furious. He stopped talking to Nitze entirely. When Nitze walked past him in the office or rode with him on an elevator, the Baron wouldn't even acknowledge his presence. "I became a non-person in the firm," Nitze recalled.

The disaster was humiliating, but it soon turned to Nitze's advantage. Before, the partners had hardly talked to him. Now, humbled by defeat and exiled from Dillon's sight, Nitze began making friends in the firm. He became part of the team, working with those who did the firm's pick and shovel work, men like Dean Matty, Bill Phillips, and James Forrestal. Clarence Dillon had introduced Nitze to the world of investment banking as practiced from the president's office. Now Nitze's new colleagues showed him another side of Wall Street, ushering him deep into the fast-paced world of the deal, and teaching him how to survive and prosper. "Becoming a non-person was the best thing that ever happened to me," Nitze said later.

Jim Forrestal was the most compelling of the people that Nitze met. Intensely energetic, with beads of sweat perpetually forming on his forehead, Forrestal was the son of Irish immigrants and had grown up in the Hudson Valley. At Princeton he had been a major figure on campus and was voted "Most likely to succeed." By the early 1930s Forrestal was already fulfilling the expectations of his classmates as one of Dillon, Read's rising stars. Forrestal's hard-driving style and relentless ambition became a model for Nitze.

Turning 23 at the beginning of the new decade, Paul Nitze may have had a job, but he was living modestly. At Harvard Nitze had been surrounded by wealthy young men. On Wall Street he worked mostly with older men who had already begun making real money. The friends he had made in Paris led rich and carefree lives. Yet as Nitze started his career in an industry known to spawn great fortunes, he himself had comparatively little money. Of course, he had far more than the thousands of men in shabby coats who walked listlessly through the city, hungry and unemployed. He had more money than the many college-educated men his age who labored in tedious clerical jobs for meager wages. Still, it wasn't enough. Having glimpsed the estates and great houses of America's rich and dined under their crystal chandeliers, Nitze longed for the glamorous life of parties and travel and power that wealth bought.

What he had instead in 1930 was a tiny apartment on East Eighty-Second Street that he shared with a friend from Chicago, Sidney Spivak. Spivak ("Spiv" as his friends called him) was a charming man with a strange background. Running away from home at the age of 12, he had been adopted as a mascot by an army regiment in Boston. Eventually, he was taken in by foster parents who sent him to boarding school, which he found frightfully dull. His illicit adventures got him kicked out of several prestigious prep schools in succession, and he finally dropped out altogether.

Spiv made his way to France, where he worked in a department store and mastered Parisian French. One day an old classmate came into the store and offered him a job in Chicago. It was in Chicago at a party that Nitze first met Spivak. In time they became great friends, and when Nitze was at Dillon, Read and Spivak was working for Lehman Brothers in New York, they got an apartment together. Spivak was a bright student of politics and his views were decidedly to the left. "I'm not sure that he wasn't a member of the Communist party," Nitze said later. In 1932 Spivak was an ardent supporter of Roosevelt and worked on his campaign. Partly as a result of Spivak's prodding, Nitze supported the New York governor in 1932 and 1936. It was only after Roosevelt tried to pack the Supreme Court in early 1937 that Nitze grew disgusted with him and became a Republican like most of his Wall Street colleagues.

Despite their cramped apartment, Nitze and Spivak entertained often. One of their dinner guests was William Bullitt, a former Wilson aide at the Versailles peace conference and a man of wide international experience. Nitze met Bullitt on the Lexington Avenue subway and invited him to the apartment for dinner. A large and gregarious man, Bullitt entertained Nitze and Spivak with tales of his adventures and talked with particular passion about the Bolshevik government in Russia. In 1919, two years after revolution had brought Lenin to power, Wilson sent Bullitt on a secret mission to meet with the new leaders in Moscow. Bullitt was inspired by what he saw and recommended that the United States recognize the Bolshevik government. Wilson rejected the advice and sent American troops to join an Allied effort to crush the revolution in Russia.

In the early 1930s Bullitt continued to believe that the United States had made a tragic error by initiating hostilities against the Bolsheviks.

He wanted the United States to reverse its mistake by establishing diplomatic relations with the Soviet Union. After Roosevelt won the White House in 1932, Bullitt had his wish fulfilled when the new president established diplomatic relations with Moscow and made Bullitt the first U.S. ambassador to the Soviet Union.

Listening to Bullitt's stories in 1932, Nitze was undecided about relations with the Soviet Union. As a Wall Streeter, he was highly skeptical of a system that repudiated the free market. He also had difficulty accepting Bullitt's optimistic views about a political system that the newspapers portrayed as repressive. Nitze would have to learn far more about communism before he established strong views on the Soviet Union.

After being settled for a while, Spivak's inherent instability caught up with him. Following a hard night of partying, he showed up drunk for work at Lehman Brothers in white tie and tails. He was fired. Over the next weeks Nitze watched as Spiv went "off his rocker" and finally left for Paris. Returning to the United States and entering a mental institution, Spivak eventually recovered and got a job working on the business affairs of Joseph P. Kennedy. "He was a charming person when he wasn't nutty," Nitze recalled.

Although Spivak was homosexual, he also pursued women. The most intense object of his desire was Dorothy ("Dot") Dillon, Clarence Dillon's daughter. Nitze had met Dot shortly after going to work for Dillon, Read and soon was introduced to her friend Phyllis Pratt, the attractive granddaughter of Standard Oil's first president and heiress to a multimillion-dollar fortune. Together, Nitze and Spivak courted two of New York's wealthiest women.

Phyllis Pratt was born into a world of wealth and power on March 24, 1912. She was the fourth child and youngest daughter of John Teele Pratt, a financier and philanthropist. Her mother was Ruth Sears Baker Pratt, an ambitious woman who successfully ran for Congress a year after Mr. Pratt died in 1927. Like her husband and his entire family, Mrs. Pratt was a Republican and a good friend of President Herbert Hoover; some even said they were lovers.

In New York City the Pratts lived in a sumptuous upper East Side mansion near Central Park. On Long Island's North Shore they shared a vast estate with John Teele Pratt's siblings. The estate was dominated by the great Pratt manor house, and across it were scattered smaller guests houses, huge gardens, and stables. Among Congresswoman

Pratt's friends were some of the richest and most powerful people in the city.

Phyllis Pratt was 19 when she met Paul Nitze; he was 24. Phyllis's mother was initially appalled by the romance. No one who mattered in New York City had ever heard of Paul Nitze or his family. A professor's son was definitely a step down on the social ladder for a Pratt. He had no great fortune, not even much of a trust fund. His job at Dillon, Read was a good one, but in depression New York that could quickly change. What drew Phyllis to Nitze were his good looks and his self-confident air, which conveyed strength but didn't entirely cloak insecurity. By most accounts it was Phyllis who pushed the affair forward, falling madly in love with Paul and pursuing him relentlessly.

For Nitze, Phyllis's devotion was flattering. At the age of 21, everyone knew, Phyllis Pratt would inherit a great deal of money. Exactly how much was never quite clear, perhaps up to seven million dollars. Even Phyllis didn't know for sure because the money was mixed up with other Pratt money in a wide array of accounts and investments. In any case, the precise amount didn't much matter. In depression America, a few million dollars was a huge fortune that could buy a young couple nearly anything they wanted.

Paul and Phyllis were engaged in late October 1932 and married on the afternoon of December 2. Despite Phyllis's wealth and position, it was a small wedding held at her mother's home on East Sixty-first Street. The house was decorated with autumn flowers, palms, and cybotium ferns.[4] Nitze's family came from Chicago and his friend Walter Maynard was the best man. There were no ushers. Phyllis was dressed in a gown of ivory-colored satin. Her cousin, Barbara Pratt, was her maid of honor and only attendant.

Following their marriage, the newlyweds left for a short trip to Europe. When they returned, they moved into a spacious apartment (complete with servants), which Phyllis paid for, on East Sixty-first Street, just a few blocks away from Mrs. Pratt's house.

By 1933 Paul Nitze was living the way he wanted. Phyllis's wealth forever changed his life, allowing him to enter the rarefied world of America's wealthiest families. Evenings not spent at their own apartment were spent at the theater and at New York's most fashionable clubs and restaurants. They met the powerful people who were frequent guests at Congresswoman Pratt's elaborate dinner parties (one night they dined with President Herbert Hoover.) On weekends it was out to the Pratt estate in Glen Cove, where the young couple had a sizable house on the grounds.

Life was also better at Dillon, Read. By 1933 Nitze was back in Clarence Dillon's good graces, and his education at the feet of the master financier continued. Like his hero Napoleon, the Baron was a small man (about five foot seven) who thought of himself as someone who depended on cunning and intelligence to outwit more powerful foes. His influence on Nitze was immense. "I had never seen anybody who had a more clear, analytical mind combined with this radical and brutal decisiveness in taking the course of action which flows from the analysis," he said. Dillon had a unique gift for sorting through masses of information in an objective and systematic fashion and developing a logic chain to deal with it, Nitze recalled. Once he had arrived at a decision, "he would then suddenly switch from being an analyst to being a man of action." In the fast-paced world of Wall Street Dillon's gift made him enormously successful. In government Paul Nitze emulated the Baron's style with similar results.

In April 1934 Phyllis gave birth to a daughter, Heidi. A year and a half later the family grew with the birth of a son, Peter. In 1937, not long after his thirtieth birthday, Nitze was promoted to vice-president at Dillon, Read. It is often said that Nitze was a millionaire in his own right by the age of 30, but this is not true. His talent and his ten- to twelve-hour days on Wall Street earned him the respect of the partners at Dillon, Read and led to his promotion, but he still had not made a massive fortune. This was his great goal as a businessman, which he thought to achieve by toiling away, looking for the magic investment, and developing the skill to master his trade. It was a challenge that Nitze thought would consume him for years, if not for his entire life.

And then he went to Germany.

For some time the newspapers had been running disturbing articles about developments in Nitze's ancestral homeland. In January 1933 Hindenburg bowed to Hitler's growing power and made him chancellor. A month later the German Reichstag was consumed by a suspicious fire. In March Hitler and his National Socialist party triumphed in nationwide elections. Less than three weeks later the new majority party forced the Enabling Act, granting Hitler dictatorial powers, through the government. By the mid 1930s, Germany, in violation of the Versailles treaty, had begun to rearm. Europe was on the road to war.

Even for the depression, 1937 was a remarkably slow year on Wall Street, and with business down, Nitze decided it was a good time to take Phyllis and the two children on a vacation to Europe. He hadn't had a real vacation since 1929.

The Nitzes' trip lasted six weeks, with much of that time spent in Germany. Renting a Model A Ford, they drove from city to city and saw a country that had been fundamentally transformed since his last visit in 1929. Gone was the uncertainty and malaise of the Weimar Republic. In its place was a steely nationalism and messianic dogmatism. Berlin's wild and decadent clubs, which had been the talk of Europe in the 1920s, were long closed. In Adolf Hitler's Germany jazz was banned and homosexuals were shot. Prostitutes no longer paraded on the streets. Instead, it was the day of Nazi youth, with their prim uniforms and stiff salutes. At giant rallies and in torchlit parades the apostles of the new order celebrated the rise of the Third Reich holding aloft hundreds of long red banners bearing swastikas. "Berlin was fascinating during that period," Nitze recalled. Changes that were redefining the political climate of Europe were "happening in front of you."

For Nitze the transformation of Germany triggered mixed emotions. He found the Nazi youths "tough, arrogant, and damned impressive." He was also awed by the way the German economy had turned around. While the rest of the world remained hobbled and demoralized by the Great Depression, Hitler had put Germany back to work and resuscitated the spirit of the German people. To Nitze and many others, the Nazis had to be given credit for the miracle they had created in the center of Europe.

But if Nitze saw the good side of the Third Reich, he also saw its ugliness. In Berlin he and Phyllis dropped by the office of a German business associate. The secretaries nervously explained that he wasn't there because he had been arrested by the gestapo. A Jewish banker who was an old acquaintance of Nitze refused to meet with him out of fear. Throughout Germany there were signs of the devastating effects that the 1935 Nuremberg laws were having on the nation's Jews.

The militarization of Germany was evident everywhere. A year before Nitze's visit Hitler had marched troops into the Rhineland. In April 1937 German bombers, aiding the fascist army of Francisco Franco in Spain, had turned the town of Guernica into rubble, killing sixteen hundred civilians. Now, in Hamburg, Munich, and Berlin, the number of fresh army recruits on the streets made it apparent to Nitze how far the Nazi leadership had moved Germany toward a war footing. "There wasn't any doubt but that they were creating military forces of obvious capability," he recalled. Nitze also got a chance to see firsthand the man who was leading this revolution. In Nuremberg and Munich he and Phyllis went to see Hitler speak. His upper body convulsing in artfully honed gesticulations, the führer's words poured forth in a raging torrent. "He screamed an awful lot," Nitze said later, "but he certainly managed to convey emotion to his audience."

By the end of the trip Nitze felt that Adolf Hitler had done wonderful things for Germany for which he deserved praise. Less encouraging was the overwhelming evidence that the Nazi leader would not be content to limit the Third Reich to Germany alone. "He clearly had aggressive intentions," Nitze said.

Back in the United States, Nitze found himself fascinated by the larger questions raised by the political phenomenon occurring in Europe. On a fishing trip in Canada he read Oswald Spengler's *The Decline of the West.* Nitze had gone through the book in college; now he studied it intensely. A lengthy, dense, and nearly mystical work, Spengler's basic thesis was that the existence of western democracies was fatally threatened by the discipline and power of authoritarianism. In the late 1920s Spengler's work was of academic interest. A decade later, as Britain and France waffled in the face of growing German aggressiveness, *The Decline of the West* could not have been more timely. Profoundly affected by the book, Nitze wanted to pursue its arguments further. "I was firmly of the opinion that Spengler had missed the main point," Nitze recalled, "but I couldn't quite figure out where he had missed it." Nitze decided to take a leave from Dillon, Read to do graduate study at Harvard.

Clarence Dillon told him that the idea was "asinine, crazy."[5] People in the investment banking business did not leave Wall Street to enter academia, especially somebody who had just been made a firm's vice-president. But Nitze had made up his mind. After eight years at Dillon, Read, he didn't need to prove his worth to anybody. There was no question now that he could reel in investment profits as well as the next man. More compelling for him was the challenge of understanding the changes sweeping the world in the late 1930s. "I loved the investment banking business, but there were things going on in the world that the investment banking community just wasn't interested in and that you didn't learn about by being in the investment banking business," Nitze recalled.

Moving the family to Boston, Nitze plunged into the study of religion, sociology, and politics. It was here that he first grappled with the problems of communism. One of his chief tutors on the subject was Pitirim Sorokin, a White Russian emigré who been the minister of labor in the revolutionary government of Aleksandr Kerenski. With a deep antipathy toward the Bolsheviks, who had ousted him from office, Sorokin preached an alarming message of impending doom. He agreed with, and updated, Spengler's argument that authoritarianism posed a mortal threat to the western democracies. Pointing to the rise of Nazism and Stalinism, Sorokin prophesied that the day of the west might already be coming to an end. While Nitze came to believe that Sorokin was "really a screwball," he found his ideas uncomfortably convincing.

Two other professors who influenced Nitze were Robert Merton and George Sawyer Pettee. Merton, a sociologist, awed Nitze with his intellectual brilliance and taught him about Marxism-Leninism. Pettee, a political thinker, complemented this education in the foundations of communism with his work on revolutions and the behavior of revolutionary states. Pettee's chief point was that revolutionary states were predicated on repression and were inherently aggressive. He saw close parallels between Hitler's Germany and Stalin's Russia.

Nitze stayed in Cambridge for two semesters. "I learned a lot from spending that year in Harvard," he recalled. But Nitze had no interest in pursuing a doctoral degree. Except for a few unusually bright professors and graduate students, he wasn't impressed by academics. Nor had Nitze's assessment of their impact on world affairs changed since the time that he had decided not to follow in his father's footsteps.

On Nitze's last day of class with Sorokin, the professor asked whether anybody had any final questions. Nitze raised his hand and reminded Sorokin that he had been lured into the class with the promise that Spengler's work would be explained. Nitze wanted to know what had happened to that promise. "Oh, Mr. Nitze," Sorokin replied, "Spengler was a great man. I was just trying to make this course interesting."

"I came to the conclusion," Nitze said later, "that the people at Harvard didn't really know more about this than I did. They knew a lot of background, a lot about the structure of the Communist party, a lot about the theory of the Communist party, and a lot about what people had written about fascism, but when you got down to the inwardness of what was going on, I came to conclusions that they weren't really that good." Nitze returned to Wall Street.

For the rest of his life Paul Nitze would prefer the realm of action over the realm of thought. During the 1930s Nitze was inspired by the public works projects of Robert Moses in New York. The speed with which Moses built the massive Triborough Bridge filled Nitze with envy. He wanted to get things done in the way that Moses got things done. Even as he lived the life of confirmed doer, though, Nitze retained a keen interest in placing his actions in a theoretical framework. "Many people who are just doers live on a given theory for a long time without really checking it against reality," Nitze would say later. To be relevant, people have to reassess their value system and political philosophy continually. If they ceased to do this, if they stopped learning and became static, if they repeated the same old arguments uncritically, their views would no longer be relevant. And in the realm of action, such people would become useless.

Back in New York, Nitze attempted to launch his own investment firm. An experienced financier by this point, he still had not made his fortune, and set out to do so now. The flagship of this effort, Paul H. Nitze and Company, was a failure. Although he found being his own boss "great fun," a bad case of strep throat and the "nervously exhausting" strain of being on his own forced Nitze to return to Dillon, Read. Before he went back to his old firm, however, Nitze made an investment that would net him great wealth. He put $5,000 into the creation of the U.S. Vitamin Corporation. With Americans just discovering the wonders of pharmaceutical nutrition, the company was an immediate success and began to make money right away. Following World War II, U.S. Vitamin was merged with Revlon and Nitze and his partners got roughly one million shares of preferred stock that eventually came to be worth over $100 each. What had been a collective investment of $100,000 was turned into $100,000,000. Along with other investments, the creation of U.S. Vitamin would make Paul Nitze a multimillionare before the age of 40.

On September 1, 1939, the war that had been so long in the making broke out with devastating fury when German troops began pouring onto Polish territory in a surprise attack. Two days later Britain declared war on Germany. France soon followed. For months following the fall of Poland, there was no fighting between Germany and the west. Then, on May 10, 1940, a wave of German tanks and infantry— the vanguard of an invasion force of two million men—surged over the borders of Holland, Belgium, and Luxembourg. In less than three weeks all of the low countries had surrendered, France tottered on the brink of collapse, and 300,000 French and British troops had to be ignominiously evacuated from the port of Dunkirk. On June 22 France surrendered.

On that same day the White House announced that James Forrestal would take a $10,000-a-year job as one Roosevelt's six assistants, known as the "silent six." Although he had been promoted to president of Dillon, Read after Clarence Dillon retired in 1938, Forrestal was tired of Wall Street. When Nitze returned from Harvard, Forrestal expressed a strong interest in the lessons Nitze had learned there, and the two men had long conversations about communism and the tumult in Europe. Like Nitze, Forrestal was bored with making money and wanted to pursue power in a broader arena.

Early in 1940 Forrestal made it clear to Roosevelt's confidant, Harry Hopkins, that he was interested in a government post. With the war heating up in Europe, Roosevelt needed people who could help him deal with the challenge of financing America's rearmament program. Forrestal was a natural choice.

The president's new assistant, in turn, needed help in coping with his job. He wanted an aide who would follow orders and get things done, who was a Wall Streeter, and who was used to working the way Forrestal liked to work. He knew just the man.

Nitze was in Louisiana on a business trip when he received the telegram: "BE IN WASHINGTON MONDAY MORNING. FORRESTAL."[6]

CHAPTER 2

Rubble and Ruin

C LARENCE DILLON had been right when he predicted in September
1929 that the dominance of Wall Street was coming to a close.
In the 1930s many investment firms flourished, despite the broader
economic disarray of the depression, but America's destiny was no
longer shaped by New York's financiers. Instead, the New Deal ushered
in an era of big government and created a new strain of American
power broker: the Washington bureaucrat. With mobilization for war,
this trend accelerated. In New York, Boston, and Philadelphia banks
and law offices began losing their brightest people to federal agencies.
Connoisseurs of power can detect its unique aroma from nearly any
distance. And in 1940 the aroma was coming from the once sleepy
southern city on the banks of the Potomac River.

Promptly obeying Forrestal's summons, Nitze took a train to Washington and showed up at his boss's new office in the Executive Office
Building next to the White House. Nitze asked what he was there for.

Forrestal pointed to an empty desk and said he wanted Nitze to sit
there.

"What do you want me to do?" Nitze asked.

"I want you to help me," Forrestal said.

Nitze asked who would pay his salary. Forrestal said that because he wasn't entitled to hire any assistants, Dillon, Read would continue sending Nitze a paycheck.

What about living quarters? Nitze asked.

Forrestal said Nitze would live with him.

The arrangement and Nitze's position were "all totally illegal and improper," he recalled. But in an age before legislation on government ethics, nobody seemed to care. Moving in with Forrestal, Nitze went to work.

Following his trip to Germany, Nitze had believed that the United States should stay out of the coming cataclysm in Europe. After the German invasion of Poland, his views had changed little. Given the moral flabbiness and the appeasement of Britain and France, Nitze could see no overriding reason to support those two nations in a confrontation with Hitler. As a German-American, he was hesitant to rally against Germany. Moreover, Nitze could not recognize any outstanding moral virtues of Great Britain or France. They may have been more democratic than Germany at home, but both nations had vast colonial empires in which basic human liberty was systematically repressed. The greatest imperial power on earth was not Nazi Germany, but Great Britain. Having only glanced through *Mein Kampf*, Nitze failed to appreciate the scope and madness of Adolf Hitler's macabre dream. Perhaps part of him was also trying to ignore the truth about the diseased mentality that had taken hold in his ancestral homeland, a country long known for its refined civilization. Among friends, Nitze often argued that Germany was being unfairly condemned. At one small dinner party with the financier Vincent Astor, for example, Nitze surprised a group by saying that he would rather see America under the dictatorship of Hitler than under the British Empire.

In Washington's espionage-conscious environment, these views caused difficulty for Nitze. As an American of German descent, Nitze was already singled out for special attention by FBI agents conducting background checks on government officials, and the revelation of Nitze's sympathy for Nazi Germany prolonged this investigation. Nothing turned up to disqualify Nitze from handling classified information, but the episode was discomforting.[1]

What made the investigation a particularly sensitive matter for Nitze was the specter of Paul Hilken.

Following the tremendous explosion at the Black Tom munitions terminal in the summer of 1916, responsible newspapers and government officials had dismissed speculation that foreign agents had blown up the plant. But after the war details began emerging that linked a German spy ring to acts of sabotage in the United States, including the blast at Black Tom. In 1928 Paul Hilken, a suave and aristocratic Baltimore shipping official, confessed his role as a paymaster for the German agents who had blown up Black Tom. Over the next decade more information about the conspiracy and Hilken's role would come to light as American lawyers sought reparations from Germany for the destruction wrought by spy rings.

For the Nitze family the episode was a source of unending embarrassment; Hilken was Anina Nitze's brother. To most Americans, loyalty and patriotism were matters taken for granted and seldom thought about. But to Paul Nitze, haunted by the high treason of his uncle, patriotism became a sensitive topic for decades to come.[2]

By the time Germany leveled Rotterdam and smashed into France, Nitze's commitment to neutrality had evaporated, and when he arrived in Washington, he saw that America could not remain impassive in the face of German aggression.

Forrestal found the job of coordinating rearmament activities unsatisfactory. Essentially, the president wanted him to mediate between agencies and officials, to speed rearmament by lubricating bureaucratic machinery. But as a man used to being in command, Forrestal didn't want to facilitate action, he wanted to direct it. Nitze was even more aggressive, so aggressive that even Forrestal thought he was moving too fast.

One area that Forrestal and Nitze worked on was Latin America. With Germany and Japan conquering much of the world, the vast raw materials of the South American continent came to be seen as a key strategic asset by U.S. officials. However, while the U.S. government's Latin American policy was in disarray, German and Italian intelligence agencies were gaining a foothold on the continent. To bolster U.S. efforts in the region, Forrestal moved to create an office to coordinate inter-American affairs. Assisted by White House aides, Nitze drafted a charter for the office. All that remained was to get the president's signature. But in an early lesson in bureaucratic politics, Nitze watched with frustration as his boss tiptoed around the matter.

Responding to Nitze's exasperation, Forrestal said that Nitze always wanted to move too fast, that he wanted to do things right away. "And down here in Washington you can't get things done that way," Forrestal said. Forrestal explained that a number of players were involved in

Latin American affairs. These people had to be consulted and persuaded. To go over their heads and appeal directly to the president would insure that the Office of Inter-American Affairs would be doomed to failure. After nearly a month of talking, Forrestal finally had the full support of all the players, and Nelson Rockefeller was chosen to run the new office with a Texan named Will Clayton as his deputy. For Nitze the episode was instructive. Unlike financial activities in Wall Street, in Washington action by consensus would yield the best results.

In 1940, after two months in Washington, James Forrestal was appointed under secretary of the navy. Out of a job, Nitze drifted back to Dillon, Read. He had been back in New York for only a short time when he was asked by another friend at the firm, Bill Draper, to return to Washington and work (again on the payroll of Dillon, Read) on setting up a military draft. This operation was headed by one of America's foremost military leaders, General George C. Marshall. Working with Marshall was an inspiration for Nitze because the general had an intuitive understanding of the nature of America's governmental system, something Nitze felt he lacked. On Wall Street one learned how to "think something through faster" and be willing to make a decision, Nitze said, "but it has nothing to do with a broader understanding of the American system and how you worked within it and how you get things done within it and what will last. Marshall really understood these things and had all the character, principle, that was inherent in being a great public figure in the United States."

Following his work on the draft, Nitze went to work for Nelson Rockefeller as finance director at the Office of Inter-American Affairs. For the first time he was put on the government payroll. Settling into his new life as a government bureaucrat, Nitze made arrangements for Phyllis and the children to join him in Washington. Together with another family, the Nitzes stayed at Nelson Rockefeller's sprawling house on Foxhall Road. To get downtown each morning, Nitze joined a car pool with several other government officials, including a Harvard man named Alger Hiss. Following the Japanese attack on Pearl Harbor, it was hard to imagine being any place besides the capital. "Washington at that point was where the action was, absolutely fascinating," Nitze said.

With the American war effort gaining momentum, Nitze's work on Latin America increased in importance and in 1942, his office was absorbed by the Board of Economic Warfare (BEW), a mobilization agency headed by Vice-president Henry Wallace. Nitze's job at the BEW was to procure strategic materials, such as zinc, copper, manganese, and chromite, from Latin America. At first this meant coordinating the private U.S. companies that imported these materials. But when President Roosevelt signed an executive order that placed responsibility for procuring key resources in the hands of the BEW, Nitze suddenly found himself working as the government's point man on strategic materials. Because modern war is as much a clash of industrial might as of military prowess, feeding America's war machine was a task of the highest priority. As head of the Metals and Minerals Branch of the BEW, Nitze was in charge of an organization that pursued materials in every part of the world not occupied by enemy armies. It was his first experience running a large bureaucracy. And it meant making changes in the way he worked.

Throughout his career, Nitze had been an operations man, a person who works on the details of a problem. Now he was an administrator, worrying about procedures and promotion and fighting for his organization. To be effective, Nitze had to learn to delegate authority, to resist handling interesting problems himself. He found it was a skill that came naturally.

In September 1943 President Roosevelt abolished the BEW and created a new organization to handle economic resource matters, the Foreign Economic Administration (FEA). Heading it was a Wisconsin political hack named Leo Crowley. Henry Wallace had won Nitze's respect, despite Wallace's left-wing views, for his good nature and intelligence. Crowley seemed devoid of both qualities. "He was a total incompetent," recalled George Ball, a young Chicago lawyer who worked at the FEA. And he was corrupt, too. Crowley used politics and his political connections to further the personal ambitions of his former business associates.

Life under Crowley was at first unpleasant and in time intolerable. In the summer of 1944 Crowley refused to sign a policy directive Nitze's staff had written because Crowley thought a bureaucratic rival, Will Clayton, would get credit for the action Nitze was recommending. Saying he couldn't work under such circumstances, Nitze resigned on the spot. "I don't want you to resign, Paul," Crowley said. It was too late, Nitze replied. Incensed at the prospect of losing his metals man, Crowley became threatening. "You know I'm an important figure in the Democratic party," he fumed, "and I will guarantee you that if you do this you will never again get a job in a Democratic administration."[3]

Handing in his written resignation, Nitze took a taxi over to the recently built Pentagon building, and within two hours he had been offered a job working for a new organization called the U.S. Strategic Bombing Survey.

Founded to assess the impact of the massive bombing of Nazi Germany, the Strategic Bombing Survey was chaired by Franklin D'Olier, an amiable insurance executive from New Jersey. The vice-chairman was Henry C. Alexander, a polished vice-president of J. P. Morgan. Its staff was to be made up of civilian and military personnel who would be unbiased judges of air power.

Injecting tremendous energy into the survey during its formative stage was George Ball, who had fled the FEA shortly before Nitze. When Ball joined the survey, he found that the organization "was totally inadequate for the job that had to be done." There was a desperate need for serious professionals who could analyze complex economic and military data.

Nitze had impressed Ball at the FEA as a "man of considerable competence." What he knew of Nitze's skills and background convinced him that Nitze would be ideal for the survey. "He had been working on supply problems so he understood a good deal about the supply needs of the Germans as well as the Americans," Ball recalled. Nitze also had "quite a little acquaintance with Germany."

When Nitze accepted a job on the survey, he became one of its nine directors. As head of the Ball Bearing and Machine Tool Division, later renamed the Equipment Division, Nitze's job was to assess the effect of bombing on these components of the enemy's industrial base.

Strategic bombing was a new and untested concept in the 1940s. During World War I planes had been used mostly for reconnaissance. With the development of larger and faster aircraft capable of carrying powerful bombs, it became possible to reduce modern cities to rubble through concentrated aerial raids. The 1937 bombing of Guernica was an early and grisly example of this capability. In 1940 the Luftwaffe's attack on Rotterdam and the nightly pounding of Britain firmly established strategic bombing as a mainstay of twentieth-century warfare.

Once the Allies recovered from the shock of Hitler's initial successes, they unleashed their own bomber forces in terrible retaliation. At a meeting of the Allied command in Casablanca in January 1943, it was determined that a cross-channel invasion of France would have to wait, but in the meantime a bomber offensive would be launched immediately against Germany. The aim of the attacks, the Allies agreed, was to bring about "the progressive destruction and dislocation of the

German military, industrial, and economic system, and the undermining of the morale of the German people to a point where their capacity for armed resistance is fatally weakened."[4] Military officials, bristling with charts and graphs and brimming with confidence in technology had high hopes for the raids. Some argued that bombing would quickly bring the German war machine to its knees and pave the way for Allied victory. The first targets would be German submarine yards, aircraft plants, and oil refineries.

Night after night, waves of RAF bombers swept across the North Sea and dropped thousands of tons of bombs on Germany. During the day American planes took over the bombardment. The devastation that resulted was unlike anything the world had ever seen. Aerial reconnaissance showed vast industrial complexes reduced to wastelands of rubble and twisted steel. Oil refineries burned for weeks and months. Once the proud masters of Europe, the German leadership now spent nights in underground bunkers.

No one disputed that the bombing caused massive destruction. Advocates of the bombing produced before and after photographs documenting the demise of targeted factories and shipyards. But were the raids helping the Allies win the war? Were they worth the men and planes lost to German antiaircraft artillery and fighter and interceptor planes? No one knew for sure. In October 1944 D'Olier was told that "One of the fundamental purposes of the survey is to determine whether the results obtained were commensurate with expenditures of men and material."[5]

It was a sensitive task. In helping to organize the survey, Assistant Secretary of War Robert Lovett had envisioned a study that would vindicate his personal crusade to make strategic bombing central to the Allied war strategy. Military officials who favored a postwar emphasis on air power had a keen desire to prove that the long-range bomber would be the magic weapon of the future. In the survey itself were military officers who believed it was their duty to formulate a ringing endorsement of strategic bombing. And there was great pressure on all survey members to affirm that the vast bombing effort was not in vain.

D'Olier fought this pressure from the beginning. When the survey was finally established in London, he vowed that the organization would not allow its conclusions to be distorted by any ulterior motives or preconceptions. Assembling his entire staff in December, D'Olier said that "we shall proceed in an open-minded manner, without prejudice, without any preconceived theories, to gather the facts. We are simply to seek the truth. . . . We have no intention, nor should we at this stage, of commending or criticizing any individual, group, or organization in any way except as the final facts and the real truth might so require."[6] Although he functioned for the most part, in the words of one director, as "an amiable figurehead," D'Olier largely stood by this pledge.

The survey established headquarters in London in a seven-story residential building at Grosvenor Square in Mayfair, a section of the city almost entirely taken over by Americans. Working out of an office that had once been a Londoner's apartment, Nitze recruited new staff members. Philip Farley was a U.S. Army sergeant and a clerk in a bomb disposal unit in Britain. In response to a letter requesting that experts on bombing be released to work on the survey, Farley's unit sent him to London for an interview. There he met with Nitze, George Ball, and Ball's aide, a gregarious Chicago lawyer named Adlai Stevenson. Nitze took an immediate liking to Farley and asked him to be his assistant.

During the first months survey members struggled to find a workable approach to their assignment. The task proved daunting. Because strategic bombing had just been invented, there was no literature on the subject and few real experts. Moreover, the scope of the project was immense. By late 1944 much of industrial Germany lay in ruins, and it was this vast wasteland that would be the survey's laboratory. Yet to make the study useful, it was not enough to tally up the square miles of rubble and make sweeping estimates of how bombing had affected overall German production. Assessing the effectiveness of precision bombing meant looking at specific industries and factories. And this is where the job became most difficult.

"In the original plan . . . teams would inspect the burned and battered factories," recalled John Kenneth Galbraith, a lanky economist Nitze's age who headed the economics division. "And specialists were deployed to do so. They learned only that the factories were very burned and battered. Such inspection did not show when or by how much production had been curtailed. For this the production records were needed, and even these told little of the effect on the output of the industry as a whole or of the ultimate effect on weapons production or, beyond that, on military operations."[7] If a plant suffered a shortage of labor, electricity, or raw materials and was also periodically hit by bombs, who could say how much of any change in production could be attributed to bombing? For all of its engineers, economists, and statisticians, the survey practiced a highly inexact science.

Still, while precise conclusions remained elusive, some themes became instantly clear. When the bombing began, many Allied officials believed that striking at certain key factories could cripple the German war machine. Phil Farley's main assignment for Nitze was to look at what effect this kind of selective targeting had on German antifriction bearing production. "One school of thought was that if you could just pick a key segment like that, you could bring much of the German industry to a halt," Farley recalled. Allied planners had launched numerous raids, with great losses in planes and men, against antifriction bearing factories.

The effort was a failure. Poring over captured data, Farley found that antifriction bearing production had not been significantly curtailed. "Essentially what I showed was how the Germans quickly learned what we were trying to do and they hid and dispersed key elements so they could keep antifriction bearing production going," he recalled. In one case Farley's team found a factory operating at peak capacity amidst the destruction inflicted by early bombings. From the air the factory looked like rubble and was taken off the target list. On the ground it was producing bearings. Such examples of German resourcefulness were everywhere.

Farley also discovered that the Germans rapidly adapted to the bearing losses that they did sustain. Reassessing their military requirements for antifriction bearings, German planners found that the average life of a plane in combat was less than a week. "You obviously didn't need a lot of antifriction bearings to make the plane work for a week," Farley said. Production could be scaled back without hurting the Luftwaffe's ability to field an air force.

Other analysts reached similar conclusions. As Allied armies pushed into Germany in the winter and spring of 1945, advance survey teams followed closely behind, gathering reams of new data. Captured papers—which would total over 200 tons—poured into a special analysis center that the survey set up in Bushy Park, a town twenty miles from London. As the information was analyzed, a surprising discovery was made: In several critical areas arms production had actually increased during the time of heaviest bombing. What had happened was that the blind, night-time bombing of German cities had destroyed large sectors of commercial industry. This meant that the fuel, labor, and raw materials slated for those industries could be channeled into military production at arms factories which the Germans had begun to disperse and place underground.

Hamburg was a typical example. On three summer nights in 1943 the RAF came in from the North Sea and laid waste the center of the city. A terrible firestorm caused the deaths of thousands of civilians.

But did war production in Hamburg cease? Not at all. It increased. While the restaurants and department stores and banks of Hamburg were destroyed, the factories and shipyards on the outskirts of the city survived. "Before the holocaust these had been short of labor," recalled Galbraith. "Now waiters, bank clerks, shopkeepers and entertainers forcibly unemployed by the bombers flocked to the war plants to find work. . . . The bombers had eased the labor shortage."

When the final figures were compiled, it was clear that despite the greatest aerial bombardment in the history of warfare, despite months of supposedly pinpoint raids on key factories, tank and aircraft production actually increased between 1943 and 1945. In 1942 the average monthly production of panzer vehicles was 516. In 1943, after heavy bombing had begun, production was 1,005. And in 1944 it was 1,583. Captured German documents showed that panzer vehicle production peaked in December 1944, a time when the allied bombing campaign was also reaching a crescendo.

In the realm of aircraft the story was the same. During the last week of February 1944 every known aircraft plant in Germany was attacked; 3,636 tons of bombs were dropped. The attacking American bombers suffered heavy losses. But again, Galbraith and his analysts found that the raids had achieved nothing. "In January, before the attacks, 2,077 combat aircraft—fighters and bombers—were produced by the Germans," wrote Galbraith. "In March, the month after the attacks, production was up to 2,243. By September 1944, when the peak was reached, production was nearly twice what it was before the raids. . . . It could be argued that the effect of the air attacks was to increase German airplane output." The effect also was to misdirect Allied energies. "The aircraft, manpower and bombs used in the campaign had cost the American economy far more in output than they had cost Germany," Galbraith concluded.[8]

Nitze's equipment analysts were reaching the same conclusions as Galbraith's economists. Farley's findings for antifriction bearing production were repeated for the ball bearing industry as a whole. As Nitze said later, "not one end item of German war production had been delayed a single day by virtue of the attacks on the ball bearing industry." The ball bearing plants had been blasted into rubble repeatedly, and each time the surprisingly durable machines that made the bearings would be dug out and put into action in another location. As long as an enemy had the time and labor force to repair and relocate its factories, production could continue. "The basic lesson was that there were no easy ways to win a war," said Farley. Ambitious plans to obliterate specific industries were bound to fail, and therefore the basic theory of precision bombing, exuberantly expounded by Robert Lovett and others, proved largely unworkable.

Also without foundation was the idea that bombing could undermine enemy morale. Given the example of the heroic defiance displayed by the British people during the London blitz of 1940, Allied officials should have realized that the wholesale slaughter of civilians would not break their will. But this lesson was ignored. In a doomed and bloody effort to smash the German spirit, waves of Allied bombers struck at civilian targets. On a single night in February 1945 the city of Dresden—a cultural center in Germany and one of the world's most beautiful cities—was laid waste by incendiary bombs. Thousands of civilians were killed, many asphyxiated when air was sucked out of underground shelters by a raging firestorm.

This kind of carnage might have been warranted if it helped to end the war or shorten it. But a special division of the survey studying German morale found little indication that bombing civilians had undermined the Third Reich. Briefing a Pentagon group in 1945, George Ball said that "we have found little evidence up to this point to indicate that the efficiency of the German worker materially decreased. He may not have liked his situation and he may have wished that the war would end, and he even may have thought that the war was lost, but he still went to work and he still did his job."[9]

To most survey members, it was clear that strategic bombing had not achieved the goals laid out by military planners. For the Allies it was a vast waste of men and resources. For the Germans it was a ghastly inferno that consumed hundreds of thousands of lives. But while the bombing failed in its intended mission, survey members found that it contributed to winning the war in unforeseen ways.

To take back the continent of Europe, Allied forces had to cross the English Channel and fight their way though France and western Germany. This operation could have turned into a disaster if German fighter bombers had been free to cut up the invading force and pummel armored columns on the roads. However, by the time of the Normandy invasion of June 1944, strategic bombing had helped the Allies capture the skies over France. The bombing did so not by paralyzing German aircraft assembly lines, but by knocking German fighters out of the air.

Day and night Allied planes rumbled in from the North Sea. Determined to stop them from unloading their deadly cargos, the Luftwaffe sent fighters to intercept. In blazing dogfights over Germany, thousands of Allied bombers were shot down. But the losses to the German air force were also staggering, and when the invasion finally came, the Germans did not have the air power to repel it. In this roundabout way, Ball recalled, the bombing "gave us command of the air for the invasion."

Perhaps the most intriguing episode of the survey's work in Germany was the interrogation of Albert Speer. While still in his thirties, Speer had risen to become Hitler's chief mobilization planner. Tall and slender and far more urban than other top Nazis, he was the German leader that survey members most wanted to interrogate.

Nitze was in London when Speer was finally located near the north German coast by an army intelligence unit. Flying to Germany, Nitze joined Galbraith and Ball for what would be a ten-day interrogation of Speer. Every afternoon around two, survey members would drive to a castle with a large moat where Speer was living and would talk with him until six or seven in the evening. For the three veterans of Washington's wartime bureaucracy, these sessions provided a fascinating, and ultimately unsettling, glimpse at the inner workings of Germany's military-industrial complex.

Among top U.S. government officials, Speer had come to be seen as a figure of near mythic proportions during the later years of the war. He was "the German miracle man," recalled Galbraith. "He had worked wonders with German production."[10] During his interrogation Speer expressed great pride at what he had accomplished. But what deeply affected Nitze, Galbraith, and Ball were Speer's points about what the Third Reich could have accomplished. Speer's argument was persuasive: Because of the stupidity and incompetence of Hitler's inner circle, and because of the regime's endemic overconfidence, Germany failed to take the mobilization steps that would have allowed it to maintain a winning edge. "Unlike Britain and the United States," Nitze said later, "Germany suffered no critical defeat early in the war—no Dunkirk or Pearl Harbor—to focus attention on the problem or galvanize the country."[11] Embracing their own propaganda slogan "Victory is certain," top Nazi leaders—many of whom had started out as small-time thugs—fell prey to the material temptations of power, becoming lazy and corpulent. As Speer put it, "The soft men and the weak were never sorted out and discarded as they were in Britain and the U.S. The weak remained in positions of responsibility to the last."[12]

The implications of Speer's statements were disturbingly clear: If Adolf Hitler had been more rational and methodical, if he had purged his inner circle of reprobates like Goering and Bormann and relied solely on men like Speer, and if he had fully mobilized the country in 1941 instead of 1944, Germany might have won World War II.

Unlike Ball and Galbraith and other directors of the Strategic Bombing Survey who preferred to be close to the front lines, Paul Nitze spent most of his time in London handling administrative and policy issues. As finally constituted, the survey included 350 military officers, 500 enlisted men, and 300 civilians. These people had to be housed and paid and given assignments. The data they collected had be categorized and analyzed. Reports had to be written and memorandums sent to Washington. The paper flow was enormous, but thanks to D'Olier, everything ran smoothly.

A sturdy Irishman, D'Olier was a good-natured man who could drink eight whiskeys and sodas in an evening and not appear to be affected. When Nitze and the other directors occasionally tried to keep up with him during an evening of hard drinking, they found themselves slobbering drunk. What made D'Olier so easy to work with was that he readily delegated authority. He concentrated on relations with Truman and top military officers and viewed himself as the survey's facilitator rather than its manager.

As vice-chairman, Henry Alexander took on most of the administrative work. Still, there was only so much paper he could push, and Nitze stepped forward to help out. At Grosvenor Square, Nitze took an office next to Alexander's and worked as his assistant. When Alexander was away, Nitze took over his functions, sitting at D'Olier's elbow and running the survey's meetings. "Due to his ability," one survey member remarked about Nitze at the time, "Mr. D'Olier has leaned very heavily on him and I feel that many of the policies of the survey are definitely set by Mr. Nitze due to the confidence that higher authority has in him."[13] When both Alexander and D'Olier were away, which was often, Nitze led the discussions at the daily staff meetings and served as acting chairman.

After the German surrender in May 1945 the survey established a forward headquarters in the Park Hotel at Bad Nauheim, a town twenty miles from Frankfurt. Every weekend the chairman and the directors would meet there to discuss plans and operations. In London Nitze had been removed from the destruction of Germany; now he viewed it firsthand.

In 1937 Nitze had seen Nazi youths parading proudly in the streets of Germany, their uniforms crisp and pressed, their faces healthy and intense. In Bad Nauheim and in other towns he again saw young Germans on the street, but they were no longer proud. Now many of them hobbled on crutches, their legs blown off in battle. In 1937 the youths had looked at foreigners with arrogant contempt; in 1945 they glared sullenly at their conquerors with hatred.

Touring Hamburg, Berlin, and the cities where the damage was most serious, Nitze saw for himself how wanton the bombing had often been. He was most shocked by the destruction of Darmstadt, a small city south of Frankfurt. One night RAF bombers had launched a raid in the area. Unable to find their initial target or their secondary target, they unloaded their incendiary bombs over Darmstadt and headed home. A firestorm engulfed the city. "This had been an unexpected raid," Nitze recalled. "There had been no warning and all the people in the shelters had been burned to death or died of carbon monoxide." The sole war-related target in the city, a chemical plant on the outskirts of town, came through the bombing undamaged.

There were many Darmstadts.

In June several top members of the survey were summoned back to Washington to advise the U.S. high command on the bombing campaign against Japan. Now one of the survey's most influential officials, Nitze would be closely involved in this work. On June 19, D'Olier, Alexander, and Nitze met with General Marshall and the secretaries of war and the navy to discuss the bombing in Europe and plans for the stepped-up bombing effort against Japan. Survey members also held several long meetings with the Pentagon's Joint Target Group (JTG), which handled the details of the raids.[14]

The sessions were intensive. "I might say that we are here and prepared to stay here and are available morning, noon or night until you are through with us," D'Olier declared at the first meeting. Briefed in depth on the bombing campaign planned against Japan, survey members were disturbed to learn that the JTG had decided to make massive incendiary raids against Japan's highly flammable cities the cornerstone of the new air offensive. In their zeal to destroy Tokyo's war machine, America's military leaders intended to perpetrate dozens of Darmstadts and Dresdens.

Arguing vehemently against incendiary raids, Nitze urged the JTG to go after three main targets: power, steel, and transportation. "The destruction of one of these segments alone is sufficient to completely disrupt their war effort," Nitze said at an early session. Unlike ball bearing machines or tank factories, these targets couldn't be rebuilt or dispersed. Drawing on the interrogation of Speer, Nitze said that the German war planners "were of the opinion that it would have been absolutely impossible for them to disperse either their chemical or oil plants or their power facilities or their steel or their transportation." When the Allies had hit these systems, the impact had been dramatic. "The transportation attack shut down three quarters of the rest of the industrial system for lack of coal," Nitze told the group.

Ball echoed this assessment, saying that "even if the German economic system had been in a healthier position, still the effect of [attacks on] oil and transportation in our judgment would have been decisive." Producing arms and supplies was virtually impossible without fuel, and such materials would be of little use if they could not be moved to the field. Investigators in Germany had often found war materials piled up inside and outside of factories that could not be shipped to the armies. Nitze and the others argued that raids against Japan should seek to undercut its war effort by striking at the primary railroads and loading yards.

Summoning additional experts from Europe, the survey directors stayed in Washington through June and hammered away at the thinking of the Joint Targeting Group. In early July Nitze was asked by D'Olier to write a report outlining an alternative strategy for the bombing of Japan.

Over the July 4th holiday Nitze took his work up to New York, where he spent Independence Day at Jones Beach with his family and some friends. While everybody else frolicked in the sand and waves, Nitze scribbled away on a yellow pad, his mind lost in the details of aerial bombing. On the way back to their house on the Pratt estate at Glen Cove, Nitze received a scare when Phyllis lost the papers he had been working on. Retracing their steps, they found the top secret documents on the floor of a drugstore.

"Japan's position as a strong military and industrial power is already terminated," Nitze's report said. Reflecting the views of the survey members, Nitze argued that the United States could bring about Japan's surrender by November 1945 through a blockade of the Japanese home islands "coordinated with an overwhelming attack on the Japanese rail network and on coastwise shipping." Such attacks would isolate the islands from each other and make it impossible for Japan to continue the war. Nitze's report also recommended attacking Japanese ammunition dumps and plants that produced oil and nitrogen. It stressed that urban attacks should be only a last resort.

During the long sessions in Washington, military officials on the

Joint Targeting Group had sat raptly as survey members unveiled their tentative conclusions. Deferring to more informed judgment, the JTG was willing to accept in part the recommendations made in Nitze's report. But while they changed their position and proposed that attacks on transportation be given top priority, they were unwilling to stop the carnage being wrought by incendiary bombing. In their own report the JTG argued that such raids "will produce chaotic conditions in administration and control which will accelerate the disintegration to be achieved through attacks upon transportation." On July 23 a new targeting directive was approved by the Pentagon's top command which leaned more toward the survey's recommendations and de-emphasized the role of incendiary bombing.[15]

It was too late. The wholesale slaughter of Japanese civilians had begun in March with the incineration of 83,700 people during the firebombing of Tokyo. For the rest of the war General Curtis LeMay's XX Bomber Command patterned most of their raids on the Tokyo success, burning over sixty Japanese cities.

After the atomic bombing of Hiroshima and Nagasaki, Japan surrendered on August 14. Its work finished in Europe, the Strategic Bombing Survey headed for the Pacific.

Studying the bombing of Japan was a far different project than the survey's work in Europe. In scope the devastation was smaller. Over 1.3 million tons of bombs had been dropped on Germany: only 161,377 tons were dropped on Japan. But tonnage meant little. What was different was the use of A-bombs. The product of an enormous scientific project, the A-bomb fascinated Washington's civilian and military leaders. Aerial reconnaissance showed that Hiroshima and Nagasaki had been leveled, but few details were available on the precise power of the bomb. Paul Nitze and his colleagues were the first Americans to look closely at what this awesome new weapon could do to an urban center.

Before the survey left for Japan, Henry Alexander announced that he was returning to J. P. Morgan. Alexander had been a dominant voice in the European study, writing the survey's final report. Although he would continue in an advisory role, he said that his responsibilities in New York could no longer be avoided. George Ball also left the survey. Nitze was the logical choice to become the new vice-chairman. With D'Olier playing the same detached role as before, Nitze quickly emerged as the chief manager and leading theoretician of the Pacific study.

In late September Nitze flew to Guam and then to Japan. Immediately upon arriving in Tokyo, he was summoned to a meeting with General Douglas MacArthur, the chief of U.S. occupation forces. A vain and imperious man, MacArthur treated his sphere of command like a personal fiefdom. He also had his own opinions on airpower. For nearly four hours he lectured Nitze about the role of airpower in the Pacific. When he was finished, MacArthur invited Nitze back to his court in two days. Nitze returned and again sat quietly as the general held forth on the subject of airpower for several hours. Before dismissing Nitze, MacArthur made a final point: He didn't want to see or hear from Nitze's organization the entire time it was in Japan.

Three days after being told to disappear, Nitze was invited to dine with MacArthur. During the next two months the general regularly asked Nitze to dinner and to his office to talk about the Pacific war. One day MacArthur announced that his deputy was leaving and asked Nitze to take the job and help run occupied Japan.

Nitze said he would consider the offer. Over the next few days he developed a number of conditions that would have to be met before he took the job. He wanted to recruit several aides and assure them of decent housing. He also wanted to have somebody working for him in Washington. When Nitze presented these conditions, MacArthur flew into a rage and refused to make any guarantees.

"Well, I have my answer, General," Nitze recalled saying. "I will stay with the U.S. Strategic Bombing Survey."

The survey's headquarters in Tokyo were fitting for conquerors. They were in the Mejei Seimei building overlooking the grounds of the Imperial Palace. Instituting daily staff conferences, D'Olier and Nitze immediately put the survey to work. The study proceeded far more smoothly in Japan than it had in Europe. Even in defeat, Japan was an orderly nation. Its local and national governments were largely intact, and unlike Germany, it had been occupied by a single army rather than several. Once the arrogant villains of East Asia, Japan's people were now remarkably docile and friendly toward the American occupiers.

With its vast burned-out tracts, the city of Tokyo was a chilling testament to the power of the incendiary bomb. In only one night of raids, 63 percent of Tokyo's commercial area had been burned and 267,171 buildings had been destroyed.[16] It was the most devastating air attack in history.

But the obliteration of Tokyo had required 334 B-29 bombers carrying 2,000 tons of bombs. In the attacks on Hiroshima and Nagasaki it had taken only a single B-29 carrying one bomb to level most of the city.

Spending time at the survey's regional offices in Hiroshima, Nitze looked closely at the damage done by the first A-bomb. After what he had seen in Europe, it was nothing spectacular. Hiroshima was the seventh largest city in Japan, with a population of about 245,000 people in August 1945. Located on a flat delta whose seven mouths divided the city into six islands, its commercial, military, and residential areas were intermingled in a 13-square-mile built-up area. Most of the houses in the city were made of wood and covered by black tile roofs. With antiquated fire fighting equipment, many neighborhoods in the city were firetraps even in peacetime.

Nitze arrived in Hiroshima over two months after the blast. From the center of the city, where the bomb had exploded, one could see little besides rubble. Like lonely tombstones, there remained standing parts of a few concrete buildings and the twisted skeletons of a few steel frame buildings. Otherwise, the blast and the firestorm generated by the bomb had consumed all that lay in their paths.

What made the devastation less than overwhelming, however, were the signs of Hiroshima's recovery. From his investigators, Nitze learned that railroad service in much of the city had been functioning since August 8, only two days after the attack. Electric power was available in some areas on August 7. Located on the outskirts of the city, the bulk of Hiroshima's industrial capability survived the blast. As for casualties, there was no sure count, but it was estimated that 70,000 to 80,000 Japanese were killed in Hiroshima on the first day. The number was about half that in Nagasaki. Many more would die later of radiation sickness, and four decades later Japanese would still be dying at a steady pace from the long-term effects of the A-bombs.[17]

As appalling as the human toll was, the survey's job was to measure the effects of strategic bombing on the enemy's war effort population. And through this chilly lens the atomic bombing did not appear decisive. In the survey's final report on the Pacific war, Nitze wrote that "the damage and casualties caused at Hiroshima by one atomic bomb dropped from a single plane would have required 220 B-29s carrying 1,200 tons of incendiary bombs, 400 tons of high-explosive bombs, and 500 tons of antipersonnel fragmentation bombs."[18] Bombing raids of this size or greater were common during the war.

Nitze noticed something else that mitigated his awe of the A-bomb's power. In both Hiroshima and Nagasaki the bomb had struck without warning. Normal air raid precautions had not been taken. In Nagasaki, however, some four hundred persons were in tunnel shelters at the time of the explosion. These consisted of rough tunnels dug horizontally into the sides of hills with crude, earth-filled blast walls protecting their entrances.[19] Even in the tunnels close to ground zero, all the occupants had survived the initial blast. (It is not known how many died later of radiation sickness.) Nitze was impressed with the survival rate. "The tunnels had a capacity of roughly 100,000 persons," he wrote in the final report. "Had the proper alarm been sounded, and these tunnel shelters been filled to capacity, the loss of life in Nagasaki would have been substantially lower."[20]

As 1946 began, what Nitze feared most was a repetition of the events that had produced World War II. The United States had vanquished Hitler and Tojo, but Joseph Stalin had emerged from the war with a powerful army that now occupied half of Europe. Although Russia had suffered twenty million dead following the German attack in June 1941, and much of the country's industrialized western region lay in ruins, few American leaders doubted that the Soviets could rebuild. And when they did, the Soviet totalitarian system—a system that had killed millions of its own people through collectivization and purges and one that Nitze had come to equate with Nazism during his studies at Harvard in 1938—would be more powerful than ever.

In 1944 Nitze had received an early warning about the emerging Soviet threat from a charming and intense foreign service officer he met in the dining car on a train from Washington to New York. "We got into a discussion about the USSR in the war and the postwar world," Nitze recalled of his first meeting with George F. Kennan. The message from Kennan, who was on his way to serve in the Moscow embassy, was chilling. He believed that the alliance between the United States and the Soviet Union would not survive the war and that Moscow's relentless search for security would soon lead to a confrontation. "I thought everything he was saying made very good sense," Nitze said later.[21]

Anticipating new tensions in the postwar period, Nitze included recommendations for safeguarding American security in his Pacific Summary Report. Central to his blueprint was the notion of peace through strength. Despite the advent of atomic weapons, Nitze argued, traditional weapons of war such as ground troops and naval forces would remain of paramount importance in the new age. A-bombs did not make war obsolete. Instead, they increased the stakes of war and made the danger of another Pearl Harbor many times greater. Nitze recommended that the United States pursue a military research and development program so that in the "field of military weapons and tactics" the United States was "not merely abreast of, but actually ahead of any potential aggressor." Vigilance and superiority would be the keys to security in the postwar world, he felt. And to survive atomic war if it came, the United States should have a program of civil defense.

To Paul Nitze, the searing lesson of World War II was that western weakness led to aggression. Now, as the most powerful nation on earth, Nitze argued, the United States could never again neglect its armed forces. The best way to prevent a war was to prepare for one. "The United States must have the will and strength to be a force for peace," he wrote in conclusion.[22]

Around the same time that Nitze was writing the Pacific Summary Report, he read a speech Stalin had given in Moscow in February 1946. The speech called for a heroic effort to rebuild the Soviet Union in the postwar period, but Nitze and other Americans discerned a more ominous message: They believed that Stalin was calling for a holy war against capitalism. Visiting his former boss James Forrestal, who by this time had become secretary of the navy, Nitze compared Stalin's speech to a declaration of war. Forrestal agreed and suggested that Nitze take this message to Under Secretary of State Dean Acheson.

Nitze had first met Acheson years ago when Acheson worked for the New York law firm Covington and Burling. With the carefully groomed mustache of an English gentleman and a biting wit, Acheson was already establishing a reputation as one of the more colorful characters around town.

Still optimistic about the Soviets, he was unpersuaded by Nitze's words of gloom. "Paul, you are just seeing mirages," Nitze remembered him saying.

The work of assessing strategic bombing in World War II would continue into 1947, but after finishing the Pacific Summary Report, Nitze decided that the interesting part of the survey was over and cast about for another job. The parents of three children by this time—William was born in 1942—Nitze and Phyllis bought a large house on Woodley Road in Washington's Cleveland Park section. Washington may have lacked the glitter, high society, and wealth of New York, but it compensated with the raw excitement that surrounds the exercise of power. He had not been in the capital for long, Nitze later confessed, before he "soon caught Potomac fever."[23] In the dawning postwar era, with the old colonial empires in their death throes, the center of the political world, it was clear, would be Washington. Paul Nitze was going to stay right where he was.

Turning down a lucrative offer to become managing director of a firm in New York, Nitze soon landed a job working for Will Clayton, who was now the under secretary of state for economic affairs. Nitze's official post was deputy director of the Office of International Trade Policy. The director of the office was Clair Wilcox. Within three days of Nitze's arrival, Wilcox headed off to a trade conference in Havana, Cuba. This would be the pattern for much of the next year. With Wilcox overseas, Nitze worked as acting director of the office with Clayton as his direct superior.

At six foot three, Will Clayton towered over Nitze. Before the war he had been a hard-driving entrepreneur who built the largest cotton trading company in the world. It was a record of success that impressed Nitze. But what made Clayton even more impressive was his integrity and kindness. "He was the only fellow I respected in the government," Nitze said later. Accustomed to the action-packed world of business deals, Clayton liked to make things happen—to see a problem, identify the solution, and implement that solution immediately. And because he made things happen, Clayton created an aura of excitement around him, a feeling among his subordinates that they were in the center of the action and that the opinions they voiced and the memorandums they wrote could make a difference.

The problem that obsessed Will Clayton in late 1946 and early 1947 was the economic crisis in Europe. With its governments in turmoil and its people drained from years of war, Europe was an economic disaster zone. A shattered agricultural system was unable to feed the continent and millions went hungry in the cities. Basic consumer goods were scarce. During the winter of 1946–1947, one of the coldest in decades, people froze in their homes because there was no fuel. And after so much upheaval, many nations' monetary systems lay in shambles.

As an international businessman, Clayton saw that Europe's recovery was inextricably linked to America's prosperity. If Europe wasn't economically sound, who would buy American cotton? Who would buy American automobiles and a thousand other exportable goods? "We need markets—big markets, in which to buy and sell," Clayton said.[24]

For Nitze this argument was compelling. Yet his commitment to rebuilding Europe went far deeper. As a young child before World War I, his parents had taken him through the great cities of Europe and taught him where his roots lay. Between the wars Nitze had enjoyed the culture of the continent while watching it lumber toward apocalypse. His sense of what the world was—of who he was—would be forever tied to Europe. Nitze felt that if the United States turned its back on Europe, there was the risk of chaos, destitution, and worse still, Soviet domination.

In early 1947 the term "Cold War" was still new to the Washington lexicon. However, with the Good War and the Grand Alliance less than two years past, the rivalry between the United States and the Soviet Union that George Kennan had predicted in 1944 was rapidly reshaping the world's political geography. To Nitze the perils of the late 1940s were ominously reminiscent of those of the late 1930s. Once again, a totalitarian power with a tremendous military force loomed over a weak and divided Europe. That much of Russia lay in ruins was immaterial to Nitze, as was the fact that Stalin had little incentive to spark a war with the United States, a nation that had just outproduced the Axis war machines with resources to spare and that possessed the most powerful weapon in the world. If it was at all possible for the Red Army to push across Europe, Nitze felt that the threat had to be taken seriously. Even more real, many thought, was the threat that internal subversion would bring the Communist party to power in Italy and France, as was already happening in the nations of eastern Europe. The best defense against a future of conquest and domination for the people of Europe was to usher in a new era of order and prosperity, Nitze felt.

Strangely, the country that crystallized Nitze's emerging thoughts about Europe was not one ravaged by war, but rather neutral Sweden. In the months following the war Sweden had proved too generous in giving assistance to its neighbors, and by late 1946 it found itself with a major balance of payments problem, that is, it was spending far more money buying foreign imports than it was earning through exports. Appealing to the United States for help, the Swedish government sent their chief economist, Dag Hammarskjöld, to Washington for consultations. In long meetings with Nitze, Hammarskjöld laid out the economic situation in Sweden: Unless Sweden was provided with some relief, its economic situation would continue to unravel.

Nitze arranged for Sweden to receive trade concessions from the United States. But no sooner had he finished with that problem than it became clear that Canada was in the same bind. Again Nitze's office found a way to alleviate the situation. Curious as to how many other countries faced the same problem, Nitze talked to officials at the U.S. Treasury Department. Their analysis was disturbing. The officials explained that the United States was running an annual $5 billion trade surplus with the rest of the world. The situation was particularly bad vis-à-vis Europe. Unless the Europeans revitalized their economies, unless they began producing goods, they would have to keep spending their reserves of gold and American dollars to buy products abroad.

In a memorandum to Clayton, Nitze said that the amount of this wealth flowing to the United States would add up to almost $25 billion over five years. When these reserves ran out, as they surely would, Europe would be broke. And if Europe went broke, the United States would have no place to sell its surplus goods, its factories would close, and unemployment would skyrocket. European war debts, especially the money borrowed by the British, would never be repaid. "There was the probability of a bankrupt world," Nitze recalled. "Thus we had to give priority to an aid program."[25]

During May 1947 Clayton toured Europe to observe the economic situation. Over the last year he had been fighting for loans and other assistance of the kind that had been given to Sweden and Canada. Now, as he traveled through the still devastated continent, he realized that these piecemeal efforts fell far short of what was needed.

When Clayton returned from Europe, he invited Nitze and three other top State Department economic officials to join him for lunch in the Blue Room of Washington's Metropolitan Club. As he talked to the group, it was clear that Clayton had been shaken by his trip. He talked of the great calamity in the making and stressed that time was of the essence in formulating a response.

After lunch Clayton returned to his office and dictated a memorandum. "It is now obvious that we grossly underestimated the destruction to the European economy by the war," he said. The United States had understood the extent of the physical damage, but it hadn't appreciated the far-reaching effects of dislocation, the nationalization of industry, and the demise of commercial firms. "Europe is steadily deteriorating," Clayton warned. "The political position reflects the economic. One political crisis after another merely denotes the existence of grave economic distress. Millions of people in the cities are slowly starving."[26]

Before the war Europe had been self-sufficient in coal, it had imported little food from abroad, and far-flung merchant fleets had brought in the goods the continent did need. But with the coal mines empty and farmers broke, with factories quiet and ports in disarray, Europe was forced to import vast quantities of goods from the United States and to pay high rates for U.S. ships to bring those goods across the Atlantic. To stop Europe from going broke and allow it a chance to stagger back to its feet, the United States had to provide assistance.

And it had to do so without delay. In his memorandum Clayton ridiculed suggestions that the government should set up a commission to study ways to help Europe. The time for study was long past, he said. The time for action had come. "The problem is to organize our fiscal policy and our own consumption so that sufficient surpluses of the necessary goods are made available out of enormous production, and so that these surpluses are paid out of taxation and not by addition to debt," Clayton wrote. The idea was not radical. Instead of driving the European nations to bankruptcy by forcing them to spend their dwindling national treasure on imported American goods, the United States would simply give Europe those goods.[27]

In the short term the program would be expensive. Clayton estimated that the U.S. government would have to give Europe about $6 or $7 billion worth of goods over three years. American taxpayers would bear the burden of this generosity. In the long term, however, the aid would pay for itself many times over. If Europe prospered, America would prosper. But if it starved and sank into chaos, America could face another depression.

In March 1947 President Truman had asked Congress to approve assistance for Greece and Turkey. Couched in biting cold war language, his request had provoked a hostile reaction from the Soviet Union and had drawn criticism from Americans who thought he was needlessly forcing a confrontation. Nitze and other policy makers working on the European aid program wanted to avoid this mistake. Not only did cold war rhetoric heighten tensions, it warped American policy by misstating the problem facing Europe. In late May George Kennan, now heading the newly created Policy Planning Staff at the State Department, wrote that U.S. aid to Europe "should be directed not to the combatting of communism as such but to the restoration of the economic health and vigor of European society."[28]

With a consensus solidified in the administration, a decision was made in late May to press for a massive aid program for Europe. Charles ("Chip") Bohlen, Nitze's old clubmate at Harvard and now a State Department official, was given the task of writing a speech to be delivered by Secretary of State George Marshall at the Harvard graduation in June. The speech reflected Kennan's emphasis on the nonideological rationale for aiding Europe. "Our policy is directed not against any country or doctrine but against hunger, poverty, desperation and chaos," Marshall said.[29] In the weeks and months following the speech, U.S. officials offered to allow the Soviets and their eastern European allies to join the program. It was a shrewd gamble. Had Moscow joined, there would have been no chance of pushing the Marshall Plan through Congress. Blatantly excluding the Soviets, however, would have worsened tensions in Europe. U.S. officials counted on the Soviet Union's xenophobia to insure that it would turn down the offer. They were right; the Kremlin declined.

To Washington's policy makers, the Marshall Plan embodied all that was good and noble about American foreign policy. But to Josef Stalin and the men in the Kremlin, it was another declaration of Cold War, a hostile bid to transform western Europe into a cluster of American satellite states.

Among Paul Nitze and his colleagues at the State Department's Office of International Trade Policy, Marshall's speech generated enormous excitement. After watching Europe sink slowly into an abyss, it was a relief to hear a call for action. Yet there was also confusion. "The 'Marshall Plan' has been compared to a flying saucer," wrote one official at the office. "Nobody knows what it looks like, how big it is, in what direction it is moving, or whether it really exists. Nevertheless, all of us here must cope with this mysterious phenomenon."[30]

The European response to Marshall's speech took the State Department by surprise. Throughout the summer of 1947 European officials flocked to Washington to spell out their needs. Working to synthesize the European requests with American ideas about how aid should be distributed, Nitze began to spend all his time, working late night after night, on the Marshall Plan. As he pored over data about crops and fertilizers and coal and factory output in the sixteen nations designated for aid, Nitze rapidly became one of the government's leading experts on the economy of Europe. And as the Marshall Plan took shape, an increasing share of the government's organizational work for it fell into Nitze's hands. Working with a small group of economists, Nitze placed Clayton's economic division at the forefront of the assistance effort. The people in the division were "a particularly creative group," recalled Lucius Battle, who worked on Canadian affairs. "They were really, I thought, the most creative down-the-line brains in the department at that time. I thought what came out of the economic bureau had more snap to it than most of the other bureaus."

Nitze became Clayton's special assistant in August and was now more visible as he helped set the tone of the economic bureau's work.

"He had brains and he was fairly aggressive," remembered Battle. "He was regarded as a rather intellectual elite even then." He was noticed by Clark Clifford, the suave and influential assistant to President Truman who was working on public relations for the Marshall Plan. "I got to know him and came rather early in our relationship to have a very real respect for his dedication, knowledge and contribution that he was making to the government."

So impressive was Nitze's work on the Marshall Plan that when a conference was held in Paris to hammer out a comprehensive aid program, Clayton asked him to brief America's key ambassadors on the most recent thinking in Washington.[31] "I don't remember anything I've worked on that has given me more pleasure," Nitze said forty years later. "Organizations were expanding from nothing, and someone would pick you up by the neck and put you in the job."[32] To provide a central meeting ground and place to work for the European representatives and U.S. experts who would be coming to Washington to work on the project, Nitze rented a Connecticut Avenue office building and filled it with rental furniture and telephones. He then persuaded Paul Hoffman, president of Studebaker, to run the Marshall Plan's Washington operation.

By early fall the long days and nights of work were beginning to produce results. In June the Marshall Plan had been nothing more than a few paragraphs in a commencement speech. By the time the heat began to lift from Washington in September, hundreds of officials from a half dozen agencies were working on the program and a new bureaucracy was taking shape.

Without question, the most daunting part of the enterprise was extracting the needed funds from the Republican-controlled Congress. Spearheading the effort for the State Department was Under Secretary of State Robert Lovett. Once again, however, the burden of working out the details fell to the economic division. Clayton put Nitze in charge of the job. Preparing the aid requests for Congress was a massive project. Before skeptical and stingy Republican committee chiefs, the administration had to justify an aid program extending over several years and totaling more than $10 billion. Every request for every country had to be explained in detail. To do the math, Nitze borrowed all the calculating machines of the Prudential Life Insurance Company in Newark. Driving himself relentlessly through the fall of 1947 and into 1948, Nitze produced a series of "brown books" that documented the balance of payments deficit of all sixteen nations and gave a precise statement of the assistance needed by each country.

It was an impressive accomplishment, and when hearings on the aid began in front of the House Committee on Appropriations, Nitze confidently presented the brown books to John Taber, the committee's chairman. Before becoming a congressman, Taber had been a lawyer and farmer in upstate New York. He was not impressed with the product of Nitze's labor.[33]

At the first hearing Taber announced that he had seen the brown books and was not going to use them. Instead, he said that the committee would go country by country alphabetically and ask Nitze to justify every commodity that was to be shipped. Nitze was flabbergasted. The brown books were the only coherent summary of the administration's aid requests. Without them, one would be lost in a vast sea of numbers.

As Nitze remembered the episode, the discussion got as far as "P" in Austria, the first country. Taber demanded to know why the United States should send twenty-five thousand tons of pulse beans. Nitze asked whether he could call experts from the Agriculture Department.

No, he could not, Taber said. Nitze had to explain himself. After Nitze mumbled something about nutritional levels, Taber stood up. "This man knows nothing!" he said. Aid to Europe would have to be delayed until the State Department got organized, Taber announced before stalking from the room.

Nitze was stunned. The story of how bold ideas are killed by stubborn committee chairmen was an old one in Washington. Could this be the fate of the plan to rescue western Europe? It was not at all unimaginable after Taber's tirade.

Then something strange happened. A half hour after leaving the room, Taber returned. He calmly told Nitze that when the hearings resumed the next morning, he could call other experts to bolster his testimony.

Afterward Nitze went to Bob Lovett and asked him why Taber had turned around. Lovett explained that he had been studying Taber's character, and when the congressman called him in a rage, Lovett knew that the best thing to do was just let Taber blow off steam. For fifteen minutes Taber fulminated about State Department incompetence and Paul Nitze's ignorance. When he was finished, Lovett, an old Pentagon hand, asked Taber how many rivets were in the wing of a B-29. Taber replied that he obviously wasn't an expert on aircraft. "That's just the point," Lovett said. "Now, why don't you let Nitze call those experts." Taber relented.[34]

Over the next months Nitze testified before Congress several dozen times. Before the ordeal was over, Nitze, already a lean man, had lost

15 pounds. With the help of a war scare generated by a communist-backed coup in Czechoslovakia, the Marshall Plan was approved by Congress and aid began flowing to Europe by the end of 1948.

Will Clayton was not at the State Department to celebrate the victory. Through September, as the battle in Congress heated up, Nitze had heard rumors that Clayton might leave government and return to Texas because of an illness in the family. Still, Nitze was stunned when Clayton called him into his office one day in October and announced that he was leaving the department. "When I get back to Houston they'll give me a great big office and give me respect," said Clayton sadly, "but there won't be a thing for me to do." Nitze walked out of his boss's office with tears in his eyes. A few days later Clayton cleaned out his desk and left town.

The excitement and triumph of working on the Marshall Plan solidi-fied Paul Nitze's commitment to a life in government. Two decades earlier he had set out from Harvard to have an impact on the world, to make things happen. Helping to organize a massive aid program for Europe against great odds was a dramatic confirmation that an individ-ual could make a difference. Along with a small elite in the U.S. government, Paul Nitze had a hand in altering the course of history. More than anything, he wanted to continue this involvement.

In the foreign policy establishment of the late 1940s, one of the most intense centers of activity was the State Department's Policy Planning Staff. Late in the spring of 1947 George Marshall had summoned George Kennan to his office and asked him to put together a staff devoted to long-range foreign policy problems, particularly the situa-tion in Europe. Marshall had only one piece of advice: "Avoid trivia."[35]

In his search for staff members, Kennan wanted a deputy who knew economics. He asked Nitze to take the job. Nitze was open to the suggestion, but Kennan's plan was quashed when he asked for the approval of Dean Acheson, the under secretary of state. Acheson said that he knew Paul Nitze and he was not the kind of deep thinker that Kennan wanted. Nitze was a practical operator, Acheson said, and that wasn't what the Policy Planning Staff needed. It ought to be thinking about broad policy, not concrete operations.

Following his impressive work on the Marshall Plan, Nitze's reputa-tion in the State Department grew. When Acheson was made secretary of state in early 1949, he began to reassess the value of the man he had dismissed as a Wall Street operator. During an exhausting conference in Paris on the issue of currency in Germany and Austria, Acheson found Nitze's advice immensely valuable. He also liked the direct manner and crisp analysis of this practical operator.

Following the conference, Acheson asked Nitze to take the job of Kennan's deputy at the Policy Planning Staff. In August Nitze moved into his new office, only a few yards from Acheson's own. There, on the fifth floor of the State Department as the postwar empire of the United States came of age, Nitze would not only watch the exercise of power, he would wield it himself.

C H A P T E R 3

A Weapon
So Powerful

O
N SEPTEMBER 3, 1949, a B-29 flying a routine reconnaissance
mission over the north Pacific detected high levels of radioactivity
in the air east of the Kamchatka peninsula in Soviet Russia near the
Bering Sea. Around the same time a scientist working for the navy
discovered telltale signs of fission products in rainwater samples taken
from ships in the Pacific. The air force hurriedly assembled a panel of
experts to evaluate the findings. After intensive study they concluded
on September 19 that the phenomena "are consistent with the view
that the origin of the fission products was the explosion of an atomic
bomb whose nuclear composition was similar to the Alamogordo
bomb."[1]

The Soviet Union had detonated its first atomic weapon.

At the State Department, George Kennan called top members of
the Policy Planning Staff into his office and told them that the government had "learned of an atomic explosion in Russia." Truman would
soon announce the news, he said, and the staff was to start work on
questions that might be asked when the news became public.[2]

On the morning of September 23 President Truman told the nation of the Soviet explosion. Anticipating that Americans would be stunned by Russia's leap into the atomic age and knowing also that there would be accusations and recriminations, Truman tried to play down the event. "Ever since atomic energy was first released by man the eventual development of this force by other nations was to be expected," he said. Privately the President, like most Americans, had thought that "eventual" meant years, many years. Still, he assured the nation that "This problem has always been taken into account by us."[3]

In a statement issued from New York where he was visiting the United Nations, Secretary of State Dean Acheson reiterated the president's soothing theme of inevitability, saying "we have been fully aware that sooner or later this development would occur."[4]

But like the president, Acheson had thought it would be later rather than sooner. The common wisdom among many in the United States—high government officials included—was that the Soviets did not have the technological prowess to develop an atomic bomb before the early 1950s. It was believed that Stalin's Russia was too backward, too much of a peasant land, and not yet recovered from the wartime damage to its industrial base. While the U.S. government might have "taken into account" the possibility of a Soviet atomic capability, it was only in the most general sense. At the State Department, for example, little or no substantive work had been done to prepare for the eventuality. "We hadn't been that foresighted," recalled Gordon Arneson, Acheson's special assistant for atomic affairs.

Still new to the Policy Planning Staff, Paul Nitze was not in a position to contribute much to the speculation that rippled through the government. He was not an expert on Soviet affairs who could prophesy how a Kremlin with atomic arms might behave. Nor was he a military expert who could say which way the new balance of power would tip or even whether there was a new balance of power. With the exception of his year and a half on the Strategic Bombing Survey, Nitze had spent most of his adult life thinking about money and resources. His three years as a State Department expert on U.S. foreign economic policy rarely placed him in contact with military or Soviet-related issues. He was interested in them, but he was not involved in decision making on such matters.

But if Nitze was not an expert on national security policy in the fall of 1949, he was, at the very least, a promising student of the subject. When Nitze first came on the staff, some of its members had been uneasy about his appointment. With a wide, generous face and large and expressive eyes, Nitze projected a friendly air. Had it not been for the streaks of white and gray in his full head of hair, he would have looked far younger than his age of 42. In this group of rumpled foreign service officers and career bureaucrats, Nitze stood out in his neatly tailored Wall Street suits and freshly starched shirts. Some staff members were aware of his work on the Marshall Plan, but others had never heard of him before. "He was not known to us," recalled John Paton Davies, an Asia expert who had joined the staff when it was founded and who assumed that Nitze was being groomed to replace Kennan. "We wanted to see what he was like."

It did not take long for Nitze to impress his new colleagues favorably. Intelligence and drive were valued above all else at the staff, and Nitze had both. "I thought he had a very clear mind," said Davies. "He was very serious and hardworking. He concentrated on the subject matter. He was, intellectually, very competent." Nitze might not have had any experience with some of the arcane strategic matters that so absorbed Kennan's small group of experts, but in the government of the late 1940s, when the national security bureaucracy was small and real expertise was rare, newcomers learned fast.

Nitze's first major assignment as Kennan's deputy was as liaison with the Pentagon on military preparedness. It was not the choicest job, but it was unusually edifying. In long talks with military officials—men who recited statistics and assessments of all kinds, the sort of concrete material that an economist's mind could consume and retain—Nitze rapidly acquainted himself with the military issues of the day. In the opinion of John Kenneth Galbraith, who had watched his eager colleague become captivated with the work of the Strategic Bombing Survey, this adaptability stemmed from the fact that Nitze was a "Teutonic martinet happiest in a military hierarchy."[5]

Perhaps more accurately, Nitze was a financier happiest in an environment that, at least in some respects, resembled an investment firm with its heavy emphasis on quantifying problems. In Germany and Japan Nitze had assessed the destruction wrought by strategic bombing through the compilation of mountains of data. In working on the Marshall Plan, he had sought to break down the economic needs of Europe by producing little books that showed the balance of payments deficit in each country. The work on military preparedness was more of the same: comparing statistics, estimating costs, and making recommendations based on the concrete reality of numbers.

Far different, and decidedly less familiar, were the issues that arose in the wake of the explosion of the Soviet A-bomb. No amount of statistics or graphs could lead to the answers to the difficult questions now being asked about Soviet intentions and the psychological impact of their new atomic capability on world affairs. Like so many others in the government who lacked Soviet expertise, Nitze was not equipped to cope with these questions.

A week after President Truman made his announcement, Nitze received a report that represented the State Department's first attempt to make sense of the Soviet explosion. Prepared by the Estimates Group, Office of Intelligence Research, the report concluded that "There is no immediate change in the military capabilities of the USSR. Although the Soviet Union has revealed its ability to produce an atomic weapon, it is still behind the U.S. in this production." United States nuclear superiority was not threatened nor was the overall security of the west jeopardized, the report stressed. "Soviet military capabilities of overrunning Western Europe and the Near and Middle East have not increased, neither have its immediate capabilities of prosecuting a war successfully against the U.S."

As for the psychological component of the Cold War, the report stated that the Soviet A-bomb explosion had not dealt any kind of crushing blow to the morale of noncommunist peoples: "In western-oriented countries, there will be no important weakening in resistance to the USSR. In some, in fact, the resistance potential may be strengthened by acceleration of moves towards common defense."[6]

Not everyone in the government or even the State Department agreed with the Office of Estimates. Many officials, especially in the Pentagon, were panicked by the Soviet A-bomb explosion. To them, it heralded the beginning of a new and dangerous age, an age of insecurity unlike any the United States had ever known. And in this new age, with the great oceans no longer providing a buffer from foreign aggression, many felt that America's own atomic weapons program, a program already producing about four new bombs a week, had to be accelerated.[7]

Like his counterparts in the Pentagon, Paul Nitze was deeply alarmed by the explosion. His immediate reaction was to link Soviet possession of the A-bomb to the possibility of Soviet aggression in western Europe. And unlike the Office of Estimates, Nitze concluded that a Soviet Union armed with atomic weapons would have a greater capability for overrunning western Europe. Lacking the seasoned judgment of a strategy specialist or the intuition of a long-time diplomat,

Nitze came to this disturbing conclusion essentially by quantifying the problem. In August he had traveled to Europe with a Pentagon group at the invitation of British military planners. The British were examining the problem of defending western Europe against a Soviet invasion and the results of their studies were grim. "It was apparent that the planners faced a real problem," Nitze said later. "They estimated that the cost of the military equipment for a force strong enough to hold at the Rhine was $45 billion. . . . That was triple the cost of the entire Marshall Plan."

And the Marshall Plan had barely survived attacks by a stingy Congress. What were the chances of winning approval for spending requests that were far greater? "It was my view," Nitze recalled, "that the maximum we could support and have any hope of getting through Congress was $1 billion a year."[8] But even that figure was viewed as politically difficult. It was clear that the money was simply not there for any kind of major military buildup. To deal with the problem more realistically, Acheson later wrote, Nitze recommended "reversing the process and working backward from attainable figures to an appraisal of the military results they would produce." The modest goal that Nitze proposed to Acheson was the deployment of a force in Europe that would "preclude a quick victory by sudden marches backed up by an American capability for punishing blows against an aggressor's homeland."[9]

Now, with Soviet acquisition of an A-bomb, Nitze saw this modest goal as dangerously inadequate. Punishing blows against the Soviet Union could be administered only by American bombers carrying atomic weapons. But if the Soviets had their own atomic weapons, wouldn't they be able to deliver retaliatory blows? And if that were the case, wouldn't the United States be forced to abstain from atomic weapons use lest such a move bring Soviet bombs raining down on American or western European cities? And if such restraint were necessary for survival, wouldn't the west's paltry conventional forces, in the final analysis, be the only thing stopping the Soviets from conquering western Europe?

At a meeting of the Policy Planning Staff on October 11, Nitze voiced these concerns. The Soviet atomic capability, he said, "might make conventional armaments and their possession by the western European nations, as well as ourselves, all the more important." Obtaining these forces would mean making sacrifices. Since the price tag for building adequate conventional forces was over $35 billion, Nitze said, "it might be necessary . . . to lower rather than to raise civilian standards of living in order to produce arms as against consumer goods."

But such a buildup—if it could be funded at all—would take time, and in the interim the United States would have to rely on atomic weapons to deter a Soviet attack. To make this deterrence credible, to convince the Soviet Union that it was dead serious, the United States had to make clear its intention to use the A-bomb, even in the face of possible retaliatory blows. Nitze thought that building an "effective civilian defense in this country" would be a good first step toward enhanced credibility.[10] Acheson agreed. The Soviets had to believe that the United States would respond to conventional aggression with atomic attacks, he said.

George Kennan was not so sure. After two decades of studying Soviet behavior, he did not believe that the Kremlin had any plans to launch a blitzkrieg against western Europe. Historically, Russia had been the victim rather than the initiator of bold acts of aggression, a country more concerned with securing its borders than extending them. Under the Bolsheviks this defensive mentality had, if anything, grown more pronounced. Despite early rhetoric about fomenting revolution worldwide, the Soviet government's primary concern had always been safeguarding its own internal power. Invading western Europe would jeopardize Soviet security and Bolshevik power by engaging the Soviet Union in a protracted struggle with the United States, a nation armed with atomic weapons and possessing the greatest industrial base in the world. Such a prospect, Kennan knew, was wholly unappealing to Stalin and his lieutenants. As a consequence, Kennan was not concerned about Soviet conventional capabilities in Europe or with the credibility of America's atomic deterrent. Why grow obsessed with deterring an attack that would never come?

But what Kennan did worry about were the dangers of an atomic competition between the superpowers, a race that could assume its own momentum and produce perils unrelated to the political conflict that spawned it. At the top of the U.S. foreign policy agenda, Kennan believed, should be a bold effort to stop this race before it began. In a comment that must have shocked the high officials gathered that day in the State Department, Kennan suggested "there might be some advantage in . . . agreeing with the Russians that neither of us would use it [the bomb] at all."[11] Thirty years before the idea would enter the political mainstream, the director of the Policy Planning Staff was suggesting that the United States pledge never to be the first nation to use nuclear weapons.

* * *

In some ways George Frost Kennan was an unlikely candidate to mount a fundamental challenge to the prevailing notion that the United States should be ready to obliterate Russia if its tanks rolled into western Europe.

Kennan was born in 1904, the only son of a Milwaukee couple. His mother died shortly after his birth, and his father, a quiet and reserved man, was not very attentive. Kennan was raised mostly by his three older sisters and his childhood was not a pleasant one. Shy and insecure for most of his life, he was a timid and aloof boy who shared little of his schoolmates' enthusiasm for rambunctiousness. Sent to St. John's Military Academy for secondary school, he was picked on and accused of being a sissy.

If the discipline and loneliness of the academy was unpleasant, Princeton University, Kennan's choice for college, was not much better. Inspired, as he later wrote, by "the excitement and sense of revelation derived from reading Scott Fitzgerald's *This Side of Paradise*," Kennan had high expectations of Princeton. But for him, Princeton would not be the dazzling place it had been for Fitzgerald. "I was hopelessly and crudely Midwestern," he later wrote. "I had no idea how to approach boys from the East. I could never find the casual tone. My behavior knew only two moods: awkward aloofness and bubbling enthusiasm. I was afflicted from the start, furthermore, by a quality that has pursued me all of my life: namely, of being slowest and last to learn the ropes in any complicated organizational structure."[12] After four lonely years in which Kennan was, in his own words, "an oddball on campus, not eccentric, not ridiculed or disliked, just imperfectly visible to the naked eye," he joined the foreign service.

Early in his career Kennan focused on the Soviet Union. In 1928 he began training as a Russian specialist. By 1931 he had secured a position with the Russian section of the American legation in Riga, Latvia. In describing his time there, Kennan wrote that his job "involved no operation duties, no active responsibility. No one, in particular, could have been further than I was from the making of policy."[13]

Despite all of its outward insignificance, Kennan's stint in Riga was an important turning point in his life. Before Riga, his feeling toward the Soviet Union had been one of vague yet certain hostility. After two years in the chilly city, barely a hundred miles from the Soviet border, that feeling hardened into an intense anti-Sovietism. "The present system of Soviet Russia is unalterably opposed to our traditional system," he wrote a friend in 1931, ". . . there can be no possible middle ground or compromise between the two."[14]

Kennan's growing Soviet expertise landed him a job in the Moscow embassy when the United States established diplomatic relations with the Soviet Union in 1933. William Bullitt, Nitze's old dinner guest, became the first U.S. ambassador. During on and off postings at the embassy over the next decade, Kennan's attitude toward the Soviet Union became more antagonistic. By 1946 he was one of the leading skeptics about close postwar ties with the Soviet Union.

In February of 1946 Kennan sent from Moscow to Washington an eight-thousand-word telegram. Later known as the Long Telegram, the document delved into the question of Soviet intentions and concluded that "World Communism is like a malignant parasite which feeds only on diseased tissue" and which had to be opposed by a sustained western effort to check or contain Soviet expansion.[15]

The Long Telegram was sent to the right place at the right time. In 1946 Washington was a city on the verge of cold war. "Six months earlier," wrote Kennan, "this message would probably have been received in the Department of State with raised eyebrows and lips pursed in disapproval. Six months later, it would probably would have sounded redundant, a sort of preaching to the convinced."[16] As it was, the Long Telegram helped galvanize an emerging consensus and was accepted as gospel by many top government officials, including, most fervently, Navy Secretary James Forrestal, who sent a copy to everyone he knew.

Kennan now became a man with a status rare even in Washington, that of prophet. He enjoyed the sort of meteoric rise that often accompanies the timely articulation of fashionable views. He returned from Moscow a celebrity. Aloof and a bit stiff, Kennan was barely more charismatic than he had been during his school days, but in conversation he was intense and compelling. His eyes alternately darting from the listener to some far point in space, Kennan spoke with the same grace and fluidity with which he wrote. Because of his uniquely incisive analyses of the Soviet Union and world events, Secretary of State Marshall found Kennan fascinating and, in time, indispensable.[17] Within a year of its birth in May 1947, the Policy Planning Staff had become one of the most influential groups in the national security establishment. Kennan worked as a close advisor to Marshall and Truman and drafted sweeping statements of policy that were embraced at the highest levels of government.

Yet somewhere along the road to the top, George Kennan began to stray. A brilliant man with a subtle and discriminating intellect, Kennan soon found himself deeply disturbed by the simplistic thinking that came to dominate U.S. policy toward the Soviet Union. He worried that he had created a monster, a hysterical anti-Sovietism that was blind to the complexities and nuances of Kremlin decision making and that, in its shallow and alarmist analyses, distorted Soviet intentions beyond recognition. Containment became something Kennan had never wanted it to be. He had envisioned a political and economic effort to strengthen the west, to purge its dead tissue so that the communist parasite would have nothing to feed on. But Washington policy makers understood containment differently. Transfixed in horror by Pentagon scenarios for a Soviet all-out attack and limited lightning thrusts, many officials were soon clamoring for a huge military buildup to prepare for Soviet aggression. To some extent, Kennan went along with these calls, but he was anguished by the crude and inaccurate thinking that underlay them.

As he explained later, Kennan had wanted the west only to "cease at that point making fatuous unilateral concessions to the Kremlin, to do what we could to inspire and support resistance elsewhere to its efforts to expand the area of its dominant political influence, and to wait for the internal weaknesses of Soviet power, combined with frustration in the external field, to moderate Soviet ambitions and behavior." Kennan wanted the west to stand up to the Soviets "manfully but not aggressively and to give the hand of time a chance to work."[18]

With the 1948 Soviet-inspired coup in Czechoslovakia, the war scare that ensued, and the 1949 Russian blockade of Berlin, U.S. policy makers lost their patience. The military component of containment was increasingly emphasized, and as Kennan disagreed more frequently with the direction of U.S. policy, his influence began to dwindle.

Dean Acheson's rise to the post of secretary of state in early 1949 sealed Kennan's fate. "My Foreign Service experience was not only strange to him but was in his eyes, I suspect, of dubious value as a preparation for statesmanship or anything else," Kennan wrote later.[19] Lucius Battle, Acheson's special assistant, watched the relationship between the two men deteriorate. "They admired each other enormously but there was just not a meshing either of goals or of thought processes." Differences in personality also alienated the secretary of state from his planning chief. "George Kennan had a sense of being the philosopher king," recalled Dorothy Fosdick, a staff member who was close to him. "He felt he had special insights . . . he felt he should make policy." That sort of lofty arrogance didn't work in Acheson's State Department. "It was impossible for Acheson to deal with Kennan toward the end," said Fosdick. "You couldn't help feeling sorry for Dean."

In September 1949 Acheson and Under Secretary James Webb moved to undercut Kennan's influence by instituting new guidelines for how Policy Planning Staff papers were to be handled. Instead of going directly to the secretary of state, staff papers would be subject to the veto of any of the chiefs of the operational division in the department. Kennan was appalled. "The whole raison d'etre of this staff," he wrote in his diary, "was its ability to render an independent judgment on problems coming before the Secretary or Under Secretary."[20] If the staff was no longer to be trusted to give that kind of advice, Kennan questioned whether it should exist at all. On September 29 he told Webb that he wanted to leave the department at the end of the year. By November Acheson had decided that Paul Nitze would take Kennan's place.

Free from the burden of currying favor, Kennan could now promote his heretical dogma. He knew it was unlikely that anyone would pay much attention to his efforts, but he hoped his ideas would at least make people stop and think. Following the Soviet A-bomb explosion, Kennan began spending most of his time writing a lengthy paper calling for a renewed effort to control atomic weapons. It was a project that would occupy him for the next three and a half months. The result, he later said, was "one of the most important, if not the most important of all the documents I ever wrote in government."[21]

Even as Kennan wrote this paper, however, Nitze moved deftly to cut his superior loose from the inner circle at State. With Kennan spending more time writing in a little office he kept at the Library of Congress, his deputy aggressively sought the ear of the secretary of state. In the battle that was now beginning at the State Department over the future of America's nuclear weapons policy and, indeed, its entire national security policy, Kennan would find Paul Nitze to be his single greatest foe. And while the meditative diplomat would wage his campaign with an elegant pen and the force of his Soviet expertise, Nitze, the former Wall Street operator and wartime administrator, would rely largely on his growing skills as a master bureaucrat.

The first round in the debate over how the United States should respond to the Soviet bomb came in mid October when the Policy Planning Staff began a reassessment of the prospects for the international control of atomic energy. It was, explained Kennan at the first meeting, to be a far-reaching undertaking that "would of course examine the military implications of the atomic explosion in Russia."[22] The reassessment would be Nitze's first major exposure to the problems of controlling atomic weapons.

In summoning top strategic experts to brief the Policy Planning Staff, Kennan may have thought that he could help jolt the government into sober thinking about atomic weapons. He may have hoped that once the dangers of an unrestrained arms race and the folly of relying on atomic weapons were made clear, U.S. officials would move boldly in the realm of disarmament. He was wrong.

The tone of the reassessment was established early on by the first experts who met with the staff. Three strategic specialists from the Pentagon told the group that the threat to use nuclear weapons was essential for the defense of western Europe. Ridiculing Kennan's idea of a no-first-use agreement, the men expressed little doubt that "Russia would use the atomic bomb in war if she found that it would be desirable and effective."[23] Controlling atomic weapons was out of the question for the moment, they said. Instead, a program for civilian defense should be initiated immediately.

The next experts ushered into the Policy Planning Staff's office were from the Atomic Energy Commission (AEC). Their concern was with the mechanics of a possible disarmament agreement. "As the nature of the Russian police state is not likely soon to change," they argued, "there seems little possibility that the Russians will accept the majority U.N. plan for the international control of atomic energy." The AEC officials also recommended that the United States "should inaugurate a program for civilian defense."[24]

And so it went. The reassessment involved eight briefings held over two and a half weeks. Each expert had essentially the same message: Even if it was desirable, which was questionable given the military situation in Europe, the international control of atomic energy would be impossible because of the closed nature of the Soviet state. The prevailing attitude toward disarmament was summed up at the final meeting by Vannevar Bush, president of the Carnegie Institution. No United Nations plan for international control was likely to succeed anytime soon, he said. In any case, "We cannot maintain national security without the atomic bomb in view of Russia's marked superiority in conventional armaments."[25]

The chances for progress toward disarmament, the experts agreed, were slim to nonexistent.

Ignorant about controlling atomic weapons before the reassessment, Paul Nitze now knew all that he needed to know. Again and again over the coming months he would repeat the arguments that had been voiced during the reassessment. Only a few months into his education on strategic affairs, he became a confirmed and hard-line skeptic of arms control. He would remain one for over a decade.

The critical question of whether to press anew for the control of atomic weapons was only one part of a wider debate triggered by the explosion in Siberia. The more contentious issue that now arose was whether the United States should try to offset the Soviet move by building a thermonuclear weapon, known as the hydrogen bomb, or the super. By late October 1949 the battle lines were already being drawn for what would be one of the most impassioned national security debates of the postwar era.

On the gray and wet Saturday morning of October 29, the General Advisory Committee of the Atomic Energy Commission met in Washington to begin deliberations on the H-bomb. The GAC included some of the most distinguished physicists in the nation: Robert Oppenheimer, Enrico Fermi, and Isador Rabi were among its members. It was also a group that included many tortured souls, men who in Oppenheimer's words "had known sin" for their participation in the Manhattan Project.

Gathering at the AEC's headquarters on Constitution Avenue, the group engaged in two days of emotionally charged debate. By Sunday they reached the unanimous conclusion that the United States should not develop thermonuclear weapons. In a report issued October 30, the GAC emphasized that at stake in the H-bomb debate was the very future of humanity. In their view that future would be uncertain if the United States introduced a weapon "whose energy release is 100 to 1000 times greater and whose destructive power in terms of area of damage is 20 to 100 times greater than those of the present atomic bomb."[26]

In language almost unknown to the bureaucratic world, the GAC pleaded against building a bomb "that might become a weapon of genocide." Rejecting the contention that the H-bomb was an inescapable response to Soviet possession of the A-bomb, they argued that the "extreme dangers to mankind inherent in the proposal wholly outweigh any military advantage that could come from this development." Oppenheimer and his colleagues argued further that the United States should not be stampeded into a crash program to build the H-bomb simply on the chance that the Soviets might take this step. It is, they wrote, "by no means certain that the Russians will produce" an H-bomb. And even if the Soviets did build such a weapon, it would be of little significance, the GAC said. For should the Soviets "use the weapon against us, reprisals by our large stock of atomic bombs would be comparably effective to the use of the super."[27]

To members of the GAC—men who had spent years working for advances in the realm of atomic energy—backing away from one of the great physics problems of the day must not have been easy. But that is precisely what they did. The H-bomb, they said, should never be built.

Dean Acheson received the GAC's report with a mixture of relief and bewilderment. Emotionally, he wasn't ready for the H-bomb. His instinctive reaction was to oppose development. He felt relief because the committee had made a vehement case against the bomb. Yet if the case was strongly worded, it was not, in Acheson's view, cogently argued. Soon after the report was released, he invited Oppenheimer to his office to elucidate the GAC's arguments. After a long session with the physicist, Acheson remained perplexed. "You know," he said to his assistant Gordon Arneson when Oppenheimer had left, "I listened as carefully as I knew how, but I don't understand what Oppie was trying to say. How can you persuade a paranoid adversary to disarm 'by example'?"[28]

Acheson could no better fathom Kennan's views on the matter. As he toiled away at his paper, alone and pensive, Kennan pondered the prospect of a world with thermonuclear weapons and grew increasingly repulsed by the idea. He believed that if anyone was going to introduce such an odious device it should be the Soviet Union. Let them bear the moral responsibility for this ugly and irreversible step toward human self-destruction; let Moscow, not Washington, face the opprobrium of the civilized world.

To Acheson, Kennan's thinking seemed divorced from reality. He found it so vague, so clouded, so absolutely irresponsible that, as he later recalled, "I told Kennan if that was his view he ought to resign from the Foreign Service and go out and preach his Quaker gospel but not push it in the Department."[29] Acheson could sympathize with Kennan's moral revulsion toward the H-bomb, but could not respect it. "Those who shared this view," he wrote in his memoirs, "were, I believed, not so much moved by the power of its logic . . . as by an immense distaste for what one of them, the purity of whose motives could not be doubted, described as the 'the whole rotten business.' "[30]

Yet while Acheson believed there was little room in the policy-making process for moral convictions—at least for the convictions of Kennan and Oppenheimer—he resisted the idea that immediate development of the thermonuclear weapon was necessary. At a November 3 meeting of the Policy Planning Staff, Acheson suggested a renewed effort to control atomic arms, and in the meantime, he said, "perhaps the best thing is an 18–24 month moratorium on the super-bomb— bilateral if possible, unilateral if necessary." During such a moratorium it might be possible to "come to an agreement with the Russians," and if that proved impossible, at least the United States would have done its best to avoid an H-bomb race.[31]

Compared to the secretary of state, Paul Nitze was far less intimidated by the scope and implications of the H-bomb debate. Nitze determined early in the debate that the problem was not a moral one to be solved through anguished philosophizing. The world of weaponry and ideology was a world of power politics, a harsh world in which idealism had no place and even a morally repugnant course of action was often the only course that made sense. He insisted that the H-bomb issue was best dealt with by rationally weighing the risks and identifying the options—as if it were nothing more than a complex Wall Street deal.

To Nitze, the greatest risk to be taken into account was that the Soviet Union would get the H-bomb first, and that possession of the weapon would grant them a huge psychological advantage in the Cold War and a military advantage should there be a hot war. He believed that this consideration should be central to the decision-making process. At the November 3 Policy Planning Staff meeting, Nitze remarked about the H-bomb that "the burden of proof should fall on those who say that there would be no power advantage to the country developing it." In his mind evidence was already accumulating that the H-bomb would bestow such an advantage, but the precise nature of this edge remained unclear. To his colleagues at the Policy Planning Staff that day, Nitze said that "further study obviously is called for on the answers to the Secretary's question as to whether we would really be at a disadvantage if they developed it and we did not and why."[32]

In the meantime, there was the more immediate question of feasibility. Ultimately, feasibility was the most critical issue in the entire debate. If there was no more than a slim chance of building an H-bomb, a major effort to do so would be a waste of resources and political capital. But to the policy makers at the State Department, the question of feasibility was one of the most mystifying. Officials who hadn't studied physics since college, if they had studied it at all, were hardly qualified to make sense of the theoretical scientific debate about the construction of thermonuclear devices. David Lilienthal, the chairman of the AEC, had told Acheson that the chances of success "seemed about even."[33] But how reliable was that estimate? Nobody really knew.

Nitze was determined to find out. Having immersed himself in the technical aspects of atomic weaponry during the Strategic Bombing Survey, he felt at least some familiarity with the subject. Also, Nitze had come to see himself as a man adept at digesting and applying new information, a man who could lug home a briefcase full of specialized documents for a few nights and have the subject mastered by the end of the week. It was a judgment founded on experience. Over the last two decades Nitze had conquered the complexities of Wall Street, run several different wartime agencies, unraveled the mysteries of strategic bombing, and become an expert on the difficult subject of foreign economic policy. He was a man of considerable self-confidence—egotism even—who saw no reason why he couldn't understand the scientific aspects of the H-bomb debate.

One of Nitze's first steps in his investigation was to invite Robert Oppenheimer to the Policy Planning Staff. A tall and fragile man with deep-set, sensitive eyes, Oppenheimer had directed the Manhattan Project during World War II. It was a job that had won him accolades throughout the government. But following the obliteration of Hiroshima and Nagasaki, Oppenheimer had become increasingly anguished over his role in developing the atomic bomb. The atom had yielded enough ugliness for one century, he believed. Why harness it to produce an even deadlier weapon? With passion and eloquence Oppenheimer crusaded against the H-bomb.

Oppenheimer presented Nitze with an array of objections to the H-bomb: It was not technically feasible, it would consume more fissionable material than it was worth, and U.S. work on the weapon would accelerate Russian efforts in the area.[34] If they were sound, the scientist's arguments constituted a powerful case against going ahead with the H-bomb.

But was Oppenheimer right? When Nitze related Oppenheimer's thoughts to Robert LeBaron, one of his Pentagon contacts and an avid supporter of the bomb, LeBaron replied: "Talk to Dr. Teller."

Edward Teller, a brilliant physicist, had come to the United States from Hungary in 1935. He had worked with Oppenheimer on the Manhattan Project, and the two had remained friends following the war. Unlike Oppenheimer, Teller felt little guilt about his role in developing the A-bomb. Instead, he had been fascinated with the work, and even when the focus had been on making the fission atom bomb,

Teller had grown obsessed with the possibility of developing the far more powerful thermonuclear hydrogen bomb. After the war ended, that obsession had been repeatedly frustrated. There was neither official support nor government funds for such a project. When the Soviets exploded their A-bomb, Teller saw a new chance to press his thermonuclear agenda. Within days he was on the phone with Ernest Lawrence, Luis Alvarez, and other scientists, talking excitedly about a crash program on the super. Teller was convinced that the H-bomb was feasible, and in early October he set out to win converts to this view.

At Nitze's invitation, Teller visited the Policy Planning Staff office. For two hours he stood before the blackboard and tutored Nitze in his thick Hungarian accent on two possible methods of producing thermonuclear weapons. Nitze was impressed by the presentation. He was more than impressed; he was convinced.

"Ed Teller knew his subject so well that he was able to explain why this thing would work in just two hours time," Nitze said later. While Oppenheimer's technical doubts had seemed disjointed to Nitze, Teller had no question about feasibility and exuded total command of the scientific aspects of the problem. By the end of their meeting Nitze had become one of his converts. "After listening to Teller," Nitze said later, ". . . I was persuaded that there was substantial possibility that it was possible to make the process work."

As it later became clear, Edward Teller did not know what he was talking about. The methods that were used to build a H-bomb over the next three years bore little resemblance to the methods that Teller was promoting in 1949. Many of his colleagues regarded Teller's ideas on the super with skepticism; they were seen more as a product of excessive zeal than of careful research. "He wanted it to work and so he thought it would work," said Arneson.[35] Few in the scientific community were entirely convinced that a thermonuclear weapon could be built. But Paul Nitze believed him—believed him so absolutely that he dismissed other views. With little or no knowledge of physics, Nitze thought that he had followed Teller's calculations, and that those calculations proved the super's feasibility.

Having resolved the question of feasibility in his mind, Nitze turned next to one of Oppenheimer's other objections: that American work on the H-bomb would spur the Soviet program. On this issue he consulted Ernest Lawrence, another staunch advocate of the bomb. Lawrence claimed that it was possible for the Soviets to solve the H-bomb puzzle, that their progress in doing so had nothing to do with U.S. actions, and that they were probably working on it already. Once again, Nitze was convinced. If there was a good chance that a thermonuclear bomb could be built, the United States had to assume that the Soviets were trying to produce one.

The only lingering question now was whether the Soviets would actually want to develop such a weapon. To Nitze, there was little doubt about this. If the H-bomb could confer power on its possessor— and Nitze was almost certain that it would—then men who were disciples of power, like those in the Kremlin, were sure to pursue it. And if the H-bomb were pursued singlemindedly, with the same zeal, say, as collectivization, the Soviets could probably obtain it. As Nitze said later, "it was just question of time until the Russians would get" the H-bomb. He agreed that U.S. work on the bomb would speed Soviet efforts in the area, but felt that this was a risk the United States had to take; it was critical to stay a step ahead.[36] "What position would the world be in," Nitze later asked, "if the Russians had this weapon and we didn't even know what the process was or how to make such a device?" A bad position, indeed, he decided. Without question "they would have hegemony right away."[37] At stake, Nitze believed, was the "future political orientation of the world."

In resolving the questions of feasibility and Soviet intent, Nitze believed that he had arrived at a sound basis for supporting development of the bomb. But he had not rebutted a key argument made by the GAC scientists: the contention that, even if it were armed with a thermonuclear weapon, the Soviet Union would be adequately deterred by the United States's stock of less powerful but more numerous fission bombs. By 1949 the United States had some 250 A-bombs of equal or greater power than the weapon that had destroyed Hiroshima. With bomb production accelerating, that arsenal nearly doubled by 1950, and by 1952 the United States possessed about 1,000 fission bombs. Without the diversion of huge amounts of money and material to the H-bomb program, the U.S. A-bomb stockpile undoubtedly would have been even larger by 1952. In the face of such an arsenal—with its capacity to destroy every major city in the Soviet Union several times— it is unclear how Soviet possession of the hydrogen bomb would have guaranteed instant "hegemony."

In any case, Nitze's argument that the Soviets would have a monopoly on the hydrogen bomb was weak. If the Soviets developed it, the more technologically advanced United States would quickly follow suit. Any Soviet monopoly would last, at best, for only several years, during which time their thermonuclear capability would be offset by the

American arsenal of fission bombs. Nitze's picture of the H-bomb as a weapon that could fatally disrupt the balance of terror was simply not accurate.

For a man so concerned with comparing risks, Nitze appears to have given scant attention to the risks outlined by Oppenheimer and the GAC. They argued that the survival of humanity would be jeopardized if thermonuclear weapons existed. Every weapon made by human beings had been used in war. Why would the H-bomb be any different? And if predictions of the H-bomb's power were accurate, large arsenals of these weapons would have the capability to wipe out entire nations in an intentional or accidental war. Wasn't this risk greater than the risk of the Soviets' gaining a transitory psychological edge in the Cold War? Shouldn't there be an effort to work out a moratorium on the testing of such weapons?

Nitze didn't think so. The scientists on the GAC argued that a ban on testing thermonuclear weapons would effectively prevent the development of such devices and could be easily monitored. Acheson himself had once suggested the idea. But Nitze did not take the idea seriously and failed to investigate the details of a possible ban. He was irritated by the very tone of the scientists on the GAC. He found it shrilly emotional, morally patronizing, and detached from the dictates of reality. Dismissing the scientists almost entirely, Nitze argued that the critical issue, the issue of all-consuming importance, was the possibility of a Soviet monopoly on the H-bomb. The most immediate threat was not humanity's self-destructing, but the Kremlin's gaining a winning hand in the game of superpower rivalry.

By the end of November, Nitze had concluded that the "lesser risk was for us to go forward with the development of a thermonuclear weapon hoping that it wouldn't work."

Dean Acheson had a far more difficult time making up his mind. He liked to think of himself as a moral man, a man of peace. Along with David Lilienthal, he had helped draft the first U.N. plan for the international control of atomic energy. Acheson was uncomfortable with a unilateral move by the United States which would so clearly repudiate the spirit of the disarmament effort, however doomed that effort was. He was also uneasy about dismissing the voices of dissent. At times Acheson even found himself agreeing with them.[38]

In a memorandum of November 18 George Kennan asked a series of penetrating questions about thermonuclear weapons development: "Would the use of the super-bomb constitute a menace to civilization itself through the possibility that it would pollute the earth's atmosphere to a dangerous extent?

"Would our development of the super-bomb increase our military capacity as compared with increased production of atomic bombs?

"Should our decision on the question be determined by what Russia may or may not do with respect to developing the super-bomb?

"What would be the moral effect in the United States and throughout the world of our developing this weapon of mass destruction, the ingredients of which have no peaceful applications whatever?"[39]

Acheson was troubled by these kinds of questions. Unlike Nitze, he had difficulty navigating in the murky world where politics and morality overlapped. Nitze's compass was reductive logic; he simply dismissed the moral component of the hydrogen bomb debate. But as America's leading statesman, Acheson bore a heavier burden. The H-bomb, he wrote in memoirs, was opposed by "men of the highest standing in science, education, and government."[40]

How could the secretary of state ignore these people?

On November 19 the pressure on Acheson to make a decision mounted when Truman designated the secretary of state, the secretary of defense, and the chairman of the AEC "as a special committee of the National Security Council to advise me on this problem."[41] This three-man committee had worked together earlier in the year to make a recommendation to Truman on the pace of the U.S. nuclear weapons program. It had been an easy job followed by an easy decision (to step up production). But now the issue was more difficult and the committee was deeply divided. With David Lilienthal against the H-bomb and Defense Secretary Louis Johnson strongly for it, Acheson held the swing vote. His decision, quite possibly, would be the government's decision.

On November 28 Acheson appointed Paul Nitze to head the group that would represent him on the Working Group of the Special Committee.[42] The other State Department officials chosen were Gordon Arneson and Adrian Fisher, two advisors who had also decided that the United States should build the H-bomb. The Working Group had been set up because neither Acheson, Lilienthal, or Johnson had time to assess all the facts of the H-bomb debate. As a result, the truly important work on this weighty matter would be done not by the top officials Truman had designated, but by their trusted lieutenants.

In selecting Nitze, Arneson, and Fisher to take the lead on this issue, Acheson, whether he realized it or not, had taken a major step toward making the decision to support the H-bomb. Any new arguments, perspectives, or information that came before the Special Committee would be filtered through these H-bomb advocates. And because much of the work of the group would remain highly classified and limited to only these three men, there was little chance of dissenting views being voiced in the department. In principle, Acheson may have remained committed to an objective review of the hydrogen bomb issue. In practice, such a review could never take place.

On December 3 the secretary of state took a further step toward supporting the bomb. In a memo to Nitze, Arneson, and Fisher, Under Secretary Webb wrote "Secretary Acheson expressed the view that the working group and the NSC subcommittee probably should not direct its efforts toward the ultimate moral question at this time." Instead, Webb wrote, the Working Group should focus on specific questions arising from H-bomb development, issues such as government expenditures, military capabilities, and Soviet responses. While Webb did note that Acheson was "troubled about the possibility that a decision to go ahead would be interpreted all over the world as a decision that war is inevitable," he did not direct the group to look into the matter.[43]

This was a critical move. By eliminating from consideration one of the most compelling objections voiced by opponents of the H-bomb, Acheson was not only strengthening Nitze's hand—who didn't want to ponder moral questions in any case—but was also giving the Pentagon an advantage in the debate. The Defense Department would have little difficulty constructing sophisticated military rationales for the bomb, arguments that the State Department and the AEC would be hard pressed to rebut. If the debate were a technical one, the Pentagon would probably win.

On December 16 the Defense members of the Working Group fired their first salvo. In a memorandum given to Arneson, who in turn circulated it to Nitze and Fisher, they argued that "In time of war sole possession of the thermonuclear weapon coupled with tremendous superiority of conventional military forces would provide the Soviets with the necessary balance to current Western unity and to our superior fission weapons stockpile to enable them to risk hostilities for the rapid achievement of their objectives." If, however, only the United States had the weapon, there would be distinct benefits: "Possession of such weapon by the United States will provide an offensive weapon of the greatest known power possibilities, thereby adding flexibility to our planning and to our operations in the event of hostilities." The memorandum concluded, "There is an imperative necessity of determining the feasibility of a thermonuclear explosion and its characteristics. Such determination is essential for U.S. defense planning, preparations for retaliation, and direction of research."[44]

Neither the State Department nor the AEC prepared a paper rebutting this assessment.

In mid December Nitze began work on a memorandum that he hoped would solidify the State Department's position on thermonuclear weapons. Later in the month Dean Acheson would be meeting with Lilienthal and Johnson and he needed to be clear on where the State Department stood. He also needed to know where he stood himself, for Acheson had yet to make up his mind.

In drafting his memorandum Nitze had two overriding considerations: He wanted to allay Acheson's uneasiness about the H-bomb and to devise a compromise package that the secretary of state could sell to David Lilienthal. The result of this effort was short but ingenious.

Beginning with the assumption that there was a 50 percent chance that thermonuclear weapons were feasible, Nitze outlined what he saw as the central considerations in the debate:

1. That the most immediate risks facing the security of the free world and ultimately of the U.S. are in the ideological, economic, and political aspects of the Cold War;

2. That emphasis by the U.S. on the possible employment of weapons of mass destruction, in the event of a hot war, is detrimental to the position of the U.S. in the Cold War;

3. That, even though it is probable that the USSR would actually use weapons of mass destruction only in the event of prior use by others, it is essential that the U.S. not find itself in a position of technological inferiority in this field. . . .

The last consideration, in Nitze's mind, was the most pressing. The United States could not risk sole Soviet possession of the H-bomb. While it was true, Nitze wrote, that there was more to be feared from "a possible thermonuclear capability on the part of the USSR than is to be gained from the addition of a thermonuclear possibility to our growing stockpile of fission bombs," the United States still could not afford to delay research and development. Accordingly, Nitze made the following recommendations:

1. That the President authorize the A.E.C. to proceed with an accelerated program to test the possibility of a thermonuclear reaction;

2. That no decision be made at this time as to whether weapons employing such reaction will actually be built beyond the number required for a test of feasibility.

3. That the N.S.C. reexamine our aims and objectives in the light of the USSR's probable fission bomb capability and its possible thermonuclear bomb capability.[45]

Nitze was holding out the promise of a thoughtful look at where the United States was headed in the nuclear realm, and he hoped the last recommendation would win over Lilienthal. If all went well, this formula would break the bureaucratic stalemate.

In preparing for his December 22 meeting with the Special Committee (dubbed the Z Committee by Lilienthal), Dean Acheson dictated a long memorandum filled with talking points. Reading the memorandum over on the evening of December 20, shortly before leaving for Christmas vacation, Nitze found that his boss's thinking on nuclear weapons was still unsettled, even incoherent. The memorandum was a thoughtful, almost agonized, effort by Acheson to sort out the problem of nuclear weapons and national security. It was filled with sweeping questions about America's reliance on such weapons, the prospects for international control, and the dangers of Soviet aggression. Nitze was pleased that Acheson was pondering questions that went to the heart of the nuclear imbroglio, but for the most part the questions had no answers. Acheson hadn't dictated any. More troubling still, the memorandum did not directly address the H-bomb issue at all.[46]

The first meeting of the Special Committee was only two days away and the secretary of state had prepared no detailed position on the subject to be discussed. It appeared that Nitze's memo had had little or no impact on Acheson. He still had not made up his mind on the bomb.

Nitze's memo also failed to produce the early compromise he had hoped for among the members of the Z Committee. Instead of presenting Nitze's recommendations and trying to win Lilienthal over with the promised reexamination of national security policy, Acheson opened the meeting by saying that they were "not here to reach a decision, but to think together." His proposed discussion on basic strategic questions, however, did not get far. Almost immediately, Johnson and Lilienthal began arguing bitterly over what was at stake in the H-bomb decision. Johnson contended that the issue was a "very limited one," while Lilienthal insisted that the "purpose and course of mankind [was] wrapped up in this."[47] The session achieved nothing.[48]

So badly frayed were relations between Lilienthal and Johnson following the meeting that the Special Committee would convene only once again—just two hours before the final meeting with President Truman. Paul Nitze's compromise formula—and his key memorandum which outlined it—would receive scant attention.

As the H-bomb debate dragged into the new year, the extraordinary secrecy that had initially marked the proceedings began to break down. By mid January, the work of the Z Committee had not only become public knowledge, but was generating intense interest and partisan posturing. The H-bomb became a Washington obsession. Shrouded in uncertainty, the debate had the required elements for political intrigue: a powerful and futuristic weapon, a hulking enemy with unclear motives, and, juiciest of all, a steady stream of rumors about acrimonious bickering in a divided administration. On January 15 the Washington columnist Drew Pearson talked about the H-bomb debate during his Sunday evening radio broadcast. Two days later the *New York Times* ran a front page story on the issue.[49]

Pressure mounted on Truman to proceed with development. In November Senator Brien McMahon of Connecticut, chairman of the Joint Committee on Atomic Energy, had written the president an impassioned letter saying, "if we let Russia get the super first, catastrophe becomes all but certain—whereas, if we get it first, there exists a chance of saving ourselves."[50] In January the powerful senator renewed his lobbying. The Joint Chiefs of Staff also stepped up their efforts. Despite the understanding that deliberations on the H-bomb would be carried out solely through the Special Committee, Johnson transmitted to Truman a January 15 memorandum by Omar Bradley, chairman of the JCS, that strongly favored development. Rebutting the arguments made by the GAC scientists and others, Bradley wrote that "it is difficult to escape the conviction that in war it is folly to argue whether one weapon is more immoral than another. For, in the larger sense, it is war itself which is immoral, and the stigma of such immorality must rest upon the nation which initiates hostilities."[51]

The pressure on Truman produced results. As his biographer Robert

Donovan has written, the president made up his mind about the H-bomb at least ten days before the Z Committee came to him with their report.[52]

By mid January, Acheson, too, had made up his mind. In a January 19 telephone conversation with Admiral Sidney Souers, Truman's consultant on national security affairs, Acheson said that he "had about reached the position that we should advise the President to go ahead and find out about the feasibility of the matter."[53] It had not been an easy decision, but as Acheson later wrote, "I could not overcome two stubborn facts: that our delaying research would not delay Soviet research, contrary to an initial hope I had briefly entertained; and that the American people simply would not tolerate a policy of delaying nuclear research in so vital a matter while we sought for further ways of reaching accommodation with the Russians after the experiences of the years since the war."[54]

For George Kennan, the H-bomb debate climaxed too early. By the time his seventy-nine-page memorandum on the international control of atomic energy was released, it was clear where the discussion on thermonuclear weapons was leading. Long before the president made his final decision, Kennan said, "I knew that my labor had been, once again, in vain."[55]

That Kennan's paper failed to have an impact on the debate is not surprising. As he himself later noted, "The views put forward here conflicted with what was already established military policy. They conflicted with the ideas we had formed as to where the essentials of our own defense were to be found. They conflicted with the reaction of Congress, the military establishment, and the public to the news of the detonation by the Russians of an atomic weapon. . . . They conflicted, finally, with the growing tendency in Washington . . . to base our own plans and calculations solely on the capabilities of a potential adversary, assuming him to be desirous of doing anything he could do to bring injury to us, and to exclude from consideration, as something unsusceptible to exact determination, the whole question of that adversary's real intentions."[56]

What were these heresies that clashed so violently with the wisdom of the day? What was it that this thoughtful and anguished diplomat had written that was so far out of the mainstream? Essentially, Kennan argued that if the United States was truly serious about abolishing atomic weapons, it had to stop relying on such weapons as a primary defense against possible Soviet aggression. Kennan stated further, as he later summarized, "that before we decide to proceed with the development of the hydrogen bomb, thus committing ourselves and the world to an indefinite escalation of the destructiveness and expensiveness of atomic weapons, we reexamine once more, in the most serious and solemn way, the whole principle of the 'first use' of atomic weapons."[57] With all the force and eloquence he could muster, George Kennan provided a glimpse of the future, arguing that the United States had to stop the arms race before it began.

In his memoirs Kennan writes that he "cannot remember that this paper was ever seriously considered or discussed. Nor can I recall what was the reaction to it of the Secretary of State. If I had to make a guess, I should think it was probably one of bewilderment and pity for my naiveté."[58]

In fact, the reaction was that and more. There was an edge of contempt in the rebuttals to his paper that Kennan failed to recall. Even before the paper was officially circulated, the attacks on it began. Some officials "didn't want to offend Kennan," recalled Gordon Arneson. "I didn't mind offending him because he was nuts." On December 29 Arneson wrote that the "paper is based primarily on a fundamentally incorrect assumption; namely that it is possible to achieve prohibition of atomic weapons and international control of atomic energy that has any meaning, without a basic change in Soviet attitudes and intentions, and, in fact, in the Soviet system itself."[59] Two weeks later another State official, John Hickerson, wrote that "the better assumption would be that the only way to prevent the use of atomic weapons and other weapons of mass destruction is to prevent the outbreak of war between countries possessing such weapons."[60]

On January 17, with Acheson yet to see Kennan's paper, Nitze sent his own criticisms to the secretary. Nitze agreed with the argument that the United States would benefit from a policy of "no first use." He wrote that there were several considerations "in favor of a use policy based solely on retaliation in the event of prior use by an enemy. These include the deep abhorrence of many of the people of the United States to the use of weapons of mass destruction, the improvement in our public stance toward atomic energy throughout the world if we are able to adopt such a policy, and the greater possibility of achieving our political objectives during and at the conclusion of a war if it is possible to avoid the use of weapons of mass destruction during such a war." Nitze also sympathized with Kennan's argument that America's first-use policy was a somewhat belligerent stance, one that "may impede the establishment of those conditions under which a more general relaxation of tension between the U.S.S.R. and ourselves might be possible."

Yet while Nitze agreed with some of the points in Kennan's paper, even some of the most important points, he dismissed the paper's central argument that the United States should refrain from developing the H-bomb until it first sorted out its nuclear arms policy. "There are considerations which make it advisable to accelerate the program to determine the feasibility or non-feasibility of a thermonuclear weapon," Nitze wrote. Paramount among these, he again argued, was the Soviet Union. "It must be assumed that the U.S.S.R. is proceeding with a program in this field, and it would seem that the military and political advantages which would accrue to the U.S.S.R. if it possessed even a temporary monopoly of this weapon are so great as to make time of the essence."[61]

That Nitze didn't respond more aggressively to Kennan's paper is not surprising. The memorandum was not going to be classified as a Policy Planning Staff report as Kennan had originally intended. On the cover memo Kennan attached when he sent the paper to Acheson, he wrote: "Since Paul and the others were not entirely in agreement with the substance and since I was afraid that this report might be an embarrassing one to have on record as a formal Staff report, I have re-done this as a personal paper."[62]

A more thorough criticism of Kennan's paper was not worth Nitze's time. By mid January 1950 George Kennan and his views on the H-bomb were no longer relevant. Neither he nor his paper posed a challenge to Nitze's personal influence or the influence of the ideas he championed. Not only had Kennan ceased to figure in the State Department's policy-making process several months earlier, but, as of January 1, he ceased to be even a daily presence. After a small and touching farewell party with the Policy Planning Staff, Kennan left the office for good. He remained in the department for a while as counselor, but would never again wield major influence. As one staff member who had been with Kennan since 1947 recalled, "Mr. Kennan was going to have a very honorable and respectable job but he wasn't going to see very much of Mr. Acheson."

It was a sad ending to the saga of Mr. X. As containment was transformed into a policy increasingly dependent on U.S. military power, its principal originator grew to be so irrelevant to State Department deliberations that, toward the end, he came to see himself as a "gadfly" and a "court jester."

And to Kennan, his replacement at the staff embodied all that he had fought against. "Paul was in one sense like a child," Kennan said later. "He was willing to believe only what he could see before him. He felt comfortable with something only if it could be statistically expressed. He loved anything that could be reduced to numbers. He was mesmerized by them. . . . He'd have a pad before him, and when he wrote down the numbers, it was with such passion and intensity that his pen would sometimes drive right through the paper. Of course, the numbers were predicated on a total theoretical hostility that had to be assumed to give these figures meaning. He had no feeling for the intangibles—values, intentions. When there was talk of intentions, as opposed to capabilities, he would say, 'How can you measure intentions? We can't be bothered to get into psychology; we have to face the Russians as competitors, militarily. That's where I come in; that's where I'm in my element.' He accepted the characteristic assumptions of the Pentagon about the Soviet Union; he was enamored of Pentagon phraseology, which was stiff, meaningless, without nuance or political sensitivity."[63]

That such a man would be making policy disturbed Kennan. It was clear that Acheson had been right when he vetoed Nitze's appointment to the staff in 1947, saying that Paul Nitze was an operations man whose Wall Street methods made him unsuited to long-range policy planning. Equally clear, however, was the fact that the times had changed, and that with the intensification of the Cold War, official Washington was no longer interested in the nuances of Soviet intentions. The "total theoretical hostility" that formed the foundation of Nitze's thought was increasingly the starting point of all national security analysis.

Nitze and Kennan would remain friendly over the years even as their differences widened. The two had been friends before working together, and they would remain friends afterward. Passionate though he was about his views, Paul Nitze was not one who couldn't talk to those with whom he disagreed. Kennan was much the same way. Sensitive and thoughtful, he did not bear many grudges. "My relations with Mr. Nitze have never been marked by anything other than mutual respect and warm friendship," he would later say. Still, Kennan felt he had been "defeated" by Nitze. "Paul never accepted the premise that I have always started from, and that is that there is no defense against nuclear weapons, therefore once both sides had them, there was no use for them. Paul regarded the atomic bomb as the decisive weapon, whether used or not used, since it could provide the basis for nuclear blackmail. I did not believe, and never have believed, in the reality of nuclear blackmail. These people—and Paul was one of them—would have their way. I didn't expect any good to come of it."[64]

Over thirty years after the H-bomb battle, Paul Nitze attended Kennan's eightieth birthday party. In a toast that touched Kennan deeply, Nitze praised his old boss as a "teacher and an example for close to forty years." "George has, no doubt, often doubted the aptness of his pupil," Nitze continued, "But the warmth of his and Annelise's friendship for Phyllis and me has never faltered."[65]

The exit of Kennan and the conversion of Acheson did not solve all of Nitze's problems. David Lilienthal was still opposed to H-bomb development. If the Special Committee was to present a unanimous decision to Truman, Lilienthal had to be won over. But how? On January 26 Acheson met with the AEC chairman and worked out a general framework for a compromise.

From the beginning one of Lilienthal's chief qualms about going ahead with a thermonuclear weapon was that it would serve to accelerate the U.S. dependence on nuclear weapons. To Lilienthal, the national security policy of the United States was already so unclear, so egregiously incoherent, that the nation was in no position to make a decision on something as important as the H-bomb until that policy was thoroughly reexamined. Acheson and Nitze sympathized with this sentiment. At his meeting with Lilienthal, the secretary of state made a suggestion that Lilienthal found appealing. As Lilienthal wrote later, "Acheson indicated his belief that the President should direct the AEC to go ahead," but that "this could be combined with what I believed was needed before a commitment to the H-bomb was made by the President, namely a serious re-examination . . . of the prevailing policy of almost exclusive military reliance on big bombs."[66]

With Lilienthal amenable to this suggestion, Nitze dusted off his December 19 memorandum, rewrote most of the recommendations, but stopped short of specifying what sort of review of national security policy would be conducted. He then went to see Lilienthal with the paper.

Repeating the complaints he had made to Acheson, Lilienthal reportedly said, "I don't think that the executive branch has thoroughly thought through what its policies would be in a world in which such nuclear weapons as thermonuclear weapons were part of the arsenals of the world."

Nitze agreed, saying that he was not at all happy with the way in which basic foreign policy problems have been addressed.

"Well," said Lilienthal, "I don't want to go forward with this until that problem has been thought through. I think one first ought to think through the political consequences of this course before they try to go through with it."

"I can't quarrel with that," Nitze remembered saying. "But I think they ought to be done concurrently rather than one delayed until after the other."

Lilienthal objected. He did not want to begin a crash program before completing the policy review. As he wrote later, "I felt that such a direction by the President, prior to that reexamination and perhaps resetting of the course would be highly prejudicial to the examination itself." Still, Lilienthal knew that he didn't have many choices at this point. H-bomb development was going to proceed with or without his consent. As this was probably the best deal he would get, Lilienthal accepted Nitze's compromise.

"And so," Nitze recalled, "I wrote a last paragraph into this piece of paper which was a directive from Mr. Truman to the secretaries of state and defense to conduct a basic review of national security policy, taking into account the existence of nuclear weapons and the possibility of thermonuclear weapons." Nitze then showed the directive to Acheson, who approved it.

Paul Nitze was not in Washington to brief Acheson for the final session of the Z Committee on January 31, 1950, or the fateful meeting with Truman that followed immediately afterward. Instead, Nitze was in Boca Raton, Florida, addressing the annual convention of the National Association of Manufacturers. It was a dull event, but as it turned out, Acheson's meeting with the president was not much more exciting. It lasted only seven minutes.

Addressing no one in particular, Truman asked only a single question: "Can the Russians do it?"

All heads nodded, "Yes, they can."

"We don't have much time," said Admiral Souers.

"In that case," the president said, "we have no choice. We'll go ahead."[67]

The president approved the directive Nitze had given to Acheson. And as he initialed the accompanying press statement, he said he "recalled another meeting that he had had with the National Security Council concerning Greece a long time ago. . . . at that time everybody predicted the end of the world if we went ahead, but we did go ahead and the world didn't come to an end."

Harry Truman was right when he predicted that "it would be the same case here."[68] His January 31 directive did not bring the world to an end. But the State-Defense review group the president authorized that day triggered a series of fundamental changes in the national security policy of the United States which, in time, would make the world a very different place.

CHAPTER 4

The Threat Assessed

SHORTLY BEFORE leaving on an extended tour of South America in February 1950, George Kennan wrote a final memorandum to Dean Acheson and the members of the Policy Planning Staff. "There is little justification for the impression that the 'cold war,' by virtue of events outside of our control, has suddenly taken some drastic turn to our disadvantage," he wrote. The fall of China was "the culmination of processes which have long been apparent." The Soviet acquisition of the A-bomb "likewise adds no new fundamental element to the picture." Nor did the possibility of the Soviets' developing the H-bomb. "The idea of their threatening people with the H-bomb and bidding them 'sign on the dotted line or else' is thus far solely of our own manufacture." To Kennan, the nature of the east-west conflict had changed little since 1945. "In so far as we feel ourselves in heightened trouble at the present moment, that feeling is largely of our making."

Given this, Kennan wrote that there was no reason to alter the policy of containment. Originally, that policy had been based on the premise that the west did not need to meet the Soviet threat tank for tank or division for division in a mindless attempt to create military parity. Instead, the Soviet Union's ideological offensive was best countered "by a movement on our part equally comprehensive, designed to prove the validity of liberal institutions, to confound the predictions of their failure, to prove that a society not beholden to Russian communism could still 'work.' " In thwarting Moscow, the policy of containment had sought to bolster the cohesion and appeal of the western democratic system. One of the principal axioms of the policy was that "communism had to be viewed as a crisis of our own civilization, and the principal antidote lay in overcoming the weaknesses of our own institutions." While western military power had to be strengthened to offset the threat of intimidation by the Kremlin, such measures as the Atlantic Pact and the Arms Program, "were not part of a policy of military containment." Containment was a political program, not a military one.

In conclusion, the author of the Long Telegram and many of the most important national security documents of his day warned that "There is no reason, to date, to doubt the validity of this approach. In fact, any serious deviation from it could easily lead to the most appalling consequences."[1]

Like so much of what he had been saying throughout the last year, Kennan's memorandum conflicted with the common wisdom of the day. His notion that nothing had changed in the Cold War, that there was no cause for alarm, and that policy could proceed as usual must have seemed outlandish to Acheson, Nitze, and other top State Department officials. To these men everything had changed. Even as Kennan completed his memorandum, the atmosphere of crisis that had begun with the fall of China and the Soviet explosion of an A-bomb was nearing a crescendo. And feeding the mounting panic was a new and virulent breed of anticommunism at home.

The latest round in the battering of Truman's State Department had begun on January 22. On that day Alger Hiss was convicted of perjury. A smooth Harvard graduate and former State Department official, Hiss had been found guilty of lying when he denied passing classified documents to a communist agent. Sentencing was set for January 25, a day on which Acheson had coincidentally scheduled a press conference. The night before the conference Acheson confided to his special assistant, Lucius Battle, that he would speak in the defense of Hiss. Battle, who could smell a disaster brewing, immediately contacted Nitze. "We've got to stop him," he said. Nitze agreed. The next morning, the two men warned Acheson to tread carefully. The secretary assured them that he was only going to read from the Sermon on the Mount.[2]

Instead, Acheson—ever loyal to his class—made a statement that would cause a small sensation and haunt him for the rest of his term as Secretary of State. "I should like to make it clear to you," he told reporters, "that whatever the outcome of any appeal which Mr. Hiss or his lawyers may take in this case, I do not intend to turn my back on Alger Hiss."[3] From that point on life at the State Department would never be the same. As right-wing senators demanded the scalp of "Red Dean," new developments at home and abroad intensified the climate of crisis.

On February 2, 1950, Klaus Fuchs, chief of the Theoretical Physics Division of the British Atomic Energy Research Establishment, was arrested and charged with engaging in espionage for the Soviet Union. Fuchs had worked on the Manhattan Project during World War II. He had access to some of the west's most sensitive atomic secrets and there were concerns that he had given the Soviets information that would accelerate their thermonuclear weapon program.

One week later, in Wheeling, West Virginia, Joseph McCarthy, the junior senator from Wisconsin, charged in a dramatic speech that the State Department was teeming with communists—eighty-one, to be precise. What Acheson came to call "the attack of the primitives" reached new heights.

On February 14 Mao Tse-tung, the leader of communist China, signed a treaty with the Soviet Union. Now the world's largest country and the world's most populous country were bonded in an alliance against the United States.

In this atmosphere George Kennan's soothing theme of continuity carried little weight at the State Department. Paul Nitze was the man of the hour. With his intense distrust of the "men in the Kremlin," his focus on the psychological dimension of the Cold War, and his perception of a military balance rapidly shifting in favor of the Soviet Union, Nitze's thinking was in step with official Washington. And as director of the Policy Planning Staff beginning January 1, 1950, he was in a position to turn that thinking into policy. No longer was Nitze a newcomer to the national security realm, unsure of his judgment and groping for an understanding of complex geopolitical issues. The long discussions with his Pentagon contacts, the work with Arneson and Fisher on the H-bomb question, and the many hours of study to master the issues of the time had rapidly established him as one of the leading military specialists in the State Department. "He learned a lot," recalled the staff's executive secretary, Carlton Savage. "He was driven by the substance of problems," recalled Dorothy Fosdick. His whole state of mind was geared toward maximizing his knowledge. "He was all business," she said.

Nitze still knew little about the Soviet Union and perhaps did not have the perspicacity or seasoned political judgment of a long-time diplomat. But what he lacked in knowledge and experience, he made up for in intellectual forcefulness, fierce self-discipline, and an instinct for the bureaucratic jugular. If some of the staff had initially questioned Nitze's ability to handle national security work, they did no longer. "Paul certainly redeemed himself," recalled Savage.

Dean Acheson found him impressive. The work Nitze did on the H-bomb issue was solid, and he had proved to be an effective liaison with the Pentagon at a time when State-Defense relations were nearing a point of crisis. Clearly, this was a man who could handle any job thrown his way, a very thorough and informed man. He could give Acheson what he wanted when he wanted it. "In intellectual terms, Dean found Paul very rewarding," recalled Battle. "He was decisive; he was clear; he was thoughtful; he was an outsider but was also an insider in the sense of knowledge and intellect and associations." For one who loathed mediocrity, Nitze's intelligence and unabashed workaholism was refreshing. He was, Acheson later wrote, "a joy to work with because of his clear, incisive mind."[4] In a very short time the secretary of state found a nearly endless number of uses for his planning chief. He came to rely on Nitze for daily advice, inviting him to the morning meetings, calling him into the office for a few words, asking him to look over a speech or comment on an idea. Nitze, in turn, came to view Acheson as a mentor. He found his boss shrewd and intelligent, cultured and elegant. Though outwardly arrogant, he was not one to belittle subordinates. Nor did his staunch principles prevent him from being flexible in his thinking or amenable to persuasion. Acheson's patrician bearing and haughty wit inspired seething disdain in many. Right-wing senators from the South and the Midwest considered him self-righteous and corrupt, a symbol of all that was wrong with the eastern establishment. Yet to Nitze, he was a person to respect and emulate. He was also someone to impress. "From the time Paul became head of the Policy Planning Staff he was on Acheson's wave length," said William Bundy, the secretary of state's son-in-law.

During the fall of 1949 Nitze had worked hard to meet all the secretary's needs—to have a paper prepared on time, to get the information Acheson needed for a meeting, to be on top of things continually. Now he pushed himself even harder. "If the matter was high on Mr. Acheson's agenda," recalled former staff member Robert Tufts, "it tended to be high on Mr. Nitze's agenda. Whatever Acheson was deeply concerned with, Nitze tended to get involved with." As Nitze's relationship with Acheson became closer, his power in the department grew. People knew he had the secretary's ear, that he was on his way up. He became a man to cultivate, someone who could take one's idea or request right to the top of the department and see that it got proper attention. And because Nitze could do favors, he could ask them. He could tap resources in the department that would be otherwise unavailable. With Acheson behind him, he had real influence in the most important bureaucracy in the government besides the White House. It was more power than Nitze had ever had in his life.

This power flowed not just from his closeness to the secretary of state. As director of the Policy Planning Staff, Nitze now had his own organization. And as soon as it became his on January 1, he started to alter the way it did business. As Tufts recalled, there were "very big changes" when Nitze took over. With Kennan, the staff had often been a one-man show. "He wanted a court," recalled Fosdick. "Our role was to help him make up his mind." And once he had done so, Kennan, and Kennan alone, would write the papers that went to the secretary. "Kennan produced papers so fast you could hardly keep up with the drafts," said Tufts, "and staff meetings tended to take the form of verbal comments on the paper that Kennan was at the moment writing."

With Nitze as director it was "a very different operation," remembered Tufts. "Mr. Nitze didn't like to write and didn't write except when he had to." So rather than Nitze's handing down nearly finished products, "I and other members of the staff would produce papers which he then criticized." Instead of a director who felt he had special insights and superior knowledge, who felt that after due consideration he would pronounce his judgment, the staff had a team player at the helm. "Paul was interested more in a consensus view," said Fosdick. "He didn't think he had the answers, he felt that he had to use the wisest brains." With Nitze staff members felt more engaged; they felt like the foreign policy experts they were rather than the editors Kennan had often asked them to be. If the Policy Planning Staff had once been George Kennan's court, it now became Paul Nitze's seminar.

Even as Nitze dismantled much of what Kennan had left behind, however, he capitalized on what the former director had built. Nitze did not have to carve out a role for himself or his staff; it already existed.

Kennan had been one of the most powerful men in the State Department, and it was expected that Nitze would be as well.

Important as the bureaucratic reasons were for Nitze's rise, the fundamental source of his growing influence remained his articulation of timely views. While Kennan had awed the government with his brilliance and eloquence in outlining the concept of containment, Nitze's effectiveness stemmed from the forcefulness of his argumentation and his command of the facts. "He wasn't very articulate compared to George Kennan," said Carlton Savage, but he was more concise. "Kennan was inclined to be rather cosmic in his outlook," recalled John Paton Davies. "Nitze on the other hand was much more pragmatic and much more issue focused." By eliminating the intuitive and scholarly approach to international affairs that had often characterized Kennan's work, and reducing national security problems to simple comparisons of military might and blanket statements about western morale, Nitze brought a compelling concreteness to State Department decision making.

Nowhere was this more apparent than in discussions about the adequacy of the U.S. military effort to deal with Soviet aggression. Two days after Truman signed the H-bomb directive, Nitze met with the Policy Planning Staff to discuss Soviet behavior. He brought up a question that had been raised at Acheson's morning meeting: Was there an increased possibility of Soviet aggression? In Nitze's opinion there was. The chance of war, he told the group, was "considerably greater than last fall." Reporting the views of his contacts on the Joint Chiefs of Staff, Nitze said that it was their opinion that "the Soviet Union could begin a major attack from a standing start so that the usual signs of mobilization would be lacking."[5]

Over the next week Nitze worked on a paper analyzing recent Soviet moves. Completed on February 8, it was his most substantive attempt to date to assess Kremlin intentions. In sweeping terms he depicted postwar Soviet policy toward the west as unrelentingly hostile. "In seeking to interpret Soviet tactics," Nitze began, "it is always useful to remind ourselves that during the course of the war, the Kremlin concluded that the US would emerge as the citadel of the non-Soviet world and therefore the primary enemy against which the USSR would have to wage a life-and-death struggle." In the years following the war, Nitze wrote, "the USSR has shown a willingness to employ at any given moment any maneuver or weapon which holds promise of success." Subversion, intimidation, invasion—the Kremlin made little distinction among modes of aggression. It was concerned only with expedience, never losing sight of its overall goal. "As the USSR has already committed itself to the defeat of the US," wrote Nitze, "Soviet policy is guided by the simple consideration of weakening the world power position of the US."

With the fall of nationalist China, the acquisition of an A-bomb, and continuing economic revitalization, Nitze argued that the Soviet Union was now positioned as never before to move aggressively against the west. "The USSR," he concluded, "considers this a favorable and necessary moment for increased political pressure, and, when feasible, taking aggressive political action against all or most soft spots in its periphery."[6]

For a man who had no formal training in Soviet issues, who had never been to Russia, and who had been involved in national security matters for less than seven months, such judgments on Soviet intentions were strikingly audacious. Winston Churchill once commented that "I cannot forecast to you the action of Russia. It is a riddle wrapped in a mystery inside an enigma."[7] Most Soviet experts agreed. People like Averell Harriman, Charles Bohlen, and George Kennan had spent years in Moscow studying the Kremlin, poring over Soviet newspapers, analyzing Stalin and his lieutenants firsthand. But rarely were they sure about what the Soviet Union might do next. Among such men there were bitter disagreements over what motivated Stalin's foreign policy.

Yet to Nitze there was little ambiguity. "Soviet actions," he wrote with certainty, "make clear that Moscow's faith in the inevitable disintegration of capitalism is not a passive faith in automatic historical evolution. Instead it is a messianic faith that not only spurs the USSR to assist the transformation of the Marxist blueprint into a reality, but also gives the Soviet leaders a sense of confidence that in whatever particular course they follow they are riding the wave of the future."[8] Nitze's assertions were all the more bold in that they contradicted the consensus of top experts at the Central Intelligence Agency. In a lengthy report on Soviet intentions issued two days after Nitze finished his paper, the CIA portrayed Soviet foreign policy very differently. The dominant theme in Soviet dealings with the outside world, the CIA said, was not a "messianic faith," but rather a terrible insecurity. "The lack of secure frontiers, resulting in an immemorial experience (since the Tartar invasion) of being overrun by more civilized and technologically advanced foreigners, constitutes the basis for a morbid sense of national insecurity and psychological inferiority." Far from increasing its confidence to an almost religious zealotry, as Nitze suggested, the CIA argued that "Communist doctrine has reinforced this basic sense of insecurity inherent in the experience of the Russian people and the early years of the present Soviet regime."

As for predicting Soviet actions with certainty, the CIA stated that it was a difficult if not impossible task. In a rather astounding admission from an organization dedicated to keeping the United States a step ahead of its enemies, the CIA report stated that "there is no factual information on any decisions or plans of the Politburo which would permit a definite and authoritative answer with respect to the timing and methods which the USSR will employ in pursuit of its objectives. *Lacking such evidence it would be as unjustifiable to assume that the USSR definitely intends to resort to aggression involving the United States as it would be to assume the contrary.*"[9]

Neither America's leading Soviet experts nor its most advanced intelligence-gathering organization could confidently predict Soviet actions. But Paul Nitze felt that he had such an understanding of Moscow's thinking as to state—without the use of qualifiers such as "might" or "possibly"—that the Soviets would begin "taking aggressive political action against all or most soft spots in its periphery."[10] George Kennan, it appeared, did not have a monopoly on mysticism. At times, his successor outdid him on this score.

Nitze's views on Soviet intentions were symptomatic of the attitude he preached to his staff: systematic pessimism. "On the Policy Planning Staff under Paul we always used to look at everything in the worst light," commented former member Louis Halle. "In this kind of thinking, everything is a victory for those infallible geniuses in Moscow, a defeat for us." The fusion of Nitze's certainty of Soviet aggressiveness with a deep pessimism about the future produced an analytical framework within which the most terrifying scenarios could be conceived and believed.

In better times it was a framework that might have been ridiculed as a doomsayer's delusion. But with the Cold War at its height, Nitze's approach was destined to alter history.

The basic review of national security policy that Truman approved on January 31 was not a new idea. The National Security Council had attempted such a review in March 1949.[11] Four months later it had revised that paper.[12] In December it was decided to mount a more ambitious effort. On December 20, 1949, Admiral Souers recommended to James Lay of the NSC "that the Council now direct the

NSC staff . . . to prepare a report for Council consideration assessing and appraising the objectives, commitments and risks of the United States under a continuation of present conditions or in the event of war in the near future."[13]

George Kennan had opposed the idea of a review from the beginning. When the NSC revised its March paper, Kennan had caustically written that "The basic assumption apparently underlying this paper: namely, that it is possible to describe in a few pages a program designed to achieve U.S. objectives with respect to the U.S.S.R., gives a misleading impression of the nature of our foreign policy problems."[14] By January Kennan's views had changed little; and he was disappointed when the NSC acted on Souers's recommendation and initiated the review. Paul Nitze was disappointed as well, although for different reasons. Nitze believed that the review should be conducted by State and Defense, not the NSC. Since these were the two departments that dealt with the Soviet threat on a daily basis and would have to implement any recommendations made in such a review, their officials should be the people undertaking the study and making the recommendations.

In signing the January 31 directive, Truman finally accepted this reasoning. Written mostly by Nitze, the document recommended "That the President direct the Secretary of State and the Secretary of Defense to undertake a reexamination of our objectives in peace and war and of the effect of these objectives on our strategic plans, in light of the probable fission bomb capability and possible thermonuclear bomb capability of the Soviet Union."[15]

Nitze's success in shifting responsibility for the review from the NSC to State and Defense was a deft stroke. Ever since the Soviet explosion in Siberia, he had pressed for a fundamental rethinking of U.S. national security policy. "It was obvious," Nitze said later, "that Soviet development of atomic energy bore directly on the policy of containment, and would require a re-assessment of the means necessary to carry that policy through with hope of success."[16] As the debate over the H-bomb made clear, there were innumerable inconsistencies and weaknesses in current U.S. policy, what Nitze called "political, psychological and moral imponderables."[17] Without the use of nuclear weapons, many believed that western Europe could not be defended. Yet now that the Soviets had the A-bomb, U.S. atomic weapons would no longer be the defensive panacea they had once been. As Nitze wrote later, "I was . . . persuaded that, over time, the U.S. atomic monopoly, and the strategic significance thereof, would progressively decline," and thus the United States "would eventually have to move away from primary reliance upon nuclear weapons." This would be difficult given the multibillion-dollar price tag of building up to military parity in Europe. "So the question remained," wrote Nitze, "what should the United States do to avoid complete reliance upon nuclear weapons?"[18]

This troublesome question lay at the heart of the defense debate in early 1950. To build a defense that could repel a Russian invasion of Europe—a scenario many Soviet experts considered farfetched—would require tens of billions of dollars. But with a fiscally conservative Congress and a $5.5 billion deficit estimated for 1950, Truman was in no position to request defense funds above the existing ceiling of $13.5 billion. Nor was Defense Secretary Johnson, who was so politically committed to the ceiling that he earned the nickname "Secretary of Economy," inclined to press for greater funds.[19] The only hopeful sign was an emerging consensus in the national security establishment that much greater defense outlays were needed. "Everyone started from the assumption that the Defense Department budget was inadequate for the world commitments that we assumed," recalled Townsend Hoopes, who worked for the Joint Chiefs of Staff. "Everyone thought that it had to be revised up—primarily on the conventional side."

Nitze believed that if this was going to be done, if the budget ceiling was to be abandoned, a compelling, even shocking case had to be made for more defense spending. The NSC was not about to make such a case. It was too closely tied to the White House and too conservative in its thinking. Nitze's success in getting the review changed to a State-Defense venture was a major triumph because it assured that a strong argument for higher defense spending would be made. As Acheson's natural choice to chair the review group, Nitze would personally see to that.

From the beginning it was obvious that the greatest threat to Nitze's grand scheme was Louis Johnson. Stout and balding with a pale, pudgy face, thin lips, and deep-set eyes, Johnson had a severe and unsettling appearance. He was a professional politician who made no secret of his ambition to be president, and he was not the kind of man whom Acheson and Nitze preferred to work with, not one of the dedicated public servants like Robert Lovett or John McCloy who had left their banks and law offices to join the government during World War II.

The eldest child of a struggling Virginian grocer, Johnson had made politics the focus of his life. After graduating in law from the University of Virginia, he moved to West Virginia and began practicing corporate law. In 1916 he ran for the state assembly and won. From there he went on to win a seat in Congress. Johnson served only one term in the House. After failing to win reelection, he began working on veterans' issues. In 1937 he became assistant secretary of war, where he soon distinguished himself as an extremely difficult man. He feuded bitterly with Secretary of War Harry Woodring until 1940, when Henry Stimson took over the department and fired Johnson. After the war Johnson went into business, and in Truman's 1948 reelection campaign he emerged as one of the president's strongest supporters. Late in the spring of that year, with campaign contributions down and the president in clear trouble, Johnson took over Truman's finance committee and performed miracles. His efforts were decisive in saving the president from defeat. In March 1949 Truman fired James Forrestal and rewarded Johnson with the post of secretary of defense.

Johnson hoped to use the Defense Department to catapult himself to the presidency. "His primary loyalty and whole future lay at the White House," recalled a Pentagon official, Najeeb Halaby. Johnson's scheme for achieving this goal was simple: By keeping the Pentagon budget low, he would emerge as the hero of the Truman administration and then mount a presidential campaign on the theme of economy. Dean Acheson, with his advocacy of higher defense budgets, posed an obstacle to this plan, and Johnson and the secretary of state were almost immediately at each other's throat. "A more dissimilar pair could not have been placed in the same harness than the urbane, intellectual, lawyerly Acheson and the abrasive, cocksure, hyper-ambitious Johnson," wrote one historian.[20] Their relationship deteriorated throughout 1949, and by March 1950 they were hardly on speaking terms.

In early February the State-Defense Policy Review Group began taking shape. From the Policy Planning Staff, Nitze selected his brightest colleagues to work on the review. Foremost among these was Robert Tufts. A member of the staff since 1947, Tufts was a talented writer with a gift for hard-hitting and lucid prose. Nitze could count on him to produce a persuasive final report. The staff's secretary, Carlton Savage, also joined the review, as did two other trusted members, George Butler and Harry Schwartz.

Defense Secretary Louis Johnson had a different criterion for membership on the review group: total and unquestioning loyalty to the Pentagon. This came as no surprise. Since taking office, Johnson had stunned Washington's national security establishment with his territorial behavior. So obsessive was he about maintaining control of the ideas that flowed into the Pentagon, that in August 1949 he took the unprecedented step of decreeing that there be no contacts between State and Defense except through Major General James Burns, his hand-picked liaison officer.[21]

As a trusted aide who shared Johnson's suspicions of the State Department, Burns was the obvious choice to head the Pentagon team and oppose calls for increased military spending. Because of failing health, however, Burns lacked the energy to carry out his assigned role. Johnson's other choices for the team, Robert LeBaron and Najeeb Halaby, were no more reliable. LeBaron was a cantankerous man in his seventies whose vague and imprecise manner had earned him the nickname "the artful dodger." State officials considered him brilliant and personally agreeable, but impossible to do business with. "By the time he'd finished talking you didn't know what the hell he had said or what he wanted to do," recalled Gordon Arneson.

Halaby was more solid. A graduate of Stanford and Yale Law, he had worked in the State Department's Office of Intelligence Estimates after the war. Still in his early thirties, Halaby joined Forrestal's staff when the Department of Defense was formed. Like Nitze, he admired Forrestal tremendously and was appalled when President Truman handed the top Pentagon post to Louis Johnson as a campaign trophy. "It was an utterly shattering blow to all of us working on Forrestal's staff to have Louis Johnson—a big, arrogant, humorless, bull of a man," recalled Halaby.

With Burns ill, LeBaron incompetent, and Halaby a quiet dissident, Johnson's team had neither the ability nor the inclination to carry out their unwritten orders to sabotage the review group.

What Johnson hadn't counted on, also, was the role of the Joint Chiefs of Staff. The chiefs wanted a man from the Joint Strategic Survey Committee to be on the review group, and Major General Truman ("Ted") Landon was selected. Not directly answerable to the defense secretary and not reflexively committed to the budget ceiling, Landon was not a Johnson lackey. And he was no saboteur.

The group decided that the officials from Defense and State would write separate papers and attempt to reconcile their positions in a final draft. Landon agreed to do the paper for Defense, and Nitze began working on the one for State. Landon's was completed first. It reflected Johnson's budget-conscious defense thinking: Atomic weapons were deemed an adequate deterrent, the military balance between the United States and the Soviet Union was portrayed favorably, and no dramatic defense increases were recommended.

Nitze and the Policy Planning Staff members immediately attacked the paper. They bore in on the status quo assumptions and optimistic assessments. They asked question after question, probing for inconsistencies and weaknesses. And as they hammered away, a surprising fact emerged. It became clear that Landon did not really believe what he had written. The general could obediently recite official Pentagon dogma, he could cite official Pentagon data to defend that dogma, but ultimately he could not defend the position in debate. Nor did he wish to try. The passion of State's attack made it clear to Landon that the review group was not just another exercise in bureaucratic politics, not another forum in which he should mindlessly defend Pentagon turf. Landon saw that the Policy Planning Staff was sincerely interested in questioning basic assumptions.[22] With that realization, Nitze later recalled, the general "became thoroughly persuaded of the honesty and sincerity of what we were trying to do and became very much a full member of the group." Landon's conversion was a crucial turning point in the review. "Through him," Nitze remembered, "it was possible to mobilize the complete support of the Joint Staff and all the resources of the JCS organization."

Landon's turnabout was surprising. Even more stunning was Burns's failure to intervene. As Johnson's point man on the group, Burns could easily have been an intractable exponent of official Pentagon policy. But this never happened. "Had he done so," wrote historian Paul Hammond, "had he performed a role in the committee comparable to that played by Nitze in behalf of the Secretary of State, the whole project would have deadlocked."[23]

Burns apparently harbored his own doubts about the $13.5 billion budget ceiling. "He was a wonderful man caught between his own convictions, which lay with State, and his loyalty to Louis Johnson," recalled Halaby. As the pace of the review picked up, Burns failed to be the obstructionist that Johnson wanted. He would come late to the meetings at the State Department and leave early. While there, Burns said little and made no effort to derail the group's work. It was, as Tufts observed, "a rather risky role for him to play." It placed him in a "delicate situation, a situation that could have blown up in his face."

With Burns's nod of approval, Defense members Halaby and Le-Baron joined Landon in his commitment to the review. As Nitze commented later, "there was, in fact, a revolt from within" the Pentagon against Johnson's policies.[24]

* * *

With Defense Department opposition nullified, Nitze was presented with a historic opportunity to restructure U.S. national security policy. For years the United States had relied on nuclear weapons to defend western Europe. For years the government had disagreed bitterly about how to change this situation. Now a strange calm had suddenly settled over the bureaucratic battlefield.

Nitze was determined to move fast before something shattered this rare moment. Taking almost complete control of the group, he began working at a killing pace, day and night, driving himself as he had while working on the Marshall Plan. It was "a gruelling experience," he said later.[25] By February 20 Nitze had his own draft paper on the table. It was fundamentally different from Landon's. It portrayed the United States and the Soviet Union as locked in a mortal struggle for control of humankind's destiny. It suggested that unless the Soviet military buildup was matched, the western world would face a major threat to its survival. It stated that the Cold War was not just an occasional exchange of propaganda blasts, but a battle of life or death, a struggle between freedom and slavery.

From the Pentagon representatives there came no major challenge to Nitze's draft. By late February arguments over basic principles had ended and the group began showing its work to outside consultants.

Nitze had won round one.

Robert Oppenheimer was the first outside expert consulted. Summoned to Washington by a mysterious letter from Acheson, a surprised Oppenheimer was handed a lengthy paper on cold war policy when he arrived at the State Department. He spent an hour reading Nitze's draft and then met with the full review group to give his criticisms. Oppenheimer's reaction was mixed. He was uneasy about the manner in which the paper treated the issue of nuclear weapons; so many questions were left unanswered. If it could be built, should the United States stockpile the H-bomb? What were the prospects for international control? What about the issue of first use? Oppenheimer thought that none of these problems had been addressed in the draft. This was a major weakness, he said, for what the United States "did about the A-bomb could be an inspiration for most other considerations."

Like Kennan, Oppenheimer thought that how and when the United States would ever use nuclear weapons was of overriding importance. He believed that a no-first-use policy was most desirable, but noted that "we seem to have slipped into our present military posture by default because obviously right now without the atomic bomb we would have

no military posture." The question then arises, continued Oppenheimer, "whether we could build up our strength during the next five
years, for example, so as to get away from complete dependence on the
atomic bomb."

Nitze was deeply pessimistic about this prospect. He pointed out
that "to supply Western Europe alone with a reasonable amount of
conventional armaments might cost $40 billion and even then you
would only have around sixty divisions as compared to about 200 of the
Soviet Union." Nitze believed that this goal was virtually unreachable
and that a more feasible short-term objective of the United States was
to "strengthen the moral fiber of the people."

To this idea Oppenheimer was sympathetic. He expressed the hope
that the group's work would help alert the American people to the facts
and prod them to act on that awareness. But the scientist did have one
major objection. He felt that Nitze's draft was too crude in its depiction
of the Soviet Union. He wondered if the paper would present a recog-
nizable picture to the average citizen of the Soviet Union and asked
if the group was so sure that the comparison was one between "jet black
and pure white."[26]

Nitze dismissed this criticism, but in the coming months—and
decades—he would hear it again and again. To many, Nitze's attempt
to cast the Soviet Union as a slave state while portraying the United
States as a model of freedom and democracy was the single greatest
weakness of the paper that would become known as National Security
Council memorandum 68 (NSC 68). It gave the document a tone of
propagandistic self-righteousness and an intellectual shallowness that
suggested that the author was blind to the inequities and injustices
found in the west and its client states. As one critic of the period wrote,
"The neat dichotomy between 'freedom' and 'slavery' is not a realistic
description either of the situation today or of the alternatives as they
appear to present themselves to large areas of the world. . . . Are the
Indo-Chinese free? Can the peoples of the Philippines be said to be
free under the corrupt Quirino government? . . . To classify as "free"
all of those people whose governments oppose Russia, or we seek to
have oppose Russia, is a travesty of the word."[27]

Defending the freedom versus slavery approach years later, Nitze
claimed that "NSC 68 was very much a product of its times."[28] In his
view "the style in which it was written was appropriate to that period
of 1950. . . . A good deal of the discussion about the contrasts between
the Communist system and the Communist ideology and doctrine
vis-a-vis the Western ideas, the Western culture, was, I believe, wholly

appropriate for the mind of 1950." Townsend Hoopes put it another way: "We were all the children of the Cold War."

The next consultant to take a look at the review group's work was James Conant, president of Harvard University. His criticism was more blunt than Oppenheimer's. What Conant found most disturbing was the paper's aggressive liberation theme (an idea later dubbed "rollback"). The stated goal of "restoring freedom to the victims of the Kremlin," was in Conant's view, "much too large a task." And it was too risky as well. He suggested instead "that for the next 20 years our objective should be to live on tolerable terms with the Soviet Union and its satellites while avoiding war."

Later in the draft Conant again came upon the rollback theme and asked sharply what the phrase "forces required for victory" meant? "If victory consists in liberating the peoples in the satellite countries, that is one thing," he said. To Conant, the entire thrust of the paper in this area was dangerously misguided.

Nitze disagreed vehemently. The latent resistance of the peoples under Soviet domination was a major asset of the west, he argued. The United States had to keep that desire alive and give those behind the iron curtain some hope of salvation. "A purely defensive objective may deny us their assistance," Nitze said.

Conant scoffed at this notion and pointedly asked how far the United States should go to attain victory. "Should we crack the monolithic Communist party control?" he asked. The phrases "restore freedom" and "choosing own governments" seemed meaningless, Conant said. He again stressed that U.S. objectives should be "confined to containing the Soviet Union." Nitze replied that "if we had objectives only for the purpose of repelling invasion and not to create a better world, the will to fight would be lessened." The two men were stalemated.[29]

When writing the final draft, Nitze partly heeded Conant's advice and cut out some of the rollback rhetoric. But the changes were only in style, not in substance. In its final form the paper suggested that the United States "take dynamic steps to reduce the power and influence of the Kremlin inside the Soviet Union and other areas under its control. The objective would be the establishment of friendly regimes not under Kremlin domination."[30] Partly as a result of NSC 68, the rollback theme would remain entrenched in official American national security thinking for almost a decade.

* * *

Oppenheimer and Conant were the only outside consultants to raise serious objections to the content of Nitze's draft paper. A week after Conant's visit Chester Barnard and Henry Smyth, two experts on atomic energy, received the paper with effusive enthusiasm. Smyth's only critical comment was that he found the paper lacking "a gospel which lends itself to preaching." Nitze replied that the group had given that matter some thought, but had concluded that such rhetoric "might be more appropriate in the form of a speech written for the President than as an integral part of the study."[31] Later, Nitze and his colleagues would change their mind on this point.

No outside consultant was more supportive of the call to arms than Robert Lovett. Like Nitze, Lovett had started out on Wall Street and had been lured into government by the exigencies of world war. Like Nitze also, the experience of Nazi and Japanese aggression had shaped many of Lovett's beliefs about political and military power. After the war Lovett became under secretary of state. In that position, as crisis followed crisis, he became deeply disillusioned with Soviet conduct. Lovett was a quiet man, discreet and controlled, with a placid face and a pleasant wit. Yet beneath his poised exterior was a burning anticommunism and a militant antagonism toward the Soviet Union.

"We must realize," Lovett told the group, "that we are now in a mortal conflict; that we are now in a war worse than any we have ever experienced. Just because there is not much shooting as yet does not mean that we are in a cold war. It is not a cold war; it is a hot war. The only difference between this and previous hot wars is that death comes more slowly and in a different fashion." Lovett said that the grim reality of the world situation should be stated simply, clearly, and without reserve. The Soviet Union had to be depicted as the naked aggressor that it was. "Soviet expenditures on their military establishment," said Lovett, "are obviously too large to be for defensive purposes. The Soviet Union's military establishment is obviously designed for offense. The Russians have demonstrated a willingness to use threats, compulsion, and force to accomplish their ends. They have been and are now using invisible means of aggression."

To meet this threat, to defend the west and its way of life, Lovett stressed that the United States had to tell the real story to its own people and to the world. A much "vaster propaganda machine" was needed to get out the truth about communism. "If we can sell every useless article known to man in large quantities," Lovett noted wryly, "we should be able to sell our very fine story in larger quantities." But publicizing the Soviet threat was only the beginning. A far more ambitious military effort had to be mounted to meet that threat. This would take time, and the west, Lovett stressed, didn't have much time. It needed to act swiftly and ruthlessly to counter Soviet aggression. The United States had to behave "as though we were under fire from an invading army," Lovett said. "In the war in which we are presently engaged, we should fight with no holds barred. We should find every weak spot in the enemy's armor, both on the periphery and at the center, and hit him with anything that comes to hand. Anything that we do short of an all-out effort is inexcusable."

Lovett agreed wholeheartedly with Nitze's emphasis on rollback. "There are plenty of partisans and dissidents on the enemy's borders and within his camp who are willing to fight with their lives if we give them some leadership and if they are convinced that we are going to stick with the job until we have finished it," he said.[32]

The review group would meet with one more consultant, Ernest Lawrence. Together they met with six experts in the field of national security. Among them, it was Lovett who made the greatest impression. With his impeccable credentials and reputation for incisive analysis, Lovett's passionately expressed views carried tremendous weight. His comments were very much in line with Nitze's, and when the final draft was completed, it included much of Lovett's polemical intensity and many of his policy recommendations.

Perhaps as significant as who the review group consulted was who they ignored. Despite the in-depth analysis of Soviet intentions included in its report, not a single expert on the Soviet Union met with the group. George Kennan would have been a logical choice, but he was in Latin America. Charles Bohlen, the State Department's other leading Soviet expert, was also overseas. Whether the review group sought the input of any other Soviet experts is not clear. What is evident, however, is that Nitze's analysis of Soviet intentions in NSC 68 again revealed the intellectual shallowness with which he commented on this most difficult of subjects. The Kremlin's design, stated the document, "calls for the complete subversion or forcible destruction of the machinery of government and structure of society in the countries of the non-Soviet world and their replacement by an apparatus and structure subservient to and controlled from the Kremlin."

Nitze and his colleagues argued that this design was motivated by a Soviet fear of freedom. "There is a basic conflict between the idea of freedom under a government of laws, and the idea of slavery under the grim oligarchy of the Kremlin." Sustaining this conflict was the

Kremlin's determination to eliminate the very concept of freedom. "The existence and persistence of the idea of freedom," said NSC 68, "is a permanent and continuous threat to the foundation of the slave society; and it therefore regards as intolerable the long continued existence of freedom in the world." The drive to abolish all traces of freedom, suggested the paper, was at the heart of the Kremlin's expansionist policy.[33]

Where Paul Nitze got these ideas is not apparent. Few Soviet experts of the period believed that Moscow's expansionism was motivated by a zealous desire to eliminate the idea of freedom. Few even agreed that expansionism was at the top of its foreign policy agenda. Instead, experts argued that Soviet history, geography, and ideology contributed to expansionist tendencies that were rooted in a defensive mentality. As the February CIA report on Soviet intentions stated, "the Russian expansion which took place prior to the advent of the Communist regime was based essentially upon a search for defense in depth within the context of the exposed Russian geographical position. The process of expansion was marked by caution and opportunism and not by the Germanic type of venturesome aggression. The sense of insecurity which this reflects has doubtless been reinforced by the Communist estimate of a continuing danger of attack from hostile capitalist powers."[34]

Charles Bohlen, who had spent considerable time in the Soviet Union, didn't share Nitze's analysis either. Like the CIA, he believed that the primary objective of the Kremlin's foreign policy was to maintain control over its own country and its satellite states in eastern Europe. Bohlen was disturbed by Nitze's rather curious notion that Moscow was driven to eliminate freedom because its very existence posed a challenge to the foundation of the Soviet slave state. The two men had been members of the Porcellian Club while at Harvard and had kept up their friendship over the years. Tall and handsome, with the kind of angular face and perfect combed-back hair that other men envied, Bohlen had a debonair style unusual for a career foreign service officer. Women found him immensely appealing, and his reputation for hard partying was legendary. But when it came to his work, Bohlen took great pride in accurate and balanced foreign policy analysis. In November 1949 Nitze had visited Bohlen in Paris where the two engaged in "long and gloomy debates."[35] While Bohlen didn't agree entirely with Kennan's view of Soviet intentions, he thought Nitze was even further from the truth.

In late March Bohlen returned from Paris and discovered what

Nitze was up to. Bohlen had no quarrel with NSC 68's advocacy of higher defense budgets and found the report "excellent in the whole." But he took strong exception to Nitze's analysis of Soviet intentions. "It is open to question," wrote Bohlen in a memo to Nitze, "whether or not, as stated, the fundamental design of the Kremlin is the domination of the world." Such a conclusion would imply that Moscow was willing to run great risks to achieve this aim, and that, Bohlen argued, was simply not the case. Stalin and his cronies were far more concerned with holding on to their power than with toppling foreign governments. He suggested that NSC 68 would be more accurate if it stated that the "fundamental design of those who control the USSR is (a) the maintenance of their regime in the Soviet Union, and (b) its extension throughout the world to the degree that is possible without serious risk to the internal regime."[36]

When writing the final draft, Nitze heeded Bohlen's suggestion—at least cosmetically. He wrote that the aim of the Soviet Union was "to retain and solidify their absolute power, first in the Soviet Union and second in the areas now under their control." But he went on to say that the Soviet leaders felt that these aims could not be achieved without "the ultimate elimination of any effective opposition."[37] Bohlen would remain unsatisfied.

By the first day of spring 1950 the State-Defense Policy Review Group had completed the bulk of its work. Now the more difficult job began. If the six weeks of grinding labor were to have any impact at all, it was critical to win the approval of Acheson, Johnson, and, finally, the president himself. Failing this, the paper would simply disappear into the bureaucracy without a trace.

Acheson would not pose a problem. Nitze had made a point of keeping his boss closely apprised of the group's work, meeting with him almost daily. Acheson supported the review from the beginning, and he had kept the president informed as the work progressed.[38] Reading over Nitze's drafts, Acheson expressed few of the objections voiced by Oppenheimer, Conant, and Bohlen. He was not upset by the paper's hyperbole nor disturbed by its analysis of Soviet intentions. "The task of a public officer seeking to explain and gain support for a major policy is not that of the writer of a doctoral thesis," Acheson later explained. "Qualification must give way to simplicity of statement, nicety and nuance to bluntness, almost brutality in carrying home a point." Analytical accuracy and honesty was not the point. "The purpose of NSC 68," wrote Acheson, "was to so bludgeon the mass mind of 'top government' that not only could the President make a decision but that the decision could be carried out."[39]

One member of top government who proved resistant to bludgeoning was Defense Secretary Johnson. Because the review challenged the $13.5 billion budget ceiling, it threatened his authority. To have the Department of State shove a new military policy down the Pentagon's throat would be humiliating. Johnson had hoped that he could sabotage the review group by placing his most trusted lieutenants on it. But this strategy had failed. Burns and the others didn't have the stomach to voice Johnson's dogma, giving Paul Nitze an opening to dominate the review.

And dominate he did.

Nitze was the group's chairman. His boss was fully behind him. He was arguing the more fashionable position. The entire proceedings took place in his Policy Planning Staff conference room. Also, Nitze was on the offensive, crusading for a cause which was compelling and straightforward.

He was an effective crusader, a natural at the art. Leaning forward in his chair, hunched and intense, chopping with his hands for emphasis, it wasn't exactly eloquence that made Nitze a forceful presence at the conference table. It was his incisiveness, his ability to follow a line of thinking and then tick off his objections. Leading the questioning of the consultants, Nitze never hesitated to argue a point with vigor, and when he did so, he tried to focus the debate on a concrete fact or assumption, something—preferably a number—that he could work with. Nitze didn't always win the arguments, but his persistence allowed him to control the direction of the discussion.

Nitze had spectacular success in winning over the Defense representatives on the review group. But there was little he could do to sway their boss, and it was Johnson's opinion that ultimately mattered. No recommendations on America's defense policy would go anywhere without the support of the secretary of defense. In mid March, Nitze asked Landon whether Johnson was being kept abreast of the group's work. "Well, I'm not sure that he is," said Landon, "I report to General Burns in Louis Johnson's office, but I myself don't see the secretary."

Suspecting that a cowed Burns might not be conveying the full story of the group's work to Johnson, Nitze confronted the general. "Don't you think we ought to brief your secretary? I've been briefing my secretary every day. Don't you think Secretary Johnson should know where we are right now because the report will have to be signed by him and Mr. Acheson."[40] Burns agreed, and on March 13 he sent a memo to the defense secretary reporting on the group's work and stating bluntly their conclusion that it was imperative to "build up strength in non-atomic weapons."[41] A meeting of the review group was set for March 22 to brief Johnson and General Bradley in greater detail.

Nitze had no illusions about the importance of the March 22 briefing of the secretary of defense and the chairman of the Joint Chiefs of Staff. It would probably be his only chance to present the merits of the review group's paper to Johnson. He was determined to make a convincing case and wanted everything to go smoothly. To prepare, Nitze drew up a memo for Acheson carefully choreographing the meeting. It suggested that the secretary of state open with a few remarks about the importance of the group's work. He was to emphasize that the president wanted "a thorough and fresh review unfettered by considerations of existing policies or commitments." He was to remind Johnson that the White House had "participated in the study from the beginning." After these introductory remarks, Acheson was to ask Nitze and General Landon to outline the group's work. Then there could be a general discussion of where the review should go next.[42] Nitze was leaving nothing up to chance or even to his boss's judgment. He mapped the meeting down to the final detail of providing State and Defense press officers with an alibi for why the two secretaries were meeting (to discuss NATO affairs, they were told to say).

Johnson and Bradley arrived at the State Department on a cold and rainy Wednesday afternoon. Worried that his presence might attract attention, Johnson insisted on entering the State Department through the garage and taking a service elevator up to the Policy Planning Staff's conference room. The meeting was large—fourteen men in all. Acheson, Nitze, Under Secretary of State Dean Rusk, and four members of the staff represented the State Department. James Lay and an aide were there for the National Security Council. Admiral Souers, Truman's consultant on national security affairs, had decided to sit in. And Burns, Landon, and Halaby from Defense were present. The group crowded around the staff's table that afternoon constituted nearly all of the high-level officials in the national security establishment.

After friendly greetings, Acheson started to explain the purpose of the meeting as Nitze had suggested. He had not gotten far when Johnson interrupted to ask Acheson if he had read the group's paper. Acheson replied that he had. The secretary of defense said that he hadn't and neither had General Bradley. Even though Acheson had sent a copy over a week earlier, Johnson claimed that the paper had not been given to him until ten o'clock that morning. Neither he nor Bradley, said Johnson sharply, "was going to agree to anything" which they had not read. He said further that he did not like "being called to conferences without having had an opportunity to read the appropriate material, that this was the fourth time the Department of State had done this to him, and that he did not want any more of it."

As a feeling of impending doom crept into the room, Acheson explained that the meeting's sole purpose was to judge whether the review group was properly carrying out Truman's January 31 directive. No decision of any kind would be made. Acheson made the mistake of saying further that Nitze and Burns had tried to schedule the meeting at the most convenient time. Johnson then turned on Nitze. "Any arrangements for meetings should be made only through the secretary of defense," he snapped. Nitze had better "remember that in the future." General Burns, Johnson added, "has no authority to arrange such conferences."[43]

The group had been together for less than five minutes and already they appeared poised for interdepartmental bloodletting. Dispensing with his introductory remarks, Acheson asked Nitze to begin outlining the group's work. Nitze did so, speaking first about the group's tentative conclusions. Johnson settled down. As Acheson recalled, the defense secretary "listened, chair tilted back, gazing at the ceiling, seemingly calm and attentive." Perhaps the meeting would go smoothly after all. Nitze appeared to have Johnson's ear and began to discuss the substance of the group's work. "Suddenly," Acheson recalled, Johnson "lunged forward with a crash of chair legs on floor and fist on the table scaring me out of my shoes. No one, he shouted, was going to make arrangements for him to meet with another cabinet officer and a roomful of people and be told what he was going to report to the president. Who authorized these meetings contrary to his orders? What was this paper which he had never seen?"[44]

Sputtering about conspiracies, the secretary of defense charged that "plans had been made to issue a press release after the meeting which presumably would indicate that agreement had been reached on this matter." Johnson stormed that he was "not going to agree to anything." After he had carried on a bit longer about how his authority was being undermined, Acheson curtly told Johnson that "there did not seem to be anything more to discuss at this meeting."[45] He suggested they adjourn. Johnson agreed and stalked out of the room with Bradley and Halaby.

Acheson described the group as "shell-shocked" after the Defense people had left. And no one was more stunned than General Burns, who had stayed behind in the conference room. Putting his head down on the table, Burns burst into tears. "I consulted with the secretary about this," he sobbed. "He agreed to it. He agreed to everything. He never told me he was going to blow up like this."

As Burns wept and talked of resigning, Acheson was summoned into his office next door where Louis Johnson continued to storm at him, saying he had been insulted. "This was too much," recalled Acheson. "I told him since he had started to leave, to get on with it and the State Department would complete the report alone."[46]

When Acheson rejoined the group, Nitze had convinced Burns not to resign and Souers and Lay were leaving to inform the president of Johnson's outburst. No effort was made to continue the meeting. The entire episode had lasted only fourteen minutes. Within the hour Truman called the secretary of state and expressed his outrage. The review group was to continue its work as before. "From this time on until the President later felt it necessary in September to ask for Johnson's resignation," wrote Acheson, "evidence accumulated to convince me that Louis Johnson was mentally ill. His conduct became too outrageous to be explained by mere cussedness. It did not surprise me when some years later he underwent a brain operation."[47]

If Johnson thought he could destroy the review with his antagonism, he was wrong. He only strengthened Nitze's hand. As the tale of Wednesday's stormy meeting flashed through the government, Johnson's obstructionism was laid bare for all to see. Officials could now appreciate the kind of obstacles that Nitze had been struggling with, and they came to view his efforts with more sympathy. Through his own obnoxiousness, the defense secretary had nullified the Pentagon's vast powers of dissent.

Nitze had won round two.

During the last days of March Nitze struggled to put the State-Defense review into final form. It was a tremendous job and one of the biggest reports he had ever put together. Robert Tufts did much of the writing, but Nitze's input was the greatest. By March 30 the paper was ready to be circulated.

Reading over NSC 68 decades later, three aspects of the paper stand out: its moral righteousness, its economic logic, and its emphasis on the psychological dimension of the Cold War.

The moral righteousness is found principally in the section that compares the United States and the Soviet Union. Nitze's analysis of Soviet intentions was so bewildering to Russian experts like Charles Bohlen because it was not a rigorous or academic analysis. Instead, it was a broadly moralistic effort to illustrate the inherent evil of Soviet communism. NSC 68 emphasized that the existence of the iron curtain, the secret police, and a whole array of other repressive mechanisms was evidence that every aspect of Moscow's rule was antidemocratic and illegitimate. "Being a totalitarian dictatorship the Kremlin's objectives in these policies is the total subjective submission of the peoples now under its control," the report stated. "The concentration camp is the prototype of the society which these policies are designed to achieve, a society in which the personality of the individual is so broken and perverted that he participates affirmatively in his own degradation."

These grim realities of Soviet rule dictated that there could never be true coexistence between the United States and the Soviet Union. "No other value system is so wholly irreconcilable with ours, so implacable in its purpose to destroy ours, so capable of turning to its own uses the dangerous and divisive trends in our own society, no other so skillfully and powerfully evokes the elements of irrationality in human nature everywhere, and no other has the support of a great and growing center of military power." To Nitze, a rigorous analysis of Soviet intentions—the kind preferred by Sovietologists—was unnecessary. The language of NSC 68 implied that Soviet aggressiveness was self-evident; it was such an integral part of their entire system that it should be obvious to even the most casual observer.

Just as plain, suggested NSC 68, was the moral superiority of the United States. "The fundamental purpose" of the United States "is to assure the integrity and vitality of our free society, which is founded upon the worth of the individual." In its world view the United States hoped to preserve and promote the idea of freedom and the expression of freedom. "For a free society," wrote Nitze and Tufts, "does not fear, it welcomes, diversity. It derives its strength from its hospitality even to antipathetic ideas. It is a market for the free trade in ideas, secure in its faith that free men will take the best wares, grow to a fuller and better realization of their powers in exercising their choice."[48]

Some years later a former government official remarked to Dean Acheson that when he first read NSC 68 he thought it was "the most ponderous expression of elementary ideas" he had ever come across. Responding to this criticism in his memoirs, Acheson quoted Oliver Wendell Holmes, Jr., who said that often "we need education in the obvious rather than investigation of the obscure."[49]

Nitze agreed with this view. For years he would begin speeches much the same way he began NSC 68: by contrasting the objectives of the United States and Soviet Union. Time and time again during the Cold War he would justify U.S. actions and policies by citing the inherent worth of the western way of life. And with varying degrees of hostility—depending upon the political climate—he would condemn the despotism of the Soviet state. To Nitze's critics, it was a simplistic view of the world. Lost in the black and white comparison between good and evil was the gray reality of America's acquiescence to, or active role in, the violation of human rights by U.S. client states, violations that were often more savage than those of Soviet client states. Lost also was a recognition that the "worth of the individual" was not always championed in the United States itself, where economic inequities and racial prejudice reduced millions of Americans to a state of poverty and degradation. Nonetheless, the framework articulated in NSC 68, with its clash of diametrically opposed moral absolutes, became one of the principal axioms of Nitze's philosophy of international relations.

Since both Nitze and Tufts were trained as economists, it is not surprising that NSC 68 was replete with statistical data. What is surprising is the importance such data played in the paper's argument. George Kennan had been right when he said that his deputy was never happy until he got numbers down on paper. Even when producing an essentially ideological treatise, Nitze leaned heavily on numbers. Several charts presented data that showed the decisive economic lead that the United States had over the Soviet Union. "Even granting optimistic Soviet reports of production," NSC 68 stated, "the total economic strength of the U.S.S.R. compares with that of the U.S. as roughly one to four." The United States had a gross national product of $250 billion as compared to $65 billion for the Soviet Union. The United States produced far more steel, aluminum, oil, and electric power than the Soviet Union. Most importantly, the U.S. economy was functioning at only a fraction of its actual potential while the U.S.S.R. was "on a near maximum production basis."

What all of this meant, Nitze explained, was that the United States could easily afford to field a military machine far superior to the Soviet Union's. Moreover, if the nation expanded its entire economy, it could do so without a decline in the standard of living. Money was not an obstacle to meeting the Soviet challange, NSC 68 stated. Dismissing the critics who charged that military spending would reduce American productivity in the long run and that it would drain away crucial resources needed for civilian research and development, Nitze argued that the United States could spend much more on defense without hurting its economy. He would make this point for decades to come.

What NSC 68 failed to explain was how the Soviet Union fielded an alleged force of two hundred military divisions in Europe if its GNP was only $65 billion a year, especially given the continuing costs of rebuilding its war-devastated industrial base. The economic data in NSC 68 purported to show that the Soviets need not have conventional superiority in Europe. But to a careful analyst like Nitze, who had estimated that it would cost the west $40 billion annually to deploy forces that could match the Red Army, these statistics should have cast doubt on the claim that such superiority existed at all.

Of all the aspects of NSC 68, perhaps none was of more lasting significance than its conception of the psychology of the Cold War. As Nitze had stressed repeatedly during the H-bomb debate, he deemed the morale of the western world to be a critical component in the east-west confrontation. His support for the bomb had been based partly on the belief that unilateral Soviet possession of the weapon would trigger widespread despair. In NSC 68 Nitze again emphasized the importance of safeguarding western morale. He argued that if free people believed that the Soviets were winning the Cold War, if they perceived the United States as weak and vacillating, they might lose their will to resist. "The assault on free institutions is world-wide now," said NSC 68, "and in the context of the present polarization of power a defeat of free institutions anywhere is a defeat everywhere." The communist-inspired coup in Czechoslovakia was an example of the psychological tremors that could be set off by Soviet aggression. "The shock we sustained in the destruction of Czechoslovakia was not in the measure of Czechoslovakia's material importance to us. In a material sense, her capabilities were already at Soviet disposal. But when the integrity of Czechoslovak institutions were [sic] destroyed, it was in the intangible scale of values that we registered a loss more damaging than the material loss we had already suffered."

If the Kremlin's program of aggression was to be checked, Nitze believed that the United States had to move decisively to enhance western morale. "As we ourselves demonstrate power, confidence and a sense of moral and political direction, so those same qualities will be evoked in Western Europe. . . . In the absence of affirmative decision on our part, the rest of the free world is almost certain to become demoralized." Nowhere was affirmative decision more readily demonstrated than in the realm of military power, Nitze believed. NSC 68's proposed buildup of U.S. military forces was intended to not only repel communist aggression wherever it should occur, but to prove to the western world that the United States was committed to its defense.

What NSC 68 called for was an American promise, backed up by military might, to support anticommunist governments throughout the world. It was to be a sweepingly ambitious promise, one predicated on the notion that the struggle between east and west was a simple clash of right and wrong.

It was to be a promise that would come back to haunt Paul Nitze.

Despite its extremely sensitive nature and top secret classification, NSC 68 was widely distributed throughout the government. In the State Department alone, Under Secretary Webb had fifteen copies sent to various officials and advisors.[50] A day later, with Johnson away at a NATO meeting in Europe, his office distributed copies of the report to the JCS and the service secretaries.[51] Over the next week Nitze's office was flooded with comments.

Generally, the response to the group's work was positive. Few officials challenged the notion that more defense spending was needed. But some did question the report's methodology and logic. State official Llewellyn Thompson wrote that the "the conclusions reached do not appear to flow logically from this analysis and some of the most important suggestions in the paper are not directly supported by the analysis."[52] Charles Bohlen echoed this view: "I believe my chief suggestion concerning this report, which is excellent in the whole, is that conclusions do not in every case stem directly from the argumentation."[53] Bohlen felt that insufficient evidence was presented to back up the claim that the gap between U.S. and Soviet military power was widening.

The harshest criticism came from Edward Barret, the assistant secretary of state for public affairs. Eventually, his office would have to sell any military buildup to the public and he wondered how it could be done. "The whole paper seems to me to point to a gigantic armament race, a huge buildup of conventional arms that quickly become obsolescent, a greatly expanded military establishment in being. I think that, however much we whip up sentiment, we are going to run into vast opposition among informed people to a huge arms race."[54] Some of the programs recommended in NSC 68 could be sold, said Barret, but not all of them.

With the exception of these complaints, no one—at least in the State Department—questioned the overall validity of NSC 68's conclusions. Even Barret wrote that "I consider this a remarkable job of analyzing the problem." Although the policy of containment was literally being rewritten, there was no grand debate about the changes. With George Kennan gone, his belief in a containment policy predicated on political and economic resistance to communism had no defenders. There was now remarkable unanimity in the State Department over the need to militarize containment. With few flourishes but undeniable finality, the Kennan era had come to an end.

At the White House there was acute uneasiness about NSC 68. Truman didn't disagree with the basic tenor of the report; he had long felt a deep antipathy toward the Soviet Union. What he did question, however, were its fiscal implications. The State-Defense review group was suggesting that billions more be spent on defense. By the Spring of 1950 Truman seems to have accepted the inevitability of this proposition. But the president, who had a sign on his desk saying "The buck stops here," was not about to sign a report whose precise budgetary implications were unclear. Five days after receiving NSC 68, he passed it on, unsigned, to the National Security Council for further review. "I am particularly anxious," Truman wrote to James Lay, "that the Council provide me with a clear indication of the programs which are envisaged in the Report, including estimates of the probable cost of such programs."[55]

After two months of labor with the review group, Nitze was not pleased to have the final report sent on to the NSC. If he and Tufts had had their way, the cost estimates that NSC 68 had originally included would have been kept in the paper. But when Nitze went to Acheson in late March and told him that the report called for a defense budget of $40 billion a year, the secretary panicked. "Paul, don't you put that figure in this report," he said. "It is right for you to estimate it and tell me about it and I will tell Mr. Truman, but the decision on the amount of money involved should not be made until it is costed out in detail. One first ought to make the decision as to whether this is the policy one wants to follow, and then the degree to which one actually implements it with appropriations is a separate question . . . but don't you get into this figure."

Acheson feared that NSC 68 would be doomed if it were burdened with a number like $40 billion. Every service and every department connected with national security would start demanding a piece of the pie. Nobody would be able to agree on a breakdown of the numbers. To have attempted an estimate, Acheson wrote later, would have "prevented any recommendation to the President."[56]

To carry out Truman's request to estimate the costs of NSC 68, Lay organized an ad hoc committee made up of an unusual array of government officials. It included Nitze and Burns from State and Defense, Under Secretary of the Army Tracy Voorhees, Hamilton Dearborn of the Council of Economic Advisors, Richard Bissell from the Economic Cooperation Administration, and officials from the CIA, the Bureau of the Budget, and the Treasury.

Whereas the drafting of NSC 68 had taken place under Nitze's direction in his own conference room, the fight over implementation would be different. It wouldn't be easy to dominate the Ad Hoc Committee, where Nitze was only one voice among eleven. In determining the fate of NSC 68's recommendations, he would have to contend with people who knew little about defense but a lot about economics—officials who had grown accustomed to Truman's fiscal austerity, whose reputations were riding on those policies, and who were wary of schemes to make radical increases in government expenditures. The Ad Hoc Committee had been in existence for less than a week when Nitze got a taste of the obstacles that lay ahead.

Among the most ardent supporters in the government of the $13.5 billion ceiling on military spending were officials from the Bureau of the Budget. They were not at all receptive to NSC 68 and its attempt to rewrite the rules of fiscal common sense. On May 8 the bureau's representative to the Ad Hoc Committee, William Schaub, mounted the most vehement attack on the paper yet made. In a lengthy memorandum prepared for the committee's second meeting, Schaub questioned the military, political, and economic thinking underlying the report. Among other things, he did not share Nitze's sanguine assessment of the economic implications of increased military spending. "There is no doubt that a larger share of resources could be devoted to security purposes," wrote Schaub, "but such a course is not without its cost under any circumstances, and the extent of diversion is crucial to an analysis of consequences."

The idea that military spending could be dramatically increased without affecting the nation's standard of living or economic well-being was simply false, said Schaub. "Large and growing military expenditures not only would divert resources from the civilian purposes to which they should be put but also would have more subtle effects on our economic system. Higher taxes, if necessary, would have a proportionately dampening effect on incentives and on the dynamic nature of the economy. . . . There would be a continuing tendency to reduce public expenditures for developmental purposes which are highly desirable for the continual strengthening of our economy."[57] For Schaub and the people at the Bureau of the Budget, the prospect of tripling military budgets was their worst nightmare come true. As Schaub later said, the bureau was "not against defense spending in particular. It was against spending that was not productive." And they could think of few things less productive than shoveling money into the Pentagon. Money "disappears pretty fast when it gets into the hands of that system," Schaub observed.

Schaub was not the only economist on the Ad Hoc Committee, however. Nor was the Bureau of the Budget the only economic agency represented. Hamilton Dearborn sat in for the Council of Economic Advisors, and neither he nor his boss, Leon Keyserling, thought that greater defense budgets would be catastrophic. Keyserling, an influential advocate of Keynesian economics, had been consulted on the question of military spending when the review group was first drafting NSC 68. "Keyserling and I discussed these matters frequently," Nitze recalled. "Though he wanted to spend the money on other programs, he was convinced that the country could afford $40 billion for defense if necessary."[58] Keyserling's views were reflected by Dearborn, who in a memo to the Ad Hoc Committee wrote, "In the Council's view, the United States economy's capacity for growth is such that substantial new programs could be undertaken without serious threat to our standards of living, and without risking a transformation of the free character of our economy."[59] As long as the nation proceeded cautiously, there would be no disaster.

By the fourth meeting of the Ad Hoc Committee a deadlock was emerging. During a discussion on May 12 it was agreed that the Ad Hoc Committee could not come to a conclusion on what the economic implications of NSC 68 were until the programs and estimates had been formulated in detail. The National Security Resources Board was the first agency to attempt this job. In late May it submitted a series of proposals to the Ad Hoc Committee for upgrading U.S. defense capabilities. Although spending for some programs such as civil defense would be greatly increased, the suggested military expenditures for the next five years fell far below the increases that NSC 68 had suggested.[60]

Meeting with top State Department officials on a warm and sunny day in early June, Nitze pointed out that the planning assumptions underlying the NSRB document and NSC 68 were very different. The group agreed that the recommendations in NSC 68 were going to meet substantial resistance.[61] It appeared that opposition to higher defense spending was just getting under way. In all likelihood, it would continue to grow.

By mid June it seemed that the recommendations of NSC 68 were destined to be forgotten and ignored. Tripling defense budgets was too radical an idea. Even if the different agencies could stop squabbling and decide how to spend the money, Congress was sure to reject such increases. For two months Paul Nitze and the Policy Planning Staff had existed in a kind of dream. Sitting around a conference table discussing geopolitical trends, the need for higher defense budgets seemed self-evident. Even Louis Johnson's lieutenants had accepted the idea. In making the case for more military spending, the State-Defense review had been a phenomenal success. It had also been a personal triumph for Nitze, whose position and authority at the State Department seemed stronger than ever.

But suddenly the dream ended. With NSC 68 remaining unsigned by the president, the battle lines were being drawn for a struggle over defense outlays. The best that could be hoped for was several billion dollars more per year. Like so many policy papers, NSC 68 seemed destined to sink quietly from sight.

Nitze, it appeared, had lost the final and most important round.

C H A P T E R 5

The Best Job
in the World

AT 9:26 P.M. on June 24, 1950, an urgent telegram arrived at the
State Department from John J. Muccio, the U.S. ambassador to
South Korea. "According [to] Korean army reports . . . North Korean
forces invaded ROK territory at several points this morning," Muccio
wrote. Areas on the Ongjin peninsula had been hit by heavy artillery fire.
North Korean infantry had invaded at three different places along the
thirty-eighth parallel. Amphibious landings had been staged on the east
coast of South Korea. By daybreak five American military advisors with
a Korean regiment near the border reported that the regiment was about
to be overrun. "It would appear from the nature of the attack and
manner in which it was launched," wrote Muccio, "that it constitutes
[an] all out offensive against ROK."[1] The Korean war had begun.

Paul Nitze was salmon fishing in New Brunswick when the attack
came. Far up the Upsalquitch River, he learned of the North Korean
move when the news came crackling over a radio brought along by one
of the guides. Nitze headed downstream as fast as possible, got into his
car, and drove at top speed to an airport, where he caught the next
flight to Washington.

Unlike many in the government, Nitze was not entirely surprised by the North Korean aggression. A few months earlier he had discussed the possibility with Alexander Sachs, an economist with Lehman Brothers. It was Sachs who had introduced Albert Einstein to President Roosevelt and helped to organize the Manhattan Project. Visiting Nitze at the State Department, he brought along several papers that argued that the Soviets viewed the "correlation of forces" as shifting in their favor. There was little question, Sachs believed, that the Kremlin would try to exploit its growing advantage in the months to come. As Nitze recalled later, the economist argued that "Moscow was naturally cautious, and would try to minimize risks by acting through a satellite. He predicted a North Korean attack upon South Korea sometime late in the summer of 1950." Immersed in writing NSC 68, Nitze found Sachs's prophecy plausible. "It did not seem a silly analysis," he said later.

The problem was how to prepare. Nitze thought that at the very least the United States should bolster the South Korean military. Working with Ambassador Muccio, he searched for ways to do this, with little success. As Nitze recalled later, "Muccio . . . and I managed to put together a $10 million program to give the South Koreans some additional fast patrol boats. That was the limit our aid program of those days would support."[2] And even that program was difficult to get through. Ever penurious, Defense Secretary Johnson opposed the military aid. In May the head of the Mutual Defense Assistance Program wrote to Dean Rusk that "Defense has maintained, and still maintains that there is no military justification for military assistance to Korea."[3]

To Nitze, the North Korean invasion was further confirmation of the Pentagon's irresponsibility. But it was more than that. This act of "naked aggression," as he termed it, appeared to confirm the basic analysis of NSC 68. Nitze had no doubt that the entire invasion was inspired and orchestrated by the Soviet Union. "It had been apparent from the first," he said in November, "that the North Korean aggression was not a product of North Korean resources and intentions. It was conceived in Moscow. It was conducted with Moscow-supplied weapons."[4]

It would later become clear that Nitze was wrong on this point. The invasion was conceived not in Moscow, but in the North Korean capital of Pyongyang. Rather than masterminding the operation, Joseph Stalin was a reluctant co-conspirator. In the panicked days of late June, however, this was not known. To Nitze, the chilling implication was that the Soviets were pushing at the soft points on its periphery, just as NSC 68 had predicted. Throughout the H-bomb debate and the State-Defense review, Nitze had contended that the Soviet Union would act more boldly now that it had atomic weapons. With the invasion of Korea, this prediction seemed to be borne out. "We were badly scared." Nitze said later. "It had been demonstrated that the Communist leaders were prepared to launch organized satellite military forces across recognized boundary lines in surprise attack to achieve their objectives. If they were prepared to do this in North Korea, why not in other areas?" More frightening still, couldn't this sort of boldness go beyond regional aggression? NSC 68 had suggested that on some dark night in the future the Soviets might use their atomic arsenal to "strike swiftly and with stealth" against the United States. Their apparent recklessness in Korea deepened Nitze's fear. If they didn't hesitate to so brazenly challenge U.S. interests abroad, "might they consider launching a surprise attack directly against the U.S. if they thought that this would give the attacker a decisive advantage?"[5]

Whatever the theoretical implications of the incursion, the immediate problem was how to contain the communist forces racing down the peninsula. One day after the attack, Acheson briefed Truman on the situation and recommended that he allow General MacArthur to send military supplies to South Korea. The president consented. He also ordered the U.S. Seventh Fleet to steam north from the Philippines and directed the air force to prepare plans to destroy all Soviet air bases in the Far East.

These measures did nothing to slow the North Korean onslaught. On Monday, June 26, President Syngman Rhee and his cabinet fled Seoul to a naval base in the south. Across the peninsula Republic of Korea troops fell back in the face of superior communist tanks and artillery. Late in the afternoon the North Koreans captured a strategic town near Seoul. The road to the capital now lay open.

That evening Truman and his advisors reassembled at Blair House. Acheson again took the lead in recommending a military response. He suggested that "an all-out order be issued to the Navy and Air Force to waive all restrictions on their operations in Korea and to offer the fullest possible support to the South Korean forces, attacking tanks, guns, columns, etc., of the North Korean forces in order to give a chance to the South Koreans to reform." The president immediately approved Acheson's recommendation, but directed that no forces be used above the thirty-eighth parallel in North Korea, "not yet."[6]

The next day the United Nations Security Council voted to assist the South Korean government in driving back the attack. The Soviet representative on the Security Council had walked out months earlier and was not present to veto the resolution. This was a critical mistake on the part of the Soviet Union. For the duration of the war, U.S. forces would operate as U.N. forces.

Despite MacArthur's use of every aircraft in Japan against the North Korean forces, the invaders rolled relentlessly southward. On Wednesday morning high State Department officials gathered in Under Secretary Webb's office and were told that "Seoul is lost."[7]

The following day, June 29, Truman escalated U.S. involvement a step further and directed that MacArthur extend air attacks into North Korea. At 1:31 A.M. on June 30 Washington received an urgent memo from MacArthur: "The Korean Army is entirely incapable of counteraction and there is grave danger of a further breakthrough. If the enemy advance continues much further it will seriously threaten the fall of the Republic. The only assurance for the holding of the present line, and the ability to regain later the lost ground, is through the introduction of U.S. ground combat forces into the Korean battle area."[8]

After receiving MacArthur's telegram, Army Chief of Staff General Pace called Truman to relay the request for combat troops. At 5:00 A.M. President Truman acceded to MacArthur's wish. When the country awoke that morning, it learned that the United States was about to go to war in Korea.

Paul Nitze supported the hard line from the beginning. Obsessed with the psychological dimensions of the Cold War, Nitze agreed with Acheson that the United States had to stand firm against aggression in Korea. Failure to do so would send a signal to the world that the United States was either unable or unwilling to defend its interests and its allies. The entire thrust of U.S. and U.N. policy, Nitze felt, dictated an armed response to the North Korean move. "The terms of the Charter and the logic of our own position," he said later, "left no choice. We had to react by counter military measures. The entire program for collective security was at stake."[9]

By itself, South Korea was not integral to U.S. security. Acheson himself had excluded it from a Pacific "defensive perimeter" that he had outlined in a speech earlier in the year. But like Czechoslovakia, South Korea suddenly became a symbol of communist aggression and the west's will to resist Kremlin belligerence. Nitze was convinced that the United States had only two options: demonstrate resolve or absorb a devastating defeat in the Cold War. "The assault on free institutions is world-wide now," he had written in NSC 68, "and in the context of the present polarization of power a defeat of free institutions anywhere is a defeat everywhere."[10]

Still, Nitze wanted the United States to move with caution. He watched uneasily as General MacArthur took control of U.N. forces fighting in Korea. Just days after the attack, as the U.N. resolution naming MacArthur commander was being drawn up, Nitze had a disturbing talk with one of his new staff members, Charles Burton Marshall.

A few years before, Marshall had worked closely with T. J. Davis, a former aide to MacArthur, and the two men became friends. In long talks Davis told Marshall hair-raising stories about his former boss— stories about his arrogance, his disregard for higher authority, and his compulsive risk taking. "The man he described to me was a real fruitcake," Marshall said later. Davis was sure that it was only a matter of time before MacArthur "blew a fuse."

When he learned that the general was to be given the Korean command, Marshall related his talks with Davis to Nitze. "You can't trust this fellow," he said. Nitze agreed, remembering well MacArthur's disturbing resemblance to a Roman consul. Getting hold of John Hickerson, State's U.N. man, Nitze tried to stop the appointment, but it was too late. The resolution had already begun circulating. MacArthur would be the U.N. commander.

And there were other danger signs. As U.S. troops and supplies began to flow onto the Korean peninsula, talk in the government turned to the possibility of carrying the ground war into North Korea. In July the discussion remained hypothetical, since U.S. troops were pinned down on the end of the peninsula. But no one doubted that the tide would soon turn, and as communist troops were pushed back, the United States would have to decide whether to move into North Korea and crush Kim Il-sung's communist regime. General MacArthur pushed the idea, as did many others in the government. But Nitze dissented. Crossing the thirty-eighth parallel could prove disastrous, he felt. The risks of triggering a wider war with China or the Soviet Union were simply too high. Nothing the United States might gain from crushing Kim would be worth a global conflagration. In mid July Nitze began calling for a stated U.S. policy of remaining below the thirty-eighth parallel. In this effort he found an unlikely collaborator: George Kennan.

Kennan had been on his Maryland farm when the attack came. Returning to Washington, he found the State Department gripped by frenzied excitement. For the first time in many months, Kennan fell in step with the mood of the moment. "It was clear to me from the start that we would have to react with all necessary force to repel this attack and to expel the North Korean forces from the southern half of the peninsula," he later wrote.[11] Although Kennan felt "relegated to the sidelines" because he wasn't invited to the Blair House war councils, he came to play a central role in State Department deliberations. During the first week of the war the secretary of state invited his old policy director and Nitze to lunch. "When I left Washington," Kennan quipped, "it never occurred to me that you two fellows would go ahead and make policy on behalf of the United States without consulting me."[12]

In the tumult that followed North Korea's attack, Kennan rebuilt his rapport with top State Department officials. Predictably, however, he soon found himself disturbed by the direction of the government's war policy. Kennan felt it was critical to make it clear that the United States had no intention of crossing the thirty-eighth parallel. He argued that "the further we were to advance up the peninsula the more unsound it would become from the military standpoint." He held that the United States should terminate its operations once it drove the North Koreans from the South, and that "it was desirable that we did not frighten the Russians into actions which would interfere with this."[13]

Acheson, in a dark and angry mood, was inclined to go north, go north and grind Kim Il-sung's army into the dust. But for the first time in many months, Nitze sided against his boss and with George Kennan. During the second week of July Nitze and Kennan and the Policy Planning Staff began drafting a paper which called for a U.S. policy of not advancing beyond the thirty-eighth parallel. Most of the staff supported this view. "There was a general consensus that Acheson was going in the wrong direction on this," recalled Dorothy Fosdick. Nitze and the staff felt that Acheson, by supporting a step that would mire the United States in a land war in Asia, was ignoring his better Atlanticist instincts. He was playing right into Soviet hands. "If we were going to pick a quarrel with the Russians," observed John Paton Davies, "Manchuria was the last place to choose. As far as the Russians were concerned it was a very useful diversion against us. It would leave Europe easy picking for them. It was a distraction."

Only Charles Burton Marshall felt that MacArthur's forces shouldn't, and couldn't, stop. Marshall had worked on Korean matters for the House Committee on Foreign Affairs. He was familiar with the geography of the Korean peninsula and had also been in the army. He disagreed strongly both with Kennan ("one of the most ignorant bas-tards I ever saw on this kind of question") and with Nitze, whom he considered a great strategic mind, but not much of a tactical thinker. "There wasn't any way of stopping at the thirty-eighth parallel," Mar-shall argued almost forty years later, his voice rising and rich with scorn, his large wrinkled hands chopping the air. "It was a civilian delusion that you can stop along some geometric line. You can't. The nature of battle is determined by the mountains, by the rivers, by the accesses," and by the need to protect one's flanks. To stop the drive north at an abstract point, said Marshall, could leave U.S. forces vulnerable to devastating counterattacks.

To Nitze and Kennan, however, this risk was more palatable than a possible war with China. They ignored Marshall. It was harder to ignore the rest of the government. The mood in Washington was militant and vindictive. Even before their memorandum was com-pleted, the Policy Planning Staff came under blistering attack.

In a letter to Nitze, John Foster Dulles—a leading Republican who had been brought in as a consultant to Acheson in the name of biparti-sanship—lashed out at the idea of leaving the North Korean regime intact. "The 38th Parallel, if perpetuated as a political line and as providing asylum to the aggressor, is bound to perpetuate friction and ever-present danger of new war," Dulles argued. "If we have the oppor-tunity to obliterate the line as a political division, certainly we should do so." Not only would the elimination of the communist regime bolster security in the region but it would teach a lesson to other would-be aggressors. "If there can be armed aggression under condi-tions such that failure involves no permanent loss, then that puts a premium on aggression," Dulles said.[14]

A day later John Allison, the director of the Office of Northeast Asian Affairs, also blasted the Policy Planning Staff. "At the very least we should destroy the North Korean Army," he wrote. Echoing Dulles, Allison argued that "A determination that the aggressors should not go unpunished and vigorous, courageous United States leadership to that end should have a salutary effect upon other areas of tension in the world."[15]

Despite his belief in rolling back communist influence, Nitze was unmoved by the arguments put forward by Dulles and Allison. He may have found rollback a compelling theory, but when confronted with the prospect of triggering a third world war, Nitze balked. In practice, a central reality made rollback unworkable: The Soviet Union would never tolerate a U.S.-backed regime within its orbit. Completed by July

25, the Policy Planning Staff memorandum, heavily influenced by Kennan's thinking, stressed this point. "There is ample evidence of the strategic importance to Russia of the Korean peninsula," the paper stated. "It is unlikely that the Kremlin at present would accept the establishment in North Korea of a regime which it could not dominate and control." For this reason, there was a grave risk that "U.N. military action north of the 38th parallel would result in conflict with the U.S.S.R. or Communist China."

Nitze and his colleagues believed that it was dangerously naive to think that Korea could be unified during the war. They argued that the situation was far too complex to be dealt with through military force and "that a satisfactory permanent solution of the Korean problem can be hoped for only when and if a substantial accommodation is reached between the U.S.S.R. and the non-communist world."[16]

During his years under Truman, Paul Nitze won almost every bureaucratic battle he fought. This would not be one of them. The staff's call for restraint on the Korean peninsula was ignored. On September 15, 1950, General MacArthur staged a bold amphibious landing at Inchon, a city near Seoul, two hundred miles behind enemy lines. A few days later the Eighth Army, which had been pinned down near Pusan at the end of the peninsula, broke through North Korean lines. Afraid of being trapped by MacArthur's advancing forces, North Korean troops fled in disarray toward the thirty-eighth parallel. They took heavy losses but managed to get back to North Korea with twenty-five thousand troops. The tables had turned. Seoul was quickly recaptured, and MacArthur was authorized, with Acheson's support, to pursue the enemy forces into North Korea. On October 9 the general mounted a full-scale invasion across the thirty-eighth parallel.

During the first few weeks of the counterinvasion, victory followed victory. United States troops conquered almost half of North Korea in just seventeen days. At a mid October conference on Wake Island, MacArthur told Truman that "It is my belief that organized resistance throughout Korea will be ended by Thanksgiving."[17] When the president asked whether Chinese intervention was possible, the general assured him that Mao did not have the forces available for such a move. Truman returned to Washington relieved. The war seemed near an end.

An issue that had lurked in the background of the government's deliberations since the first day of North Korean attack was the use of atomic weapons. In the initial war council at Blair House, General

Vandenberg had mentioned the possibility of using atomic weapons to destroy Soviet air bases in the Far East.[18] Nobody liked the idea, and the issue was rarely raised at high-level meetings during the summer and fall of 1950.

Nitze suspected that the matter would come up again. On November 4 he invited General Herbert Loper of the Defense Department to his office to discuss the subject. Loper worked on atomic weapons matters for the army, and he and others in the Pentagon had long pondered the problems of using atomic weapons on the battlefield. Detailing how the bomb might be used in Korea, Loper said that it would be employed for "tactical purposes against troop concentrations and artillery support positions." The result might be to deter "further Chinese participation in the war." Also, "If the bomb were used for tactical purposes, it is unlikely there would be large destruction of civilian life." Militarily, said Loper, the use of atomic weapons in Korea would be effective, but not "decisive."

Politically, however, use of the A-bomb would be a nightmare. Following the meeting, Nitze wrote that there was a "serious possibility that its use might bring the Soviet Union into the war" and "would help arouse the peoples of Asia against us." Whatever the case it would be critical to win U.N. approval to use atomic weapons, and the protracted debate surrounding such a request "would be of military value to our adversary." Taken together, Nitze thought it doubtful that the United States would gain from using nuclear weapons in Korea.[19]

Later in the war the United States would again consider using nuclear weapons, but in November such drastic action seemed unnecessary. As MacArthur drove the tattered remnants of North Korea's armies toward the Chinese border, he appeared close to his goal of destroying all opposition on the peninsula.

On November 24 the general launched a final offensive. "If this operation is successful," he said with customary cockiness, "I hope we can get the boys home for Christmas."[20] The next day China ripped into the Eighth Army with 300,000 troops which had secretly infiltrated North Korea. MacArthur's final offensive had landed U.S. forces in a deadly trap. The Eighth Army suffered one thousand casualties in the first forty-eight hours of fighting. "We face an entirely new war," the general told the JCS.[21]

While Nitze might have felt vindicated for a brief moment when he heard the news, his dominant reaction was alarm. The United States was now doing battle with the Sino-Soviet bloc itself. "This development presents our nation with one of the greatest challenges in its history," he said a few days later.[22] Another world war was not inconceivable.

On November 28 Nitze accompanied Acheson to the White House for one of the gloomiest NSC meetings of Truman's presidency. Although he retained his customary poise, the secretary of state was in anguish. He felt that he had failed the president in not leading a move to restrain MacArthur, and he was deeply distressed by China's intervention, telling the group that the United States was "much closer to the danger of general war."[23] A CIA report issued several days later echoed this view: "The USSR is prepared to accept, and may be seeking to precipitate, a general war between the United States and China, despite the inherent risk of global war."[24]

Following the Chinese onslaught, the U.S. position in Korea rapidly unraveled. Early in the morning of December 3, an ominous telegram arrived from MacArthur: "This small command . . . is facing the entire Chinese nation in an undeclared war, and unless some positive and immediate action is taken, hope for success cannot be justified and steady attrition leading to final destruction can reasonably be contemplated."[25] When Acheson and Nitze arrived at the Pentagon a few hours later, the mood was somber. The secretary of defense and the chiefs of staff—men who had been confident and often brilliant leaders in World War II—expressed despair and helplessness about the events unfolding halfway around the world. With MacArthur's forces pinned down near the Yalu River and fresh Chinese troops pouring into the combat zone, it appeared that the United States was heading for a major military defeat.

Talk turned to bombing China, calling for a cease-fire, or evacuating the peninsula. Acheson was adamantly opposed to evacuation. "There is danger of our becoming the greatest appeaser of all time if we abandon the Koreans and they are slaughtered," he said. Admiral Sherman of the JCS went even further. The United States had to prepare for war with China to salvage its prestige, he argued. "If we don't take this course, others will begin to push us around. If any one can kill that many Americans and not be at war, we are defeated."

Sherman's logic was straight out of NSC 68. But Nitze wondered whether the United States wanted to push the stakes so high. "Are we ready to follow the chain of events if the Soviet Union puts in its forces in support of the Chinese?" he asked the group. The NATO alliance might not stick together in such an event, Nitze warned. "There would be a slight chance of holding our European allies. It is not possible to hold the UK in line for early hostilities with the Soviet Union. . . . If we carry hostilities against China and the Soviet Union comes in, what do we do?"[26]

The result of a hasty or ill-conceived action could be global war. Yet Nitze believed that the United States had to move decisively to avoid humiliation. It was a delicate balance. "A mistake," he remarked on November 30, "a failure to weigh all the implications of an act, a failure to act to the limits of our capabilities, a failure to act prudently and in time, might involve our nation in the greatest ordeal of its history."[27]

Two days later, as the situation continued to deteriorate, Nitze reluctantly began leaning toward the idea of hitting China. At a State Department meeting on December 5, he suggested that the U.S. should make every effort to obtain a cease-fire, but if this didn't work and Chinese forces continued to press MacArthur, the United States should give "consideration to blowing up the dams on the Yalu River." Kennan was in agreement. The Chinese, he said, "have committed an affront of the greatest magnitude to the United States. . . . we owe China nothing but a lesson."[28]

The United States did not extend the war into China. MacArthur held his position on the peninsula and the military situation stabilized. On December 15 President Truman declared a national emergency, telling the American people that "Our homes, our nation, all the things we believe in are in great danger. This danger has been created by the rulers of the Soviet Union."[29] In Korea, neither China nor the Soviet Union moved to push the United States too far.

As new supplies flowed to U.S. forces in Korea, the Eighth Army and the Tenth Corps slowly revived. They retreated back under the thirty-eighth parallel and managed to hold a line some fifty miles south of Seoul. For the next two years the war would be virtually stalemated.

Because it seemed to confirm the analysis of NSC 68, the invasion of South Korea was a boon to Nitze's crusade to overhaul American national security policy, allowing him to achieve the bureaucratic victory that had so recently seemed beyond reach. In September Truman finally approved the State-Defense review group's report. Over the next several months NSC 68 would be revised three times in an effort to hammer it into a more specific policy guidance document. Most of the cold war rhetoric was chopped out. The sweeping comparison between the United States and the Soviet Union was eliminated. NSC 68/3, the final draft, concentrated instead on detailing how much money would be spent and where it would go.

The armed forces, it specified, would be increased to 3.2 million men by June 1952. Military assistance to NATO countries would be stepped up. Civil defense funding would be increased by almost half a billion dollars, and stockpiling of strategic materials would continue. An expensive propaganda campaign would seek to lionize the United States and vilify the Sino-Soviet bloc. Finally, the government would make a greater effort to root out communist subversion in the United States.

Not every measure Nitze wanted was approved, but when Truman signed NSC 68/3, he extended the Policy Planning Staff's mandate to continue its work. In a separate memo the president instructed the secretary of state and the secretary of defense "to undertake immediately a joint review of the politico-military strategy of this government with a view to increasing and speeding up the programs outlined in NSC 68/3."[30]

With the Korean war all consuming, no action was taken on this directive until June 1951. Beginning in that month, Nitze helped draft a successor to NSC 68 designated NSC 114. Again the tone was ominous. Almost every trend in the Cold War boded ill for the United States, the new paper said. Since April 1950 "the Soviet rulers have continued in relentless pursuit of the Kremlin design." Not only were they psychologically steeling their nation for war, but militarily they were ever more able to actually wage it. "The U.S.S.R. . . . is substantially stronger than in April 1950," the document stated. While the United States ignored its rearmament goals, Soviet capabilities grew unabated. "The strength in being of the United States and its allies has probably increased in absolute terms less than that of the Soviet system since April 1950."

In its grim summation NSC 114 warned that "Review of the world situation shows that the danger to our security is greater now than it was in April 1950. . . . Fifteen months ago 1954 was regarded as the time of maximum danger. It now appears that we are already in a period of acute danger which will continue until the United States and its allies achieve an adequate position of strength." The paper recommended an accelerated effort to implement the military buildup called for by NSC 68/3.[31]

In the climate of barely controlled panic and ferocious anticommunism that characterized 1951, there was little opposition to NSC 114. Yet while Truman quickly approved the document, not everybody agreed with its assumptions. Charles Bohlen was particularly disturbed by the new paper. What he saw in NSC 114 was a grossly distorted picture of the Soviet threat, the same picture he had seen in NSC 68. Bohlen had been in Paris when NSC 68 was being drafted. By the time he returned to Washington, the study was virtually completed. Because he agreed with the general thrust of the recommendations, Bohlen chose not to pick a fight over the issue of Soviet intentions. Now, in his new post as Counselor to the secretary of state, Bohlen was determined to set the record straight.

Writing to Nitze in late July, Bohlen explained that he wholly supported the goal of rearming, but was uncomfortable with the picture that NSC 114 painted of the Soviet Union. It didn't make sense. What bothered him most, was "the presentation of the Soviet Union as a mechanical chess player engaged in the execution of a design fully prepared in advance with the ultimate goals of world domination." This was not the way the Soviets worked, Bohlen felt. Nor did he agree with the alarming notion that Korea "represented a new phase in Soviet general policy indicating a willingness to accept the grave risk of precipitating global war which was not present before Korea."

As a Soviet expert who had spent years trying to divine the real nature of Kremlin decision making, Bohlen could not endorse this kind of speculative analysis. Certainly Paul Nitze had no basis on which to make such a sweeping judgment, he felt.[32]

When Nitze failed to act on Bohlen's memo, the counselor took his case to Acheson. In an impassioned August memorandum Bohlen argued that State should work to "introduce more precision and accuracy in the analysis of the Soviet Union's international policy." A vital first step was to abandon the distorted view of Soviet intentions contained in NSC 68.

Assaulting Nitze's central thesis, Bohlen stated, "The chief purpose of the Soviet Union is not the world wide extension of communism to which all other considerations are subordinated." The men in the Kremlin were self-centered. They had no inclination to risk their position of power to extend communism. Echoing the judgments expressed a year earlier by the CIA, Bohlen argued that "Ever since his accession to power the guiding thought of the Stalinist Group has been that under no circumstances and for no revolutionary gains must the Soviet state be involved in risks to the maintenance of Soviet power in Russia."[33] International adventurism posed such risks by increasing the chances of a global war with the United States. Because the Soviets feared war with the United States, Bohlen believed they would remain committed to a cautious foreign policy.

In September, as NSC 114 was being revised, Bohlen drafted another memorandum suggesting specific changes in the document that would reflect this reality. Again he attacked Nitze's groundless assumptions and cautioned against engaging in "metaphysical speculation" about Soviet intentions.[34]

Nitze decided that he'd had enough of the Counselor's cavilling. In a rebuttal, he argued that the entire government must agree on one interpretation of Soviet intentions, the one contained in NSC 68. "If we accept as facts," Nitze argued, "that the USSR is implacably hostile, that they have dangerously superior relative capabilities for local or limited actions, and that they will act opportunistically, then it seems to me that the USSR will exercise their capabilities at any time and place they conceive to be favorable to them." Such an assumption, Nitze added, hardly constituted "metaphysical speculation."[35]

Bohlen was increasingly angry with Nitze's insistence on putting forward a judgment he wasn't qualified by training to make, and he told Acheson so. Nitze's interpretation of Soviet intentions "is not a true picture of how the Soviet Union operates insofar as I have observed it and studied it," Bohlen wrote. Paul Nitze didn't know what he was talking about.[36]

Several weeks later, as Nitze and his staff continued revising NSC 114 without incorporating any of Bohlen's suggested changes, the counselor intensified his attack. Again writing to Acheson, Bohlen complained that the latest draft "totally ignores, except for one brief phrase buried on page 20, the role of the Soviet internal situation in Soviet policies and actions." Such an omission was intolerable. The internal situation was perhaps the "single greatest controlling force in its foreign policy; yet this is virtually ignored in the entire 68 series." Just as egregious, Bohlen wrote, was the paper's treatment of Soviet perspectives on war. "No attempt whatsoever is made to analyze the great body of Soviet thought in regard to war between states or the even more elementary fact that any war, whether the prospect of victory be dim or bright, carries with it major risks to the Soviet system in Russia." Bohlen urged Acheson to restrict Nitze and his colleagues to studying U.S. military programs and to direct qualified consultants to undertake a thorough study of Soviet intentions.[37]

No such study ever took place. With Acheson and most of the State Department ready to assume the worst about the Soviets following Korea, Nitze was free to ignore Bohlen. It was a victory he relished. Almost thirty-five years later, settled into a comfortable armchair in his State Department office to discuss current arms control questions with a reporter, Nitze digressed into an account of his feud with his old clubmate Bohlen. "I turned out to be right and Chip wrong," he concluded with an air of vindication.[38]

More accurately, it was not a matter of who was right and who was wrong; Nitze had the secretary's ear and Bohlen did not.

Less than two years after Paul Nitze had first engaged the question of U.S. policy toward the Soviet Union, his singularly alarmist assessment of the Kremlin's intentions reigned unchallenged in the government. His victory on this point was remarkable. Supported by neither the intelligence agencies nor any Soviet experts, Nitze had dealt a crippling blow to the assumption—originally propagated by Kennan and ably defended by Bohlen—that the Soviet Union was a cautious power unlikely to risk a direct confrontation with the United States. Not until the blossoming of detente a decade and a half later would this view again receive a serious hearing within the U.S. government.

Nitze's victory over Bohlen underscored his growing power. By 1951 Paul Nitze had become one of the most active and influential foreign policy officials in the Truman administration. A decade on Wall Street and a decade in government had made him a bureaucrat of unusual adroitness. Working Washington with élan and confidence, Nitze cultivated ties everywhere. After Louis Johnson was fired in September 1950, he made a special effort to expand his contacts across the Potomac. Consultations on Korea brought Nitze to the Pentagon as often as three times a week. He solidified his longtime relationship with Department of Defense civilians and built a rapport with the Joint Chiefs of Staff. As Acheson's point men on the war, he and Robert Tufts spent long hours in the "tank"—the JCS's bug-proof conference room. By January 1951 relations between the Policy Planning Staff and the JCS were so good that Nitze organized regular weekly meetings with JCS officials at the State Department. There was no rigid agenda. Rather, the meetings were informal gatherings for exchanging information and maintaining open lines of communication.[39]

In the small national security establishment of the early 1950s, Nitze's brand of bureaucratic activism was extremely effective. He had a great capacity for identifying and filling power vacuums. At a time before there existed legions of national security experts from a half dozen agencies, Nitze and his small staff were able to wield influence on a wide range of policy questions, from disarmament policy to U.S. relations with Iran.

By 1951 the Policy Planning Staff's standing in the State Department could not have been better. Acheson relied heavily on the staff and made an effort to keep Nitze's people in the loop. "You weren't off in a corner," recalled Charles Burton Marshall, "you really were involved." Located next to Acheson's office, the staff's conference room pulsed with excitement. Top officials from the White House, Pentagon, and CIA dropped in regularly for visits or briefings. Acheson himself would often slip through the side door to sit in on the staff's contentious discussions, and most members of the staff could expect occasionally to be called into the secretary's office for a one-on-one briefing. "You were right at the top of the policy-making process," said Dorothy Fosdick, her face lit up by the memory. "It was a wonderful time for all of us." Never in his life had Paul Nitze more thoroughly enjoyed himself. "It was the best job in the world," he said later.

With Korea, McCarthy, and the Cold War, there was a new upheaval nearly every week. At times the staff worked more like Acheson's personal crisis management team than as a policy planning group. As Robert Tufts recalled, the staff had a tendency "to be diverted from long-range strategic considerations and to get involved with whatever the current crisis was." Their work reflected the needs of Acheson. And for that assistance, he rewarded the staff and its director with power.

But it was not solely the willingness of Acheson to listen to the planning group that mattered; his own position in the administration counted as well. With Truman solidly behind him, this position could not have been much stronger. Unlike most of the secretaries of state who succeeded him, Acheson did not have to engage in exhausting guerrilla warfare against the secretary of defense or the national security advisor to protect his turf. To the end of his presidency, Truman regarded Acheson as his chief advisor on national security affairs. With the secretary of state's power unchallenged, the planning staff's position was secure as well.

Personal relationships in the State Department also contributed to Nitze's influence. Acheson's natural affinity for his planning director was accentuated by the distaste with which the exacting statesman viewed others in the department. In particular, Acheson had little confidence in his under secretary, James Webb. Picked by Truman, Webb was not Acheson's choice for the job and the two men never worked well together. "It wasn't that these men were at each other's throats or wouldn't speak to each other, but there not close collaboration between them," recalled Burt Marshall. Foreign affairs was not Webb's strong point, and Acheson, impatient with the less gifted, was not inclined to be his tutor.

The secretary of state was no more enamored of his assistant secretaries. Chiefly foreign service officers, a profession for which Acheson had little use, the assistant secretaries tended to concentrate on their own areas, emphasizing narrow concerns over larger policy goals. To shape a coherent national security policy, Acheson felt he needed broader analyses. Normally, such broader analyses might have been done by the deputy under secretary of state for political affairs. But that official, H. Freeman Matthews, failed to deliver. "Doc was a small-staff man," recalled Lucius Battle. "He didn't want much of a staff for himself. The result was that he had about two people working for him." The result also was that his breadth of knowledge was limited.

Nitze's base was far stronger. His staff, comprised of roughly a dozen members, was small enough to allow for intimate collaboration, yet large enough to include experts in a range of fields (with the unfortunate exception of Soviet affairs). Oriented toward long-range planning and overall policy, the staff provided precisely the sort of global thinking and sweeping guidance that Acheson found lacking in the rest of the department. It was also an easygoing group. Nitze sought to create a working environment free of rigid hierarchy and senseless bureaucracy. He had a "great capacity for making collaborators out of his subordinates," recalled Marshall. Nitze fostered an atmosphere where debate mattered, where the exchange of ideas was real, and where staff members could change their boss's mind or broaden his thinking. "He really was open to suggestions very much, more so than Kennan," said Carlton Savage. Even if he disagreed with a point, added Tufts, he was "certainly prepared to hear the argumentation out." And when Nitze lost an argument—as he sometimes did—he lost it gracefully.

Fierce debate was the norm at staff meetings. At times the debate raged so intensely that outsiders came away from meetings thinking that Nitze's group was riven with animosity. After one typical meeting, Hans Morgenthau, a consultant to the State Department, left the conference room shaken. Taking Tufts aside, he said that "things must be in terrible shape." In fact, the group was as close knit as ever. "We just didn't have to be polite with each other because we knew each other so well and could be frank, not hesitating to tell each other if something was a lot of nonsense," said Tufts.

Nitze encouraged an atmosphere of openness, but he also drove his people hard and had little patience for a staffer who failed to perform. If you weren't prepared when you went to see Nitze, said Savage, "he wouldn't have much time for you." Nobody can remember Nitze's firing anybody, but "some people were very, very rarely consulted," said Tufts. And the time such people spent on the staff was "short lived."

Nitze demanded everybody's maximum input for a simple reason: He wanted the staff to wield influence on as wide an array of issues as possible. He also wanted to insure that the staff's ideas were not lost in the bureaucracy. Having an impact on policy meant, above all, that good plans were translated into concrete actions. "The best plan," Nitze observed in 1951, "is of little but academic interest until it is acted upon. We have found that it is important to participate in this follow-through so that . . . we don't lose touch with the actual operators and become an ivory-tower organization."[40] Nothing was worse than becoming irrelevant, Nitze felt. Kennan had suffered that fate; people had just stopped listening.

By making himself invaluable to Acheson, by opening up channels throughout the administration, and by concentrating on "follow through," Nitze insured that he never became isolated.

In his pursuit of influence under Truman, few issues were more important to Paul Nitze than atomic weapons. Here, he was particularly determined to be a dominant voice in administration councils. Ever since the H-bomb debate Nitze had sought to exert as much personal control as possible over atomic weapons policy. In a sense, he didn't trust other officials to handle this grave matter. He doubted many of his colleagues had the sobriety and nerve to think rationally about atomic weapons. The near hysterical opposition to the H-bomb underlined this point in his mind. Nitze believed that only dispassion and realism—two qualities he felt he possessed in abundance—could produce a sound atomic policy.

Until 1951 Nitze had spent much of his time working to increase the American atomic stockpile. In the spring of that year he became involved in a unique effort to limit such weapons.

Although NSC 68 had dismissed disarmament negotiations with the Soviet Union as futile, the Truman administration was not ready to give up on the idea. Acheson still hoped that an intelligent deal could be struck with the Soviets. Other administration officials believed that arms control had to be pursued for propaganda reasons. Truman himself had publicly committed the United States to disarmament negotiations in a speech to the United Nations in late 1950. Accordingly, on February 23, 1951, the National Security Council directed the departments of State and Defense to begin work on a "plan for the reduction and regulation of armaments and armed forces."[41] Nitze was chosen to coordinate the effort.

With Johnson's exit from the Pentagon, and George Kennan no longer pestering State with his heretical memos, assembling a consensus on disarmament policy was much easier than it would have been a year earlier.

Meeting with State Department officials on March 7, Nitze outlined ideas already under consideration at the Policy Planning Staff. The most promising plan for reducing armaments, he suggested, was one that would tie limits on both conventional and atomic armaments to each country's population and gross national product. No country, for example, would be allowed to put more than 1 percent of its population under arms or devote more than a certain amount of its GNP to armaments. While such a scheme was ambitious, Nitze argued that it might work if coupled with a broad effort to ease tensions between east and west.[42]

In a March 10 memorandum Nitze set out his thinking on this matter in greater detail. Repeating the arguments made in NSC 68, he wrote that success in arms control depended entirely on the state of U.S.-Soviet relations: "International tensions have become so acute and so widespread that it seems unlikely that important progress can be made on any major issue except in the context of a comprehensive approach to the general reduction of tensions." Negotiating an Austrian peace treaty, unifying Germany, and terminating the war in Korea could all be part of a broad effort to foster better ties.

If cooperation in these areas produced successes, and if the superpowers got to the point where they could talk to each other and trust each other, Nitze wrote, a bid to reduce armed forces might work.

The disarmament plan he proposed was sweeping. It would cover "all weapons and armed forces" of almost all the nations in the world. In the realm of conventional armaments, his plan would establish ceilings on the size of armed forces, the proportion of gross national product used for military purposes, and the number of tanks, aircraft, and naval vessels that each nation could deploy. Nitze recommended further that chemical and biological weapons be banned completely and that atomic weapons be dealt with "in accordance with the U.N. plan or with some other plan which is equally or more satisfactory."[43]

With this memorandum Nitze once again set the terms of a major policy debate. On March 15, JCS Chairman Omar Bradley met with State Department officials and established a working group under Nitze's direction to study his recommendations. By early July the working group had produced NSC 112, an extensive inquiry into the problems of arms control. That document would serve as a foundation of U.S. negotiating policy for the next two years.

Expanding on Nitze's memorandum, NSC 112 stated that any program for reducing armaments must first establish a system for the "disclosure and verification of armed forces and armaments." Once such a system was in place, the parties involved could begin working toward the overall goal of bringing about the "regulation, limitation and balanced reduction of armed forces and armaments to a level which would decrease substantially the possibility of a successful initial aggression." If all went as planned, the result would be a safer world.[44]

NSC 112 was well received in the Truman administration and approved on July 19, 1951. In one sense it was another bureaucratic victory for Paul Nitze; his disarmament plan rather than someone else's had been accepted by the president. At the same time it was not a victory at all. In the tense climate of the early 1950s, with the Americans and Soviets hardly speaking and a war raging in Korea, it was clear that such a plan was doomed to fail. Even Nitze never took his own proposal seriously. "I knew perfectly well that the Soviets would never buy the idea; nor, even if they did, would we have any way of getting a true account of how much they were spending or how many men they were keeping under arms." On a more fundamental level, Nitze didn't take the plan seriously because he did not yet believe in arms control. Just a year before, in NSC 68, he had written that "it is impossible to hope that an effective plan for international control can be negotiated unless and until the Kremlin design has been frustrated to a point at which a genuine and drastic change in Soviet policies has taken place."

With Stalin securely ensconced in the Kremlin, no such change was on the horizon. And, as Nitze himself was quick to point out, the Soviets were, if anything, more belligerent now that they had atomic weapons.

Additional evidence that Nitze was not yet committed to arms control came a year after NSC 112 was approved. By 1952 the United States had developed the technology to build a thermonuclear weapon. But before going ahead with testing, Truman wanted to take another look at the consequences of exploding a weapon that could have a thousand times the destructive power of the bomb that leveled Hiroshima. In June he once again directed the Special Committee of the NSC, made up of the secretaries of state and defense and the chairman of the AEC, to examine the H-bomb issue.

Nitze wasted no time in jumping into the debate. Within a few days of Truman's directive, he dispatched a memorandum to Acheson urging him to oppose any delay in testing thermonuclear weapons. Dismissing the notion that the United States should try to head off a more deadly arms race by seeking a moratorium on H-bomb testing, Nitze wrote that such a move "would not bring a halt to thermonuclear development programs." Instead, "each side would attempt to put itself in a position that would assure the greatest probability of being able rapidly to manufacture successful weapons in the event of a violation of the agreement."

To Nitze, the arms race was a symptom rather than a cause of the superpower rivalry. Stopping the march of technology would not ease the clash of ideology. "The confrontation that has led us to put so much of our energy and such quantities of our resources into the atomic and thermonuclear programs will not be altered by a standstill arrangement," he told Acheson. Again, Nitze stressed that arms control would be possible only if there were fundamental changes in the Soviet system. Until such changes came about, until the Kremlin dismantled its totalitarian machinery and abandoned its expansionist dreams, the United States should spare no effort and be restrained by no moral qualms in its pursuit of technological superiority over the Soviet Union. "If the U.S. atomic capability is dramatically increased in the near or medium term through the development of thermonuclear weapons, this accretion of effective power may serve as an instrument for securing the objectives expressed in NSC 68 without war," Nitze wrote.

Bluntly stated, Nitze believed that the H-bomb might give the United States the coercive edge it needed to protect western security interests and roll back Soviet power in eastern Europe. On the strength of these arguments, he recommended proceeding with plans to test thermonuclear weapons in November of 1952.[45] This position did not go unchallenged in the Truman administration. As the thermonuclear age drew closer, many experts became uneasy about the impending tests.

In early September the Panel of Consultants on Disarmament released a report that summarized the arguments for and against testing the new weapon and recommended a postponement. Made up of experts ranging from Robert Oppenheimer to Allen Dulles, the panel was a new but respected group within the administration, and it was unwilling to rubber-stamp a step as potentially destabilizing as the testing of a new type of weapon. The group warned that the United States was rushing too impulsively into a spiraling arms race. And the H-bomb, with its unfathomable capacity for destruction, was a significant escalation of that race. The panel urged Truman to step back from the abyss. "The arguments for a postponement of the projected thermonuclear test seem to us persuasive," the report said. Rejecting Nitze's dire forecasts, they stated, "We are not persuaded by the claim that postponement would bring unacceptable dangers, and while we admit that it is not clear where a postponement would lead, we have to note that this ignorance applies to any effort to limit the current power struggle."[46] Certainly refraining from the development of the H-bomb would not undermine America's nuclear deterrent. By 1952 the United States had over a thousand A-bombs and was producing new warheads at the rate of nearly one a day. The ability of the United States to destroy the Soviet Union was unquestioned. Developing a new and powerful weapon would only multiply that capacity.

Despite the passion of their plea for caution, the panel's counsel was ignored. The real power on this matter lay in the hands of the Special Committee. At a meeting late on the bleak and rainy afternoon of October 9, the committee voiced unanimous support for H-bomb testing.

In marshaling the arguments against postponement, Secretary Acheson, who by this time had overcome his uneasiness about the H-bomb, asked Nitze to expand on the case for early tests. Attacking the panel's moratorium proposal, Nitze said that it "took only superficial analysis to conclude that such a proposal would not be to the advantage of the United States inasmuch as in all probability even if the Soviet Union were to agree to such a moratorium they would doubtless proceed in every way possible short of tests to improve their thermonuclear as well as atomic position against the day they were prepared to violate the moratorium." Two years earlier Nitze had dismissed a moratorium because it might leave the United States behind in the race for a thermonuclear weapon. Now that the United States had developed such a weapon, Nitze's argument changed little. Not only did he see advantages in possessing the bomb, but he continued to believe that no cooperative measures could stop the forward motion of the arms race. As before, it was an argument that was based on the premise of total theoretical hostility. Gordon Arneson, another subscriber to this pessimistic gospel, backed Nitze. He suggested to the group that "any proposal for an approach to the Soviets had to be viewed in the light of the basic analysis of NSC 68."

Robert Lovett, now secretary of defense and still a dedicated hard-liner, was aghast at the mere mention of a moratorium. In comments presaging darker times to come, Lovett said that such an idea "should be immediately put out of mind and that any papers that might exist on the subject should be destroyed." The likes of Oppenheimer, he fumed, were no doubt responsible for this dangerous suggestion and it appeared that the physicist's motivations in these matters were "suspect."[47]

After the October 9 meeting, a test ban was never again seriously discussed in the Truman administration. Three weeks later, on the island of Elugelab in the remote Eniwetok atoll, a thermonuclear device designated MIKE shattered the Pacific calm with an explosion roughly one thousand times more powerful than the blast that had destroyed Hiroshima.

In November 1952 Dwight Eisenhower defeated Adlai Stevenson in the presidential election and brought two decades of Democratic rule to an end. For Nitze, the future was suddenly uncertain. He had worked for Roosevelt and then Truman since 1940. In the minds of Republicans, he was closely associated with both presidents. Worse still, the director of the Policy Planning Staff was known to be a protégé and principal advisor to the most reviled Democrat in Washington: "Red" Dean Acheson.

Despite all of this, Nitze toyed optimistically with the notion that he might not lose his job in January. Like many who had grown accustomed to a steady supply of classified information and regular access to the most powerful people in Washington, Nitze was hopelessly addicted to government work. More than anything, he wanted to continue shaping global strategy and was determined to press his campaign for greater vigilance toward the Soviets. He feared that the ideas of NSC 68, with their core axiom of greater defense spending, might be ignored by the fiscally conservative Republicans. He hoped that the new secretary of state, John Foster Dulles, would recognize that Nitze was as tough on communism as anyone else and let him continue at the Policy Planning Staff.

On January 20, 1953, Nitze was informed of his fate. After the inaugural luncheon at the White House, Dulles called Nitze into his office. "You know, Paul," Nitze recalled Dulles saying, "I really don't disagree at all with the Acheson policies, or those policies you've been working on. I'm in general agreement with what you and Acheson have been trying to do." As for the Policy Planning Staff, Dulles continued, "I really admire the work that has been done by the staff under your leadership."

Nonetheless, the secretary said, Nitze would have to give up his post. He was too close to Acheson and the Republicans had fought the election campaign on the thesis that they would implement a new foreign policy.

Nitze said he understood. Politics was politics. When should he leave?

Dulles replied that he hadn't yet found a replacement for Nitze, but he had talked to Bedell Smith, the under secretary of state, and Smith would head the search for a successor. Dulles suggested that Nitze should work with Smith and see whether he could find someone to take over the staff.[48]

Nitze remained in his post for some three months following his inaugural day chat with Dulles. It was not a pleasant period. Nitze had never liked Dulles. Even on Wall Street, when Dulles was with a prominent law firm, Nitze had viewed the future secretary of state with distaste. During the 1952 campaign Nitze had been incensed by Dulles's cutting attacks on the Truman administration's foreign policy, especially his charge that Truman had acted unwisely in driving beyond the thirty-eighth parallel, a move that Dulles had enthusiastically supported. On a personal level, Dulles didn't have the polished manner and easy wit that made men like Acheson and Lovett so easy to deal with. The product of a rigid Calvinist upbringing, Dulles came across as stiff and overbearing. His thin lips seemed turned down in a perpetual frown, and his bad breath kept one at a distance. The new secretary of state trusted only a few aides and made little effort to reach out to either the career diplomats or political appointees like Nitze. During the first few months he considered his office a lonely outpost in enemy territory. Relations between him and Nitze soured quickly.

One of Dulles's first obligations as secretary was to appear before the House Committee on Appropriations to give his general views on the state of the world. Whenever Acheson had gone before the committee, Nitze and his staff had prepared an outline of important points. Shortly before Dulles was to testify in February, Nitze sent over the usual outline.

Several days later, Rod O'Connor, one of Dulles's high-strung assistants, appeared in Nitze's office. Who had asked Nitze to send over the outline? he demanded.

Nitze replied that no one had requested it, but he thought it might be useful.

"Don't ever send in a paper again unless the Secretary asks for it," O'Connor snapped.

A few days after testifying, Dulles called Nitze into his office. He explained that he had made a major blunder in front of the committee. Unfamiliar with the routine of congressional testimony, Dulles had been under the impression that his remarks were off the record. Only later did he realize that they were only off the record for one day, and that when the hearings were printed, his statements would be reproduced in full. Fearing that he had been too "flamboyant," Dulles ordered Nitze to go to the committee clerk, ask for a transcript of the testimony, and rewrite the entire thing based on the unused outline.

Nitze explained that this wasn't possible, that the committee didn't allow radical changes because then the questions of the committee members don't make sense. "It corrupts the record," Nitze said.

Dulles told Nitze to do what he could.

When Nitze got in touch with the clerk, he was told that the committee didn't care if the whole transcript was rewritten. It was the worst testimony they had ever heard, the clerk said.

Nitze gave the job of reviewing the transcript to Burt Marshall, who stayed up until three the next morning going over it. "I was absolutely amazed," Marshall said later. "I couldn't believe my eyes." In his review of the world, the secretary of state had jumped from country to country, making one outrageous statement after another, ridiculing friends and enemies alike. Canada, he had said, was not much to speak of but was a good piece of real estate. England was all washed up, a fallen empire. It, too, however, was a good piece of real estate.

France, Dulles continued, gaining momentum, was filled with prurient men who kept mistresses and bought dirty postcards, but since it had all those canals and highways leading to Germany, relations should be kept civil. The Italians weren't much good for anything; they had been a liability to their allies in every war they had fought.

Moving to South America, Dulles said that aid to that continent was like opium, and suggested that the United States cut it off slowly to ease withdrawal pains.

Had Dulles's remarks been published, Nitze said later, "it would have built up the Communist propaganda line for the next twenty-five years." After hours of work, Nitze and Marshall completely revised the transcript—even making up new questions from the congressmen—and sent it back to the committee clerk, who entered it into the record without complaint.[49]

Throughout February Nitze's rapport with Dulles remained poor. The more he knew of the man, the more he disliked him. Particularly infuriating to Nitze was the cavalier fashion in which Dulles treated State Department officials. In the summer of 1952 Bob Tufts had left the Policy Planning Staff to advise Adlai Stevenson on foreign policy. Following the election, Nitze asked his top draftsman to come back to work on the staff. Tufts agreed, quietly returning to his old job of putting more punch into calls for greater vigilance toward the Soviets. Soon after settling into Acheson's wood-paneled office, however, Dulles learned that Tufts remained on the staff. He was furious. "He was so upset," recalled Tufts, "that he wanted me to resign as of 4:30 that day." With Nitze unable to save him, Tufts did so.

In almost every office in the department, the same thing was happening. Before, Nitze had disliked Dulles; now, he came to loathe him.

Early in March the death of Josef Stalin provoked a head-on clash between the two men. When the Soviet leader died, Eisenhower asked for a speech that would extend a friendly gesture to Stalin's successors. Dulles opposed the idea. He saw no reason to call off his holy war against communism simply because there were some new faces in the Kremlin. Nitze, on the other hand, thought that such a speech was a good idea. In NSC 112 he had recommended a broad effort to improve relations with the Soviet Union, however doomed the attempt might be. The death of Stalin presented an ideal opportunity for such a move. Also, Nitze could see that Eisenhower was committed to the speech. And since, ultimately, he served in the new administration at the president's indulgence, if Eisenhower wanted a speech that warmed up to the Soviets, Paul Nitze would produce one.

Working with White House speech writer Emmett Hughes, Nitze began drafting the first conciliatory speech by a U.S. president since the beginning of the Cold War. Dulles, in the meantime, took off for the weekend with his wife Janet to Duck Island, their vacation spot on Lake Ontario. With a telephone deliberately left off the list of the island's amenities, the secretary of state was cut off from events in Washington.

On Sunday morning, the day before Eisenhower was to give his address, Nitze arrived at the White House to go over the final draft. Showing up early for the eleven o'clock meeting, Nitze was given directions to the Oval Office by a White House attendant who was apparently new on the job. "I was told to take the elevator to the second floor and go straight ahead," Nitze recalled. "So I go up alone and walk into a room, and there is Eisenhower in his BVDs, almost stark naked. Mamie grinned but the President looked embarrassed, and tells me: 'No, you're in the wrong room, go up to that oval room in the far corner.'"

When the meeting got started, no one objected to Nitze's proposed draft. The next day, before the American Society of Newspaper Editors, Eisenhower gave what many would call the best speech of his presidency. "Every gun that is fired," he said, "every warship launched, every rocket fired signifies, in the final sense, a theft from those who hunger and are not fed, those who are cold and are not clothed. The world in arms is not spending money alone. It is spending the sweat of its laborers, the genius of its scientists, the hopes of its children."[50]

After seven years of cold war, the president's message of peace and hope was greeted with acclaim in both the United States and the Soviet Union. But when Dulles heard the speech he was furious. It was clear that Paul Nitze had overstayed his welcome.

In April Robert Bowie was brought in from Harvard to take over as head of policy planning. Finally, Dulles could afford to do without Paul Nitze. The question now was where to put him. Despite their differences, Dulles wanted to give Nitze a chance to stay on in a less politically sensitive post. To this end, Dulles offered Nitze the job of assistant secretary for Middle Eastern affairs. Worried that his German background would get him in trouble with the "Jewish element," Nitze turned the job down.

A more appealing opportunity arose unexpectedly. In April Chancellor Konrad Adenauer of West Germany came to Washington to confer with the new administration. Attending a reception for him, Nitze ran into the new secretary of defense, Charles Wilson. Although he had never met Wilson, the secretary pulled Nitze aside for a private chat. Explaining that the assistant secretary of defense for international security affairs (ISA), Frank Nash, was in poor health, Wilson suggested that Nitze should come over to the Pentagon and accept a job at ISA with the thought of eventually assuming Nash's post.

Taken by surprise, Nitze said, "You don't know anything about me."

Wilson replied that Dulles had suggested the idea and that he had already checked Nitze out.

Nitze was not going to argue. He asked only for a month's vacation before taking the job. Wilson agreed.

After a much needed rest, Nitze showed up at the Pentagon in early June and discovered that Nash was still sick and had not been in for some time. Installing himself in the office next to the assistant secretary's, Nitze assessed the situation at ISA. The immediate problem was morale. With Nash ill and a former auto executive heading the Defense Department, ISA was not a cheery place.

Things quickly brightened. After three years of building bridges between State and Defense, Nitze had a good reputation at the Pentagon. Known as a hard-liner and a pragmatist, he was well received at

ISA. "Everybody was just delighted to have a live body—someone who was going to do something," Nitze recalled. In a few days Nash was healthy enough to return to work. The two men were old friends and worked well together. Things began picking up at the agency. Following months of worry, it looked to Nitze that he would be staying on the inside after all.

He had been in the new post for only a short time when the ax fell. On June 13 an article written by a McCarthy supporter appeared in the *Washington Times-Herald* which said: "Paul H. Nitze, 46, one of the principal shapers of the European recovery plan, is the latest Truman-Acheson lieutenant contemplated for retention in a powerful position under the Eisenhower Administration." The article implied that Nitze had pushed the Marshall Plan to increase profits for Wall Street.[51]

Around the same time Eisenhower's legislative liaison, Major General Wilton Persons, and Vice-president Richard Nixon reportedly went to Capitol Hill to ask Republican Senator William Knowland if there were any Congressional opposition to Nitze's appointment. Without mentioning Nitze's name, Persons asked Knowland what he thought of appointing a high-level Truman administration official assistant secretary of defense for ISA. Knowland replied that it would be a poor idea. Several months earlier there had been a bitter and protracted battle in the Senate when Eisenhower nominated Charles Bohlen to be the U.S. ambassador to Russia. Giving a top Pentagon post to another former Truman official might trigger a similar clash.

Persons went back to the White House and told the president that there was strong opposition to Nitze's appointment. Charles Wilson was then called and told to fire Nitze.

Ignorant of all of this, Nitze showed up at Wilson's office with Frank Nash to brief the defense secretary for an NSC meeting. The briefing had barely begun when Wilson interrupted to relay the bad news. "I am told," Nitze recalled the secretary's saying, "that if I send your name to the Senate it will be in violation of this agreement the President has made with the Republican leadership that there won't be any more Bohlen cases. This has become a controversial issue. And what's more, even if we win this confirmation fight, it may act against our ability to get the defense appropriations that we otherwise could get."

Nitze was stunned and angry. "Mr. Wilson," he said, "you remember, I didn't ask for this job. You took me aside, said you knew all about me, and wanted me to do this job. You'll have my resignation next Monday."

Over the weekend Nitze wrote up his letter of resignation. But before sending it to Wilson, he dropped by to see Dulles. Ever the lawyer, Dulles went over the letter with Nitze, completely rewrote it, and made it much more pointed.

"I want the record to be completely clear," the letter read, "that I have at no time sought or asked for any appointment in the Defense Establishment. . . . I now understand that there is certain Congressional opposition to my appointment and that you are concerned thereby. I therefore request that I be relieved of my agreement to accept an appointment in the Defense Department."[52]

Nitze sent the letter to Wilson and left town.

CHAPTER 6

The Outer Darkness

N ITZE DROVE out to his farm in Maryland. Located near the town of La Plata on 2,000 acres along the Potomac River, the farm provided a much needed antidote to the heat and pressure of Washington.

Nitze and Phyllis had begun looking for a place in the country after eight years in the capital. Climbing into the car on Saturday and Sunday mornings, they scoured the area north and south of Washington. Finally, in 1949 they stumbled upon Causein Manor, a two-thousand-acre stretch of land on the Potomac, and only a forty-five-minute drive down Route 301. The farm had stalls for horses and fields for planting. Its price was under $200,000, but the costs of renovating the manor house and grounds were far higher. Still, it was an investment that would pay off many times over. For Nitze it was "one of the great beauty spots in the world," a place to decompress and concentrate on the therapeutic business of the gentleman farmer. For the children, by now four of them, the farm was a place to sprawl out and cool off.

Causein Manor was loved most by Phyllis, who sought to re-create the joys she had known on the great Pratt estate in Glen Cove. There, in the aristocratic paradise that the Standard Oil fortune built, Phyllis had developed a passion for riding and the calming rhythms of country life. In Maryland she saw that the stables were filled with fine horses, some brought down from Glen Cove. Over the years Phyllis would take great pride in the world she and her husband built at Causein Manor.

But for all its beauty, Nitze felt the farm was best when it served as a temporary escape from the hectic world of the State Department. To Nitze, suddenly purged from government, this quiet spot in the country now seemed like a place of exile.

Back in Washington, there was confusion about what had happened to Nitze. "An air of mystery cloaked the answers to many of the charges, denials and counter-denials," said the *New York Times* in an article on Nitze's "disappearing job."[1] Columnists Joseph and Stewart Alsop realized immediately what had happened to their good friend, and like many others, they were furious. "The Eisenhower administration has just added another major surrender to the long tale of its surrenders to the Right or anti-Eisenhower wing of the Republican party," the Alsops wrote. By sacrificing Nitze, they argued, Eisenhower had sacrificed the principle of continuity and experience in American foreign policy. "Nitze is a conspicuous, unimpeachably non-partisan member of the small group of high civil servants who alone supply these indispensable ingredients, experience and continuity."[2] How could such a man be fired? What did this say about the courage and integrity of the new administration?

With McCarthyism at its height, the answers to these questions were self-evident. As an Achesonian, Paul Nitze was a marked man.

Nitze soon found a position heading the Foreign Service Educational Foundation at the John Hopkins School for Advanced International Studies (SAIS) in Washington. During World War II he had founded SAIS with Christian Herter, a well-known Republican who was married to Phyllis's cousin. Located near Dupont Circle, SAIS was home to a number of well-known experts on international affairs. Although it lacked the key intoxicant of power, the atmosphere at the school was congenially political. It would be Nitze's base for the next seven years.

As he worked to accommodate himself to life in what he called "the outer darkness," Nitze sought out the company of those with whom he had shared the ordeal of fire under Truman. And of them all, none was more important to him than Dean Acheson. A few months after

Eisenhower took office, Nitze invited his former boss to lunch at the Metropolitan Club. Acheson was delighted. "You know," he said, "you're the first person in Washington who has asked me to lunch since I was Secretary of State."[3]

Still bitter about his own ejection from power, Acheson was incensed by the way the new administration had treated Nitze. "I understand that he is being sacrificed to the Hill demand that all who worked with me be changed or fired," he wrote to Truman in April. "This seems to me plain cowardice and utter folly."[4]

To the former statesman, Nitze's dismissal was a telling symptom of the new sickness infecting Washington. Everything Acheson had worked for was being dismantled, he felt. "Like the man who was getting deaf and warned against alcohol," he wrote a former aide, "I find that I like what I drink better than what I hear." What Acheson heard was precisely what Nitze had experienced during his final days at Foggy Bottom: The new secretary of state was turning the department upside down. "Dulles's people seem to me like Cossacks quartered in a grand old city hall, burning the panelling to cook with," Acheson wrote.[5]

For the remainder of the 1950s, Nitze and Acheson would be co-conspirators in a common cause: to undermine the Eisenhower-Dulles regime and return the Democrats to power.

Throughout 1953 there were few changes in U.S. foreign policy. In October 1953 Eisenhower approved NSC 162/2, a document that affirmed many of the concepts articulated in the NSC 68 series.[6] Superficially it looked like the new administration would be just as vigilant as Truman's when it came to opposing communism. The God-fearing Dulles spared no vitriol in denouncing what he viewed as the moral degeneracy and political bankruptcy of the Soviet system. Nor, at first, did it seem that he would spare any amount of U.S. toil and treasure to stop this system from expanding. "If Soviet communism is permitted to gobble up other parts of the world one by one," Dulles warned in his first televised address, "the day will come when the Soviet world will be so powerful that no corner of the world will be safe."[7]

Aside from the "chance for peace" speech, delivered after the death of Stalin, Eisenhower also projected the image of a hardened cold warrior. Before coming to the White House, he had served as supreme commander of NATO. It seemed unlikely that a man who had personally supervised the defense of western Europe could be soft on the

Soviet threat. Although Eisenhower had attacked Truman's foreign policy during the election, there were grounds for guarded optimism on the part of Nitze and others that the new administration would continue the military buildup.

That optimism evaporated on a cold evening in January 1954, when Nitze went to New York to hear Dulles deliver a major policy address at the Council on Foreign Relations. In a highly partisan tone, Dulles attacked Truman's defense policy as a formula for national bankruptcy. He charged that the policy implied a readiness to fight "in the Arctic and in the tropics; in Asia, the Near East, and in Europe; by sea, by land, and by air; with old weapons and with new weapons." In a clear attack on NSC 68, Dulles condemned this limitless and open-ended commitment to do battle anywhere and everywhere, saying that it could not possibly be sustained "without grave budgetary, economic, and social consequences."

He proposed an alternative defense strategy, one that in Nitze's mind set the clock back to 1945 and nullified years of painstaking labor by the Truman administration. "We keep locks on our doors," said the secretary of state, "but we do not have an armed guard in every home. We rely principally on a community security system so well equipped to punish any who break in and steal that, in fact, would-be aggressors are generally deterred. That is the modern way of getting maximum protection at bearable cost." Dulles believed that through similar means western security could be preserved in an era of totalitarian adventurism. Instead of deploying huge military forces around the globe, he argued that the United States should rely on the "deterrent of massive retaliatory power," specifically, the threat of devastating nuclear strikes, to keep communist forces in check.[8]

Nitze was furious. By suggesting that the United States rely principally on nuclear weapons for its defense, Dulles had exhumed a strategic concept that Nitze had worked to entomb since 1949. Gathering in the council's bar after the address, Nitze and a few other Truman veterans grumbled about Dulles's idiocy. "It was not a step forward," Nitze concluded, "it was a step backward—a step back dictated not by new strategic considerations but by domestic political and budgetary considerations."

Shortly after the speech, Nitze dispatched a ten-page critique to Robert Bowie, his successor at the Policy Planning Staff. The important thing, he wrote, was not Dulles's "condescending tone with respect to the accomplishments of the United States during the last seven years but an analysis of the reasoning by which he justifies a major reversal of those developments of policy which were so hard won after much trial and error, bitter experience and arduous thought."

Nitze's analysis was blistering. All the resentment that had been building up for months came spilling out in page after page of broadside attack on Dulles and the new strategic policy.

Disgusted that fiscal constraints should dictate American strategy, Nitze blasted the notion that the United States could not afford to build both a conventional and nuclear defense. "Can one say today when our population is living better than any people on earth have ever lived, when our steel plants are only being used to 75 percent of their capacity, when we feel threatened by the magnitude of our agricultural surpluses, that we are even close to the economic limits of what we could do if we were called upon with clarity of purpose and nobility of vision to do it?" Money was not the issue when it came to defense, Nitze felt. "It is perfectly clear," he argued, "that the problem is one of leadership and will, not of dollars and cents."[9]

In addition to Robert Bowie, Nitze sent his critique of Dulles's speech to Adlai Stevenson. A year after losing the election, the former governor of Illinois remained the leader of the country's Democratic opposition. He, too, was disturbed by the new defense policy, feeling that it would do little to stem communist aggression in the third world. As he wrote to one friend, "How we can 'retaliate' against 'civil wars,' which most of us have to come to feel . . . is the approved Communist method, I hardly see." Stevenson read Nitze's critique "with the utmost interest," pronounced it a "splendid memo," and asked for "further refinements." He said also that he would probably "lift portions of it for a forthcoming oratorical effort."[10]

If Dulles's "massive retaliation" speech seemed to promise more perilous U.S.-Soviet confrontations in the years ahead, other developments during the mid 1950s pointed in the opposite direction. Stalin's successors in the Kremlin, Nikolai Bulganin and Nikita Khrushchev, were taking a less xenophobic approach to the west. In July 1955 the two leaders met Eisenhower in Geneva for the first superpower meeting since Potsdam. The talks went well, and the relaxation of tensions that followed the summit came to be known as the "spirit of Geneva."

Nitze was skeptical about what had been accomplished at Geneva. Despite the new atmosphere of cordiality, he doubted that there had been any fundamental change in the relationship between east and west. He was not sure that Stalin's death signified the beginning of a new era. Shortly after the Soviet leader died, Nitze had argued that "the nature of the system is the same. The basic hostility to everything that the United States stands for is the same. I think the basic nature of the threat remains unchanged."[11] One friendly meeting altered nothing.

His instincts on this matter seemed to be confirmed during a visit to the Soviet Union shortly after the summit. Nitze stayed at Spaso House, the Ambassador's residence, at the invitation of Chip Bohlen and through the Ambassador's influence, was allowed to sit in at the meeting of the Supreme Soviet at which Khrushchev and Bulganin were to report on the Geneva meeting. For six hours the two leaders presented their views of the summit and assessed the state of U.S.-Soviet relations. With Bohlen quietly translating the speeches, Nitze watched the reactions of the delegates to what was said. "Whenever the speakers dwelled on the Geneva conference, its apparent success and the spirit of Geneva," he recalled, "the audience was dead; people yawned, some actually fell asleep. Whenever Khrushchev or Bulganin launched into an impassioned description of western faults, errors and shortcomings, the necessity for *mir* and the actions the party proposed to take to achieve *mir*, the audience became animated and broke into loud applause."

After the speech Nitze asked Bohlen to explain *mir*. Bohlen said that as the Soviets used the word, it "meant a condition in the world in which socialism, the first stage of communism, had triumphed world-wide, class tensions had thus been removed, and the conditions for true peace under the leadership and preeminence of the Soviet Communist Party had come to pass." The reaction of the audience, continued Bohlen, "indicated a lack of interest in the relaxation of tensions exemplified by the spirit of Geneva, but enthusiasm for the continuing struggle for *mir*."[12]

To Nitze the message was clear: As long as eastern Europe was under Soviet control, and the basic thrust of Soviet foreign policy remained aggressive, there would be no genuine thaw in the cold war. The spirit of Geneva was illusory, he felt.

Nitze was not alone in opposing Eisenhower's defense policies. Many strategic experts were disturbed by the decision to increase U.S. reliance on nuclear weapons at a time when the Soviets were developing their own strategic arsenal. They felt that the United States should be moving in the opposite direction by building a credible conventional defense. They argued that without such forces, the American and Soviet nuclear arsenals would simply cancel each other out, leaving the

Soviets free to exploit their huge armies on the Eurasian land mass for local aggression.

In late 1954 strategic experts William Kaufmann and Bernard Brodie attacked the policy of massive retaliation in two widely read works. By 1955 the army was also expressing uneasiness about the administration's nuclearcentric policies. And three thousand miles from Washington, at the RAND Corporation in Santa Monica, California, a mathematician named Albert Wohlstetter was systematically analyzing U.S. nuclear military plans and developing revolutionary alternatives to massive retaliation.

In January 1956 Nitze joined this rising chorus of dissent with an article on nuclear strategy in *Foreign Affairs*. Departing from the popular view that the ultimate result of the U.S.-Soviet arms race would be an atomic stalemate, Nitze argued that emerging armaments technology made it possible that "in a general nuclear war one side or the other could 'win' decisively." Although a nuclear exchange might destroy civilization, Nitze believed that this would not occur unless the war was fought in an "entirely irrational way." In a nuclear war fought with "some degree of reason," success in a classical military sense would be possible: "The victor will be in a position to issue orders to the loser and the loser will have to obey them or face complete chaos or extinction."

How would such a victory be possible? Why wouldn't a nuclear confrontation mean the end of the world, as many had suggested? Nitze's explanation was simple. In a nuclear war neither the United States nor the Soviet Union would want to destroy cities. Instead, the nation that started the war by striking first "would logically concentrate the full power of its initial attack on the military—primarily the retaliatory—capabilities of the other side." The aggressor's leader would do so because he would "have much in mind the postwar problem of building a world which he can control and manage. He will want destruction of that world to be held within reasonable limits. He will wish his own country to be spared as far as possible. He will also want to destroy only as much of the enemy territory as is necessary for him to impose his will and get on with the job of making of the world what he wants and can make of it." Given all of this, it would be illogical for an attacker to destroy cities.

Similarly, the nation on the receiving end of the initial attack would be hesitant to strike back at the aggressor's cities. "It may still have the capability of destroying a few of the enemy's cities," Nitze wrote. "But the damage it could inflict would be indecisive and out of all proportion to the annihilation which its own cities could expect to receive in return." Nitze believed that if the United States were ever the victim of a first strike in which its airfields were destroyed and its nuclear arsenal was greatly depleted, it would be faced with two choices: commit suicide by striking at Soviet cities with whatever bombs were left or capitulate to Soviet demands.

Stalemate, then, was not inevitable in the arms race. Far more likely, Nitze felt, was the rise of what Wohlstetter would later call a "delicate balance of terror"—a balance in which both sides were eternally on the verge of gaining a first-strike capability. To avoid the terrifying possibility that the Soviets would tip the balance first, Nitze suggested that the west "maintain indefinitely a position of nuclear attack-defense superiority versus the Soviet Union and its satellites." He also recommended that the Pentagon prepare for other forms of communist aggression by building up conventional forces.[13]

The thrust of Nitze's thinking, in short, was that the United States should return to the principles of NSC 68 and get on with the job of building a military that could cope with Soviet aggression at every level of violence, from a limited incursion in a faraway country to a full-scale nuclear strike at the American heartland.

Underlying this updated prescription for security was the same premise of total theoretical hostility that had characterized Nitze's thinking at the Policy Planning Staff. And if anything, this axiom was even more flawed now that Stalin had died. To Soviet experts it seemed highly unlikely that Moscow would ever attempt a nuclear first strike. Such a move would entail an unprecedented, and nearly unimaginable, level of Kremlin risk taking. Even in the best of circumstances, an attack on the United States would leave open the possibility that among the thousands of American nuclear warheads, several would survive and end up on Moscow and Leningrad.

For all of its logic, Nitze's scenario for victory in nuclear war suffered from the same weakness as his earlier strategic thought. It lacked a meaningful analysis of intentions and existed instead within a narrow framework defined by capabilities. In this sense, Nitze's view of national security was not a complex and thoughtful vision that mirrored geopolitical reality. Rather, it was more a mathematical model in which comparisons of military hardware constituted the starting point for almost all further analysis.

Because no Republican president would ever support the huge defense budgets that Paul Nitze wanted, he threw his considerable energies into returning the fiscally liberal democrats to power. In 1956 this meant working for Adlai Stevenson.

Nitze had great affection for Stevenson, who had been a friend to Nitze and his sister for many years. When it came to national security, however, neither Nitze nor Acheson viewed Stevenson as the ideal leader of the Democratic party. While he seldom departed from the Cold War orthodoxy of the day, Stevenson showed a distressing penchant for questioning the rigidity of the Acheson-Nitze line. In April 1956, for example, Stevenson declared that the United States "should give prompt and earnest consideration to stopping further tests of the hydrogen bomb."[14] Such heresies were encouraged by Chester Bowles, Arthur Schlesinger, Jr., and other close advisors who represented the liberal wing of the Democratic party. If Stevenson became president, it was doubtful that he would be another Harry Truman.

But hard-liner or not, Stevenson was the preeminent Democrat of the 1950s and the party's likely nominee to challenge Eisenhower in his bid for a second term. With little chance of another high-level appointment, Dean Acheson could afford to turn his caustic wit on Stevenson. Nitze had no such luxury. The former governor represented his best hope for getting back into government, and Nitze worked hard to become one of Stevenson's foreign policy advisors, joining an informal group that included not only Bowles, but George Kennan as well.

Like so many others, Stevenson was quickly impressed by Nitze's thoroughness, coming to view him as among "our best people" in foreign affairs. In late 1954 Stevenson told his advisor Thomas Finletter that he would like to have Nitze working for him full time. Nitze "would be ideal were he available to help us whip in shape ideas on all manner of domestic as well as foreign problems," Stevenson wrote.[15] No formal offer of this sort was ever made, but Stevenson turned often to Nitze for foreign policy advice.

As the election approached, Nitze's role in Democratic party politics grew. Acheson, too, became more involved. Although Stevenson's chances of victory looked slim against a popular incumbent, the election presented a chance for both men to blast Dulles and the Republicans. The principal vehicle for their attack was the Democratic party platform. As a member of a group that the *New York Times* dubbed "the party eggheads," Nitze worked through the summer with Acheson, Bowles, and six members of Congress fashioning the foreign policy planks in the platform.[16]

In a paper submitted to the platform committee, the group called attention to an increasingly hot foreign policy issue: communist gains in the third world. Earlier in the year Nitze had written that political tumult and antiwestern sentiments made the former colonies of Asia and Africa "a fertile field for communist exploitation."[17] The platform paper echoed this view. If the United States was not vigilant, if it failed to combat communist subversion and piecemeal aggression in the third world, the west could face a new strain of Soviet satellite states around the world. "Peace can be lost without a shot being fired," the paper said.[18]

More than anything, Acheson and Nitze wanted to toughen up the Democrats. McCarthyism had been a bitter experience for both men. Watching the attacks on friends like Charles Bohlen and former Policy Planning Staff member John Paton Davies, Nitze had come to develop a deep loathing for McCarthy, whom he considered "crude, ugly, and brutal."[19] Emotionally scarred by anti-German witch-hunts of the past, Nitze was acutely sensitive to the brand of demagoguery that McCarthy practiced. Even in 1956, with the Senator's power shattered, Nitze and Acheson were stung by charges that Truman had been soft on communism. Acheson especially had reacted to right-wing attacks by becoming an ever more rigid cold warrior. And although Nitze adjusted his views to remain inside the Stevenson camp, he also was determined to leave no opening for those who might impugn his patriotism.

Despite the hard-line foreign policy positions that the "eggheads" formulated for the 1956 election, Stevenson was buried by another Eisenhower landslide.

After a second electoral defeat, Paul Butler, the chairman of the Democratic National Committee, decided to create a more formal, and more formidable, opposition structure. In January 1957 he organized the first meeting of a group called the Democratic Advisory Council. Described by one member as a "kind of cabinet in exile," the DAC was an uneasy mix of sitting Democratic governors, unemployed Democratic statesmen like Harriman and Acheson, and liberal academics like John Kenneth Galbraith and Arthur Schlesinger, Jr.[20] The organization met at least four times a year and often more frequently.

The advisory council was divided into two committees: one on domestic policy and one on foreign policy. Galbraith was quickly chosen to head the group on domestic policy, and Acheson maneuvered for the other job. The DAC leaders hesitated. "He wasn't considered an asset," the group's director, Charles Tyroler II, said later. "The Republicans had done an incredible knife job on him. He was, to say the least, a controversial character." But with Truman's backing, Acheson got the job.

As close to his former boss as ever, Nitze was Acheson's logical choice for vice-chairman of the foreign policy committee. Tyroler approved the appointment and both men began pouring tremendous energy into the council, rarely missing the weekend meetings that the group held at its suite of offices on Connecticut Avenue.

As Galbraith later said, the DAC's discussions on domestic policy were interesting, but "our foreign policy discussions were the true portents." At each meeting, he recalled, Acheson and Nitze "produced a paper attacking whatever John Foster Dulles had done in the preceding weeks. The attack was always for being too lenient toward Communism and the Soviet Union." In response, Stevenson usually led an effort to moderate the paper. "He wanted to soften the line all the time," Tyroler remembered. A battle-scarred veteran of the Cold War himself, Averell Harriman also was irritated by the shrill inflexibility of the Acheson-Nitze line. "You know, Dean," he said one day, "I don't agree with your declarations of war."[21]

What Galbraith found so disturbing about the DAC discussions, especially in hindsight, was that, short of such occasional challenges, the positions taken by Acheson and Nitze were never fundamentally questioned. "Here, early and in miniature," he wrote, "were the fatal politics of Vietnam. It was not that the issue was debated and the wrong decision taken; it was rather that there was no debate. The old liberal fear of being thought soft on Communism, the fear of being attacked by professional patriots and the knowledge of the political punishment that awaits any departure from the Establishment view . . . all united to eliminate discussion."[22]

To many in the liberal wing of the Democratic party, Dean Acheson had simply lost touch with the times. "Acheson was a prisoner of the past and of his critics—always trying to prove how tough he was on Communism," recalled DAC member Newt Minnow. But very few on the DAC were bold enough stand up to him. Caustic and intimidating, with years of experience to back up his arguments and with Nitze, statistics in hand, always at his side, the haughty old statesman could put up an incredible fight in a head-on debate about U.S. foreign policy. Passing out his latest cold war tirade at the DAC meetings, the former secretary of state would effortlessly obliterate anybody who questioned his work. "Acheson dominated the foreign policy discussion to such an extent that I don't recall substantive changes being made in any of his stuff during this entire period," recalled Tyroler. "Acheson always carried the day."

Following his time with the DAC, Acheson would be permanently tagged by many influential Democrats as an overzealous hard-liner. And since Nitze was known to be his chief lieutenant, or "amanuensis" as Galbraith disdainfully labeled him, he also came be viewed with uneasiness. Years later Robert Kennedy would remark that Nitze's rise on the New Frontier was hampered by the fact that he had a "good number of enemies."[23] In large part, Nitze made these enemies during the late 1950s, when the Democratic foreign policy consensus first began to crumble. Like Acheson, William Foster, and other Truman veterans, Paul Nitze was resented for attempting to shackle the Democrats to an anachronistic cold war dogma, a dogma that seemingly had not changed since the days of Korea and Stalin. This resentment—and the division within the Democratic party it underlined—would linger for decades.

Of course, to Nitze, it was not he and Acheson who had lost touch with the times, but rather Eisenhower, Dulles, and the liberal wing of the Democratic party. In his view the basic message of NSC 68 was as timely as ever. In October 1956 Moscow brutally suppressed an uprising in Hungary. Throughout the third world nationalist and communist-backed insurgencies were challenging western preeminence. And, most disturbing of all, the Soviet Union continued to increase its nuclear arsenal.

In NSC 68 Nitze had urged that the United States wage an undeclared war against the Soviet empire. To succeed, such a crusade needed to generate momentum and hope. High defense budgets had to be approved year after year and the people behind the iron curtain had to believe that freedom was possible. The dream was that a no-holds-barred fight against communism would eventually sap its vitality.

The reality under Eisenhower proved far different. Despite Dulles's frequent talk of rollback, it was obvious to Nitze that few in the government continued to take seriously the notion of winning the Cold War, if they ever had at all. In lectures across the country Nitze decried the loss of hope and condemned U.S. passivity in the face of Soviet perfidy. "In essence my position is that although I agree that we should be following a policy of limited objectives rather than unlimited objectives, it is my view that our policy should be basically offensive and not merely defensive," Nitze told a group at the Air War College at Maxwell Air Force Base. Repeating the arguments of NSC 68, Nitze said that "a purely defensive policy can result in the gradual erosion of hope in central Europe, can lead to the atrophy of NATO, and to the eventual political and military isolation of the United States."[24]

Precisely what kind of "offensive policy" Nitze had in mind was unclear. Past attempts by the CIA to foment revolt behind the iron curtain had failed dismally. Moreover, it was exactly this kind of behavior that was most likely to increase Soviet xenophobia and insecurity. Rollback may have been appealing in theory, but in reality the idea had become ever more farfetched since the days of NSC 68.

During the mid 1950s, Paul Nitze had a chance to expound his thoughts on national security in a study group sponsored by the Council on Foreign Relations. The topic was nuclear weapons and foreign policy, and the participants were former government officials and independent experts. With his vast reservoir of expertise, Nitze was a dominant voice at many of the sessions. One point he stressed often was that a nuclear war could be kept limited, and even won. Such a war might be fought in Europe with small, tactical nuclear weapons used against troops and tanks on the battlefield. Or it could be an exchange of attacks on air bases in the USSR and the United States. Whatever the case, the United States had to prepare for such a war and plan to win. "Even if war were to destroy the world as we know it today, still the U.S. must win that war decisively," Nitze declared.[25]

One member of the study group impressed by Nitze's thesis was a young Harvard professor with a heavy German accent and horn-rimmed glasses named Henry Kissinger. During the second year of the study group, Kissinger had been named study director. Almost immediately, Nitze pegged the academic as a consummate know-it-all, a man with a tremendous intellectual ego who pontificated on subjects beyond his grasp. He resented the swaggering manner in which Kissinger chaired the study group. "Henry managed to convey that no one had thought intelligently about nuclear weapons and foreign policy until he came along to do so himself," Nitze said later.[26]

At one meeting Nitze and Kissinger disagreed about limited war, with Kissinger suggesting that once a war became nuclear, it would be difficult to set any limits. But it wasn't long before Kissinger came around to Nitze's point of view—a view far more fashionable among defense analysts of the time. And in a book that Kissinger wrote after the study group was finished, the professor warmly embraced the theory of limited nuclear war. The book, *Nuclear Weapons and Foreign Policy*, was published in 1957 and, despite its turgid prose, became a bestseller. Kissinger's proposal for keeping nuclear war limited entailed designing a set of military tactics and geographic zones for confining nuclear exchanges to certain areas of Europe and thus being able to defend western Europe against Russian invasion without triggering a worldwide conflagration. Many hailed the book as a ground-breaking work. To Nitze, however, Kissinger's tome was a ponderous example of its author's naiveté and a work that hopelessly jumbled the theory of limited nuclear war.

In a review for *The Reporter*, Nitze savaged the book. "I find the picture Kissinger presents oversimplified and overdrawn," he wrote. Nitze said the book was hard to read and filled with errors. "There are several hundred passages in which either the facts or the logic seem doubtful, or at least unclear." He also criticized Kissinger's proposal for limited war in Europe as totally unworkable.[27]

Satisfied with the review, Nitze dispatched a copy to the editor of *The Reporter* and another to Kissinger. He then left for his summer home on Mount Desert Island. Some time later he received a call from *The Reporter*'s editor. The editor asked if there was anything libelous in the review. No, there was not, replied Nitze. Why would the editor worry about libel in an article on strategic affairs?

Well, explained the editor, Henry Kissinger was unhappy with the review. Very unhappy. In fact, both he and the Council on Foreign Relations had threatened the magazine with a libel suit if the review ran.

Nitze was shocked. He went back, reread the review, and assured the editor that it contained nothing libelous. On September 15 *The Reporter* published Nitze's piece. No libel suit ever materialized. Nitze later learned that Kissinger had offered a deal to the magazine: He would refrain from suing if he were allowed as much space as he wanted to print a rebuttal. The magazine agreed.

About a month later, Kissinger met Nitze at a conference in Rome. "You know what," he said, "I got up to page 147 of the rebuttal and I decided there was something wrong with my position." Kissinger's response was never printed.

As the heat eased in Washington that fall, Paul Nitze received his first real opportunity to influence policy since leaving government in 1953. A large ad hoc group had been assembled to reassess U.S. strategic doctrine and Nitze was asked to join as a consultant. Chaired by Rowan Gaither, the Security Resources Panel, or the Gaither committee as it was soon dubbed, had its origins in a report put out by the Federal Civilian Defense Administration earlier in the year. The report had recommended to Eisenhower that the United States spend $35 billion on civil defense measures to protect the American people from nuclear attack. The proposal was taken up by the NSC, which decided to form a committee of prominent citizens to assess the idea.

Gaither chaired the boards of the Ford Foundation and the RAND Corporation. Robert Sprague, who was named as his deputy, was an industrialist and defense expert. Other private citizens with background in defense were invited to sit on the panel. The Gaither committee was heavily populated with representatives of what Eisenhower would come to call the "military-industrial complex." For the most part people who reflected administration opinion were selected. By now a well-known critic of Eisenhower and Dulles, Nitze did not meet that criterion. He received no official invitation.

Once the Gaither committee began work, its political mood changed rapidly. One of Gaither's first moves was to consult his associates at RAND on how to organize the group. In doing so, he opened the door to dissent. Albert Wohlstetter convinced Gaither that to be effective, the committee had to broaden. Civil defense was only a peripheral issue in a broader debate, said the RAND analyst. The more pressing problem was the growing vulnerability of U.S. bomber bases to a surprise attack by the Soviet Union. Any examination of the strategic situation must grapple with the challenge of maintaining deterrence, Wohlstetter said. A study confined to civil defense would miss the real issue.

Eisenhower clearly had not asked for, and did not want, a sweeping review of his administration's strategic policies. But Gaither and Sprague agreed with Wohlstetter that the issue of deterrence had to be addressed. When the committee stepped up its work in early September, Sprague—who took over the group when Gaither became ill—ordered studies on a wide range of strategic matters.

With this new mandate came the need for greater expertise. James Phinney Baxter, the president of Williams College and a member of the committee's steering panel, knew a man with a wealth of firsthand experience forming strategic policy, his good friend Paul Nitze. Sprague was also familiar with Nitze, and panel members Robert Lovett, John McCloy, and William Foster did not need to be convinced of his talents. Although Nitze the Democrat was persona non grata in the administration, there were no major obstacles to his quietly joining the committee. On September 4 Nitze wrote to Acheson that a group had been set up to conduct "yet another agonizing reappraisal of our budget and defense position. They have asked me to work with them and I have agreed to do so."[28]

Working on the study turned out to be nearly a full-time job. The committee's purview was narrower in scope than that of the group that produced NSC 68, but the operation was far larger. Legions of defense experts were tapped for advice; a large scientific staff worked on technical questions; mountains of documents from the CIA and the Pentagon informed the group's analyses; several think tanks contributed to the project; and a staff of fourteen secretaries handled the committee's administrative work. In all over one hundred people worked on the study.

Though only a consultant, Nitze attended almost every one of the top secret steering panel meetings held throughout September in the Executive Office Building. It was here, next door to the White House, that the organizational and theoretical work for the committee was done. Here the panel struggled to make sense of the many studies the huge staff produced. To Nitze, the work was profoundly disquieting. Sifting through the documents and listening to the briefings, he saw a striking difference between what the administration said about America's strategic position and the views of outside experts.

Albert Wohlstetter's view of the strategic balance was particularly at odds with administration statements. For several years he had been poring over intelligence data, analyzing the Soviet ability to launch a surprise nuclear attack. His conclusions, presented in RAND Staff Report R-290, gave frightening substance to the fears that Nitze had voiced seven years earlier in NSC 68. Echoing the State-Defense report, R-290 stated that "it is a painful fact that the risks to the Soviets of attempting a surprise attack on the United States are much lower than generally estimated."[29]

In a dramatic briefing to the steering committee, Wohlstetter stated that according to air force intelligence, the Soviet Union would deploy some five hundred intercontinental ballistic missiles (ICBMs) by 1960. This would provide them with more than enough firepower to decimate the Strategic Air Command (SAC) in a first strike and hold U.S. cities at risk. Without immediate remedies, implied Wohlstetter, American security would be fatally compromised within three years.

In early October Nitze took a break from Gaither committee work to attend a conference in Rome on transatlantic relations. The trip was not to prove relaxing. On October 4 the Soviet Union stunned the world by launching a 184-pound satellite into space. Like most of the

Americans and Europeans at the meeting, Nitze was shocked by Sputnik. It seemed to indicate that the Soviets were closer to developing ballistic missiles than previously estimated.

The next day Nitze had lunch with a British official who was part of his country's loyal opposition. Over a bottle of Italian wine, the two men hammered out the general lines of a policy which they felt the west should adopt in light of Sputnik. "The wine happened to be a bottle of Suave," Nitze recalled, "and so our consensus became known as the 'Suave plan.' In its rough outline the plan called for an intensive effort on the part of the United States to increase both the capability and credibility of our strategic deterrent, to effect close collaboration between the United States and its NATO allies in the development of adequate forces in Europe."[30]

Since neither Nitze nor his British companion were in power, the Suave plan was unlikely to become policy. But upon returning to the United States, Nitze was given an opportunity to stress many of the plan's components when he was asked to write the Gaither committee's final report.

Robert Sprague had assigned the job of writing the report to Baxter, the lone academician on the steering panel, but Baxter felt uncomfortable with the task. Trained as a historian, he didn't feel qualified to synthesize a huge mass of sophisticated defense analysis. Baxter asked Nitze to write the report instead.

It was a prayer answered. For five years Paul Nitze had been an exiled prophet in the wilderness, decrying the strategic heresies of Eisenhower and Dulles. Now, backed by high priests of the defense establishment, Nitze had found a pulpit. And from it he would denounce massive retaliation.

In "Deterrence and Survival in the Nuclear Age" (or the Gaither report), Nitze avoided the ideological bombast of NSC 68 and devoted only one sentence to Soviet intentions: "We have found no evidence in Russian foreign and military policy since 1945 to refute the conclusion that USSR intentions are expansionist, and that her great efforts to build military power go beyond any concepts of Soviet defense." He then moved to the centerpiece of his argument: "The evidence clearly indicates an increasing threat which may become critical in 1959 or 1960." With each passing year, wrote Nitze, the Soviet Union was becoming more powerful. They were catching up to the United States economically and could afford to devote more resources to their military sector. Already, he argued, they were spending more than the United States on defense. The next decade could see Soviet military spending climb to twice that of the United States.

In terms of actual military forces, Nitze found the picture particularly unsettling. Over the previous decade, the report stated, the Soviet Union had made "spectacular progress" in bolstering its military might. It had developed and deployed a substantial nuclear arsenal, produced hundreds of long-range bombers, constructed a vast air defense system, and, more recently, made dramatic progress toward deploying intercontinental ballistic missiles. On top of all this, Nitze claimed, the Soviet Union had "maintained and largely reequipped their army of 175 line divisions" (a figure that later turned out to be greatly inflated).

The Gaither report warned that to counter this buildup, the United States must take prompt action, especially in the realm of strategic weapons. Reflecting the conclusions of the steering committee, Nitze argued that the United States should protect its population from nuclear annihilation by strengthening deterrence rather than investing billions in civil defense. Since vulnerable U.S. air bases would invite communist aggression, protecting the Strategic Air Command's ability to retaliate had to be a top priority. The report recommended a number of steps.

First, the reaction time at U.S. bases had to be reduced "so an adequate number (possibly 500) of SAC planes can get off, weapons aboard, on way to target, within the tactical warning time available." To do this, the United States had to improve its early warning radar system in the frozen reaches of Canada and Alaska.

Second, before the Soviet long-range missile threat became a reality in late 1959, drastic measures would have to be taken to protect SAC. America's long-range bombers would have to be dispersed to bases around the country and be able to get off the ground in under twenty-two minutes. A program to build hardened shelters for the planes would also lessen their vulnerability.

But simply protecting bombers was not enough, the report said. The United States had to enhance its own offensive striking power. The panel recommended increasing the number of intermediate-range missiles in Europe from 60 to 240, increasing the number of planned ICBMs from 80 to 600, and speeding up efforts to hide nuclear weapons under the seas by building Polaris missile-carrying submarines.

In addition to this massive acquisition of nuclear striking power, the report pressed for limited-war forces. Ever since the early 1950s Nitze had argued that the United States should prepare to fight small wars in the third world. Earlier in 1957 he had told a Senate subcommittee that "we run a grave risk of piecemeal defeat if we do not develop the capability of handling limited situations with limited means."[31] Now Nitze repeated this argument, writing that the capability to mount limited operations would "enable us to deter or promptly suppress small wars which must not be allowed to grow into big ones."

The cost of all these measures was tremendous. The panel estimated that defense outlays would have to be increased by $44 billion over five years. As in NSC 68, Nitze stressed that money was immaterial: "These several defense measures are well within our economic capabilities. The nation has the resources, the productive capacity, and the enterprise to outdistance the USSR in production and in defense capability." With higher taxes, a larger federal debt, and cuts in other government expenditures, the burden would be bearable. "The American people," contended Nitze, "have always been ready to shoulder heavy costs for their defense when convinced of their necessity."

And the necessity was not in question, Nitze stressed. The nation's very survival was at stake. "By 1959 the USSR may be able to launch an attack with ICBMs carrying megaton warheads against which SAC will be almost completely vulnerable under present programs," the report stated. In the spring of 1950 Nitze had forecast the coming of grave peril, a time of maximum danger. In the fall of 1957 he again looked into the future and divined an equally ominous threat. "The next two years seem to us critical. If we fail to act at once, the risk, in our opinion will be unacceptable."[32]

On November 6, the day before the Gaither report would be officially submitted to Eisenhower, Nitze was invited to a meeting at the State Department to advise Dulles and other officials on the upcoming NATO conference in Paris. Almost immediately he began lecturing the group about more fundamental questions. The United States, said Nitze, could not deal with its allies effectively unless it was ready to deal with the broader strategic situation. A host of questions had to be addressed: "How seriously do we view the threat presented by Russian technological achievements? What level of effort do we think this threat merits on our part? What percentage of our gross national product do we think should be devoted to defense and to the support of our foreign policy? How much reliance should we put upon SAC to preserve local situations against pressure around the periphery of the communist world? Should we not reverse the trend toward inadequate ground, sea, and tactical-air forces?"

Preaching the freshly minted gospel of the Gaither report, Nitze offered an answer to all of these questions. He argued that "the current threat warranted an increase in our effort, that the strategic situation indicated that we should both improve the security of SAC and simultaneously reverse the trend toward inadequate ground, sea, and air forces for limited military operations."

It was a familiar argument coming from Paul Nitze, and when he finished, Dulles was unmoved. In savaging the secretary of state behind his back, Nitze often dwelled on how Dulles behaved like the same mercenary lawyer he had known twenty years earlier on Wall Street—a lawyer who represented his clients' interests regardless of the truth. When it came to defense, Dulles's client was a president who wanted to keep spending low. For five years the stolid and plodding secretary never forgot that point.

And he wasn't going to forget it now.

Ignoring Nitze's main arguments, Dulles commented dryly that his remarks were not much help in preparing for the NATO conference since it would be "impossible to get complete agreement on all the details of such a comprehensive program within the time limit necessary."[33] Nitze found this attitude inexcusable. By refusing to take off his lawyer blinders and recognize the coming danger, Nitze felt that Dulles was abdicating his responsibility as secretary of state.

Almost seventy people attended the NSC meeting at which the Gaither report was submitted to Eisenhower. The president listened with interest as the committee's findings were outlined. He appeared impressed, but as always, Ike worried about the money. "If the budget is too high," he had told his new secretary of defense, Neil McElroy, in October, "inflation occurs, which in effect cuts down the value of the dollar so that nothing is gained and the process is self-defeating." Moreover, added the president, there was a point "at which the additions to military strength resulting from additional funds diminish very rapidly."[34]

Dulles expressed open contempt for the report's recommendations and frequently interrupted members of the committee who were presenting them. He was not worried about money; he was worried about prestige—his prestige. Central to the Gaither report was an attack on the policy of massive retaliation and the secretary of state was not about to let it go unchallenged.

Nitze left the meeting appalled and his loathing for Dulles climbed to a new high. A week later he sent Dulles a cordially disdainful letter. "Your remarks at the White House on this November 7 can hardly be said to constitute support by the Secretary of State even for the highest priority recommendations of the Security Resources Panel," Nitze wrote. "The Panel had formulated an integrated program, which had been discussed with your Policy Planning Staff and which incorporated their suggestions, a fact of which you seemed uninformed even though Mr. Gerard Smith, Director of the Staff, was sitting with you at the White House meeting."

To Nitze, Dulles's inability to comprehend the political and stategic realities confronting the nation was puzzling. He suspected that the secretary of state had never come to recognize how weighty was the burden of directing American foreign policy. Mentally, Dulles was still a partisan Republican unable to see beyond tomorrow's headline. The result, in Nitze's view, was the degrading spectacle of a U.S. secretary of state consistently sacrificing the national interest to his ulterior Republican agenda.

Nowhere did Nitze find Dulles's thinking more oblivious to reality than in the realm of nuclear weapons policy. Accusing him of "failing to face fully the concrete factors" surrounding nuclear weapons, Nitze attacked Dulles for clinging to illusory security in his reliance on massive retaliation. "It has long been foreseeable that in the absence of a much more vigorous defense program in both the active and passive aspects, a time would come when massive retaliation against the Soviet Union could not be undertaken without inviting the loss of a huge portion of the population of the United States—perhaps as much as half and certainly enough to destroy the fabric of our society and ruin the nation as a going concern." That time was now upon us, said Nitze, and a fundamental revision of U.S. strategic policy was necessary. "In the longer run we shall have no alternative to the development of conventional military strength and to holding to a minimum the strategic tasks beyond deterrence of nuclear attack by the enemy, to be allotted to our nuclear capabilities."

Paul Nitze had long believed that John Foster Dulles was not competent to hold the post of secretary of state. Now, for the first time Nitze told him so. "I should ask you to consider, in the light of events of recent years, whether there is not some other prominent Republican disposed to exercise the responsibility of Secretary of State in seeking a balance between our capabilities and our unavoidable commitments, equipped to form persuasive policies, and able to secure the confidence and understanding of our allies."[35]

As influential as Dulles was in the administration, his resignation would have changed little. Ultimately, Eisenhower made the decisions, and he was firmly opposed to most of the Gaither report's recommendations. Intimately familiar with American defense policy, the former general didn't share Nitze's apocalyptic vision of the future. As supreme commander of NATO forces in Europe, Eisenhower had pondered the Soviet threat day after day. He knew firsthand from his military experience the risks, uncertainties, and tremendous costs of mounting large invasions. As NATO commander, he didn't believe that the Soviets would gamble everything in a surprise attack on Europe. As president, he worried even less that they would take the far more risky step of launching a nuclear first strike. Consequently, Eisenhower felt that the chief value of the Gaither report was not as a blueprint for an arms buildup, but rather as a prod to keep people on their toes. As he wrote in his memoirs, "it acted as a gadfly on any in the administration given to complacency and it listed a number of facts, conclusions, and opinions that provided a checklist for searching examination."[36]

Nitze and other members of the Gaither committee found the president's complacency maddening. The nation was at risk, they felt. Some way had to be found to force the administration's hand.

On December 9 Nitze attended a dinner at the home of William Foster to discuss how to keep the committee's recommendations alive. Also present were Laurence Rockefeller, former Under Secretary of the Air Force Roswell Gilpatric, and pollster Elmo Roper. Vice-president Richard Nixon sat in for the administration.

After briefing Nixon, the group took up the question of how to promote the committee's recommendations. Foster made two proposals. He said, first, the group should convince Eisenhower to publish a "sanitized" version of the report and, second, a committee should be formed to alert the public to the nature of the Soviet threat. The meeting ended without a firm decision on whether to form a committee, but everyone agreed that the report should be made public.[37]

Eisenhower would not countenance publicizing the Gaither committee's findings. He was not going to approve an arms buildup, and the publication of a report calling for one would only damage him politically.

Despite the president's desire to keep the Gaither report secret, key portions of the report were inevitably leaked to the press. Eisenhower was furious. On Capitol Hill senators and congressmen charged that the president was trying to conceal U.S. weakness and called for the full report to be released. Democrats sniffing about for a political cudgel with which to attack the Republicans in the 1960 election seized on the report as evidence of a "missile gap." Over the next three years charges of Republican laxity on defense would become a cornerstone in the Democratic campaign to recapture the White House.

Paul Nitze derived intense pleasure from authoring an influential attack on an administration he despised. And if the experience was disappointing in that most of the Gaither committee's recommendations were not implemented by Eisenhower, it was clear that the ideas of the report would receive a more sympathetic hearing if and when a Democratic president was elected.

Twenty years later, when the Gaither report was finally declassified and Nitze's role in writing it became known, many pointed to the report as another example of his proclivity for alarmist analysis. The missile gap that the document warned about never materialized. By 1961 the Soviets had only four ICBMs, not the hundreds that the Gaither report had predicted.[38] The vulnerability of SAC had been wildly exaggerated. If anyone was vulnerable, it was the Soviet Union.

Nitze defended his role in drafting the Gaither report in a contradictory manner. He correctly pointed out that the committee had no choice but to rely on intelligence data about the Soviet missile program which later turned out to be wrong. "We could not then anticipate all the problems the Soviets might have in the development of intercontinental missiles," Nitze said later.[39] At the same time, despite subsequent revelations about the nonexistence of the missile gap, Nitze stubbornly stood by the report's forcasts of vulnerability: "I think that there was no doubt about the fact that we were running into a period of potential instability, dangerous instability which if not corrected could have increased the danger of war in the period of 1956 to 1961."[40]

And Nitze never reversed his thinking about one of the Gaither report's most controversial recommendations: that the United States should structure its strategic forces on the assumption that the Soviets might launch a surprise nuclear attack (or "bolt out of the blue") in a time of peace. This assumption carried the mind set of total theoretical hostility to new heights. Despite the myriad uncertainties of launching a fleet of missiles and bombers in an intercontinental attack, and despite the gut-level fear of nuclear war that any sane leader would have, Nitze seemed to believe that when the math was right and a first strike became hypothetically possible, the United States must assume that the Soviets would take the gamble. Or, even if they did not, that the perception in the world of U.S. vulnerability, however abstract, would prove fatal to U.S. interests. Eight years after the hydrogen bomb debate, Nitze continued to believe that the strategic nuclear component of the U.S.-Soviet competition was of overriding significance.

To others, however, worrying about the precise balance of nuclear forces made little sense in the face of a spiraling arms race and ever mounting levels of overkill. By 1957 the United States had nearly six thousand nuclear bombs and over two thousand medium- and long-range bombers.[41] This destructive capability, coupled with research programs to develop new weapons technologies, seemed more than sufficient to the president. It gave the United States "a superiority overwhelming enough to deter the Soviet leaders from aggression," Eisenhower later wrote.[42]

Nitze's old colleague George Kennan also believed that the United States had more than enough nuclear weapons. In his fifties now, Kennan had grown quite comfortable in the role of outside heretic and had lost none of his eloquence or intensity over the years. He still talked as he wrote, in elaborate and beautifully constructed sentences. And from his base at Princeton's Institute for Advanced Study, Kennan continued to fight the militarization of containment, a hint of vindication in his arguments. He had warned about a military competition of ever mounting danger. He had said that if the United States pushed forward with the H-bomb, if it abandoned the quest for arms control, and if it built more and more weapons, it would find itself mired in a deadly game of enormous stakes and unacceptable risks.

Now, with Soviet production of nuclear arms picking up speed, Kennan could see his prophecy coming true. During the H-bomb debate Paul Nitze had talked about the super as a coercive instrument that could help roll back Soviet influence. But that promise had proved illusory. Instead, the weapon had helped usher in a new phase of the arms race in which nuclear weapons became more unusable than before.

What so disturbed Kennan was the failure of U.S. policy makers to learn from their mistakes. As he saw it, the stockpiling of increasing numbers of weapons was a product of the defense establishment's continued misjudgment of the political significance of the nuclear balance. "These people seem unable to wean themselves from the belief that it is relative changes in the power of these weapons that are going to determine everything," Kennan stated in his well-publicized Reith lectures of 1957. In an attack that struck at the heart of Paul Nitze's strategic philosophy, Kennan continued: "They evidently believe that if the Russians gain the slightest edge on us in the capacity to wreak massive destruction at long range, they will immediately use it, regardless of our capacity for retaliation; whereas, if we can only contrive to get a tiny bit ahead of the Russians, we shall in some way have won; our salvation will be assured."

To Kennan, Nitze's approach to deterrence was mindless folly. Deterrence was not a concept that could be mathematically determined, he felt. One could not sit down with a sheet of statistics listing each side's nuclear forces and decide whether deterrence existed. Nor could one enhance deterrence by building more weapons. "So far as the effectiveness of the long-range atomic weapon as a deterrent is concerned, it is not the indefinite multiplication of its power which is important or relevant to our problem," Kennan wrote. "It need only be terrible enough to make its use against us an irrational and self-defeating act on the part of any adversary. This it has been, in my opinion, for many years; and its effectiveness for this purpose is not going to be enhanced by its being made more terrible still."[43]

To some jaded observers, the debate over America's strategic position in the late 1950s was no different from the debates that had preceded it. The technology of the arms race was more advanced and the perils of a surprise attack seemed more acute, but the fundamental questions were the same: Was the Soviet Union a brash and adventurist power? Would it exploit a strategic advantage to launch a bolt-out-of-the-blue attack on the United States? Was a military buildup the answer to America's security problems?

As before, those who believed that the Soviet leadership was more interested in preserving its internal power than in conquering new territory answered no to these questions. To Paul Nitze, however, this optimism seemed as dangerous in 1957 as it had in 1949. The assumption of total theoretical hostility remained most compelling to Nitze, and what frustrated him to distraction was his inability, in the late 1950s, to "bludgeon the mass mind" into accepting this gospel of pessimism. During the strategic debate of the late 1950s it was not anguished men like Robert Oppenheimer who led the opposition to Nitze's thinking, but rather a skeptical president with impeccable military credentials.

Even within Nitze's own party and among his friends there was doubt that the axioms of NSC 68 were still relevant. After over a decade of the Cold War, many believed that it was time to take a new approach to the east-west conflict, to negotiate with the Russians, and perhaps to even take risks in the pursuit of peace. Still, as powerful as these unsettled voices of dissent were becoming, they would seldom hold sway during the tumultuous days that lay ahead.

PART II

IMPLEMENTING AN IDEOLOGY

To the Pentagon

I N APRIL 1959 Paul Nitze traveled to Africa. In no other place were the changes sweeping the world more apparent. As Belgium, France, and Britain gave up their colonial territories on the continent, numerous independent nations came into being. The opportunities for the United States to make new friends and the dangers of acquiring new enemies were tremendous. The decolonization of the third world was the greatest challenge for U.S. diplomacy since the end of World War II. To Nitze and many others, the first priority in this dawning era was to prevent the new nations from turning to the Sino-Soviet bloc. This meant reorienting America's cold war strategy. It meant recognizing that with the exception of Berlin, Europe would no longer be the focal point of east-west tensions. The iron curtain was now more than a decade old. Hope of rolling back Soviet influence had died, and NATO and the Warsaw Pact had reached a military standoff. It was not a desirable status quo, but it appeared to be a stable one.

In contrast, the third world was boiling over with revolutionary ferment and passionate anticolonial feelings. With centuries of oppression to answer for, the western nations had little influence. Instead, Russia and China were the champions of these new nations. Ten years after the Marshall Plan had won over western Europe, the Cold War had shifted to a new battleground.

Nitze went to Africa as part of a delegation sent by the Council on Foreign Relations. Beyond seeking to enrich the council's understanding of the continent, the ten-person group had no special mission. Each member had a different itinerary and each was asked by the council to focus on a different aspect of African affairs. Nitze was to spend most of his time in West Africa, but his "focus" was hardly specific. "I was asked to look into basically political questions," he recalled, "into the relationship between the tribal organization and party organizations, the military, personal leadership, how the dynamic of these political factors might interrelate and then other questions."

Nitze's first stop was French West Africa. In the newly independent state of Guinea, he received a jolting introduction to the problems of the continent. When the French had pulled out seven months earlier, they left the country in utter disarray. The departing colonists had whisked all their administrators back to France, removed the files and the filing cabinets from the government office buildings, stripped the police of their guns and uniforms, taken the ambulances from the hospitals, and even broken the toilets in the president's palace, Nitze remembered.

The withdrawal was hardly an auspicious start for the country of two and a half million people. In desperation, Sekou Toure, Guinea's new leader, asked the United States for assistance. None was forthcoming. Without even an embassy, the United States was ill prepared to help out the new nation. When Nitze visited Guinea, there were only three Americans in the entire country.

Toure turned to the Soviet bloc nations. Czechoslovakia responded immediately with a shipload of guns and ammunition for Guinea's police. Soon other ties were formed. Within months most of Guinea's exports were to eastern Europe. When Nitze arrived at his hotel in the capital city of Conakry, he found it "filled with East Germans, Czechs, Poles, Bulgarians, Russians and so on. The place was swarming with Communists of one variety and another."

Nitze believed that Guinea's new friendships reflected the shortcomings of America's foreign policy. The United States simply lacked the initiative to tackle the challenges of the emerging nations, and Guinea was a classic example. "I think we have lost a great deal by not having been on the spot, not having had some mobility of action when this first took place," Nitze said when he returned. "The upshot has been that the Communists moved in hammer and tongs."

In Nigeria the situation was more hopeful. While the illiteracy rate was a crippling 98 percent, and the nation of nineteen million produced only twenty-five high school graduates a year, Nigeria had the advantage of having been a British rather than a French colony. When Nitze visited, Britain was working to prepare Nigeria for self-rule. Asked later about the prospects for democratic government in Africa, Nitze responded that "The only place that I went where there is a possibility it could work for a period of time was Nigeria."

In Kenya, Sudan, the Ivory Coast, and elsewhere, there was little hope for democracy, or even cohesive central governance. The end of colonial rule had left most of the continent in chaos, and in that chaos, Nitze saw a disturbing potential for communist gains. His judgment was that the Soviets and Chinese were making a "maximum effort" throughout Africa. He believed that failure by the United States to respond could have an adverse impact for decades to come.[1]

Another figure in Washington with a keen interest in the third world was Senator John F. Kennedy, Democrat from Massachusetts. As a young congressman in 1951, Kennedy had traveled to Southeast Asia and India. The poverty, misery, and colonial decay he encountered greatly alarmed him. America's foreign policy challenge of tomorrow, he came to believe, would be to deal with the developing nations.

A member of the Senate Foreign Relations Committee by the mid 1950s, Kennedy argued that the United States must make a concerted effort to win over the hearts and minds of the millions of people emerging from the bonds of colonialism. For the most part, these people were uncommitted to any political ideology. If the United States ignored their hopes and dreams, Kennedy believed that upon becoming independent, the masses of the third world could well turn to communism. The problem, he stated in 1959, "is one of timing—and whether once that freedom is achieved they will regard the United States as friend or foe."[2]

When the State Department created the post of assistant secretary of state for African affairs in 1957, the Senate Foreign Relations Committee set up a Subcommittee on African Affairs. Kennedy became its first chairman and took the lead in focusing attention on the momentous changes sweeping the continent. "Call it nationalism, call it anti-colonialism, call it what you will," he said in 1959, "Africa is going through a revolution." For the United States to turn its back on that revolution would be a great mistake, Kennedy argued. Instead, he advocated political support and economic aid to build "a strong Africa."[3]

For all his rhetoric about Africa, the infrequency with which Senator Kennedy convened his subcommittee became a campaign issue in 1960. One such rare convention, in early June 1959, was to hear testimony from Paul Nitze, who had recently returned from his month-long trip. The hearing marked the first real contact between Nitze and Kennedy.

Naturally, Nitze knew about Kennedy. He had seen him in action during the Chicago convention, when Kennedy first came to national prominence with a strong but unsuccessful bid for the vice-presidential nomination. Nitze also knew of Kennedy through his association with the Democratic Advisory Council.

From a large family of combative and quick-witted people, John F. Kennedy was generally impatient with lazy thinkers and ponderous speakers. He valued spirited discourse and wanted crisp and concise advice. He was annoyed by sycophants. In this sense Nitze was his type of person. Well organized, informed, and economical with words and time, Nitze was refreshingly substantive in comparison to many of the would-be advisors who proffered their ideas on Capitol Hill.

Intellectually, the two men were similar. Arthur Schlesinger, Jr., observed that Kennedy "was a man of action who could pass easily over to the realm of ideas and confront intellectuals with perfect confidence in his capacity to hold his own." He wasn't what Schlesinger called an "authentic intellectual" because the realm of ideas was not his primary habitat. His habitat was the world of power. What made Kennedy seek to go beyond his world and into that of the intellectuals, wrote Schlesinger, was his "inexhaustible curiosity . . . Vague answers never contented him."[4]

Nitze was much the same way. He had spent his childhood among intellectuals and was accustomed to their methods of discourse. Like Kennedy, Nitze was an avid reader and a cultured man who could converse easily about history or art if he chose. As his longtime friend Charles Burton Marshall said, Nitze was "a man with a raging curiosity," a person who took up the piano and learned music "to see how it worked technically, to see how Bach could be Bach." Yet while Nitze enjoyed ideas and art, he shared Kennedy's lust for action; he wanted to change the world, not simply observe or enjoy it.

What differentiated the two men was the way they wielded ideas in a policy-making forum. As a senator used to lengthy and freewheeling committee hearings, Kennedy preferred a loose style of discussion. Even if a particular point of view seemed muddled and the most logical course of action was already evident, he often liked to hear out all sides before making up his mind on an issue.

Nitze's approach was different. Ten years on Wall Street and thirteen years in government had drilled into him the value of conciseness. In discussing policy, Nitze still worked like the investment banker he had once been: analyzing the available data, identifying the possible options, and making the best choice. Often there was little time left for musing over philosophical subtleties. Nor did he seem to have any inclination to do so. Many people came away from their first discussion with Paul Nitze feeling uneasy about the steely and mechanistic man they had just encountered. With a speaking style that could be bluntly dismissive and choppy hand movements that grew more intense as he tried to cut apart a person's argument, Nitze was an intimidating figure. Some took an instant dislike to him. Old friends came to understand and accept him. "One thing I've learned about Paul Nitze over the fifty years that I've known him is that you don't engage in some academic debate about a point of view," said Roswell Gilpatric. "You express yourself, put your case forward while in the decision-making process."

Kennedy and Nitze also differed in their personalities. Kennedy was a gay and gregarious man with an easy and casual wit. He was relaxed and self-confident. Nitze, too, was self-confident and he could be charming, but when he plunged into the policy world, Nitze was not often relaxed. He gave people he dealt with the sense that they should get straight to the point. "He's sort of angular," remarked Gilpartic, "and he doesn't make any effort to ingratiate himself. You just take him as he is."

In 1959 John F. Kennedy was willing to take Paul Nitze as he was. In the months following their encounter at the African affairs committee hearing, the senator began soliciting Nitze's advice on national security matters. Nitze's chief contact in the senator's office was Deirdre Henderson, a staff aide. With Kennedy's campaign for the presidency heating up, Nitze provided material for speeches on military and foreign policy.

Despite this new advisory role, Nitze did not immediately commit himself to Kennedy's candidacy. At first he supported Senator Hubert Humphrey, an old friend and a reliable hard-liner. As the primaries got under way, however, Humphrey proved a lackluster candidate. When he dropped out of the race in May 1960, Nitze gravitated toward

Kennedy. To some eastern establishment stalwarts, the young senator seemed a dubious choice. Ever since Kennedy had made the outrageous suggestion that France should recognize "the independent personality of Algeria," Dean Acheson had suspected him of insufficient maturity when it came to foreign affairs.[5] "This impatient snapping of our fingers" was no way to treat a NATO ally, Acheson wrote in a bitter attack on Kennedy.[6] Acheson had his own candidate for president: Senator Stuart Symington, former secretary of the air force and fellow Yale man.

But while his old mentor remained disdainful of a man whose family had made its fortune bootlegging, Nitze found much that was appealing about Kennedy. Young and vibrant in Eisenhower's dreary Washington, Kennedy personified the potential of the Democratic party. More decisive than Adlai Stevenson and more magnetic than Humphrey, Symington, or Lyndon Johnson, the Pulitzer Prize–winning senator seemed like the man who could lead the Democrats out of the political wilderness in which they had wandered for almost a decade. Most importantly, J.F.K. passed the Nitze litmus test: He was tough on defense.

During Eisenhower's first term, Kennedy had been an early and vocal critic of massive retaliation. Echoing Nitze's own sentiments, he told his senate colleagues in 1954 that "Our reduction of strength for resistance in so-called brushfire wars, while threatening atomic retaliation, has in effect invited expansion by the Communists in such areas as Indochina through those techniques which they deem not sufficiently offensive to us to risk the atomic warfare for which we are so ill-prepared defensively."[7] In the late 1950s Kennedy spoke often of the strategic situation. "We have been driving ourselves into a corner," he warned, "where the only choice is all or nothing at all, world devastation or submission."[8] To bolster America's position, Kennedy supported higher defense spending, a new nuclear strategy, and the development of stronger conventional forces.

He was Paul Nitze's kind of candidate.

At the 1960 Democratic National Convention, Kennedy narrowly edged out Stevenson and Johnson. In his acceptance speech before a crowd of eighty thousand in the Los Angeles Coliseum, the senator pledged to lead America into a new frontier, "the frontier of the 1960s, a frontier of unknown opportunities and paths, a frontier of unfulfilled hopes and threats."[9] If Nitze had any remaining doubts about who he would back for president, they were erased by Kennedy's ascendancy.

The task before him now was to help put the Democratic nominee in the White House and bring his long years of exile to an end.

In late August Kennedy showed Nitze how much he respected his advice. Determined to make a smooth transition if he won in November, Kennedy decided to set up a panel of national security experts to lay the groundwork for his foreign policy. He asked Nitze to be its chairman.

On August 30, 1960, Kennedy and Nitze appeared together at a Washington press conference. Handsome, tanned, and immaculately dressed, Nitze projected the image that Kennedy capitalized on so heavily during the election: new, intelligent, healthy, and rich—everything that the elderly Eisenhower and his heir apparent, Richard Nixon, were not.

Kennedy spoke first. He announced that he was forming a Committee on National Security Policy that would be chaired by Nitze. The task of the committee "would be to undertake nonpartisan consultations on the security problems" faced by the United States. The committee's work, said Kennedy, "would be divorced entirely from the partisan campaign." Nitze's group did not exist to churn out clever speeches on defense policy; its aim was to help a Democratic administration move swiftly during its first few months in a crisis-torn and "dangerous" period of world history.

In Nitze's remarks, he explained how the group would operate. By consulting with experts in the field of national security, the committee would determine which problems were most pressing and what sort of solutions existed. Advice would be sought from Democrats and Republicans alike, "some of whom had served on Eisenhower administration committees."[10]

Besides Nitze, the committee included Roswell Gilpatric, David Bruce, and James A. Perkins. All four had worked in Republican as well as Democratic administrations and their contacts in the foreign policy world were extensive. To a man, their views on national security were hard-line.

In early September Nitze's group set up shop in the Senate Office Building, next door to Henry Jackson's office. Jackson was a conservative Democrat from the state of Washington and a longtime acquaintance of Nitze's. He had strongly supported the idea of the committee and, like Nitze, wanted to insure that the Democrats remained the party of vigilance. During the following weeks Jackson engaged the committee's members in long, intense discussions on national security.

As the Kennedy campaign raced from stop to stop across the country, Nitze scheduled meetings with various experts. He turned to the usual people. Former Truman hands Dean Acheson, Robert Lovett, and William Foster were consulted. Others that the committee talked to included Robert Bowie, Colonel George A. Lincoln, and James Conant. Nitze also invited in analysts from RAND, the Institute for Defense Analysis, and the Washington Center for Foreign Policy Research. Those who might have offered a less militant perspective on the Cold War, people like George Kennan and Averell Harriman, were not consulted. Nitze's aim was to set an agenda, not sponsor a dialogue.

Kennedy's narrow victory over Richard Nixon in the November election imbued Nitze's committee with a new sense of mission. No longer were they debating what a Democrat might do if he were elected; they were debating what the next president would do.

Nitze was elated by the turn of events. Ever since being sacrificed on the altar of McCarthyism in 1953, he had longed to get back into government and continue his crusade for the goals of NSC 68. Now the United States would have a president who was committed to these goals, who was ready to spend more on defense, to close the alleged missile gap, and to do battle with burgeoning nationalist movements in the third world. Moreover, he was a president who personally approved of Nitze, who called on him regularly for advice, and who had put him in charge of an important policy group. That Nitze would get a high position in the Kennedy administration was a foregone conclusion. Even the post of secretary of defense seemed within reach.

During the 1950s Paul Nitze had hovered in the outer darkness. In the 1960s he would sit in the inner circle.

By early December Nitze's group had finished its work. Under twenty pages in length, but broad in its analysis, the Report of Senator Kennedy's National Security Policy Committee was written largely by Nitze and grappled mostly with the difficult question of nuclear weapons policy.

It considered first whether the United States should strive for a "win" capability. The ability to fight and win a nuclear war had long appealed to U.S. policy makers and military officials, Nitze not excluded. NSC 68 had argued that military superiority was a critical component of containment. By the late 1950s, however, Nitze had come to believe that a "win" capability was unattainable and probably undesirable. The policy committee's final report reflected this: "It is doubtful whether such a capability is possible within presently foreseeable technology. It would probably require a first or preemptive strike by our side to capitalize on its 'win' capabilities. Furthermore, such a capability would probably be destabilizing—in other words would increase the danger of a nuclear war."

Still, while Nitze recognized that total nuclear superiority was a dangerous fantasy, he was not content with having merely an assured retaliatory capability, that is, enough nuclear warheads to destroy Moscow and a host of other vital targets in response to a Soviet nuclear attack. A nuclear weapons strategy geared toward retaliation, with no coercive potential, was almost useless, Nitze felt. Such a posture "undermines the credibility of the deterrent and gives little or no support to the political aspects of our policy." The committee didn't spell out the solution it favored, but the implications of its suggestions were clear: The United States had to build a large, reliable, invulnerable, and accurate force of strategic nuclear weapons that could be used in a controlled and "rational" manner to destroy selected military targets in the Soviet Union should deterrence fail. In short, the president's nuclear options had to be expanded.

In the realm of arms control the report counseled caution. Dramatic, sweeping disarmament proposals held little promise and should be avoided, it said. "We believe that the most feasible intermediate term objective is not complete and total disarmament but a more stable nuclear relationship between the two blocs."

Nitze's thinking had been moving in this direction for some time. He believed that the best way to rein in the arms race was to convince the Soviets that there were sensible alternatives to endless competition. "The most feasible and practicable route to such a relationship lies through reciprocal action and counter action between the two blocs," the report stated. Showing restraint in introducing new types of weaponry, dispersing bombers, hardening missile silos, and placing quantitative and qualitative caps on the arms race were all examples of this type of action.

The committee's report was widely circulated among Kennedy's advisors and praised for its clear vision. By proposing to channel the superpower competition into a more manageable framework, the report challenged none of the assumptions of the time. It reflected Nitze's desire to update America's cold war policy, not rethink it.[11]

Shortly after his triumph at the polls, John F. Kennedy began the search for people to help him settle the New Frontier. It was not an easy job. "People, people, people!" exclaimed the president-elect in exasperation, "I don't know any people. I only know voters."[12] In truth, the Massachusetts politician was not well connected. He was not an eastern establishment figure who could place a few calls to New York banks and the Council on Foreign Relations and have a cabinet in a week. One of Kennedy's earliest moves was to recruit Clark Clifford to help him manage the transition. Having retired from the Truman administration to become a well-paid Washington lawyer—some said the most highly paid in town—Clifford had the kind of insider status that made him an ideal headhunter.

The two most important posts were the top positions at State and Defense. Since Kennedy intended to make foreign policy a major focus of his presidency, it was crucial to have a secretary of state who could spearhead a new political offensive. Just as indispensable was a secretary of defense who had the cunning and endurance to take control of the Pentagon's sprawling empire and manage Kennedy's military buildup.

To fill either of these posts, Kennedy turned first to Robert Lovett. A staunch anticommunist and leading stalwart of the New York financial and legal community, Lovett was a figure of immense prestige. But he was also a tired man, telling Kennedy that "My bearings are burnt out."[13] Kennedy would have to look elsewhere to for his secretaries of state and defense.

In late November Clifford invited Nitze to his office to discuss appointments. The president had yet to settle on a secretary of state, said Clifford. Did Nitze have any suggestions? Nitze said that he thought Dean Rusk would be an excellent choice. During the darkest days of the Korean War, Rusk had selflessly volunteered to take the hot seat of assistant secretary of state for Far Eastern affairs. After leaving government, he served ably as president of the Rockefeller Foundation. A quiet and somewhat bland man, with a bald head and a round, impassive face, Rusk projected the image of an anonymous bureaucrat. Unlike many of his stature, he had not been born to wealth and position, but had clawed his way up from a boyhood in rural Georgia to become a mainstream establishment figure with impeccable credentials.

On November 28 the president-elect called at Acheson's home in Georgetown to talk about the problem of selecting a secretary of state. Sitting in the living room sipping tea—the first of their famous teas— Kennedy told Acheson that he was not going to appoint either Adlai Stevenson or Chester Bowles, two of the leading candidates for the job at the time. Instead, he was thinking that perhaps Senator J. William Fulbright, head of the Senate Foreign Relations Committee, would be right for the post.

Acheson scoffed at the suggestion. The old statesman had ideas of his own. David Bruce would make an excellent secretary of state, he said, and Paul Nitze should be appointed under secretary with the aim of eventually elevating him to the top slot. "Paul has great qualities," Acheson told Kennedy. Unfortunately, "he's wholly unknown—it would be impossible to appoint him secretary of state now, but after a year or so he might develop into a very useful man."[14] Kennedy said nothing about Nitze and had no enthusiasm for Bruce. Acheson then suggested Rusk. Kennedy didn't know Rusk, but Acheson assured him that he was "strong and loyal and good in every way." The former secretary of state recommended him "without reservation."[15]

After thinking it over for many days, Kennedy decided to offer Rusk the job. Ever pensive, Rusk said he would consider it.

Besides offering ideas for cabinet appointments, Nitze served Kennedy in other ways during the transition. When Robert Anderson, the outgoing secretary of the treasury, asked Kennedy to send one of his representatives with him to Bonn to discuss the gold problem with the Germans, Kennedy declined and directed Nitze to receive Anderson's report on his return. When the State Department sought Kennedy's advance approval of a proposal for a multilateral nuclear force to be submitted to the December meeting of the North Atlantic Council, Kennedy again declined. Instead, he asked Nitze and David Bruce to talk quietly with the NATO director general, Paul-Henry Spaak.[16] Nitze also briefed Kennedy on disarmament issues the evening before he was to meet with President Eisenhower at the White House.[17]

By early December the president-elect still had made no official offer to Nitze. Amidst the swirl of transition rumors, it was widely believed that Nitze was a candidate for secretary of defense. While this was true, Nitze was never a leading contender for the job. In the view of Kennedy and his confidantes, Nitze had great strengths, but equally great liabilities. "He was considered as under secretary of defense and also, I believe, the secretary of defense," recalled Robert Kennedy. "But he was turned down because of the fact that he had made a good number of enemies. And there were those who had worked with him who didn't feel that he had the personality to carry that job, carry the position— although he is supposed to be a very bright person."[18]

In making his appointments, Kennedy sought the approval of the New York financial and legal establishment above almost all else. He knew that many of these power brokers viewed him with distrust, and he desperately wanted to instill in them confidence in his presidency. While Nitze was an old Wall Street hand himself, he hadn't worked in the private sector for two decades and lacked the prestige of someone like Robert Lovett or John McCloy. Acheson was right: Nitze was virtually unknown. And in one of the few circles in which he was known—the Democratic party officials he had met at the DAC—Nitze was viewed with mixed feelings. Party liberals identified him with Acheson, and they associated the former secretary of state with static cold war beliefs unsuited to the dawning era.

Kennedy's search for a defense secretary with credibility but few enemies was frustrating. "I'd like to have some new faces here," he told Schlesinger in early December, "but all I get is the same old names. It's discouraging. I suppose it will take a little while to develop new talent."[19]

New talent soon appeared in the form of Robert Strange McNamara, the president of Ford Motor Company. Suggested by Lovett, who called him "the best of the lot," and endorsed by Galbraith, McNamara appeared ideal for the top post at either Treasury or Defense. When Kennedy offered him the Pentagon job, McNamara insisted the president-elect was speaking to the wrong man, arguing that he knew nothing about defense issues. But Kennedy persisted and eventually McNamara agreed on the condition that he be allowed to choose his own top staff.

Nitze's call from the president-elect finally came one evening in December as he sat having cocktails with Phyllis. As Nitze would later tell the story, Kennedy offered him the choice of three jobs: national security advisor, deputy secretary of defense, or under secretary of state for economic affairs.

"Well, how long have I got to make up my mind?" Nitze remembered asking.

"Thirty seconds," replied Kennedy.

"All right," said Nitze, "I'll make up my mind in thirty seconds if that's what you say." Without more hesitation he continued, "What I would opt for is the job of deputy secretary of defense. I've done the economic job in the State Department, and I don't think the job of the head of the NSC staff can be done unless there is someone in the Department of Defense that you can really work with, and the real job is in the Department of Defense not in the NSC staff."

In Nitze's view his choice was a good one. As deputy secretary of defense he would be in the Office of the Secretary of Defense (OSD), the Pentagon's nerve center, an ideal position from which to orchestrate the military buildup for which he had so long pressed.

Moreover, if the defense secretary didn't last—and they never did—Nitze would be in a position to move to the top. The next four years looked promising.

A few days later Nitze received a call from McNamara.

"Paul," he asked, "will you become head of ISA? I know that Mr. Kennedy offered you the job of deputy secretary, but I want Roswell Gilpatric for that job and I want you to be assistant secretary."

Nitze was stunned. The Office of International Security Affairs (ISA) was primarily concerned with foreign military aid. Heading ISA would mean relegation to an obscure third-level post in the Pentagon. It was not what Nitze had expected or what he'd been promised. And it was not what he felt he deserved. "Let me call you back," he told McNamara.

Hanging up the telephone, Nitze dialed the number of Kennedy's private phone in Palm Beach. But when an aide informed Kennedy who was calling, the president-elect refused to take the call.[20] The message was clear: assistant secretary of defense for international security affairs or nothing. Over breakfast with McNamara on a bright Monday morning, Nitze accepted the job.

That Paul Nitze would turn down the post of national security advisor to become deputy secretary of defense seems incredible in hindsight. But in 1960 the NSC job was not considered of great importance. The dominance of the secretaries of state under Truman and Eisenhower had left the NSC head with little power. Under both administrations his chief function was to coordinate policy, not make it. And Paul Nitze was not interested in being a coordinator. McGeorge Bundy of Harvard University (William Bundy's younger brother) was given the job instead. What Nitze did not foresee was the new role the national security advisor would play in an administration notable for both its informality and its weak secretary of state.

Kennedy's behavior in the episode was puzzling. Since McNamara had been given the top Pentagon post before Kennedy called Nitze, the president-elect must have known that he could not guarantee Nitze the job of deputy secretary. That decision was left to McNamara. Trying to unravel the situation later, one of Kennedy's talent hunters, Adam Yarmolinksy, wrote that "we talked about whether Nitze should be Deputy Sec'y. and Gilpatric should be A/S for I.S.A. or vice versa." In the end, "The question of Gilpatric vs. Nitze was resolved on the basis of what McNamara learned about their personal characteristics and the impression he had was that Gilpatric was more of an administrator and longer on judgment, and perhaps Nitze was more of an ideas man." In running the Pentagon, McNamara sought a deputy who would be his alter ego, not a debating foe. Subdued and agreeable, Roswell Gilpatric fit the bill; Nitze did not. When Kennedy was told of the final arrangement, his response was, "Sure go ahead."[21]

Nitze's appointment to ISA was hailed by the press and the foreign policy world as a move of major significance. As one high-level Kennedy official later recalled, "That was a very important post . . . and it was perceived as an important post by everybody thinking about the new administration."

On Christmas Day the *New York Times* announced the Nitze appointment with a two-column headline on the front page. The "scope" of the ISA post had been "widened," the story said. Nitze's job would be to "develop new disarmament plans and proposals." Perhaps feeling guilty about the double-dealing that had landed one of his closest national security advisors in a third-level post, Kennedy made a point of emphasizing Nitze's significance to the press. "I cannot too strongly stress the importance of the post which Mr. Nitze has accepted," said the president-elect. "I am glad he has agreed to join the Defense Department in this capacity. His wealth of experience will be of great assistance to both Defense Secretary McNamara and to me."[22]

On a cold, bright day in late January 1961, John F. Kennedy was sworn in as the thirty-fifth president of the United States. From the steps of the west portico of the Capitol, the new president let it be known that the Eisenhower years had come to an end. Nowhere was the passing of the torch more keenly evident than in the realm of national security policy. Speaking in his choppy way, the Boston accent still pronounced after fourteen years in Washington, Kennedy announced a new beginning in the foreign policy of the United States. In sweeping terms he embraced an approach to world affairs of nearly limitless scope and ambition: "Let every nation know, whether it wishes us well or ill, that we shall pay any price, bear any burden, meet any hardship, support any friend, oppose any foe to assure the survival and the success of liberty."

For the first time, Kennedy promised, the United States would devote attention to the threat of communism in the third world. As for the U.S.-Soviet competition, Kennedy suggested "that both sides begin anew the quest for peace, before the dark powers of destruction unleashed by science engulf all humanity in planned or accidental self-destruction." At the same time he called for a nuclear weapons buildup. "For only when our arms are sufficient beyond doubt can we be certain beyond doubt that they will never be employed."[23]

In many ways the president's foreign policy vision suffered from the same tension that marked Nitze's own ideology. It invited a heightened cold war antagonism by embracing the vigilant militarism of NSC 68, yet emphasized new efforts to resolve the differences between east and west.

It was a balancing act that had never been tried before. But both the president and his assistant secretary of defense thought it could be done.

About a week after the inauguration, late in the afternoon of January 29, Paul Nitze and other high-level members of the new administration were sworn in at the White House. As finally constituted, the Kennedy administration contained an impressive array of national security hardliners. Many of those who had worked under Truman and captiously lambasted Eisenhower now held high posts—men like Roswell Gilpatric, William C. Foster, John McCloy, and Jerome Weisner. There were also some new faces. McGeorge Bundy at the NSC and Walt Rostow, head of the Policy Planning Staff, were the most prominent of the many who left academia for a stint in Washington. Arthur Schlesinger, Jr., became a special assistant to the president. But whether they were veterans or newcomers, few who worked for Kennedy questioned the need to bolster American military might and prepare for battle in the third world. This was the consensus Nitze had long wanted. Yet it was also a cold war orthodoxy of profoundly dangerous dimensions.

From Nitze's point of view the most important new addition was Robert McNamara, the man who would be his boss at the Pentagon. Nearly a decade younger than Nitze, with a round face, round rimless glasses, and slicked-back hair, McNamara was an intense and driven man. Joining the Ford Motor Company after World War II, he was one of Henry Ford II's brightest "whiz kids"—working his way up to become the company's president in 1960. He was not, however, one of the company's most loved executives. Many in Detroit found him cold, aloof, and mechanistic. It was a reputation that followed him to Washington. McNamara's problem, remarked one Pentagon official, was that he was "kind of underdeveloped in some areas and overdeveloped in others . . . like some engineers who don't know anything about the social sciences." A human computer, some called him—the ultimate technocrat.

In reality, McNamara was not, as Richard Barnet charged, "the leading speciman of homo mathematicus."[24] Those who knew him best saw a very different person. "Despite McNamara's reputation as a human robot, he was really a very kind as well as a loyal friend," recalled a Ford colleague, Lee Iacocca.[25] He was also a learned and open-minded man. Unlike most automobile executives, McNamara had little interest in car talk. He lived near the University of Michigan in Ann Arbor and preferred to socialize with intellectuals. He contributed to the NAACP and, despite his Republican affiliation, voted for Kennedy. The notion that McNamara had no interests other than number crunching was false. "He would far rather discuss existentialism or Rouault, climb up a mountain or ski down one, play squash or drink a martini, than crank out statistics on the number of air sorties flown against North Vietnam," said Pentagon official Phil Goulding.[26] McNamara's aloof abrasiveness was something he couldn't help. "His intelligence was so formidable and so disciplined," remarked Iacocca, "that it often overshadowed his personality." He was, concluded Iacocca, "one of the smartest men I've ever met, with a phenomenal IQ and a steel trap mind. He was a mental giant."[27]

When he took the job at the Pentagon, McNamara had read only one book and one article on the subject of nuclear weapons: Kissinger's *Nuclear Weapons and Foreign Policy* and Wohlstetter's "A Delicate Balance of Terror."[28] He knew little about how the Defense Department operated and nothing about the dozens of sensitive matters in which the U.S. military was involved. By his own judgment, McNamara was "an ignorant automobile executive," and he wasn't at all sure that he belonged in one of the most demanding posts in the government. "I felt in my heart that my appointment as secretary of defense was wrong," he said later.[29] Nuclear strategy, counterinsurgency, antisubmarine warfare, weapons systems procurement—the list of subjects that had to be mastered went on and on.

A less intense man might have bowed his head in humble despair and thrown himself at the mercy of his top aides for the first year or two. But that was not McNamara's way. In the month following his appointment he leaped into the complex issues of national security with disciplined zeal. Roswell Gilpatric was his chief tutor during this time. An old friend of Nitze's—the two had gone to Hotchkiss together— Gilpatric had been under secretary of the air force during the Truman years and a keen student of military policy throughout the 1950s. He was one of the sharpest experts in his field, and he was awed by the facility with which McNamara mastered defense issues. He was "a very quick study," recalled Gilpatric. "We spent a month together before he took office . . . I never saw anybody who seized to the subject so quickly."

The relationship between McNamara and Nitze got off to a curious start. In some ways they were very similar. Both attacked their work with singular thoroughness and precision and were unrelenting in their demand for quality and efficiency. "From a very early point they came to have a considerable sense of kinship and common energy drives," recalled William Bundy, Nitze's top deputy. "And they both had the temperament to just throw themselves into something. I think that was a considerable common bond. Another common bond was that they wanted to find new and better ways of doing things."

But the differences between the two men were as great as the similarities. The former head of Ford Motors was not unlike Nitze had been when he entered government twenty years earlier. "McNamara was a charger and an issuer of orders and a ramrod," recalled one of Nitze's special assistants, Timothy Stanley. He brought to the Pentagon the same swaggering managerial style that had boosted him to the top of the corporate world. Nitze, in contrast, had mellowed considerably over the years. In 1940 he shrugged off Forrestal's warning that one must move cautiously in Washington. By 1961 Nitze had come to see the wisdom of that advice. He had learned better than most how to get things done, how to turn proposals into decisions and decisions into actions. He had come to see that the best way to achieve results was by slowly building a consensus through persuasion rather than by imposing a policy through superior bureaucratic firepower.

It was a decision-making approach that was foreign to McNamara, and it made him uneasy. "I think McNamara regarded Nitze as a kind of restless spirit," recalled Stanley. "He could never be quite sure where Paul Nitze was coming from or going to." Had the circumstances been different, the chemistry might have been better. But the circumstances only made things worse.

It was no secret that Nitze wanted to be deputy secretary and that McNamara had prevented him from getting what the president had offered. This created an awkward situation right off. "McNamara had quite a problem with Paul Nitze because he wanted my job," recalled Gilpatric. Tension also arose from the fact that Nitze was in some ways better qualified than McNamara to be secretary of defense. He had thirteen years of experience in government, he was familiar with national security issues, and he knew how to get things done in Washington. Understandably, McNamara was uneasy about having an older and more competent defense expert as a subordinate. He had to walk a fine line that enabled him to benefit from Nitze's insight without allowing Nitze to become a dominant voice in Pentagon councils.

From the beginning McNamara chose not to depend on Nitze for day-to-day advice. The phone in Nitze's office would ring all day with McNamara on the other end asking questions, and Nitze was constantly making the brisk six-minute walk to McNamara's office, but the brunt of the defense secretary's education was handled by Gilpatric, who was closer at hand and less of a threat. As disciples of hierarchy, McNamara and Nitze could work together; rarely would they think together. This distance wasn't troubling to Nitze. "Nitze had a lot of respect for McNamara at this stage, a lot of respect," recalled Bill Bundy. "He felt that this guy had such fantastic energy and managerial talents and experience that all and all this was a very worthy Secretary of Defense to be working for."

Throughout February Nitze worked to get settled in. With seventeen miles of corridors and twenty-five thousand employees, the Pentagon was Byzantine compared to Foggy Bottom. It was a bureaucratic empire of unparalleled vastness, and as assistant secretary of defense for international security affairs, Paul Nitze had his own fiefdom.

Whereas the deputy secretary was directly tied to the Office of the Secretary of Defense (OSD), the assistant secretary for international security affairs had considerable autonomy.

Established in December 1950 by President Truman, the Office of International Security Affairs was an outgrowth of the Mutual Defense Assistance Program passed by Congress in the fall of 1949. Quickly named the "little State Department," ISA coordinated the foreign and military aspects of U.S. national security policy. By the beginning of Eisenhower's presidency—when Nitze had spent his ill-fated days at ISA working for Frank Nash—this task included administering military aid, helping to manage NATO affairs, facilitating interagency work, and providing advice to the secretary of defense on politico-military issues.[30]

During the Eisenhower years ISA grew in size and importance. Only the shadow that John Foster Dulles cast over the entire national security establishment stopped the office from realizing its potential. When Kennedy came to power, he saw in ISA a workhorse for his foreign policy agenda.

The President intended a new activism in the third world. As the office in charge of doling out military aid, ISA would be a versatile instrument of that activism.

Kennedy wanted armed forces that had a coercive and limited-war potential, forces that could be actively employed in the pursuit of political objectives. As the office designed to integrate military and foreign policy, ISA could cater to that desire.

Kennedy wanted arms control. And as an office well positioned to bring together feuding officials from the CIA, NSC, State, and Defense, ISA was an ideal instrument for creating the bureaucratic harmony so crucial to the success of arms control.

Finally, Kennedy sought a more relaxed chain of command in his administration, a setup that would allow him to solicit advice from officials below the cabinet rank. ISA flourished under this arrangement because it was a natural breeding ground for policy initiatives.

With a prominent director and a broadened mandate, ISA would become more influential than ever.[31] And far from losing power by not getting the Pentagon's number two post, Nitze was in a better position to turn ideology into policy than he would have been as McNamara's deputy.

As head of ISA, Nitze directed some three hundred people. This included a principal deputy assistant secretary and six regular deputy assistant secretaries. A little over a third of those who worked at ISA were military officers. Eight separate departments, ranging from the Office of Europe and North Atlantic Affairs to the Office of International Logistics Negotiations, helped run America's global military empire.[32] Whether the task was selling small arms to Morocco or negotiating a test ban treaty with the Soviets, ISA was involved.

As he had done at the Policy Planning Staff, Nitze leaned heavily on his staff. William Bundy was Nitze's principal deputy assistant secretary. Colonel Thomas Wolfe was director for Sino-Soviet affairs. Admiral Luther Heinz ran the office for Far Eastern Affairs. And in ISA's planning office, Nitze had RAND analyst Henry ("Harry") Rowen. Originally trained as an economist and engineer, Rowen began studying strategic affairs in the early 1950s under the tutelage of Albert Wohlstetter and became intimately familiar with the arcane details of America's nuclear war plans. By bringing Rowen into ISA Nitze tapped a vast reservoir of expertise. Intense and articulate, with an appetite for fourteen-hour days, Rowen would help place ISA at the forefront of the revolutionary changes in American defense policy.

To manage his massive paper flow, Nitze had two special assistants, Timothy Stanley and Lawrence McQuade. A young defense intellectual, Stanley had met Nitze at Harvard in 1956 and became, he said later, "an instant convert to the Paul Nitze fan club." Four years later Stanley was working as an assistant to Nitze's predecessor at ISA, John Irwin. He fully expected to be fired when the new administration came in. Instead, Nitze not only asked Stanley to stay, he asked him to review the office's administrative staff and determine who should remain. Stanley complied, and when he had finished, Nitze accepted all his recommendations.

Because of ISA's immense compass, Nitze delegated vast authority to his deputies and immersed himself in those issues he considered most important. During his years at ISA Nitze would become so consumed with the bigger issues that when it came to carrying out one of ISA's principal functions—managing military assistance programs—Nitze was almost invisible. "He did not see it [military assistance] as a major policy tool," recalled Stanley. There were only so many hours in a day and Nitze was not about to spend time on the latest aid package for Turkey. He turned most of this work over to Bill Bundy. Williston Palmer, the cantankerous general who worked for Bundy on military assistance, hardly ever saw Nitze during the early 1960s. "Nitze was always off in something else," Palmer recalled scornfully. "He was a kind of secretary of something without a portfolio."[33]

To those at ISA who worked closely with Nitze, however, there was no scorn. For the young staffers and deputies who were at Nitze's side during the tumultuous Kennedy era, the days at ISA would be some of the best days of their lives. "It was an exciting intellectual time," recalled Stanley. And it was exciting, in great part, because of who Paul Nitze was. In 1961 Nitze was not a man who needed to engage in an extended introductory policy debate before taking action. If McNamara was unsure about where his assistant secretary was coming from or going to, Nitze's vision of change was strikingly clear. His goals were those he had articulated in NSC 68, in the Gaither report, and in his writing during the late 1950s.

Paul Nitze's challenge was not to create an ideology; it was to implement one.

In pursuing his agenda, Nitze worked at a punishing pace. He expected his subordinates to work at the same pace. But he also treated them fairly and with compassion. Although he might be distant and impersonal while in a meeting or giving out assignments, his deputies found him approachable. He was tough, but rarely mean. He would push his staff, but never bully them. "I think that Mr. Nitze has a feeling for people," remarked Luther Heinz, "an understanding of people's capabilities and abilities, that he can get the most out of people; he works with them. He certainly is a very personable man, a very delightful man."[34]

Moreover, Nitze was a man one could argue with. If he had a keen sense of where he was taking ISA, Nitze did not know precisely how to get there. The staff he picked was unusually bright, and they knew far more about many matters than he. When they saw that their boss was off target in his analysis or wrong with his facts, they told him so. "He was open minded," said Wolfe. "I think he listened." Nitze wanted to get a wide range of opinions, and the only way to get these opinions—to have them stated frankly, bluntly, and frequently even if they went against the common wisdom—was to create an environment in which people were not afraid to speak. Nitze created that environment.

He created, also, an environment in which his people felt that when they did speak, their voice would be heard not only by Nitze, but by McNamara and possibly the president. As a general rule government officials work harder when they believe they are making an impact. Nobody enjoys slaving over ideas and papers that simply vanish into the bureaucracy, and few people will put in overtime for long if they feel isolated and irrelevant.

With Nitze heading their office, the staff at ISA felt that they counted. Access is the currency of influence, and Nitze had access. "It was clear that Paul Nitze was not just a figurehead sitting at a desk," said Wolfe, "but that he was an active participant in, and had access to, and the ear of, and the respect of, people who were making decisions in government right up to the President. This, in turn, obviously had some effect on the way people in ISA at lower rungs of the responsibility ladder felt about him and the way they worked."[35] Everybody knew that Nitze attended National Security Council meetings. They knew that if they did an exceptionally good paper or came up with a particularly creative policy proposal, there was a chance that it would be presented to the president, that it might, in fact, become the policy of the United States government.

The evidence that ISA counted could be even more immediate. Late one night during a crisis, ISA staffers were toiling away at the Pentagon when the telephone rang. Harry Rowen answered it, and the caller said he was Jack Kennedy. "Yeh, and I'm Joe Stalin," Rowen said as he hung up. A minute later the phone rang again; it *was* the president, calling to talk over a problem.

The fact that he treated them well, that he listened to them, and that he had influence in the government made Paul Nitze a boss the people at ISA were willing to work hard for. If that meant staying at the Pentagon to finish a report long after everybody had left, they would do it. If it meant coming in before the parking lots had filled to analyze new intelligence data, they would do it. And if it meant hardly seeing their wives and their children for weeks or months because some part of the world was heating up, they were willing to make that sacrifice, too. "The worst thing would be to be allowed to go home at five o'clock," remarked Larry McQuade.

To coordinate their wide range of projects, Nitze held weekly staff meetings. These meetings were attended by all of his deputy assistant secretaries, their deputies, and representatives from the Joint Chiefs of Staff. The aim was to keep everybody informed about all the activities at ISA so the organization could work more smoothly.

Other than the weekly staff meetings there was no formal method of operation. In the morning the staff would read the cable traffic that pertained to their part of the world and then get to work on whatever the current problem was. If they ran into difficulties or had questions, "of course, we had free access to both Paul Nitze and Bill Bundy," Admiral Heinz remembered.[36]

In the larger scheme of things, Nitze's position in the government did not evolve the way many had expected. Two weeks after he was appointed, an article appeared in *U.S. News & World Report* that stated, "A powerful role, lodged in an unimpressive title, has been assigned to one of Kennedy's top aides—Paul Nitze." The article went on to say that McNamara would be concerned with administration and Gilpatric would deal with the public. Given an apparent vacuum in the realm of policy formation, the article went on to predict that "Mr. Nitze is to wield influence of large and growing proportions in the new Administration," and would "emerge as one of the real decision makers in the new Government."[37]

During the first few months of the Kennedy presidency it became apparent that this would not be the case. The reason was Robert McNamara. Although Nitze was the most knowledgeable and experienced top official in the Defense Department, McNamara's role would not be limited to "administration." With his incredible intellect, the defense secretary mastered most national security issues by early spring. "The senior man in the Pentagon on all subjects turned out to be Robert McNamara," recalled McGeorge Bundy. "McNamara did not confine himself to procurement and management but became the

President's primary defense advisor on every subject." Coming from his job as chairman of Kennedy's National Security Policy Committee, Nitze may have originally been perceived as a primary player, but "As time went on," said Bundy, he became instead, "a valued member of the McNamara force in the government and not an independent force."

This stemmed as much from Nitze's own perception of his job as from the circumstances imposed on him. Controlling the Pentagon had historically been a daunting task, and Nitze felt that if he displayed too much independence, he might weaken McNamara's position by creating the impression that dissonance existed within the department. He was particularly hesitant to cultivate his own relationship with Kennedy. Hierarchy was essential to the management of the Pentagon, Nitze believed, and if people started breaking the chain of command, chaos could ensue. McNamara's natural insecurities about Nitze also might be heightened if Nitze independently conferred with Kennedy. "I felt I would destroy my usefulness to the President if I were to short circuit Mr. McNamara and go directly to the President," Nitze said later.[38]

Nitze saw Kennedy often, but rarely, if ever, talked with him alone. After a short time in the White House, Kennedy complained that Nitze was not maintaining a personal relationship with him. Even at NSC meetings Nitze did not directly advise the president. McNamara spoke for the Defense Department and if either Nitze or Gilpatric spoke, it was invariably in support of McNamara. Paul Nitze "would never have been found coming down on a side different from the secretary in a public meeting," Bundy recalled. "Once there is a McNamara policy there is not a separate Nitze policy." If Nitze disagreed with McNamara on an issue, and he often did, he made his differences known in private before the NSC meetings.

Because he made a point of not asserting himself too vigorously, Nitze never became a part of Kennedy's closest inner circle. His exclusion was subtle but clear. Early on, the president began to have informal sessions with McNamara and Gilpatric to which Nitze was not invited. The two men were often asked to linger after an NSC session for private conversation. Kennedy would also invite McNamara and Gilpatric to small dinners at the White House or have them fly up to Hyannis or down to Palm Beach. Nitze rarely socialized with the president.

Had Nitze been closer to McNamara, he might have played a more direct role in advising Kennedy. But the two men remained distant.

They were uncomfortable with each other personally and, more important, philosophically.

Paul Nitze came to the Pentagon a committed ideologue. Since writing NSC 68, his opinions had changed little. He still viewed the Soviet Union as an implacable foe committed to world conquest. In 1961 Nitze had no doubt that Khrushchev was "striving for what he considered to be superior military power"[39] and that the "men in the Kremlin" could still not be trusted. While fluent in Russian, their mother tongue was force.

To many of Kennedy's young advisors, Nitze's views on the Soviet Union seemed extreme and anachronistic—a dogma better suited to the 1940s than to the 1960s. The foreign policy differences that divided the Democratic Advisory Committee had not been settled by the 1960 election. On the one hand, again, were Nitze, Acheson (who kibbitzed from the outside), and other Truman veterans like Arms Control and Disarmament Agency head William Foster, who believed that little had changed with the death of Stalin and that the communist goal remained world domination through military belligerence. Opposing these views, as before, were men like Stevenson, Harriman, and now Bundy. They were more sanguine about the Soviet Union and believed that Stalin's death had ushered in a new era in which Soviet behavior might change.[40] Underpinning this debate was the enduring controversy over intentions and capabilities. As always, Nitze believed that if the Soviets had the military force to mount aggressive action, it must be assumed that they would do so. Others contested this assumption of total theoretical hostility, arguing that the question of Soviet intentions was far more subtle and complex.

McNamara arrived at the Pentagon knowing little about the Soviet Union. But he was by no means an anticommunist ideologue and, in time, came to ally himself with the Stevenson-Bundy view of Soviet intentions. Gilpatric was of a similar mind set. And while Nitze's disagreement on this critical point did not interfere with the work of running the Pentagon, it reflected a conceptual gulf that separated him from McNamara.

A gulf also yawned between Nitze and the rest of the Kennedy crowd. The men closest to the president were younger and brasher. Many had never worked in Washington before. Kennedy's rhetoric about a New Frontier infused them with a kind of exaltation and arrogance. In their minds the torch had indeed been passed to a new generation and they were not about to hand it back. Nitze was not part of their generation. He had helped manage World War II, not fought in it. He had been on the scene in Washington when Kennedy and McNamara were barely out of college. Like Dean Rusk, Nitze was a holdover, a member of the old, stodgy, striped pants elite with whom some of Kennedy's younger advisors felt a keen rivalry.

Had he worked harder to ingratiate himself with Washington's new illuminati, these difference might not have mattered. But that was not Nitze's way. "He was always unfailingly polite and courteous and states-manlike," said Tim Stanley, "but this was a man who had everything. He had money, he made money, he married money. . . . I don't think he ever felt the need to ingratiate himself with anybody." With clear blue eyes and a compact, immaculate appearance, Nitze was a hand-some man. His weekends at the farm kept him fit and perpetually tan, and over the years, as his hair turned almost entirely white by the age of 50, Nitze had grown better looking. His eyebrows now slanted less severely and his nose lost its sharp curves, softening his face.

But while Nitze's countenance had changed, his manner had not. To many, he still came across as stiff and chilly. His thin lips rarely broke into a smile, and the press seized on his stuffy aristocratic bearing to back up claims that Nitze was "arrogant," "abrasive," and worst of all, "intellectual." Nitze could be charming, of course. Those who met him at a dinner or drove out to the farm for a day would often come away captivated by his charm. Yet it was a charm he used selectively. And during meetings in McNamara's office or the White House, it was frequently not used at all. "Nitze's not affable," complained one of McNamara's men, "he's not warm or congenial."

Nitze was not one for the fanfare of the New Frontier balls. Skipping the party circuit, he preferred more intimate gatherings with old friends like columnist Joseph Alsop. Phyllis felt the same way. A prod-uct of New York's old-money social set, she felt uncomfortable with the glitter and informality of the Kennedy crowd. More so than her hus-band, Phyllis wanted to stay on home territory.

In an administration where social access often translated into politi-cal influence, Nitze cultivated few friendships among top officials. He didn't want to be pushed into Bobby Kennedy's pool at Hickory Hill, and he simply never made the effort to join the president's social circle. "They were not his type of people," said Bill Bundy, who was also turned off by the Camelot hoopla.

Despite all of this, Nitze managed to position himself as a major player in the government. This was made easier by the State Depart-ment's passivity. Early on it became clear that Dean Rusk would serve more as a lieutenant than as a leader. He lacked the energy to vigorously inject himself into the policy process. Instead, wrote Arthur Schlesinger, Jr., "Rusk would sit quietly by, with his Buddha-like face and half smile, often leaving it to Bundy or the President himself to assert the diplomatic interest." Again and again, Rusk would fail to take a stand on critical questions. "Indeed," wrote Schlesinger, "nearly every time Kennedy faced a major foreign policy decision the views of his Secretary of State remained a mystery."[41] On a personal level, there was little warmth or rapport between the president and his secretary of state. Kennedy didn't even address Rusk by his first name as he did his other cabinet officers.

The State Department's passivity meant that the Defense Department often took the lead in foreign policy. At first, it was a role that made McNamara uncomfortable. Riding back to the Pentagon from an NSC meeting one day, Nitze began outlining his latest plan for filling the void left by State. McNamara blew up. "Just keep your sticky fingers out of foreign policy," he snapped. In time, though, McNamara grew to relish his greater power. And as the branch of Defense geared most toward diplomacy, ISA's role in foreign policy grew. From his experience in the State Department, Nitze had an excellent feel for the kind of work that had an impact on diplomacy. When Kennedy made an early overseas trip, for example, he turned to the State Department on short notice for briefing papers. Nothing materialized. He then asked ISA to put something together and quickly received a complete, concise, and thoroughly indexed briefing book. Days later State finally sent over several cardboard boxes filled with unsorted cables on the countries listed in the president's itinerary.[42] It was a minor incident, but telling.

During the Truman era Nitze had elevated bureaucratic activism to a fine art, developing a knack for identifying and filling vacuums. Now he brought these skills back into play. When it became evident that the State Department was not pushing Kennedy's foreign policy agenda, Nitze seized the initiative. During the spring of 1961 his office became deeply involved in crises in Cuba, Laos, Berlin, and the Congo. Again and again ISA became enmeshed in diplomacy. "Over at ISA," Nitze later boasted, "we thought that task wasn't really being done, and I had a good competent staff, and so, so far as it was done, I think we did it."

At the Defense Department itself, ISA was often on top of things. With his small staff of deputies, Nitze could forge a consensus quickly, whereas the JCS, for instance, could not. "It sometimes would take them three days to blow their nose," Nitze said. "We would sometimes

Nitze's work on the U.S. Strategic Bombing Survey in Europe and Japan was an early education in the destructiveness of modern warfare. As vice-chairman of the Survey he supervised the U.S. teams that assessed the impact of the atomic bombs dropped on Hiroshima and Nagasaki and wrote a report that outlined the requirements for security in the new atomic age. Nitze received the Medal of Merit for his work on the Survey.

A single atomic bomb destroyed all of Hiroshima, yet Paul Nitze was hardly awed by the destruction. He estimated that 220 bombers carrying conventional bombs could have done just as much damage and disagreed with those who concluded that the atomic bomb was an "absolute weapon."

Like Nitze, James Forrestal harbored an intense distrust of the Soviet Union, and in the aftermath of World War II, he advocated hard-line anticommunist policies. Forrestal served as the nation's first secretary of defense before suffering a mental breakdown and committing suicide in 1949.

Nitze rejected Robert Oppenheimer's advice to postpone H-bomb development and sided with H-bomb advocate Edward Teller in the bureaucratic battle over whether to build the bomb. Both Nitze and Teller believed that possession of the H-bomb could bolster America's position in the Cold War.

As director of the Manhattan Project during World War II, the physicist Robert Oppenheimer helped build the atomic bomb. However, in 1949 he firmly opposed research on the far more powerful hydrogen bomb, believing that it was a genocidal weapon that would make the world a more dangerous place.

George Kennan was the principal architect of the U.S. policy of containment and founder of the State Department's Policy Planning Staff in 1947. A diplomat by training, Kennan took a nuanced view of the Soviet threat, believing that Moscow's political intentions were far more significant than its military capabilities. At the height of the Cold War in 1950, Kennan lost influence to Nitze, who argued that capabilities were of overriding importance.

Charles Bohlen was one of America's top Soviet experts in the early 1950s. Like Kennan, he disagreed sharply with the dire assessment of the Soviet threat that Nitze presented in the Cold War treatise NSC 68, labeling it "metaphysical speculation." Bohlen believed the Soviet leadership was cautious by nature and would not risk surprise attacks against the west.

Nitze's influence as director of the Policy Planning Staff was due in great part to the support of his boss and mentor, Secretary of State Dean Acheson. Acheson's power, in turn, derived from his excellent rapport with President Harry S Truman.

As President Eisenhower's secretary of state, John Foster Dulles exiled Paul Nitze from the State Department and opposed the expensive defense buildup advocated in NSC 68.

The nerve-wracking crises in Berlin and Cuba consumed much of Nitze's time at ISA. In both showdowns, Nitze believed that U.S. nuclear superiority enabled the United States to prevail over the Soviet Union. He felt this was particularly true in Berlin, even though he and his staff at ISA could devise no sane plans for using nuclear weapons in the event that the crisis escalated to war.

Nitze was a top advisor on national security affairs to John F. Kennedy during the 1960 campaign, but he never became part of the president's inner circle.

Nitze did not want to become secretary of the navy. Yet once he took the job in 1963 he immersed himself in the details of naval strategy and became fascinated with U.S. sea power, which he saw as a highly flexible instrument of American foreign policy.

In 1965 Robert McNamara invoked the logic of NSC 68 when he rejected Nitze's advice to not escalate the war in Vietnam. But by 1967 the secretary of defense had come to agree with Nitze that no amount of firepower could win the war.

In punishment for his growing disillusionment with the war, McNamara was ousted from his job by President Johnson in February 1968 and bade farewell to the Pentagon during a rainy ceremony.

Instead of elevating Nitze to secretary of defense, Johnson appointed his longtime friend Clark Clifford to the post. Clifford was a hawk on Vietnam when he took the job, but after a month of intensive briefings on the war by Nitze and other Pentagon officials, Clifford came to advocate a rapid U.S. withdrawal.

To counter what he felt was a dangerous decline in the U.S. strategic position, Nitze joined with Eugene V. Rostow *(second from right)*, Charles Tyroler II *(first from right)*, and other former government officials to form the Committee on the Present Danger in 1976. Among those influenced by the committee's work was California governor Ronald Reagan *(center)*.

During Nitze's crusade to bolster U.S. military strength during the 1970s, many of his old friends and former colleagues felt that he was being unduly pessimistic and receiving poor advice from hard-line strategic analysts like T. K. Jones. Jones helped convince Nitze that the Soviet Union could survive a U.S. nuclear attack involving 2,000 warheads.

In February 1977, Nitze badly damaged his reputation in Washington by questioning the patriotism of Paul Warnke during Senate hearings to confirm Warnke as a top arms control official in the Carter administration.

Armed with elaborate charts on the strategic balance and inside information about arms control policy, Nitze emerged as the most formidable opponent to the SALT II treaty signed by Jimmy Carter and Leonid Brezhnev in June 1979.

Senator Henry ("Scoop") Jackson was a longtime friend of Nitze's and among his chief allies in the fight against the Warnke nomination and SALT II treaty. Like Nitze, Jackson worried about the possibility of a Soviet first strike and felt that the Carter administration was not doing enough to lessen this threat to American security.

Carter's secretary of defense, Harold Brown, was as committed to U.S. security as anybody in Washington and felt that Nitze's assessment of the strategic situation was overly alarmist. In his view, SALT II was a good deal for the United States.

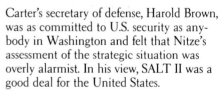

Ralph Earle, like many other friends and former colleagues in Washington, felt confused and betrayed by Nitze's implacable opposition to SALT II.

As INF negotiator, Nitze cultivated close ties with European officials like West German foreign minister Hans Dietrich Genscher.

Nitze shared the concern of top European leaders that citizen protests could derail U.S. deployment of INF missiles and result in a major blow to the cohesion of the NATO alliance.

Nitze's chief rival in Washington was Assistant Secretary of Defense Richard Perle. Deeply skeptical of arms control agreements, Perle sought to limit Nitze's flexibility in Geneva and opposed the walk-in-the-woods compromise formula.

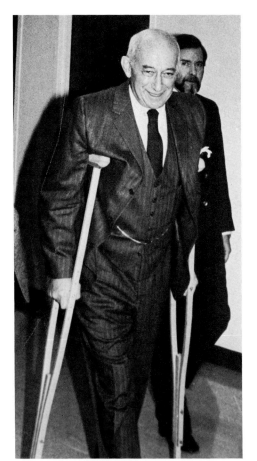

As head of the Arms Control and Disarmament Agency in the early 1980s, Eugene V. Rostow was Nitze's closest ally in the government. He backed the walk-in-the-woods formula and had his staff fight for the proposal in Washington. Rostow was recovering from a hip operation when he was fired from his post in January 1983.

Another of Nitze's allies in government was Richard Burt, the young assistant secretary of state. Burt had a keen grasp of how policy was made at the sub-cabinet level and battled Richard Perle for control over U.S. arms control policy.

In the battle over arms control policy during the Reagan years, Secretary of State George Shultz *(far left)* competed with Secretary of Defense Caspar Weinberger *(third from left)* for influence over President Reagan's thinking. In December 1984, Shultz bolstered his position in this competition by making Nitze his special advisor.

In the opening meeting of the 1986 Reykjavik Summit, Soviet leader Mikhail Gorbachev put forward sweeping arms control proposals. President Reagan suspected that the hidden Soviet agenda was to stop SDI, and the summit foundered when the two sides could not reach agreement on the question of strategic defenses.

For Nitze the weekend at Reykjavik was one of the high points of a long career. Although no formal agreements emerged from the summit, teams led by Nitze and Soviet Marshal Sergei Akhromeyev made dramatic breakthroughs on intermediate and long-range weapons during an all-night negotiating session.

In his bid to turn the progress made at Reykjavik into concrete arms control agreements, Nitze was consistently opposed by Reagan administration hard-liners like Kenneth Adelman *(above)* and Edward Rowny *(below)*. As director of the Arms Control and Disarmament Agency (ACDA), Adelman had an official mandate to serve as the institutional advocate of arms control in the government. In practice, he often sided with anti–arms control officials in the Pentagon.

By the final year of the Reagan administration, the exit from government of hard-liners like Perle, Weinberger, and Adelman allowed Nitze and Shultz to exercise tremendous influence in shaping U.S.–Soviet relations. With Gorbachev proving a compliant negotiating partner, a START treaty cutting long-range arms by half was virtually completed by the time Reagan left office.

be able to get a position together within an hour. When you get into a rapidly moving situation, when the house is burning down, every president likes to see something reasonable put forward for his consideration promptly."[43]

Although Nitze's office worked hard to fill the void left by State, it also made a point of forging ties with that department. Nitze was proud of the State-Defense relationship he had fostered as director of the Policy Planning Staff. It had yielded great successes, most notably the NSC 68–114 series. A decade later the need for collaboration between the military and diplomatic branches of the government had, if anything, grown more acute. A heavily armed alliance had to be held together, complex arms control negotiations were under way, and a new cold war arena had emerged in the third world. Managing these problems required a finely tuned politico-military decision-making apparatus; as an old State Department hand, Nitze was uniquely qualified to work toward that goal.

From the outset he began to cultivate extensive contacts with people at State. As Wolfe recalled, there was "a very studied, conscious, deliberate effort to bring the State Department as closely into working on the kind of problems that were identified as could be."[44] Nitze's main contact in the department was Deputy Under Secretary of State Alexis Johnson. The two men had known each other during the Truman years and shared a commitment to improved State-Defense relations. But while Nitze's effort in this area encountered little opposition from the Defense Department, Johnson ran into trouble at Foggy Bottom. Too often, he later wrote, State Department officials "looked upon the Pentagon as a hostile force to be defended against."[45] Contact during the Eisenhower years had been scarce and frosty, and when Kennedy took power, deep divisions between the two departments remained.

To Nitze, this was an intolerable situation and he and Johnson "saw eye to eye on the need to build respect and easy rapport between military and foreign service officers."[46] They initiated an ambitious program of exchanging mid-level Pentagon and State Department personnel. And in an attempt to keep the lines of communication between the two departments continually open, Nitze organized a series of Monday planning sessions and luncheons at the State Department, usually held in the office of the Policy Planning Staff.

* * *

For Paul Nitze the dawn of the Kennedy era was an exhilarating time. Back in government after eight years of Republican dominance, Nitze no longer had to watch helplessly while Eisenhower and Dulles chipped away at the accomplishments of the Truman years. The dissidents of the 1950s had seized the reins of power and no aspect of Eisenhower's national security policy escaped review. The changes advocated by his opponents on the outside were now being implemented on the inside. Under Kennedy the principles of NSC 68 again held sway in Washington. Economics would no longer determine the scope of the U.S. defense effort; few challenged the need for greater defense spending. Nuclear weapons would no longer be viewed as crude instruments of mass destruction. In the third world the communist threat would be granted no quarter. A defeat for democracy anywhere, Kennedy's advisors agreed, should be seen as a defeat everywhere. Counterforce nuclear targeting was discussed at the highest levels of government. Conventional forces designed for limited war were suddenly in vogue.

During the 1960s Nitze would finally see his ideology put to test. Hardly had he settled in at ISA when the first upheaval of the Kennedy era occurred.

Bluffing at the Brink

I N THE predawn hours of April 17, 1961, fourteen hundred Cuban exiles led by CIA advisors clambered out of amphibious landing craft onto Cuban soil. Their goal: to topple Fidel Castro's revolutionary government. The point chosen for the invasion was a small inlet on the south coast of Cuba known as Bahia de Cochinos, or Bay of Pigs. Despite the exile force's year of training by CIA operatives in Guatamala and months of planning, the invasion started to fall apart almost as soon as it had begun. Beach assault boats crashed into reefs that U-2 reconnaissance planes had reported as "seaweed." A local militia immediately offered stiff resistance, and Castro's regular army was instantly alerted by communications equipment that intelligence reports had said did not exist. Shortly after sunrise the invasion force came under attack by government warplanes that were supposed to have been destroyed by B-26 attacks launched against Castro's air bases from Nicaragua. At 9:30 A.M., the ship carrying most of the ammunition and communication equipment for the exiles was sunk.

In Havana Castro's police rounded up thousands of dissidents. The popular insurrection the exiles hoped for never materialized. By Tuesday afternoon the invasion force was under attack by twenty thousand government troops armed with Soviet tanks and heavy artillery. By early Thursday, April 20, it was all over. Some twelve hundred exiles had been taken prisoner and the rest were either dead or wounded.

Anti–United States demonstrations broke out in Latin America and Europe. The Soviet Union protested vigorously. At a Friday morning press conference in the State Department auditorium, President Kennedy took total responsibility for the debacle. "There's an old saying," he commented, "that victory has a hundred fathers and defeat is an orphan."[1] It was his first foreign policy disaster. The question in the White House, in Washington, and around the world was how could such a catastrophe have occurred. A well-circulated joke answered, "Caroline [the president's 4-year-old daughter] certainly is a nice kid, but that's the last time we shall let her plan a Cuban invasion."[2]

Paul Nitze, like most people in the administration who might have been able to head off the calamity, felt he had failed the president. Had Nitze studied the plans closely, talked the matter over with his contacts on the Joint Chiefs of Staff, and raised objections to McNamara and Kennedy, he might have forced a real debate about the invasion. Nitze did none of these things. The plan was a legacy of the Eisenhower administration, which had set up camps in Guatemala to train Cuban exiles. When it first came to Nitze's attention during his early days at ISA, he was absorbed with the problem of Laos and asked his deputy William Bundy to handle it. As the invasion date grew closer, however, Nitze was drawn into the planning and saw that the enterprise was a dubious one.

At ISA, Nitze was visited by General Edward Lansdale, the renowned counterinsurgency expert who had helped suppress the Huk rebellion in the Philippines and worked as a political advisor to President Diem in South Vietnam. Lansdale argued that the ragtag group of exiles would never succeed in their mission and that he saw no evidence that the Cuban people would back such an invasion. He suggested that the whole thing be called off.

This message was amplified in late March, when Arthur Schlesinger brought John Plank, a Harvard expert on Latin American affairs, down to Washington and asked him to assess the invasion's chances of success. Schlesinger, who had his own doubts about the operation, set up a dinner meeting between Plank and Nitze at the home of Tracy Barnes, one of the CIA officials involved in planning the invasion. As they ate, Plank told Nitze that any U.S.-backed effort to unseat

Castro would almost certainly fail. While it was true that many Cubans disliked Castro's rule, they did not want to return to the Batista days. A popular insurrection against Castro, especially one sponsored by the United States, was not about to happen. Nitze was partly inclined to agree with Plank that evening. The logic supporting the invasion did appear flimsy, he conceded.[3]

But Plank's argument also seemed weak. An immediate uprising was not critical to the success of the enterprise, Nitze had been told. "It was not estimated by anybody who heard discussion of this thing that there would be an immediate rising of the Cuban people against the Castro regime," Nitze said later. The plan, as advertised by the CIA, was premised on no such assumption. Rather, explained Nitze, "it was thought that there was a possibility that if this landing could become established and held for a period of time . . . there then would be some accretion to it from the militia who seemed not to be too satisfied with the Castro regime." Once the militia rebelled, "there would be a growth in sabotage and guerrilla operations around the country, and that if this began to grow, then a large part of the Cuban population would rather be on the winning side than on the losing side."[4]

Or so the CIA had said.

And while Nitze's usual response to any argument was to hunt for holes, he remained curiously uninterested in cross-examining the advocates of the Cuban venture, even after the warnings from Lansdale and Plank. A similar covert action had succeeded in Guatemala seven years earlier and Nitze saw no reason to oppose the exile invasion in the face of strong optimism on the part of the CIA and numerous other officials. While no evidence argued overwhelmingly for success, no evidence seemed to doom the invasion either. Moreover, as presented by the CIA, the operation had an escape hatch. "The plan provided if this kind of accretion to the landing did not begin to really grow soon enough, that then it was thought possible for this group to cut through to the mountains and join the guerrillas," Nitze said.[5] Even if the invasion did not spark an uprising of any kind and even if it did not win over the militia, then at the very least, the United States would have laid the foundation for a large anticommunist insurgency in Cuba.

Or so the CIA had said.

But what the CIA did not say was that the "mountains" that were to provide a nearby haven for any failed invasion force were in fact eighty miles away from the Bay of Pigs across a tangled swamp. Nor did the CIA mention that its invasion force was poorly trained, inadequately armed, and decidedly unmotivated. Finally, the CIA concealed from Nitze and others their ignorance of Cuba's internal situation. In reality, the CIA had done little intelligence work on the prospect of an anti-Castro uprising in Cuba. And even if it had done this work, the agency probably would have neglected to mention its conclusions. For as Schlesinger later wrote, independent experts on Cuba believed that "Even a sizable middle group, now disillusioned about Castro would not be likely to respond with enthusiasm to an invasion backed by the United States because we were so thoroughly identified in their minds with Batista."[6]

Like most others, Nitze was misled by the CIA and failed to ask the tough questions that would have exposed fatal weaknesses in its plan. With the chances of success presented as better than even, Nitze believed it was worth risking an invasion to topple Castro.

Late in the afternoon of April 4, Nitze was summoned to the State Department for a key meeting on the question of whether to proceed with the Cuba venture. Crammed into a small conference room behind the secretary of state's office, the president and most of his top advisors weighed the various options. Senator William Fulbright, chairman of the Senate Foreign Relations Committee, who had earlier written a memo to the president opposing the operation, also attended. When writing his memo, Fulbright had thought of the invasion as a somewhat distant prospect. Now, as Richard Bissell of the CIA briefed the group on the combat preparations, it became clear that the invasion was imminent. Hundreds of exiles were armed and waiting, the CIA and the navy had most of the operational details worked out, and the president's White House advisors stood ready to deal with the publicity.

When Bissell had finished his briefing, Kennedy turned to Fulbright and asked for his opinion. Fulbright strenuously repeated what he had said in his memo: The operation was totally out of proportion to the threat; it would violate several treaties; it would cause a furor in Latin America and the United Nations; and it would severely compromise the moral authority that the United States so regularly employed against the Soviet Union. "He gave a brave, old-fashioned American speech, honorable, sensible and strong," recalled Schlesinger, "and he left everyone in the room, except me and perhaps the President, wholly unmoved."[7] Turning to the rest of the group, Kennedy went around the table asking what each person thought and whether he voted for or against the invasion.

Nitze was disgusted with the way the meeting was run and felt a "deep unhappiness" about the entire affair. Here were a dozen top officials sitting in a little conference room at the State Department with the chairman of the Senate Foreign Relations Committee, being asked to vote on a crucial policy decision. Nitze was particularly annoyed by Fulbright's insistence on turning the discussion into a moralistic evaluation of the plan. In Nitze's mind there was no question that the United States had a moral right to invade Cuba. "The Soviet Union had inserted itself in our backyard by stealth and deception in the form of the Castro regime in Cuba," he said later. "Like a spreading cancer, it should, if possible be excised from the Americas."[8] The rules of diplomacy and international law were irrelevant in the Cold War. Right and wrong was not the issue, Nitze believed. "The real issue was: Would it succeed?"

When Nitze's turn to speak came, he commented only briefly, rebutting Fulbright but saying that he had been leery of this operation because "it did seem to depend upon an estimate of its potentialities for success." Nonetheless, he had come to the conclusion that it should be done; that the pros, in spite of the risks, were greater than the cons. Later Nitze would regret his shallow response. "I should have had the guts to give a complicated answer."[9]

With none of his key foreign policy advisors stating any objections, the president gave the go-ahead to the plan.

On the morning of the landing, Nitze and Bill Bundy received an unexpected visit from Lansdale and an army general. Sitting in Nitze's office, the four men talked anxiously about the operation in Cuba. Finally, Nitze and Bundy bluntly asked what the chances were of the invasion succeeding.

About 35 percent, one of the visitors replied.

Thirty-five percent? Nitze and Bundy were appalled. The CIA's estimate had been far more optimistic. Now, as fourteen hundred Cubans fought a doomed battle against Soviet tanks, both men began to see how badly they had been deceived. It was a searing experience. "Never again would we let an action decision be taken on the basis of fuzzy statements or military judgments," Bundy said later. More than all others, Paul Nitze should have seen a disaster in the making. A decade earlier Nitze had watched Douglas MacArthur lead the United States into a quagmire on the Korean peninsula. "He had experienced this and seen the consequences of ambiguity more than anybody else in the administration," remarked Bundy. But like the others, Nitze had suppressed his doubts and kept silent.

On Thursday afternoon, April 20, after most of the exiles had been either killed or captured, Kennedy turned to Theodore Sorensen, an aide and speechwriter, as they strolled across the White House lawn. "How could I have been so far off base?" he asked. "All my life I've known better than to depend on experts. How could I have been so stupid to let them go ahead?"[10]

On Saturday Nitze attended a National Security Council meeting at the White House that had been called in part to answer this question. The mood was somber as the president launched into a long monologue about what had gone wrong and why. He was not going to blame anybody and accepted full responsibility. He announced that he would have General Maxwell Taylor, Allen Dulles, Admiral Arleigh Burke, and Robert Kennedy work as a commission to look into what went wrong and why.

As for future policy, the president directed that two groups be formed: one to look into the problems surrounding Cuban refugees and the other to study future policy toward Cuba. Turning to Nitze, Kennedy said, "You'll take charge of developing a paper for my consideration on what our policy for Cuba will be from here on out." Nitze objected that such a job was best handled by the State Department.

"Oh, nonsense, Paul," said Kennedy. "Go ahead and figure out how it's to be done and do it." Nitze's reply was that he would move over to the State Department and form a task force over there. "I really don't think this ought to be done by the Defense Department," he protested. In the end, this was exactly what Nitze did; he turned over most of the project to people at State.

The study did nothing to change policy toward Cuba, and over the next year the Kennedy administration stepped up covert attacks on Castro's regime. This campaign drove Cuba further into the Soviet orbit, and with his own life in constant jeopardy from assassins hired by the United States, Castro became willing to take even the most dire measures to protect his country from U.S. actions.

May was a busy month for Paul Nitze. As head of ISA he played the role of diplomat more actively than expected. A NATO conference in Oslo demanded his participation. After that he went to Geneva to participate in a conference on Laos. Hardly had Nitze recovered from these trips when the president invited him to the Vienna summit with Khrushchev in early June. Nitze welcomed this invitation. Only three other members of the administration—McGeorge Bundy, Dean Rusk, and Assistant Secretary of State for European Affairs Foy Kohler—were asked along on the trip.

After a brief stopover in Paris for talks with General de Gaulle, the presidential party flew on to Austria in *Air Force One*. Touching down at the Vienna airport on a gray and rainy Saturday morning, the group was whisked through the city's streets to the American embassy where talks with Khrushchev were scheduled to be held. For more advice on how to deal with the Soviets, Kennedy had asked that Llewellyn Thompson, the U.S. ambassador to the Soviet Union, and Nitze's old friend, Chip Bohlen, now ambassador to France, join him in Vienna.

Despite a wide-ranging ideological argument between the two leaders, the first day's discussion was relatively good natured. But on Sunday morning the conversation turned combative when the issue of Berlin arose. World War II had been over for sixteen years and still the former capital of the Third Reich remained divided among the four powers—Great Britain, the United States, France, and the Soviet Union—that had occupied it in 1945. Deep in the Soviet satellite state of East Germany, Berlin was a striking symbol of a divided Europe. Half of the city was under Soviet control, and the other half was occupied by NATO troops. While the eastern sector was drab and depressing, West Berlin glowed with capitalist prosperity. It stood as a beacon for disaffected East German citizens who streamed into the western sector at the rate of ten thousand people a month.

To the Soviet and East German leadership, this was intolerable. In November of 1958 Khrushchev announced that in six months he would sign a peace treaty with East Germany declaring the borders established after World War II permanent and giving the East Germans free reign over all of Berlin. To western leaders, such a blatant maneuver to eject the NATO powers from Berlin was unacceptable. When Khrushchev visited the United States in 1959, Eisenhower met with him at Camp David and managed to get the peace treaty idea dropped for the time being. But two years later, with a youthful new president in the White House, the Soviet leader again began to press for a peace treaty. In a speech on January 6, 1961, Khrushchev declared his intention to remove the western presence from Berlin.

When the topic arose at Vienna, the Soviet leader remained intransigent on this point. Speaking intensely, he told Kennedy that the German situation was intolerable. The Soviet Union wanted to reach an agreement on the status of Berlin, but if this proved impossible, Khrushchev warned that the Soviets would sign the treaty with East Germany alone. Such a treaty would cancel all existing agreements. The western powers would have no special rights in Berlin beyond those the Democratic Republic of Germany granted them.

Kennedy replied that Berlin was a vital U.S. interest, and if the United States allowed itself to be expelled through Soviet pressure, American promises and commitments throughout the world would be viewed as worthless. The United States could accept no ultimatum from the Soviet Union. Pressure on Berlin would disrupt the equilibrium of power. The president reminded Khrushchev that he had come to Vienna to improve relations.

The Soviet leader did not relent. The United States had no use for Berlin, he said. After a treaty was signed, Berlin would be a "free city," accessible to all countries interested in having relations with it. If the United States insisted on trying to maintain its position, it would violate the sovereignty of East Germany. With or without U.S. participation, said Khrushchev, the Soviet Union intended to sign the treaty by December 1961. If the United States wanted a war over Berlin, there was nothing the Soviets could do about it. Kennedy responded to Khrushchev's threat by stating that the Soviet Union was unilaterally precipitating a crisis by threatening a change in the existing situation. "Is this the way to achieve peace?" the president asked in exasperation.

After lunch, in a final conversation before ending the summit, Khrushchev charged that the United States wanted to humiliate the Soviet Union. If the west insisted on occupation rights after the treaty was signed, and if East German borders were violated, the Soviet Union would respond with force. "I want peace," said Khrushchev, "but if you want war, that is your problem." The Soviet Union had no choice but to go ahead with signing the treaty in December, he declared.

"It will be a cold winter," Kennedy said as the two men parted.[11]

Kennedy, Nitze, and the rest of the U.S. delegation returned to Washington sobered by the summit. It was all too easy to imagine a confrontation over Berlin escalating into war. With each side feeling its credibility was at stake and each believing it was in the right, neither was prepared to back down. If Khrushchev carried out his threat to sign a treaty with East Germany and moved to cut off access to Berlin, the United States leadership would face a choice: respond with force or accept humiliation.

Kennedy moved quickly to deal with the impending crisis. On June 13 Nitze accompanied McNamara to an NSC meeting on the subject of Berlin. The secretary of defense explained that the U.S. position was fatally weak. Troops in Berlin had enough ammunition and combat rations to hold out in a conventional conflict for only eighteen days, and the options for dealing with a Soviet move against the isolated city were not attractive. The president was deeply disturbed by these findings and ordered an interdepartmental group to develop a viable strategy to deal with the Berlin crisis. Foy Kohler would chair the group, and Nitze was to direct the Pentagon's work on the project.

From the beginning, Paul Nitze was a hard-liner on Berlin. Some in the administration believed that the Soviets were genuinely unhappy about Berlin and saw Khrushchev as trying to consolidate his hold on eastern Europe for security reasons. (Much as the United States wanted Castro removed from its orbit.) They felt the confrontation could be defused through negotiations.

Nitze thought this was nonsense. In his opinion negotiations or concessions of any sort were dangerous. He had seen this kind of belligerent posturing before when the Soviet Union had blockaded Berlin in 1948. Khrushchev's security concerns were without foundation, he believed. To Nitze, the Soviets were behaving in a manner consistent with the analysis of NSC 68. Their primary goal in putting pressure on Berlin was to humiliate the west and score a major cold war victory. "Speaking personally," he said at one point during the crisis, "I am convinced that there is . . . a much broader Communist objective involved, of which Berlin is merely a proving ground. This is to impose on the West and on the U.S. by the application of threats of force and terror tactics, a psychological defeat by purporting to demonstrate our impotence in the face of the much advertised Soviet power."[12]

And such a defeat would only be the prelude to a much wider campaign of Soviet aggression. The Soviets would not stop at Berlin. "Concurrently, by a combination of threats and cajolery, they hope to break up the unity of the NATO alliance and undermine the will of some or all of its members to resist the Communist program," Nitze predicted. "If the Communists were to succeed in these objectives the effects would invariably be felt not only in Western Europe but throughout the world—in Indochina, in the Far East, in the Near East, in Africa and in Latin America."[13]

At stake in Berlin, then, was not the status of a single city, but the fate of the entire world. Berlin was only a symbol, a piece of real estate which by itself was of no overwhelming value to the United States. Yet as Nitze had stated in NSC 68 a decade earlier, perception was the key to victory in the Cold War. If the United States failed to show resolve in Berlin, if it failed to prove to people everywhere that it could stand firm in the face of Soviet aggression, the stage would be set for a string of communist victories around the globe.

Underpinning this grim scenario was not only the immutable axiom of total theoretical hostility, but another assumption Soviet experts hated: the portrayal of Moscow as a mechanical chess player angling relentlessly for global checkmate. Within this framework there was no such thing as legitimate Soviet security concerns—only pure evil that had to be resisted with superior force.

On this point Dean Acheson and Paul Nitze naturally saw eye to eye. A bit older and grayer now, but no less aggressive, the former statesman had been asked by Kennedy to help manage the Berlin crisis. By early July he had come—typically—to dominate the debate over Berlin. Three weeks after Kennedy returned from Vienna, Acheson presented him with a long paper that Nitze had helped write. Khrushchev was only looking for a pretext to test the American will to resist, Acheson argued. The Soviet goal was to shatter American power in Europe, and in that sense the Berlin crisis was simply a conflict of wills. There was nothing to negotiate, the paper stressed. Indeed, going to the bargaining table would signal U.S. weakness and exacerbate the crisis. The only solution was to convince the Soviet leadership that the United States would risk war to protect its stake in Berlin. To that end, Acheson recommended an immediate buildup of conventional and nuclear forces. Moreover, if the Soviets signed a treaty with East Germany and attempted to cut off access to Berlin, the United States must respond with military force. While it was possible that such a strategy might spark nuclear war, Acheson deemed the risk worth taking.[14]

Nitze also judged the risk worth taking. As he explained later, "the costs to the West of losing Berlin clearly seemed to be much higher than the value to Moscow of gaining Berlin. So it was justifiable for the United States to take somewhat greater risks in a situation where the stakes were higher for the U.S. than they were for the Russians."[15] As for actual nuclear war, Nitze believed that every effort should be made to avoid it, but he was not ready to rule out the possibility. As he commented in 1963, "A full scale nuclear exchange would in all probability—if not certainty—devastate the West so badly that the outcome might be 'victory' in the technical military sense only. Hence use of nuclear weapons by us only becomes rational if the alternative would be even worse than nuclear war—such as the capitulation to the Communist program of aggression."[16]

And in 1961 it appeared to Nitze that relinquishing Berlin would mean just such a capitulation.

*   *   *

In late June and early July, as the interdepartmental group on Berlin (later called the Berlin Task Force) came together, management of the crisis was divided between State and Defense. While Kohler and his aides concentrated on a set of diplomatic responses to Khrushchev's challenge, Nitze's staff began developing contingency plans for a military confrontation.

It was a daunting task. Militarily, the situation seemed hopeless. "Berlin is so vulnerable because it is so isolated," said Harry Rowen. "It was easy to see how they could restrict access." Lying 110 miles inside East German territory, Berlin was connected to West Germany by a single artery: the Helmstedt Autobahn. To cut off overland access, the East Germans had only to close the Autobahn. This could be done easily with either barricades or military forces. It could also be done slowly. Some traffic could be let through, some stopped and harrassed. A telephone pole that "fell" across the road might tie up traffic for hours. With numerous Warsaw Pact divisions stationed nearby, it was hard to imagine a better place for the Soviets to challenge western interests. Berlin was the "one area where the local Soviet cards were always much stronger than those in the western hand," observed Nitze's Soviet specialist Thomas Wolfe.

At ISA Nitze entrusted the search for military options to Colonel DeWitt Armstrong. In ISA's hierarchy Armstrong worked nominally under Rowen. But as the crisis began to heat up after the Vienna summit, Nitze supervised the colonel's work directly. Thin and intense, with an admiration for Nitze verging on hero worship, Armstrong was not new to contingency planning for Berlin. He had arrived at the Pentagon in 1959 and been involved in the planning work that followed Khrushchev's original Berlin ultimatum. At that time, little was accomplished. There had been some preparation for testing a blockade with military probes on the Autobahn, and existing plans for an airlift were updated and refined, but beyond this, few military options were developed. Instead, U.S. war plans dictated that if Warsaw Pact troops repelled a NATO military probe, the United States would launch an all-out nuclear strike against the Soviet Union.

To Armstrong, this all or nothing approach was sheer lunacy. "I was acutely disturbed by the nuclear component of the plans," he said later. An expert on the use of ground forces, Armstrong believed that U.S. military planners had too hastily dismissed the conventional military options for defending Berlin. He thought the situation was not nearly as hopeless as the common wisdom suggested.

In the fall of 1960 Armstrong began work on a major paper which examined the problem of how to keep Berlin free without resort to nuclear weapons. He organized his paper into action-reaction scenarios. "I wrote up a politico-military sequence of events," he explained, "talking in concrete terms about what could happen" in various situations. The study confirmed Armstrong's instincts that nuclear war was not the only alternative. "My point was that it was by no means impossible to do something with conventional forces . . . there were some alternatives between abject collapse on the one hand, and nuclear warfare on the other."

Armstrong thought it was obvious that NATO forces could not fight their way through East Germany. Rather, a strong show of force on the Autobahn and a willingness to use it in creative ways could convince the Soviets to restore access. "My suggestion was that there was a pretty good possibility that they would back off well before we got to the point where no longer did we have forces that we could use," he recalled. Armstrong referred to his proposal as "a program of mounting pressures."

Nitze found the colonel's logic persuasive. In July he and McNamara flew to Europe to consult with General Lauris Norstad, the NATO supreme commander. Norstad had just set up a special Berlin planning unit in Paris know as "Live Oak." What disturbed Nitze and McNamara was that Norstad's plans for defending Berlin envisioned the early use of nuclear weapons. When Nitze asked about sending a probe down the Autobahn if the Soviets cut off access, Norstad scoffed at the idea. The general thought that even with substantial reinforcements a probe would be cut to shreds. Still, before Nitze and McNamara left Europe, they insisted that Norstad not rule out armed probes.

Armstrong's work was of such value because it gave Nitze the facts he needed to challenge skeptics like Norstad. Nitze had long believed that a demonstrated willingness to use force could achieve results, even if those forces were inferior to an opponent's. Like a surprise blow to a bully's nose, simply showing resolve could make an enemy back down. Nitze recognized, also, that in Berlin there were not many alternatives. "Brinkmanship may have been discredited, but that was our policy," he said later.[17] Other ISA staff members agreed. "It was sort of a game of chicken," said Rowen. "The idea wasn't that we could mount enough force to push our way in without getting into a substantial war; the idea was that the Soviets would not want to have a substantial war."

The idea also was to display firmness before the situation ever became a military confrontation. To safeguard access, the Soviets "had to be confronted by the willingness of the United States and the other powers to maintain that access," said Rowen.

"And the question was, who was going to blink first?"

On the stiflingly hot evening of July 25, President Kennedy went on national television and somberly told the American people that "We cannot and will not permit the Communists to drive us out of Berlin, either gradually or by force." The city, he said, was the "great testing place of Western courage and will, a focal point where our solemn commitments stretching back over the years since 1945, and Soviet ambitions now meet in basic confrontation." To deal with the crisis, Kennedy announced he would request an additional $3.2 billion in military appropriations, and call up some 200,000 reserve troops. He added that besides bolstering the defense effort, "we have another sober responsibility." Nuclear war was a real possibility, he said. Because of that possibility, the president asked Congress to allocate new funds to civil defense programs so that "In the event of an attack, the lives of those families which are not hit in a nuclear blast and fire can still be saved—if they can be warned to take shelter and if that shelter is available."

While Kennedy did not declare the national emergency that Acheson, Nitze, and others had pressed for, his tough talk of military measures and nuclear war intensified the atmosphere of crisis.[18]

By the time of Kennedy's speech, Paul Nitze had turned over much of the running of ISA to Bill Bundy and was spending almost all of his time on the Berlin crisis. As his staff grappled with the details of contingency planning, Nitze immersed himself in the work of the Washington Ambassadors' Group. The Ambassadors' Group included the British, French, and, by August, German ambassadors and had been formed during the first Berlin crisis. Its purpose was to coordinate the west's stance on Berlin. In 1961 Kohler became the U.S. representative to the group.

While the four top officials met frequently, the real work of the Ambassadors' Group was done by the highly secretive Political-Military Subgroup. The director and guiding force of the subgroup was Paul Nitze. Throughout the summer the subgroup met continually to work out a basic outline of the west's military and diplomatic policy on Berlin. In late July and early August this work was taken up at a four-power foreign ministers conference in Paris.

Aimed at updating the west's strategy on Berlin, the conference was the scene of an intense struggle over the plans that the Washington Ambassadors' Group had been debating. Working the delegations with

Kohler and the other Americans, Nitze lobbied hard for the program of mounting pressures. At his side was Armstrong, feeding him the arguments and data to strengthen his case. The Europeans were hesitant about adopting the program. Ironically, they feared that bolstering NATO conventional forces would weaken deterrence because it might signal a U.S. unwillingness to use nuclear weapons and hence invite Soviet aggression. In any case, the Europeans were reluctant to adopt a strategy that might mean higher defense budgets. But with few viable strategies for defending Berlin, the other three powers grudgingly acquiesced to the plan.

A NATO Council meeting had been scheduled for after the foreign minister's conference to present the work of the four powers to the rest of the alliance. Working frantically, Armstrong began drafting a speech for Rusk that described the new strategy. In his exhaustion, Armstrong couldn't think of an ending. Nitze wrote the rest. Presented by the secretary of state of the United States and backed by Britain, France, and Germany, the new doctrine was adopted as NATO strategy.

As the west met to plot strategy, the situation in Berlin continued to deteriorate. More than a thousand refugees were fleeing East Germany every day, many of them skilled workers. On August 1 the East German government moved ominously to place new restrictions on overland travel between East and West Germany. Several days later, Walter Ulbricht, the East German leader, flew to Moscow to plead for Soviet help in staunching the massive hemorrhage of people. On August 4 Warsaw Pact representatives met in secret session and voted to allow Ulbricht to seal the East Berlin border.[19]

Nine days later, in the cool early morning hours of August 13, as Nitze vacationed in Maine—his first vacation since taking office—East German troops occupied the border area separating East and West Berlin and began erecting a brick and barbed wire barrier. Harry Rowen and Tim Stanley were at the Pentagon the day the wall went up; almost everybody else was out of town. "It was directly clear, right within hours that we weren't going to do anything," recalled Rowen. "That was that."

Placing a call to Stanley, Nitze asked what was going on. Nothing was happening, Stanley said. "You should take a few more days and I'll call you if something happens."

"If nothing's going on in Washington, I'm coming back on the next plane because something should be," Nitze snapped over the phone. Back in his office within twenty-four hours, Nitze swung ISA into action. He was too late. The White House would not change its decision to take no action. Nitze was furious. "He saw this as simply a first step in the eventual Soviet control over all of Berlin," recalled Stanley. He couldn't believe that the United States would let the Soviets get away with such a move.

Others saw things differently. Some thought the wall helped ease the crisis by solving the volatile refugee problem. Many suspected, also, that the building of the wall represented the furthest extent of Moscow's bullying. Still, the cruelty, swiftness, and symbolism of the move cast a chilling shadow over an already tense region. Never had the United States and the Soviet Union seemed so close to war.

As the crisis escalated, the Kennedy administration sought to bolster its credibility through menacing references to the use of nuclear weapons. In mid August Nitze invited the Soviet ambassador, Mikhail Menshikov, to lunch. In the quiet elegance of Washington's exclusive Metropolitan Club, Nitze reminded the diplomat that there would be little left of the Soviet Union after a U.S. nuclear strike.[20]

Back at ISA, Nitze was less cocky. The actual use of nuclear weapons involved myriad imponderables. Grappling with the nuclear component of the Berlin crisis was RAND strategist Thomas Schelling, a consultant to Harry Rowen. Schelling shared the view, popular among Nitze's staff, that a consistent show of resolve over Berlin might compel the Soviets to back down. In early July he wrote a paper examining the role that nuclear weapons could play in demonstrating American will if the confrontation turned violent.

Entitled "Nuclear Strategy in the Berlin Crisis," Schelling's paper argued that if military hostilities ensued, and nuclear weapons were used, the aim should not be to gain a military edge in the sense of knocking out air bases or destroying armored columns. Rather, Schelling believed that they should be part of a high stakes game of chicken. "We should plan for a war of nerve, of demonstration, and of bargaining, not of tactical target destruction," he wrote.[21] The point of this game would be to convince the Soviets that the United States would do anything to prevail and that further hostilities might lead to global war. Becoming more specific, Schelling proposed at one point that the United States prepare to detonate nuclear warning shots to convey U.S. resolve if the Berlin crisis turned into a military confrontation.

DeWitt Armstrong and a few others initially favored the concept. Looking into the feasibility of using a nuclear-armed antiaircraft missile to fire a warning shot high over the Autobahn, Armstrong thought that such a step could send a sobering message to the Soviets. He believed that "the Soviets might, after a warning shot, knock it off." On the other hand, they might simply raise the stakes: "We shoot one high burst, they shoot two high air bursts. So what do we do now?"

The United States could push the game of chicken even further. But what if the Soviets wouldn't back down? "If we used three they might use six," Nitze remarked. Moreover, once nuclear weapons starting flying, one side might go beyond warning shots. "When that happens," he said, "then you know that you're in for keeps and you've lost a hell of a lot."[22]

Nitze dismissed the idea of warning shots.

In late August Nitze began working on another approach for dealing with an escalation of the crisis. He wrote to McGeorge Bundy that "ISA is sponsoring a game-type analysis of the Berlin situation to be prepared by the RAND Corporation under its ISA contract, to be conducted with the participation of high level officials from the White House, State, Defense and CIA."[23] While Nitze himself did not participate, Henry Kissinger, Walt Rostow, Harry Rowen, Carl Kaysen and other officials took part in the three-day simulation held at Camp David in early September. To the relief of all, Thomas Schelling, the analyst in charge of the game, could not get a war started between the two teams representing the United States and Soviet Union.

Still, to many who went to Camp David that weekend, the lessons of the simulation were unsettling. Nitze's new Berlin man, John Marshall ("Squidge") Lee, recalled that the game underlined the weakness of the western position. "You simply can't defend an object that is 120 miles down a road from your border. It is an untenable military situation," he said. "With the Soviet team it was possible to put the initiative on the NATO side—we would have to do something and the Soviets didn't have to do much of anything, they just sort of got in the way. . . . The idea of sending a battalion down the Helmstedt Autobahn in order to test their enthusiasm was fine, but they wouldn't even have had to shoot at it. They could have just blocked its passage with their forces on the road. If we had endeavored to force our way through twenty Russian divisions, you're taking on a major war. And furthermore, you're taking it on in an absolutely losing position because you couldn't do anything. The upshot was that there simply wasn't anything much to do except to say this is intolerable and we will oppose everything with force."

In other words, there was nothing the West could do except continue the policy of bluff and brinkmanship. And the best chance of making that policy work, of convincing the Soviets that the United States would employ all means at its disposal to keep Berlin free, was to have a credible hard-liner tell the Soviets bluntly that the United States was ready to resort to nuclear weapons. Such a person would have to be known to the Soviets as a hard-liner, and he would have to occupy a government post where detailed work on nuclear weapons strategy was done. He would have to be believable.

Paul Nitze was given the job.

On September 7 Nitze spoke to the Association of the United States Army in Washington. "It is clear for all to see," he began, "that the current crisis is Mr. Khrushchev's crisis. He has taken the initiative. He has chosen the timing. He has made the demands. He has issued the threats. He has specified the deadlines. He could call off the crisis if he wished to. He is acting in the classic role of the aggressor."

The United States would not allow itself to be bullied by an aggressor, Nitze said. It would not allow itself to be humiliated. The Soviets might be militarily stronger in East Germany, but they were not superior everywhere in the world. They had weak points around the globe. And if the Soviets struck in Berlin, said Nitze, the United States might choose to strike back elsewhere. "The point is that we can offset a local preponderance of Communist strength by a determination to apply Western strength on terms other than those selected by the Soviets."

There were other options, too. "We have great nuclear capabilities," Nitze said. "We have a tremendous variety of warheads which gives us the flexibility we require to conduct nuclear actions from the level of large-scale destruction down to mere demolition work . . . the number of nuclear delivery vehicles of all types which the U.S. possesses provides the flexibility for virtually all modes and levels of warfare."[24]

Including, of course—although Nitze didn't say so directly—the sort of warfare that might stem from a confrontation over Berlin.

Nitze's September 7 speech was nuclear saber-rattling of the first order. No American official had ever talked so explicitly about using nuclear weapons to defend Berlin. Reported on the front page of the *New York Times,* the speech was undoubtedly read with interest by the Soviet leadership.

But if Nitze could bluff persuasively in public, he was in private acutely aware that the nuclear threat was exactly that: a bluff. Not only did he reject proposals that warning shots be considered, but he also opposed a much more ambitious plan put together by Harry Rowen.

Earlier in the year, before the situation in Berlin had begun to heat up, William Kaufmann, one of Rowen's RAND consultants, made an interesting discovery while going over new intelligence data. The vaunted missile gap of the recent election did not exist, it turned out, and the Soviet nuclear arsenal was in poor shape. New U.S. satellite reconnaissance photographs revealed only four operational ICBMs in the Soviet Union, and information about those missiles indicated that they would take at least six hours to launch. In addition, the Soviet bomber force was not on alert and the Soviet air defense network was riddled with gaps. It appeared that a small U.S. bomber force could fly into the Soviet Union undetected and destroy nearly its entire nuclear arsenal on the ground. A disarming first strike seemed feasible.

Working with great secrecy, Rowen and a few others put together a detailed memorandum explaining how a first strike would be executed and arguing that it was doable. Nitze was appalled. Even if the United States successfully struck first, he said later, the "casualties suffered by the U.S. would almost certainly number in the millions and even more in Western Europe from the surviving Soviet nuclear forces." Such casualties were unacceptable. Nitze dismissed the first strike option.[25]

In fact, Paul Nitze dismissed most talk of nuclear weapons use during the Berlin crisis. Rowen's memory is that with the exception of his first strike plan, which was put together with great secrecy and never became a part of ISA's Berlin contingency plans—the issue of nuclear action was seldom discussed in detail among Nitze's Berlin staff. At "some point in the listing of the options there would be some mention of nuclear weapons, never specific," recalled Rowen. "I don't think anyone ever did get specific. It wasn't taken that seriously as a possibility." Squidge Lee agreed, "Nobody sat down and blocked out what we would do if this thing goes nuclear because that was clearly the ultimate step down the line."

One reason that ISA staffers tried to downplay nuclear use in the crisis was because it conflicted with their crusade to move the military away from massive retaliation. Another reason was that talk of nuclear war in Europe made the Allies uneasy. Most of all, the ISA staff didn't dwell on the nuclear options because their boss found them inherently unattractive. Still, while rarely discussed, a nuclear exchange remained a persistent specter. "Nuclear war *was* possible," said Lee. "I think subliminally it loomed over the entire picture."

And while Nitze rejected specific proposals for the use of nuclear weapons, he and his staff embraced the notion that American nuclear superiority could moderate Soviet actions. In blunt remarks to the Radio-TV Directors Association in Washington in late September,

Nitze said that "the preponderant Western advantage lies in our nu-clear striking power and the Russian fear that if they provoke us sufficiently by encroaching on our vital interests, we shall bring it to bear. . . . we could inflict a much greater level of damage on the Soviet Union—even if they struck first—than that which they could inflict on us."[26]

Of course, determining how much the Soviets feared the American nuclear arsenal was one of the great imponderables of the Berlin crisis. Rowen was skeptical about making such a judgment: "What compo-nents of western strength the Soviets most feared is hard to say." But Nitze's Soviet expert Thomas Wolfe strongly promoted the idea that Kremlin actions were influenced by its perception of the strategic balance. The central point he stressed to Nitze was that the Soviets "were not in a position to risk pushing too hard to the point of provok-ing a strategic military response from the United States."

Lee shared this assessment. And he also agreed with Nitze's macabre analysis that the United States would emerge from a nuclear war in better shape than the Soviet Union. "If a war went major nuclear," Lee said later, "first, the Soviet Union would be destroyed; second, NATO Europe would be destroyed; and the USA would be damaged but not destroyed. That was sort of the ultimate end of the line. We could have eaten what they threw back at us. They couldn't have eaten what we were able to throw at them."

Nuclear weapons may have been unusable in the crisis, and the flexibility Nitze boasted about may have been fictitious, but on a psychological level the ISA staff felt that U.S. strategic superiority made all the difference. This contradiction between *concrete* reality and *perceived* reality had long lay near the heart of Paul Nitze's strate-gic philosophy. After Berlin he would view perceived reality as ever more important. However, Nitze's view, whether correct or incorrect, became outdated almost immediately, for never again, not even by 1962, would the United States have the degree of nuclear superiority that it had in 1961. And as the strategic balance stabilized, it became ever more difficult to envision such a thing as meaningful superiority.

As the Berlin crisis stretched into the fall, Nitze's contingency plan-ners began molding their work into final form. It was an exhausting job. Armstrong's original paper on potential Soviet actions and possible western responses was the starting point for the work, which was directed by Lee. In a short time, however, Armstrong's list of scenarios began expanding at an almost uncontrollable rate. At first it was felt that every plausible Warsaw Pact action had to be taken into account and several different response options provided. The code name for the plan was "Horse Blanket"—the number of scenarios was so great, the reasoning went, that it would take a piece of paper the size of a horse blanket to write them all down.

Despite weeks of work by Lee and Armstrong, the Horse Blanket was never finished. It "got to nitpicking about things down several layers of probability," Lee said later. "It got unreal because there was this immense row of: if this, then that, and then this and then that, and each one of these multiplied by five or ten." At that point, said Lee, "you're not really planning, you're niggling. It was meaningless." Nitze agreed. He worried that it was too complicated to be of use to the Allied leadership. He instructed Lee and Armstrong to take it back and thin it down.

A revised version of Horse Blanket, code named "Pony Blanket," proved a far more manageable undertaking. "Pony Blanket took the possible actions they might take," said Lee, "and instead of trying to think of every goddamn thing we could do from A to Z . . . it cut it down to a usable size by picking out the possible actions they could take, only those that sounded reasonably possible to us and that would be the most difficult to deal with."

The Pony Blanket was used by Nitze in discussions with NATO officials in the military subgroup of the Washington Ambassador's Group. It placed the program of mounting pressures into an organized and coherent framework, one in which the Allies could have more confidence.

Yet even Pony Blanket was not succinct enough for Nitze. He wanted a set of options that could be summarized on one page; he wanted a "Poodle Blanket." Lee and Armstrong complied.

When the detailed contingency planning was largely finished, and almost every plausible scenario for Soviet aggression had a set of western responses, Nitze made an additional request of Lee. He asked him to write a summation, a statement of strategy and policy. Lee went to work. Sitting down at eight in the morning, Lee wrote steadily all day and into the night. When the sun came up, Lee's secretary arrived to type the five-thousand-word paper. That same day the paper was circulated to officials at ISA and the Joint Staff for comment. When comments came in the following day, Lee spent another night at the Pentagon doing revisions.

The next morning Nitze read the paper and found it excellent. He took it to McNamara who in turn had Kennedy read and tentatively approve it within two hours. As Lee said later, the aim of the paper was to "make a coherent policy statement . . . to take the Pony Blanket problem and express what was the U.S. position as to what should be done under these various contingencies and how it should be graduated up and how it should be played." He succeeded brilliantly. McNamara liked the paper so much that he would hand it out to visiting Allied defense ministers and then read it aloud. But the administration considered the document so sensitive that it would not allow the ministers to keep a copy. On October 23, 1961, President Kennedy approved a revised draft as National Security Action Memorandum 109.

In addition to altering western strategy toward Berlin, ISA's work had a significance that went beyond the crisis. In 1961 a fundamental debate over NATO's overall defense doctrine was underway. Central to this debate was the question of whether western policy in the case of a Soviet invasion of western Europe should be to use U.S. strategic forces immediately in an all-out attack on the Soviet Union or to respond gradually and flexibly at a far lower level of violence. Nitze had been an advocate of flexible response since the early 1950s. Now, in long discussions with the European defense planners in his military subgroup, he saw an opportunity to promote this new strategy, and with the writing of the Pony Blanket and the Poodle Blanket, Nitze's arguments became more persuasive. Western Europeans had long taken it for granted that the use of nuclear weapons was the only way to deal with Soviet aggression. During the Berlin crisis they saw that the creative use of conventional forces could forestall the rush toward Armaggedon. And "while it may not have been until 1967 that NATO officially adopted the flexible response concept," Nitze said later, "the seeds that led to its germination were sown in 1961–1962 at those meetings of the military subgroup."[27]

As finally constituted and accepted by the Allies, the contingency responses were divided into four phases. The starting assumption was that the Soviets had cut off access to Berlin and a major crisis situation had developed. Phase One involved immediate Allied reaction to the Soviet move such as diplomatic protests, airlifts, and attempts to reinforce Berlin with ground troops.

Phase Two detailed actions that NATO might take should the Soviets respond to Phase One measures with force. Mobilization of the United States for general war was its chief provision.

Phase Three assumed that the United States had completed mobilization and that the Soviets were persisting in their aggressive behavior.

It envisioned sending several divisions down the Autobahn, strengthening the airlift, or attacking airfields in East Germany. Each of these steps was considered a viable option. Each was designed to demonstrate that the United States was serious, yet not trigger general war.

If the troops sent down the Autobahn were thrown back or the Warsaw Pact launched air strikes against West German air bases, NATO would move to Phase Four. Essentially, this was general war. But because of myriad uncertainties, plans for a war stemming from a conflict over Berlin were never articulated in interdepartmental papers or during Allied consultations. "Phase Four was generally always left blank," Nitze recalled.

In private McNamara and Nitze did discuss in detail what nuclear actions they might recommend to Kennedy if the Berlin crisis led to war. It was a problem that the two men had grappled with at length during their early days in office. They had come up with few acceptable options then and they came up with few now. "I would say the nuclear options were very unattractive when you looked at them in detail," Nitze recalled. "Not impossible, but very unattractive."

Because the options for controllable Phase Four actions were so sparse, the ISA staff toyed with a few rather unusual ideas. One suggestion was to promote the tough-talking Air Force General Curtis LeMay to secretary of state. "We felt that would really jolt the Soviets," quipped a Nitze aide. A more serious proposal was to impose a NATO maritime blockade of the Soviet Union in response to any move on Berlin. Intrigued by the idea, Nitze and his ISA staff went to work on the details. As it turned out, however, U.S. naval power was poorly designed for such a mission. "We had a maritime superiority," remembered Lee, but it didn't mean much. As Nitze explained later, "The main problem was that we didn't have the appropriate torpedoes and they didn't work. Nor did we have the appropriate sonars and those that we did have were unreliable." There was no way a blockade would be successful.

Although Nitze had alluded in his September 7 speech to weak points on the Soviet periphery where the United States could make the Soviets pay for cutting off access to Berlin—a concept later known as horizontal escalation—his staff had trouble finding those points. "There was no equivalent thing on the other side," said Lee. There was no way that they "could pinch this and we could pinch that."

Phase Four remained blank.

*   *   *

In early fall 1961 Nitze traveled to Germany with his assistant, Larry McQuade. They visited Bonn to talk with the U.S. ambassador and with Chancellor Konrad Adenauer. From there it was on to West Berlin where Nitze and McQuade had dinner with the city's charismatic mayor, Willy Brandt. During the crisis Brandt had emerged as a symbol of western resolve. After dinner the mayor suggested that everybody go out and have a drink. They went to a restaurant on the top floor of the Berlin Hilton, and when Brandt entered the room, the crowd applauded him. At one point in the evening Brandt led Nitze and McQuade onto the restaurant's terrace. Glimmering below were the bright lights of West Berlin. Fifteen years after being turned into rubble by Allied bombers, West Berlin had been transformed into a vibrant metropolis.

But looking east, Nitze and McQuade saw an eerie sight. Beyond the wall and past the coils of barbed wire and guard towers, the lights suddenly stopped. Except for a few street lights which shined dimly in the night, East Berlin was dark. It would remain so for decades to come.

By the time the elaborate contingency plans were coming together, the Berlin crisis began to abate. In mid September, after the U.N. General Assembly, the United States initiated talks with the Soviets. On October 17 Khrushchev told the twenty-second Congress of the Soviet Communist Party that "the Western powers were showing some understanding of the situation, and were inclined to seek a solution to the German problem and the issue of West Berlin." Accordingly, Khrushchev continued, "we shall not insist on signing a peace treaty absolutely before December 31, 1961."[28] Over the next year harassment of traffic on the Autobahn would continue, and Khrushchev would make occasional threats, but the greatest danger had passed.

After the grueling showdown in Berlin it was hard to imagine a more difficult crisis. Yet within just a year the United States and the Soviet Union would be locked in a far more perilous battle of wills.

CHAPTER 9

Khrushchev's Gamble

O N THE EVENING of October 15, 1962, Paul Nitze attended a dinner for the German foreign minister, Gerhard Schroeder, in the State Department's eighth-floor dining room. Seated across from him at the table was the minister's intelligence officer, Hans-Albert Reinkemeyer, and as the evening wore on, he and Nitze fell into an animated discussion about what the Soviets would do next. Nitze argued that Khrushchev would try to recoup the losses he had sustained in the Berlin crisis. To do so, he would need to win a showdown elsewhere in the world, and Nitze predicted a crisis in Cuba. Reinkemeyer thought that this was nonsense. The two men were so engrossed in their argument they hardly noticed when Secretary Rusk was called from the table by his security officer.[1]

Returning to the room, Rusk looked slightly pale. A short time later he signaled Nitze to join him on the terrace. Roger Hilsman had just been on the phone, Rusk said. It appeared that recent U-2 reconnaissance flights over western Cuba had revealed a ballistic missile installation under construction near San Cristóbal.[2]

Nitze was surprised by the development, but not totally. For some time there had been suspicion in Washington that the Soviets were shipping missiles to Cuba. Over the past two months at briefings in the "tank" with the Joint Chiefs of Staff, Nitze had learned of bits and pieces of intelligence that hinted at this new threat. Just a few days earlier, on October 11, at such a briefing McNamara and Nitze had listened to a report that French embassy officials in Havana had seen trucks which appeared to be carrying missiles rolling through the Cuban capital at night. "I thought—and I thought so at a time before we had photographs—the factual evidence indicated that missiles were there in Cuba," Nitze said later.[3]

The weekend before the crisis began, Chip Bohlen and his wife visited Causein Manor. Over the years Nitze's friendship with his debonair old clubmate and bureaucratic foe had never faltered, and Bohlen's family often stayed at the large guest house on the farm. But the differences that divided the two men in 1951 still remained, and when Nitze expressed his suspicions about missiles in Cuba, Bohlen was predictably skeptical. He didn't believe the Soviets would take such a risk. This view was shared by most other officials in the administration.

In August the staff at ISA had pondered the prospect of nuclear weapons in the Caribbean after Nitze received a mysterious memo from McGeorge Bundy. Without saying what prompted his inquiry, Bundy asked ISA to look into the consequences of a Soviet bid to place ballistic missiles in Cuba. Harry Rowen wrote a paper saying that such a move would be extremely destabilizing and would precipitate a major crisis.

Now, as Rusk told Nitze, the CIA had photographic proof that the Soviets were moving missiles into Cuba. And as the two men stood talking in the cool October night about how to inform the president and what to make of the Soviet move, it was clear that the United States was facing another great crisis.

At six o'clock the next morning, a groggy Elmo ("Bud") Zumwalt answered his telephone. It was Nitze, his boss at ISA. Zumwalt was told to report to the Pentagon immediately.

Zumwalt was a navy captain who had come to ISA in July to work on Soviet matters. Nitze had recruited him after a visit to the National War College during which the school had been abuzz with talk about a speech that Zumwalt had recently given on the problems of Soviet succession. Nitze didn't get a chance to meet the navy officer, but he remembered the name. Always on the lookout for new talent, he spoke with his military executive a while later: "There's a guy over at the National War College named Zumwalt who's supposed to have become a hotshot on the Soviet Union," said Nitze. "Get him into ISA for duty." Brash and self-possessed, with close-cropped hair and the intense, direct manner typical of ambitious military officers, Zumwalt was advised by friends that working under a civilian at the Pentagon would derail his career. He accepted Nitze's offer nonetheless, and in a short time had become one of the top deputies at ISA.

When Zumwalt arrived at the Pentagon early on the morning of October 16, its acres of parking lots were nearly empty and the long corridors were quiet. But in the wing of the building known as the "little State Department," Paul Nitze was in his office with several other staff members. After first pledging them to absolute secrecy, Nitze revealed the news. So concerned was he about the danger of leaks, that on this first day and over the next two weeks, Nitze gave Zumwalt, Rowen, and the others only a general sense of what was happening, letting them know the minimum needed to get their assistance on selected parts of the problem.[4]

During the first day of the crisis, while his deputies prepared for the ordeal that lay ahead, Nitze maintained the appearance of normalcy by flying to Knoxville, Tennessee, for a speech on the uncomfortably timely topic of civil defense. On the flight he took out a pad and tried to think through on paper what it was that the Soviets were up to, what it could be that Khrushchev wanted. "What process could have gone through the Soviets' minds in deciding to do this?" Nitze wondered. "And what might be their maximum objectives and minimum objectives? And then what general courses of action were appropriate for us?"

It just didn't make sense. Not yet at least.

Back in Washington President Kennedy summoned his top advisors to the White House. The immediate inclination of most who met with the president on the first day was to knock the missile sites out with an air strike. But Kennedy was cautious. Once before he had moved too hastily on a Cuban matter, placed too much faith in his advisors, and the result had been the debacle at the Bay of Pigs. Now he wanted to take time, to look at all the options, and to avoid perhaps an even greater disaster. He also was inclined to let his advisors hash out the problem largely by themselves. A presidential presence, he had learned during the Bay of Pigs episode, tended to impede open debate.

The group who met with Kennedy on that first day comprised most of the top officials in the national security establishment. In time, they would come to be known as the Executive Committee, or "Excomm." For the next twelve days these sixteen or so men would handle all matters related to the missiles in Cuba.

On Wednesday, October 17, Nitze joined Excomm for a meeting in Under Secretary of State George Ball's conference room. It was a day of heated discussion. Nobody disagreed that the missiles were politically unacceptable or challenged the notion that the credibility of the United States was on the line. Nor did anyone question the necessity to go to the brink of war to get the missiles out of Cuba. But on other questions, there was little harmony.

Robert McNamara took the view that it would be a major political defeat to allow the missiles to stay in Cuba, but that they had little impact on the strategic situation. A "missile is a missile," he argued, and it didn't make a difference if it was launched from Cuba or the Soviet Union.[5] The Cuban deployments "didn't change the strategic balance one bit," he said later. "Look at Khrushchev in the missile crisis. I mean: if he thought—or knew, as we knew by that time—that he was numerically behind by seventeen-to-one or thereabouts, do you think an extra forty-three missiles in Cuba, each carrying one warhead, would have led him to think he could use his nuclear weapons? No way!"[6]

Seldom did Nitze disagree openly with his boss. But this was no time for bureaucratic loyalty. "Everybody knew that he [Nitze] was going to speak up and call the shots as he saw them," recalled Gilpatric. And Nitze's views on the missiles were profoundly different from McNamara's. Yes, the United States had overwhelming strategic superiority. Yes, it could be argued that a mere forty-three missiles made little difference quantitatively. But there was more to nuclear strategy than numbers. The missiles in Cuba were dramatically closer to the SAC bases in the Midwest, Nitze said. Their flight times to U.S. targets would be half that of the long-range missiles stationed in the Soviet Union. If allowed to remain, they would fundamentally alter the strategic equation. "Militarily it would be a major step towards nuclear parity—effective nuclear parity, not in numbers but in military effectiveness—because their capability in an initial strike from those sites would be tremendous," Nitze said. The specter of American vulnerability that had so haunted Nitze for over a decade was suddenly made frightfully real by Khrushchev's bold gamble.

The consequences of that vulnerability were only too clear. As the Soviets established a position of nuclear superiority and moved to control the oceans with a stronger naval force, Nitze wrote later, "The free world would shrink slowly to within the boundaries of the United States, and we, in time, would be isolated. In a unipolar world, the United States would be forced to yield to Soviet influence."[7] Placing missiles in Cuba was only the first step in this grand design.

As always, Nitze's assessment of Soviet intentions hinged on the premise of total theoretical hostility. While many experts speculated that Khrushchev's move was aimed at shoring up Moscow's desperately weak strategic posture and protecting Cuba from U.S. invasion, Nitze saw it as the Kremlin's latest bid for global hegemony. Again, he saw no such thing as legitimate Soviet security concerns—only pure evil. And because Nitze imagined that the fate of the world was once more at stake, he deemed the missile deployment as a virtual declaration of war.

In spite of the sharp disagreement between Nitze and McNamara, their dispute would remain academic. To the members of Excomm, the crisis was primarily political, and all agreed that there was only one question of real importance: How could the United States remove the missiles from Cuba? To this question there were no easy answers.

As on the day before, most believed that an air strike should be launched without delay. Since the missile deployment was such a clear provocation, the reasoning went, it merited an equally clear response. And nothing could be clearer than American fighter planes sweeping across the Caribbean to wipe out the nearly completed missiles sites. Yet as attractive as many on Excomm found this idea, the problems with an air strike became immediately apparent.

First there were the political problems. Many felt that an attack out of the blue on Cuba—whatever the reasons—would reflect poorly on the United States, handing Castro and Khrushchev a propaganda victory. Even a hawk like Treasury Secretary Douglas Dillon shuddered at the thought. A surprise attack on Cuba would have looked "too much like the Japanese attack on Pearl Harbor," he said later.[8]

But to Nitze, the "everlasting debate on the morality of a big country [attacking] a small country" was "all nonsense." As in the Bay of Pigs, he didn't give a damn about international law. The important issue was not one of morality, but of political expediency, "of who does what, with what, to whom, and when." To this end, Nitze initially favored a surgical air strike. He felt that destroying the missiles would nullify the Soviet bid for effective nuclear parity and teach a sobering lesson to Khrushchev. He believed further that it would be a perfectly moral action since the new missiles posed a grave threat to U.S. security.

But there were other problems with an air strike—not moral or political problems, but military ones, problems that Paul Nitze could appreciate. At ISA Nitze assigned Harry Rowen to analyze the air strike option. Working with Seymour Weiss at the State Department and members of the Joint Staff, Rowen quickly discovered that the air force had little sense of restraint, and that if they went in, they would go in with everything they had. Plans for taking out the missiles called for an initial attack consisting of five hundred sorties, striking all military targets, including the missile sites, airfields, ports, and gun emplacements.[9] The proposed strike, it turned out, was about as "surgical" as an amputation performed with a dull ax.

And Nitze hesitated.

If the United States went in with that kind of firepower, numerous Cubans and their Soviet advisors would be killed. "There was no way of destroying those missiles without destroying Soviet technicians," said Rowen. Soviet retaliation on a comparable level would be almost inevitable. They might move on Berlin. They might hit the U.S. intermediate-range missiles in Turkey. Or they might do something unexpected, something irrational. It was hard to say. As Nitze remarked later, "You can never tell what people like the Soviets will do."

Only one thing was clear. Once Americans started killing Russians, the crisis would move into what had been called Phase Four during contingency planning for the Berlin crisis, the phase in which full-scale war between the superpowers could no longer be prevented. And even Nitze, as confident as he was in the superiority of U.S. nuclear forces, did not want to enter that phase. "We did not want to trigger hasty nuclear acts or irretrievable lunges into a pattern of escalation unrelated to the issues initially at stake," he said later.[10]

Why force Khrushchev's hand if it could be avoided? Thomas Wolfe, Nitze's Soviet specialist, had retired from ISA in late September. But during the first days of the crisis, Nitze summoned him back to the Pentagon. Wolfe's advice was that the United States should move cautiously and not "back Khrushchev up against a wall and not give him a way to make a face saving retreat." Nitze agreed: "It was perfectly clear that what you needed to do policy-wise was to use the minimum force or threat of force necessary to accomplish the result." He concluded early in the crisis that the United States should try to avoid any actions that might precipitate a global war. As Zumwalt recalled, "Paul Nitze was always in the middle saying 'we've got to do enough to get the missiles out; we've got to make a small enough commitment of power that the Russians can save face and have a way to back out.'" McNamara came to share this position. "I felt we should reduce the risks as much as we could to achieve our necessary objective," he said later.[11]

And the best way to do this, Nitze and others decided by the second day of the crisis, was to blockade, or "quarantine," Cuba. This move would keep the Soviets from shipping additional missiles and preserve the option of more severe action. It would place the U.S. response at the bottom of the ladder of escalation rather than near the top.

But would it get the missiles out of Cuba? Nitze wasn't sure. "I was uncertain as to where we ought to go," he said later. "I was uncertain about whether or not an air strike would be better than a blockade."

At a Thursday morning Excomm meeting with Kennedy, the sense of crisis intensified when the group was told by the CIA director, John McCone, that the missiles in Cuba might be operational within eighteen hours. The president made it clear that this could not be tolerated, but he stopped short of pressing his own opinion on how to prevent such a development. Later in the afternoon, the group moved over to the State Department to formulate options to present to Kennedy when Excomm reconvened at the White House that evening.

During this discussion the advocates of an air strike suffered a setback when new intelligence data confirmed the tentative conclusions reached by Rowen and others: Taking out the missiles would be a large and bloody operation. "This more detailed intelligence made it plain that an air strike to destroy all the offensive missiles would be a major effort, not an affair of a few bombs and a few minutes," stated the administration's 1963 *History of the Cuban Crisis.* [12] In addition, there was no assurance of total success. When pressed, the air force admitted that some missile sites might survive an air strike. "They might get 85 to 90 percent of them but they wouldn't get them all," recalled Dean Rusk.[13]

And there was another disturbing imponderable. "There was a key question," said Rowen, "of whether there were Soviet nuclear weapons in Cuba and if they survived what would be done and would these things be launched." Nobody had the answer to this question.

By the end of the meeting the group agreed that a quarantine made the most sense. At 10:00 P.M. on Thursday, Excomm met again at the White House and Kennedy tentatively approved the quarantine proposal.

* * *

By the fourth day of the crisis Paul Nitze had established himself as a key official on Excomm. With the exception of Dean Rusk, who had shared the ordeal of Korea, Nitze was the most experienced member of the group. He was also among the most controlled. After being in the "tank" with the JCS during some of the darkest moments of the Korean war, when MacArthur's forces were pinned down on the frozen terrain near the Yalu River, Nitze remained unruffled in a situation where the United States held such a strong position. "It seemed to me," he said later, "that we had both tactical superiority in the area of Cuba and we had overall strategic superiority under those circumstances, and we were really not running that great a risk."

This feeling that war between the superpowers was not imminent and that the situation was less out of control than it seemed gave Nitze the coolness to work on the Cuban missile crisis as if it were any other problem. On the first day of the crisis he had begun to put together a group of ISA staff to deal with the various questions that arose. By the end of the week this group had evolved into the main body within the Defense Department working on the crisis. "The group in ISA was sort of a focal point for the people on the Joint Staff who were concerned with this problem, and anybody else in the Pentagon," recalled Wolfe. Not everybody at ISA was involved in the crisis, but for those who were, the work never stopped. As Wolfe said, "during the period of the intense crisis, right to and through the President's address, this group was just on call, night and day, grinding out inputs."[14]

The papers produced by the group helped Nitze play a key role in Excomm's deliberations. Since neither the State Department nor the NSC had a comparable resevoir of military expertise, Nitze often came to the Excomm meetings best prepared. With his staff on call constantly, Nitze could get substantive answers to complex questions prepared within hours. Also, as one of the only Excomm members who took extensive notes, he could keep close tabs on the debate's evolution and respond to key questions as they arose. Upon returning from Excomm meetings, he would determine the main issues that had come up and ask his staff to analyze them. Working furiously, the members of the group would often dictate their answers directly to a typist. Twenty or so copies of each memorandum would be mimeographed, given to Nitze, and off he would dash to the next meeting. On the way to the White House or State Department, Nitze would read through the papers and decide which were worthwhile. When the Excomm meeting began, Nitze would pass out the memos to the group. "Time after time," said Zumwalt, "he sort of captured the high ground in the sense that they were starting from his position."

Despite Kennedy's tentative endorsement of a blockade, the air strike option remained popular with some members of Excomm, and debate raged through Friday. "I was trying to keep the air strike alive," McGeorge Bundy explained later, "not so much because I was sure it was good, but because I wasn't a bit sure the blockade was good and I thought we ought to keep the option going."

What Bundy saw as a useful dialectical exercise, Nitze condemned as fruitless bantering. "It wasn't really a planning session," he complained later, "it was kind of a sophomoric seminar." As construction on the launching pads continued, and the time moved closer when Soviet technicians would put warheads on those missiles, Nitze grew more anxious to start planning the details of a U.S. response. It was time to end the seminar.

After the Friday afternoon meeting in Ball's conference room (the "think tank," as it had been dubbed), Nitze approached Deputy Under Secretary of State Alexis Johnson and suggested that they write up a scenario for U.S. action. With the crisis in its fifth day, and the United States still lacking an agenda for action, Nitze suggested to Johnson that they work together to "develop a specific plan for the blockade detailing exactly what to do and when to do it."[15] Johnson agreed.

That evening the two men met in Johnson's office at the State Department to consider how they should proceed. As Johnson recalled, "We needed some centralizing concept to impose coherence on the detailed scenario we wished to draft, and decided upon the President's speech announcing the missiles' presence and our blockade response." Kennedy had tentatively scheduled the speech for Monday night. Nitze and Johnson chose to write their quarantine scenario as a number of steps that the United States would take in the twenty-four-hour period leading up to Kennedy's announcement of a quarantine.

Laboring through the night, Johnson developed all the diplomatic steps to be taken "before, during, and after the speech to make sure that support was obtained from the appropriate governments and organizations." Nitze worked on all the military moves. Everything was coordinated to the president's speech, which was labeled "P hour." By midnight the two men had put together a comprehensive quarantine plan that combined the two strands into one document. They were so nervous about security that they did not even give the paper to their secretaries to type. They wrote it out in longhand.

After a long and sleepless night—"sleeping was not a part of the schedule," Johnson quipped—Nitze was back in Ball's conference room with Excomm on Saturday morning. Once again the air strike advocates were on the offensive. Stiffly unyielding, Acheson would not let the idea die. But Robert Kennedy and others remained passionate in their opposition to an air strike. The United States had never been the country that started wars, Kennedy argued. "A sneak attack is not in our traditions," he argued.[16]

Throughout this debate Nitze and Johnson kept their blockade scenario a secret. There was no point in having it torn apart before even reaching the president. Moreover, the two men faced one last obstacle: They did not yet have a draft of a speech for their scenario to revolve around, and without a speech the scenario made no sense. To solve this problem, Nitze approached Kennedy's speech writer, Ted Sorensen, early Saturday morning and asked if he would prepare a draft. "Well, I don't know what the policy is," Sorensen said. "It's still being argued."

"I don't care about that," said Nitze. "No speech is going to be given by the President until the President has gone over it and everybody else has gone over it. Whatever speech is given is going to be thoroughly vetted before it's given. The thing is we need a first draft." Sorensen relented.

"And the moment we had an initial draft of the speech and a scenario, a time phase scenario," recalled Nitze, "we had the elements for translating what up to that time had been a bull session into a planning session."

When the full Excomm assembled at the White House that afternoon, Nitze and Johnson were ready to execute their end run. Passing out copies of Sorensen's speech and their blockade scenario, they outmaneuvered the advocates of an air strike and discussion became focused on the detailed plan now before the group. The air strike advocates had no plan to offer. Kennedy made his final decision: A naval quarantine of Cuba would be announced on Monday night.

Though he was instrumental in winning approval for the quarantine option, Nitze saw it only as a first step. He professed himself fully prepared to climb further up the ladder of escalation. For the Sunday morning meeting with the president, Robert Kennedy suggested that each member of Excomm write on a slip of paper a recommendation for how the United States should follow up the blockade. Nitze wrote: "We should follow the blockade with the offer of a political plan in the UN. If in two or three days we have continuing evidence of progress [on the Soviet missile bases] we should strike on a minimum number of targets. I believe it highly unlikely the Soviets would strike SAC, with SAC fully alerted. If the surviving missiles are used against us, I would invade Cuba, without using nuclear weapons. We might then have to make a purely compensatory attack on the Soviet Union. I do not believe effective action against the missiles in Cuba complicates the Berlin problem. If we permit this to go unanswered, we will be accepting coexistence on Khrushchev's terms."[17]

And even a full-scale war was preferable to that, Nitze felt.

Twenty-four hours before Kennedy went on the air, all military commands were ordered to DEFCON 3. This meant that the Strategic Air Command was to put all forces on a higher level of air and ground alert, ready to unleash nuclear strikes at the president's command. Atlantic-based naval forces were mobilized to impose the blockade and to protect U.S. shipping. United States military forces in the Caribbean were instructed to prepare to furnish riot-control support to selected Latin American countries.

Twelve hours before the speech, or P hour minus 12, special intelligence briefings were given to the United Kingdom and Canada. At P hour minus 6 the navy began reinforcing the lonely U.S. outpost on Cuba, the base at Guantanamo Bay. At P hour minus 2 congressional leaders were informed. At P hour minus 1 Allied embassies in Washington were given full briefings and a text of the president's speech. Dean Rusk also met with the Soviet ambassador, Anatoly Dobrynin, to give him a copy of the speech. "I saw him age ten years right in front of my eyes," Rusk remembered.[18]

At seven o'clock on Monday evening, October 22, John F. Kennedy appeared on national television and in a grave but calm manner told the country that another great crisis was underway. The Soviet deployment of missiles in Cuba, said the president, was a "deliberately provocative and unjustified change in the status quo which cannot be accepted by this country if our courage and our commitments are ever to be trusted again by either friend or foe."[19] Once more, Americans were told, U.S. credibility throughout the world was at stake. And once more Kennedy and Khrushchev were locked in a dangerous battle of wills.

As McGeorge Bundy said later, the Cuban missile crisis actually involved two debates. "There is the debate over what the first step should be and then there is the debate in the week of the open crisis as to what we're going to do next which comes almost every day." It was during this second phase, as the fatigue of a week with little sleep set in, as nerves became frayed, and as tempers grew short, that the United States and the Soviet Union moved closer to war than at any time since 1945.

On Tuesday morning Kennedy met with Excomm in the cabinet room to discuss where to go next. Twenty-seven Soviet ships were still steaming toward Cuba, the group was told. Moreover, according to a disturbing intelligence report presented by the CIA, nine offensive missile sites had been identified. Of these, "The two MRBM sites at Sagua la Grande and sites 1 and 2 of the four MRBM sites of the San Cristóbal complex are fully operational. Sites 3 and 4 have emergency operational capability." Altogether, the memorandum concluded, "We now have counted a total of 24 launchers and 33 missiles at the 6 MRBM sites."[20]

It was not yet clear whether these missiles were armed. But it now seemed obvious that even if the quarantine were 100 percent effective in keeping new missiles out of Cuba, the Soviets probably still could make the remainder of their missile sites operational.

Once again discussion turned to an air strike. McNamara said that the military was maintaining aircraft on alert for prompt action and that preparation for an invasion was proceeding at "full speed."[21]

Worried that U.S. military action against Cuba might prompt a Soviet move on Berlin, Kennedy approached Nitze after the morning meeting and asked him to chair a subcommittee of Excomm for Berlin contingencies. Many Excomm members felt the possibility that the Soviet mights squeeze Berlin was dangerously high. Nitze's staff was divided on the question. Wolfe believed that if there were an air strike or invasion, Khrushchev would have to respond. "What he would have done would be to look someplace else where the strength relationship was more equal or in his favor and stirred up some problems there." And there were few places where the Soviets had a greater advantage than in Berlin. As Wolfe said later, "if they felt impelled to use forceful measures, that might be the place, the most likely place, for them to apply them."

But others at ISA thought the chances of a Soviet move on Berlin were slim. "That would have changed this from a very local and focused sphere to involve all of Europe," said Rowen. "And it just didn't look like it would make sense. . . . It was very unlikely." DeWitt Armstrong felt the same way. As one of the key people on Nitze's Berlin subcommittee (or "Excomm-Subcomm"), Armstrong's assignment was to prepare for the worst. But while he took the threat to Berlin "very seriously indeed," he believed that the previous year's showdown in Germany had eliminated Khrushchev's appetite for playing chicken on the Autobahn. Nitze agreed. It would have been "an irrational act, a totally irrational act on the Soviet side, to respond with an invasion of Berlin or even the institution of a blockade of Berlin," Nitze said later.[22]

But then again, in times of such tension—unprecedented tension—nothing could be ruled out. As Nitze said afterward, "You could well imagine that some irrational act would take place."

On the morning of October 24, as Excomm met at the White House, reports came in that some Soviet ships en route to Cuba appeared to have stopped or turned back, but some were still steaming ahead toward the line of interception for the quarantine which had been extended 500 miles from the island. It was estimated that two Soviet ships, the *Gagarin* and *Komiles,* would arrive at the line between ten thirty and eleven o'clock. At that fateful point, the United States would either have to intercept the ships or back down. War between the United States and the Soviet Union had never appeared more imminent, and the pressure in the cabinet room had never been so intense.[23]

Shortly after ten o'clock the navy reported that a Soviet submarine had moved into the area near the two Soviet ships. Grim and intense, McNamara said that the submarine posed an unacceptable threat to U.S. naval forces in the area. The aircraft carrier *Essex* was going to signal the submarine by sonar to surface and identify itself. If it refused, he continued, depth charges would be used until the submarine surfaced. McNamara's statement had a chilling effect on the room. No one seemed more disturbed than the president. "His hand went up to his face and covered his mouth," Robert Kennedy wrote. "He opened and closed his fist. His face seemed drawn, his eyes pained, almost gray."

"Isn't there some way we can avoid having our first exchange with a Russian submarine?" the President asked.

"No," replied McNamara, "there's too much danger to our ships. There is no alternative. Our commanders have been instructed to avoid hostilities if at all possible, but this is what we must be prepared for, and this what we must expect."

"We must expect that they will close down Berlin—make the final preparation for that," the president said.[24]

For the first time, the crisis seemed out of control. Nobody in the cabinet room knew what to do or say. There was a sense of helplessness, a feeling that it shouldn't have come to this. And as the minutes ticked slowly away, the members of Excomm waited for news from U.S. naval forces far out in the Atlantic ocean.

At 10:25 a messenger arrived with a note for CIA director McCone. "Mr. President," he said, "we have a preliminary report which seems to indicate that some of the Russian ships have stopped dead in the water. . . . Six ships previously on their way to Cuba at the edge of the quarantine line have stopped or have turned back toward the Soviet Union." The group breathed a collective sigh of relief. A short time later the Office of Naval Intelligence presented a report to Excomm stating that the twenty Russian ships closest to the barrier had stopped and were dead in the water or had turned around.[25]

Yet while most of the Soviet ships headed toward Cuba had stopped, the crisis was by no means over. Intelligence data presented later in the day indicated that work on the missiles was continuing at a furious pace. On Friday it was revealed that technicians were uncrating IL-28 nuclear-capable jet bombers and preparing them for action. The quarantine was doing nothing to stop the Soviet nuclear buildup in Cuba.

Once again the talk in Excomm turned to military action. In fact, such action now seemed nearly inevitable.

At a meeting on Friday morning, October 26, Kennedy ordered the State Department to step up its crash program for a civil government to be established in Cuba after the invasion and occupation. McNamara reported that much of the invasion force was in place but said that high casualties could be expected. Nitze told the group that his subcommittee was at work preparing for a possible Soviet move against Berlin.[26] He also stressed the "importance of getting the Soviet missiles out urgently."[27] The mood in Excomm was one of mounting impatience. McCone, among others, pushed strongly for an invasion. "Even if the Soviet missiles are removed," he said, "Castro, if he is left in control, will be in an excellent position for the Communization of Latin America."[28]

When talk turned to the goals of negotiations, most agreed that their aim should be to force the Soviets to abandon work at the sites, stop military shipments, defuse the nuclear weapons in Cuba, and allow for U.N. inspection. Nitze emphasized that the single most important short-term objective should be to obtain a guarantee that the "nuclear missiles be disassembled from their launchers."[29] Since some of the sites were nearing operational status, a guarantee only to stop further work and end military shipments would not eliminate the threat. Every missile had to be taken apart, Nitze said.

Later that day a CIA intelligence report seemed to confirm Nitze's original assessment that the Soviet missiles in Cuba substantially altered the strategic picture: "We estimate that it would cost the USSR more than twice as much and take considerably longer to add to its ICBM strike capability from the USSR as great an increment as the potential salvo from Cuban launching sites."[30]

On Friday evening a solution to the crisis suddenly appeared within reach when a long letter from Khrushchev arrived. After writing emotionally about the dangers of a nuclear catastrophe, Khrushchev hinted at a bargain: "If assurances were given that the President of the United States would not participate in an attack on Cuba and the blockade lifted, then the question of the removal or the destruction of the missile sites in Cuba would then be an entirely different question."[31] As Excomm met late into the night, Khrushchev's letter was examined and debated. Was Khrushchev really offering to trade his missiles for a U.S. promise not to attack? Or was he just stalling, buying time so that all the missiles could become operational? No one knew for sure.

On Saturday morning, October 27, the twelfth grueling day of the crisis, Excomm reconvened at the White House. The previous evening's optimism evaporated in the face of new developments. The FBI reported that Soviet personnel in New York were preparing to destroy all sensitive documents, apparently under the assumption that war was imminent. Also, a new letter had arrived from Khrushchev. While the previous letter had clearly been written by the Soviet leader himself, Saturday's very formal letter appeared to have come from the Foreign Office of the Kremlin. The deal that Khrushchev had proposed on Friday was not mentioned. Instead the Soviets had a different settlement in mind: They would remove their missiles from Cuba if the United States withdrew its missiles from Turkey.

Ever since the crisis had begun, the possibility of such a trade had loomed in the background. During the first few days Nitze had asked Bill Bundy to prepare an analysis of the Jupiter missiles in Turkey. His report had concluded that they were obsolete, vulnerable, and practically useless.[32] This surprised no one. As Dean Rusk later said, "We joked about which way those missiles would go if they were fired. They were first generation intermediate missiles with rather primitive guidance systems, and we were told that tourists driving down a public highway with .22-calibre rifles could pass by these missiles sites and put holes in them and put them out of action."[33]

The president himself had long pressed for a unilateral withdrawal of the missiles. Earlier in the year he had instructed the State Department to make it clear to the Turkish government that the United States was intent on removing the Jupiters. At a NATO meeting in Oslo just four months earlier, Rusk and Nitze had sounded out the Turks on the idea. The response from Turkish Foreign Minister Selim Sarper was that Turkey considered the missiles an indispensable symbol of American commitment. Still, Kennedy insisted that the United States get the missiles out. Nitze again talked to the Turks, this time with George Ball, and again their reaction was negative.[34] Finally, late in the summer of 1962, Kennedy decided that the United States would eventually withdraw the missiles no matter what the diplomatic costs.

But when Khrushchev, or the Soviet Foreign Office, suggested a trade involving the Jupiters, the issue took on new meaning. Voluntarily discarding the worthless weapons was one thing; taking them out under Soviet pressure was a wholly different matter. "The President could not risk anything resembling a public trade," McNamara said later. "People would have interpreted this as caving in."[35] However, President Kennedy hinted to the members of Excomm that caving in would be preferable to war and that he might be willing to trade the Turkish missiles for the Cuban ones if it would defuse the crisis.

Nitze adamantly opposed the idea. Turkey would be furious if the United States decided on its own, without consultation and in response to Soviet pressure, that it was withdrawing the Jupiters, he said. And there was a larger issue to consider, continued Nitze heatedly. If the United States agreed to trade away the Jupiters, the possibility existed that "the next Soviet step would be a demand for the entire denuclearization of the entire NATO area." Who could say how far Khrushchev would go in his demands? Once the United States started giving in to Soviet bullying, where would it all end? By now almost lecturing the president, Nitze said that the United States must not let the Soviet Union broaden the debate over Cuba to include other countries. McGeorge Bundy agreed that "we cannot get into the position of appearing to sell out an ally."[36]

The debate over the Jupiter missiles ended without decision, but Nitze thought that it appeared as though the president might accept a trade. He could barely contain his fury. Returning to the Pentagon, he railed against the absence of resolve. Nitze's aides were equally upset. "It was an appalling thought," said Rowen. "It would look like we were trading off the security of Europe for the defense of the United States."

Nitze's unwillingness to relinquish useless missiles in exchange for a reduced risk of war underlined his enduring sensitivity to the psychological component of the Cold War. As in Berlin, he felt the issue in Cuba was not the disposition of a piece of real estate, but rather the political orientation of the world. Trading away the Turkish missiles would not only show a lack of resolve, Nitze felt, but would undermine NATO and bring Khrushchev one step closer to breaking up the alliance. Again, Nitze's operative image was of the Soviet Union as a mechanical chess player trying to eliminate a key piece so it could move inexorably on to checkmate. By opposing a militarily insignificant concession, Nitze was pushing his views of cold war psychology to a new extreme.

When Excomm reconvened at four o'clock on Saturday afternoon, McNamara had brought along the Joint Chiefs of Staff. They told the president that they had originally opposed the quarantine plan as far too weak. Now the fruits of that policy were apparent: Missile construction was continuing and the threat was increasing. An air strike followed by an invasion, argued the chiefs, had become the only alternative. McNamara agreed, saying that a limited air strike was now impossible because U.S. reconnaissance planes were being fired on and that the United States must now plan for a major air strike followed by an invasion. Rusk recommended that the president immediately authorize mobilization measures.[37]

In the middle of this discussion a disturbing message arrived. General Maxwell Taylor announced that he had just received a report that a U-2 had been shot down over Cuba and the pilot killed. Taylor suggested an air strike be launched immediately against the surface-to-air-missile site responsible for the attack. McNamara was furious. He told the president that the United States must now be ready to attack Cuba. An invasion had become almost inevitable. All the forces were in place and the attack could begin Sunday if the president gave the authorization. This would probably mean a Soviet strike against Turkey, McNamara added, and the United States should prepare for war in the NATO area.

The tension in the cabinet room was tremendous. Pressure mounted on Kennedy to make a decision, and he groped for a response to the insistent militancy of McNamara and the JCS. "It isn't the first step that concerns me," the president said, "but both sides escalating to the fourth and fifth step—and we don't go to sixth because there is no one around to do so. We must remind ourselves we are embarking on a very hazardous course."[38] No, the president finally decided, the United

States would not attack on Sunday. Another effort would be made to communicate with Khrushchev.

Ted Sorensen and Robert Kennedy left the cabinet room to compose a letter to Khrushchev. The letter ignored the more formal communication that had come in during the morning and responded instead to Friday's offer that the Soviets would remove the missiles from Cuba if the United States pledged not to invade the island. By seven o'clock the letter had been typed, approved by the president, and transmitted to Khrushchev.

Two hours later a weary Excomm again assembled in the cabinet room. McNamara recommended that the Pentagon call up twenty-four air reserve squadrons, fourteen thousand additional military personnel, and three hundred navy troop carriers. He also suggested that mobilization of private U.S. shipping beginning on Sunday to "have sufficient ships available for an invasion."[39] Kennedy approved all of these steps and also authorized the first military action of the crisis: Air strikes against surface-to-air missile (SAM) sites in Cuba would be carried out the next day.

On Sunday morning, October 28, Nitze was fortifying himself for another day of crisis when the news came. Khrushchev had accepted the latest offer. The Soviets would immediately begin dismantling the missiles under U.N. supervision and inspection. The worst was over.

Hurrying to the White House for an eleven o'clock Excomm meeting, Nitze found his colleagues transformed. For the first time in thirteen days everyone was relaxed. Their mood was exultant. Secretary of State Rusk, usually placid and reticent, perked up and gave a little speech. Everyone present had helped to bring about the highly advantageous resolution of the Cuban missile crisis, he said. Bundy broke in to say that there were hawks and there were doves, but "today was the doves' day."[40]

In the days and weeks following the ordeal, Nitze helped oversee the postcrisis cleanup work. While the missiles were out for the time being, Nitze was unwilling to assume that the Soviets would not attempt a similar move again. To insure that the United States could quickly detect any future missiles in Cuba, he put together a paper on long-term surveillance requirements that was circulated at one of the final Excomm meetings in early November.[41]

The Soviet Union never returned missiles to Cuba. Both Khrushchev and Kennedy were traumatized by the crisis. They had been to the brink, and neither wanted to be there again. More and more the president turned his attention to the challenge of defusing the nuclear competition. With Berlin secure and the Cuban crisis over, Nitze also began to grapple more intently with the question of how to control nuclear weapons. In his mind it was the critical issue of the day.

It was an issue that would consume him for most of his remaining years in government.

CHAPTER 10

A Game Called Arms Control

As PAUL NITZE saw it, the favorable outcome of the confrontations in Berlin and Cuba would have been impossible without American nuclear superiority. The lesson of these crises was that nuclear weapons were not phantom chess queens never brought into play. Rather, Nitze felt they dominated the board and made the difference between victory and defeat.

In Berlin American interests had been threatened 120 miles inside of communist territory. Despite elaborate contingency plans for keeping the Autobahn open, it was clear that Warsaw Pact troops would have prevailed in a shootout over Berlin. Yet when the crisis heated up, Moscow had backed down. Nitze attributed this collapse of Soviet resolve to America's massive edge in nuclear forces.

The same was true in the Cuban missile crisis, he felt. "We knew perfectly well that if there was a nuclear war, this country would be severely damaged," Nitze said. "However, we knew that our capability to destroy the Soviet military was much greater than theirs to destroy ours . . . we had meaningful superiority at that time." This superiority "was one of the reasons why we went into the Cuban Missile Crisis with such confidence."[1]

Nitze took the outcome of the Berlin and Cuban crises as a vindication of his thinking about nuclear weapons. Although he had largely abandoned the idea that the United States should strive for a capability to disarm the Soviet Union in a first strike, he still argued for some measure of nuclear superiority during the early 1960s. His position was that it was not enough to retain only enough nuclear bombs to strike back at the Soviet Union in the event of a sneak attack. This posture— known as "minimum deterrence"—had the advantage of being inexpensive and nonthreatening. But to Nitze it was fatally flawed.

The most glaring of its many shortcomings, Nitze felt, was that it would be useless in a crisis or in the face of piecemeal Soviet aggression. A minimum deterrent arsenal was fine for blowing up Soviet cities, but what if the United States wanted to use nuclear weapons to take out a small air base or military headquarters in East Germany during a crisis? What if the Soviets moved troops into Iran and the United States wanted to strike at selected military targets in the southwestern portion of the Soviet Union? Such attacks would be difficult to mount using an arsenal designed to destroy Soviet cities. To keep Soviet expansionism in check, Nitze believed that the United States had to back up its commitments with nuclear weapons that could be used selectively. A posture of minimum deterrence, Nitze wrote in 1960, was "not a very solid foundation for our political aims."[2]

And minimum deterrence presented other problems.

To Nitze, having just enough nuclear weapons to destroy most major Soviet cities was nearly the same as having none at all. If for some reason the Soviet Union launched nuclear weapons at the United States, it would be national suicide for a U.S. president to strike back at Soviet cities. To do so would insure that even more Soviet nuclear weapons would rain down on the United States in response. This was the grand strategic failure of minimum deterrence. It assumed that an American president would mindlessly sacrifice the United States to a lost cause. Only if the Soviets believed this bluff would minimum deterrence work.

But what if the Soviets didn't believe the bluff? What if they determined that the United States would act rationally and not suicidally in a nuclear confrontation? And what if they moved to chip away at American security knowing that the U.S. leadership could do nothing to stop them? What would be the U.S. response, Nitze asked, if "four Polaris submarines failed to report and we suspected Russian action, or if ten Minuteman installations in Alaska were sabotaged? All-out retaliation would be suicidal while the ins and outs of limited reprisal are far from clear."[3]

To some observers, it was plausible that minimum deterrence could work for years—that it could work and save the United States billions of dollars in the process. As long as there was even a remote chance that Mother Russia would be obliterated, they contended, the Kremlin would be deterred. They argued further that the real risk of nuclear war came not from a Soviet plan to launch a surprise nuclear attack, but rather from a paranoid Soviet leader who, in a crisis, might launch Soviet missiles so that they wouldn't be destroyed on the ground in a U.S. first strike. Because a minimum deterrent force could not be used in a first strike, it would lower Soviet insecurities and therefore reduce the risk of nuclear war.

Paul Nitze accepted the argument that vulnerability produced instability. But to him, the benefits of a nuclear arsenal that could cope with limited aggression outweighed the risk of rash Soviet actions. From the beginning of Kennedy's presidency, Nitze strongly supported the administration's move toward flexible response, a policy he had advocated since the mid 1950s. The instrument of this policy would be a large and varied nuclear arsenal that could be used to strike at a wide range of military and civilian targets. The guiding theology was that such an arsenal could be used in a limited fashion without triggering a global conflagration. "The failure of deterrence need not inevitably lead to uncontrollable nuclear war," Nitze said in 1962. "There is no reason why each side has to fire its nuclear weapons indiscriminately, no reason why a distinction can't be drawn between civilian and military targets."[4]

This line of thought, embraced by the president and his closest advisors, represented a major departure from massive retaliation. Under the top secret plan for waging nuclear war left in place by Eisenhower—known as the Single Integrated Operational Plan, or SIOP-62—the president had few options. If the Soviets invaded western Europe, the United States could either unleash thousands of nuclear weapons on the Soviet Union and its allies or do nothing.

Kennedy quickly junked this doctrine. After a series of internal policy changes, McNamara revealed the change in policy to NATO's leadership in May 1962. In a speech written by ISA's RAND consultant William Kaufmann, edited by Harry Rowen, and reviewed by Nitze, McNamara told NATO officials gathered in Athens that "our principal military objectives, in the event of a nuclear war stemming from a major attack on the Alliance, should be the destruction of the enemy's military forces while attempting to preserve the fabric as well as the integrity of allied society."[5] Known as counterforce targeting, or no-cities, this new strategy embraced the notion that nuclear war could be fought in a limited and controlled manner, not unlike an artillery duel between two mature and discriminating gunners.

The abandonment of massive retaliation was a triumphant event for Paul Nitze. Since hearing John Foster Dulles expound that policy on a cold night in January 1954, Nitze had strived to move America toward what he considered a more rational nuclear strategy. Now these ideas were being implemented, and in the wake of the Berlin and Cuban crises, Nitze felt that the more flexible policy was already yielding dividends.

But if massive retaliation had problems, so did the new strategy. The talk of waging limited nuclear war leaking out of Washington made Moscow nervous. The Soviets stepped up missile production. In the United States the military, particularly the air force, saw in the new strategy an opportunity to request ever more expensive nuclear weapons. A chief criticism of massive retaliation was that it allowed nuclear stockpiles to become bloated beyond reason. Counterforce targeting only accelerated this trend.

Moreover, there was scant evidence that the shift to flexible response was worth the price. Nitze felt that nuclear weapons were the key to NATO's success in the Berlin crisis. But was this true? The ISA staff had searched in vain for some way to use nuclear weapons in the event that the crisis escalated. No sane plan was devised. Nitze had rejected the contingency plan put together by Harry Rowen and others that called for a first strike on the Soviet Union. He had also backed away from more modest suggestions for nuclear demonstration explosions. When the contingency plans for Berlin were completed, they contained no recommendations on how to use nuclear weapons.

This dismissal of nuclear options was particularly striking in light of the Soviet strategic posture. At the time of the Berlin crisis, the Soviets had only four ICBMs. Never again would the United States possess such an overwhelming superiority in nuclear striking power. Yet even after months of hypothesizing, neither Paul Nitze nor his aides could find a realistic way to take advantage of that power.

By the time of the Cuban missile crisis the Soviet Union had 75 ICBMs and a total of 536 warheads they could theoretically put on U.S. soil.[6] What were the hopes of finding "attractive" nuclear options in the face of this far larger arsenal? Would Paul Nitze, always cautious, really be willing to ponder the "selective" use of nuclear weapons if there were even minute chances that a few of those warheads might end up falling on New York, Washington, and Chicago? The Berlin crisis proved to Nitze that nuclear superiority made a difference. But because overwhelming U.S. superiority evaporated nearly instantly, this proof—if ever valid at all—became irrelevant.

Nitze's claim of usable superiority is even more dubious in regard to Cuba. Among the veterans of the Cuban missile crisis, Nitze stands almost alone in his belief that American nuclear superiority made a difference during the tense thirteen days in October. In 1982 six veterans of the crisis—McGeorge Bundy, Dean Rusk, Robert McNamara, Ted Sorensen, Roswell Gilpatric, and George Ball—signed a statement that said: "The Cuban Missile Crisis illustrates not the significance but the insignificance of nuclear superiority in the face of survivable thermonuclear forces."[7] Even Maxwell Taylor, a hawk during the crisis, commented that "The strategic forces of the United States and the USSR simply cancelled each other out as effectual instruments for influencing the outcome of the confrontation."[8]

For all of its great expense, for all of its destabilizing effect, there was little evidence that flexible response—with its presumption that nuclear forces could be used coercively—made more sense than minimum deterrence.

By 1963 Nitze himself seemed confused. "Perhaps there are no clear-cut answers to the issues I have been discussing," Nitze said after winding up an anguished comparison between minimum deterrence and flexible response before an audience at the Air War College.[9]

McNamara was having even greater doubts. The adoption of counterforce targeting had turned into a nightmare for the defense secretary who had staked his reputation on carefully managed military spending. As the Soviet nuclear arsenal grew, the number of military targets grew as well. Because each target of importance had to be covered, the new strategy proved a bonanza for the air force, providing its generals with a powerful rationale for requesting new weapons.

By January 1963 McNamara had had enough. He told his staff that counterforce would no longer be the Pentagon's official strategic doctrine. In search of another solution, he ordered his whiz kids to determine how many nuclear weapons it would take to destroy enough of Soviet society in a retaliatory strike to stop the Soviets in their tracks. By the end of the year a doctrine known as "Assured Destruction" would be born. In its essence, it was a doctrine of minimum deterrence.[10]

* * *

Because the fighting of a nuclear war was an unpracticed art, bolstering American security through changes in strategic doctrine was a purely cerebral exercise.

The game of arms control was far more concrete.

When Kennedy announced Nitze's appointment to ISA, he emphasize that Nitze would be a key player in the arms control field. The president hoped that Nitze could use the pivotal ISA post to bring together the many agencies that dealt with arms control and impose unity where there could easily be chaos.

The hot arms control issue in the early 1960s was nuclear testing. As a senator, Kennedy had made the test ban a personal theme, pushing the idea among his colleagues on Capitol Hill. As president, he was determined to negotiate a comprehensive test ban treaty.

Paul Nitze came to the Pentagon with mixed feelings about a test ban and about arms control in general. In NSC 68 Nitze had written that controls on atomic armaments could help eliminate the risks of surprise attack. But he had dismissed hopes for negotiating such controls with Moscow, saying that "the absence of good faith on the part of the USSR must be assumed until there is concrete evidence that there has been a decisive change in Soviet policies. It is to be doubted whether such a change can take place without a change in the nature of the Soviet system itself." He continued to reiterate this argument throughout the Truman years: For arms control to be possible, the Kremlin would have to modify its totalitarian system at home and mitigate its aggressive policies abroad.

By the late 1950s Stalin's death and the detente fostered by Khrushchev and Eisenhower had brought some relaxation in tensions. Advances in spy technology had also made trusting the Kremlin less important; technology could insure that they stuck to their promises. In principle, Nitze was ready to give arms control a try, but in practice, he still saw many obstacles to making the process work.

In April 1959 Nitze traveled to Geneva for an international disarmament conference. There, five western delegations and five communist delegations haggled over comprehensive disarmament proposals. The conference was going nowhere, and Nitze was struck by the folly of such sweeping negotiations. Radical disarmament plans would never work, he decided. They were too hard to negotiate and too complex to implement. Moreover, there was no guarantee that such plans would enhance anybody's security. Making the delicate balance of terror more stable was a formidable task. It meant reducing the risk of surprise attack, but not cutting the nuclear arsenals that both sides felt they needed to safeguard their security. It also meant embarking on lengthy and exhausting negotiations, talks that could go on for years and could easily break down should the climate of U.S.-Soviet relations worsen.

If everything went as planned, the final product of this strenuous effort would be finely tuned and narrowly focused agreements that made the world a safer place. But once those treaties were in place after many years of hammering out the most minute details, what would stop either superpower from reneging? As Nitze wrote in 1960, "it cannot be assumed that the agreements will continue to be honored unless honoring them continues to be in the interests of each of the parties." And what would guarantee that?

Getting ideological enemies to agree on anything was difficult. Keeping them talking for years to achieve agreements on the most sensitive of topics seemed nearly impossible. But Nitze was ready to try. "If we can see any possibility of working out reciprocal actions with the Russians whereby deterrence can be made substantially more secure, we should continue to strive for that goal," he said.[11]

A ban on all nuclear testing would strengthen deterrence. By slowing the march toward smaller, more powerful nuclear warheads—weapons that made a first strike more feasible—a test ban would help safeguard the arsenals of both superpowers from surprise attack. One of the greatest sources of momentum in the arms race was technology. With each side pouring vast amounts of national treasure into developing more effective weapons, there was an intense fear in both Washington and Moscow of falling behind. By closing off at least one direction in which technology could spin out of control, a test ban would help allay that fear.

And such an accord would contribute to peace in other ways. Throughout the world nations were seeking entry to the nuclear weapons club. By 1960 Britain and France had become members, and Mao's China was knocking insistently on the door. American leaders feared that when nuclear weapons became standard equipment, regional arms races would break out in volatile areas such as the Middle East. To slow this trend, to keep the nuclear club exclusive, the United States hoped to pressure other nations into forsaking the bomb. Yet how could the United States or any other nuclear power ask a nation to eschew nuclear weapons if it was constantly improving its own arsenal? Who would listen to such hypocritical sermonizing? "If the USSR and the United States are continuing unlimited testing themselves, we think it would then be very difficult to persuade other countries not to test," Nitze said in 1962.[12]

For those around the world who longed for peace, a test ban was revered as a symbolic first step. For the people who worried about the fallout from atmospheric testing, a ban held out the promise of a safer environment. For security experts in both east and west, an agreement would make a palpable contribution to stability in the way that more weapons could not.

There was even something in it for the hard-liners at the Pentagon. In the early 1960s the United States held a major lead in warhead technology. American laboratories were producing more powerful and more compact warheads than their Soviet counterparts. A test ban agreement would help freeze that advantage. This was especially true in the realm of tactical nuclear forces. "Toward the lower end of the yield spectrum, the U.S. advantage would persist over a longer time than would be the case with testing," Nitze said. And overall, America's nuclear advantage would "dissipate more slowly under a comprehensive treaty."[13]

To the new president anxious for diplomatic successes, a test ban had the appeal of being achievable. Since November 1958 the United States, Great Britain, and the Soviet Union had been negotiating at the Geneva Conference on the Discontinuance of Nuclear Weapons Tests. While these talks moved at an excruciatingly slow pace, they had produced general agreement on a major sticking point: the kind of control system needed to monitor a comprehensive test ban. During the summer of 1958 scientists from NATO and Warsaw Pact nations had produced a report proposing a control system that would place seismic monitoring posts throughout the world, including inside the Soviet Union and the United States. Seismographic readings at these posts would be able to detect most underground nuclear explosions. When it was impossible to tell whether a seismic event was an earthquake or an explosion, international teams carrying only monitoring equipment were to travel directly to the spot of the suspicious seismic event for on-site inspections.

Throughout 1958, 1959, and 1960 the Soviet Union accepted the monitoring report and it served as the basis of the conference. With a committed U.S. President, there was no obvious reason why the test ban negotiations could not produce a final agreement.

The main group in the administration that dealt with arms control issues was the Committee of Principals. Formed by Eisenhower in

1958, the group included the government's top national security officials. Nitze was not an official member, but he attended almost every meeting and became a key participant.

Early in March 1961 the committee met to prepare for the next session of the Geneva conference. The most contentious issue was the number of on-site inspections the United States should demand. Shadowing this debate was a keen awareness of Soviet xenophobia; the Soviets had endorsed the report calling for on-site inspections, but it was not certain they would stand by their endorsement. President Kennedy considered on-site inspection crucial for verifying the treaty and for achieving its ratification. No test ban accord would survive in the Senate without airtight measures to stop the Soviets from cheating.

On March 4 the committee assembled at the White House with the president to make a final decision about on-site inspections. Earlier, the group had proposed requiring a minimum of ten on-site inspections per year with the option of ten more visits in case of heightened seismic activity. But now the Joint Chiefs of Staff were having second thoughts. JCS Chairman Lyman Lemnitzer argued that the number of inspections should be proportional to the number of suspicious seismic events, with no ceiling at all.

Kennedy asked for Nitze's view.

The number of on-site inspections was not so important, Nitze replied. What really mattered was the administrative mechanism for determining which seismic events were to be investigated. If the Soviet could dictate which events were inspected, if they could stop the United States from investigating some alleged earthquakes but not others, the system would be meaningless. The Pentagon saw loopholes that might "negate the purposes of the treaty," Nitze said.[14]

When the U.S. ambassador to the Geneva conference, Arthur Dean, left for the first round of negotiations in mid March, the JCS position was ignored and he took with him the proposal for twenty annual inspections. To those who longed for an agreement, Dean's instructions seemed to be a victory over Pentagon hard-liners and a hopeful sign that the most daunting obstacle to a test ban—the power of Washington's hawks—could be kept in check.

The hopes that ran so high when Dean left for Geneva were shattered on the opening day of the conference when the Soviet chief negotiator, Semyon K. Tsarapkin, gave substance to the exact fears Nitze had voiced. He demanded that the control system set up to verify the test ban be administered by a three-man council, or troika. It had been assumed previously that the control system would be headed by a single official from a neutral country, an official sure to be impartial. What the Soviets now wanted were three officials—one from NATO, one from the Warsaw Pact, and one from a neutral country—each of whom could veto any inspection of a suspicious seismic event.

The American delegation was flabbergasted. Such a system of optional verification was a virtual license to cheat. It was so unacceptable that it called into question the Soviet commitment to a test ban.

By early April other disagreements emerged. The U.S. proposal of twenty on-site inspections was met by a Soviet counter offer of three. The Soviets wanted fifteen detection stations on their soil; the United States insisted on nineteen. The Soviet delegation argued that the detection stations and inspection teams should be manned mostly by host country personnel; Dean ridiculed that idea, demanding neutral verification officials.

In Washington Nitze followed the opening stages of the test ban talks with interest. The Soviet hard line on verification seemed to confirm his suspicions that a comprehensive test ban might be out of reach and that if a treaty were achieved, it could be filled with dangerous loopholes.

When a test ban was discussed at the Vienna summit, Khrushchev insisted that three on-site inspections a year would be adequate. Any more would constitute espionage. As for the control system, the Soviet leader argued that U.N. supervision was out of the question because of that organization's recent prowestern activities in the Congo. He remained adamant about a troika.[15]

By late summer 1961 hopes for a comprehensive test ban were fading fast. Tensions over Berlin helped poison the atmosphere in Geneva, and the talks were stalemated. On the evening of August 30 the Soviet Union announced that it was breaking the joint moratorium on atomic explosions and resuming atmospheric testing. Two weeks later the United States followed suit, but confined its tests to underground sites. With the paralysis in superpower relations and the all-consuming crisis in Berlin, an agreement on nuclear weapons was nearly unimaginable. In Siberia mushroom clouds blossomed into the sky as the Soviets mounted a vigorous test series. By early October Nitze and other Pentagon officials were pushing for a renewal of atmospheric testing. State Department officials opposed the idea. Did the United States really wish to emulate Khrushchev's atomic saber rattling? And wouldn't such a move accelerate the diplomatic rigor mortis setting in at the Geneva conference?

At an October 7 meeting of the Committee of Principals, the two factions clashed bitterly. McNamara led off by urging that the United States meet the Soviet blustering by preparing to resume atmospheric testing. Nitze backed him up, arguing that the extensive Soviet tests were weakening the U.S. political position. If the Berlin talks failed and the international situation further unraveled, Nitze said, the United States had to begin testing in the atmosphere; not to do so would signal a lack of resolve. Later in the meeting Nitze also said that with another testing series the "Soviet might increase their military capabilities by a factor of three to five over the U.S." Was the State Department prepared to live with this?[16]

Presented with the specter of a modest diminution of U.S. military power and the unsettling thought that U.S. "resolve" might appear faint, the committee backed preparations to resume atmospheric testing. In an administration ready to take great risks to topple Castro and keep Berlin free, there was not yet a willingness to take any risks in the pursuit of arms control.

When the Geneva talks resumed on November 28, hopes for a comprehensive test ban were dealt a further blow when the Soviets proposed a draft treaty to ban only atmospheric tests. To the American delegation, banning explosions in the atmosphere would ease concerns about radioactive fallout, but it wouldn't do much else. The Soviet offer dragged the talks in the wrong direction, and Ambassador Dean denounced it as nothing more than a "propaganda proposal" and "a piece of sheer effrontery."[17]

By late January 1962 the negotiations broke down completely. No date was set for the next meeting. The Geneva Conference on the Discontinuance of Nuclear Weapons Tests never resumed.

The termination of the conference was not the end of test ban negotiations. In early March 1962 the Eighteen Nation Disarmament Conference convened in Geneva, and the Americans, Soviets, and British took up negotiations where they had left off. The change in the title of the meetings was of no help, and when the conference ended in June, nothing had been accomplished. In July the administration decided to undertake a major review of U.S. test ban policy.

Through most of 1961 the Berlin crisis had consumed Nitze's attention. When the crisis abated, he focused his enormous energies on the test ban debate. Nitze worked on the test ban much as he had on the Cuban missile crisis, but in "slow motion," as Bud Zumwalt put it. After a Committee of Principals meeting, Nitze returned to his office at ISA and called in key staff. From the notes he had scrawled during the meeting, Nitze tried to distill what had been said. With a lucidity that always impressed his staff, Nitze pinpointed the key questions that had arisen at the meeting. After some discussion about where things were going, Nitze assigned the questions to members of the staff.

Zumwalt handled a lot of this work, but the brunt fell to John McNaughton. A sharp, Harvard-trained lawyer, McNaughton had been Nitze's second choice for the job of arms control deputy. Nitze had first tried to recruit Thomas Schelling, but Schelling refused and recommended McNaughton. For the next three years, McNaughton would head ISA's arms control office and serve as Nitze's point man on the test ban question.

Bureaucratic power, Nitze had learned long ago, often stemmed as much from knowledge as from position. In the test ban debate he had influence because he had information. On the crucial question of verification, for example, Nitze's easy access to arcane data gave him a special edge. "A lot of the analytical work that went on had to do with how good were the seismic capabilities," recalled Zumwalt. With its close ties to the JCS and contracts with RAND, ISA could answer questions that the State Department and other agencies could not. If Nitze wanted to know how a particular verification program was progressing, he knew who to call. If he wanted an analysis of the latest Soviet test series, it could be on his desk in days, if not hours. And if he wanted answers to broader political questions, he could get those as well. As the Pentagon's liaison with the State Department and NSC, Nitze's office had access to high quality political intelligence and analysis. It also had a well-rounded staff to make sense of this material.

By bringing all of this thinking together, Nitze was instrumental in imposing order on the government's test ban deliberations. "I believe it is true to say that the person President Kennedy and Mr. McNamara put the burden on to work out the formula that finally resulted in the test ban treaty was myself," Nitze later boasted. "I headed what I believe to have been the critical staff work."[18]

One of Nitze's most important acts was to establish the basic operating assumptions that would guide United States officials in the test ban debate. Since the first meetings of the Committee of Principals, high administration officials had been perplexed and irritated by the maddening diversity of views on basic factual issues. How could they hope to debate a new verification device, for example, if every agency had a different view of what the device did? What good was it to talk about the average number of earthquakes in a particular region of the Soviet Union if each official had been given a different number by his experts?

To end this chaos, McNamara gave Nitze the forbidding assignment of identifying all the factual disagreements on the test ban that existed within the administration. McNamara thought that once the major differences were clear, they could be resolved, and once they were resolved, the meetings of the Committee of Principals would no longer degenerate into arguments about basic facts.

Nitze worked on this problem for months. He got nowhere. Despite his knack for bringing people together and making complex issues clear, Nitze was unable to find a method for getting dozens of experts to agree on dozens of facts. Exasperated, he went to see McNamara for advice. Within minutes, the former auto executive produced a deft solution.

Following McNamara's directions, Nitze identified what he thought to be the fifty principal issues of fact in the debate. He wrote each issue on a three-by-five index card. Then he talked to all the scientific experts at all the different agencies, listened to their conflicting views, and made up his mind on what the balance of evidence indicated to be the truth. He wrote down his conclusions on the other side of the card.

When he had completed all fifty cards, he sent them to all the relevant agencies and solicited comments. The results were striking. Despite months of bickering, there turned out to be few substantive disagreements. Fueling the battles over factual data had been a lack of clarity rather than intractable divisions of opinion. With a common frame of reference now established, debate over the test ban flowed more smoothly.

The administration's review of test ban policy occurred in late July 1962. Consisting of four consecutive meetings of the Committee of Principals, three of which the president attended, the review revived planning for a comprehensive test ban. At the first meeting a new seismic detection system called VELA was described by Glenn Seaborg, chairman of the Atomic Energy Commission. VELA could detect nuclear explosions as small as 15 kilotons. The system would make possible a cut in Soviet-based control posts and reduce the number of on-site inspections needed.

McNamara was encouraged by the breakthrough and told the group that he was still very much in favor of a comprehensive test ban. Dean Rusk was less optimistic. What was the point of talking about the number of on-site inspections, he asked, when it was clear that the Soviet Union would tolerate none? He suggested that the time may have come for the United States to settle for an atmospheric test ban.

Nitze was thinking the same thing. His index card review of test ban data had revealed deep pessimism on the part of the government's technical experts about verifying a comprehensive treaty. The JCS in particular voiced doubts that it could ever support such an accord. Nitze himself was skeptical. "I agreed with General Taylor's claim that the Soviets could conduct 80 percent of the testing they wanted to do without being detected," he said later.[19] Nitze recommended to the committee that the United States offer the Soviets an atmospheric test ban with the understanding that it "would be made comprehensive if and when agreement could be reached on inspection."[20] This move would not kill the dream for a world free of nuclear explosions, only delay it.

Still, even a delay was undesirable. While the security risks of a test ban were high, Nitze believed the foreign policy rewards would be great. At the committee's meeting with Kennedy on July 30, Nitze presented a report on nuclear proliferation that provided a convincing argument for a comprehensive test ban, an argument that reminded the group why it was a dream that shouldn't die. Reading aloud from the paper, Nitze said that within seven to ten years many nations might possess nuclear weapons. Sweden, India, West Germany, Italy, China, and South Africa might all have nuclear arms by the early 1970s. A comprehensive test ban was essential to prevent a world in which nuclear weapons were standard ordnance in military arsenals around the globe. It would not be a final solution—much work would remain to stop proliferation—but a test ban was a necessary first step. And the ban would have to be on *all* nuclear testing. An atmospheric test ban would not stop the spread of nuclear weapons.

These points weighed heavily on President Kennedy. "I see the possibility in the 1970s of the President of the United States having to face a world in which fifteen or twenty nations may have these weapons," Kennedy said in early 1963. "I regard that as the greatest possible danger."[21] The result of the administration's internal review was a renewed commitment to a comprehensive test ban. At a press conference on August 1, Kennedy announced that the United States was prepared to accept a smaller number of control posts. He hoped this concession would move the talks forward.

Despite a new determination to push on, however, the pessimism expressed by Dean Rusk had begun to take hold in the administration. Many officials suspected that the Soviets would never moderate their position on verification. Many could also see that it might be impossible to get the Joint Chiefs of Staff to support a comprehensive ban. And even if a comprehensive test ban were negotiated, White House aides familiar with the mood on Capitol Hill said there might not be enough Senate votes to ratify it.

By the spring of 1963 hopes for a comprehensive test ban were dead. In Geneva negotiators turned their efforts to negotiating an atmospheric ban, but even this modest goal proved difficult. With the limited treaty nearing completion by the summer, McNamara, Nitze, and McNaughton had to spend long hours in the tank with the chiefs of staff to convince them to back the agreement. Using an anti-arms control argument that would become popular in later years, JCS Chairman Maxwell Taylor told the Senate Foreign Relations Committee that "the most serious reservations" of the chiefs had to do with "the fear of a euphoria in the West which will eventually reduce our vigilance."[22] In exchange for supporting the treaty, the JCS demanded and received the right to step up underground testing and to resume atmospheric testing on short notice. The effect of this deal, wrote one observer, was to turn "an agreement intended to limit nuclear testing into a limited warrant for increasing nuclear testing."[23]

In July 1963 Averell Harriman traveled to Moscow to put the final touches on the Limited Test Ban Treaty. The failure to achieve a comprehensive test ban was a major disappointment for the president, although he hailed the treaty he did get as a "step towards reason."[24] Nitze regarded the treaty as a worthwhile experiment in mutual cooperation. It proved that the United States and the Soviet Union could sit down at a negotiating table and make something happen, however modest. Beyond that Nitze saw little value in the Limited Test Ban Treaty. "When it came to really carrying out the objective of arms control—reducing the risk of war—it really wasn't effective in bearing on that at all," he said later. Another observer was more blunt: "It wasn't an arms control treaty; it was a public health treaty."

For Nitze, the lessons of the Kennedy years were mixed. The Berlin and Cuban crises seemed to be confirmation that nuclear superiority could bolster American security, and by 1963 he still believed that the United States should maintain a nuclear edge over the Soviet Union. He argued that only by maintaining "superiority of strategic and non-strategic military force can the United States have the optimum opportunity to use its military power short of war to support its foreign policy."[25]

An escalating arms race did not cure Paul Nitze of his infatuation with a larger, more flexible nuclear arsenal. Even when it became clear by 1962 that the United States already had a massive lead over the Soviet Union in strategic striking power, Nitze recommended that the administration push on with a program to build a thousand Minuteman missiles and large numbers of submarine-launched missiles.[26] To Nitze, the benefits of American nuclear superiority outweighed the risks of triggering a dangerous Soviet arms buildup.

And even that negative side effect could now be dealt with.

With arms control now a more plausible, if still imperfect, mechanism for promoting mutual security, Nitze believed that talks with the Soviet Union could help reduce the instability that accompanied the arms race. Even though the test ban negotiations were largely a failure, they proved that a sustained dialogue between the superpowers was possible. By 1963 it was also clear that arms control was destined to become a permanent part of the U.S.-Soviet relationship. To Nitze, the question was no longer whether to pursue arms control; it was how to pursue it most intelligently.

Nitze believed that the guiding motivation behind arms control should be the same as that underlying military policy: to enhance U.S. security. Arms control must not to be viewed as a far-reaching, idealistic attempt to foster U.S.-Soviet detente and bring about world peace. Instead, it should be a limited and pragmatic effort to achieve military goals through nonmilitary means.

Following the completion of the Limited Test Ban Treaty, Nitze was dismayed by the administration's failure to channel the arms control effort into new areas. He thought that the Arms Control and Disarmament Agency wasn't saying anything interesting, and he was disappointed by the thinking in the Pentagon.

Early in the fall of 1963 Nitze found time to put his own ideas in writing. While recovering from a hernia operation, he sat in his hospital bed and began to write. "Nobody had ever thought of bilateral negotiations," Nitze would say later. "Everybody had always thought about negotiations through the U.N. or other multilateral bodies." Nitze claimed that the report he wrote in the hospital, entitled "Considerations Involved in a Separable First Stage Disarmament Agreement" (SFSDA), was "the first paper written in the U.S. government on the subject of bilateral arms control negotiations with the U.S.S.R."[27]

Excited about the idea, Nitze returned to ISA and enlisted Bud Zumwalt's assistance in working out the technical details. Stumped by the question of tactical nuclear weapons, Zumwalt struggled for long hours to smooth out the paper's rough edges. Finally, the paper was ready to be circulated. In October Nitze sent out copies to McNamara, Raymond Garthoff at State, and Adrian Fisher at ACDA.

Months passed and Nitze received no comments from anybody. Finally, Garthoff returned his copy, and then McNamara's came in. The secretary of defense had read the paper with great interest, and the margins were filled with scrawls in his barely legible handwriting. Nitze used the comments to revise the paper and then circulated it back through the bureaucracy.

For twenty-five years the SFSDA paper would remain Nitze's most comprehensive statement on the subject of arms control.[28] In the second great crusade of Nitze's life, the crusade to stabilize the nuclear arms race, this document would be a blueprint akin to NSC 68.

The premise of the paper was that the disarmament effort could benefit both sides, but it was also very much a "zero sum game; what improves the relative position of one side harms the relative position of the other." The challenge of arms control, said Nitze, was to pursue its "non-zero sum aspects," to forge agreements that benefited both sides, while simultaneously improving the strategic position of the west. In its essence, arms control was both a cooperative and a competitive endeavor.

Since neither the United States nor the Soviet Union was prepared to bargain away its security, arms control could only yield gains to each side that were nonthreatening in nature. For the United States the goal of arms control should be "To reduce the size, weight, and likelihood of success of a Soviet strike against the United States and its allies." The best way to achieve this goal was to increase the survivability of strategic arsenals in both nations and reduce the overall megatonnage within those arsenals. As a result of this process, Nitze said, "major instabilities resulting from the psychology of the arms race should diminish. Decreased concern on either side about the survival of its retaliatory force should remove lingering incentives toward, or fears of, premeditated attack against one another." Reducing the danger of a surprise attack would lower the chance that the United States would be engulfed by a nuclear war. Clearly, this would enhance American security.

But this security came at a price.

If the Soviet leadership knew that its arsenal was safe from an American first strike, if they knew that enough weapons would always survive to devastate the United States, then the menacing edge of U.S. nuclear superiority would be lost. And lost with it would be the ability to force the Soviets to back down in future crises. For Nitze, fresh from the traumas of Berlin and Cuba, this was a dubious trade-off. To avoid shearing the United States of all its coercive nuclear potential, Nitze wrote, "Compensations would have to be sought in arrangements either contained in the disarmament treaty or permissible under the treaty. These might involve (1) a full spectrum of deterrence below the strategic level, and/or (2) capabilities for deliberate, selective, controlled response."

In advancing ideas for what a bilateral arms control accord might look like, Nitze's paper was far ahead of its time. It delved into the problems of how to restrict increases in warhead accuracy, how to limit the size of ballistic missiles, and how to insure the survivability of missile-carrying submarines. Nitze also put forward radical views on the subject of verification, arguing that limits on antiballistic missiles, civil defense measures, and intercontinental missiles hidden in silos could all be verified without on-site inspection.

Tackling the difficult question of how conventional forces and short-range nuclear weapons in Europe might fit into the arms control equation, Nitze wrote that these forces had to be limited if the Soviets were to be denied military superiority in Europe. Without an overall military balance between NATO and the Warsaw Pact, strategic nuclear parity would be unacceptable. Nitze thought that bringing about a military balance in Europe would be exceedingly difficult, but that it could be done.

Just as important as achieving mutual security in Europe was the need to deescalate the overall cold war confrontation. Nitze wrote that as long as the Soviets sponsored paramilitary aggression in Vietnam, made Cuba a military client state, and resisted a settlement to the Berlin problem, "no major political detente is foreseeable and therefore significant arms control reductions would be unlikely." Negotiating elaborate arms control accords would require that the United States and the Soviet Union resolve their political problems. Whether this would happen anytime soon remained to be seen.

The SFSDA paper brought together many strands of Paul Nitze's early thoughts on arms control and strategic weapons. The premise of the paper was that a stable strategic balance was integral to U.S. security and that such a balance could be achieved through arms control. But the document was also strewn with Nitze's more hard-line views, the views of NSC 68. It showed that Nitze was not quite ready to forsake the dividends of American nuclear superiority for the stability of strategic parity. He still viewed the Kremlin's international policy as unacceptable and believed that the United States could not truly negotiate with the Soviets until they changed their system. It advocated real arms control, but only after the Soviets had capitulated to America's diplomatic agenda and only if that control allowed for a coercive U.S. nuclear arsenal. In Moscow's view this was hardly a formula for a non-zero sum outcome.

By late 1963 Paul Nitze had gone further than almost anyone else in the U.S. government in arguing that arms control should play an integral role in American defense policy. But exactly how large that role should be was a question that Nitze still could not answer.

CHAPTER 11

His Own Ship

IN MAY 1963 an exhausted Roswell Gilpatric announced that he would leave the Pentagon. The money wasn't good, a war was brewing in Southeast Asia, and Gilpatric wanted out. Nitze was in Great Britain with Kennedy when the news came. "Gilpatric is leaving," the president reportedly said, "and you're my next deputy secretary of defense." Elated, Nitze placed a transatlantic call to Bud Zumwalt and said to get the necessary clearances to accompany him to the Office of the Secretary of Defense.

Because Gilpatric planned to stay on for several months, official Washington had ample time to mull over Nitze's promotion. The reaction was not favorable. Over the past two and a half years, Democratic pundits had winced as an abrasive McNamara alienated power brokers on Capitol Hill. Now they blanched at the thought of placing an equally aloof figure in the Pentagon's number two slot. What Nitze's appointment means, wrote columnists Rowland Evans and Robert Novak, "is that McNamara will be reinforced at precisely those points where he needs no reinforcement."[1]

There were other reasons for discomfort with Nitze. By 1963 his unwillingness to ingratiate himself with the Kennedy crowd had taken its toll. While men like McGeorge Bundy and McNamara became close friends and confidantes of the president, Nitze drifted further from the inner circle.

His hawkish talk during the Cuban missile crisis served to increase this distance, and both Kennedy and his brother Robert had resented Nitze's patronizing sermons against trading away the Jupiter missiles in Turkey. "The President didn't like Paul Nitze very much," said Robert Kennedy in 1965. "He thought he was an effective fellow. . . . But he was rather a harsh figure, and he didn't please the President very much in some of the answers he gave at the time of the Cuban missile crisis. The President wasn't very fond of him."[2]

In another crisis, Nitze's views as deputy secretary would carry more weight, and from such a high-level post he would have more power to fight for those views. Also, with the president favoring rapprochement with the Soviets by 1963, the time was not right to promote one of the government's most vocal hard-liners.

If President Kennedy did have second thoughts about elevating Nitze, he found a convenient escape hatch when trouble erupted in the Department of the Navy. Secretary Fred Korth, a Texas lawyer, was caught in a conflict of interest scandal involving weapons contracts. President Kennedy moved quickly to fire him and hoped to name a replacement simultaneously. He decided that Nitze should fill the post and had McNamara relay the bad news.

Nitze was stunned. He reminded McNamara that he had been promised the deputy secretary job. It was the job he wanted. McNamara told him to go see the president.

Nitze went over to the White House and told Kennedy that he had come into the Pentagon to do policy work. He liked doing policy work and wanted to continue doing policy work. The right place for him was in the post of deputy secretary of defense. Nitze argued further that everybody in Washington would consider his being made secretary of the navy a demotion.

Kennedy laughed. He told Nitze that he didn't understand Washington at all. Nobody would consider the appointment a demotion. That may be true, Nitze replied, but he still didn't want the job.

Kennedy was unmoved. "I promise to you," he said, "that if you take this job—and I want you to take it—I won't keep you in it for more than a year." Nitze reluctantly agreed. When he went home and told Phyllis what happened, she burst into tears.

*   *   *

Being secretary of the navy was a dreary prospect. When Nitze asked Zumwalt what he thought of the job, the navy captain had been predictably upbeat. "It's all the difference in the world; it's your own ship to command, as opposed to a staff job being a second guesser of McNamara." Still, Nitze was depressed. There would be no more NSC meetings, no more Committee of Principals meetings, and few trips to the White House. The days of pondering grand strategy would be over. Essentially an exalted numbers cruncher, the secretary of the navy was concerned with personnel administration, weapons development, procurement, budgets, and congressional relations. The service secretaries were rarely consulted about broader questions of national security policy, and unlike assistant secretaries or deputy secretaries in State and Defense, they were not part of the chain of command that led to the president. At the age of 55, after sixteen years in government, Paul Nitze would have less influence over policy than he had under Acheson more than a decade earlier.

And if this were not depressing enough, Nitze faced a tough confirmation fight in the Senate. Three ultraconservative members of the Armed Services Committee—Barry Goldwater, Strom Thurmond, and Harry Byrd—were determined to kill the nomination. To them and to many other right-wingers, letting a Harvard graduate, Wall Street operator, and Acheson associate into the navy department was sheer insanity. Nitze embodied the supercilious eastern establishment that had "lost" China and refused to turn its back on Alger Hiss. A patrician appeaser in a high-level policy-making slot was bad enough; allowing him to get right inside the guts of the military establishment was out of the question. A service secretary was about as close as a civilian could come to being part of the military, and Congress's residual McCarthyite elements wanted to reserve these posts for the hardest of hard-liners.

In the days following Nitze's nomination, there were doubts about whether he would be confirmed. The descendants of the "primitives" who had demanded "Red" Dean Acheson's resignation a decade earlier now drew a bead on his protégé. Joe D. Waggoner, Jr., the right-wing congressman from Louisana, sent a newsletter concerning Nitze to the president and every senator. "His confirmation," warned Waggoner, "would be a giant step down the road in the appeasement, no win, surrender policy eating away at the security and the defenses of this nation."[3]

There were letters from concerned citizens to both the White House and Senate. A handwritten note to the president from a Chicagoan read: "I am convinced this man [Nitze] harbors strong sentiments to (1) pass control of U.S. arms to the U.N. and (2) disarm the U.S. in the face of growing Soviet might."[4] In a letter to Senator Byrd, the commander-in-chief of the Veterans of Foreign Wars repeated this allegation, writing that Nitze had "proposed we unilaterally hand over the Strategic Air Command and NATO to the U.N. and give the U.N. Assembly ultimate power of decision on the use of these systems."[5]

What both letters were referring to and the incident that would sustain the right's attack on Nitze was a speech he had given at the Asilomar National Strategy Seminar on April 28, 1960. Asked by the chairman of the seminar to say something provocative to stimulate debate, Nitze wrote a speech in which he put forward the proposal that "we multilateralize the command of our retaliatory systems by making SAC a NATO command, and . . . that we inform the United Nations that NATO will turn over ultimate power of decision on the use of these systems to the General Assembly."[6]

Nitze made his stance on the proposition clear five times during this speech by referring to his proposal as a "Grand Fallacy." Less subtle minds, however, had trouble understanding the baiting nature of Nitze's hypothesis, and mistook it for a serious policy proposal by a man with dangerously dovish predilections.

To push through the nomination, McNamara put two aides to work on the problem. Their initial inclination was to take on the three objecting senators publicly. Nitze's record on defense matters was impeccable, and he would surely be vindicated in a public debate. But before triggering a confrontation, McNamara's aides wanted someone to sound out other senators on the committee. Bud Zumwalt was asked to do the job, and although he thought it highly unusual to get involved in partisan politics, he agreed.

Ushered into Senator Henry Jackson's office, Zumwalt was told that the votes to confirm Nitze were there and that it made no sense to stir up the three dissenters. Jackson suggested instead that affidavits be collected from those who could defend Nitze and placed in the record. It seemed that confirmation wouldn't be much of a problem after all.[7]

On the wet and windy morning of November 7, 1963, Nitze took a seat at the witness table in the Armed Services Committee room. In his opening statement he tried to impress the eleven senators with his commitment to a strong defense. "I am a strong believer in the importance of maintaining superiority over the Communist bloc in every element of our military power," he said. "I believe that the United States must maintain its strategic superiority over the U.S.S.R. I believe that the U.S. Navy plays a vital part in the maintainence of that strategic superiority through its invulnerable Polaris submarine missile system and its attack carrier strike forces."[8]

Nitze ridiculed the charge that he favored appeasement. For over a decade he had been making the same hard-line arguments, and to substantiate this claim, Nitze presented numerous excerpts from his speeches and writings. All pointed to what should have been obvious to anyone who knew Paul Nitze: The author of NSC 68 was no appeaser. Still, some members of the committee remained belligerent. Chairman Richard Russell led off the questioning by asking Nitze about his participation in the 1958 Fifth World Order Study Conference of the National Council of Churches and the Asilomar seminar speech. The conference had produced a report critical of U.S. defense policies and had questioned the morality of deterrence. Nitze tried to make it clear that although he had chaired the conference, he had disagreed with the conclusions of the report and had been particularly disturbed by the parts on deterrence. As for the Asilomar speech, Nitze assured the senators that he had no intention of trying to turn SAC over to NATO.

After close questioning, Chairman Russell seemed satisfied that Nitze would be a responsible steward of the navy. Senator Saltonstall was similarly satisfied. Senator Byrd from Virginia, however, had a much harder time distinguishing a dove from a hawk. He also had difficulty distilling the meaning of the Asilomar speech, but suspected the worst. Again and again, his patience at times wearing thin, Nitze explained that he had proposed the internationalization of the U.S. arsenal only to provoke debate among the scholars assembled at the seminar. "This speech," said Nitze, "in part was meant to shock people into a realization of what the requirements of our security were, and what unpalatable alternatives we might have to face if we did not do things, many of which we subsequently have done, to improve our defense posture." Obviously, it would be preposterous to carry out any scheme to multilateralize SAC forces, Nitze said. Byrd remained mystified.

When Senator Jackson's turn came, he sought to bolster Nitze's position by having him explain his participation in the drafting of NSC 68 and the Gaither report. After his questioning, Jackson effusively praised Nitze. "Mr. Chairman, I have known Mr. Nitze for many years. In all of my conversations with him and discussion, and so on, I can say to the committee that he has always taken a hard, tough position in dealing with the enemies of this country. I have personally great faith in his integrity, his honesty, and his tough-minded devotion to this awesome job of national security."

Strom Thurmond, senator from South Carolina, remained unconvinced. "Mr. Chairman, has the witness been sworn?" he drawled pugnaciously before starting his questioning. After Nitze had been sworn—something rarely asked of a presidential nominee—Thurmond cross-examined him for nearly half an hour. It was the severest grilling Nitze ever experienced before a congressional committee. But in the end, the senator could reveal no dark, pacifist secrets that suggested that Nitze would betray the navy or the United States.

On November 29 Paul Nitze finished moving his growing collection of framed photographs and memorabilia through the long Pentagon corridors and into his new office at the Navy Department. With Kennedy's death seven days earlier, the promise of a one-year stint was forgotten. Nitze would stay in his post for almost four years.

As *Navy* magazine later commented, Nitze's appointment not only generated concern among the Thurmonds and Goldwaters of Congress, but also caused anxiety among navy officials: "Frankly, there were immediate misgivings in the ranks. Here was a man, many Navymen felt, who was being sent to accelerate the Navy's indoctrination in Defense Secretary McNamara's management techniques."[9]

Urbane representatives of the eastern establishment were not appreciated in the navy. Many naval officers tended to share the right wing's suspicions of Harvard and Wall Street. Like most military men, they were protective of their territory, obsessed with getting their piece of the budgetary pie and slow to welcome changes in the bureaucratic status quo. McNamara's managerial activism was viewed with contempt and hostility. Navy people did not appreciate having a hotshot corporate executive surrounded by snotty whiz kids trying to change the way things had been done for years.

And now here came Paul Henry Nitze—Harvard '28, former Wall Streeter and Acheson lieutenant, a multimillionaire aristocrat whose chief knowledge of things nautical came from vacationing in Maine's finest yachting waters, a man, moreover, who was considered a major leader of the McNamara revolution. The common wisdom in the Pentagon was that Nitze had spearheaded the whiz kid invasion. While there was some truth to this charge—Nitze had recommended RAND analyst Charles Hitch to McNamara and made ISA a haven for RAND's ideas—he hardly merited the nickname "king of the whiz kids." Nonetheless, the rumors persisted. The patrician lilt in Nitze's voice, his finely tailored suits, and his penchant for smoking a pipe did nothing to offset the impression. Even if some navy people knew that the blame for the whiz kid influx lay elsewhere, it was still obvious to them that Paul Nitze was not a typical secretary of the navy and certainly not a good old boy from Texas like his two immediate predecessors. They saw him as an officious intruder bearing the McNamara banner.

Nitze was aware of the hostility. He had been in the Pentagon long enough to know where his sort were not welcome. When he assumed his new position, Nitze made a special effort to put the navy brass at ease. On his first day in office he sent a letter to all flag and general officers: "I am aware that despite my years of public service, I have much to learn about the organization, the people, and the mechanics of getting things done in the Department of the Navy." In a humble tone he said that his first weeks would be spent getting educated about the business of running the navy. "It is my intention and desire," he concluded, "to have the closest possible relationship with the senior military leadership of the Department. I am looking forward to becoming acquainted with as many of you as possible during the ensuing months and I assure you that you will have my confidence and support."[10]

Paul Nitze had been a keen student of military matters for years, but it was not until he entered the Navy Department that he became truly immersed in the military world. At ISA the majority of the staff had been civilians. Most of his top advisors had been civilians. The big issues he had dealt with were largely political in nature. At the Navy Department the environment was strikingly different. Zumwalt had been right when he said "it's your own ship." Nearly as old as the Republic, the Navy Department had its own traditions and legends, heroes and villains. Despite its headquarters in the Pentagon, the department was fiercely autonomous. Its high officials bonded closely with their fellow Annapolis alumni. They chafed under civilian control. They viewed the other services with suspicion and militantly promoted the navy way of war. While the secretary of the navy and the chief of naval operations (CNO) answered to higher authorities, they had remarkable independence and almost absolute control over their own realm.

The independence of the Navy Department made the secretary's job intimidating, but it also made it tolerable and, in time, enjoyable. Because Nitze now had his own ship, he had to master all the details of its operation. It was an intellectual and managerial challenge unlike any he had faced before. It was a challenge, however, that Nitze had spent his entire career preparing for. Settling into his new office, he felt instantly at home in the department's technocratic milieu. If Nitze had been dependent on numbers in the past, he became totally absorbed by them now. Numbers and statistics, on an almost mind-boggling scale, dominated the technical world of weapons procurement, personnel policy, and budget requests.

And if Nitze was accustomed to proffering advice on tough decisions, he would now be making those hard choices himself. He had been in his post for less than two weeks when the first major decision came hurtling his way.

As the Pentagon prepared its annual budget request to Congress, quarrelsome debate arose over whether the navy would get funds for a new aircraft carrier. In his quest for a more cost-effective military, McNamara had long been skeptical of new carriers. But by late 1963 the navy's clamor for a larger carrier force could no longer be ignored and there was evidence that McNamara was softening his stand. At the urging of navy officials, Nitze brought the navy's case to the defense secretary, arguing at their regular Friday meetings that another carrier was needed immediately. Finally, McNamara agreed to the request. But he told Nitze that he wanted the carrier to be nuclear, and since nuclear carriers were more expensive than those powered by fossil fuels, funding would have to be delayed for another year.

Nitze took McNamara's offer back to the uniformed navy officials. They didn't buy it. In their view McNamara was using the promise of a nuclear carrier to stall the carrier advocates until he could amass enough bureaucratic power to crush them outright. In meetings with Nitze the navy officials said that they would prefer to have funding for a fossil-fueled carrier immediately rather than a nuclear one the following year.

Nitze accepted their arguments. He returned to McNamara and, in a move that made a decidedly good first impression on his new colleagues, won approval for the fossil-fueled ship.

On January 9, 1964, top navy officials gathered in the department's Pentagon auditorium to hear Nitze's inaugural speech as secretary.

Nitze knew that if his tenure was to go smoothly, he had to convince the skeptics in the audience of his sincerity and intelligence. Through December he had spent long hours poring over the details of U.S. naval activities and it paid off. When he went before the Navy brass that winter day he sounded surprisingly coherent.

The theme of the speech was developments in U.S. naval policy, and it reflected some of Nitze's long-standing concerns. Since the Truman era, Nitze had advocated the buildup of military might that could be used by a president without igniting a nuclear war. Now, as navy secretary, he vowed to push for "politically usable seapower." In his view there was no better instrument of limited war than the aircraft carrier. Capable of being shifted to trouble spots around the world, the carrier could threaten varying levels of military force—from strafing runs by attack aircraft to devastating assaults with tactical nuclear weapons. Its mere presence in a region was a display of tremendous military power. "There is a growing realization," Nitze told his audience, "that the political invulnerability of attack carrier forces is vital to our success in supporting foreign policy in all phases of peace and war." As secretary of the navy, Nitze promised to keep the carrier force strong.

A less glamorous but equally important part of a limited-war arsenal was antisubmarine warfare (ASW) forces. Nitze's interest in ASW went back to contingency planning during the Berlin crisis. While investigating McNamara's suggestion that the United States be prepared to blockade the Soviet Union, Nitze and his staff discovered that U.S. naval forces would not be able to execute such a mission. The problem, in great part, had been with U.S. submarine and antisubmarine forces. Many of the torpedoes had proved worthless and the sonar systems critical for waging antisubmarine warfare were inadequate and unreliable. As a result, Nitze recalled, "there was no way we could blockade the Soviet Union." As secretary of the navy, Nitze vowed to change this. "Here is an aspect of seapower peculiarly adapted to the concept of usable power," he said.[11]

Nitze's speech was a success. And as the navy saw that he was not going to launch a zealous campaign to press the McNamara reform agenda, it slowly became more comfortable with its new secretary. Nitze's most valuable ally during this delicate time was the Vice-chief of Naval Operations, Claude V. Ricketts. A solid and dignified man steeped in navy tradition, Admiral Ricketts came to the conclusion that Nitze was sincere and urged the other admirals to give the new secretary a chance, saying that Nitze was a man they could work with. By the time he died of a sudden heart attack in July 1964, Rickettts had opened a lot of minds. Slowly, the navy brass began to see that Paul Nitze was not all that bad.

Slowly, also, Nitze began to see that his new job was better than expected. Naval strategy turned out to be fascinating. It was far more concrete than nuclear strategy because naval forces were more likely to be employed in a limited-war situation. "When one looks at what is most probable," Nitze said in 1965, "I . . . think it more likely that there will be conflicts at a lower level than all-out nuclear war."[12] Because of the perils and destructiveness of a war on land, Nitze felt that a future conflict between the superpowers might be confined, at least initially, to the seas. He believed that the navy should place a "particular emphasis on readiness to fight the kinds of war most likely to occur."[13]

Even without actual war, American and Soviet naval forces were constantly in contact. In the uneasy standoff of perpetual cold war, the U.S. Navy was forever in motion, tracking enemy submarines, shadowing Soviet destroyers, and playing naval war games. United States naval forces were not like ICBMs which would languish in dark silos until Armageddon. Nor were they like the mass of armaments that sat in West Germany waiting for Soviet tanks to come rumbling through the mist of an apocalyptic dawn. Naval forces were different in a way that appealed intensely to Paul Nitze: They were usable.

Ever since the late 1940s Nitze had been disturbed by America's overreliance on nuclear weapons. Like others in the Pentagon, he had advocated spending more money on limited-war forces. Yet even though Nitze had long been a fierce partisan in the quest to make American military forces more usable, his contact with the issue had always been theoretical. At ISA Nitze sought to implement the ideology of NSC 68 through broad and sweeping strokes. At the Navy Department he concentrated on the details.

Used creatively, the potential striking power of naval forces was nearly limitless. As Nitze pointed out to the Senate Armed Services Committee during his maiden testimony as secretary, "Excluding the Soviet Union, nearly 90 percent of the remaining area of the world lies within 500 miles of sea coasts. This geographic fact of life, in combination with the carrier's progressively improving limited war effectiveness, suggests logically that sea based air power will assume greater significance in the future."[14] Mobile naval forces offered almost instant military options for U.S. policy makers faced with a crisis almost anywhere on the globe. The carrier-launched air strikes against North Vietnam in late 1964 were an example of this. The events in Southeast Asia, said Nitze in early 1965, "produced positive evidence of the immediate readiness, usable capabilities and controllable combat potential now available in the Navy-Marine Corps team."[15] Nitze believed that the possibilities for using the navy as an interventionary force in the third world had not been fully realized in the past. He was now determined to turn the navy into a highly flexible and coercive instrument of U.S. foreign policy.

Before he could pursue any of his dreams, Nitze had to get a handle on his new job. In winding up his speech to the navy's top Pentagon officials, he commented, "You who are manning the ramparts of one of the great battle areas in the world today—the Washington bureaucracy—are the ones who must help me both to learn and act."[16] As he settled into the Navy Department, that help would come, but Nitze would also encounter opposition to his rule.

Nitze's first priority was to cultivate close ties with Chief of Naval Operations David L. McDonald. In many ways the CNO has more power over the navy than the secretary. He is in charge of day-to-day naval operations and represents the navy on the Joint Chiefs of Staff. He is also in touch with the uniformed men. To accomplish anything in the Navy Department, one has to go through the CNO. Bud Zumwalt, who followed Nitze to the Navy as his executive officer, stressed this from the beginning and advised Nitze to form a "duumvirate" with McDonald.

Admiral McDonald was a southerner and a consummate navy man. He harbored a deep distrust of the political establishment and considered the *Washington Post* akin to *Pravda*. McDonald had close ties with the conservative elements in the Senate that had sought to torpedo Nitze's nomination, and if he wanted to, the Admiral could make Nitze's life unbearable.

Early on Nitze moved McDonald's office next door to his own and began constantly soliciting his advice, talking to him almost hourly. Nitze tried to convey to the admiral—or Dave as he soon called him— that he was not McNamara's haughty commissar, but a hard-working and willing student of naval affairs who was genuinely interested in building a better navy. His efforts yielded results. By 1965 Nitze would comment that he and McDonald worked "hand in glove." Zumwalt— later CNO himself—called their relationship the "best Secretary of the Navy/CNO partnership in history."

Nitze impressed McDonald and the other admirals with his avid interest in naval affairs. The number of issues to be mastered, from global strategy to personnel policy, was huge. In 1964 the navy had 650,000 uniformed personnel, 190,000 marines, and hundreds of thousands of civilians working in laboratories and naval shipyards. Its annual budget was $15 billion to $20 billion. Paper flowed into the top office in an unending deluge. As he had done at ISA, Nitze tried to immerse himself in seminal questions and delegate much of the drudgery to his subordinates.

Antisubmarine warfare was Nitze's first focus. Unlike massive aircraft carriers and sleek destroyers, the ASW hardware was unglamorous, and the job of tracking submarines could be frustrating and tedious. During much of the postwar period the navy had been lax in its antisubmarine warfare effort. Nitze was determined to change that. He believed the sea would be a decisive theater of battle in any war with the Soviet Union because the United States would have to supply Europe over the sea lanes of the North Atlantic. It would be decisive also because the United States might seek to bleed Moscow through a blockade of Russian ports. To control the course of World War III, the United States had to control the seas. Yet, Nitze stressed, with an estimated three hundred subs, the "Soviet submarine fleet constitutes the major threat to such control."[17]

In the spring of 1964 Nitze had lunch with Admiral Page Smith, commander of the Atlantic fleet, in Norfolk, Virginia. Smith was deeply disturbed by the vulnerability of his ships to Soviet submarines. The admiral told Nitze that he wanted to have a fighting fleet, but what he commanded instead was "just a goddamn bunch of yachts." Smith explained that the SQS-26 sonars on his ships were perpetually malfunctioning and that without this key submarine-detecting instrument, the fleet was at the mercy of Soviet subs. During a trip to the Sixth Fleet in the Mediterranean, Nitze heard similar complaints. "The Soviets could have made hash out of our fleets," he said later. "We were sitting ducks."

Navy bureaucrats at the Pentagon saw things differently. "They really didn't believe in their gut that we would ever fight the Soviet Union," recalled Zumwalt. And when they did worry about war with the Soviets, navy brass reasoned that if the United States had a strong carrier force that could pummel Soviet land targets and Soviet ships, Soviet subs wouldn't dare raise the stakes of a war at sea. Nitze's ASW crusade would mean less money for the force these officials wanted, and in the daily infighting over budget requests, navy officials resisted increases for ASW. There was indifference to the program among those in a position to push it.

Nitze's response was to appoint an ASW manager and an ASW "czar" in the spring of 1964. The manager, Rear Admiral Karaberis, had the job of overseeing the navy's antisubmarine research, development, and procurement programs. The czar, Vice Admiral Martell, was given full authority to coordinate the entire ASW program. As Nitze said, "Admiral Martell is Mr. ASW."[18]

With his task forces in place, Nitze's ASW crusade swung into high gear. One of his first moves was to add to the navy's understanding of the sea. He ordered oceanographic studies of the circulation of ocean currents, the nature of underwater acoustics, and the landscape of the ocean's bottom. Nitze wanted the navy to be intimately familiar with the battlefield of the future. And to find the enemy on that murky battlefield, Nitze ordered an overhaul of the SQS-26 sonars.

Of course, locating enemy submarines was of little use if they could not then be destroyed. Quiet and maneuverable, submarines were elusive targets; pinpointing their location was not enough to assure a kill. They could suddenly dive or rise, slow down or speed up. To destroy a submarine one had to predict its course and either hit it with a torpedo or detonate a charge close enough to disable it. But torpedoes were complicated and cantankerous weapons. And the navy's main torpedo, the Mark 43, was ill suited to the ASW mission, Nitze felt. One of his early projects was to find a new torpedo.[19]

During the first part of 1964 Nitze made detailed, personal reviews of the principal ASW weapons systems. He studied their shortcomings and the managerial and technical obstacles to making the antisubmarine effort succeed. It was difficult terrain, but Nitze had mastered equally arcane matters while working on the Strategic Bombing Survey and the European Recovery Plan. He knew the homework would pay off. Long ago, Nitze had realized that most bureaucratic battles were won not by having the secretary of whatever on one's side in a tense interagency meeting but by being better prepared and more informed in the day-to-day wrangling over the details of policy. In the mid 1960s, Paul Nitze came to know as much about the minutiae of antisubmarine warfare as some of the navy's experts on the subject. And when Nitze left the Navy Department in 1967, antisubmarine warfare forces were an important part of America's naval fleet.

Inevitably, Nitze's work on ASW led him into broader issues of naval warfare. In his view the U.S. Navy was ill prepared for sustained conventional combat with the Soviet Union. The common wisdom in the navy held that war between the superpowers, if it ever came at all, would be a spasmodic affair resulting in nuclear annihilation. Nitze moved to alter navy thinking by initiating a comprehensive "War at Sea" project. Its premise was that the United States might respond to limited Soviet aggression by trying to bottle up the Soviet navy through a blockade. The result of such an action, Nitze thought, would be a drawn-out conflict at sea. Neither side would rationally want to escalate in Europe and risk nuclear strikes against its homeland, yet both would seek military advantages. Attacking the other's naval forces would be the most logical way to hurt the enemy but not risk blowing up the world. "War at sea," commented Nitze, "can be bitter and grim but it seldom results in lasting harm to real estate."[20]

Nitze envisioned ASW forces as playing a critical role. In outlining his limited-war strategy at the Naval War College, Nitze said that the Soviet submarine forces could be used to devastating effect against both ships enforcing a blockade of the Soviet Union and Allied merchant ships supplying NATO. However, the submarine threat could be mitigated if Allied forces had the ability to mine and patrol key straits that Soviet subs traversed. By squeezing these chokepoints, NATO naval forces could produce "very great attrition upon enemy submarines in a limited war at sea," Nitze said.[21] That attrition could cripple the Soviet navy and leave the United States in total control of the seas.

Looking beyond the superpower confrontation, Nitze pressed for U.S. capability to put ashore two marine divisions anywhere in the world by the early 1970s. Such a formidable array of usable military might would have awesome coercive potential. Third-world threats to U.S. interests, he thought, could be resolved by just threatening the use of force. And if that didn't work, there were a host of steps short of actual war—such as harassment, surveillance, blockade, and interdiction—that could be taken in a confrontation with a smaller nation.

Nitze's ideas for enhancing the navy's limited-war capabilities were received enthusiastically in the Pentagon. McNamara incorporated the concepts into his annual strategy statements and backed up Nitze's requests for the funds needed to implement his ideas.

In NSC 68 Paul Nitze had called for a U.S. promise to defend anticommunist states anywhere and everywhere. As navy secretary he lobbied for the military hardware to carry out that promise.

As much as Nitze preferred to concentrate on strategy, he was soon drawn into management questions. The most pressing of these concerned personnel. In the mid 1960s life for people in the United States Navy was trying and unpleasant. The pay was low, the housing dismal, and the opportunities for advancement small. In 1964 the resignation rate among officers was twice what it had been in 1963, and retention of enlisted men was also dropping. For a service so dependent upon technical expertise, this exodus was devastating.

The root of this problem was that huge sums of money were being spent on sexy new weapons systems, while people were neglected.[22] Unless the navy became more attractive, it would never compete against the civilian world. "Many segments of industry," Nitze noted, ". . . more than match the salary, fringe benefits, and retirement benefits of a military career without demanding long hours and unpaid overtime, family separations or personal hazards."[23] To solve this problem, Nitze established and chaired a Personnel Policy Board in December 1964.

Nitze's work on personnel issues was eye opening. Through most of his life, Paul Nitze traveled in a rarefied world of wealth and power. He had gone from Hotchkiss to Harvard to Wall Street to Washington's Northwest, without ever seeing how most of America lived. He did not see Washington's vast slums from the government car that chauffeured him to work. In his drives to the farm or to Maine he may have passed through small towns that existed on the brink of poverty, but he was not aware of the daily lives of the people in these towns. Nitze had seen the insides of thousands of plush homes and hotels around the world, but he had never seen the way millions of Americans lived. Until he became secretary of the navy.

In many trips to U.S. naval installations Nitze finally came into contact with the trials of lower middle-class life. Peering into the world of the enlisted man, he was angered by what he found. He was appalled to learn, for example, that eleven thousand navy men were separated from their families for lack of housing.[24] The families that did have housing were not much better off, living in quarters constructed in the 1940s. "Those buildings were considered flimsy and austere by personnel of World War II," Nitze pointed out. "In 1965, they are deplorable."[25]

Navy people also had to cope with low pay, long work hours, and long family separations. All were taking a toll. The divorce rate among navy people was skyrocketing. There were "morale problems and drug problems," recalled Nitze's assistant John Rhinelander. There was also a major recruitment problem. "You had problems in the kind of people you were getting. You were getting a less educated, poorly trained person." And for the person who did perform well, the archaic promotion system offered few rewards.

To make a navy career bearable, Nitze's Personnel Policy Board instituted a series of changes. It offered spot promotions to promising junior officers, modernized the personnel data management system, won approval for a 5 percent base pay increase for all personnel, and instituted a system of reenlistment bonuses. It also initiated a five-year program to accelerate navy housing projects and to insure that the housing was inhabitable. Finally, in an effort that *Navy* magazine praised as "persistent and persuasive," Nitze managed to win congressional approval for hazardous duty pay.

The result of these efforts was an increased retention rate and higher morale. The result, also, was to establish Paul Nitze's reputation as the best navy secretary in years. "He had enormous respect by the time he left," remembered Rhinelander. "They [the navy men] came to accept him and they came to admire him." *Navy* magazine may have still ridiculed the whiz kids in its editorials, but it no longer raised questions about the man whom it had once called the "king of the whiz kids." "Paul Nitze has accomplished much for the United States Navy and Marine Corps," the magazine said in 1966.[26]

The affection was mutual. For Nitze the years as secretary of the navy were surprisingly rewarding. Even for an accomplished problem solver like Nitze, it was an unusually satisfying time. As director of the Policy Planning Staff, he had won acceptance for the broad policy proposals contained in NSC 68. As head of ISA, he had made critical contributions to resolving the crises in Berlin and Cuba and to the test ban negotiations. But in running the navy, Paul Nitze was in control of his own bureaucracy. The navy's victories were his victories, and because of that, those victories were some of most rewarding of his career.

Despite his successes, there were problems in the navy that even a master bureaucrat like Nitze could not solve. Admiral Hyman G. Rickover was one such problem. Like J. Edgar Hoover, Rickover was a public servant so deeply entrenched in the government and so obdurate that no president could remove him or control him. Like Hoover, also, Rickover was a legend in his own time. Joining the navy in 1918, Rickover had gone on to become a pioneer in naval nuclear propulsion. His efforts as "father of the nuclear navy" earned him a lasting place in navy lore. By 1963, however, many in the navy thought the time had come for the old admiral to retire. In early 1962 Rickover had reached mandatory retirement age, but had used his powerful connections in Congress to get a two-year active duty extension. By February 1964 Rickover would be 64 years old and legally required to give up his job. Nitze was determined that this should happen. But by taking advantage of a loophole in the retirement rules, Rickover again managed to get an extension. Throughout Nitze's tenure as secretary, the admiral would prove a troublesome adversary, especially with his dogged insistence on building expensive nuclear-propelled naval vessels at a time when McNamara was seeking a more cost-effective mix of nuclear and nonnuclear vessels.

Because attempts to retire Rickover elicited loud protests from his many admirers, Nitze saved his most determined effort to remove the admiral until his last few weeks in office. Nitze sought the assistance of President Johnson himself, visiting him at the White House and describing the situation in detail. Johnson totally agreed with the idea of getting rid of Rickover, but feared the political fallout. Firing an old man with a grand reputation was not an appealing prospect. Johnson told Nitze first to get the approval of the Joint Committee on Atomic Energy. "Tell them I'm all for this," said the president.[27]

With Johnson behind him, Nitze sought out Senator John O. Pastore, chairman of the joint committee. Pastore also agreed, saying, "I've thought for a long time that Rick's outlived his usefulness." Still, Pastore wanted to think about the issue for a few days and talk to some of the other committee members. When Nitze called him back, Pastore suggested he come up to Capitol Hill. Upon entering Pastore's office, Nitze found several prestigious members of the Committee. Seated among them was Hyman Rickover.

"I understand that you are trying to get me fired," Rickover said. Nitze was ambushed, and realizing that the hunter had become the prey, he retreated.

"Everybody agrees," Senator Jackson told Nitze, "that at some time Rickover might be relieved—but that time has not come yet."[28] Rickover remained in the navy for another decade and a half. Secretaries of the navy could come and go, and even a few might be as determined as Nitze, but some things would never change.

By the spring of 1967, Cyrus Vance was ready to leave the position of deputy secretary of defense to return to private life. A bad back now caused him so much pain that when Nitze met with Vance, he often conducted their meetings from a cot in his office. Vance planned to return to his law practice by midsummer.

For the third time in seven years, the Pentagon's number two slot was open. Curiously, Nitze did not move aggressively to secure what was rightfully his. He was part of a generation that waited to be called rather than openly maneuver for a post. Some of Nitze's friends, however, were from a different generation. "When I learned that Cy Vance was getting ready to leave," recalled Bud Zumwalt, "I went to Paul

Nitze and said, "Look, the president has promised you the deputy secretary's job twice . . . I think you ought to get in there and make it known that you want it." Nitze finally did.

By now more secure, and having warmed to Nitze a bit, McNamara agreed.

On June 30, 1967, Nitze left the navy post and moved over to the Office of the Secretary of Defense. In a final memorandum to the Navy Department's officers, he wrote: "I look upon my association with the Navy and Marine Corps with appreciation and a sense of privilege. . . . You have my thanks for the profitable experience of the past three years."[29] In 1963 Phyllis had cried when Nitze took the navy job; now she cried when he left it.

Three and a half years after being torn from the world of policy making, Nitze's internal Pentagon exile had come to an end. The navy job may have been more of a diversion than expected, but Nitze never forgot where the action was. In moving to the OSD, he entered the nerve center of the Pentagon. Once again he would be wielding real influence. Again, he would sit in the inner circle. But Nitze also knew that in moving to this new post, he was moving to one of the hottest spots in the government, for halfway around the world in a country most Americans could not even locate on a map, the United States was fighting a losing war.

CHAPTER 12

Debacle
in Southeast Asia

VIETNAM. By 1967 the conflict in that tortured and divided land had come to consume the lives of Washington's national security managers. When Nitze became deputy secretary of defense, nearly half a million American troops were bogged down in an endless battle against an elusive enemy. Over ten thousand miles away from Washington, Vietnam was an unlikely place for the United States to commit its prestige and national treasure to a war of attrition. It boasted no natural resources of particular value, shared few traditions with the west, and was not of overriding strategic importance to the United States. Politically, it would be difficult to envision a more unstable ally than the corrupt and authoritarian Saigon regime. Geographically, there were few places less hospitable to Americans than the steaming jungles of Southeast Asia. Culturally, the peoples of Vietnam and the United States couldn't have been more dissimilar.

Yet beginning under Eisenhower, the United States had propped up the prowestern government of Ngo Dinh Diem with military and economic assistance. Despised by many in South Vietnam for his repressive policies, tolerance of corruption, and deceptive land reform programs, Diem ruled with little popular support. By late 1961 a communist insurgency—the National Liberation Front (NLF), or Vietcong—controlled almost half the country. The insurgency was backed by Ho Chi Minh, leader of North Vietnam. The Kennedy administration's response to NLF gains in South Vietnam was to step up military involvement. By the time of John F. Kennedy's death in November 1963, seventeen thousand U.S. military "advisors" were fighting the Viet Cong.

As head of ISA, Nitze did not view Vietnam as a priority issue and turned the matter over to Bill Bundy. When General Maxwell Taylor and Walt Rostow traveled to Southeast Asia on a 1961 fact-finding mission, Bundy was involved in the policy review that followed and accompanied McNamara to the critical Honolulu meeting in December that resulted in an increased U.S. commitment to Diem's regime. "I became in a sense the honcho of that policy for Secretary McNamara," Bundy recalled, "that is, all the things that were supplied under it, the additional military aid, the equipment for the strategic hamlet program, were all funneled through my office."[1]

Even as Nitze's deputy and ISA became enmeshed in the war, he remained aloof, concentrating his energies on Berlin, Cuba, and the test ban negotiations. If Bill Bundy could manage ISA's role by himself, and he clearly could, Nitze saw no reason to spend his time on the issue. When Roswell Gilpatric formed the first administration task force on Vietnam, Nitze did not join it. Nitze "just didn't figure" in the policy-making process regarding Vietnam, Gilpatric recalled.

But while Nitze didn't focus on Vietnam, he did have views on the matter, very strong views. When Taylor and Rostow returned from their mission, Nitze strongly opposed their recommendation that the United States dispatch two divisions to South Vietnam. He labored hard to persuade McNamara and Rusk that sending troops "wouldn't be decisive, it would just get our tit in the wringer." Bill Bundy also argued against troops. "We all agreed that the Taylor-Rostow force recommendation didn't make any sense," he said later. At a tense interagency meeting at the State Department, Nitze vigorously argued this point, and for the moment his side prevailed; only "advisors" were sent.

Nitze opposed the idea of committing troops because he appreciated something that most of his colleagues did not: A western power could not determine the future of Vietnam. When Robert McNamara was a mid-level executive in Detroit and Walt Rostow was a professor of economic history at MIT, Nitze had closely followed France's bid to retain control of Vietnam from his post in the State Department. Even then Nitze saw that it was a no-win situation for the United States. "To support Ho," he later wrote, "was to support the transfer of the Indo-chinese people from colonialism to Communist tyranny. To support the French uncritically was to support an effort bound to fail in the face of forces confronting it."[2]

After the debacle at Dien Bien Phu and France's withdrawal, Nitze read some of the literature on the French experience. The more he learned about France's war against the Vietminh, the more pessimistic he became about the ability of the United States to shape the destiny of Vietnam. Also, Nitze had absorbed some bitter lessons from Korea about waging a land war in Asia. To supply troops in Korea, the United States had to ship supplies halfway around the world; the North Ko-reans, in contrast, could rely on overland supply lines from China that proved impossible to sever. In Vietnam the situation would be the same.

Had Nitze been promoted to deputy secretary of defense in 1963, he would have been in a strong position to argue against escalating the war. But his transfer to the Department of the Navy left him with scant influence over national policy. When the administration began plan-ning to escalate the war, Nitze counseled restraint. To McNamara, Vance, McNaughton, and others in the Pentagon, he argued that Vietnam was the wrong place to take a stand against communist expansion. Every Thursday afternoon Nitze gathered with Zumwalt and other top aides to discuss his Friday meeting with McNamara, and every week the men debated what Nitze should say about the war. Then, at the meeting alone with McNamara, Nitze tried to highlight the signs of impending disaster. Nitze's line of argument, recalled Zumwalt, was that "undesirable as a communist takeover of the whole of Vietnam surely was, it did not pose an immediate or direct threat to the safety of the United States, nor did we have a treaty, or any other commitment to fight for South Vietnam, that would make a failure to send troops a failure to keep a promise."[3] Nitze also believed that if any forces were to be committed to South Vietnam, they should not be ground troops, but rather sea and air forces used to provide support for the operations of the South Vietnamese army. He realized that without major ground action against North Vietnam, a decisive victory would be unlikely, but such action would probably trigger Chinese or Soviet intervention, result in staggering American casualties, and drain U.S. military strength from other vital areas of the world. Keeping the

Saigon regime afloat was not worth these costs.

McNamara disagreed. So did the president. Step by step, like a gambler trying to regain lost winnings, the United States became more embroiled in the war in Southeast Asia. Following the Gulf of Tonkin incident in August 1964, during which North Vietnamese patrol boats allegedly fired on an American destroyer, U.S. involvement in Vietnam grew rapidly. After a Vietcong mortar attack on the Pleiku air base in early February 1965, the United States initiated Rolling Thunder, a massive bombing operation against North Vietnam. By October 1965 there were 148,000 U.S. ground troops in South Vietnam. For the second time in fifteen years the United States was at war on the Asian mainland.

As secretary of the navy, Nitze was not entirely excluded from decisions surrounding the war. With American naval forces and marine troops bearing the brunt of the early fighting, Nitze was drawn into the policy-making process. He advised McNamara and the president on the forces that the navy needed to prosecute the war. He asked Congress for the funds to build and support those forces. And, in time, Nitze took a keen personal interest in the problems of naval strategy in Vietnam.

He quickly became conversant with the new language invented for the war, with its myriad acronyms and morbid euphemisms. But despite the flood of cables and reports Nitze felt detached from the conflict, and wanted to see for himself what was happening. In mid-June, 1965, he took a one-week trip to South Vietnam to tour navy installations and assess the military situation. It was a disturbing expedition, confirming his worst fears about duplicating France's folly.

From the vantage point of the aircraft carrier *Midway*, which was stationed in the South China Sea off the coast of Vietnam, the war seemed under control. Nitze spent a day on the ship. He inspected the giant bombs that were to be loaded onto planes, listened as young pilots were briefed about their targets in North Vietnam, and watched as the planes roared off the carrier deck. When they returned from their mission, Nitze talked with the exuberant airmen. Still wearing their jumpsuits and parachutes, the pilots described a dogfight in which they had shot down two North Vietnamese MIGs. With such military might and combat expertise, it was hard to believe that the United States would not win the war.

But on the ground, in the rice paddies and jungles of South Vietnam, the situation was strikingly different.

Across the gleaming South China Sea, far from the security of the

U.S. Seventh Fleet, was Chu Lai, a small outpost on the coast. Here, Nitze found American marines attempting to capture enough land on the coast to build an airstrip. Despite sustained efforts and ample firepower, however, the marines could not hold enough of the surrounding jungle to begin their job. The guerrillas in the area were too strong.

From Chu Lai Nitze took a helicopter north to Da Nang, a large port city not far from the North Vietnamese border. The U.S. position here looked even more perilous. The city was under siege by NLF troops, who dominated the surrounding mountains and most of the countryside. The U.S. air base in Da Nang was surrounded by barbed wire and bunkers, and the marines controlled a strip of land around the base only three miles wide on one side and a half mile on the other. In the city itself Vietcong infiltrators were everywhere. Even with reinforcements arriving weekly, it looked doubtful that the marines could secure the area.

From Da Nang, Nitze flew by helicopter to the isolated outpost of Pleiku in the central highlands. Deep in the interior of South Vietnam, Pleiku was surrounded by jungle and NLF guerrillas. Its only source of overland supply from the coast was one long road that passed through territory controlled by the insurgents. It was a military planner's nightmare.

After Pleiku, Nitze traveled to the Mekong delta in the southern part of South Vietnam. This maze of waterways was rife with NLF activity and heavy fighting. Here again, the situation was rapidly deteriorating. The South Vietnamese army was losing two or three battalions a week, and no position was secure from NLF infiltration.

In the capital city of Saigon chaos had become a way of life. The new government of Nguyen Cao Ky, recalled Nitze, was "in very poor shape and had little public support." There was rampant political repression and the economy was in shambles. To Nitze, the situation in South Vietnam seemed akin to that in China during the late 1940s: A dedicated rural communist insurgency with popular support was pushing against a corrupt and unstable government. The parallels with the French experience were even closer. As Nitze commented later, the "whole position in Vietnam looked to me dangerous in the extreme, looked very much like the situation must have appeared to the French in Dien Bien Phu."

As strong as the NLF obviously was, Nitze became suspicious during his trip that U.S. military officials in South Vietnam were exaggerating the size of the insurgent forces—both to justify requests for additional troops and to rationalize the ineffectiveness of the troops already in the field. While staying at the Saigon quarters of General William Westmoreland, the commander of U.S. forces in South Vietnam, Nitze confronted him about the possibility of deception. Westmoreland was incensed. Later he wrote that Nitze's charge "shocked me, both because he made the accusation while a guest and because it seemed inconsistent with his reputation as a man of prudent judgment."[4] Despite Westmoreland's denial, Nitze and many others remained suspicious about the general's estimates of enemy strength for the duration of the war.

Upon returning to Washington, Nitze went to see McNamara. The war was almost lost, he said. Short of "an absolutely immense effort," Nitze saw no hope of of saving the Saigon government. Even if the president went all out and sent the additional 200,000 troops that many in the Pentagon were recommending, Nitze doubted a communist victory could be prevented.[5] McNamara, who was the chief architect of the U.S. intervention, responded to Nitze's report by drawing his views out to their logical conclusion.

Was Nitze recommending that the United States withdraw from Vietnam? he asked.

Nitze replied that he was. At the very least, he said, the United States should not send the 200,000 troops. "I don't think we ought to do that unless we are prepared to go much further and I don't think that even if we go much further this would be sound," Nitze recalled saying.

McNamara then asked what would happen if the United States withdrew from Vietnam. Did Nitze think the communists would test us someplace else?

Nitze said they probably would.

Can you predict where? pressed McNamara.

Nitze said he couldn't.

If that were true, continued McNamara, could he be certain that the difficulties of stopping them there won't be greater than the difficulties of stopping them in South Vietnam?

Nitze couldn't be certain.

Well, McNamara concluded, "you don't really offer us an alternative."

At that point, recalled Nitze, "I could see McNamara's mind shut off. I could always tell when McNamara had gotten bored with a given discussion because he felt he had totally defeated the person talking to him and there wasn't any point in carrying on the discussion further."

The great irony, of course, was that Nitze had been defeated by his own ideology. Had McNamara been inclined, he could have quoted from NSC 68 to back up his argument. In that document a younger Paul Nitze had written that "a defeat of free institutions anywhere is a defeat everywhere." He had emphasized that perception in the Cold War was of paramount importance, and that a setback for U.S. interests, even if strategically insignificant, could shatter the morale of the free world.

The pioneers of the New Frontier may have constructed the disaster in Southeast Asia, but it was Paul Nitze who helped lay the foundation.

The U.S. intervention in South Vietnam was a classic application of NSC 68's logic. By itself the nation was of no great importance to the United States. Allow the communist insurgency to triumph, however, and NSC 68 dictated that U.S. credibility would decline worldwide. As Nitze himself said in early 1966, "The entire world is using it [Vietnam] as a gauge of our ability to resist so-called wars of national liberation."[6] Having been well schooled in cold war dogma during his early years at the Pentagon, this was Robert McNamara's fervently held belief in 1965. And as long as Nitze embraced the ideology on which this belief was based, his arguments against the war could be effortlessly cut to shreds.

As a veteran bureaucrat, Nitze knew when further opposition to a course of action was futile. Moreover, as a public servant who championed loyalty to the president, he usually fell into line once a policy became inevitable. At a critical meeting in July 1965 with President Johnson and the Joint Chiefs of Staff, Nitze suppressed his uneasiness over the war and supported McNamara's position. "We have two alternatives, Mr. President," Nitze said. "Support the Vietnamese throughout their country or stick to the secure positions we do have. We need to make it clear to the populace that we are on their side. Then gradually turn the tide of losses by the ARVN [Army of the Republic of Vietnam] at certain points."

"What are our chances of success?" asked Johnson.

"If we want to turn the tide, by putting in more men it would be about sixty-forty," Nitze replied. "If we gave Westmoreland all he asked for, what are our chances? I don't agree that the North Vietnamese and China won't come in. Expand the area we could maintain. In the Philippines and Greece it was shown that guerrillas can lose."

"Would you send in more forces than Westmoreland requests?" the president asked.

"Yes, sir. It depends on how quickly the—"

"How many?" interjected Johnson. "Two hundred thousand instead of 100,000?"

"We need another 100,000 by January," replied Nitze.

"Can you do that?" asked Johnson.

"Yes, sir," said Nitze.[7]

By early fall 1965 President Johnson agreed to send an additional 230,000 troops to South Vietnam over a one-year period. By the end of 1966 there would be some 385,000 U.S. troops in Southeast Asia. Initially, the United States had sent troops to aid Saigon's fight; now it took over the war entirely.

At the Department of the Navy, Nitze gave up attempts to change policy and plunged into the job of implementing it. Within a year he would be deeply involved in the management of navy operations in North and South Vietnam. Privately Nitze remained skeptical about the prospects for victory, but publicly he joined the chorus of administration voices who promoted the political and military thinking that fueled an escalating U.S. commitment.

Ever since the 1950s Nitze had called for the use of limited-war forces to oppose nationalist and communist advances in the third world. Under Kennedy he had endorsed the new emphasis on counterinsurgency and embraced the black and white vision of third-world conflicts that underpinned that policy. "The Communists," he said in 1961, "are . . . using political pressure and subversion to capture the minds of men and to extend their control of other nations from within as well as by the pressures from without."[8] To counter this worldwide movement, Nitze had strongly backed U.S. assistance to the third world during his years at ISA. Like so many others of the time, he believed that the United States could win the political struggle for the "hearts and minds" of those emerging from the bonds of colonialism. In the same way America had won the Cold War in Europe, it could triumph on this new battlefield.

Predictably, it was in the military realm where Nitze's faith was strongest. Early in his tenure as secretary of the navy, Nitze pressed for the acquisition of large interventionary forces such as aircraft carriers and amphibious landing equipment. Following the Tonkin Gulf incident, it was precisely these forces that swung into action. Nitze may have learned the lessons of the French experience better than

most, but with the war heating up, he seemed to forget them. Like
the generals in Paris who had failed to comprehend the strength and
commitment of the Vietminh, Nitze came to believe that the creative application of American military power could weaken and even
defeat the Vietcong.

In 1965 Nitze began putting together an ambitious plan that he
hoped would help strangle the insurgency. During his visit to Vietnam
he had been alarmed by the military situation in the Mekong delta.
Lying just south of Saigon, the delta was of critical significance, but
controlling the delta was a tactical nightmare. Overland travel was
difficult and the region's main lines of transportation were canals and
rivers. With its isolated villages and thick jungles, the watery labyrinth
provided an ideal stronghold for the NLF, and by the early 1960s they
controlled most of the region. This gave the insurgency a major foothold in the south. From bases in the delta, food, arms, and fresh troops
were sent to guerrilla units all over South Vietnam. The food came
from the many farms in the area, and the arms were either made locally
or smuggled in by sea from North Vietnam. The supplies coming out
of the delta were essential to Vietcong operations.

In 1965 the navy began a program, code-named "Market Time," to
stop the flow of arms into the delta region by boat. Within months U.S.
naval forces were tracking hundreds of small junks daily and seizing
ships laden with war materials.

Navy officials soon decided that stopping infiltration was not
enough. Nitze believed that the United States could send forces deep
into the delta, take control of the waterways, and smash the NLF's
delta strongholds. In April 1966 the navy began the "riverine warfare"
program, code-named "Game Warden." Its objective was to patrol
inland channels, conduct visit-and-search operations, and do battle
with the Vietcong. "As the noose is tightened," Nitze predicted in
June, "it will deny them their vital supply system and their main source
of food and manpower."[9] With the delta pacified, victory in the rest
of South Vietnam would come more easily. Game Warden included
230 river patrol boats, a half dozen helicopter detachments, and numerous landing craft.[10]

Like other U.S. military operations in South Vietnam, the navy's
scheme relied on the creation of "free-fire zones" to achieve its objectives. As Nitze explained to a congressional committee in March 1967,
"We think if during the daytime traffic is permitted by the South
Vietnamese and they monitor it, and at night there is a curfew and our
river patrol can then fire at anything that moves on the rivers, this is

having a very important effect down in the delta."[11] No mention was made by Nitze, and no congressman asked, what might happen to innocent Vietnamese who were either unaware of the curfew or unable to get off the river by sundown. By 1967 some two thousand South Vietnamese civilians were being killed each month in free-fire zones.

In early 1966 the cables and field reports to the Pentagon indicated that the military situation in South Vietnam was improving. The presence of over 200,000 U.S. troops was beginning to yield results. Still pessimistic about the possibilities for a decisive victory, Nitze again wanted to see firsthand what was happening. Traveling to the same places he had visited in 1965, Nitze found himself "very much surprised with the progress that the Marines had made." American soldiers still lived with "mud, heat, rain, loneliness and the shock of sudden and violent death," but now it seemed they were winning.[12] The beleaguered outpost of Pleiku had been secured. The air base at Chu Lai had been built. And the mountains surrounding Da Nang, once controlled by the Vietcong, were now in U.S. hands. Monumental problems remained, but it looked like the tide was turning.

The effect of Nitze's second visit was to impress on him the possibility of actually winning the war. In 1965 the picture was one of utter hopelessness, but tens of thousands of U.S. troops had changed that picture. They had saved South Vietnam. "Had we not done in fact what we did do militarily in 1965," Nitze said later, "South Vietnam would simply have been defeated by the communists. That is clear."[13]

The lessons of 1965 seemed so clear, in fact, that Nitze fell prey, if only momentarily, to the illusion that yet more U.S. military power could continue to yield results. "As troop strength increases, in conjunction with Vietnamese and other friendly forces," he told Congress in March 1966, "we can expand Vietnamese government political and military control over key population and food producing areas."[14] And as everybody knew—or thought they knew—controlling the population was the key to victory.

The virtual command over U.S. naval forces during wartime had an almost intoxicating effect on Paul Nitze, who had long been fascinated by military power. At times he sounded as enthusiastic as any admiral in describing how the U.S. Navy was helping to win the war. To a receptive audience at Annapolis Nitze boasted that "Naval river patrols, amphibious operations, carrier air strikes, gunfire support, and anti-infiltration coastal patrols are contributing in ways, many of them quite novel, to the successful accomplishment of military objectives in the Republic of Vietnam."[15] To another audience he recounted how the "destroyer USS *Wilsey* placed some eight rounds of 5-inch shells into the 15-foot mouth of a Vietcong cave," and how "All told, more than 50,000 5-, 6-, and 8-inch shells have been fired on enemy targets."[16]

But if Nitze could now see a bright side to the war, he was haunted by its ugly side. To visit Vietnam was to enter another world. It was a stifling, tropical world where temperatures hovered over 95 degrees week after week and the humidity soaked a person's clothes and twisted the brain. It was an ancient land with a delicate ecosystem and a fragile rural culture. As America's great war machine lumbered and lurched through the countryside, Vietnam was being devastated. The United States was making progress in the war, but at a tremendous cost. Reports of American atrocities in the field were common: Unarmed civilians were regularly shot by infantry patrols; entire villages were needlessly destroyed; U.S. troops and their South Vietnamese allies used torture systematically.

On a larger scale wanton artillery shelling and aerial bombardment was taking a terrible toll on the rural populace. Nitze felt that such tactics created far more enemies than they eliminated. Officers in the field, he learned during his trip, regularly called in artillery barrages against civilian targets.

While touring the southern part of Vietnam, Nitze witnessed an example of this practice firsthand. From a distance he watched as shells rained down on a village where NLF guerrillas were suspected of hiding. An hour later he made his way to a local hospital that was flooded with maimed and bloody children who had been caught in the barrage. "It was the most horrible thing I had ever seen," Nitze later remarked.

Upon his return to Washington, Nitze was asked to give a press conference comparing his impressions on this trip with those of a year earlier. He told the press, "The progress in all phases of our Navy and Marine operations has been much more dramatic than I expected before I left Washington."[17]

As 1966 came to an end, Nitze acknowledged that gains were being made in the war. At times a gleam may have come into his eyes when he talked about how much punishment navy and marine forces were inflicting on the Vietcong. As secretary of the navy, part of Nitze's job was to be a cheerleader. At American naval bases in the United States and around the world Nitze spoke to thousands of enlisted men and officers about the courage of servicemen under fire and about the importance of fighting communism. During misty-eyed ceremonies at the White House and the Pentagon, Nitze stood with President Johnson to pin medals on the chests of heroes and to read accounts of their valor in his soft patrician voice.

But when he wasn't cheering, when he relaxed in private and talked bluntly about the war, Nitze saw defeat in Vietnam. He could see it in America's long-range strategy for victory.

Since the first days that U.S. warplanes had thundered over the DMZ and swept in from the South China Sea to pound North Vietnam, the Johnson administration had contended that the aim of the bombing was to destroy Hanoi's ability to aid the Vietcong and to force Ho Chi Minh to sue for peace. Nitze harbored doubts about this strategy from the beginning, believing it was naive to think the North Vietnamese would come groveling to the negotiating table or capitulate in the face of American firepower. "It didn't seem to me that the Russians and the Chinese could permit that to happen," Nitze said later. "Just as we couldn't permit the South Vietnamese to be overrun by forces from across the border, they couldn't permit it either."[18] Also without foundation, he felt, was the hope that bombing could stem the flow of supplies, either from China into North Vietnam or from there into South Vietnam. This notion was revered as gospel in parts of the Pentagon. The right bombs dropped on the right places would win the war, officials said, unfurling elaborate charts to prove their point.

It was a gospel Nitze had heard before. During his work on the Strategic Bombing Survey, Nitze had listened to military officials exaggerate the efficacy of aerial bombing, with their confident talk of surgical strikes and glib assumptions of waning enemy productivity and morale. He had not been fooled then and he was not fooled now. While Nitze granted that "our attacks in the north have contributed to at least putting a ceiling upon the degree of infiltration in the south," he doubted that bombing could do more than that.[19] It was one of the great myths of the war, and during his final days as secretary Nitze was given a chance to debunk it.

Throughout 1966 Robert McNamara had become increasingly sickened with the ugly business of fighting a war in Vietnam. Despite the Pentagon's elaborate formulas for curbing infiltration, upping interdiction, and raising body counts, it was not clear that victory was possible. And as more troops and supplies crossed the Pacific, McNamara feared that the struggle was a vast waste—a waste of time, energy, money, and human life. Recruited to the Pentagon to cut fat, McNamara had helped orchestrate the greatest boondoggle in American history. His growing dismay over the course of the war took a tremendous emotional toll on McNamara, and it was a strain made greater by his effort to mask his anguish and plod onward.

The only evidence of the defense secretary's growing doubts was that he began asking harder questions. One day in May 1967 he called Nitze and Secretary of the Air Force Harold Brown into his office. McNamara explained that officially neither of them was part of the chain of command that forwarded advice to the president. In terms of the decision-making process, their opinions carried little weight. Nonetheless, he wanted both of them to undertake independently inquiries into the efficacy of bombing to interdict war supplies. McNamara wanted to know what could be done to improve the effectiveness of U.S. bombing and what, in the long run, was the maximum potential of such bombing. The studies were to be undertaken quietly and forwarded to his office when they were completed.

Brown worked with air force analysts and Nitze used the navy staff. Nitze's staff put together models of the various target systems and simulated attacks on them. They found that if the United States concentrated its bombing in specific areas of southern North Vietnam, it could stop more supplies destined for the Vietcong. But the rise in the amount of supplies destroyed would be "by an uncertain increment over an undefinable base."[20]

Nitze's analysts also concluded that if the United States wanted to strangle North Vietnam itself to make Hanoi sue for peace, it would have to cut off foreign imports, and this would be nearly impossible. North Vietnam's long border with China greatly complicated interdiction efforts. Even stopping only the supplies that came in by rail would be a tremendous job. The analysts estimated that it would take four tons of munitions delivered for every ton of supplies destroyed.

As for interdicting war materials that flowed into North Vietnam by sea, Nitze's study found that if the United States mined Haiphong harbor and all of the other main ports, sufficient supplies to sustain the war effort would still get through. An American attempt to cut off imports could make the North Vietnamese people suffer, place a tremendous strain on their government, turn their ports and bridges and railways into rubble and twisted steel, but it could not force North Vietnam to stop supporting the National Liberation Front. "There was really an impossibility," Nitze said later, "no matter what you did, of improving the effectiveness to such a level that the North Vietnamese would not have enough supplies for their efforts in South Vietnam."[21]

Nor could bombing stop supplies from flowing out of North Vietnam to the south. The Vietcong, Nitze learned, could sustain their level of combat operations with only a trickle of supplies coming down from the north. It was estimated that only eight to ten trucks a day, or fifteen tons of supplies, were required to keep NLF forces in the field. Given South Vietnam's long border with Laos, it was unlikely that any level of bombing could cut off such a minute flow of material. Aerial reconnaissance over the border area, Nitze recalled, revealed the futility of the bombing. "You looked at the photographs of the Mui-Gia Pass and it looked like Verdun. It wasn't that the air attack wasn't effective. It was effective as hell. It knocked the bejesus out of the places that we were trying to knock the bejesus out of. And yet, all the time you'd see little paths going through the jungle someplace else, where they'd been weaving through the craters."[22]

To Nitze, the implications of the bombing study were clear: "If it were impossible to stop the sending of supplies from North Vietnam to South Vietnam to support forces fighting there, then it was dubious to fight a war of attrition and hope for a military victory within five years." To Robert McNamara, the consummate numbers man, the Nitze study coupled with similar data pouring in from other sources provided the evidence to confirm what he had dreaded: No amount of firepower could win the war.

Nitze's promotion to the post of deputy secretary of defense in June 1967 finally put him into a position to exert real influence over America's war policy. He now had ready access to McNamara and to the reams of classified information that flowed into the Office of the Secretary of Defense (OSD). Once again he was part of the national security establishment's inner circle.

When Nitze arrived at OSD, any consensus on the war that might once have existed at the Pentagon lay in ruins. High Defense officials were now bitterly divided over Vietnam. On one side were civilian officials led by an increasingly disillusioned McNamara. His view was that the bombing should be confined to tactical strikes in South Vietnam to support infantry operations, and that if any strikes were going to be launched against North Vietnam at all, they should be limited to the southern portion of that nation, specifically to the panhandle south of the twentieth parallel. Before he had left, Cyrus Vance had supported McNamara in this position, as did John McNaughton, head of ISA, and his successor in that post, Paul Warnke. When Nitze became deputy secretary, he became a member of the antibombing faction at the department.[23]

Strenuously opposing this view were ranking military men, including General Earle Wheeler, chairman of the JCS. The military hawks in the Pentagon wanted to expand the war with more extensive air strikes and big increases in ground troops. To support their contention that victory was possible, these men invoked the words and optimism of General Westmoreland, one of Wheeler's strongest supporters. Tired of fighting a defensive war, Westmoreland had a concocted a grand scheme for victory. By the spring of 1967 he was advocating an "optimum force structure" of 670,000 troops that would enable the United States to take the "strategic offensive."[24] This strategy would include intensified bombing, incursions into Laos and Cambodia, and perhaps an amphibious landing north of the demilitarized zone. Such a step-up in the U.S. effort, argued Westmoreland, would bring the war to an end in three years.

But skeptical civilian officials believed that Westmoreland's "optimum force structure" would produce only a wider war and greater losses. Seventeen years earlier Nitze had stood almost alone in opposing MacArthur's crusade to go north in Korea. Now, in opposing Westmoreland's zealotry, he stood with some of the most powerful men in the government.

But if Nitze saw himself as having allies in this fight, most with whom he sided did not yet view the deputy secretary as an ally. One of the most important forums in which high administration officials debated the war was something known as the "Non-group," so named because it did not officially exist. Chaired by Under Secretary of State Nicholas Katzenbach, the Non-group met almost every Thursday for informal discussion about Vietnam. This was a time for officials to air concerns and put out feelers, and Nitze attended regularly. Another member of the Non-group was Nitze's old deputy Bill Bundy, now assistant secretary of state for Far East affairs. Bundy had been a key architect of America's war policy, but after three years of pushing for more forces in Vietnam, he was beginning to have doubts. "We certainly weren't making the kind of headway we had hoped for, but were we making any headway at all? It was hard to say. I tended to think we were inching ahead, but only inching," Bundy said later.

Bundy listened closely to members of the Non-group. Paul Nitze was not one of the more vigorous dissenters that he heard. Nitze expressed concerns in the Non-group, Bundy recalled, but they were "never really pursued to the point of saying we should change course, never pursued even near that point."

At the Pentagon Nitze was equally discreet. As the battle lines were being drawn for the most bitter military-civilian clash in Pentagon history, Nitze carefully kept his views secret. "You never knew where he stood," said Leslie Gelb, then a young Pentagon official. Even Nitze's military assistant, James Wilson, was unclear about his boss's sentiments on the war. "He shared with me nothing that I could characterize as his innermost thoughts on the subject," said Wilson. Only after long months of picking up hints and gathering clues could Wilson finally discern the general outline of Nitze's views. "He was first of all a European hand. He saw the war as taking resources and concentration away from what he regarded as the major problem, which was the relationship with Soviet Russia." Also evident to Wilson was Nitze's skepticism about the bombing. "Nitze at no time had any confidence whatever that through the use of bombing we could substantially interdict the flow of supplies into Vietnam." Although he never heard Nitze say so directly, Wilson slowly realized that the deputy secretary of defense "had concluded that this war could not be won in any conventional sense and that it was time to withdraw."

Until the summer of 1967 Robert McNamara, too, had kept quiet about his growing doubts. But as he grew disturbed and then tortured by the carnage he had helped unleash in Vietnam, the defense secretary began telling the truth. On August 25, 1967, he told the Senate Armed Service Committee's Preparedness Subcommittee that no amount of bombing would end the NLF's war effort in South Vietnam. "Enemy operations in the south cannot, on the basis of any reports I have seen, be stopped by air bombardment—short, that is, of the virtual annihilation of North Vietnam and its people."[25] The administration's official rationale for continued bombing, implied McNamara, was without foundation. When he heard about the testimony, President Johnson was furious. The time was approaching when the increasingly dovish McNamara would have to go, he decided.

Even as Johnson plotted the removal of his defense secretary, however, McNamara was searching for a way to salvage the country's prestige by developing a formula for peaceful disengagement. While administration hard-liners doubted that a peace agreement could be forged in Vietnam, McNamara and Nitze saw a settlement as the only alternative to defeat.

Late in the summer of 1967 the two began working on a negotiating proposal. Assisting in this effort were Paul Warnke and Nicholas Katzenbach. As presented by President Johnson on September 29 in San Antonio, Texas, the proposal stated that the United States would be willing to stop all bombing when North Vietnam was ready to negotiate and not take advantage of the cessation to increase infiltration. In not demanding a total end to infiltration it was a significant departure from past U.S. negotiating positions.

The plan received little response from Hanoi. Since the North Vietnamese did not recognize the right of the United States to bomb their nation, they were unwilling to let the administration use that action as a bargaining chip.

With peace proposals going nowhere and Americans worrying about a wider war, more members of the administration began pressing for a unilateral reduction in the bombing. The issue became a focal point in the much broader debate over where the war was leading. More and more the lines were drawn between hawks and doves, probombers versus antibombers. Even Dean Rusk, ever stoical, ever loyal, began to toy with the idea of a bombing reduction. At an NSC meeting in the autumn of 1967, Rusk passed a slip of paper to Nitze: "What would you think of calling off the bombing to the nineteenth parallel?" Nitze had not heard that specific suggestion before. Still, it did not go far enough. "If you're going to do it, you really ought to do it all the way," he wrote back.[26]

At the White House the circle around President Johnson became smaller and tighter. Fewer and fewer people could be trusted. Walt Rostow, who had been head of the Policy Planning Staff under Kennedy, was now National Security Advisor. Like most who became confidantes to Lyndon Johnson, Rostow's most important qualification for the job was unquestioning loyalty. At meetings of the Non-group, Rostow's presence—and his reputation for reporting everything to the president—dampened open debate. A hawk to the end, Rostow saw his job as nudging dissenters back into line, not exploring their reasons for dissent.

With his presidency slowly disintegrating, Johnson seethed with anger at each new sign of betrayal. In mid November the president ousted the most prominent turncoat when he announced that Secretary of Defense McNamara would become head of the World Bank in early 1968. The announcement came as a surprise to a nation which had seen Robert McNamara as a model of loyalty and efficiency. At the Pentagon it was greeted with anger.

Another Christmas passed and the war dragged into the new year. Over half a million soldiers were now fighting in Vietnam, and the stream of body bags coming back from Southeast Asia was heavier than ever. By the end of 1967 over twenty thousand Americans had died.

Every week the casualty lists grew longer, and as the war touched the lives of more Americans, opposition to it swelled. Something had to change.

On January 31, 1968, the Vietcong launched the dramatic Tet offensive, simultaneously attacking more than a hundred cities and towns in South Vietnam. Pouring out from their underground tunnels and jungle strongholds, the guerrillas struck at U.S. and South Vietnamese forces throughout the country, infiltrated the U.S. embassy in Saigon, and took over Hue, the third largest city in Vietnam. The bloodiest fighting of the war engulfed South Vietnam for three weeks and took the lives of over a thousand Americans. The overall result of the offensive, however, was not the mass uprising that the communists had hoped for. Instead, the insurgents achieved few of their objectives and lost some thirty thousand dead. It was the single largest defeat suffered by the NLF.

Militarily, Tet may have been a disaster for the guerrillas, but politically it was a turning point. Throughout the United States, Americans watched the pitched street fighting in Saigon on television and wondered how the NLF could mount such an offensive. For years U.S. officials had been saying that the insurgents were losing and the tide was turning. Just two months earlier General Westmoreland had said, "The ranks of the Vietcong are thinning steadily."[27] Some administration official reiterated this sanguine message nearly every night on the news.

But if this were true, where did the resources for the Tet offensive come from? Unable to suspend disbelief any longer, the *Wall Street Journal* summed up the sentiments generated by Tet: "We think the American people should be getting ready to accept, if they have not already, the prospect that the whole Vietnam effort may be doomed."[28]

The offensive underscored long-held doubts within the administration about the military's optimistic assessments of the war. In the Pentagon Nitze let down his guard to comment on the "unsoundness of continuing to reinforce weakness." Paul Warnke was more blunt, saying that Tet showed that U.S. military strategy was "foolish to the point of insanity."[29] Before the offensive, even skeptical officials had given credence to reports that the insurgency was being slowly destroyed. After Tet, it was clear that the enemy retained enormous vitality and strength. Perhaps their numbers could be thinned. Perhaps more countryside could be secured. Perhaps ever larger tracts of the Ho

Chi Minh trail could be scorched and cratered. But decisive military victory now appeared implausible.

By late February General Wheeler had determined that the United States should call up an additional 206,000 troops in response to the Tet offensive. In his final act as secretary of defense McNamara argued vehemently that such a move would be disastrous, proposing instead a total bombing halt and an extensive review of U.S. military operations in South Vietnam. When Clark Clifford took over the department on March 1, the stage was set for a major showdown.

Few civilians in the Department of Defense were enthusiastic about having Clifford take over McNamara's job. To those who had worked in the Pentagon since the Kennedy era—and few were left— McNamara represented competence and continuity. He may have been domineering at times and his curtness may have bordered on rudeness, but he was probably the best secretary of defense to occupy the office. Nitze thought it a shame that a brilliant public servant should be fired for opposing a bankrupt policy. The irrationality of the Vietnam war, by 1967, had brought Nitze and McNamara closer. During their entire seven years in the Pentagon together, it was one of the few major issues on which the two men agreed. "On the Vietnamese war," recalled Nitze, "McNamara and I saw eye to eye. There I did not have any disagreements with McNamara."

Had one of the old hands at the Pentagon taken McNamara's place, his passing might not have generated undue discontent. But to fill Defense's top post, the embattled president had picked his close friend Clark Clifford, a Washington insider with notoriously hawkish views on Vietnam and little knowledge of defense issues. The son of a Missouri railroad executive, Clifford had made his reputation as a special assistant to Truman during the early days of the Cold War. In 1946 he had issued one of the first calls for a policy of worldwide containment when he had written a report for Truman that said the United States should "support and assist all democratic countries which are in any way menaced or endangered by the U.S.S.R."[30]

Johnson had met Clifford when he was at the peak of his influence, working as counselor to President Truman in the late 1940s. After Clifford retired from the government in 1950, Johnson relied on him for political and legal advice. He knew him as a man of competence and discretion with a special knack for taking care of sensitive matters. He knew Clifford also as a man who had the trust and respect of two forces whose support the president could not do without: the Democratic party and the eastern establishment.

But while the president and his political advisors viewed Clifford as a friend and possible savior, Pentagon civilians saw him as an intruder. "They didn't know much about me," Clifford said later. "I was a rank outsider." The new defense secretary's sole qualification, it seemed, was that he shared the president's dogged determination to continue the war at any cost. Clifford's selection was seen by some as an insult not only to the Defense Department, but to Nitze particularly, since he was the most qualified candidate to succeed McNamara. When Nitze walked out of the press conference the day Clifford's appointment was announced, a reporter asked "What are you going to do now?" The implication was that he might resign since he wasn't moving up. Paul Nitze had no such plans. "I'm going back to work," he replied.[31]

In private Nitze's bruised ego could not be concealed. After so many years in the Pentagon, he had desperately wanted the top post and not getting it left him depressed for months. Phyllis brought home two white canaries, but their melodious singing could do little to ease Nitze's frustration at seeing a deserved promotion slip away once again.

In early February Clifford made his first visit to the Pentagon to consult with McNamara, Nitze, and the assistant secretaries. Tall, soft-spoken, and wearing an expensive double-breasted suit, Clifford was too smooth for the weary Pentagon veterans. "The word for the new man was elegance—elegance of movement, style and manners," recalled Pentagon public affairs official Phil Goulding. "This was a silent screen star, with his handsome profile and his evenly waved hair." In contrast, the outgoing defense secretary was a wreck. "Sitting across from him was McNamara—needing a haircut as he so often did, wearing a frayed, white, button-down oxford shirt with a sewn tear over the pocket."[32] Seven years after leaving Detroit, the government's premier technocrat had reached the limits of his endurance. During a departure ceremony at the White House McNamara became choked up as he was awarded the Medal of Freedom. A day later Nitze stood beside him and the president in the cold February rain for a final farewell at the Pentagon. It was a dreary occasion. When Nitze spoke to praise McNamara, the public address system died.

In the view of DoD's top people, their exhausted boss had undergone an ordeal by fire. They had watched him learn the hard way that military power could produce death and destruction in Vietnam, but never victory. They thought that Clark Clifford was naive to think otherwise, and they resented his suave self-assurance.

Nitze was more positive about Clifford than his colleagues. The new defense secretary may have been too analytically shallow and overtly partisan for Nitze's taste, but the two men had known each other since the Truman years and Nitze considered Clifford a "very impressive, very able fellow."[33] Clifford was glad to have Nitze as a deputy. "I did not want to go into government," he said later. But few could refuse Lyndon Johnson when the president put his heavy arm over a friend's shoulder and pleaded and cajoled a few inches from his face. Clifford reluctantly took the Pentagon post. McNamara had called the Pentagon a "jungle" in peacetime. With a war raging, Clark Clifford felt that he had left the comfortable and insulated world of his law office and been "thrown in with the snakes." It was reassuring, therefore, to have a veteran snakekiller at his side. "I was gratified that Paul Nitze was there," Clifford said.

On the morning of March 1, 1968, Nitze watched in the East Room of the White House as Clark Clifford took the oath of office as secretary of defense. During the reception that followed the swearing in, Clifford asked Nitze to join him for lunch at the Pentagon.

As they ate, Nitze made clear his position on the war, presenting Clifford with a memorandum he had written for McNamara a few days earlier. The paper made two recommendations. First, the bombing should be stopped all the way down to the seventeenth parallel, the border between North and South Vietnam. Nitze believed this was a critical move. "The thing that was really hurting us was the concern— the legitimate concern—in this country and in the world that the Vietnamese war could escalate to something larger," he explained later. "If you could get rid of that bombing, then from the domestic and worldwide point of view you would at least diminish that concern."[34]

Second, Westmoreland should not get the 206,000 additional troops that he had requested, but only limited reinforcements of 50,000 men. As Nitze saw it, the objective of U.S. negotiating efforts should be an agreement that the United States would not use military force north of the seventeenth parallel if Hanoi promised not to send its forces south. However, Nitze did not think that Washington would have much of a negotiating position unless it recovered from the setbacks suffered during the Tet offensive. "Tet was a disaster for both sides," he said. "So I thought the critical question was who could pick themselves up fastest. Time was of the essence. From Tet to June 30 was the critical period. If the South Vietnamese didn't pick themselves up fast, then we would be forced to the alternative of disengagement."[35] Fifty thousand troops would do the job, Nitze argued.

Nitze also tried to impress on Clifford the broader context of the war. The United States had commitments all over the world. It was crucial not to lose sight of long-range objectives and let national security policy become distorted. The country could not afford to pay too high a price to achieve any single foreign policy objective.

"Clifford gave no sign of agreement," Nitze said later of the lunch, "but he listened." Still, even though it appeared possible to educate Clifford, Nitze was alarmed that a man with so little defense experience should rule the Pentagon at such a pivotal moment in the war. As Nitze commented later: "He didn't understand what was going on in Vietnam, didn't understand what the problems of the Defense Department were, didn't understand the overall strategic problem apart from Vietnam, the degree to which our position vis-à-vis the USSR was weakening, and the degree to which support for our position in Europe and elsewhere had declined."

Despite his ignorance, Clifford impressed everyone with his desire to learn. One of his first steps was to continue the daily morning meetings that McNamara had held with Nitze and Goulding. Originally the aim of the meetings was to review press reports on defense issues and insure that the Pentagon's positions were clear and consistent. Clifford soon expanded the group to include Paul Warnke and two aides, George Elsey and Colonel Robert E. Pursely. "It was really an advisory council," he said later. Vietnam was almost the sole topic of discussion.

Every morning at half past eight the five men would meet and take up the latest developments in the war. Clifford would lead off by reviewing the facts without disclosing his own opinion. He would then give each person, beginning with Nitze, a chance to talk. It was an unusually candid exchange of ideas. "Each man expressed his opinions without reservations and without fears that he would see them in print or that he would be quoted to others in the government," recalled Phil Goulding. "I am aware of no instance of internal or external leaks from the 8:30 group."[36] The meetings always lasted at least an hour and often would consume most of the morning. "That was *the* most important meeting of the day," Clifford said.

Nitze used this time to hammer away at the defense secretary's optimism about the war. "We used to argue, argue, argue," recalled Nitze. "He would try to perfect his case and I would try to tell him why this was wrong and that was wrong. The upshot was that we would spend hours, day after day after day, arguing about the various fine points of our policy toward Vietnam." It was an exhausting and often bitter dialogue. Nitze had hoped that a review of the facts would quickly change Clifford's thinking. He was wrong. After days of intensive discussion, Clifford's views hadn't changed. "I came to the conclusion that I was not making much progress," Nitze said.

Clifford's ingrained hawkishness would not be easily overcome. "I supported President Johnson on Vietnam," he said later. "I believed in our policy. I accepted the original domino theory."[37] Clifford had been appointed secretary of defense because Johnson considered him a dependable hard-liner. To change now would destroy his relationship with the president. Nitze, Warnke, and others felt that only a relentless barrage of evidence would wear through Clifford's bond of loyalty. They hoped that the interdepartmental task force set up to evaluate the Wheeler-Westmoreland troop request would provide the ammunition for such a fusillade.

Suggested by the president himself, the top-level task force, which began meeting in late February, included representatives from the Pentagon, State, Treasury, and the White House. Clifford, Nitze, Warnke, Taylor, Rostow, and Wheeler were all members. Across the oval table in the secretary of defense's dining room, hawks faced doves in what would turn out to be a critical debate in determining U.S. policy on Vietnam.

Nitze wanted the task force to make a fundamental reassessment of U.S. policy toward Vietnam. For too long America's war policy had consisted of nothing more than periodic and narrow debates over whether to send more troops. It was a policy of incrementalism that avoided the big questions and squelched real dissent. Nitze hoped that after a genuine and gut-wrenching debate, the need to get out of Vietnam would become ineluctably obvious to Clifford and other administration officials.

Meeting every day and evening through early March, the task force argued about the future of the war. Nitze produced two papers for the group, one laying out his views on how the Vietnam war was weakening the U.S. global position and the other analyzing U.S. strategy in the war. He wanted to make two points. First, there was little chance of winning the war, and second, there *was* a great chance of losing ground in the struggle with the Soviet Union.

Nitze also asked Air Force Secretary Harold Brown to prepare a paper on options for escalating the bombing of North Vietnam. Brown's response was nauseating. The most effective option, he stated, would be to intensify bombing of North Vietnam's military and government headquarters, railways, and ports. "The present restriction on bombing NVN [North Vietnam] would be lifted so as to permit bombing of military targets without the present scrupulous concern for collateral civilian damage and casualties," Brown wrote. "The aim of this alternative campaign would be to erode the will of the population by exposing a wider area of NVN to casualties and destruction." The aim also would be to bring the economy to its knees and to cut off the flow of supplies to the guerrillas in the south. "In time," Brown predicted, "these cumulative pressures would be expected to bring NVN to negotiation of a compromise settlement, or to abandonment of the fight in SVN."[38]

Six months earlier McNamara had said with a snort that bombing would win the war only if the United States was ready to destroy the North Vietnamese as a people. Now there was talk of doing just that.

Brown's arguments were familiar. Cut the NLF's umbilical cord, bomb Haiphong harbor, smash Hanoi's will to resist—Nitze had heard these suggestions again and again. But though Brown's latest memo was accompanied by over fifty pages of detailed analysis, Nitze had yet to see the facts to substantiate the claim that bombing would work. Heavy bombing had not been decisive when used against industrial powers during World War II. It would have even less of an impact on a rural nation.

To Nitze's dismay this basic axiom never became central to the task force's deliberations. Instead, most of the sessions were spent debating the details of the Wheeler-Westmoreland troop request. It was an exercise in microanalysis. "We spent hours determining which units could be sent, what the mix would be, that is how many Marines, how many Navy, how many Army, what the impact would be upon our reserves situation," Clifford recalled.[39]

The costs of escalation were sobering. To find the troops Wheeler and Westmoreland wanted, the Pentagon would have to move American soldiers from their posts around the world to duty in Southeast Asia; extend involuntarily the enlistments of tens of thousands of servicemen; and call up more reserve units in the United States. The draft—long a focal point for the antiwar movement—would have to be expanded. Taxes would have to be raised to pay for the wider war. Tentative estimates indicated that war expenditures would increase from $30 billion in 1968 to roughly $42 billion in 1969. And, sending more troops to Vietnam would insure that the flow of body bags coming back would rise even further.

As the editors of the Pentagon Papers later wrote, "A fork in the road had been reached. Now the alternatives stood out in stark reality.

To accept and meet General Wheeler's request for troops would mean a total U.S. military commitment to SVN—an Americanization of the war. . . . To deny the request for troops, or to attempt to cut it to a size which could be sustained by the thinly stretched active forces, would just as surely signify that an upper limit to the U.S. military commitment in SVN had been reached."[40] And neither action would assure victory.

Johnson's national security team made no changes in the policy of incrementalism. After a week of inconclusive argument, the task force sent a memorandum to the president that did not reassess U.S. strategy in the war. It did not contain any concrete suggestions for how the United States might achieve victory. It did not even assure the president that victory was possible. It did not propose a revised negotiating strategy that might produce a political solution. The memorandum contained only one recommendation for real action: It said that the United States should send 22,000 additional troops to South Vietnam.

In the administration as a whole the task force merely deepened a deadlock, but for Clark Clifford it triggered second thoughts. "Until the day-long sessions in March, I had never had the opportunity of intensive analysis and fact finding," Clifford recalled. "Now I was thrust into a ruthlessly frank assessment of the situation by the men who knew the most about it. Try though we would to stay with the assignment of devising means to meet the military's requests, fundamental questions began to recur over and over again."[41] With those questions came growing doubts for Clifford. "I could not find out when the war was going to end; I could not find out the manner in which it was going to end; I could not find out whether the new requests for men and equipment were going to be enough, or whether it would take more and, if more, when and how much."[42] Presenting the task force report to the president, Clifford voiced these doubts, but he stopped short of arguing for withdrawal. He was still not convinced that the war was unwinnable.

The turning point came when J. William Fulbright, the chairman of the Senate Foreign Relations Committee, requested that Clifford testify before his committee. Fulbright was a vocal critic of the administration's Southeast Asia policy. He was expected to be out for blood. On Friday, March 15, Clifford and Nitze went to see Johnson to discuss the hearing. The president thought that Clifford had not been at the Pentagon long enough to articulate the administration's position on the war and that Nitze should testify instead. Nitze protested vigorously, arguing that the defense secretary had a good enough grasp of the situation to go before the committee. But Johnson's mind was made up. His good friend Clark Clifford would not be fed to the sharks after less than a month in office. The deputy secretary of defense would represent the administration.

Over the weekend Nitze imagined himself in Fulbright's packed committee room, hot under the glaring klieg lights, television cameras rolling. To support the administration's position on the war, he would have to regurgitate the standard pap that the bombing was working, NLF forces were thinning, and the tide in the countryside was turning. Yet if Nitze told the truth—as McNamara had finally begun to do—he would seriously damage the administration's credibility and probably lose his job.

After agonizing through Saturday, Nitze decided that the only honorable alternative was to resign. On Sunday he wrote a letter of resignation to the president stating that further troop deployments to Vietnam would threaten U.S. commitments elsewhere in the world. For this reason he could not defend the administration's policy before the Fulbright committee. He concluded saying that in light of his position he could understand if the president wanted him to resign.

On Monday morning he showed Clifford the letter. The secretary of defense was shocked. "I had no idea that you felt so strongly about this," Clifford said.

Nitze replied that he had been trying to make his feelings clear for the last twenty days but Clifford hadn't really been listening.

Clifford said he did not want Nitze to resign.

"I have no desire to resign." Nitze said. "But I thought the President would want me to resign and that you would want me to resign." The secretary asserted firmly that he did not feel that way. Nitze could send the letter to Johnson, but he should delete the last paragraph.

Nitze followed Clifford's suggestion. He redrafted the letter and had his assistant James Wilson deliver it by hand to the White House. The president did not demand Nitze's resignation, but in the following months he made it clear that Paul Nitze was no longer a man to be trusted.

Years later Nitze remarked that he would have been "perfectly prepared to accept an administration decision which, from a narrow ground, I might have disapproved of but on which I could see that higher authority with a broader grasp could have considerations in mind that I didn't have in mind, and defend that." But Nitze did not feel the administration had a broader grasp of the situation in early

1968. "I felt that I understood the problem as well as the next man, and nobody was prepared to explain to me what these broader considerations were. In fact, I felt the situation was reversed, that I was paying more attention to the broader considerations than higher authority was. ... It wasn't a great break with the administration. It was just that you operate in a certain way, and that's the way you are going to operate. I couldn't do it any other way."[43]

The incident heightened Clifford's growing doubts about the war. "That was very impressive," he said later of Nitze's resignation threat. If a public servant of Paul Nitze's integrity and intelligence was ready to leave government rather than defend the Vietnam policy, something was dangerously wrong. If most of the other top civilians in the Pentagon were convinced that the war was futile, then perhaps Clifford had been misled. "I supported Johnson's policy because I had been informed, as had the rest of the American public, that that policy was succeeding."

Now Clark Clifford wasn't so sure.

In his meetings with the Joint Chiefs of Staff, there was a new and sharper edge in Clifford's questions. The former attorney began to cross-examine the top brass about how and when the war could be brought to end.

"Six months?" he would ask the JCS.

"Oh, no. It can't be done in that period."

"A year?"

"Well, no."

"Two years?"

"Well, we'll have made a good deal of progress in two years."

"Well, is that the date that we're aiming for?"

"Oh, no."

"How much longer than two?"

"Well, nobody knows."

"Three years, four years?"

"Nobody knows."

"All that we had," Clifford later remarked, "was the advice of the military that if we continued to pour troops in at some unknown rate and possibly in an unlimited number for an unknown period of time, that ultimately it was their opinion that the enemy would have suffered the degree of attrition that would force them to sue for some kind of peace."[44] Clifford could no longer deny what Nitze and others had been telling him all along: The military did not know what it was talking about. Once the most hawkish of hawks, Clark Clifford decided that the time had come to get out of Vietnam.

Nitze was pleased with Clifford's conversion. Soon, though, he found himself frightened by the totality of it. Rapidly abandoning his past position, the defense secretary swung radically over to the other side of the debate. He now wanted to get out of South Vietnam as soon as possible. "I did not believe that we were ever going to win in Vietnam," Clifford said later. And if victory was impossible, how could the deaths of any more Americans be justified? He had, in Nitze's words, "suddenly flipped from being an extreme hawk to being an absolute incontinent cut-and-runner."[45]

Even in his moments of greatest despair about the war, Paul Nitze had never believed that the solution was to evacuate Vietnam overnight. "He felt that to abandon South Vietnam was an unprincipled piece of work that the United States would suffer from in terms of its relationship with all countries," recalled James Wilson. Instead, Nitze favored sending fifty thousand more troops in response to Tet, solidifying the U.S. position, and then deescalating within a negotiated framework. He also wanted to see a major effort to improve the South Vietnamese army to the point that it could take over the war. It was a program for withdrawal that would take several years to implement. But Nitze believed it was the only real choice. "You just can't pull out arbitrarily without paying for it forever after," he said.[46] In a strange reversal, Nitze found that he and Clifford were once more on the opposite sides of the debate. "I suddenly found myself being the principal hawk spokesman and, again, thoroughly disapproving of what Clark was proposing. Thus all the roles were reversed."

Paul Warnke also favored a quick withdrawal. Intelligent and eloquent, with a wit that could be biting, Warnke had come into the Defense Department after practicing law in Washington for almost two decades. He had taken over ISA when John McNaughton was killed in a plane crash. Like so many others who initially supported the escalation, Warnke had come to view the Vietnam war as "constituting a massive mistake by the United States—an understandable mistake, but nonetheless a miscalculation."[47] More so than Nitze, Warnke had been at Clifford's elbow continually since March telling him that the war was hopeless. And like Clifford, Warnke opposed a slow withdrawal, in part because it would mean that thousands more American soldiers would die in Vietnam.

At the 8:30 meetings Nitze now faced two advocates of rapid disengagement. But while his relationship with Clifford would remain warm, his ties with the head of ISA began to deteriorate. "There was a tension between Warnke and Nitze," recalled James Wilson. As deputy secretary, Nitze was in a position to approve or kill many of Warnke's proposals for managing the war. He took advantage of that power to try to reduce Warnke's influence. "Much of the paper that was coming from Warnke's office," remembered Wilson, got nowhere. "His recommendations were rarely approved, unlike the case with Nitze's relationship with other assistant secretaries and people at that level."

Warnke would not be silenced. Cultivating a strong and independent relationship with Clifford, he gradually began to bypass Nitze. Instead of sending war-related memorandums to the deputy secretary, he would send them straight to the secretary. As Wilson said, "that kind of paper came much less frequently, and knowing this tension existed, I kind of assumed that Warnke had shifted his guns and was directing his recommendations directly to the Secretary of Defense."

Wilson was right. By mid-1968 it was Paul Warnke, not Paul Nitze, who was Clark Clifford's closest advisor in the Pentagon.

With Clifford's conversion, things began moving quickly. On March 19, the Senior Advisory Group, or "wise men," met with Johnson and expressed their opposition to the war. Consisting of political heavyweights like Dean Acheson, John McCloy, and Douglas Dillon, the wise men spoke for the eastern establishment and their advice was of tremendous significance to the President.

Exhausted by the war, uncertain about his chances of winning reelection or even nomination with Bobby Kennedy now in the race, and realizing that his foreign policy lay shattered beyond repair, Johnson shocked the country on March 31 by announcing that he would stop the bombing of North Vietnam and would not seek reelection. The long journey to complete withdrawal from Southeast Asia had begun.

PART III

A NEW ARENA

A Unique Endeavor

F OR CLARK CLIFFORD the last ten months of the Johnson presidency were devoted almost exclusively to disengaging the United States from South Vietnam. "I was consumed by the problem of Vietnam," he said later. "I was giving maybe 80 percent of my time to Vietnam." To make this single-minded focus possible, Clifford largely abdicated his other responsibilities as secretary of defense. He did not deal with the myriad day-to-day management problems. He spent little time poring over budget requests. He stepped away from the relentless dueling with Congress.

Clifford turned these jobs over to Paul Nitze. As Nitze explained to reporters, "He has left me the detailed administration of programs, the five-year financial plan, the concept formulation papers, the handling of money programs, and technical decisions."[1] It was a work load that Clifford was happy to be free of. "He practically ran the Defense Department during the time I was Secretary of Defense," Clifford said of Nitze later. "It was a great comfort to me to have an experienced man in the number two position."

And if Clifford was relieved to give up his management role, Nitze was glad to take it over. After seven years in the Pentagon he finally had the job—though not the title—he had coveted since the first days of the New Frontier. The only price was that Nitze became a slave to the paper flow as never before. Days at the Pentagon began by eight o'clock every morning and rarely wound down before seven in the evening. And the week often ended on Saturday, not Friday. Ray Furlong, Nitze's military assistant, was awed by his boss's discipline. "He was absorbed with his job." James Wilson was impressed as well. The amount of work that demanded the deputy secretary's attention every day was stunning—piles of paper, constant phone calls, streams of visitors. But it didn't overwhelm Nitze. "He could move lots and lots of paper," said Wilson. "It was a rare day when anything of importance was not dealt with by the end of the day and was in the basket on his desk." After eleven hours or more at the office, Nitze sometimes went home with a briefcase of papers. "I don't know how many hours a day the man worked," Furlong said. But after serving four deputy secretaries, Furlong was sure of one thing: Paul Nitze "worked harder than any deputy whom I observed."

More than most other officials, also, Nitze was effective. "He was enormously competent," Furlong recalled, competent to the degree that he sometimes intimidated high military officials. More than once, for example, Nitze corrected the commandant of the Marine Corps about facts relating to his command. "Mr. Nitze was a challenge to a lot of people because he knew the business in an extraordinary way," said Furlong. And there was no part of the business that he knew better than the strategic nuclear component.

During his years at the Navy Department, Nitze hadn't been involved in arms control issues. Service secretaries were rarely consulted on such matters. But he had never lost his fascination with the problem of how to rein in the arms race and promote strategic stability. Nor had the United States government as a whole lost its commitment to arms control. Following the completion of the Limited Test Ban Treaty, the process had temporarily stalled as the war in Vietnam consumed the time and energy of Washington's policy makers. By 1966, however, things began to move again. ISA head John McNaughton took the lead in pushing for bilateral negotiations with the Soviet Union on strategic nuclear weapons. To bolster his efforts he recruited Morton Halperin, an academic from Harvard who had done early theoretical work on arms control.

In December 1966, at a meeting on his ranch in Texas, Johnson approved a suggestion by Robert McNamara that the United States initiate a strategic arms control dialogue with the Soviets. Half a year later the president met with Soviet leader Aleksei Kosygin in Glassboro, New Jersey, and agreed on the need to impose greater restraints on the arms race. This move surprised no one. To government officials and independent observers, Americans and Soviets alike, there was a growing fear that the arms race was out of control.

Between 1960 and 1967 the United States developed and deployed one thousand intercontinental ballistic missiles (ICBMs) and over six hundred submarine-launched ballistic missiles (SLBMs). In the same period the Soviet Union deployed almost eight hundred ICBMs and began developing its own SLBMs.

During the mid 1960s both sides began developing anti-ballistic missiles (ABMs), which offered the possible promise of a shield against nuclear attack, but also guaranteed instability by raising the specter that one side would achieve a shield first, nullifying the other's retaliatory capability.

Finally, there was the ominous development of multiple independently targetable reentry vehicles (MIRVs). Although they had not yet emerged from the laboratories in 1967, MIRVs had the potential to transform the strategic balance by allowing more than one warhead—and as many as twenty—to be placed on a single missile.

What all of this added up to, in the words of Robert McNamara, was a "kind of mad momentum." It seemed that human beings no longer controlled technology; rather it was technology that had come to rule the destiny of human beings. And the best hope for restraining this powerful force, of stopping it from wasting vast resources and possibly triggering a nuclear holocaust, was arms control agreements between the United States and the Soviet Union. By 1968 bilateral arms control was near the top of the Johnson administration's diplomatic agenda. The president wanted it, the Russians were amenable to the idea, and half a dozen agencies were working on the problem.

Nowhere was the excitement surrounding the arms control effort greater than at the Department of Defense. Although John McNaughton had been killed in a plane crash in July 1967, Morton Halperin continued to spearhead the Pentagon arms control efforts under the direction of Paul Warnke, the new head of ISA. Warnke himself knew little about the complexities of the issue and concentrated heavily on Vietnam. But Halperin found a valuable ally in Paul Nitze. On the issue of arms control especially, recalled Halperin, Nitze functioned "as if he were secretary of defense." Moreover, because of an involvement in arms control going back to the Truman administration, he functioned with enormous competence. "His command of the substance of the issues was rare," recalled Furlong. "Among the senior civilians, he not only had a command of the facts, he had an understanding of the diplomatic side as well."

Nitze proved a valuable ally also because he had faith in the process of arms control. "Nitze was committed to the importance of the enterprise," said Halperin. Yes, there was the perpetual problem of trusting the Soviets. Yes, there was the challenge of getting agreements that truly promoted strategic stability. Overall, though, Nitze believed that arms control was a good thing. At the same time his was not a blind faith. "His basic view," recalled Halperin, "was that negotiated agreements . . . can reduce the risk of war. But whether they do reduce the risk of war turns on a much finer set of details." One detail Nitze worried about was how to make agreements ironclad. "Treaties and international agreements should be specific," he said in 1967, "but I would ask by whose interpretation? Unless there is good faith . . . is it possible to have a treaty so precise and so specific that loopholes cannot be found?"[2]

Nitze didn't know the answer to this question, but he did know that if strategic stability was to be maintained, the United States would have to take the risk. Nitze knew also that in an age where brash military actions by the superpowers were becoming less attractive, the battle for an edge in the Cold War would move to the negotiating table. And in this new arena Nitze was determined that the United States prove the more cunning contestant.

In addition to commitment, Mort Halperin and the other arms controllers at the Pentagon noticed something else about Paul Nitze, something unusual: He listened. With McNamara, recalled Halperin, "You had to watch what the first three words out of your mouth were because that might be all you got." But Nitze was different. "He was much more accessible than anybody at that level. You could see him, ask for a meeting, say you wanted to talk." And you could argue with him as if he were a colleague rather than one of the most powerful men in the government. It wasn't easy, of course. "He was very smart, he was very tough," said Ivan Selin, a young official in systems analysis. Nitze would "allow another point of view to be expressed at any time," recalled James Wilson, "but he would subject it to the most rigorous scrutiny and probe it, so that when these views were advanced, the people advancing them knew that they would be up to their ears in discussion of the details." To put it mildly, said Halperin, "you had to persuade him."

As one of Nitze's military assistants through the latter half of 1968, Ray Furlong's job was to screen Nitze's visitors and his paper flow. "The man was literally running the Department of Defense," Furlong recalled. "You tried to limit the number of people who could get in there and argue with him." But while Nitze's calendar was often closed, his mind wasn't. "He was an excellent listener," said Wilson. With Nitze, one felt one's views mattered.

On a critical issue, however, Paul Nitze didn't listen.

The issue was MIRV testing. At the same time that American policy makers were laying the groundwork for strategic arms talks with the Soviets—soon called the Strategic Arms Limitation Talks (SALT)—American weapons makers were preparing for the initial MIRV tests. SALT was to begin in fall 1968; MIRV testing was tentatively planned for August. Many felt that the testing of a major new weapons system on the eve of arms control talks would be a tragic blunder. It would send a wrong message to the Soviets, saying, in effect, arms control may be a nice idea, but the United States will continue to act unilaterally to enhance its nuclear striking power. More seriously still, MIRV tests could forever close off the possibility of a ban on such technology.

Concerned about this, Morton Halperin and Ivan Selin talked to the air force and the navy about their MIRV programs. They made the interesting discovery that it was possible to continue developing MIRVs at the same pace without testing in August. As Halperin said later, they could test "later in the development program and still have operational capability" on schedule.

Banning MIRVs was not a part of the U.S. negotiating position, but Halperin and Selin believed that it was best to keep the door open. They produced a memorandum for Nitze which, as Halperin recalled, "basically said MIRV restraints aren't in our proposal and we don't know whether the Russians are going to be interested in this or not. In order to preserve the option of responding to a Soviet proposal, it's obviously easier if nobody's ever tested a MIRV." The memorandum suggested changing the schedule of the testing program. It wouldn't affect the deployment date, "but what it will mean is that we will not have tested before the talks begin."

Nitze didn't like the idea. His skepticism about unilateral moratoriums dated back to the H-bomb debate. Still, he held a meeting on the subject. As Halperin recalled, Nitze said "that his inclination was not to delay because once you started changing U.S. programs under the theory that you might negotiate, you never start them again. You could end up in an endless moratorium." However, Nitze recognized that this was a critical issue: It was obvious that MIRVs would dramatically affect the future of the U.S.-Soviet competition. Nitze said it was an issue he should take up with Clifford and called the secretary of defense. Clifford shared Nitze's sentiment that there should be no delay in MIRV testing. Sometime later Dean Rusk reportedly raised the question of a MIRV ban at a Tuesday luncheon at the White House. But Clifford told the president that the Pentagon had considered such a ban and decided against it. MIRV testing would proceed on schedule.

Although Nitze played a pivotal role in killing the chance to stop MIRVs, the Halperin-Selin proposal met with opposition from other quarters as well. Royal Allison, the JCS's point man on arms control issues, was strongly against the ban. Allison had been a lonely voice among military officials in advocating arms control during the mid 1960s. Partly because of his arguments, the JCS had dropped much of its opposition to arms control, but not all. "There were some very basic positions approved by the Joint Chiefs," Allison recalled. "One of them was that arms control or strategic arms limitations should embrace simple limitations—those that are easily understood and verifiable with reasonable certainty and that were primarily quantitative in nature." A ban on MIRVs would violate this axiom. "MIRVs got into qualitative limitations," said Allison.

At the meeting to discuss Halperin and Selin's memo, Allison made it clear that the JCS was opposed to the banning of MIRVs. If Nitze had chosen to back a delay in MIRV testing, he would have had to tangle with the Joint Chiefs. It was not an appealing prospect. Even at the State Department where, as Philip Farley, the head of the Politico-Military Bureau, recalled, people "were very eager to see MIRVs brought under control," there was hesitation about making it an issue. "The U.S. position," concluded Farley, "was not developed because nobody wanted to go to the mat with the JCS on the extent that MIRVs might be limited."

Ultimately, it was not the testing of MIRVs that derailed the arms control process; it was the invasion of Czechoslovakia. When Soviet tanks rolled into that country in August 1968 to suppress a reform government, President Johnson canceled his planned trip to Leningrad in September. The visit was never rescheduled. SALT would not begin for another year.

*   *   *

The election of Richard Nixon in November 1968 left Paul Nitze in limbo. The high-level meetings ended, the intelligence flow dried up, and the Pentagon limousine stopped arriving in front of 3120 Woodley Road every morning. Nitze tumbled rudely back into the world of private citizenry.

Because it meant a loss of access, and thus influence, Nitze naturally chafed at life on the outside. "I'd pay a million dollars for the chance to work in the government," he once said while in exile. Still, for Paul Nitze unemployment was not what it was for other people. Right after leaving the Pentagon, Nitze caught up on his social life. He flew to Clarence Dillon's plush Caribbean hideaway in Jamaica. By now in his mid eighties, Dillon had aged with enormous grace, his mind still sharp and logical, his fortune intact. For Nitze, spending time with his old mentor was, as always, an enriching experience. He then visited the South Carolina plantation of his cousin, Mary Caroline Herter.

Back in Washington, there was no shortage of things to take up Nitze's time. Phyllis had hoped that the deputy secretary job would be her husband's last stint in government. Over the years she had grown desensitized to the intoxicant of power, coming to see Paul's work as a diversion from life's many other pleasures. Central to Phyllis's world was Causein Manor, where she wanted the family to spend more time. By 1969 the once run-down estate had blossomed into a small kingdom. In addition to the renovated manor house filled with fine furniture, the farm had a large guest house that the Nitzes rented out to friends like the Bohlens and the Zumwalts for one dollar a year. There were tennis courts, a swimming pool, a bathhouse and a small pier for a speedboat on the Potomac. The farm's stables, complete with a hired stable master, held over a dozen horses, and bridle paths meandered through the 2,000 acres.

On weekends there were plenty of guests and fierce matches on the tennis court. A Fourth of July party, which featured an elaborate fireworks display, was an annual event, and throughout the year there was a steady stream of visiting ambassadors, Washington insiders, relatives, and old friends. Although they were less enthusiastic about the farm than their parents might have hoped, the Nitze children were frequent visitors, often bringing their own children (eventually Paul and Phyllis would have eleven grandchildren.)

Although just an hour south of Washington, Causein Manor was a separate world. And if Phyllis could have her way, Paul would wind down his government work and concentrate on living the good life of being a gentleman farmer and managing the family fortune.

Nitze had different ideas. Taking an office at the Johns Hopkins School of Advanced International Studies, he cast about for something meaningful to absorb his attention.

He did not have to look for long.

The antimilitaristic mood generated by the Vietnam war not only sparked protests in the street, it spawned a revolt in Congress. Having been misled for years about the Vietnam war, Congress adopted a new skepticism toward the executive branch on national security issues. An early target of that skepticism was Safeguard, the U.S. ABM program. To many members in both parties, spending hundreds of millions of dollars on an anti-ballistic missile system was pure folly. Safeguard looked like the Vietnam of the arms race; for half a decade its mission had changed constantly while its costs inexorably climbed.

Initially, the Johnson administration had talked about an ABM system that could defend American cities from nuclear attack, but that rationale had proved flimsy. The Soviets would always be able to build enough warheads to overcome any defensive shield and obliterate American cities. So the goal was changed.

In a dramatic speech in San Francisco in September 1967, McNamara announced that the United States would go ahead with an ABM system that would be oriented toward the emerging nuclear threat from China. In explaining the decision, Nitze told Congress that the Chinese threat "cannot become actual before the early 1970s," yet when it did materialize it be would limited enough that Safeguard could provide full protection from a possible Chinese ballistic missiles attack.[3]

In time the plausibility of this rationale also wore thin, so by the summer of 1969 the Nixon administration was requesting $490 million for an ABM system that would be designed to protect Minuteman missile silos from a Soviet first strike. To congressional opponents, this latest of explanations was still not sufficiently convincing. And for the first time in the postwar era, it appeared possible that the Congress would cancel a major weapons system.

Nitze was aghast at the prospect. Hurrying over to the Senate Armed Services Committee, he argued strongly for continuation of the program. Whatever the various rationales for Safeguard may have been, Nitze believed that there was one indisputable argument in favor of the system: Without an ABM system under development, the United States would never reach an agreement with the Soviet Union to ban such systems. The United States could not bargain away something it did not have. Equally obvious, Nitze felt, were the dangers of a unilateral Soviet deployment of ABM forces. As he told the committee, "In my view a long-term relationship in which the Soviet Union proceeded with successive generations of ABMs, and we did not, could well result in an unstable situation with consequent grave dangers not only to the United States but to the rest of the world."[4]

Nitze's old mentor Dean Acheson was in full agreement. Well into his seventies now, the former statesman had lost none of his combativeness. Nor had his admiration for Nitze dimmed over the years. On the day of Robert McNamara's depressing farewell ceremony at the Pentagon, Acheson stopped at Nitze's office. James Wilson had talked with Acheson many times over the phone, but had never met him in person. Before Nitze appeared, Wilson had a chance to speak briefly with his boss's former boss. Wilson began telling Acheson how much he respected Paul Nitze and what a joy it was to work for him. Acheson nodded. "Yes," said the former secretary of state and contemporary of such men as Forrestal, Lovett, and Marshall, "he [Nitze] is the most brilliant of all of the colleagues I have worked with over time."

As the debate over Safeguard grew more heated, Nitze suggested to Acheson that they form a citizen's committee to lobby for the system. Acheson agreed, and the two men recruited another old cold warrior to their effort, Albert Wohlstetter. They named their group the Committee to Maintain a Prudent Defense Policy. To do research and draft papers, they recruited Peter Wilson, Paul Wolfowitz, and Richard Perle, three protégés of Wohlstetter who were soon being called the "three musketeers." By late May the group was ready to go public. In an interview with the *New York Times*, Nitze explained that the committee had been formed because of his concern that the ABM debate was "one sided" and that it was "awfully hard for the public to find a well reasoned argument." By writing reports, testifying before Congress, and taking part in public debates, the committee would seek to counterbalance the many liberal arms control experts and academics who were attacking Safeguard.

To get the group off the ground, Acheson sent out more than two dozen letters to establishment heavyweights, people like Arthur Dean, Henry Fowler, and Robert Lovett, people who were willing, in Nitze's words, to "stand up and be counted." "On an issue of this kind," read the letter, "connected as it is with nuclear war and nuclear coercion, it is all too easy to stimulate an emotional rather than a reasoned public response. But these issues are too grave to be governed by emotion." It was not massive defense increases that the committee would fight for, but rather "reasoned" debate over the complicated issues of national security. "Some part of our defense budget might be safely reduced," the letter explained, "but it is plain that the anti-ABM campaign has capitalized on the disenchantment with the Vietnamese war, on a general feeling of alienation from Government, and on the desire to wish away the problems of national security."[5]

The battle for Safeguard was close. A few undecided senators held the power to kill or approve the program. Predictably, Senator Henry Jackson led the fight to save the system. And in this crusade he found the committee a critical ally, Dorothy Fosdick, Nitze's former colleague at the Policy Planning Staff, was a key aide to Jackson during this time. "We were very grateful to that committee," she said later. "We drew on their expertise." Working with the three musketeers, Jackson's staff plotted out its strategy for keeping Safeguard alive. After months of intensive lobbying by both sides, a final vote was held on August 6. Safeguard survived by one vote. "It was a marginal little committee," Fosdick recalled, "but it made an enormous difference." Having accomplished its purpose, the Committee to Maintain a Prudent Defense Policy faded quietly from sight.

Even before August 6, however, Paul Nitze had ended his official association with the committee when he was asked by Defense Secretary Melvin Laird to return to the Pentagon to work on SALT issues. He jumped at the chance.

By the summer of 1969 SALT was once again near the top of the U.S. diplomatic agenda. Preparation for the talks was proceeding rapidly, and what Laird needed was a person who knew the issues intimately, who knew the Pentagon, and who could hold his own at the negotiating table. Paul Nitze was such a person. Some people might have regarded the move downward on the ladder of power as humiliating. Six months earlier Nitze had been deputy secretary of defense. Now he would have only a small, windowless office in the Pentagon and would be the direct subordinate of the deputy secretary in the emerging SALT bureaucracy. It was a career trajectory that would have driven most 62-year-old policymakers to despair. But Nitze saw the SALT job as a challenge. "It didn't seem to trouble him," said Ray Furlong, who continued to work as a military assistant at the OSD. "He handled that with great style."

Nitze handled his new job with great confidence as well. Melvin Laird knew little about arms control and left SALT policy to his deputy David Packard. But Packard was not an arms control expert either. In managing SALT, he leaned heavily for advice on a soft-spoken OSD official named Ron Easley and on a bright, young strategic expert from Stanford, William Van Cleave. Packard also made good use of the

Pentagon's technical experts, insuring that the chiefs of the Directorate of Defense Research and Engineering (DDR&E) and Systems Analysis had a say on SALT issues. Working through the SALT Guidance Committee that Packard chaired, it was this small group—which also included JCS representative Royal Allison—that shaped the Pentagon's positions on SALT. And at the group's often contentious meetings, it was Paul Nitze who proved to be the dominant voice. "If there were a chief advisor who was listened to more than any other person, it would have to be Paul," recalled Van Cleave. Although Easley, Van Cleave, and the young hotshots from DDR&E and Systems Analysis could crunch their numbers more adroitly, they could not rival their white-haired colleague in terms of experience or bureaucratic sophistication. Not only did Nitze understand the way Washington worked, perhaps better than anyone around, but he could hold his own even when it came to esoteric technical matters. "[H]e was an excellent analyst in his own right," recalled Easley. He could do his own math and make his own calculations. It was a combination that worked magic. As so often before, Nitze found himself staring from a post of modest importance into the misty reaches of a bureaucratic power vacuum. And with a savvy that only grew greater as the years passed, he stepped forward to fill it.

The confidence with which Nitze comported himself was evident in the National Security Council meetings that he now attended. "Nitze was a principal in a way that the other agency representatives were not," said one NSC official. "He did not regard his function as simply to faithfully reflect whatever the OSD bureaucracy was saying that week." Rather, he saw himself as somebody who could shape what the OSD was saying. It was an independence that Nitze found reassuring.

But even though he was in a position to wield real influence, Nitze worried. He worried that the negotiations might prove too complex, that the pursuit of real stability could prove elusive, and that the United States might find itself in a weaker position when the talks were completed. Inevitably, also, Nitze worried about the good faith of the Soviet Union. Before coming back to the Pentagon, he had commented that SALT would require "a real desire on their [the Soviet's] part to have a settling down of mutual deterrence."[6] In 1969 it seemed that this desire existed. "Our overwhelming opinion," Nitze recalled later, "was that the Soviets shared our view that in such bilateral negotiations between the two major nuclear powers, neither side could the expect the other to settle for less than parity."[7]

Still, Nitze had doubts. He always became uneasy when everybody in the government believed the same thing, especially if the matter concerned Soviet intentions. Nitze's uneasiness mounted when he was shown an intelligence report on Soviet arms control objectives that had been endorsed by the CIA, JCS, State Department, and Defense Intelligence Agency (DIA). As he recalled later, "the opinion stated in the paper was that the Soviet Union did not seek more than parity." Curious as to how this conclusion had been reached, Nitze asked DIA head Daniel Graham what intelligence data the report had been based on. Graham replied that there was no concrete evidence. The conclusion that the Soviets wanted parity, Nitze recalled, was "merely an opinion of these agencies."[8]

In the new cold war arena of arms control, trust was essential for progress. Yet because the negotiations were, in Nitze's analysis, a competitive endeavor, he found himself acutely disturbed by evidence that the trust was becoming blind.

And Nitze had other worries.

It soon became clear that President Nixon and his National Security Advisor, Henry Kissinger, had an unorthodox approach to SALT. Neither man trusted Gerard Smith, the head of the delegation. As a diplomat, Smith reported directly to Secretary of State William Rogers. In the view of the White House, however, Rogers and the State Department bureaucracy were not competent to handle SALT, and because placing faith in Smith would mean placing faith in Rogers, Kissinger hoped to circumvent the delegation head. He believed that the negotiations would move more quickly if he personally handled much of the work through secret, or "back-channel," talks with the Soviet leadership. Nixon agreed. But for this strategy to work, Kissinger needed a contact on the SALT team, someone who had a command of the issues and could pass along information about what was going on at the talks, someone whose discretion was assured, someone like Paul Nitze.

Kissinger's first overture to Nitze came less than three weeks after he had joined the delegation. In early July the SALT delegation was scheduled to visit Brussels for its first consultation with NATO officials. The night before the delegation arrived at the NATO mission, Robert Ellsworth, the U.S. ambassador to NATO, made a strange request of Ralph Earle, the defense advisor at the mission. Earle had worked with Nitze at the Pentagon during the Johnson years and the two men had become friends. Knowing this, Ellsworth asked Earle to give a message to Nitze.

It's a message from President Nixon, Ellsworth reportedly said. He wants Nitze to know that he thinks Nitze is the most capable man on the SALT delegation and really the only person he completely trusts and therefore he wants Nitze to be in the forefront of any dialogue here with the allies.

But what about Smith? Earle asked.

Nixon just has a lot more confidence in Nitze, replied Ellsworth.

The next evening Earle relayed the conversation to Nitze. Nitze became furious. His eyes darkened, getting the "opaque look" that used to make his military assistants tremble. "Gerry Smith is the chairman of the delegation," Nitze said, trying to control his anger, "and as long as I am on the delegation I will support the chairman. I will do nothing to undercut his authority or position."

Earle relayed Nitze's response to Ellsworth. Anyone who knew Paul Nitze, who knew about the values taught to him by Forrestal and Acheson—loyalty, respect, and devotion to the process of government—would have known that the message from Nixon could hardly have been conveyed to less receptive ears.

But the president and his national security advisor did not know Paul Nitze. And they would not take no for an answer.

Upon returning to Washington, Nitze was told by Rogers that Nixon and Kissinger wanted to meet with him at the White House. When he arrived, Nixon got straight to the point. "Paul," Nitze remembered the president's saying, "I don't have any confidence in Bill Rogers with respect to SALT. I don't think he understands anything about it. And frankly, I don't have any real confidence in Gerard Smith. I want you to go there and report directly to me about what's going on."

Nitze's reply was the same to Nixon as it had been to Earle. That's not the way it works, he said. "I can't go there and report secretly to you. I must have confidence in Smith and he must have confidence in me. The delegation can't keep any secrets from the Secretary and Smith."

"God damn it," the President barked. "I've told you what the channel of communication is and if anything comes up, I want you to use it." A secure, private line had been set up that would enable Nitze to communicate to the White House without Smith's knowledge. Nitze never used the line. "They knew that I was not going to do anything like that," he said later.[9]

*   *   *

Winter had already come to Helsinki, Finland, when the Strategic Arms Limitation Talks opened there on the afternoon of November 17, 1969. In the Yellow Room of the ornate Finnish State Banquet Hall, the two delegations—numbering about twenty-five people each, including technical advisors—sized each other up for the first time. The American team was a strong one. Royal Allison and Harold Brown, both high-level Pentagon officials closely involved in preparing for the talks under Johnson, had been retained by Nixon to work on the delegation. Raymond Garthoff, a Soviet expert and also a veteran of the Johnson Administration, served as executive secretary to the delegation. With the exception of Gerard Smith, the U.S. team had been working together on SALT issues for over a year before the negotiations began. The Soviets had no such advantage. Led by Vladimir Semenov, the deputy minister of foreign affairs, the team included a number of high-ranking officials, but lacked the cohesion found on the American side. "They didn't know who was going to be on their delegation until about a week before the talks started," Smith recalled.

After the reception in the Yellow Room, the two delegations retired to a sixty-foot table in the Blue Room to discuss procedural questions. With a flip of the coin it was decided to hold the first negotiating session at the U.S. embassy. After that, the negotiations would alternate between the nations' embassies.[10]

In the months before the talks opened, Nitze had stressed often that negotiating with the Soviets would be frustrating. Now he found out just how right he had been.

Twice a week at ten in the morning the two delegations would meet for formal plenary sessions. Typically, both sides would slog through prepared statements for most of the morning. Then the delegates would split up into pairs or small groups for less formal talks. Over long lunches and endless cups of coffee, they would debate the nitty gritty. Often the discussions would simply go around in circles, with each side restating past positions and rehashing old points of contention. Yet whatever was said during these conversations, however mundane or repetitive, it had to be put down on paper. In the two and half years it took to negotiate SALT I, the U.S. delegates wrote up over five hundred memorandums of conversations (MemComs).[11] Even for a veteran workaholic like Nitze, the pace of SALT was grueling. It was not what he had expected. "Originally it had been thought that this might be a kind of part-time job," he said later, "but it turned out to be more than full time, it was a job that required overtime almost continuously."[12]

When the Americans weren't negotiating with the Soviets or attending to paperwork, they were holding interminable meetings among themselves. The senior delegates usually met five days a week for two or three sessions of several hours.[13] Even in the most tightly knit government agency, it would be highly unusual for officials to spend half this much time in meetings together. High-level representatives of the JCS, OSD, and State Department—men who might have spent their time plotting against each other in Washington—worked together in an atmosphere of rare intimacy and extraordinary strain. The sense of closeness—or claustrophobia—was made even more acute by the demands of security. As Gerard Smith later wrote, "Sensitive matters could only be discussed by Americans in special quarters designed to prevent penetration by electronic measures. Small and not well ventilated, they seemed to me like the inside of a light bulb. . . . One might as well have been inside an ICBM silo."[14] Essentially, the secure conference room was "a room within a room." Ventilation was poor because air vents let out sound. Smith was particularly miserable, one delegate remembered, because he preferred his air fresh and "back then, people still smoked."

Hundreds of hours were spent in these stuffy chambers. Yet throughout the entire ordeal of negotiating SALT I, nobody cracked. Frustrated bickering, in fact, was almost nonexistent. As Smith later remarked in wonder, ". . . while the delegates held different views on a number of major issues, the surprising thing was the degree of harmony that existed between these personalities who had long been used to 'running their own shops,' whether it was a weapons laboratory, a military service or a major embassy."[15]

It was a harmony that proved vital in sustaining the group. And it existed not only in the smoky, silo-like confines of the conference room, but also when the delegation was trying to relax in hotel accommodations that were less than sumptuous. During their time in Helsinki the U.S. negotiating team lived in the Kalastajatorppa Hotel. It was a drab concrete box which, for security reasons, the U.S. delegation had taken over completely. It looked out over the bleak expanse of the frozen Gulf of Finland, and ferocious snowstorms pummeled the hotel. Seagulls screamed for most of the night, and night started in mid-afternoon. "You couldn't see out of the windows because there was so much snow and ice," said Smith. Like the working conditions, the living quarters were very close. The hotel suites of all the principal delegates were on the same floor, five rooms in a row. Smith had his room next to Nitze, and nearly every night, when the day's MemCons were finished and the long meetings had ended, Smith would hear the sound of piano music coming through the thin walls as Nitze practiced on a piano he had rented.

It was a difficult and isolating existence, made tolerable only by the fact that most of the U.S. delegates were accompanied by their wives. Smith had taken a strong position on this matter. In the past U.S. negotiators at international talks had left their spouses at home. Top officials in Washington had initially decreed that SALT would not depart from this tradition. But Smith had fought the decision, saying that "if you get a real security case involving some Soviet woman, you'll be sorry." The tradition was changed. And Phyllis Nitze, for one, rarely remained in Washington when SALT was in session.

Bridge was the diversion of choice for the Nitzes. "They both loved to play," remembered Garthoff. While conceding that bridge "was one of the few things to do up there," Gerard Smith himself didn't play much, but his wife played avidly as did the Allisons. They often played with two other captives of the Finnish winter, the French and British ambassadors. As with almost everything, Nitze took the game very seriously, concentrating intensely and becoming angry at himself for making errors.

Of course, the most demanding game that the Americans played during the last weeks of 1969 was the game of arms control. And in playing this game, with its extraordinary stakes and myriad uncertainties, the U.S. delegates could never relax, never let down their guard, never allow themselves to let a secret slip or use a fallback position too early. For it was not a friendly bridge partner who sat across the table, but an adversary who made every effort to trip up the Americans, to bring out any weakness or sloppiness that might be lurking in their character, to build them up or break them down, to gain an advantage at almost any cost.

During the first month of the talks the Soviets showed little compunction about using unorthodox methods of negotiation. The first was as hackneyed as it was transparent. When sessions were held at the Soviet embassy, they were invariably accompanied by vodka receptions. Drink up, the Soviets would say again and again. A lubricated American, they seemed to think, would be more prone to errors than a sober one. The ploy didn't work. "We were a pretty staid group of people," recalled Smith. "I don't think I ever had more than two vodkas at a time with any of the Soviets. . . . Allison hardly ever took a drink. Brown was the same." While Nitze drank regularly, he never allowed himself to be goaded into excesses, saying later, "we would drink as much as we wanted to and no more. I don't think anyone got pulled in on that kind of thing."

Also unsuccessful were Soviet efforts to foster divisions within the delegation or win over the Americans with superficial displays of warmth. In private conversations with Nitze, Semenov frequently praised Nitze's old mentor—and zealous anticommunist—James Forrestal, saying "how marvelous he thought Forrestal was, how they made a mistake in not listening to Forrestal's words of wisdom at the end of the war." Semenov also praised Nitze himself, telling him that he was the most competent member of the delegation, that the other Americans didn't fully understand SALT, and that they were not as professional as Nitze. As it turned out, Semenov tried to flatter Gerard Smith with almost the same words.

The Soviets proved far less clumsy at the negotiating table. "In the actual substantive negotiations," said Nitze, "they employed an amazing tactical versatility." They exploited the difference in nuance between Russian words and their English equivalents. They employed endless repetition to wear the U.S. team down. They attempted to create expectations that if the U.S. team conceded a given point, then other important points could be resolved. And, to the enormous frustration of the U.S. delegation, they resisted the American emphasis on detail. The Soviets strived to get agreements in principle without saying what the details would be or how they might be implemented. In contrast, the "American approach," recalled Garthoff, "was to offer a fairly complete, complex, and detailed package proposal. Arguments can be advanced for each technique, but the two are difficult to reconcile."[16]

They were so difficult to reconcile, in fact, that the first thirty-five days of SALT—over a month of intensive, grinding work—produced no more than a vaguely worded joint communiqué which said only that "an understanding was reached on the general range of questions which will be the subject of further U.S.-Soviet exchanges."

Like the Limited Test Ban Treaty, it was clear that any SALT agreement would be years in the making.

Between the end of the first negotiating round in Helsinki and the beginning of the next one in Vienna in April 1970, the SALT delegates and their superiors looked at where to take the talks. Because they were back in Washington, back in the city where turf wars were a way of life, the SALT delegates began to feud. They argued with particular ferocity about an issue that Nitze had tried to resolve, and thought that he had resolved, during the final months of the Johnson administration: the question of a MIRV ban.

Even though the United States had already begun testing MIRVs, many arms control experts believed that the superpowers could and should ban deployment. Gerard Smith was one of them. "Smith agreed with the analysis that MIRVs basically made for instability because they put a premium on first strike," recalled his deputy Phil Farley. His inclination, therefore, was to negotiate a ban on them. But from the first day of SALT, White House guidance regarding MIRVs had been sparse. Early in the talks Smith had requested permission to raise the question of a MIRV test moratorium. The White House refused. "If the Soviets presented a specific moratorium proposal," Smith wrote later, "the only thing the delegation was authorized to say was "We will refer the matter to Washington.' "[17]

Smith blamed this paralysis on high Pentagon officials. While professing their commitment to moderating the threat to U.S. land-based missiles, "these officials," Smith complained, "did not support the one measure that would have accomplished this purpose, a MIRV ban."[18] As had been the case a year earlier, it was the JCS that led the fight for MIRVs. The chiefs saw MIRVs as a key element of the U.S. strategic arsenal. As Farley recalled, "they attached importance not only to a deterrent and a survivable retaliatory force, but they saw themselves as having a mission of being able to carry out certain strategic attacks on the Soviet warfighting capability." Such attacks, the JCS believed, would only be possible if the United States deployed MIRVs.

Paul Nitze shared the Joint Chiefs' opposition to a MIRV ban, but for different reasons. Covering as many targets as possible was not his main concern. What made Nitze uneasy about a MIRV ban was the talk he was hearing from Pentagon technical experts. Briefings by people from DDR&E and Systems Analysis painted an alarming picture of a future in which the Soviets could upgrade their surface-to-air missile (SAM) systems into quasi-ABM systems capable of shooting down incoming nuclear warheads. And they could do so, said the analysts, whether there was an ABM treaty or not. The CIA chimed in with the judgment that the Soviet ABM program was further along than previously thought and that large-scale deployments were possible in the 1970s.

For these reasons Nitze saw a MIRV ban as a risky proposition. What if the United States abandoned MIRVs and then Moscow proceeded to chip away at an ABM treaty by upgrading SAMs? What if negotiations slowed or stopped the U.S. MIRV program and then no ABM treaty was achieved? What if the few ABMs allowed under the treaty were made far more effective, effective enough to, say, create a shield over Moscow? Nitze's overriding concern, remembered one member of his staff, James Woolsey, was "in being able to penetrate not only the present, but any future Soviet ballistic missile system."

Nitze had other concerns, too. Even if the ABM scenario was overplayed, there was the problem of verification. "You couldn't determine whether a Soviet missile had MIRVs," said Ron Easley. Perhaps banning MIRVs was a good idea; certainly Nitze and his colleagues could see that it would enhance U.S. security in the long run. But to take that path, to push for a ban, would not only ensure a long and difficult fight with the JCS and, when it came time to ratify a treaty, with the Senate; it would also mean taking considerable risks. In 1969 Paul Nitze, his staff, and his superiors felt the risks were too high. "From fairly early on we were somewhat skeptical of a MIRV ban," said Woolsey. By spring 1970 that skepticism had hardened into staunch opposition, and Laird's final decision was to come out against a ban.

At an important NSC meeting on March 25 the question of MIRVs was finally dealt with directly. Dismissing concerns over verification, Smith argued that an easily monitored flight test ban would effectively and verifiably stop the march of MIRVs. If neither side could test missiles with MIRVs, such missiles would never be deployed. It was a simple way to stop a dangerous escalation of the arms race.

Nitze disagreed. Pushing the Pentagon position, he argued that this wasn't the time to place MIRVs on the negotiating table. Even as he put forward this view, however, there was a disquieting edge in Nitze's voice. If the U.S. deployed MIRVs, the Soviets would soon have them as well. And because of their lead in large land-based missiles, they could use this new technology to gain a breathtaking increase in nuclear striking power. What that meant, Nitze said, was that Minuteman would soon be vulnerable and a situation of crisis instability would arise. "He did not sound very optimistic," Smith recalled.[19]

Indeed, Nitze was not optimistic. Since 1961 the United States had deployed one thousand long-range missiles on land and over five hundred at sea. It had spent tens of billions of dollars making sure that it could retaliate with devastating power if the Soviets launched a first strike. It had worked for over three years to organize far-reaching arms control talks aimed at bringing greater stability to the arms race. Yet despite all of this, the future looked bleak. If the Soviet Union put multiple warheads on their massive long-range missiles, Nitze worried that they could conceivably use them to destroy America's Minuteman force in a first strike while still holding several thousand warheads in reserve. If this happened, Nitze believed that an American president would have two choices: use submarine- and bomber-based warheads to retaliate against Soviet cities and thereby assure the destruction of U.S. cities in return or capitulate to Soviet demands.

After ten years of effort it looked to Nitze that the situation in the 1970s might be similar to what the situation had been in the 1950s.

He wasn't the only one with these fears. Members of the arms control community were nearly unanimous in the view that MIRVs would dramatically increase the Soviet strategic threat. To them, as to Gerald Smith, there was an obvious solution: ban MIRVs. But it was a solution that Nitze found unacceptable. In 1970 he joined other Pentagon officials in killing the idea by demanding that any proposal for a MIRV ban include the condition of on-site inspection. President Nixon accepted this condition. But the Soviets, with their well-known and long-standing opposition to intrusive verification measures, would not. MIRV development continued.

One reason Paul Nitze opposed a MIRV ban was that he had ideas of his own for how to mitigate the emerging Soviet land-based missile threat, ideas that he thought went directly to the heart of the problem without experimenting with risky moratoriums. During his first year on the delegation, Nitze had long brainstorming sessions with his staff and with Pentagon technical experts. The consensus early on was that the bean-counting approach to limiting strategic missiles would not bring about stability. More important than numbers was the boosting power of Soviet missiles. "The engineers tended to say that the overall parameter that really mattered, in terms of capabilities, was throw-weight," recalled Woolsey. The more throw-weight a nation had, the more powerful its arsenal could become. To limit nuclear striking power, one had to limit throw-weight.

This analysis complemented Nitze's long-held views. Since the early 1960s he had argued that in the ideal strategic world both superpowers would have ICBMs that could carry only one small-yield warhead each. Placed in hardened silos, these ICBMs could maintain deterrence, but would be unable to destroy enemy forces in a first strike. As a relatively small missile, the U.S. Minuteman largely met these requirements. Now, after his experts had driven home the urgency of the throw-weight issue, Nitze began pressing the idea that through creative negotiations, the United States could compel the Soviets to deploy similar missiles or at least make big cuts in their heavy ICBMs.

The challenge was negotiating such cuts. Forging agreement on the number of missiles that each side could deploy was one thing; banning large missiles was a more complicated matter. American satellites were able to determine how many missiles the Soviet Union deployed, but they could not see through silo covers and ascertain how heavy those missiles were or how many warheads they carried. The only way to do that was to climb down into the silos and get a firsthand look. In his 1963 treatise on arms control, Nitze had alluded to this problem. "If little on-site inspection can be negotiated, weight yield, range and accuracy limitations would be impossible," he wrote.[20]

By 1970, however, U.S. intelligence capabilities were advanced enough to determine the size of new Soviet missiles. Nitze latched onto this as a proxy for throw-weight. To those who had long said it was impossible to verify the throw-weight of a missile, Nitze now had an answer. "You could measure it," recalled Ron Easley, who worked on the problem. "If you knew the characteristics of the missile, you could project its throw-weight within a few percent accuracy."

Encouraged by this breakthrough, Nitze prodded his staff to come up with an overall approach for limiting throw-weight in the negotiations. These efforts, however, did not get far. Nitze's staff was "continually groping with him to get a handle on throw-weight" recalled Woolsey, but it never came up with a formula that was compelling enough to be sold to the bureaucracy, much less the Soviets. For the moment the technical hurdles remained too great.

And there were other obstacles to limiting throw-weight.

The uniformed military was solidly against such controls. "The JCS at home, as well as Allison in the field," recalled Garthoff, "didn't put much emphasis on throw-weight." The very idea of throw-weight controls was fundamentally antithetical to the Joint Chief's philosophy of arms control, which emphasized quantitative rather than qualitative limitations. The JCS opposed throw-weight controls because they were viewed as qualitative in nature. Controls were also opposed because the JCS didn't worry about throw-weight. As Farley later said, the chiefs "thought that the dynamics of the arms race meant that throw-weight wasn't very important to us, we could do better by getting lots of warheads through our technology rather than through big boosters." Verification was also a sticking point with the JCS. "The Chiefs felt you couldn't get a real fix on the verification of throw-weight," recalled Smith. To Nitze and the people at OSD, though, this argument was rubbish. The United States knew damn well which Soviet missiles were heavy and which weren't. "It didn't take any genius to distinguish between a 2,000 pound SS-11 and a [16,000 pound] SS-9," recalled Van Cleave.

The State Department and the Arms Control and Disarmament Agency were also chilly on throw-weight controls. "They principally opposed [Nitze] on the ground that anything that complicated would be hard to negotiate," said T. K. Jones, Nitze's technical advisor. To the diplomats, complained Jones, "negotiability was more important than defining dimensions which would actually achieve the stated purpose of the negotiations."

ACDA officials dismissed this charge. "We thought that throw-weight was something of a red herring," said Farley, "it was over-emphasized." And even if Nitze's ideas did make sense, how would such controls be negotiated? As Smith later said, "I never saw any specific negotiating proposal as to how you would do that. I think it was more or less a sort of guerrilla warfare against just having quantitative controls on launchers."

In one sense Smith was right. Paul Nitze and his colleagues at OSD were waging a guerrilla war against the SALT bureaucracy. But in another sense Smith was wrong. Maybe no specific negotiating ideas on throw-weight had ever percolated through the bureaucracy, but that did not mean they didn't exist. If the United States could identify how many heavy missiles the Soviet Union had, there was no reason why those missiles couldn't be limited by agreement. "If we could reduce the number of SS-9s to be deployed or put a low ceiling on them," explained Van Cleave, "then in those days it seemed to many people that you could resolve the throw-weight problem."

At least it seemed that way to many of the people in OSD. More so than even the people at State and ACDA, Royal Allison continued to bridle at this train of thought. During long meetings in the smoky bug-proof chambers, he and Nitze argued heatedly over whether the team should request authorization to raise the question of throw-weight controls. It was an argument, remembered Allison, "that Paul Nitze and I had forever."

In Washington the enemy was not only the JCS, but Henry Kissinger as well. From his office in the White House basement, the national security advisor decided which SALT proposals would live and which would die. Like many others, he did not share Nitze's anxieties about throw-weight. And since there was no political pressure to move on the issue, Kissinger never did. By the second year of the talks, the idea of limiting throw-weight was dead.

Desperate to stop the Soviet missile buildup, Nitze tried another approach. In the winter and spring of 1970 the arms control bureaucracy was cranking out dozens of SALT proposals in preparation for the next round of talks. To make sense of these ideas, Nixon and Kissinger ordered that all of this work be compressed into four major options to be presented to the White House. Two of the options involved freezing strategic missiles at high levels and two were more comprehensive. One called for a MIRV ban and the other entailed deep reductions that would cut superpower arsenals down to one thousand missiles on each side.

Known as Option D, the latter proposal was drawn up by Nitze and his staff. In essence, it tried to get at the throw-weight problem from another angle. It was designed to encourage both sides to reduce their land-based missiles, and it required that the Soviets make big cuts in their heavy missiles. Had it been accepted, Option D would have wrought major changes in the strategic arms competition.

Nitze's proposal, however, barely made it out of the Pentagon. In Packard's SALT Guidance Committee, there was bitter debate over the implications of the plan. William Van Cleave was firmly against it. "I didn't see any analysis as to what the impact on our own targeting requirements would be," he said later. Moreover, Van Cleave was at a loss to understand how cuts to one thousand on each side would do any good, arguing that it didn't "make sense to take a large, vulnerable force and reduce it to a small, more vulnerable force."

Nitze's reply was that under Option D the United States would be free to base its missiles on a mobile system that could elude a Soviet first strike. It would also be allowed to build limited ABM forces, known as point defenses, to protect those missiles that would remain stationary. The overall result, believed Nitze, would be an invulnerable land-based missile force for decades to come.

It was an attractive vision, but one that Van Cleave argued would never get through the government intact. He was right. When the bureaucracy was done with Nitze's proposal, the deep reductions were included, but the call for mobile missiles and point defenses was eliminated entirely. Option D no longer made sense, and the White House rejected it. Adopted instead was Option E, which essentially froze U.S.-Soviet missile levels, did not ban MIRVs, did ban point defenses, and set limits on heavy Soviet missiles that were so high as to be ineffective. The officials at OSD were appalled. "That had to be one of the stupidest arms control proposals the bureaucracy has ever churned out," said Van Cleave.

To Nitze, the direction of SALT was depressingly clear. ABM controls were still possible, but his cherished goal of reducing the Soviet missile threat was moving rapidly out of reach. SALT was beginning to smell like a failure.

On April 17, 1970, limousines carrying the U.S. and Soviet delegations and escorted by squads of white-helmeted motorcycle policemen rolled up to the entrance of the Belvedere Palace in Vienna. Once the home of Prince Eugene of Savoy, the palace was the site chosen to usher in the second session of the SALT negotiations. The session would last 120 days.

If winter in Helsinki had been dreary and depressing, spring in Vienna proved reviving, not only to the spirits of the delegates but to the pace of the talks. With procedural questions out of the way, both sides moved decisively on the issue of anti-ballistic missiles. On April 20, the United States formally proposed that ABM defenses be limited to the national capital of each country. After only seven days, the Soviets accepted the proposal. In principle, an agreement was close at hand. But the numerous and complex details of the ABM treaty would take nearly two years of negotiations—and almost continuous overtime on the part of the both delegations—to work out.

It would be an exhausting job. Nitze considered the completion of an ABM treaty to be of critical, overriding importance. With antimilitaristic sentiments more powerful than ever in the United States, Nitze worried that it was only a matter of time before America's ABM system was unilaterally canceled by the Congress. In 1969 he had helped keep Safeguard alive by a single vote. In 1970 Gerard Smith hurried back from Europe to lobby on Capitol Hill when it again appeared that Safeguard would be canceled. Nitze and the other SALT delegates worried that if progress were not made in the negotiations, the slim margin of votes that sustained Safeguard would slip away. "If the negotiations failed, we still were not going to have an ABM program because the Senate wasn't going to give it to us," Nitze said later.

While working to prevent this disaster, the SALT delegation had unusual latitude of action. While the negotiations on strategic forces were dominated by Kissinger, the delegates in Europe had almost complete autonomy on ABM issues. As Nitze recalled, "everything that was of importance in actually arriving at the ABM treaty was in fact developed by us in the delegation and recommended to Washington before it was approved. I know of no initiative that was useful in the ABM treaty which came from Washington."[21]

To Nitze, the lack of guidance—or rather interference—from Washington was a blessing. It gave him a chance to push his own ideas about what an ABM treaty should look like.

Placing ironclad restrictions on radars was one idea. In Nitze's view, an ABM treaty that the Soviets could violate, or "break out" of, after only a short period of intensive work would be worthless. It was not outlandish to imagine, Nitze thought, that the Soviets might secretly manufacture and stockpile ABM components. Nor was it implausible to think that in a time of crisis the deployment of these components could tip the nuclear balance in the Soviet Union's favor. The best way to head off such a threat was to ban the components of ABM systems that took the longest time to construct. And no component took longer than radars. From his work on the Sentinel-Safeguard program, Nitze knew that interceptor missiles and launchers were among the less complicated and less expensive parts of a comprehensive ABM system. In contrast, the giant, sophisticated radars required to track incoming enemy warheads took a long time to build. If such radars were banned, if the Soviets had to erect them from scratch, it would take years of construction—work easily picked up by satellites—for them to break out of the ABM treaty. But, said Nitze, "If you had already built the radars, you could break out rapidly and have a great big system." With these worries in mind, Nitze and his colleagues at OSD began studying ways to restrict radars as soon as SALT began. "It was the core issue," remembered Ron Easley. "We spent almost half our time on it."

The problems with banning radars were numerous. To support its massive air defense network, the Soviets depended heavily on radars. For the Soviets to give up all their large radars would be a great sacrifice, one that the United States would have to repay with a concession of its own. The alternative was to ban only those radars that could be used to track incoming nuclear warheads. Yet to do this, the two sides would have to agree on what constituted an ABM radar. This meant haggling over the details of how powerful radars could be and where they could be deployed. It meant opening up that malodorous can of worms called "qualitative limitations." And it meant even more hours, hundreds more hours, negotiating what was already a very complex treaty.

For these reasons—and for the reason that the United States had its own radars that it wanted to keep—Royal Allison and the JCS pushed for a negotiating approach that dealt only with launchers and interceptors. Among other officials, both on the SALT team and in

Washington, there was no opposition to radar controls, just indifference. Smith and Garthoff were especially apathetic about the radar issue. "They thought that too much was made of it," remembered Farley, "and if you had the other provisions, it wasn't going to make that much of a difference." The inclination at State and ACDA was to skip the radar issue. But through intense "argumentation and persistence," recalled Smith, Nitze succeeded in changing the delegation's thinking on radars. He also took the lead in negotiating controls with the Soviets. "He spent more time than any of the other senior delegates on the ABM and non-ABM radar issues," recalled Garthoff.

Nitze's chief counterpart in the talks on radar controls was Aleksandr N. Shchukin. A scientist by training, Shchukin was the Soviet Union's equivalent to Edward Teller. He belonged to the Soviet Academy and had played a pivotal role in the development of major Soviet weapons systems.[22] He was an important figure in the Soviet military-industrial complex and an influential member of their delegation.

Shchukin was also the Soviet delegate with whom Nitze got along best. Both were older, cultured men who enjoyed art and music. Both enjoyed jousting intellectually. As time passed, each found that he truly enjoyed the other's company. Shchukin appealed to Nitze because he was interested in substance; he was a diplomat who was eager to move away from the sterile rhetoric of the plenary sessions. Garthoff described him as being "able and interested and ready to talk about basic questions concerning strategic stability, going beyond the immediate issues." The relationship was made more comfortable by the fact that Shchukin and Nitze shared a fluency in French. When asked where he learned French, Shchukin said that he had had a French nanny before the revolution. "I think the language compatibility had as much to do with the Nitze-Shchukin axis as anything," Smith recalled.

In long conversations over lunch and dinner and, on at least one occasion, during a walk in the woods, Nitze and Shchukin began working out the details of the ABM treaty's limitations on radars. These talks would continue right up to the signing of the final treaty.

In August 1971 negotiations began on the question of how to deal with future developments in antimissile technology, known simply as "futures" or "exotics." On this issue as well, Paul Nitze would play an important role.

Talks on future technology were initiated by the U.S. delegation when they received instructions on the matter from President Nixon. The instructions from the White House were clear: "Our objective is to reach agreement on the broad principle that the agreement should not be interpreted in such a way that either side could circumvent its provisions through future ABM systems or components." For over nine months the delegations debated the issue, attempting to predict what kind of antimissile technology might be developed and to draw up provisions to ban it.

Such speculative work was difficult, but in the end, as John Rhinelander, the legal advisor to the delegation, later wrote, the "U.S. delegation carried out the President's instructions to the letter." Article V of the final treaty stated explicitly that "Each party undertakes not to develop, test, or deploy ABM systems or components which are sea-based, air-based, or mobile land-based." Summing up the treaty's implications, Rhinelander later wrote that "The overall effect of the treaty . . . is to prohibit any deployment of future systems and to limit their development and testing to those in a fixed land-based mode."[23]

Nitze had mixed feelings about the treaty's limitation of futures. He liked to deal with concrete issues, not hypothetical ones. As his top staff advisor James Wade recalled, Nitze believed that "you need to define what you're talking about. If you can't define it, you've got to be careful about limiting it." To the extent that futures were defined as new technology, Nitze—a technology enthusiast—wanted to leave the door open for new developments. "Nitze was in a middle position," recalled Garthoff. "He favored tight restrictions on future ABM kill mechanisms, and looser restrictions on development of future sensing devices." However, Nitze's desire to let sensors run free was not so great that he strongly pushed the point during delegation meetings. Nor was it so great that it turned him against the principle of banning futures. Like most others on the delegation, Nitze came to be solidly behind such a ban. If he did have a concern about the provisions on futures, it was the same concern that marked his crusade on radars. He wanted to be sure there were no loopholes through which the Soviets could slip, no way that some day in the future they could begin deploying new systems and justify their actions through a different interpretation of the treaty. In his discussions with Shchukin, Nitze sought to make the provisions on exotic systems ironclad.

Rhinelander recounts a particularly critical exchange that took place on December 10, 1971. Shchukin said to Nitze that if new technology were developed which could allow the mission of ABMs, "at fixed land-based sites to be carried out 'in a more efficient and less costly manner' he believed such new technology should be permitted. Shchukin suggested further that 'were such future systems to reach a stage where they could be deployed, the question would be referred to the Standing [Consultative] Commission [SCC], through which the necessary regulations could be worked out.' Nitze then asked Shchukin whether the Soviets could agree that no such deployment could take place without prior agreement in the SCC. Shchukin said yes." As Rhinelander recalled, "This discussion helped prepare the groundwork for subsequent agreement."

As finally agreed upon, Article III of the treaty specified that each side could deploy only two ABM systems: one around its national capital and one around an ICBM field. Each site could only have one hundred ABM launchers and a limited number of radars. The article stated that no other ABM systems or components could be deployed by the two powers. Still, Nitze felt that the agreement should be even more specific. On January 11, 1972, he asked if future "components were developed and could in fact be deployed in a manner to circumvent the specific limitations of Article III of the treaty, would it not be appropriate that they also be subject to agreement between our Governments?"

The Soviets thought so. And when the treaty was completed, it contained Agreed Statement D: "The Parties agree that in the event ABM systems based on other physical principles and including components capable of substituting for ABM interceptor missiles, ABM launchers, or ABM radars are created in the future, specific limitations on such systems and their components would be subject to discussion" in the Standing Consultative Committee.[24]

The treaty was exceptionally clear on the matter of futures. Thanks in part to Nitze's efforts, the language was largely free of loopholes. If he had harbored doubts in the beginning about limiting new developments, they appeared to evaporate as the delegation wound up its work and a consensus emerged on the team that the limitations were in U.S. interests. "Everybody was on board," recalled Rhinelander. "Nitze stayed on board." Smith agreed. "If Nitze had dissented, I certainly would have recalled that. There's nothing on the record that I remember which indicates he wasn't on the side of the majority."

And in 1972 there was nothing that suggested to any of Paul Nitze's colleagues on the SALT delegation that he would ever change his mind about the ABM Treaty.

The scheduling of a summit between Brezhnev and Nixon for May 23 placed intense pressure on the SALT delegations—now back in Helsinki—to finish their work. The delegates had put in overtime before; now they doubled that overtime. The strain on Nitze was especially great. His crusade for tighter controls on radars was not yet completed. As the presidential party began to leave for Moscow, the Soviet Union had not accepted the limitations that Nitze wanted. Anxious that the summit go smoothly, Washington instructed the delegation to give up on the question.

Nitze refused. In a frenzied last-ditch effort, he continued to hammer away at Shchukin, stressing the merits of his arguments, telling him that radar controls were important to the United States, and imploring him to demand concessions from his superiors. The pressure worked. On May 22 the Soviet delegation caved in and agreed to ban all large ABM-type radars except for the few allowed by the treaty. As John Newhouse later wrote, "The Americans had been on the verge of writing off this goal by unilaterally proclaiming its desirability. That they got an agreement was due mainly to the persistence of Nitze, who had forcefully argued against yielding."[25] The imperatives of summitry also played a part. "I think we kept their feet to the fire and they realized they had to have something at the summit for our masters to look at," Smith later said.

The resolution of the radar issue, however, did not mean that the entire treaty was now complete. Even as Nixon and Brezhnev sat down for their first round of discussions on the afternoon of May 23, the delegations were still working on the treaty's final draft. For three days last-minute bargaining, most of it between the higher level officials in Moscow, continued around the clock. Finally, at half past twelve on the afternoon of Friday, May 26, word reached Helsinki that most of the outstanding issues had been resolved. The delegations were instructed to fly to Moscow for the signing ceremony scheduled for eleven o'clock that evening.

They flew together on an antiquated American propeller-driven plane. Enroute the two sides worked to put the final touches on the treaty. Finally, over a round of beers, they initialed the agreed interpretations, the ABM Treaty, and Interim Agreement.

The teams recorded their thoughts in the airplane's guestbook. "It seems specially fitting," wrote Gerard Smith, "that members (and chiefs) of the Soviet delegation and the American delegation are flying together to Moscow with great trophies of our long hunt together for a start—and a very good one—on control of strategic arms." "I have a feeling," wrote Shchukin, "of completed work of great significance, which, I hope will last as a bright memory for my whole life." Nitze wrote, "From the beginning we agreed that nothing was agreed until all was agreed. Today we achieve the reward of two and one half years of patient and constructive work to bring that about. I feel that only those of us who were a part of it will ever fully know what was involved."[26]

It wasn't until nine o'clock in the evening that the plane touched down in Moscow. Before the signing ceremony, the president and his entourage had scheduled a dinner at Spaso House, the U.S. ambassador's residence in Moscow. But upon arriving in Moscow, Nitze was separated from the other Americans at the airport, and when he finally made it to Spaso House—where he had stayed with Chip Bohlen in 1955—the security guards didn't recognize him and would not allow him into the dinner. An official from the Soviet foreign ministry did recognize him, however, and invited him to ride to the Kremlin to wait for the signing ceremony to begin.

After the ceremony, Nitze was again left in limbo. Neither he nor Allison had been assigned a car. They had to walk back to their hotel from the Kremlin.

The completion of the SALT I treaty was an exciting moment for Nitze, a moment of personal triumph. He had been one of the first to conceive of bilateral negotiations almost a decade earlier. He had been a key player in organizing SALT under Johnson. He had fought to keep alive Safeguard as a bargaining chip. And he had spent two and a half years of his life in exhausting and often frustrating negotiations with the Soviets.

But even as Nitze savored all of this, he was angry. The last round of frantic bargaining in Moscow was no way to conduct a negotiation, he felt. It had been too chaotic, too risky, embodying all that was wrong with Kissinger's high-wire approach to diplomacy. In the middle of complex discussions in Moscow over limitations on new Soviet missile programs, for example, Smith had received a message from Kissinger. "You should understand," he wired, "that we are operating in a situation where we never know from hour to hour with whom we are meeting or what the topic will be."[27] Realizing how disorganized the Americans were, the Soviets capitalized on the situation. It was all very disturbing and on the plane back to Helsinki Nitze sat with a pad of yellow paper and drafted a mock memorandum that he entitled "The Last Twenty Minutes Are the Most Important," a favorite phrase of the wily Soviet diplomat Andrei Gromyko. The memo included guidelines for the Soviets on how to get the best out of those twenty minutes, and it reflected Nitze's bitterness about the final days of the talks. Sure ways to confuse Americans, the paper said, were to "arrange for the negotiations to be conducted at several levels" and "arrange to have top negotiations in your capital. Have their Delegation split between Kremlin, Spaso House and Rossiya Hotel. Use your interpreters for both sides. Have no typewriters nor Xerox machines available when needed. Give other side as minimum secure communications facilities as possible."[28]

The point was not that the Soviets were the villains. To Nitze and most others on the SALT delegation, much of the blame for the shortcomings in SALT I could be laid at the doorstep of the White House.

The ABM Treaty was a good agreement because it had been so painstakingly negotiated by experts in the field of strategic weaponry, it had the imput of a whole team of Americans working for two and a half years, and it had been scoured for loopholes and ambiguities. It was without question the best treaty ever negotiated between the superpowers.

But Nitze was not so sure about the other part of SALT I, the Interim Agreement. Unlike the pact on ABMs, the agreement dealing with strategic weapons had been worked out largely by Henry Kissinger in back-channel negotiations with the Soviet leadership. Based on the ill-fated Option E, the Interim Agreement, which froze the level of ballistic missiles for five years, was not the kind of finely tuned, ironclad agreement that the SALT team had wanted. As Gerard Smith remarked later, "All of us were uncomfortable with Kissinger's negotiations which we felt had not produced as good of a deal as if he had let the delegation do the negotiating. We knew so much more about the ins and outs of this thing."

Paul Nitze was more than uncomfortable with Kissinger's methods and the deals they produced. He believed that the Interim Agreement gave the Soviets a dangerous advantage in nuclear striking power and that it was a fundamentally flawed accord.

It was an accord, in fact, that called into question the overall value of the SALT negotiations.

Disillusionment

F OLLOWING THE 1972 Moscow summit, the strategic arms limitation talks entered a new phase. The first three years of negotiations had sought to end the escalating ABM race and freeze the construction of new strategic missiles. The objective of SALT II was far more daunting: to build a framework for lasting strategic stability. This required the superpowers to agree upon the basic features of a long-term strategic relationship and on what weapons each side could build without threatening the security of the other. It demanded a wide-ranging effort to look into the future and map out the scope and direction of the superpowers' nuclear competition. Because of its breadth and complexity, because of the ambitiousness of its goals, SALT II would make all previous arms control ventures look modest in comparison.

And already in the summer of 1972, even before the new talks had begun, there were problems. When SALT I arrived in the Senate for ratification, there was wide praise for the ABM Treaty. Almost all the senators agreed that it was a historic step toward strategic stability. But there was less enthusiasm for the Interim Agreement. Conservatives, led by Henry Jackson, blasted the agreement for granting the Soviet Union a numerical edge in strategic missiles. Jackson also expressed concern about throw-weight, the issue that so obsessed Nitze. He, too, saw ominous implications in the Soviet advantage in heavy missiles.

SALT I was ultimately ratified by the Senate, but so was a resolution sponsored by Jackson which stipulated that any future agreement, that is, SALT II, include equal levels of strategic forces.

Known as the Jackson amendment, this resolution was a comparatively mild censure of the administration. In private the senator was far more savage. Furious at the lopsided terms of the Interim Agreement, he and his top aide Richard Perle believed that nothing short of a wholesale purge of the arms control bureaucracy, especially the Arms Control and Disarmament Agency, could cure the government of its propensity for appeasement. "Kissinger and the White House were faced with a choice," recalled Philip Farley. "Who do you blame this on? Do you blame it on ACDA or do you blame it on Kissinger?" Even though it was Kissinger who had worked out most of the Interim Agreement through back-channel negotiations, the choice was obvious. "It became clear that there was going to be a night of the long knives," Farley said.

In the "ACDA massacre" that ensued, almost every top official at the agency was fired. Fred Ikle, a RAND strategist and friend of Richard Perle's, replaced Gerard Smith as director. Alexis Johnson was given Smith's other post of chief negotiator. A young hard-liner named John Lehman, also a friend of Perle's, got Farley's job of deputy director.

The purge didn't stop there. Royal Allison, the quiet and dignified JCS representative, was rudely fired and replaced by another Jackson choice, General Edward Rowny. The Nixon team was so zealous in its bloodletting that even Nitze was targeted for elimination. When he took his job, Alexis Johnson recalled, "I was told that he [Nitze] wasn't going to be on the team." When Johnson asked why his old friend was to be dismissed, he learned that the "political side of the White House, including the President himself, objected because Paul was a well known Democrat."

To the new delegation chief, the thought of losing Paul Nitze was distressing. Johnson challenged the decision. "I talked to Henry about it and I talked to Bob Haldeman," he recalled. "I said I couldn't think of anyone to take his place." Nitze was also supported by Jackson, and since Jackson was, after all, the primary wolf to whom the SALT I team was being thrown, Nitze's sacrifice was proven unnecessary.[1]

On Saturday, March 10, 1973, an air force transport carrying the U.S. SALT delegation touched down at Geneva's international airport. Settling into Geneva's Hotel des Bergues, the delegation found that their accommodations were hardly luxurious. As during SALT I, all the delegates, staff, and their wives were crammed onto a few floors. "We lived in kind of a SALT ghetto," recalled one delegate. Nitze's antidote was predictable. He rented a piano and moved it into his room.

On Sunday morning the delegation visited their offices. Housed in the old United States mission to the European office of the United Nations, the working quarters were cramped. As before, all discussions would have to take place in a stuffy, bug-proof chamber.

The new location of the talks was not much of an improvement over Helsinki. Although Geneva may be one of the most scenic cities in Europe, it also had a well-deserved reputation as one of the dullest cities in western Europe. "That's what the Swiss like," commented Johnson, who had spent considerable time in Geneva during the 1950s, "they like it dull." As in icy Helsinki, the American delegation had to rely on itself for recreation. Bridge was not very popular with the new team, but some enjoyed tennis and Nitze played with his usual competitiveness.

The first session of SALT II had been held in late fall 1972. With the U.S. SALT delegation in transition, that round had accomplished little. Now, with the new team in place, the second phase of the historic talks began. At the first meeting it was decided to dispense with the formal plenary sessions. During SALT I these ceremonious meetings had been mostly exchanges of prepared statements. With the entire staffs of both delegations in attendance, the plenaries were stiff and unwieldy forums, better suited for delivering propaganda barrages than for tough bargaining. To the relief of all, Johnson and Semenov—still the Soviet delegation head—agreed that it would make more sense to hold small meetings twice a week, with only five or six principal members of each delegation present. The critical after-session meetings between delegation counterparts would continue as usual, and informal dinners and luncheons would still be permitted.

SALT II got off to a poor start. When the American delegation left for Geneva, it had no clear instructions. Johnson was told only to propose essential equivalence and wring as many concessions as possible from the Soviets. This feeble game plan stemmed from the uncertainty in Washington. As Johnson wrote later, "Neither Kissinger nor President Nixon had a highly developed vision of SALT II."[2]

Only one thing was clear: The delegation's long-range mission was to work out a permanent strategic pact to replace the Interim Agreement. In simple terms, the Interim Agreement froze for five years the number of intercontinental ballistic missile launchers that each side could deploy. It also placed limits on submarine-launched ballistic missiles, specifying that the United States could have no more than 710 launchers on 44 submarines, while the Soviet Union could have 950 launchers and 62 submarines.

On paper it looked straightforward enough, but the Interim Agreement proved an unending source of controversy in the U.S. national security bureaucracy. No "common view of it could be forged among State, ACDA, the JCS, CIA, and the civilian officials in the Pentagon, nor within those agencies themselves," recalled Johnson.[3] If there was a consensus on the Interim Agreement, it was more political than substantive: Everybody agreed that a SALT II treaty resembling the Interim Agreement would be shot down in the Senate. To appease Jackson and his allies, SALT II would have to be a repudiation of SALT I.

Amidst this confusion, Nitze saw an opening to renew his push for deep reductions. In early 1970 he had pressed a proposal to cut launchers down to one thousand on each side and had been rebuffed. Now, as SALT II got underway, he put forward a proposal that would reduce launchers to twelve hundred. "Nitze felt that DoD [Department of Defense] should take the high ground," recalled his aide T. K. Jones. Too often the Pentagon had been a reactive player in arms control, only giving thumbs up or thumbs down to proposals that came across the Potomac from ACDA and State. Nitze felt that the Pentagon should initiate something that was "major and meaningful and that was important," said Jones. "And this proposal was important." If Nitze had his way, SALT II would pare by 40 percent the bloated nuclear arsenals that SALT I had allowed. Because strategic parity was now a fact of life, Nitze and his staff believed that "you might as well do it with less forces than with more forces—get the nuclear arsenal down to as small as possible," recalled Jones.

Nitze's proposal never made it through the bureaucracy. In the Pentagon it attracted immediate fire from the uniformed military. A 40 percent cut in strategic arms would mean overhauling America's entire nuclear posture. "The Joint Chiefs of Staff didn't want to give up the forces and therefore they were opposed," said Jones. At State and ACDA Nitze's plan was viewed as a sure way to derail SALT. Among the bureaucrats who thrived on caution and championed negotiability above all else, a 40 percent cut seemed too bold and risky. "Arms controllers said it was non-negotiable," complained Jones.

The day would come when deep cuts in nuclear arms would be the goal of American arms control policy. But in 1973, that day was still far in the future and Paul Nitze stood virtually alone.

The new SALT delegation in Geneva proved to be a fractious group. The main source of dissension was Allison's replacement Edward Rowny. A former U.S. army representative to NATO, Rowny's chief credential for the SALT post was a deep suspicion of arms control. He didn't trust the Soviets, preferring to place his faith in American technology. Rowny believed, for example, that the ABM Treaty was "an historical mistake" which "tied our hands forever."[4] After a few months in Geneva, Johnson came to the conclusion, shared by most of the other delegates, that "Ed just didn't believe in agreements with the Soviets."

During SALT I Nitze had been frustrated by his endless feuding with Allison, but he had always retained respect for the general. In Rowny, Nitze found almost nothing to respect. Solidly built, with a square face, horn-rimmed glasses, and a stoic military demeanor, Rowny was inordinately stubborn. He had no qualms about sitting in a staff meeting and repeating the same inflexible position again and again. "It was obvious that Nitze scorned Rowny," remarked one delegate. The two men argued incessantly. As Rowny recalled, "Nitze would work his pipe with his finger and then stab me (with his finger) in the chest saying, 'Rowny, Rowny, consider this.' My wife used to judge my day by the number of nicotine stains on my shirt."[5] As with Allison, Nitze's battle with Rowny was fueled by a fundamental dis- agreement over the goals of arms control. "The JCS wanted an agree- ment which protected their security interests," said Rowny. And what that meant, as before, was a modest, straightforward, and easily verified set of numerical limits. Nitze's ideas were frowned on because they were too complex. "Nitze tended to get into detail and into involved or analytical solutions which we felt were not necessary and would unduly complicate things," said Rowny. The JCS wanted to keep arms control simple.

Of course, keeping SALT II simple was nearly impossible, and Rowny's presence on the team embodied the bureaucratic paralysis that gripped the arms control process. "Rowny frustrated everybody," recalled Ralph Earle, a consultant to the team and later a member. "At our staff meetings," said Johnson, "I felt that he was trying to sabotage or block any agreement." Again and again, the JCS representative would object to negotiating proposals. "Ed Rowny was determined to prevent our getting an agreement," concluded Earle. And it was not long, remembered Johnson, until "The rest of the delegation was all arrayed against him."

Though the White House was unable to decide on how to replace the Interim Agreement, it did act decisively when faced with the prospect of huge Soviet missiles carrying multiple warheads. In the spring of 1973 U.S. intelligence agencies picked up evidence that the Soviets were about to begin testing a new generation of ICBMs, some of which would carry MIRVs. In a panicked attempt to head off this development, the White House instructed the U.S. SALT delegation to propose a freeze on the MIRVing of new ICBMs.

The new data confirmed Nitze's worst fears. Since the late 1960s he had been sounding the alarm about the lethal Soviet nuclear arsenal of the future. Now that arsenal was almost here, and if Nitze had been opposed to reining in MIRVs before—back when only the United States had MIRVs—he wasn't opposed to the idea anymore. To the floundering SALT II negotiators, the White House directive on MIRVs was an unequivocal step in the right direction. As Nitze explained later, it "would cut off the further testing or deployment of large Soviet MIRVed missiles but would also ban testing or deployment of a large MIRVed follow-on missile to the U.S. Minuteman, and would, in my view, enhance the security of both sides by helping to maintain crisis stability."[6]

But the MIRV initiative, and Paul Nitze's conversion, came too late. After struggling for years to catch up with the Americans, the Soviets had finally succeeded in emulating the technology that could dramatically boost the striking power of their strategic arsenal. Without MIRVs a heavy Soviet missile might carry a single massive warhead that could obliterate one target. With MIRVs the same missile could carry ten or more smaller warheads, each capable of hitting a separate target. Deploying MIRVs would also place the Soviet on par with the United States. What were the chances of delaying this move?

The answer will never be known. After the May instructions arrived, the SALT team solicited the help of Ralph Earle—Nitze's former colleague from the Pentagon and a lawyer by training—in drafting a treaty for a MIRV freeze that could be presented to the Soviets. As usual, the draft had to be sent back to Washington for clearance before it could be tabled. The delegation did so, expecting a speedy clearance. Weeks passed and no clearance arrived. The JCS would not give its approval to the treaty language, and the MIRV proposal never made it to the table. "The fact was that the Chiefs did not want any SALT agreement that was negotiable," complained Johnson.[7]

The missed opportunity to push for a MIRV ban was but one example of how higher authority in Washington made it difficult for the SALT delegation to operate. Besides the Joint Chiefs, the blame lay with Henry Kissinger. Now secretary of state, Kissinger was more determined than ever to exercise absolute control over the national security bureaucracy. And although his new post at Foggy Bottom was loftier, more dignified—a post that had been defined in the twentieth century by men like George Marshall and Dean Acheson—Kissinger's tactics hadn't changed. To get his way, he cunningly circumvented normal decision-making channels, leaving high officials affronted and in the dark. When it came to SALT, Kissinger not only excluded colleagues from key decisions, but also undermined the SALT delegation itself by continuing his back-channel talks with the Soviet leadership.

During SALT I those back-channel talks had been infuriating to the delegates. Now they became humiliating as well. "He would have meetings in Geneva at the Intercontinental [Hotel] which was about a mile from our headquarters," recalled Ralph Earle. "He wouldn't invite Johnson to participate." When the meetings were over, Kissinger didn't even bother to see Johnson to tell him what had happened, but sent an aide instead.

If Nitze had been uneasy about the way Kissinger operated before, he now found himself profoundly disturbed by the power that the secretary of state had amassed. The Watergate scandal was one source of this power. As Richard Nixon fought for his political life and spent more of his days responding to revelations printed in the morning papers, he leaned ever more heavily on Kissinger to run foreign policy. And run it Kissinger did.

When Nixon and Kissinger had asked Nitze to spy on Gerard Smith in 1969, Nitze had refused. He wanted nothing to do with the White House's sleazy maneuvering. As time went on, however, it became apparent that Kissinger was keeping much of importance from the SALT delegation. Most of the critical bargaining on offensive arms was not taking place in Helsinki or Vienna, but in Washington, where

Kissinger was holding secret talks with Anatoly Dobrynin, the Soviet ambassador to the United States. Nitze realized that refusing to cooperate with Kissinger at all would mean remaining in the dark about those talks.

In 1971 Kissinger offered Nitze a deal. He could see memorandums of some of the back-channel conversations if he promised to spy on Smith. Nitze refused to spy, but he did agree to conceal from Smith the existence of the back channel as his part in the bargain. Anxious to have contacts on the SALT team, Kissinger consented. For the remainder of the SALT I, the relationship between the two men was murky. "Nitze and Kissinger communicated regularly about what was going on," recalled one NSC staffer, but "it was not clear who was using who." What became known later was that Kissinger did not keep his end of the bargain. The national security advisor had his staff rewrite and alter some of the memorandums before they were shown to Nitze. "He only saw excerpts," recalled a Kissinger aide, David Halperin, "but the documents were characterized to him as being the whole record."[8]

Much of what he did see of the back-channel talks Nitze didn't like. He discovered that Kissinger and Nixon were conducting complex negotiations without doing the necessary staff work. Mistakes were inevitable. One particularly egregious error related to submarine-launched ballistic missiles. Nitze recalled reading a memorandum of a conversation between Dobrynin and Kissinger concerning the terms of the Interim Agreement. "At one point Dobrynin asked Henry whether the freeze would apply to ICBM and SLBM launchers. Henry told him, 'I don't know.' He checked with the President and came back and said, 'I don't care.'"[9] The Soviets responded by excluding SLBM launchers from subsequent discussions on the freeze. With Soviet SLBM deployments going forward at a rapid pace, it quickly became apparent that not freezing SLBMs was a critical mistake, and intensive efforts were required to restore limits on SLBM deployments.

Nitze's uneasiness about Kissinger was heightened when he learned in early 1973 that Kissinger had leaked highly classified information about SALT I. This discovery came when reporter John Newhouse asked Nitze to go over his book on the talks, *Cold Dawn*. Nitze was shocked to discover that the manuscript relied heavily on classified information. As Zumwalt recalled, Nitze realized immediately that Kissinger was the source, because "All of the highly classified material which was not supportive of Kissinger's position was not given to

Newhouse. Only the highly classified material that proved Kissinger had been right was given to Newhouse."

Newhouse admitted that Kissinger was his source. He told Nitze that Kissinger had not only given him access to many top secret documents, but had also allowed him to listen to tape recordings of verification panel meetings. This was an added source of consternation. Nitze occasionally attended these top secret policy-making meetings, but neither he nor Johnson had realized that they were being taped.

Nitze and Johnson were appalled by the sheer quantity of information that Newhouse had been given. "His information was extremely detailed, and he obviously had full access to the most sensitive records," recalled Johnson. "He revealed things that even delegation members did not know." It was one of the most blatant examples of high-level indiscretion that Nitze had ever encountered during twenty-five years in government. Hoping to bring the incident to Nixon's attention, Nitze went to see John Mitchell, the U.S. attorney general. Mitchell was too busy dealing with the escalating Watergate scandal to give any attention to the problem. In any case, Kissinger's systematic leaking to the press was old news.

Johnson was more direct and confronted Kissinger. Kissinger denied everything, saying that he had seen Newhouse only briefly and provided no information. "It was this sort of reflexive deceptiveness," Johnson later wrote, "that made the whole administration seem unworthy and difficult to work for."[10]

For Paul Nitze, the seamy reality of the Nixon administration posed a troubling dilemma. Throughout his years in government, Nitze's marching orders had always been to make the system work, to stick out the hard times and take advantage of the good times, to oppose policies he disagreed with however possible, and when that failed, prepare to resign. But these were unusual times and Nitze was in an unusual position. "No one knew better than Paul," wrote Zumwalt, "the way Henry Kissinger and his apparatus filtered all communications to the President so that, on the whole, Mr. Nixon saw and heard what Kissinger wanted him to see and hear."[11] By allowing himself to become party to these machinations, Nitze found himself in a situation where the rules by which he had always played—the rules he had learned at the feet of Forrestal, refined at the side of Acheson and obeyed under the command of McNamara—no longer mattered. All that mattered in this pitched bureaucratic battle was to restrain Henry Kissinger.

To strengthen his position, Nitze began quietly collaborating with

Bud Zumwalt—who by this time had catapulted through the ranks to become chief of naval operations and a member of the JCS—on ways to reduce Kissinger's power over the SALT process. Together the two men mounted a clandestine movement to spread views that countered Kissinger's positions. Operating outside of normal interagency channels, they tried to sound the alarm about what the national security advisor was doing. "Our actions were brought about by the way Henry Kissinger managed the National Security Council and its offspring, the verification panel," Zumwalt recalled. "He gave the Defense people who sat on those bodies as little opportunity as possible to state their opinions. Defense papers containing worthwhile ideas crossed the Potomac only to sink without a trace in Kissinger's apparatus."[12] Nitze and his superior, the secretary of defense, were not being listened to. The JCS was not being listened to. And the lower-level arms control experts throughout the government—the people whose experience and insights were so critical for avoiding errors—had been shut out of Kissinger's secret negotiations as well.

Reforming this distorted process was a noble cause. But the campaign against Kissinger also had an ugly side. In private Nitze and Zumwalt commonly referred to the secretary of state as a "traitor" and gave credence to rumors that Kissinger had been recruited by the KGB when he worked for army intelligence in Germany. Nitze once even called a friend in the intelligence world to ask about Kissinger's loyalty. No evidence ever emerged linking Kissinger to the Soviets, but Nitze remained suspicious.

At the negotiating table in Geneva, the fruits of Kissinger's handiwork were already ripening. With their usual deftness the Soviet negotiators sought to consolidate the gains that they had made in SALT I. They did this by embracing the Interim Agreement as the basis for SALT II. Conceived as a short-term freeze on the construction of new ballistic missile launchers, the Interim Agreement granted the Soviet Union 1,618 ICBMs to the United States's 1,054. Moreover, it left the Soviets with 313 heavy ICBMs, while the United States had none. This advantage had been deemed equitable by the Nixon administration because the United States held a big lead in such areas as bombers, missile accuracy, and MIRV technology. It was also considered acceptable because the Interim Agreement was to be a short-term freeze, not a permanent agreement.

On this basis Nitze had supported the Interim Agreement, testifying in favor of it before Congress in June 1972. "The Interim Agreement was a mere stopgap," he said later. "The hope was that it would provide time to negotiate a more meaningful agreement."[13] When asked by Senator Jackson whether the Interim Agreement would be acceptable as a permanent agreement, Nitze, like all the other SALT delegates, answered no.[14]

Despite its temporary status, Nitze had always been wary of the Interim Agreement. He was apprehensive about any proposal that appeared to sanction the Soviet edge in heavy ICBMs. Now that the Soviets were developing MIRVs, his wariness turned into extreme apprehension. As the SALT II negotiations got under way, Nitze hoped that a new agreement with more equitable terms could be swiftly hammered out. But after a few months in Geneva and full exposure to the bureaucratic paralysis that gripped Washington, this hope began to fade.

Early in the SALT II negotiations Nitze felt that the strategic arms limitation talks were being transformed from a useful enterprise into a dangerous venture. With mounting alarm, he watched as the Soviet negotiators began to express "quite a different view of the meaning of the Interim Agreement. It was their interpretation that the Interim Agreement was not just a temporary freeze."[15] In long and maddening negotiating sessions the Soviets argued that the terms of SALT I had been worked out to compensate the Soviet Union for inequalities in the forces of the two sides. They argued that since the Soviet Union was surrounded by hostile powers and targeted by four separate nuclear arsenals (the United States, Great Britain, France, and China) it needed larger nuclear forces than the United States. They insisted that terms guaranteeing such forces be carried over into any replacement agreement.

To allow this, Nitze believed, would leave the Soviets with a big lead in missile throw-weight that could persist into the 1980s. More missile throw-weight meant more warheads, warheads that would become increasingly accurate as the years passed. And to Nitze—his systematic pessimism still working very much as it had in the 1950s—this meant that some day not too far in the future the Soviet Union would have the capability to wipe out most of America's land-based missile force in a first strike.

If the United States possessed the will and the weapons, it could negotiate its way out of this mess. But a glance at the newspapers, with their daily chronicling of Richard Nixon's rapid demise, was evidence enough that the United States did not possess the will needed for tough bargaining.

And what about the weapons? With nearly nine thousand strategic warheads the United States had enough weapons to destroy every Soviet city with a population over twenty-five thousand many times over. Or, it had enough accurate warheads on its missiles and bombers to put two warheads on most of the important Soviet military targets. Through modernization programs already under way, it could keep this awesome array of weaponry operational and evenly dispersed on bombers, submarines, and land-based missiles through the foreseeable future.

Nitze thought this was not enough. He believed it was imperative to force deep cuts in Soviet land-based missiles. And the only way to do this, in his view, was to have equally intimidating weapons to bargain away. But the closest thing the United States had to match the huge Soviet ICBMs was something known as missile experimental, or MX. This weapon, however, was still many years away from being deployed. Without more bargaining chips, what were the hopes of getting an equitable deal in SALT II? Not very high, Nitze concluded.

Moreover, Nitze believed that the emerging SALT deadlock stemmed from factors more ominous than a lack of American bargaining chips. He believed that the Soviet Union was engaged in a bid for nuclear supremacy and that they were manipulating SALT to this end. "Soviet officials took the view that the correlation of forces had been and would continue to move in their favor," Nitze said later. "They deduced from this the proposition that even though we might, at a given time, believe their proposals to be one-sided and inequitable, realism would eventually bring us to accept at least the substance of them."[16] Continuing SALT, Nitze now saw, was like playing out a chess game after you've lost your queen.

It was a doomed proposition.

Once he had convinced himself that this was the reality of the situation, Nitze came to believe that it made no sense to keep toiling away in Geneva. The job of salvaging SALT could be done only in Washington. After nearly five years as a negotiator, Nitze was anxious to return to the bureaucratic ramparts as a policy maker.

And his new boss, Defense Secretary James Schlesinger, was eager to have Nitze back at the Pentagon on a full-time basis. A former RAND analyst and a cerebral pipe-smoking strategist, Schlesinger had immense respect for Nitze and shared his belief that the strategic nuclear balance was of utmost importance. Like Nitze, the defense secretary viewed Kissinger and his methods as a threat to the security of the United States. To fight Kissinger in the policy councils of Washington, Schlesinger needed more bureaucratic firepower. He

needed able and loyal aides who knew their way around the national
security establishment, people who could forge alliances across the
Potomac and do battle with Kissinger's legions at interagency meetings.
What the new defense secretary needed on his front line were veterans
like Paul Nitze.

In January 1974 Schlesinger offered Nitze his old post as assistant
secretary of defense for ISA. In reporting Nitze's nomination on February 9, the *New York Times* wrote that "The appointment was viewed
by many as probably strengthening the Pentagon's hand in Congress."
The *Times* had little trouble discerning the defense secretary's motives,
writing that "Nitze was expected to be skeptical, along with Schlesinger, about Kissinger's policy of giving top priority to relations with
China and the Soviets."[17] Nitze's assumption of the ISA post, many
thought, would herald a challenge to the secretary of state's omnipotence.

Ever since coming to Washington, Kissinger had worked to keep the
Pentagon powerless. His tireless campaign to undermine Melvin
Laird's credibility was well known in Washington. Presumably he had
the same treatment in mind for Schlesinger. However, if a highly
respected and wily bureaucratic operator like Paul Nitze began advising
the new secretary of defense and promoting Pentagon positions in
Congress, the isolation of Schlesinger would be more difficult. A cold
warrior with bipartisan credentials could also be devastatingly effective
if he decided to contest the manner in which SALT and detente were
managed.

There existed ample reason for Kissinger to sabotage Nitze's nomination, but ironically, one of the secretary of state's conservative detractors did the job for him. Although many years had passed since Senator
Barry Goldwater had opposed Nitze's nomination to be secretary of the
navy, and although Nitze had not tried to unilaterally disarm the
United States when he held that post, Goldwater's antipathy toward
defense officials who held degrees from Harvard and expressed fondness
for Dean Acheson proved as strong as ever.

In early March Goldwater issued a statement saying that he was
"unalterably opposed" to Nitze's nomination because he was part of "a
group interested in bringing about our unilateral disarmament."[18]
With the impeachment of Nixon a real possibility in the spring of
1974, the White House was loath to risk alienating the president's
remaining supporters on Capitol Hill. The *New York Times* reported
on March 22 that "As analyzed by White House officials, Senator
Goldwater is so strongly opposed to Mr. Nitze that he could well switch

on the impeachment issue if the White House proceeded with the nomination."[19]

Nitze's name was never sent to the Senate. For the second time in his career, he had been denied the ISA post due to irrational—indeed, bizarre—right-wing opposition. In his blindness Barry Goldwater had quashed a bid to strengthen conservative forces in the administration.

With hopes for a policy-making position scuttled by impeachment politics, Nitze searched for another way to salvage SALT. In late spring 1974 his immediate concern was limiting the damage that Kissinger might do at the Moscow summit scheduled for June. Nitze shuddered when he thought of the hasty deals Kissinger might make in the Soviet capital. Perhaps if the president knew how badly his secretary of state was mangling SALT, he might rein him in. Nitze decided to communicate his concerns directly to Nixon.

Beginning in April, Nitze spent much of his time drafting a letter that he hoped Schlesinger would endorse and deliver to the president. In retrospect, the effort was strikingly naive. As Zumwalt later wrote of Nixon, "it is obvious that writing him letters was not likely to do anything but enrage him. But even as late as Spring of 1974, a few months before the end, it seemed incredible to a veteran policy maker like Nitze that the most probable result of offering the President of the United States, in the most respectful language, a piece of thoughtful advice, would be that the author would be added to an ever growing enemies list."[20]

Written to Truman, Kennedy, or even Johnson, such a letter would have been an appropriate expression of dissent. But in 1974, with the wagons drawn close around the White House, there was no such thing as appropriate dissent. Besieged by criticism as no president before him, Richard Nixon was almost pathologically paranoid during his final days. To cross him in any way was to risk one's job. Still, Nitze labored away on his letter. By mid May, it was ready, and Nitze sent it to Schlesinger, Kissinger, and others. The Joint Chiefs of Staff expressed support for its contents, and at Zumwalt's prodding wrote a memo backing up Nitze's points. But Schlesinger never sent the material to Nixon.

The letter was Nitze's last gasp. For months he had watched Watergate engulf the capital. Nitze had been in Washington for nearly thirty-five years and he could remember nothing like it. The degree of corruption in the White House was astounding. Among his friends and family Nitze grumbled constantly about how Nixon was a crook and how he should resign or be impeached. "That was the sole subject of conversation," recalled Ralph Earle, who was staying at Nitze's home during this time.

Finally, one morning in late May, Earle found Nitze at the breakfast table in an upbeat mood. Before him was a strongly worded letter announcing his resignation from the SALT delegation. "His logic flow was that not only should he resign, but that everybody should resign," Earle recalled. In the same way that Nitze had asked Dulles to tighten up another letter of resignation some twenty years earlier, he asked Earle to cast a lawyer's eye over this letter. Earle's advice was that the wholesale condemnation of the Nixon administration should be toned down. Nitze agreed. After revising the letter he sent it to the president on May 28. Nitze also wrote up a more lengthy explanation of his reasons for leaving and sent it to Schlesinger.

For two weeks he heard nothing from the White House. With the Moscow summit less than a month away, the president was enraged that one of his senior arms control officials would choose this moment to resign. His response, therefore, was to pretend that Nitze had not resigned.

On the warm and sunny morning of June 14 Nitze took the final step and went public. His second letter to the president was one sentence long: "My request of May 28th to resign not having been accepted, I now feel compelled unilaterally to terminate my appointment effective today." The White House made no public comment on the resignation.[21]

In his statement of resignation handed out to the Pentagon press corps, Nitze bemoaned the deterioration of the SALT process and said he was leaving the SALT team because of the paralysis produced by Watergate: "For the last five years I have devoted all my energies to supporting the objective of negotiating SALT agreements which would be balanced and which would enhance the security of the United States and also of the Soviet Union, by maintaining crisis stability and providing a basis for lessening the strategic arms competition between them. Under the circumstances existing at the present time, however, I see little prospect of negotiating measures which will enhance movement towards those objectives.

"Arms control policy is integral to the national security and foreign policy of this nation, and they, in turn, are closely intertwined with domestic affairs. In my view, it would be illusory to attempt to ignore or wish away the depressing reality of the traumatic events now unfolding in our nation's capital and of the implications of those events in the international arena.

"Until the Office of the Presidency has been restored to its principal function of upholding the Constitution and taking care of the fair execution of the laws, and thus be able to function effectively at home and abroad, I see no real prospect for reversing certain unfortunate trends in the evolving situation."[22]

After giving his statement to the press, Nitze left for the farm.

Nitze's great fear during his final days on the SALT team was that Nixon and Kissinger would make unwise compromises to the Soviets in order to sign an arms control accord at the 1974 Moscow summit. From the beginning Richard Nixon—more the consummate politician than a visionary diplomat—had manipulated detente and SALT for domestic political gains. His Vietnam policy had been shaped by the same opportunism. Now, with his presidency on the verge of collapse and his thirty-year career at an ignominious end, it was conceivable that Nixon would compromise the security of the United States for a few moments of respite from his harrowing troubles. By resigning before the summit, Nitze was insuring that he would not be a prop in such a charade.

Some of Nitze's friends felt this logic was weak. Alexis Johnson had known Nitze for over twenty years and usually shared his views on most issues. This time he thought his colleague was dead wrong. Johnson could understand Nitze's "desire to dissociate himself from an administration that was appearing more unsavory each day." He could understand Nitze's longing to escape the frustration of Geneva. But he thought Nitze's assessment of Nixon's political considerations regarding SALT was way off. "I did not share his worry that Nixon would make a rash SALT agreement and told him so before he resigned," Johnson said. "It seemed to me the domestic political dynamics pointed in just the opposite direction, since a 'soft' agreement would certainly alienate the conservatives in the Senate to whom Nixon would have to turn to avoid impeachment."[23]

Johnson was right. There was no giveaway at Moscow. And had Nitze hung on for just two more months, he would have been in a new administration. Still, while Nitze's predictions of appeasement in Moscow proved unfounded, he judged that his more basic indictment of SALT remained valid. As long as Kissinger stayed in power—and President Ford ensured that he did—Nitze saw SALT as a dangerous enterprise. It was not a new president that the country needed; it was a new negotiating policy.

*   *   *

Freed from the restraints of life on the inside, Nitze knew exactly what he would do on the outside. He would work for that new policy, he would go public with his attack on SALT, and he would strive to bring the process back into line with its original principles. It was a crusade that would occupy him for the next six years.

When Nitze resigned from the SALT team at the age of 67, he had lived in Washington for almost thirty-five years and had worked in the executive branch for a quarter of a century. He had accumulated more experience in national security affairs than any person alive, serving five presidents and holding over ten different governmental posts. Nitze knew how Washington worked, knew it like few others, and he knew how to affect policy debates from outside of government. In the 1950s, as a relatively unknown dissident, Nitze had been highly effective in attacking Eisenhower and Dulles. Now, with the handicaps he had had at that time gone, Nitze would be even more effective. His well-known association with Dean Acheson was by the mid 1970s more of a historical footnote than a political liability. With the exception of a few conservative lawmakers like Goldwater—the last descendants of "the primitives"—Nitze's gilt-edged bipartisan credentials gave him considerable prestige in Congress. And if the title of "former director of the Policy Planning Staff" had not conveyed the most compelling credentials for questioning national policy, the title of "former deputy secretary of defense and SALT negotiator" did.

And Nitze the man lived up to his resume. His presence conveyed an air of authority. With a full head of white hair, a chiseled face, and clear blue eyes, Nitze looked old but by no means feeble as he approached the end of his seventh decade. His mind was as sharp as ever, and his arguments were still made with their customary crispness and economy. Whereas some people renowed as wise men rely on desultory anecdotes about a time long gone to make their points, Nitze was as intensely factual as ever. Up-to-date graphs rather than ancient memories formed the basis of his arguments. As an independent critic now unburdened of any sense of loyalty to the president, Nitze was a force to be reckoned with.

After escaping from Washington for an extended weekend following his resignation, Nitze returned with zest. Before a closed session of the Senate Armed Services Committee, he exposed the existence of Kissinger's back channel and provided details of how secret agreements had been made with the Soviets concerning the terms of the Interim Agreement. To startled committee members Nitze revealed that Kissinger had told the Soviets that by putting modern missile launchers into old submarines, they could, if they so chose, exceed the number of SLBMs that Congress had been led to believe was permissible under the Interim Agreement.

Leaked almost immediately to Leslie Gelb of the *New York Times,* Nitze's revelations touched off a brief furor in Washington. Consistent with the pattern of deception that the Watergate hearings had been exposing for months, the new charges of duplicity angered many in Congress. Kissinger issued an immediate denial. "That view must be based on a misapprehension of the negotiations by some of the witnesses," he said.[24] It was a weak attempt at evasion. And with the smell of blood already hanging heavy in the air, there was talk that the administration might have acted illegally by not notifying Congress of the secret concessions. If so, it was but one more example of lawlessness at the highest levels of government.

Having aired his secrets first—a relief after chafing in silence for years—Nitze moved on to his central point. Two weeks after resigning he appeared before a House arms control subcommittee to mount a sweeping attack on the direction of SALT. His message was one of almost unmitigated pessimism. The Soviet Union had made further progress in SALT impossible by insisting on making permanent the unequal terms of the Interim Agreement, Nitze charged. "I see no way in which essential equivalence is to be achieved unless the U.S. builds up to the Soviet levels or both sides reduce to agreed lower common ceilings," he said. For all its good intentions, the SALT II negotiations were pointless to continue within the framework insisted upon by the Soviets. Without a strategic nuclear buildup by the United States, Nitze said, "I believe it is not possible at this time to negotiate a permanent agreement to replace the Interim Agreement which would be balanced, contribute to maintaining crisis stability and lay a basis for reducing the strategic arms competition."

To be continued at all, the SALT process had to be overhauled. A good start would be to pressure the Soviets into accepting improved negotiating guidelines aimed at producing an equitable replacement to the Interim Agreement. If the Soviets balked at this, Nitze said, then the United States had to hunker down, resist signing any SALT agreements that were not in its interests, and begin a rapid strategic nuclear arms buildup. Once this was under way, Nitze suggested, the Soviets would be more compliant and the United States could negotiate a "balanced overall replacement agreement prior to the expiration of the Interim Agreement in 1977."[25]

*   *   *

With his resignation and subsequent attack on SALT, Paul Nitze was not repudiating either the concept of arms control or the SALT process itself. Instead, he was striving to bring the negotiations back into conformity with his original conception of useful arms control: not an end in itself or a part of some sweeping vision of world peace, but a highly competitive cold war process that would maximize mutual security. In Nitze's view the ammunition to sustain this competition was rapidly diminishing as the United States built fewer weapons and the Soviet Union built more. It was a sinister trend. Nitze was not so worried about the present U.S. strategic position, but "that position as it may evolve over the next 10 years in the absence of a clear understanding by the Congress and the people of the United States that there is a real problem."[26]

During the 1950s Nitze had looked into the future with a pessimistic eye and seen a time of maximum danger. Now, in 1974, he was looking ahead with the same eye. And he saw the same thing.

The Vladivostok Accord did not allay his alarm. Worked out in November 1974, at a summit meeting between President Ford and Chairman Brezhnev, the accord was a clear improvement over the Interim Agreement. It provided for equal ceilings of 2,400 strategic launchers for each side over the next ten years, specified that 1,320 of those launchers could carry MIRVs, and kept the limit on heavy land-based missiles at 313. The accord was an attempt to break the deadlock in Geneva and establish the general terms for a permanent SALT II Treaty. To many observers, the negotiations at Vladivostok had been a success. The terms of the accord represented a distinct change, and a major softening, in the Soviet bargaining position. Nitze acknowledged this, saying that "the Soviet side did make substantial concessions from their previous extreme positions."[27]

But it was not enough. Even though the Soviets had abandoned their cherished claim that they needed a greater strategic arsenal than the United States—doing so even as the Chinese, British, and French nuclear arsenals were growing—and had made other compromises, Nitze remained unsatisfied. The significance of the Soviet numerical concessions was entirely lost on him. He remained obsessed with the throw-weight issue, saying that the accord gave only the "appearance of equality." If SALT II was premised on such terms, and the United States did not begin new strategic programs, Nitze predicted that ten years down the road the United States would end up with "a half to a third of the Soviet MIRVed throw-weight."[28] And since, in his mind, throw-weight remained the single most important measure of overall strategic striking power, what the Vladivostok Accord really insured was not the fair SALT II deal that Ford and Kissinger promised, but rather Soviet strategic superiority in the 1980s.

Watching all of this from the sidelines, Nitze felt betrayed and angry. He had helped construct the bilateral arms control process during the 1960s, and had spent five years trying to make it work. He had lived in hotel rooms across Europe because he believed that the process would work. Yet in the end, as he saw it, Soviet interests were served to the detriment of western security. The United States had trusted the Soviets, only to have them take advantage of that trust. Nitze had placed his faith in a cooperative attempt to foster mutual security, only to see the United States come out, in his view, as the unquestioned loser.

As this conviction grew, Nitze groped for some way to head off the period of grave instability he saw looming in the future. And in searching for a framework in which to make sense of the unfolding situation—to make sense of it and to devise a solution—Nitze reached into his past, back to the principles of NSC 68.

CHAPTER 15

The Committee

PAUL NITZE was not the only person in Washington disturbed by the direction of SALT and American foreign policy. Among many past and present government officials, Democrats and Republicans alike, there was a feeling that the debacle in Southeast Asia had left the United States paralyzed—"a pitiful giant," as President Nixon put it. The American people no longer trusted their government. The American military no longer had confidence in itself. And almost two centuries of executive branch domination of foreign policy had come to an end, forcing the White House to share power with a fractious Congress.

To older members of America's foreign policy elite, men who had come of age at the height of the American Century when U.S. power was rarely challenged, the uncertainty of the mid 1970s was deeply troubling. While the United States wallowed in self-doubt, while it cut its defense budgets and reined in its imperial ambitions, the Soviet Union was moving in the opposite direction, many felt. Defense Secretary James Schlesinger liked to emphasize this point with a set of charts contrasting U.S. and Soviet defense efforts. The charts showed the Pentagon's budget in a nosedive while Soviet military outlays climbed steadily higher. Whether the Soviet Union's cautious leaders had any intention of using these arms was not the point. The operative assumption—well refined after twenty-five years—was total theoretical hostility.

Similar comparisons were also being done outside of government. Late in the summer of 1974 a report by the Coalition for a Democratic Majority, a group headed by former Under Secretary of State Eugene V. Rostow, blasted detente as a one-way street. It accused the Soviets of embarking on a bid for military superiority and called for the United States to respond in kind. In a letter to Henry Kissinger, Rostow argued that "it is not only wrong, but dangerous to lull western public opinion by proclaiming an end of the Cold War." Kissinger's response to these charges was curt dismissal, saying "We frankly see no evidence of a Soviet 'headlong drive for first-strike capability in both nuclear and conventional arms' that the Task Force position paper had claimed."[1]

Nitze's initial contribution to the emerging debate was cautious. After attacking the management of SALT following his resignation, he had settled back. He moved into a spacious office on the fifteenth floor of a glass-walled office building in Arlington and worked as an independent consultant. Although he kept up his normal regime of arriving at the office by eight in the morning and not leaving until after six, the job was decidedly untaxing. It was nice to be out of government, Nitze told his friends. He could go skiing in Aspen more often, spend long weekends in Maryland if he wanted, and do all those things that fourteen straight years of government service had so often made impossible.

Nitze put particular energy into his far-flung business dealings. Causein Manor, of course, required constant attention. By now worth millions of dollars, Causein Manor was not just a weekend getaway. It was a well-staffed operating farm that grew crops like corn and soybeans and raised pigs, sheep, and horses. In 1978 Nitze would incorporate Causein Manor Farms, giving $500,000 in preferred stock to himself and Phyllis and dividing the common stock among his children and grandchildren. What had started out as a $200,000 investment in 1949 had become, thanks to phenomenal increases in land prices, a cornerstone of the growing Nitze fortune.

The real estate holdings in Maine had similarly shot up in value. Located at the end of a long private road on a pine-covered hilltop overlooking Northeast harbor, the Rockridge house was less elaborate than the vast summer homes that some of America's wealthiest families had built on Mount Desert Island. But it had the advantage of being located in one of the most pristine harbor towns on the island, and along with the surrounding land, Rockridge had come to be worth a great deal of money. It was also a popular vacation spot with the children and grandchildren, who endured the day-long drive to get there. Eventually, the house at Rockridge became so overrun with relatives that Paul and Phyllis had a new house built next door.

What made Maine special was that even during the hottest days of August, temperatures remained comfortable. During the day, cool sea breezes offset the power of the hot summer sun, and at night temperatures could dip into the low fifties. The source of this relief was the icy water carried down from the arctic by the Labrador current. Because swimming was impossible in the frigid sea and heavy fog pushing in from the Atlantic could cover Mount Desert for days, socializing was the main pastime in Maine. New York socialites such as the Astors and Rockefellers added old-money glitter to the scene, while Washington stalwarts such as the Alsops and Walter Lippman made sure there was plenty of political gossip.

Besides his real estate, Nitze took great interest and pride in managing his investment portfolio. Ever since the big payoff from the U.S. Vitamin company stock in the 1940s, Nitze had had a sizable fortune independent of Phyllis's holdings. And even though he never returned to the private sector, Nitze remained fascinated with the world of finance, closely following the stock market and making sure that his investments were yielding a steady and high return.

During the 1970s Nitze's biggest business concern was the Aspen Skiing Corporation, which he had formed with his brother-in-law, Walter Paepcke, in the late 1940s. Nitze had become familiar with the mountains of Colorado from spending long summers at his parents' six-hundred-acre ranch near Longs Peak. Shortly after the end of World War II Paepcke told Nitze of a recent visit to an alpine ghost town called Aspen. Once a bustling silver mining center, Aspen's population had fallen to a few hundred when the price of silver dropped in the 1890s. Huge tracts of the town could be bought for next to nothing, and Paepcke suggested they form a partnership to turn it into a ski resort. Nitze agreed.

For its first years the Aspen Skiing Corporation barely scraped by because the ski trails it had cut on Aspen Mountain were too steep for most skiers. But after Nitze raised money to bulldoze some easier slopes, skiers flocked to the area, and by the 1970s Aspen was one of

America's most fashionable ski resorts. Walter Paepcke was dead, but Nitze remained a large stockholder in the corporation and chairman of its board. Every Christmas Nitze and his children met in Aspen for a week of skiing and socializing. Phyllis usually skipped these trips because of a long-standing rivalry with Paul's sister Elizabeth ("Pussy") Paepcke, who owned a house in Aspen and dominated the holiday social circuit there. When the family left for Colorado, Phyllis would drive to Causein Manor and brood.

In the late 1970s the motion picture company Twentieth Century-Fox offered to buy Aspen Skiing. Cutting short a visit to China, Nitze negotiated a merger between the two companies. As a result, he secured a place on the board of Twentieth Century-Fox and the Nitze and Paepcke families owned the largest block of Fox's stock. While serving on the board, Nitze worked with the actress and by then princess Grace Kelly and found the entertainment world a fascinating place. But eventually, Twentieth Century-Fox was bought out by a Denver oil tycoon, and Nitze lost the control over the Aspen Skiing Company.

Despite the diversions of private life, Nitze remained closely involved in national security affairs. Though increasingly cynical about U.S.-Soviet relations, he initially avoided sweeping attacks on detente. Instead, during his first year after resigning, Nitze put forth an agenda for rectifying the shortcomings of SALT and preserving the "special relationship" between the United States and Soviet Union. If the United States stepped up its strategic arms programs, stood firm in the face of opportunist Soviet negotiating tactics, and insisted on equitable agreements, Nitze saw no reason why SALT could not go forward. He had helped create the process. It was fundamentally sound. If pursued properly, it would work. Nitze had hope.

For others, however, the time for hope had passed. Eugene Rostow was stung by Kissinger's cavalier dismissal of the report by the Coalition for a Democratic Majority. A charming man, quick to laugh, with an expressive and friendly face, Rostow had the air of a relaxed academic ready to retire to his books and garden. Beneath this gentle demeanor, though, was a seething resentment of the political players who had replaced Washington's old establishment elite following the fall of Lyndon Johnson. Like Nitze, Rostow was repelled by the liberal McGovernite Democrats who had seized control of the party and abandoned the Truman-Kennedy legacy in foreign policy. Equally distressing to him was Kissinger's zealous pursuit of detente and arms control. Through the coalition, Rostow hoped to return the Democratic party to its traditional hard-line stance on national security. Joining him in this effort were other disgruntled Democrats such as Norman Podhoretz, Midge Decter, and Max Kampleman.

In the wake of Vietnam this crusade met with little enthusiasm. Few Americans were anxious to revive policies that had spawned the war, and Rostow and his friends felt isolated and ignored. Writing reports and making speeches wasn't having an impact. "We realized we weren't getting anywhere," Rostow said later. "The Democratic party didn't want to hear us and we weren't getting any general publicity." Something more had to be done. A group with a broader base than the coalition had to be organized, Rostow believed. With increasing seriousness, he discussed the idea through 1975 with former Treasury Secretary Charls Walker and James Schlesinger. Finally, as Walker recalled, "We all agreed that we needed a citizen's committee to beat the drums."

One day, during a visit to Schlesinger's Pentagon office, Rostow called Nitze to see whether he would be interested in a committee. "I took the view that we really should make every effort to get Paul Nitze involved, because in the first place he was Paul Nitze and second, neither Charly Walker or I were nuclear experts." Rostow phoned him to ask if he would be interested. Nitze was hesitant. "He was wary, he wanted to think about it, pursue it."

The idea of a citizens' committee was not new to Nitze. He had thought about setting one up in the late 1950s when the Gaither report was suppressed by Eisenhower, and in 1969 the Committee to Maintain a Prudent Defense Policy had met with great success. Perhaps another committee would rouse the elite from their slumberous indifference to the growing Soviet military threat. Only a bipartisan group with impeccable credentials would have the credibility to challenge both Henry Kissinger on one side and a dovish Congress on the other. Over the next months Nitze began talking to his own circle of friends about a committee. Zumwalt, who had left the navy in 1974, liked the idea. So did Nitze's former colleague from the State Department, Charles Burton Marshall.

In late 1975 Rostow brought matters to a head. Inspired by a few Bloody Marys before lunch on Thanksgiving day, he fired off a memo to Walker and Nitze. "I said we'd had preliminary discussions long enough. By God, why don't we just do it?"[2] Walker and Nitze agreed. On March 12, 1976, the first organizing meeting of the group was held at the Metropolitan Club. The work leading up to the meeting was frenzied. As Rostow said later, "It was done in an awful rush for some reason. I just sent out a lot of form letters . . . and the response was incredible." In addition to Nitze, Rostow, Zumwalt, Schlesinger, and Walker, the first meeting included Richard V. Allen, Lane Kirkland, David Packard, and Charles Tyroler II. That group became the executive committee whose job was to set the policies of the committee and recruit its members. "We never invited anyone to join in the effort without the unanimous approval of the nuclear group," explained Marshall.

As the driving force behind the group's creation, Rostow was named chairman. Fowler, Kirkland, and Packard became cochairmen. Charly Walker was a natural choice for treasurer. Charles Tyroler II, the man who had chaired a divided Democratic Advisory Committee two decades earlier, assumed the position of director. As chairman of Policy Studies, Nitze would play his usual role of ideas man.

As the committee's organization came together, it still lacked two critical ingredients for success: a name and money. "We spent endless hours on what the committee should be called," Tyroler remembered. "Thirty or forty names were considered."[3] Reaching into the past, Rostow suggested borrowing the name of another prodefense citizen's group, one which had been formed in the early 1950s by James Conant: the Committee on the Present Danger. Some members worried that the name was too alarmist, but eventually the group came to the conclusion that sounding the alarm was, after all, its principal mission. "If there is a present danger—as we all agreed there was—there's no sense in pussyfooting about it," said committee member Max Kampleman.[4]

Raising money proved more difficult. "There was much talk of large pledges and commitments," Kampleman wrote later, "but none materialized in hard cash, or for that matter, in anything else."[5] The fact that such a high-powered group had problems raising funds seemed slightly ridiculous to Walker, and he took it upon himself to "get some money." Flying to Houston, Walker and former Governor John B. Connally hosted a small luncheon and raised $37,000. It was not much, but it would pay the committee's bills until it could raise greater funds upon going public.

Exactly when to go public was a subject of heated debate. Nineteen seventy-six was an election year, and the executive committee was divided between Democrats and Republicans. Nobody wanted the committee to somehow hurt or embarrass his party. So as Rostow recalled, "We decided not to emerge until after the election because we didn't want to get caught up as proponents of either candidate."

What to present to the press on "D-Day," when the committee went public, was less controversial. Drafted and redrafted, the committee's first policy statement was blunt and simple. "Common Sense and the Common Danger" painted a bleak picture of a world imperiled by the Soviet Union. "The principal threat to our nation, to world peace, and to the cause of human freedom is the Soviet drive for dominance based upon an unparalleled military build-up," the paper stated. "The Soviet Union has not altered its long-held goal of a world dominated from a single center—Moscow." In the decade to come the struggle against Soviet power would be a battle for national survival and the values of freedom. Moreover, the battle could be won only through "higher levels of spending"—spending that was "well within our means." To pursue any other course would be disastrous. "If we continue to drift," the paper concluded, "we shall become second best to the Soviet Union in overall military strength . . . we could find ourselves isolated in a hostile world, facing the unremitting pressures of Soviet policy backed by an overwhelming preponderance of power."[6]

"Common Sense and the Common Danger" was presented to over a hundred reporters who jammed the National Press Club in Washington. Divided into three parts, it was dramatically read aloud by Fowler, Kirkland, and Packard. The committee answered questions from the press for an hour. The conference was recorded by the networks, and every major newspaper was there. Returning home, committee members anxiously awaited the results.

Nothing happened. That evening there was no mention of the committee's debut on television or radio. The next morning committee members were stunned to find that the press conference had not been written up in either the *Washington Post* or the *New York Times.* "We were just ignored," recalled Walker.

There was some foreign coverage, however. One Soviet journal stated: "Since the organization's members include extremely influential 'liberal' politicians and military figures and it is backed by strong business groups, it cannot be regarded as one of the usual anti-Soviet and anti-Communist groups which spring up with such frequency in the United States."[7]

Indeed, the committee was unusual. If the disaster in Vietnam had sundered America's political establishment, if it had spawned a deep cynicism about the uses of American power, and if it had left a divided country grappling with the specter of imperial decline, it had also generated a backlash to the backlash. By the mid 1970s a growing sector of elite opinion began to suggest—quietly at first and then with mounting vehemence—that America's self-chastisement had gone on too long. It was time to get on with the business of promoting U.S. interests. It was time to recognize, again, that an assertive foreign policy based on military power was essential to the well-being of the United States. As Jeane Kirkpatrick—a Georgetown professor known in the new lingo of the times as a "neoconservative"—put it, "a culture of appeasement which finds reasons not only against the use of force but denies its place in the world is a profoundly mistaken culture— mistaken in the nature of reality."[8] With its members ranging from Norman Podhoretz to Dean Rusk to Saul Bellow, the committee repre- sented a broad-based coalition of prodefense forces who were deter- mined to reassert American power after many long and agonizing years of self-doubt.

For Paul Nitze, the shift in the political climate necessitated no new theories. It did not take long to devise an ideological framework which would best dramatize America's predicament and strike a chord of terror in the hearts of the nation's leadership. He had developed such a framework a quarter century earlier when he had written NSC 68.

And now he brought it back into play.

In 1974 and 1975 Nitze had questioned Soviet good faith in SALT. He had called attention to their strategic arms buildup. He had won- dered aloud whether detente was a "myth." In 1976 he began to talk far more pessimistically. He spoke of a Soviet drive for superiority. "They certainly want preponderance," he told a congressional commit- tee in March. "They are perfectly frank to admit it. There isn't any argument about it. It isn't just parity or equality."[9]

And in case anyone had forgotten what preponderance could be used for in an age of nuclear overkill, Nitze reminded them. In NSC 68 he had written that "when it calculates that it has sufficient atomic capa- bility to make a surprise attack on us, nullifying our atomic superiority and creating a military situation decisively in its favor, the Kremlin might be tempted to strike swiftly and with stealth." In the Gaither report, he had written again about a first strike. Now Nitze revived the notion, writing articles in *Foreign Policy* and *Foreign Affairs* that outlined in chilling detail how the Soviets could mount a first strike. Underpinning these writings was Nitze's enduring perception of the Soviet Union as a mechanical chess player executing one risky sequence after another in a bold bid for global domination.

In view of the great shift in superpower relations brought about by detente, however, Nitze's premise of total theoretical hostility seemed out of touch with the defense debate of the 1970s. Most mainstream analysts dismissed the notion that the Soviets were seeking nuclear supremacy and took it for granted that the Kremlin was content with nuclear parity and its ineluctable offspring, mutual assured destruction (MAD).

In the fall of 1976 Nitze and a small band of dissenters were given a unique opportunity to challenge this common wisdom. The occasion was a decision by CIA Director George Bush to let an outside group of experts review the agency's intelligence work on Soviet intentions and capabilities. The move was prompted by complaints from the President's Foreign Intelligence Advisory Board (PFIAB) that the CIA was underestimating the Soviet threat. In June 1976 Bush authorized a "competitive analysis" consisting of three outside teams that would look into Soviet air defenses, missile accuracies, and strategic objectives. The CIA group currently reviewing this material was labeled Team A. The designation for the outsiders was B Team. Of the three outside teams, the most important was the one dealing with Soviet objectives; it was called simply Team B.

Chosen to head Team B was Richard Pipes, professor of Russian history at Harvard University. A Polish immigrant, Pipes was known in his field as a fierce anti-Soviet ideologue, and his selection insured that Team B would take a pessimistic view of Soviet intentions. His predisposition was shared by the team members he picked. Nitze was tapped immediately for the project, as were such hard-liners as William Van Cleave, Foy Kohler, and Thomas Wolfe. Another member, Lieutenant General Daniel Graham, former director of the Defense Intelligence Agency, had distinguished himself as one of the CIA's most outspoken critics in Washington. "There are more liberals per square foot in the CIA than any other part of government," Graham charged.[10] And what these liberals produced were overly sanguine assessments of Soviet intentions. This tendency was encouraged by Henry Kissinger, who Graham believed put pressure on the CIA to write estimates of Soviet intentions that supported detente.

Nitze's view was less conspiratorial, but it pointed to the same conclusions. He thought that the CIA felt guilty about past exaggerations of the Soviet threat and was compensating for its mistakes by consistently playing down Soviet intentions and capabilities. Reinforcing this misjudgment, he believed, "was a tendency to imagine that Soviet decision makers act or react in given circumstances in a manner analogous to the way in which the U.S. decision maker might react in similar circumstances."[11] The result was a skewed image of the Soviet

Union as rationally pursuing much the same kind of strategic policy as the United States. Because he felt the Soviets would seize any chance to move aggressively against the west, Nitze saw this outlook as dangerously naive. And like Van Cleave, Pipes and the others, he was convinced of this point well before he joined Team B.

Team B held its first meeting in late August in Arlington, Virginia. Over the next two months the group studied the same intelligence data that the CIA's Team A was using to prepare its latest National Intelligence Estimate (NIE). Some of this material was so highly classified that it could be read only at the CIA's headquarters in Langley, where Team B members were treated with suspicion and hostility.

In writing its report, Team B discovered divisions in its ranks, and debate was especially heated when it came to doing the final overall assessment of the Soviet strategic buildup. Finished by late October, the report was a predictable reflection of its authors' long-held views. As Pipes recalled, Team B "concluded that the evidence indicated beyond reasonable doubt that the Soviet leadership did not subscribe to MAD but regarded nuclear weapons as tools of war whose proper employment, in offensive as well as defensive modes, promised victory."[12] The conclusions were strikingly similar to those stated twenty-six years earlier in NSC 68. Josef Stalin may have died; superpower relations may have warmed considerably; and the rise of vast, diversified nuclear arsenals may have stabilized the arms race. But to Team B, nothing had really changed at all. In their world it was perfectly plausible that the Soviets would exploit a strategic edge to strike "swiftly and with stealth."

Once again, the central issue in the strategic debate was Soviet intentions and capabilities. Like Kennan and Bohlen in the 1950s, CIA experts saw no evidence that the Soviets sought strategic hegemony or were preparing to fight and win a nuclear war. On the contrary, Soviet history and political doctrine argued against such a notion. To Nitze and his colleagues, however, the sheer size of the Soviet strategic buildup was evidence enough. Framing this perspective was the dubious contention that capabilities dictated intentions. "The conventional wisdom used to be that capabilities and intentions have no relationship to each other," Nitze remarked in 1980. "This is not necessarily so. Had Hitler had fewer and less competent divisions and air squadrons, his intentions at any given time would have undoubtedly have been far more limited. *Intentions tend to grow with the capability to carry them out.*"[13]

On November 5 at Langley, Team B and Team A faced each other across a long table and debated. The room was crowded with curious onlookers from throughout the building. Howard Stoertz, the head of Team A, had fielded a group of young and inexperienced analysts to take on the older men. "It was an absolute disaster for the CIA," said one agency official. Pipes recalled the confrontation: "The champion for Team A had barely begun his criticism of Team B's effort, delivered in a condescending tone, when a member of Team B fired a question that reduced him to a state of catatonic immobility: we stared in embarrassment as he sat for what seemed an interminable time with an open mouth, unable to utter a sound. Later, Stoertz came to the rescue but he did not save the Agency and his office from emerging badly mauled."[14]

After the encounter between the two groups, it is believed that George Bush compelled Team A to revise its report to reflect Team B's conclusions. On December 2 Pipes and Stoertz appeared before PFIAB to present their conclusions, and Pipes listened in disbelief as Stoertz advanced views that largely agreed with the findings of Team B. Bush's effort to impose a new assessment of Soviet intentions on the CIA had succeeded.

When news of Team B leaked, its work was criticized throughout Washington. During his last days in office, Kissinger charged that the Team B report was "aimed at sabotaging a new treaty limiting arms. . . . I think it is time that we conduct a rational debate on the issue of nuclear strategy," he said. "It is too important and vital a subject to be made a subject of doctrinaire and partisan debate. Those who talk about supremacy are not doing this country a service and not doing mankind a service."[15]

To critics in Congress, the Team B episode was a blatant attempt to undermine the objectivity of intelligence and twist CIA estimates to fit an ideological agenda. Nor did the timing of Bush's undertaking—during the last months of the Ford administration—seem coincidental. Democrats suspected that Team B was aimed at saddling any incoming administration with a preordained, anti-Soviet pessimism. Three congressional committees began investigations into the affair. Summing up the sentiments of many who looked into the matter, Senator Gary Hart would write that " 'competitive analysis' and use of selected outside experts was little more than a camouflage for a political effort to force the National Intelligence Estimate to take a more bleak view of the Soviet threat."[16]

* * *

Nitze's involvement with Team B further confirmed his belief that the Soviets were close to attaining strategic superiority. To many observers, this fear seemed ungrounded given America's secure retaliatory forces. But, as in the 1950s, Nitze worked to debunk the myth of a stable nuclear balance using the specter of a Soviet first strike. Because the strategic arms race was more complex, his argument was more complex. Its thrust, however, was the same.

Nitze's scenario for how the Soviets could nullify the deterrent power of America's large and varied nuclear arsenal went like this: In a time of international crisis, the Soviet Union begins implementing a nationwide civil defense program by evacuating its cities and sheltering its population. "In some of their civil defense manuals," Nitze wrote, "the Soviets have estimated that the effective implementation of this program should hold casualties to 3 per cent or 4 per cent of their population." This would be a large number of casualties, but "not a number large enough to keep their society from being able to recover with reasonable speed."

After evacuating their cities, the scenario continued, the Soviets then use their heavy ICBMs—the missiles that had so worried Nitze during SALT—to strike at America's land-based missiles, its bombers on the ground, and its missile-carrying submarines in port. Nitze calculated that such an attack would destroy 90 percent of America's ICBMs, 50 percent of its bombers, and 35 percent of its submarine-based missiles. It would be a devastating blow. And it would leave a U.S. president with almost no options.

The logic of mutual assured destruction suggested that a president would still be able to obliterate Soviet society with his remaining forces. Several thousand U.S. nuclear warheads would survive even the most successful Soviet first strike. That force was viewed by most in the government as more than enough firepower. There were, after all, only about nine hundred Soviet cities with a population over twenty-five thousand.

But Nitze took issue with the logic of MAD. He doubted that several thousand nuclear warheads were sufficient to destroy the Soviet Union as a functioning society. Pointing out that the warheads most likely to survive a first strike were the warheads on U.S. Poseidon submarines, Nitze argued that the best way to use these weapons in a second strike would be to explode them above cities. But with civil defense measures in effect, Nitze estimated that much of the Soviet population would survive. And the Soviet leadership, deep in their hardened bunkers, would remain unscathed.

Bombers carried bigger nuclear bombs and could deliver a much more fearsome blow. But half of the U.S. bomber force would be destroyed on the ground, Nitze estimated, and the ones that did get away would face a huge Soviet air defense network.

In any case, Nitze believed that the number of nuclear weapons that the United States could drop in the Soviet Union was largely irrelevant. He made the same argument he had put forth in the 1950s: If the Soviets succeeded in destroying most of America's nuclear weapons, the only U.S. option would be to strike at Soviet cities. Yet this would trigger a Soviet nuclear attack on U.S. cities. Such a move would be suicidal. "The crucial question," Nitze wrote in 1976, "is whether a future U.S. president should be left with only the option of deciding within minutes, or at most within two or three hours, to retaliate after a counterforce attack in a manner certain to result not only in military defeat for the United States but in wholly disproportionate and truly irremediable destruction to the American people. I believe not."

Although the argument was highly theoretical, its overall thrust was simple: "If it were to be a fact," said Nitze, "that the Soviets could knock out most of our Minutemen and that many of our bombers could not successfully penetrate, there would be clear superiority on the Soviet side—just as meaningful superiority as there was in 1962 on our side."

The implications of this impending threat were clear. To deny the Soviets nuclear superiority, Nitze argued that the United States needed a carefully orchestrated strategic buildup. The objectives of this buildup, he wrote, should "not be to give the United States a war-fighting capability; it would be to deny the Soviet Union the possibility of a successful war-fighting capability. We would thus be acting to maintain a situation in which each side is equally and securely deterred from initiating the use of nuclear weapons against the other." To build this stability, Nitze argued that the United States should deploy a mobile land-based missile, step up development of a highly accurate SLBM called Trident II, and deploy a new long-range strategic bomber, the B-1.[17] It was a program of modernization that would cost tens of billions of dollars. As in the 1950s, though, Nitze believed such costs were a small price to pay for American security.

To many in Washington, Paul Nitze's perception of the threat seemed as extreme as his proposed remedies.

In the early 1950s experts on the Soviet Union had called into question Nitze's views of Soviet intentions. They now did so again.

Raymond Garthoff, a former SALT colleague and one of America's foremost Soviet experts, disagreed vehemently with Nitze's contention that the Soviets had abandoned MAD and were pursuing nuclear superiority. "Soviet military and political leaders have ceased to call for strategic superiority as an objective since the 24th Party Congress in 1971," wrote Garthoff. "Instead, mutual deterrence, a balance, parity, and equal security are advocated." Such statements were not designed for export, either. These views were reflected in internal Soviet military journals such as *Military Thought*. As Garthoff observed, there has been "a new readiness even by military commentators to accept strategic parity, mutual deterrence, and the inadmissibility of nuclear war publicly."[18]

This was not to say that the Soviet Union had abandoned efforts to enhance its nuclear arsenal. It hadn't. Garthoff and other Soviet experts did not quarrel with the claim that the Soviet Union was deploying a strategic force with a much greater counterforce capability. But they had an explanation for these deployments. "It is clear in official directives and other discussions in *Military Thought*," wrote Garthoff, "that since the mid-1960s the Soviet military command has seen a need to prepare for various possible wars, including both non-nuclear and nuclear. But this requirement is framed exclusively in terms of flexible response options to meet various Western actions."[19]

George Kennan saw things much the same way. Celebrated in many circles for his prescient efforts to head off the arms race which was now proving so calamitous, Kennan had never ceased criticizing those who championed the military component of detente. As eloquent and forceful as ever, he still saw U.S. policy as shaped by a misguided emphasis on capabilities over intentions. He believed also that U.S. policy makers had never cured themselves of their predilection to overestimate Soviet strength and confidence. In a book written to rebut the opponents of detente, Kennan argued that when the Soviet leadership "looks abroad, it sees more dangers than inviting opportunities. Its reactions are therefore more defensive than aggressive. It has no desire for any major war, least of all for a nuclear one. It fears and respects American military power even as it tries to match it, and hopes to avoid a conflict with it."[20]

In the realm of nuclear weapons the Soviets had particular cause for concern. Between 1970 and 1976 the deployment of MIRVs added over two warheads a day to the U.S. strategic arsenal, more than doubling that arsenal in six years. During this same period the United

States dramatically increased the accuracy of its strategic warheads; it modernized all three legs of its nuclear triad; it began developing several new strategic weapons systems.

And if there was reason to doubt the Soviet commitment to MAD, there was reason to doubt the U.S. commitment as well. In January 1974 President Nixon moved U.S. strategic doctrine away from MAD when he signed National Security Directive Memorandum 242. Harking back to the Kennedy years, when the ability to control nuclear war was seen as possible and desirable, NSDM 242 advocated "a wide range of nuclear employment options which could be used in conjunction with supporting political and military measures (including conventional forces) to control escalation." It also counseled that in the event of a nuclear war, the U.S. goal should be "to seek early war termination on terms acceptable to the United States and its allies, at the lowest level of conflict feasible."[21]

In light of these developments, many suggested that Nitze's picture of a one-sided arms race, with the Soviets doing all the racing, was misleading. Nor, it was argued, did Nitze's apocalyptic scenario for a Soviet first strike bear any relevance to reality.

One critic who occasionally shared the witness table with Nitze during congressional hearings in the 1970s was Sidney Drell, a respected physicist and arms control expert. He attacked Nitze's assertion that the Soviets were developing a usable nuclear edge on several grounds. First, Drell disputed the assertion that Soviet civil defense measures were meaningful. "I know of no intelligence information or technical facts on which to base a conclusion that Soviet civil defense programs are effective to the point of denying the U.S. retaliatory capability or even of threatening to disturb significantly the overall U.S. and Soviet strategic balance," he said. Nitze's assertion that the Soviets could save their population from the destruction wrought by several thousand nuclear weapons was simply nonsense.[22]

Second, Drell called into question Nitze's much repeated claim that the Soviets had an advantage in throw-weight, saying that "when total missile throw-weight and gross bomber payloads are added up, there is no projected Soviet throw-weight advantage in the decade ahead."[23] While the Soviets did have a lead in heavy land-based missiles, America's nuclear forces were far more flexible, reliable, and diversified. Like most arms experts, Drell would never advocate trading the balanced U.S. triad for a Soviet arsenal in which over 70 percent of the warheads were unwisely based on land.

In any case, Drell didn't believe that either side could launch a nuclear attack against enemy missile silos with high confidence, given the numerous uncertainties involved in such an operation. Echoing the views of many scientists, Drell argued that Nitze was deluded to think that a nuclear war could be fought with precision and control—that for example hundreds of Soviet missiles shot six thousand miles over the Arctic, a feat never attempted before, would all land on target.[24]

Taken together, Drell saw little chance that the Soviets could achieve the kind of superiority that Nitze predicted. "Our strategic nuclear forces," he said in January 1977, "are at present far more than adequate to fulfill their single vital mission of deterrence of nuclear attack."[25]

And there were other criticisms of Paul Nitze.

For some in the national security establishment, the most enduring lesson of Vietnam was that America had to reduce its reliance on military power. It had to accept the end of Pax Americana. It had to concentrate on solving economic and social problems at home and break away from the cold war mind set that kept the country trapped in an endless arms race with the Soviet Union.

Paul Warnke was one such member of the establishment. In his view Nitze and other unreconstructed hawks had failed to learn from Vietnam. They still clung to the dangerous notion that the United States should be number one. They perceived the American international role as fundamentally paternalistic, that of a world policeman. And, Warnke believed, people like Paul Nitze failed to appreciate the burden of an assertive national security policy. "The proposition that we must maintain a lead across the spectrum of strategic and conventional forces is a formula for endless escalation in defense costs," he wrote.[26]

Like so many others, Warnke had first begun to question the premises of American postwar security policy as he executed that policy during the Johnson years. On one level Paul Nitze had shared Warnke's doubts. Both men believed that the price of prestige in Southeast Asia had become too high. They shared the view that America's obsession with the war was distorting national policy. Following Tet, each had counseled against a further commitment of men and material to the war. In doing so, the two men risked their jobs under a president who demanded absolute loyalty. On a wall in his house, Warnke had a signed picture of Nitze. It read "To Paul, from your co-conspirator."

As much as they had agreed on the need to get out of Vietnam, Warnke and Nitze learned different lessons from the war. To Warnke, Vietnam was the logical outgrowth of a flawed conception of containment and a mistaken assessment of U.S. interests. If future Vietnams were to be avoided, the United States had to realize that it could not use military power to cope with every challenge to its interests. Nor should it be willing to sacrifice blood and treasure merely to sustain the appearance of American omnipotence. Wars of credibility, Warnke felt, were not worth fighting. As a consequence, the United States could safely reduce its defense budget.

Nitze disagreed adamantly. By writing NSC 68 and by promoting its conclusions into the Kennedy-Johnson era, he had been a principal architect of the strategic doctrine that had led the United States into Vietnam. Even so, Nitze believed that there was nothing wrong with the ideas of NSC 68. The problem had been in application. As the French had found out in the early 1950s, the steamy jungle of Vietnam was the wrong place to fight a war, and Nitze had counseled against U.S. involvement on that basis.

Once the war had been fought and lost, however, Nitze's response was not to abandon the ideas of NSC 68. He did not think that the United States could forget about maintaining credibility and reduce its defense budget. Nor did he believe that the Cold War was over and that nuclear superiority was no longer relevant. On the contrary, Nitze felt that because the Vietnam war had weakened U.S. prestige and eroded the country's will to fight, American interests had become easy prey for an increasingly pugnacious Soviet Union. Precisely because of defeat in Southeast Asia, the United States had to be even more vigilant and better armed to survive the years ahead.

Paul Nitze thought also that Paul Warnke was a dangerous man. At first, their dispute was an amicable one. "They were having substantive disagreements but they remained personal friends," remembered Ralph Earle. While they differed on matters of policy, Warnke and Nitze found much to like about each other. Both held strong opinions and enjoyed a good intellectual jousting match. They both were wealthy and refined, had traveled widely and read widely, and shared many friends. They could and did talk about matters besides strategic policy. Moreover, both Warnke and Nitze had been in Washington long enough not to let differences of opinion between "reasonable men" become too important. In the 1950s Nitze had continued to like Robert Oppenheimer and George Kennan despite his disagreements with them. In the 1970s he continued to like Paul Warnke. Earle remembered having a cocktail party at his Georgetown apartment in 1976. Both the Nitzes and the Warnkes were invited. "Within five minutes," he recalled, "the two Pauls were off in a corner kind of giggling and having two drinks together. They were friends."

Even when they debated deadly serious matters in front of the Congress or other audiences, they were gracious combatants. Cheerful and portly, with a sonorous voice and gift for metaphor, Warnke relied heavily on his eloquence and wit to illustrate what he saw as the many absurdities of U.S. policy. Nitze, invariably, was far more somber. Lean and austere, often humorless, he gazed owlishly over his reading glasses, reeling off numbers and facts, casting doubt on optimistic judgments, questioning conventional wisdom, and painting a grim picture in his soft voice of impending insecurity. At times the debate between the two Pauls grew fierce. At times they might have questioned each other's judgment. But they were always friends.

Until Jimmy Carter was elected President.

Prodded by his children to back someone from their generation, Nitze had become a supporter of Carter before the Iowa caucus, when he was still a dark horse ringing doorbells in Des Moines. Having made his choice, Nitze slapped a Carter bumper sticker on his Volvo station wagon and promoted the candidate to his friends. He also sent the former Georgia governor some of his speeches and made a large campaign contribution. Nitze knew little about Carter's views on defense, but what he did know was reasonably encouraging. Carter was an Annapolis graduate, he had served on a nuclear submarine, and he was known as a technocrat of sorts. He was from the South. "He had a respect for and a command of the facts and I always admire that," Nitze said later.[27] He seemed like a good bet for a hawkish president. As Rostow recalled, "we thought a fellow of that background couldn't be weak and flabby on defense and national security issues."

Nitze was further encouraged when he met Carter at a reception. The candidate said that he had read the material Nitze had sent. He had been favorably impressed and had worked some of Nitze's ideas into his speeches. Nitze was flattered, and when Carter won the Democratic nomination in July 1976, Nitze expected to be called on more frequently for advice. He was, after all, one of the party's most senior statesmen.

He didn't have to wait long. Shortly after Carter won the nomination, he invited Nitze, Vance, Brown, and Warnke—all veterans of the Johnson years—down to his home in Plains, Georgia, for a seminar on defense policy. Three younger defense experts, James Woolsey, Walter Slocombe, and Lynn Davis, were also invited.

Gathering in the Pond House, a small building that Carter had built for his mother next to a dredged pond, the group discussed the future of U.S. defense policy. When Nitze got a chance to speak, he pulled out charts on the strategic balance and proceeded to lecture Carter and the others on the perils of the Soviet nuclear threat. He talked ominously of the Soviet civil defense effort, the new Soviet emphasis on nuclear war fighting, and the massive Soviet long-range missiles that could devastate America's Minuteman force in a first strike. He spoke with intensity, brushing aside questions raised by the others. The implications of his remarks were clear: Only a massive increase in U.S. nuclear forces could secure America from impending Soviet superiority.

Carter was unimpressed. "Nitze was typically know-it-all," he said later. "He was arrogant and inflexible. His own ideas were sacred to him. He didn't seem to listen to others, and he had a doomsday approach." In the view of most others at the meeting, Nitze's performance was a disaster. Vance commented to Warnke and Brown that Nitze had "blotted his copybook" by "browbeating" and "haranguing" Carter.[28]

Only James Woolsey and Walter Slocombe saw things differently. An admirer of Nitze's, Woolsey praised his former boss's comments. "I think he just said what he thought—perhaps in a forceful way. I don't think that he tried to intimidate Carter or tried to be the only one talking." Slocombe agreed, disputing the notion that this was where Nitze and Carter parted ways. "Although it was clear that Nitze was selling and Carter wasn't buying," he said later, ". . . it didn't seem to me that there was any personal chemistry that was bad."

But when Jimmy Carter won the election and began appointing his national security team, Nitze's telephone was silent. Carter dismissed suggestions by his new national security advisor, Zbigniew Brzezinski, that he strive for "greater diversity in the defense-arms control cluster" and appoint more hard-liners.[29] "I don't think that man has the breadth or balance we need," the president-elect was reported as saying.[30] The word in Washington was that Averell Harriman, wise man and Democratic stalwart, counseled the president-elect to beware of hard-line cold warriors, mentioning Paul Nitze in particular, who could sabotage his dream for a new and enlightened American foreign policy.

Carter probably didn't realize it, but he was doing something that no president had done since Eisenhower; he was leaving Paul Nitze outside of the action. It was a critical mistake. Had Carter taken a good look at Nitze's response to being cast into the outer darkness during the 1950s, had he realized how energetically Nitze had worked to undermine the Eisenhower-Dulles regime, he might have reconsidered. But Carter was a newcomer to Washington. He didn't know about Paul

Nitze. He didn't appreciate the kind of damage that one well-connected saboteur could do. "He didn't figure out how to deal with the problem of people you don't agree with but whose support you need," recalled Walter Slocombe. And so Jimmy Carter left Nitze in his glass-walled office overlooking the Potomac. He left him to brood about the perils that lay ahead and ponder ways to get even.

When Vance was appointed secretary of state, Nitze went on television to praise the choice, recalling that "It was a continuous pleasure to work with Cyrus Vance."[31] When Harold Brown got the post of secretary of defense, Nitze was supportive. Brown was steady and well informed. Nitze, in fact, knew or had worked with most of the officials who held high-level posts in Carter's national security establishment. Many of them had been in the Johnson administration, and for these men Washington's revolving door was functioning as planned. Typically, those who held second or third echelon posts in the past were elevated to first or second echelon jobs when their party returned to power. By this tradition Paul Nitze should have had a shot at secretary of defense or state. But Nitze had blotted his copybook at the Pond House and been perceived by the president-elect as arrogant. He had bungled his courtesy call, trespassed on southern hospitality. So now, after slowly working his way up the ladder of power, after holding no less than ten jobs in Democratic administrations, after missing out on the deputy secretary of defense job in 1960, after being exiled to the Navy Department, after being passed over for the post of secretary of defense when McNamara left the Pentagon, after slaving on SALT for five years, Nitze was not getting any job at all. As Vance said later, it was "a terrible blow to Paul, because there was every reason to think it was his last chance for a senior position."[32]

At the very least, Carter could have drawn on Nitze's five years as a SALT negotiator and given him a post in the arms control bureaucracy—as head of ACDA or as chief SALT negotiator. But he didn't. And what infuriated Nitze more than anything was that the president gave those two jobs to a man he felt was totally unqualified to handle either one, much less both at the same time: Paul Warnke.

From the day the announcement was made in early January 1977, there was little doubt that Nitze would raise objections to the choice. The only question was what form such objections would take. Ralph Earle was staying at Nitze's house during this period. One morning in early February, Nitze showed him a letter at breakfast. It was addressed to Senator Sparkman, chairman of the Senate Foreign Relations Committee, and concerned the Warnke nomination. The letter stated that Warnke was too much of a knee-jerk disarmer, that he was naive about defense questions, and that, in any case, the chief SALT negotiator should not also be head of ACDA.

Earle took issue with the letter. "Paul, what's wrong with having a guy interested in arms control be head of the arms control agency?" he asked. "That seems to me illogical." Nitze amended the letter to focus more on what he saw as the rift in the foreign policy community. The Vietnam war, Nitze wrote, had left that community divided. "In one view, U.S. foreign and defense problems would continue, indeed might become more serious as a result of Vietnam, and could well call for even more emphasis and greater prudence than had been devoted to them in the past. In the contrasting view, the problems of the past had arisen largely from our own errors springing from over-emphasis on foreign policy, and particularly its defense aspects." By calling for a reduction in military spending, Nitze said, Paul Warnke had been one of the "most active, vocal and persistent advocates of this (latter) point of view."[33]

Nitze sent the letter to Sparkman, who entered it into the record. For a moment it appeared that the letter would be the extent of Nitze's objections. But the Warnke nomination was evolving into a major political battle. By bringing into focus the mounting debate over the direction of American strategic policy, it was fast becoming a test of strength for the growing antidetente coalition, the vanguard of which was the Committee on the Present Danger.

Warnke and his supporters received a taste of how bitter the battle would be when an anonymous memorandum—soon traced to the Coalition for a Democratic Majority—circulated through Congress. McCarthyist in tone, the memo accused Warnke of advocating "unilateral abandonment by the U.S. of every weapon system which is subject to negotiation at SALT." It charged him with the unforgivable sin of having been "the principal advisor to George McGovern on national security issues during the 1972 presidential campaign." And it claimed that Warnke was too far out of the mainstream, representing "views which are not shared, for the most part, by a majority of Americans."[34]

As harsh as this attack on Warnke was, it soon became clear that Warnke himself was really not the issue. As one columnist observed, "There is a peculiar, almost venomous intensity in some of the opposition to Paul Warnke; it is as if the opponents have made him a symbol of something they dislike so much that they want to destroy him."[35]

What Warnke symbolized, of course, was the dovish wing of the Democratic party, and the fight against his nomination was seen by many as an early opportunity to put the Carter administration on notice, to send the message that it would be allowed little flexibility in the realm of strategic policy and that an imperfect SALT II treaty would meet the same opposition as the man who negotiated it.

To Paul Nitze, this seemed like a sound strategy. So when Senator Charles Percy, a great admirer of Nitze's, suggested he testify against Warnke, Nitze accepted.

It was a rather odd thing for Nitze to do. In his dozens of appearances before Congress, Nitze had never spoken out against a nomination. Rarely had he even attacked another person in passing. It was simply not the sort of thing that men of Nitze's generation and background did. Much as senators treated each other with excessive deference, so did members of the establishment. Nitze's old mentor Dean Acheson may have enjoyed cutting up colleagues in private, but he seldom did so in public. Certainly Acheson would have been extremely hesitant about testifying against the nomination of a friend.

But to Nitze, the peril of the times did not allow for the luxury of gentlemanly etiquette. "He's a man out to save the state," commented McGeorge Bundy. "Nitze believes somebody like Warnke is dangerous and must be watched." Had he still been alive, Acheson would have understood these special circumstances.[36]

Nor did the dictates of honesty allow for quibbling. When Nitze appeared before the Senate Foreign Relations Committee, in early February, he was blunt: "I am concerned that Mr. Warnke, who has spoken with such certainty on matters of military requirements, weapons capabilities, and strategy, may nevertheless not be a qualified student or competent judge of any of these matters. . . . I cannot bring myself to believe that the Senate would be well advised to give its consent to Mr. Warnke's appointment."

Nitze's stated reasons for opposing Warnke were numerous. He said that he knew of only one weapons system, the Trident I, that Paul Warnke had supported over the last decade. He contended that if the United States had followed Paul Warnke's advice, it would have canceled its ABM program in 1969 and never achieved the ABM Treaty. He charged that Warnke was naive to believe that nuclear war was unthinkable and compared his strategic philosophy to that of John Foster Dulles. He accused Warnke of inconsistency, of misrepresenting his views to the Senate, of trying to moderate his positions through a poorly concealed last-minute conversion. Beyond this, Nitze kept his

attacks focused on Warnke's ideas.[37] "They were substantive antago-
nists," recalled Earle. For the first round of his testimony, Nitze appeared determined to keep it that way.

Shortly after his appearance before the Senate committee, a twenty-
seven-page anonymous memorandum circulated in Washington which
rebutted Nitze's testimony point by point. It said that Nitze had
misrepresented Warnke's positions on everything from the B-1 bomber
to the usefulness of the Marine Corps. It also counterattacked, stating
that "A basic tenet of Mr. Nitze's philosophy seems to be that a higher
defense budget automatically buys more national defense." Finally, the
memorandum called into question Nitze's motives. "Mr. Nitze's attack
on Mr. Warnke, viewed analytically, can be seen as being not a substantive, well-reasoned, carefully prepared analysis of a man representing
another point of view but as an attack on a man's integrity based on
nothing more than a reasonable difference of opinion."[38]

What bothered Nitze about the memo was not that it had rebutted
his remarks—that was fair play—but that it was anonymous and had
been prepared on the basis of a garbled and unedited transcript of the
testimony. Moreover, it was a transcript that a Warnke supporter on
the committee had clearly leaked, since Nitze himself could not get a
copy. Things were getting nasty.

And as the battle over Warnke became more heated, Nitze's comments grew harsher. He was disturbed by the possibility that Warnke
was not just a gadfly included in the administration to satisfy the
liberals, but that he truly represented Carter's thinking. "I think his
views are well considered by me," the president had said, "and I have
accepted them and I believe that Mr. Warnke's proposals are sound
and I have no concern about his attitude."[39] Nitze was disturbed also
by the way the establishment was rallying around Warnke. Clark Clifford, Robert McNamara, Melvin Laird, Gerard Smith, Averell Harriman, and numerous others voiced support for the nomination.

As one of the only establishment figures who joined the anti-Warnke
effort, Nitze found himself in unusual company. Leading the campaign
was an ad hoc organization called the Emergency Coalition Against
Unilateral Disarmament. While Nitze had worked with Daniel Graham, the group's chairman, he was less comfortable with the representatives of the many conservative organizations who sat on the coalition's
steering committee. These groups represented the side of the American
political spectrum that still talked about Alger Hiss, that continued to
believe that the Democrats had lost China, and that had played a role

in attacking Nitze himself when he was nominated to the post of secretary of the navy.

In the Senate the fight against Warnke was led by Nitze's friend Henry Jackson. Jackson's avowed strategy was to "weaken Warnke as an international negotiator to the point of uselessness by holding the vote in his favor to 60 or less."[40] To do this, he wanted to hit Warnke harder during a second round of hearings before the Senate Armed Services Committee. Although Nitze said that he had been "reluctant to appear before the Senate Foreign Relations Committee," he agreed to testify again.

At parties in Georgetown and Northwest, people began talking about the two Pauls, wondering what was happening. Was Nitze, as he claimed, simply raising substantive questions? Or had he embarked on a personal vendetta against Warnke? Following his appearance before the Senate Foreign Relations Committee, those who knew Nitze argued that his attack was substantive. But after he appeared before Jackson's committee, even his friends questioned whether his motives were pure.

Nitze began his second round of testimony by thanking the Senate for making possible "a debate which, though concentrating on the qualifications of one man to hold two most important positions, has necessarily spread to the most basic underlying issues of our proper national security policies." With that said, he was rapidly drawn into ad hominem attacks on Warnke. Nitze labeled Warnke imprudent and said, "It is this cavalier imprudence which I think disqualifies Mr. Warnke for a critical role in the search for prudent arms control, a search for which I believe many of us have been far more dedicated than the record would suggest has been true of Mr. Warnke." He called into doubt Warnke's credentials as an opponent of the Vietnam war, noting that "I cautioned against our massive intervention in Vietnam long before I recollect Mr. Warnke doing so." He challenged Warnke's arms control expertise, saying that "I don't think he has looked into the technical matters himself at all. . . . I think he talks about numbers without knowing what the numbers mean." He questioned Warnke's coherence, saying "I think he has a great ability at confusing people."

And then Nitze blundered: He impugned Warnke's patriotism. The remarks came during questioning by Senator Thomas McIntyre. Having done some research on Nitze, McIntyre came to the committee session with news clips from the *New York Times* about Nitze's own fight for a fair hearing during his nomination to be navy secretary in 1963. After reading the clips into the record, and noting wryly that some of the same senators who were now extolling Nitze's hawkishness had attacked him a decade and half earlier, McIntyre commented that the episode showed "how easily sincere disagreements about particular issues can be invalidly translated into unfortunate personal attacks on a nominee's character and even his Americanism."

McIntyre then continued: "Mr. Nitze, in your opening statement you stated that your disagreement with Mr. Warnke was not of a personal nature, because you both like and respect him."

"I didn't say that. I said I valued him as a former colleague."

"Well, if you valued him as a former colleague, it makes it pretty clear that you don't really basically object to Mr. Warnke's character."

"It does not. I said I have valued him. Frankly, I cannot understand the things that he has been saying in the last few days. I do not think they are proper."

"Are you saying that you impugn his character as an American citizen?"

"If you force me to, I do."

"That is very interesting. Do you think you are a better American than he is?"

"I really do."[41]

When the transcript of Nitze's remarks was being edited, Nitze tried to change the record to strike out his last two answers. But as he himself had once told a freshly anointed secretary of state two and a half decades earlier when Dulles had blundered during congressional testimony, witnesses were not allowed to fundamentally alter their comments. For Dulles the committee had made an exception. For Nitze they would not. The attack on Warnke's patriotism stayed in the record.

And it stayed in Washington's memory long after the Senate ignored Nitze's counsel and confirmed Warnke to be head of ACDA and chief SALT negotiator. Perhaps more than any single action in Paul Nitze's career, his character assassination of Warnke did the most damage to his reputation for fairness and integrity. "It hurt him a lot in Washington," said one friend. "There's no question," added another, "that Paul Warnke regards what Paul Nitze did in the confirmation hearings as just unforgivable." Many were shocked when they heard of the remarks. For a man so controlled, so polite, so habitually circumspect in his public statements, Nitze's attack was the equivalent of another person unleashing a string of libelous obscenities. And even in a town where public officials occasionally did this, Nitze's actions seemed unusual. "You cannot think of where anybody of his [Warnke's] stature has been so viciously attacked at a confirmation hearing," said a former SALT colleague.[42]

Nitze had violated an unwritten code of conduct. "I don't want to be old boy about it," said one friend wearing an alligator shirt and sitting in his plush apartment on New York's Upper East Side, "but it was not the thing to do." Other men might have apologized to Warnke. Paul Nitze was too proud for that. Instead he defended his actions. "I tried to restrain myself," he said later, "but some of the senators wouldn't let me, they put me in a box. If I were to answer the questions truthfully, they forced me lose my usual tact. And after I had seen what had been done to me, I asked for permission to change the record and they wouldn't give me permission."[43] Ralph Earle, who was still staying at Nitze's house through all of this, agreed. "He got painted into a corner. He got more and more strident on Warnke's substantive positions and then McIntyre nailed him with that question. Nitze made a bad mistake."

But to Paul Warnke and his many friends, there was no excuse for Nitze's action. Nor did there seem to be an explanation. Bewildered and saddened by the venom of his old associate, Warnke plaintively asked a mutual friend, "Why did he do it?"

He never learned the answer.

A Poisonous Fellow

ROM THE MOMENT Paul Nitze first arrived in the chilly city of Helsinki in November 1969, he had believed that one of the overriding objectives of SALT should be to cut the Soviet Union's force of heavy land-based missiles. He had been deeply disillusioned when the talks failed to produce those cuts and even more pained when his efforts to overhaul the U.S. negotiating posture failed dismally. With the election of a new president, Nitze believed there was an opportunity to overhaul SALT and mitigate the mounting threats to U.S. security. In the fall of 1976, he laid out his SALT remedies in a memorandum for Carter. Pointing to the Soviet lead in heavy ICBMs, Nitze said "I see no quick way of getting out of this box through negotiations."[1] The only solution was to bolster America's strategic systems while trying to force the Soviets to make negotiating concessions. With patience and resolve SALT could be resuscitated. The memorandum was ignored.

The administration found it harder to dismiss Senator Henry Jackson. Two weeks after Carter was elected, Jackson met with the president to impress upon him the need to abandon the established SALT framework. The Vladivostok Accord of 1974 locked the United States into a position of inferiority, said the Senator. If Carter negotiated a treaty based on the accord, Jackson would have to oppose it. As Jackson's aide Richard Perle wrote in a memorandum to Carter following the meeting, Carter should not pick up the negotiations where Ford had left off because "you would unnecessarily assume the burden of past mistakes, and the options available to you will be few and narrow."[2]

In March the president heeded Jackson's advice and sent Cyrus Vance to Moscow with a bold alternative to the existing SALT structure. In what he would later admit was a "long shot," Vance proposed reducing the overall missile launching ceiling from 2,400 to between 1,800 and 2,000. He suggested reducing the number of missiles allowed to carry MIRVs from 1,320 to between 1,200 and 1,100. Most importantly, he proposed reducing land-based MIRV carriers down to 550 and cutting Soviet heavy missiles from 300 to 150. The new proposals would also have placed a cap on the number of missile flight tests that each side could conduct each year with the goals of reducing accuracy and reliability. Jackson praised the proposal as a positive step away from the "Kissinger-Nixon-Ford approach."[3] But the Soviet Union immediately rejected it, labeling it an unacceptable departure from the established SALT framework.

The March 1977 proposal was almost precisely the kind of overhaul of SALT that Nitze had been advocating, but his response to it was curiously mixed. At first he commented that the Soviet Union had rejected the proposal "because it's an equitable deal, and that's what they don't want."[4] Within a few months, however, Nitze had flip-flopped, writing that "Agreement on the basis of this proposal would not assure crisis stability and mutual deterrence; and its terms would disproportionally favor the USSR as against the U.S."[5]

The negative response by Paul Nitze and the Committee on the Present Danger to a SALT proposal which even Henry Jackson had praised caused administration officials to wonder what these people wanted. On March 31 Carter said that he would consider accelerating U.S. strategic programs if the Soviets did not negotiate in good faith. Two days later Secretary of Defense Harold Brown detailed a $2 billion annual defense increase featuring the MX, B-1, and Trident II, which would be implemented if the talks continued to stall. Even the Coalition for a Democratic Majority praised Carter for his policies on human rights and arms control. George McGovern, in contrast, called the president "too conservative."[6]

What more could the committee ask for? Shortly after the committee released its report critical of the March proposals in early July, Nitze and seven other members received telegrams from Harold Brown. The president wanted to meet with the committee.

The night before the meeting committee members met to plan their approach to Carter. Rostow had called up Brzezinski to ask how the meeting would be structured and was told that Carter would say a few words of greeting and then the committee could make an opening statement. It was decided that Rostow and Nitze would both make statements.

The next day committee members met with Carter, Brown, and Brzezinski in the cabinet room. Vance was in the Middle East and Warnke was not included. It had been almost a year since Nitze had botched his visit to the Pond House. This meeting went no better. Rostow and Nitze read their opening statements, which called for a major step-up in U.S. strategic programs and a dramatic increase in defense spending. Carter's response was blunt: The American public would never tolerate the siphoning off of yet more tax dollars into Pentagon coffers. As the president spoke, Nitze began shaking his head, "No, no, no," he murmured.

"Paul," Carter said, "would you please let me finish."[7]

When the meeting ended after about an hour, the president made it clear that he wanted the committee's support. But not a single member of the Committee on the Present Danger had been given a job under Carter. Few in the group trusted the administration, and none was willing to declare a truce in a war that had clearly just begun. In his best southern drawl, Henry Fowler summed up the group's feeling. "Mr. President," he is recalled as saying, "we're a nonpartisan group and we believe in a bipartisan foreign policy and we've had a lot of experience with this set of problems. We're confident that after you've been in office a little while longer, you'll come around to our view of the Soviet Union and how to deal with it and then we'll be glad to support you."

If the administration had hoped to build some bridges, the meeting had the opposite effect. It confirmed the worst suspicions that committee members had about Jimmy Carter. "The degree of ignorance and naiveté by the President was appalling," Rostow said later. "We were stunned, just stunned. . . . In a way we could hardly talk about it. The notion that that fellow was President was just frightening." When

Carter left the room, the committee members turned their fire on Brown and Brzezinski. Disturbed by a president he found "totally naive," Bud Zumwalt plied Brown with questions about how much information Carter was getting. "Are you briefing him?" he asked the defense secretary.

Brown, of course, was briefing the president. What committee members couldn't understand was that Carter's views on national security stemmed not from poor information, but from an approach to foreign policy and defense that asked fundamental questions about U.S. interests and the resources needed to defend those interests. It was not a radical approach. Rather it was one he and many Americans felt was dictated by the disaster in Vietnam, by America's support for dictators around the world in the name of security, and by the reality of superpower nuclear arsenals so large that they jeopardized humanity's very survival. Given the ugly excesses and the high costs of U.S. security policy, Carter's new thinking was not radical at all. If anything, it was long overdue.

To America's disgruntled hard-liners, however, the president's way of thinking was so foreign as to be almost incomprehensible. And to the degree that it could be comprehended, it seemed dangerously irresponsible. To the committee members there was now little question about who the enemy was. Dangerous people were in power during dangerous times. "Every softliner I can think of is now part of the executive branch and the arms control administration," Nitze complained in August.[8] If the Committee on the Present Danger had originally been conceived as a nonpartisan group, it remained so only in name. By late 1977 it had evolved into an anti-Carter group. Public ignorance of the Soviet threat was not the main problem anymore, they felt. Instead, it was an administration that seemed blind to reality. And the solution was to push, persuade, cajole, or bully that administration into becoming more militant.

To the champions of detente, in turn, the threat posed by the committee was too clear. Not only would the administration face unrelenting pressure to raise defense spending, but it could expect to face a high-powered opposition when the time came to ratify SALT II.

Of all the members of that opposition, few posed a greater threat to ratification than Paul Nitze. When he first resigned from the SALT team in 1974, Nitze had lobbied against a SALT II treaty based on the Vladivostok Accord. During the delicate time in late 1976 when it looked possible to secure a job under Carter, he made constructive suggestions for how to fix SALT. Now, in 1977, feeling bitter and ignored, Nitze stopped advising and began crusading.

On November 2 Nitze held a press conference to release a paper on the negotiations which argued that the United States was locking itself into "a position of inherent inferiority."[9] The paper gave a taste of the arguments that Nitze would make over the next two years. It also touched off a brief flurry of accusations that Nitze had released classified information. Some supporters of the administration insisted that he had. Carl Marcy, codirector of the Commission on East-West Accord, accused Nitze of "unwise and unauthorized release of classified information, of seeking to substitute his judgment and that of the narrow group for which he speaks for the judgment of the Secretary of State, the Defense Secretary, the national security affairs advisor, the Joint Chiefs of Staff, and the President—all of whom are currently involved in the SALT negotiations."

And Marcy added another comment, one which presaged the bitterness of the battle to come. "There seem to be," he said, "a few old cold warriors who neither die nor fade away, but would brandish their sabers forever rather than help pave the way for a just and lasting peace, a reduction in international tensions, and a lessening of the possibility of nuclear war."[10]

Whether the paper Nitze released contained classified information is unclear. Nitze said it did not. But to those who debated Nitze on SALT during this time, it was obvious that he had access to a tremendous amount of inside information. The precise source of this information was always a mystery, but most suspected it came from the Pentagon. Nitze was in contact there with officials who shared his doubts about the direction of SALT, people who longed to make a case for a tougher negotiating posture, but did not want to jeopardize their jobs. For these quiet dissidents, former colleagues like Nitze and Zumwalt became a channel to the public realm. One friend recalled Nitze saying that he was getting information almost faster than when he was deputy secretary. As Rostow later put it, "he was treated very much as Churchill was treated in the thirties in London, when everybody sensed that Churchill was the center of the real opposition in the government. Paul was getting a tremendous flow of information just as Churchill did and for the same reasons: people were more and more concerned and alarmed about the drift of American foreign policy."

Hyperbole aside, Nitze got information because he had a lot of friends in government, because he had the security clearances, and because he had prestige. "If Paul Nitze calls up and asks you a question," commented one Pentagon official, "you answer it."

But while a steady input of classified information allowed Nitze to monitor closely what was happening in Geneva, his mounting opposition to the nearly negotiated treaty caused many of his friends and former colleagues to wonder about the other kinds of information that Nitze was getting. They couldn't believe that he had independently arrived at all of his highly pessimistic conclusions. They wondered who was feeding him the data and ideas that buttressed his apocalyptic claims of coming Soviet nuclear supremacy. Most wanted to continue to like and respect Paul Nitze. Since they knew that Nitze always relied heavily on his staff, some believed—or hoped—that people on his staff were responsible for his extremism. In a letter to Nitze, Richard Garwin summed up these hopes. "Paul," he wrote, "we have known one another for a long time and have worked closely together at various times during the last fifteen years. . . . I retain the greatest respect for your intelligence and effectiveness, and for your interest in the welfare and future of the nation. I fear, though, that some of those who provide you with information and analyses share your views but not your total integrity."[11]

Some who knew Nitze were quick to trace his strategic assessments to T. K. Jones. After his work with Nitze on the SALT delegation, Jones had returned to defense contract work at Boeing, where he had at his disposal a small staff of strategic experts. Still close to Nitze, who he regarded as something of a god, Jones put his experts at Nitze's disposal, helping him refine the Soviet first strike scenario for the Foreign Affairs article "Assuring Strategic Stability in an Age of Detente."

Another Jones contribution during this time was in the area of civil defense. Nitze, of course, had long been a believer in civil defense. Besides advocating greater civil defense measures in numerous government reports, Nitze had actually built his own bomb shelter at Causein Manor and kept it stocked with supplies. It was only with Jones's help, however, that Nitze was able to integrate civil defense into his critique of the strategic situation emerging in the 1970s. At Boeing Jones had done a study on the efficacy of civil defense measures. The study convinced him that the Soviets could protect up to 98 percent of their population in the face of a large-scale nuclear attack and recover in two to four years. With little analysis of his own, Nitze had largely embraced Jones's fantastical conclusions, making them central to his arguments for why the Soviets would gamble on a first strike.

More than anything else, Nitze's statements on civil defense were a tip-off to friends and colleagues that something was amiss. Did a man as intelligent as Paul Nitze really believe that the Soviet civil defense program could reduce casualties to 3 or 4 percent of their population despite the detonation of some two thousand warheads over the country? It just didn't make sense. With Jones helping to shape Nitze's SALT papers, some suspected that the ultrahawkish Boeing official was the real author of the dire forecasts of U.S. inferiority under SALT II. "What everybody always found astonishing about Paul Nitze is that he bought that junk from T. K. Jones," recalled an NSC official, Roger Molander. "T. K. Jones became his analyst, his numbers cruncher. When Paul Nitze needed numbers he went to T. K. Jones for his numbers. And you know T. K. Jones."[12]

As an aide to Harold Brown, Walter Slocombe saw much of the material on SALT that Nitze spread through the government. He reached the same conclusion as Garwin and others. "I think Nitze was misinformed about some things and relied on people who were not up to the usual quality of the people he relies on," said Slocombe. But although he and others in the government felt this to be true, they could not ignore Paul Nitze. He "was always a force to be reckoned with," Slocombe recalled. "He was . . . the most formidable opponent of the treaty. In the general process you couldn't dismiss him like you could dismiss Jesse Helms."

Nitze had a standard paper on SALT which he would periodically update. There were eighteen versions, and he sent them all to Harold Brown. When a paper came in, Brown's staff would analyze it closely. Nitze may have been seen as the enemy, his sources may have been suspect, but what he had to say was still taken seriously. Brown was reluctant, however, to be drawn into an extended debate with Nitze. "We reached the conclusion," said Slocombe, "that for the Secretary of Defense to engage in a point by point response to Paul Nitze was not likely to produce an effect which was worth the time."

On one crucial point, however, Brown and the rest of the administration were willing to debate Paul Nitze. The issue was mobile ICBMs.

Ever since the Soviet Union had begun placing multiple warheads on its massive land-based missiles in the mid 1970s, Pentagon planners had been searching for a way to overcome the projected vulnerability of America's own force of land-based missiles. By the late 1970s they believed they had found one. Their plans called for placing the ten-warhead MX missile that the United States was developing on a track system that would shuttle it between thousands of new missile silos in the Midwest. This way the Soviet Union could never know for sure which silos the missiles were in, and therefore they could not hope to destroy the majority of American land-based missiles in a first strike.

Vance and Warnke opposed the idea. Mobile missiles would be almost impossible to verify, they said, and as a result, such a "shell game" could fatally derail the arms control process. Increasingly anxious to appease administration critics, the White House overruled these objections. It ordered a step-up in the development of the racetrack system—known as a multiple point system (MPS)—and ordered Warnke to inform the Soviets that the United States considered the system allowable under SALT II.

Nitze was enthusiastic about the "shell game" concept and had been advocating it since 1976. "The objective of creating such a new system of deployment," he had written in 1977, "would be to greatly increase the throw-weight costs to the Soviets of destroying a substantial portion of our deterrent forces." To this end, "the Soviet advantage in a counterforce exchange would be drastically reduced or eliminated." The objective also would be to encourage the Soviets to follow suit and build a similar system. "Such moves by both sides would greatly improve crisis stability and thus significantly reduce the risk of a nuclear war," Nitze wrote.[13]

Some in the Carter administration thought that Nitze's advocacy of a multiple point system held out the possibility that the administration could nullify his opposition to SALT II by backing such a system. They believed that if they moved to solve the problem that Nitze worried about, with the system he supported, then he would back the administration when it came time for ratification.

They were wrong. When the SALT II treaty was finally signed by Carter and Brezhnev in Vienna in June 1979, the administration asserted that the agreement would permit an MPS. "We took the position that the MX could go forward and we notified the Russians about that," recalled Lloyd Cutler, an advisor to the President. At the summit Carter personally conveyed the point to Brezhnev, telling him that "the treaty was drafted so as to permit mobile MX missiles to be deployed."[14] While Article I of the protocol stated that neither side could deploy mobile missiles, the protocol would expire on December 31, 1981. And, explained Ralph Earle in his Senate testimony, "the draft agreement expressly provided for the deployment, after protocol expiration, of an ICBM system in which missiles and their launchers are moved from point to point."[15]

Nitze was not convinced of this. He felt that the administration had failed to extract a concrete concession from the Soviets. "I believe this is wholly dubious," he said. "I cannot see how the treaty is read to permit the multiple protective shelter system [meaning the multiple point system]. . . . I think the Russians have made it clear that in their view the multiple protective shelter system would be inconsistent with both the letter and the spirit of the treaty, and I believe we would not act to deploy such a system in the face thereof."[16]

To those who had worked to get the MPS program approved and battled to overcome objections to the system posed by Vance and Warnke, Nitze's insistence that the system was banned under the treaty was infuriating. "That amounted to saying we were lying and tended not to improve the quality of the debate or attitudes on either side," said Slocombe. Nitze's old friends shook their heads. It was not like Paul Nitze to attack on that level. His objections on the MPS question were inconsistent with the way they thought his mind worked. "He always looked first at the logic of the government's position," Jim Woolsey said later. "While the MX and the shell game was a cumbersome system, and while SALT II was far from a perfect treaty, they at least fit together logically." In Geneva Nitze's former negotiating partner Alexander Shchukin was at a loss to comprehend Nitze's crusade to tear down a structure that both men had spent years helping to build. "What has become of my old friend Paul?" he asked. "Why is he saying these things?"[17]

To those who watched Nitze in action during these acrimonious days—crisscrossing the country, appearing on television, lobbying in the halls of the Senate—it appeared that his usual zest for a fair intellectual jousting match was being clouded by his implacable opposition to the treaty. "Paul is a very compulsive man at this stage," said one friend on Capitol Hill, "It's very difficult for him to say that reasonable men can differ on issues of life-and-death importance."[18] Nitze himself put it another way. Writing in the *Fiftieth Annual Report for the Harvard Class of 1928,* he remarked that he had become a "quite poisonous fellow."[19]

If a friend pressed him to explain his actions or a senator probed his motives, Nitze would say that he was not questioning the good faith of administration officials or being compulsive. He was contributing to a substantive debate over the treaty. He was practicing the kind of systematic pessimism that he had practiced for most of his career. What bothered his opponents, Nitze suspected, was not his fanaticism, but the fact that people started to squirm as his questions grew tougher.

At the superpower summit in Vienna, Ralph Earle was asked by Richard Strout of the *New Republic* whether this was a good treaty. Earle replied that it was.

"How good is it?" asked Strout.

"Give me a copy of the treaty and two hours and I can convince any reasonable man that it's a good treaty."

"Paul Nitze is a friend of yours, isn't he?" said Strout. Earle replied that he was.

"Do you consider him a reasonable man?" asked Strout.

"By definition."

"Does this apply to him?" Strout asked.

"Yes." said Earle.

A week before the hearings on SALT II were to start, Earle received a call from Nitze inviting him to the farm for the weekend. Earle accepted. "And by the way," Nitze added, "bring a copy of the treaty."

On that Saturday afternoon in July 1979 the two men sat by the swimming pool and had a long, rational debate. Earle's impression was that Nitze was unhappy with the treaty, but not so unhappy that he would oppose it. "What I thought was that Paul had raised legitimate questions, that he was sophisticated enough to know that there was no treaty that was perfect, and that he would probably support it with some caveats."

Early the next morning Nitze carried Earle's bags out to his car. The testimony was to begin the next day. "Paul," said Earle before he left, "you're going to be testifying over the next few weeks. Your testimony is really going to be critical because you're the only person of any intellectual stature or experience who has expressed any reservations about the treaty. It's a very important thing. Don't screw it up."

That his old friend and former colleague on the SALT team could raise so many doubts about the treaty over the past few years had been painful to Earle. But what angered him most that summer morning was that Nitze didn't seem to appreciate the damage he had done.

"Well, Ralph," Nitze said as they parted, "what else would I have had to do for the last few years?"

For Jimmy Carter winning approval for SALT II was of great personal and political importance. He believed fervently in the merits of the treaty. "SALT II is the most detailed, far-reaching comprehensive treaty in the history of arms control," he told a joint session of Congress upon returning from Vienna.[20] A master of detail, Carter was intimately familiar with even the most esoteric aspects of the agreement. He was also aware of the Senate's skepticism and commented that getting SALT II signed and ratified was "the most difficult task I have assumed—more difficult than being elected President, much more difficult than Camp David."[21]

Masterminding the administration's ratification strategy was Lloyd Cutler. A lawyer and long-time Washington insider with a subdued, meticulous manner, Cutler had advised Carter regularly during his tenure, and in the latter half of 1979 he began working in the White House full time. From the beginning Cutler realized that ratification of the treaty was not assured. The conservative backlash to the social and political upheavals brought on by Vietnam was nearing an apex. Carter's popularity, in contrast, was approaching a new low.

Among many Americans there was a growing distrust of the Soviet Union. As the United States sank into a malaise of energy shortages, uncured social ills, and mounting self-doubt, it seemed that the Soviet Union was winning—winning in Latin America, winning in Angola, winning in the horn of Africa, and winning in the arms race. A complicated treaty did not appear to solve these problems. "Public sentiment for an arms control treaty was not high," recalled Cutler. "Public interest in the whole subject was rather tepid."

But Cutler himself was motivated to fight hard for SALT II by the belief that it was the best treaty the United States could hope for under the circumstances. "There were things we deserved to get," he said later. "On the other hand, we got quite a bit in that treaty . . . its most important feature was that it contained all these rules and definitions, and once you had it in place and the two sides were dealing with each other about those rules and making those rules work, the follow-on agreements for deeper cuts would come along. Indeed, SALT II contemplated that by the end of 1984 both sides would have agreed on further cuts." Cutler also believed that failure to ratify the treaty would be extremely damaging to U.S.-Soviet relations, not to mention to the political future of his employer.

Among other high administration officials, commitment to securing passage of the treaty was even more intense. Harold Brown's commitment to SALT II stretched back to the early 1970s, when along with Nitze, he had labored long hours in Vienna and Helsinki to make the first round of SALT a success. A highly intelligent man with a keen grasp of the interplay between arms and technology, Brown's strategic outlook closely paralleled Nitze's own. Like Nitze, the secretary of defense believed in maintaining nuclear forces that could be used in selective attacks on a wide range of Soviet military targets. Like Nitze, also, Brown was concerned about Minuteman vulnerability. Where the two men parted was in their perception of the degree of danger that accompanied that vulnerability. From his post in the nerve center of America's military empire, Brown did not share Nitze's intense fear of a Soviet first strike. "It bears emphasizing, because it is so often ignored," he said, "that even after a total loss of Minuteman missiles, we would not face the dilemma of surrender by inaction or mutual suicide by an all-out attack on Soviet cities and industry, provoking an equivalent attack on ours. We would instead have surviving bomber and submarine forces still fully capable of selectively attacking military, economic, and control targets, thus negating any gain the Soviets might imagine they could obtain by an attack on our ICBM force."[22]

Eventually, of course, Brown hoped to mitigate Minuteman vulnerability and in his view ratifying SALT II was a good start. While the treaty would not "solve the Minuteman vulnerability problem," he said, "it will make the solution of the problem easier than without an agreement. SALT II will limit to well below previously projected levels the number of Soviet MIRVed ICBMs. It will freeze the number of warheads on existing ballistic missile launchers, and will limit the number of reentry vehicles allowed for new ICBMs."[23] As committed to U.S. security as anybody in Washington, Brown saw the treaty as a good deal.

Part of the administration's strategy for ratifying SALT II was to appeal directly to the American people in the hope that they would put pressure on their senators. As Cutler explained, "we were trying to build support for the treaty everywhere, we were encouraging groups to organize and publicly urge support of the treaty, we brought groups from almost every part of the population into the White House to hear Harold Brown and Vance and the President talk about why it was a good treaty." And the efforts were paying off. "By late summer of 1979," recalled Brzezinski, "our campaign on behalf of SALT ratification was making steady progress."[24]

In addition to building grassroots support for the treaty, the administration tried harder to reach skeptical members of the establishment. These were people less awed by trips to the White House. They knew all of the arguments already, and as experienced political operators, they seldom gave anything without receiving something in return. And of them all, few could do more damage than Paul Nitze. "He was a leading opponent of the treaty whose views carried a great deal of weight," recalled Cutler. He was also indefatigable. "He was the committee when it came to SALT II," said Charls Walker. "He was the driving force." Not only did he write most of the committee's material on SALT, but he distributed the papers far and wide. As one State Department official complained, "He's done quite a job of getting anti-SALT facts into the hands of editorial writers and commentators. Everywhere I go to speak or meet with an editorial board, somebody has got Nitze's documents and starts asking me questions."[25]

Along with other members of the committee, Nitze mounted an effort to reach people outside of Washington and New York with his anti-SALT gospel. Accepting far more than his usual number of speaking invitations, he inveighed against SALT II in one city after another. His op-ed pieces appeared in numerous newspapers. He gave interviews on radio and television. For one man in his 70s, Nitze was doing a tremendous amount of damage. He had to be stopped.

The problem was that the administration had already tried nearly everything possible to neutralize Nitze. It had been thought that a commitment to the MX would mollify him. It didn't. Ralph Earle had hoped that a personal explanation and appeal would bring Nitze around. It didn't. Cutler had hoped that some stroking might do the trick and had many long talks with Nitze, emphasizing that "we had differences in good faith, but on the whole we had a very good treaty." It didn't. Finally, the administration and the arms control community had expected that pure common sense and a fundamental commitment to the arms control process would stop Nitze from going too far in raising questions about the treaty.

It didn't.

During the Warnke nomination hearings, Nitze had argued that "it would be tragic if the executive branch negotiated . . . a treaty with the Soviet Union and that was then rejected by the Senate. I don't think it is just a matter of 'so what.' I think that the political consequences of such an action could be really very serious indeed."[26]

Once Nitze saw the treaty the executive branch had negotiated, he changed his mind. He saw a treaty that gave the Soviet Union eight times more prompt counterforce capability than the United States, a treaty that allowed the Soviets to keep all their heavy land-based missiles while, as he read it, allowing the United States to build none, and a treaty that permitted the Soviets to build and deploy a new bomber force, while doing nothing to stop the deterioration of America's own B-52 bombers.

Throughout his career Nitze had believed that the strategic balance was among the most important factors in the U.S.-Soviet competition. And for most of his career Nitze had watched apprehensively as that balance became more favorable to the Soviet Union. Now Nitze's mind was numbed by what he felt was a treaty that locked the Soviet Union into a position of actual superiority. "From the beginning of 1978 to the end of 1985," Nitze wrote, "the number of Soviet warheads will have doubled; ours will have increased by half. The area destructive capabilities of Soviet weapons will have increased by a half; ours by a quarter. The capability of their weapons to knock out hardened targets, such as missile silos, will have increased tenfold; even if our cruise missiles, still under development, fulfill present expectations, our capability will have increased fourfold."[27] Rejecting a treaty might well be "tragic," but ratifying this particular treaty, Nitze felt, would be disastrous.

Even in his disgust, however, Nitze hesitated about opposing SALT II outright. When Nitze went before the Senate Foreign Relations Committee in July, he stopped short of asking the Senate to reject the treaty. Instead he said "that the Senate will find that amendments are necessary. I would hope that those amendments, those clarifying and improving amendments could be negotiated with the Soviet Union."

But if that didn't happen, pressed Senator Claiborne Pell, if the amendments were voted down, would "we be better off as a nation to reject the treaty as it is or to ratify it?"

"I discussed that with the executive committee of the Committee on the Present Danger," Nitze replied, "and we decided that the time has not yet come to take a position on that."[28]

Although Nitze was not ready to take a stand publicly on what the Senate should do, the tenor of his testimony was clear. "Frankly, I believe it is unwise to unequally accommodate the Soviet Union," he said at one point. "I believe we have been following a foreign policy course of weakness and inconsistency for too long. I believe the United States is being pushed around in the world by one country after another; it is time for the United States to stand up and not be a patsy."[29]

For those friends and former colleagues who couldn't understand what motivated Paul Nitze to attack SALT II, who couldn't see the point in his complicated charts or see the merit in his claims of a Soviet throw-weight advantage, things were now becoming clearer. Nitze was not so concerned with the details of the treaty, some suspected, but rather he worried that it would sap America's will. As Alexis Johnson recalled, "His concern was that the country and the Congress, if we entered into another treaty, would feel so relaxed about the strategic situation that we wouldn't do what was necessary and desirable. It wasn't so much an objection to the treaty per se, but to the mood that it would create in the country." An old hawk himself, Johnson disagreed sharply with Nitze and testified in favor of the treaty. He was annoyed by Nitze's deceptiveness. "I would have liked it much more if Nitze had stated openly and frankly his reasons for opposing the treaty—the fear of euphoria and that kind of thing," Johnson said later.

Nitze's former military assistant Ray Furlong felt much the same way. He supported the treaty and publicly debated Nitze. Like Johnson, he wasn't fooled by his former boss's emphasis on the numbers. "I think maybe deep down," Furlong said later, "one of his concerns was that the SALT treaty would generate an inaccurate perception on the part of the Congress and the American people that we were in reasonable shape with respect to our strategic forces."

Richard Garwin, also a proponent of SALT II, was disappointed that Nitze refused to make his real reservations public. He believed that Nitze's focus on Minuteman vulnerability was "misleading and a deception. He knew it was not an important question. He knew it could be remedied . . . and we could have as good a silo killing capability as the other side, and he still did not want to support SALT II even though we were not planning to do anything which would be impaired by SALT II." Instead of speaking out on the danger of lulling the American people, Garwin said, Nitze "chose this approach, this very complicated, impenetrable approach simply because who would argue with these figures? Very few people."

During the second round of testimony on SALT II before the Senate Armed Services Committee, Nitze touched more candidly on the problem of euphoria: "I think that in the past the Senate has hoped that SALT would somehow or other be the elixir which would cure our ills," he said.[30] By diverting attention from the Soviet Union's imperial expansion and its bid for nuclear supremacy, Nitze felt that SALT II fostered an artificially hopeful assessment of the relations between the superpowers. And in Nitze's world of systematic pessimism, no tint was more insidious than a rose one.

Nitze was also more forthright about what he thought should be the fate of SALT II. For the first time he publicly came out against ratification: "My view is that it would be advisable for the Senate to withhold its consent to the treaty and concurrently to do two further things." First, the Senate should dictate to the executive branch what "are the proper standards for an arms control agreement" and force them to go back to the negotiating table and get that kind of agreement. Second, it should approve a dramatically stepped-up U.S. effort to build more nuclear weapons and begin "reversing the adverse trends in our relative military posture."[31]

*   *   *

Thirty years earlier Paul Nitze had written that arms control would not be possible until there were fundamental changes in the nature of the Soviet Union. Those changes were beginning to occur. But after a decade of SALT, Nitze believed that pursuit of arms control also required changes in the United States. The United States had to have a growing defense budget, an unflinching commitment to modernizing its nuclear arsenal, and experienced negotiators with a realistic notion of the Soviet Union. Most of all, Nitze believed that to defend its interests amid the paralyzing self-doubt spawned by Vietnam, the United States had to snap out of its malaise and follow a policy of toughness and consistency.

To those who opposed Paul Nitze during the late 1970s, however, it was not the United States that needed to change, but Nitze. Many saw him as shackled to an archaic cold war dogma, his view of the Soviet Union and his doomsday predictions better suited to the 1950s than to the 1980s. "The Kremlin leaders do not want war," Nitze wrote in fall 1980 without a hint of self-consciousness, "they want the world."[32]

Yet if many in Washington came to view Nitze as an intransigent hawk, an enemy of the Democratic party, and a traitor to the arms control community, Nitze saw nothing unusual in his actions. It seemed at times that he didn't even realize what he had done. After SALT II was withdrawn from the Senate following the Soviet invasion of Afghanistan, Nitze insisted to his friends that he had not opposed ratification. Ralph Earle vividly recalled Nitze sitting in the Metropolitan Club and saying, "I was not against your treaty." He would repeat that claim many times.

And a week after Ronald Reagan was elected in November 1980, Earle remembered Nitze saying something else, something that stunned him.

"What are we Democrats going to do now that we have a Republican president?" Nitze asked.

PART IV

THE LAST CRUSADE

C H A P T E R   1 7

Back to Geneva

IN FACT, Paul Nitze knew exactly what to do now that Ronald Reagan was president: try to get a job, of course.

Being left out of the Carter administration had been a painful experience for Nitze. But by late 1979 there was mounting evidence that the Georgian would not last in the White House. Inflation, Bert Lance, new oil shortages, and Teddy Kennedy's bid for the presidency had conspired to undermine Carter's credibility on domestic issues. Abroad, there was a sense that Richard Nixon's characterization of the United States as a "pitiful giant" was being borne out with excruciating accuracy. An anti-American revolution had ousted the Shah of Iran. A revolution in Nicaragua had toppled the pro-American dictatorship of Anastasio Somoza. In Africa and Asia, the Soviet Union appeared to be on the march, bolstering Marxist governments in Angola, Ethopia, Vietnam, and Afghanistan.

For a Washington insider of forty years' experience, it was clear that the tide had turned against Jimmy Carter and that the Republicans would recapture the White House in 1980. Because a change in government was coming, Paul Nitze brooded less about his treatment at the hands of an outsider president and thought more about positioning himself to be a part of the next administration.

In early 1980 the leading contender for the Republican nomination was former California governor Ronald Reagan. Four years earlier, when the Committee on the Present Danger was in its infancy, Reagan had been invited to join. He accepted. For most of the late 1970s Reagan played little or no role in anything the committee did, but in January 1980, with his race for the presidency gaining momentum, Reagan began strengthening his ties to the committee through a series of meetings.

The first of these meetings was at Paul Nitze's home on Woodley Road.

It was a small, comfortable dinner, with Richard Allen, Charles Tyroler, and Eugene Rostow. Reagan came with two aides, Edwin Meese and Michael Deaver. Charming and amiable, Reagan was a master of light and anecdotal conversation. He could put people at ease like few other politicians. As a former governor, Reagan did not know much about foreign policy, but he knew enough to hammer home basic images about the declining power of the United States, the expansionism of the Soviet empire, and the "fatal flaws" of SALT II. The committee's themes were his themes. And in receiving advice that night on how to refine his message, the candidate could see that this group of conservative Democrats thought as he did. For five hours the men talked about national security issues. It was a "very serious conversation," recalled Tyroler.[1] Far from showing no interest in the substantive issues—as a candidate facing the Iowa caucuses in less than a month might do—Reagan was very responsive. He made it clear that he wanted to be briefed by the committee again.

It was not until July, after he had all but won the Republican nomination, that Reagan met with the committee again. As before, the conversation lasted for hours and committee members were impressed. Throughout the campaign Reagan drew heavily on the committee's ideas and literature. "The statements of the Committee have had a wide national impact," Reagan said later, "and I benefited greatly from them."[2]

On election day, 1980, Paul Nitze was at the election night party that Ella Burling held every four years at her house "Friendship." One of the other guests at the party was Timothy Stanley, Nitze's old friend and former Pentagon assistant. As the results came in, Stanley was amazed by the emerging Reagan landslide. "What do you make of this?" he asked Nitze. "I think you and I did a good enough job of educating these people," replied Nitze, feeling elated and vindicated.

Stanley was troubled by the comment. Nitze knew quite well that his former "right arm" at ISA had refused to join the committee. Moreover, when the two men saw each other, they often argued. "I felt he had become a superhawk," Stanley said. "I felt that the Russians were mellowing, that the Russians were getting out of the aggressive Khrushchev mode, and that Paul was wrong." Stanley was distressed to see one of John F. Kennedy's top lieutenants celebrating the landslide victory of a right-wing Californian.

Had Stanley known more about Nitze's political history, Nitze's ebullience on that election night might not have seemed so strange. Ever since his days on Wall Street, Nitze had been guided more by principle than by partisanship. He had stopped supporting Roosevelt when the New Deal president had tried to pack the Supreme Court. He had soured on the Republicans when they surrendered their integrity to the Neanderthal right. He had condemned the Democratic party when it veered left in the 1970s. Now, as he put it, with America facing the gravest threat to its security "at least since the Soviet threat to Berlin in 1958–62 and possibly at any time since the end of World War II,"[3] he gave his backing to the modern equivalent of the "primitives" who had driven him from the Pentagon in 1953 and tried to torpedo his Navy nomination a decade later.

Ronald Reagan may have been heir to the deeply conservative, isolationist tradition of the Republican right. He may have been an outsider from California who campaigned against the eastern establishment and condemned Harvard and the Council on Foreign Relations as bastions of elitist defeatism. He may have represented that streak in American politics of unrefined demagoguery that Nitze had so long despised. But what compelled Nitze to embrace him was Reagan's strong commitment to rebuilding American power. More than any other president in postwar history, Reagan's script on foreign policy echoed the passionate rhetoric and hard-line recommendations of NSC 68. Reagan's operative premises were total theoretical hostility and an emphasis on capabilities over intentions. His distrust of the Soviets was complete, and his reflex in the area of defense was to build more of everything no matter what the cost. In Reagan the axioms of NSC 68 would find their greatest champion yet.

As a vitriolic critic of SALT II and the leading theoretician of the Committee on the Present Danger, Nitze thought he had a good shot at landing a job in the new administration. Precisely what kind of job was unclear. There was some talk of Nitze's becoming under secretary of defense for policy, but his old enemies in the Senate, foremost among them Barry Goldwater, were sure to oppose the idea. Fred Ikle got the job instead. Considered too old and too Democratic for a major post, it seemed that Nitze would be lucky if he got a seat on the General Advisory Committee on Arms Control and Disarmament or on the President's Foreign Intelligence Advisory Board. As the months passed, however, it was not clear that he could get even that kind of consolation prize.

Nitze's fortunes changed when Eugene Rostow was appointed to head the Arms Control and Disarmament Agency. Initially, many of Reagan's advisors had wanted to appoint Edward Rowny to the post. But the president's new national security advisor, Richard V. Allen, was uneasy with the thought of Rowny in the post and believed his colleague from the committee, Eugene Rostow, would be a better candidate. Meeting with Allen and Meese at the White House, Rostow accepted the offer. But there was one condition, he said. Rostow would take the job if he could bring Paul Nitze into the arms control process.

What Rostow had in mind was making Nitze chairman of the General Advisory Committee on Arms Control and Disarmament. This way, he said later, Nitze "would be available and on tap and involved." A penthouse office in Arlington was no place for a man like Paul Nitze when there was work to be done. Meese and Allen accepted the condition.

In time Rostow had a better idea. Why not make Nitze the chief negotiator for the talks on intermediate nuclear forces (INF) that were to begin in Geneva later that year? He would be ideal. At first Nitze balked at the suggestion. The real problems lay in the realm of strategic nuclear weapons, not theater ones. Besides, Nitze had opposed NATO's 1979 "dual track" decision to deploy 572 cruise and Pershing II missiles in Europe. He remembered all too well the uproar in Europe that a similar deployment of Thor and Jupiter missiles had caused two decades before and preferred no replay of that unfortunate drama. Once the decision was made, however, Nitze reluctantly conceded that it had be carried out. To do otherwise, he said, "would appall the Europeans and confirm the impression that the United States can't be counted on for anything."[4] Nitze told Rostow he would take the job.

Rostow's next problem was to get Secretary of State Alexander Haig to endorse the idea. This proved remarkably difficult. "I ran into a terrible lot of resistance from Al Haig," Rostow said later. What made the resistance hard to overcome was Haig's lack of any concrete complaint about Paul Nitze. He voiced "a lot of objections," recalled Rostow. "They'd change every time." Rostow brought the issue up four or five times, and still Haig wouldn't budge. On the surface he was even positive about Nitze, calling him later "one of the most experienced and expert negotiators on strategic arms in the United States."[5] But respecting a man and asking him to take an important post were two different things. Haig just didn't want Paul Nitze in his State Department.

Haig's uneasiness about Nitze went back ten years. As Nixon's chief of staff during the final days of Watergate, Haig had worked desperately to keep the administration together. The resignation of a highly regarded statesman from the SALT delegation at the height of the crisis, and only weeks before a Moscow summit, had not made Haig's job any easier. And even before that episode, when Haig was Kissinger's deputy at the NSC, he had watched Paul Nitze in action. He had seen the way in which Nitze could use a low-level position in the bureaucracy as a base from which to build alliances throughout the government. Rostow sensed that the new secretary of state simply did not want that kind of operator anywhere near his territory.

In one of the first of his many bureaucratic battles, Rostow escalated the confrontation with Haig. "I insist on prevailing," he declared. Nitze's appointment as chief negotiator would be the "best possible signal to the Europeans and the Russians alike that we take these negotiations seriously."[6] Rallying support from the White House, Rostow pushed the appointment through.

Early one morning in late September 1981 Nitze received a telephone call. It was Al Haig himself asking if he would take the INF job. Nitze accepted.[7]

As a member of the SALT II delegation at a time when the talks were moribund for an entire year, Nitze might have thought that he had experienced diplomatic frustration of the highest magnitude. He might have thought that after working with someone as duplicitous as Henry Kissinger and with a bureaucracy as paralyzed as the Nixon administration was during Watergate, nothing could be much worse.

Nitze would have been wrong on both counts.

The first months that Paul Nitze spent in his seventh administration turned out to be—even for a man who had seen it all—a startling education in the politics of bureaucratic chaos. The personalities and ideologies in the new administration were strikingly disparate. From the far-right Californians who came in with the president to the moderate Washington insiders and establishment figures who find their way into every administration, Reagan's team in Washington seemed destined to set new standards for fierceness in infighting.

Nowhere were the ideological divisions more apparent than in the area of arms control. When Rostow and Nitze were appointed to head the administration's arms control effort, many Democrats howled in angry disbelief. It was like asking Jerry Falwell and the pope to spearhead a proabortion effort, some said. Weren't these the same men who had attacked SALT II just two years before? Weren't they the hawks who had ranted for four years about how the Russians couldn't be trusted? Indeed they were. But in an unsettling twist, it was not Rostow and Nitze who were the extremists in this administration. It was the other appointees who would deal with arms control, particularly Richard Perle.

Although Paul Nitze had helped acquaint a young Richard Perle with Washington a decade earlier during the ABM fight, the two men came to have dramatically different views on arms control. Soft-spoken, with a pudgy face, dark deep-set eyes, and a slightly rumpled appearance, Perle had focused his considerable intellectual energy on attacking arms control. From his years with Senator Jackson—years spent in the trenches fighting against SALT—Perle came to believe that arms control was a risky enterprise and that U.S. security could be best guaranteed though unilateral strategic modernization. Whereas Nitze wanted to tinker with the process to make it work better, Perle wanted to overhaul it, if not abandon negotiations altogether. These views were shared by Perle's influential boss, Defense Secretary Caspar Weinberger.

Many Washington insiders thought that once Perle was working for the executive branch instead of against it and was assigned to develop solutions rather than construct roadblocks, his anti-arms control sentiments would be moderated. Perle would become part of the team. The first round of interagency wrangling put such illusions to rest.

When Paul Nitze accepted the job of chief negotiator, he did so on the condition that he be allowed to negotiate seriously. In Nitze's mind this meant having the leeway to negotiate an agreement that recognized the reality of the American position, that is, the reality that the United States had little chance of trading 572 warheads for the over 1,000 warheads that the Soviet Union had deployed on its SS-20, SS-4, and SS-5 missiles. Any treaty, Nitze felt, would favor the Soviets since they were starting with such a massive superiority.

Perle's perception of the talks was far more rigid. Drawing on studies done by Pentagon analysts, Perle argued that the only way to reduce the Soviet intermediate-range missile threat to western Europe was to force the Soviets to scrap all or most of their SS-20s. He therefore proposed a bold and tough U.S. negotiating position: In exchange for the dismantling of all Soviet intermediate-range missiles, the United States would not deploy 572 cruise and Pershing missiles as planned. He called his proposal the "zero option" or "zero-zero." Perle got the backing of Weinberger at the Pentagon.

Across the Potomac, Richard Burt, head of State's Bureau of Politico-Military Affairs, had problems with the zero option. He argued that it was too inflexible, that the Soviets would scoff at it, and that the western Europeans would think that the United States was stone-walling in the talks. The zero option, said Burt, might be a good opening position, but it had to be accompanied by an implicit willing-ness to compromise. Burt called this idea "zero plus."

With his lofty new title of ambassador, Nitze kept out of this initial battle, but his instinct was to support Burt's position. Perle's hard-line position didn't trouble him too much because Rostow had guaranteed him independence and flexibility in Geneva. When the talks started everything would change, Nitze believed.

At an NSC meeting in November, President Reagan sided with the Pentagon and approved Perle's zero-zero position. On November 18 Reagan announced the plan in a speech before the National Press Club. Reaction to the speech, both in the United States and Europe, was largely favorable. Paul Warnke called it a "stroke of genius" that was "totally unassailable from an arms control standpoint." Walter Slocombe remarked that "It's a classical opening bid. It identifies genuine problems for the U.S. and offers a genuine solution to them." Most arms control experts recognized that the zero option would be rejected the Soviets, but they saw it only as an opening bid. This was Nitze's view as well. "It's hard to conceive that they'd accept it fast," he said. "But that's not the appropriate criterion for judging the pro-posal. The appropriate criterion should be, and is, 'Is it a solid basis for continuing negotiations?' And the answer to that is yes."[8] Even Wein-berger's representative on the talks, John Woodworth, assumed that there would be room for movement. "We all recognized that we were in a negotiation and that this [zero-zero] was not *the* only solution that could be acceptable to us."

What Nitze and the other arms controllers failed to comprehend were the intentions of Richard Perle. Having won the president's approval for the zero option, Perle was determined to use all the bureaucratic savvy he could muster to make sure that the United States stuck to that position, even if it meant no agreement.

When he left for Geneva in November, Nitze took no specific negotiating instructions. With the details of the U.S. proposal still being worked out in Washington, Nitze's job was to make a broad case for the zero option. Even in pursuing this modest goal, however, there were early hints of trouble. Nitze's intention was to use the first plenary meetings to stress basic themes relating to NATO and nuclear weapons. But when he began writing those statements, Richard Burt demanded that they be approved by the Interagency Group in Washington before they were delivered. Nitze reacted angrily. "This was intolerable," recalled a member of the delegation, "and Nitze fought it tooth and nail." As chief negotiator, he refused to serve as a mere mouthpiece for the bureaucracy. He had made that clear when he took the job. With Rostow's support, Nitze got Burt to agree that Nitze would only have to inform the group what he planned to say.

In Geneva Nitze adapted rapidly to the routine of the negotiations. From his five years on the SALT delegation, he had developed a tolerance for a life that many people would find dreary and mind numbing. The claustrophobic bug-proof chambers, the endless meetings, the hack work of preparing MemComs, the inconvenience of being far from home—Nitze had experienced it all before. During his years in Vienna, Helsinki, and Geneva, he had found ways to make the life of a negotiator bearable. Nitze's personal wealth allowed him to enjoy the restaurants and theaters of Europe and to go on excursions in the Alps, mountains that he had hiked since he was a small boy. As always, Phyllis was not content to remain in Washington. For most of the months that Nitze was in Geneva, she was there as well. Being the head of the delegation made a difference also. An ambassador had special privileges. This time around, Nitze would not be playing a rented piano in a SALT ghetto and laboring in the obscurity that the title of OSD representative confers. He was given an apartment of his own and treated to full VIP honors. With the international community following every move of the INF talks, Nitze found himself in the limelight as never before.

As for the element of superpower negotiations that many newcomers to the game found most frustrating—the Soviet negotiators—Nitze was used to them, too. While Aleksandr Shchukin, Nitze's chief counterpart during SALT I, had been an elder statesman like himself, his new opposite was of an entirely different generation. Only 45 years old, Yuli Kvitsinsky was too young to have been traumatized by World War II. He had come of age during the Khrushchev era and had risen rapidly through the Soviet diplomatic service during the Brezhnev years.

When Kvitsinsky's appointment was announced, there was much apprehensive talk among western officials that it was no coincidence that the top Soviet INF negotiator was an expert on West Germany. As the former number two man at the Soviet embassy in Bonn, Kvitsinsky spoke excellent German and had a keen sense of the West German political climate. Some suspected that his job was not only to negotiate with the Americans, but to manipulate the Germans.

On the first day of the talks Nitze and Kvitsinsky met alone at the Soviet mission for ninety minutes. Aware that it was far too easy for superpower negotiations to degenerate into a propaganda struggle, Nitze used this meeting to ask Kvitsinsky to agree to a news blackout. Under the terms of the blackout neither side would publicly discuss the details of the talks. In this way there would be no charges and counter-charges to jeopardize the atmosphere of cordiality. Much to Nitze's satisfaction, the Soviet negotiator promptly accepted the proposal. In an upbeat news conference after the meeting, Nitze explained that "it is only by mutual respect for the confidentiality of these proceedings that we can hope to look at the hard issues which divide us and to search for solutions that will assure security and reduce tensions."[9] Even when the talks were stalemated, the blackout would be largely observed.

Monotonously polemical at times, Kvitsinsky could be a trying negotiating partner. "From time to time," Nitze remarked, "I get thoroughly annoyed with him." Early in the talks, though, Nitze managed to cut at least partly through the ideological crust and establish the same kind of tough, dialectical relationship with Kvitsinsky that he had had with Shchukin. Able to communicate directly in French, the many informal talks the two men had were marked by slashing wit and relentless verbal dueling, "kind of a rapier thrust against rapier thrust," Nitze said. "I think he enjoys it, and most of the time I enjoy it."[10]

As could be predicted, little of substance was accomplished during the opening phase of the first round in Geneva. Both sides were feeling each other out and making preliminary arguments. It was not real negotiation, but rather an effort to determine what would be discussed when the real negotiations finally got under way.

* * *

Returning the United States in December, Nitze saw more clearly than ever that the most ferocious battles of the INF talks would not be fought in Geneva, but in the conference rooms of Washington. He saw also that his greatest opponent in the search for an INF agreement would not be Yuli Kvitsinsky, but Richard Perle.

In preparing for the second round of negotiations due to start in early 1982, Nitze and the delegation grappled with the issue of ground-launched cruise missiles (GLCMs). To be accepted by the Soviets, an agreement based on the zero option would have to contain language that banned the proposed deployment of Tomahawks by the United States. But there was a problem. Although the technology to verify arms control agreements was extremely advanced, it remained impossible to tell the difference between the twenty-foot cruise missiles that carried nuclear warheads and those that carried conventional warheads. Nitze argued that to have a ban on cruise missiles, and there could be not be zero-zero without one, the ban would have to cover both nuclear and conventional cruise missiles. Otherwise the Soviets wouldn't accept it, and with good reason.

Almost everybody in the arms control bureaucracy agreed with this view. As one ACDA official put it, "We didn't want the result, after the agreement, to be that there were lots of missiles that were ostensibly conventional but with no real way of telling that they weren't nuclear." Nor did officials want a fleet of missiles in Europe that could be armed with chemical weapons. After studying the issue, the Joint Chiefs of Staff concluded that ground-launched conventionally armed cruise missiles would probably never be deployed. Why not ban such missiles forever? Nitze and his colleagues set to work drawing up treaty language to do exactly that. The issue seemed to be simple, and it seemed to be settled.

Until Richard Perle got hold of the proposed draft.

At a meeting of the Interagency Group in January that Nitze attended, the assistant secretary of defense—or "Prince of Darkness," as he had come to be called around town—objected to tying U.S. hands on the question of conventional cruise missiles. As John Woodworth, the Office of the Secretary of Defense's man on the delegation, explained later, "The talks were about nuclear weapons, we had always taken a hard position that the talks were about nuclear weapons. . . . And we don't willy-nilly start altering our conventional posture and our conventional potential as a byproduct of agreement that is concerned with nuclear weapons." Lecturing the group, Perle said that the United States had to show more foresight in the negotiations. It was particularly important to be on the lookout for treaty language that could "come back to make us sorry later on." The proposed cruise missile language, said Perle, was an example of this kind of shortsightedness.

Being chastised about sound treaty language by a man who had never even sat at a negotiating table irritated Paul Nitze. But what outraged him was when Richard Burt suggested that the issue be taken to the president and Perle responded by threatening to reopen the question of treaty duration. During the debate over SALT II Nitze had pointed out the folly of an arms control agreement that expired in 1985. Such a short-lived agreement, said Nitze, would encourage the Soviets to plan major increases in their nuclear arsenal in anticipation of the day that the treaty expired. Nitze didn't want to see the same thing happen with an INF accord. So months earlier he had put forward, and the Interagency Group had accepted, a recommendation that the INF treaty be of infinite duration. And now Richard Perle wanted to reopen the entire issue. Nitze blew up. He attacked Perle for "talking rubbish" and accused him of trying to sabotage the negotiations. He left the meeting furious.[11]

Nitze's erstwhile musketeer in the fight to save Safeguard had not been at all moderated by his insider status, it seemed. Perle's opposition to arms control was as strong as ever. To get an INF agreement, Nitze realized, he would have to neutralize Perle. This would not be easy. While Nitze toiled away in Geneva, Perle expanded his influence in Washington under the aegis of the defense secretary. Weinberger was one of the president's most trusted advisers. By having Weinberger's ear, Perle had the president's ear.

Nitze's allies, in contrast, were weak and growing weaker. Secretary of State Haig, the most natural advocate of the diplomatic viewpoint, was rapidly accumulating enemies throughout the bureaucracy. His bid to become the "vicar of foreign policy" had been quashed immediately by Edwin Meese. Abrasive and arrogant, Haig had only limited access to the president and soon found himself embroiled in bitter bureaucratic infighting. Eugene Rostow, Nitze's other natural ally, was faring no better. Like Haig, he was seen as arrogant. More fatal still in an administration dominated by the Republican right, the ACDA head and long-time Democrat was viewed as too eager for an arms control agreement. This left Nitze with only two other hopes: the Joint Chiefs of Staff and Richard Burt.

During his years in government Nitze had had enormous success at cultivating the JCS. Through the conversion of Major General Truman

Landon, Nitze had helped win JCS backing for NSC 68. At ISA he had overcome his reputation as the "king of the whiz kids" to win the respect and support of the nation's ranking military men. As secretary of the navy and deputy secretary of defense, Nitze had strengthened that rapport. When he grew disillusioned with SALT in the early 1970s, it was to Zumwalt and the JCS that Nitze turned for help in his battle against Henry Kissinger. As pragmatists with a deep desire for predictability in the nuclear arms competition and as officials who preferred ordered hierarchy over chaotic bickering, the Joint Chiefs shared many of Nitze's basic sentiments.

But in early 1982 the four men who headed the nation's armed services were of little help to Nitze in the bureaucratic warfare surrounding the INF talks. Holdovers from the Carter years, the chiefs— led by General David Jones—had backed SALT II and, as a consequence, were viewed with suspicion by Pentagon civilians and hard-liners at the White House. On INF issues they wielded little influence, and at meetings of the Interagency Group it became clear that the JCS representative to the group, Admiral Robert Austin, was not prepared to take on Perle. Nitze would have to look elsewhere for allies.

The State Department's Bureau of Politico-Military Affairs was among the few remaining places to look. For all-out bureaucratic warfare, the 33-year-old head of the bureau, Richard Burt, might not have seemed the ideal ally. Polished and handsome, he was bright and able, but he lacked battle scars. He was new to intricacies of the national security establishment. In Washington's arms control community, Burt was considered a hard-liner. At the Fletcher School of Diplomacy at Tufts University Burt had studied strategic affairs under the tutelage of Nitze's hawkish son-in-law Scott Thompson. As a former correspondent for the *New York Times*, Burt had listened sympathetically to Nitze's tirades against SALT II. The consequence of this education was a distrust of talks with the Soviet Union. "Arms control has developed the same kind of mindless momentum associated with other large scale government pursuits," Burt wrote in early 1981. "There are strong reasons for believing that arms control is unlikely to possess much utility in the coming decade."[12]

Burt's allegiance to the anti-arms control anthem of the Reagan camp landed him a job, but it didn't guarantee influence. Coming from his position as *Times* reporter, Burt lacked the sparkling hard-line credentials that translated into power under Reagan. Moreover, he could be a difficult person to deal with. His ambition and sharp mind made people uneasy, and after only a year in government he was already acquiring enemies.

What Burt had going for him was a keen sense of how policy was made at the subcabinet level and a pragmatist's commitment to finding a way to deal with the problem of arms control. Burt realized that if he could make the Interagency Group on arms control work, he could be a guiding force in determining U.S. negotiating policy. Initially, relations between Nitze and Burt were strained. In his drive to control arms control policy, Burt wanted to control Nitze. Their November 1981 clash over whether Nitze's plenary statements had to be approved by the Interagency Group was only one example of how Burt tried to frustrate Nitze's bid for independence.

By early 1982 Nitze and Burt were getting along better. Both realized that Richard Perle was the enemy. And as the war over INF heated up, the two men realized something else: Only a united front could reduce Perle's power.

It would be an difficult fight. The weak position of the arms controllers was made painfully apparent when the issue of how to ban cruise missiles was brought before the president for a final decision. Taking advantage of his ties to hard-liners on the NSC, Perle made a last-minute lobbying effort. It worked. Reagan decided that U.S. negotiators should make no effort to ban conventionally armed cruise missiles. Burt was furious. So was Nitze. "Well, it's just one more hole we'll have to dig ourselves out of later on," he remarked when the news reached Geneva.[13]

In an early hint of insubordination, Nitze devised a way to minimize the damage. Fearing that the Soviet negotiators would see the cruise missile stance for what it was—obstruction by a hard-line administration—Nitze tried to play down the decision. At the negotiating table he portrayed it as a technical question that the two sides could deal with in the future. And to a congressional committee Nitze said that "the problem of whether or not one can reliably control and limit nuclear weapons without simultaneously limiting very similar conventional weapons is a question that we have to go into later in the negotiations."[14]

On February 2, 1982, the U.S. delegation finally presented a draft of an INF treaty based on the zero option. Two days later the Soviets tabled their own document. The distance between the proposals was tremendous.

The central premise of the Soviet position was that there was already parity in European nuclear forces. The Soviets buttressed this claim by pointing to the hundreds of nuclear weapons in western Europe maintained by France, Britain, and the United States, all of which were pointed at the Soviet Union.

At the negotiating table the Soviets said that they would be happy to reduce the number of nuclear forces in Europe. And in their February 4 document they showed how they wanted to go about this task. By 1990, the Soviet document proposed, both sides should seek to have reduced their nuclear arsenals in Europe to three hundred missiles and bombers each. The Soviets would get down to this number by dismantling their SS-4 and SS-5 missiles and some aircraft. The western powers would get to this number by not deploying the cruise and Pershing II missiles and by not expanding the French and British arsenals.

It was a forcefully presented offer. But one thing was missing. If the 1990 ceiling was set at three hundred missiles, the Soviets would be able to keep a huge arsenal of modern SS-20 missiles. And since it was precisely those missiles that the United States wanted to see dismantled, the offer was totally—almost farcically—unacceptable.

Still, while the Soviet efforts to justify this offer continued through February, Nitze had hope for the negotiations. Like the United States, the Soviet Union was starting the talks with an opening bid that reflected their interests and their interests only. "It is clear," Nitze said, "that the Soviets maintain the hope of preventing NATO INF modernization without any significant sacrifice on their part."[15] This was their baseline interest. The February 4 offer was a predictable statement of that interest. No more, no less.

What mattered most to Nitze was not the tone of the propaganda but the climate of the talks. And after the first round came to a close in March, Nitze judged the climate to be good. "Many people have thought the Soviet Union wouldn't negotiate seriously," he said when he arrived back in Washington. "We have found that that is not the case; they are negotiating, have been negotiating seriously from the very beginning." Granted, the two sides remained far apart, yet this was to be expected. "The debate in Geneva has been intense, but businesslike," Nitze said. And as for concrete progress, he remarked. "We have achieved somewhat more than might have been expected in this initial round."[16]

After a month in Washington the INF delegation returned to Geneva. Despite the lack of progress in the talks and the nagging fear that their efforts could prove in vain, morale among the diplomats was high.

And it was high because of Paul Nitze. "It was an intangible thing," said one member of the delegation. "Nitze was a grand old man. He had a great reputation, he had served in government since 1941, he was a multi-millionaire, a philanthropist. . . . And everyone who worked with him and around him placed him on a pedestal." Nitze, in turn, treated his subordinates as he always had, as if they were not subordinates at all. "Paul Nitze was very good at challenging individuals to achieve more than they thought they could achieve," recalled the team's JCS representative, William Burns. "Paul was an excellent discussant, outstanding in debate." When instructions came in from Washington, Nitze developed his own thoughts on how to follow them. He then gathered the delegates in their bug-proof chamber and opened his recommendations to discussion. Nitze listened closely, a delegate recalled, "and if some members, independently or collectively, did not wish him to implement the instructions the way he saw fit to implement them, he always deferred to the individual or the collective organization on how to proceed."

With OSD, the Joint Chiefs, and the State Department all having representatives on the delegation, the dangers of Nitze's emphasis on consensus were obvious. Yet throughout the course of talks there were few, if any, instances of obstructionism by delegates. "They held him [Nitze] in such high regard that they would not abuse the privilege," recalled a delegate. "They wouldn't undercut him, they wouldn't take advantage of him." While cutthroat bureaucratic warfare raged in Washington, a strange interagency harmony prevailed in Geneva.

To make little or no progress during the first round of bargaining was normal. SALT I had been that way and SALT II had taken six years to negotiate. Under any circumstances, arms control is a painstaking process. Patience is a basic prerequisite for success, and time to spare is the first ingredient of patience. In the spring and summer of 1982, however, the American INF delegation didn't have time to spare.

When NATO first decided in 1979 to deploy cruise and Pershing II missiles in Europe, it stated that only an arms control agreement with the Soviets could stop the deployment. The timetable for deployment specified that the first missiles would begin arriving in Europe in November 1983. This meant that as the INF negotiators began the second round in May 1982, they had about eighteen months to hammer out an agreement. On the surface, this was enough time. Most of SALT I, Nitze remembered, had been negotiated in the last year of the talks.

The catch was that Nitze did not view the date of deployment as the deadline for an agreement. On his first trip to Geneva in November 1981, Nitze had stopped to meet with West German Chancellor Helmut Schmidt. In a sobering assessment of public opinion in western Europe, Schmidt had said something that had haunted Nitze ever since. He said that if there was no progress toward an agreement by fall 1982, European support for the U.S. missile deployments would begin to evaporate. The scenario for what might then happen was both clear and frightening: If public sentiment ran strongly against deployments, one of the five western European nations that had agreed to host the missiles (Great Britain, Holland, Western Germany, Italy, or Belgium) might reverse their decision. If one pulled out, others might pull out. The consequence could be a halt to deployment plans, a collapse of the negotiations, and a major blow to the cohesion of NATO.

For the Americans in Geneva the INF was more than a bargaining game; it was a guessing game. There was constant speculation, recalled John Woodworth, about "what the political traffic was going to bear in Europe." With the speculation came grim talk of the worst case scenario: "We could erode our political situation and support by the allies" and the deployment would not go through at all.

Not since the Berlin crisis of the early 1960s had Nitze perceived such a serious threat to the unity of the western alliance. And as he slogged through week after week of negotiations in May and June, talks that were going nowhere, Nitze could see that he was fast running out of time. He was running out of patience, too.

It seemed to Nitze that there was only one way to speed up the talks and head off the impending crisis: The United States had to move away from the zero option. But how could this be done? Richard Perle and other administration hard-liners held the zero option sacrosanct. When Nitze had first left for Geneva in November, Perle had told him that he had to be ready to "tough it out for a long, long time" and that he should "resist the temptation of agreement for agreement's sake."[17] Under previous presidents Perle's insistence on sticking to an unrealistic opening position would have been naive. In the world of arms control, compromise is the heart, if not the soul, of negotiation. Without it there is no negotiating, only posturing.

But Ronald Reagan was not like previous presidents. Uninformed about arms control, he was easily swayed by superficial impressions and persuasive advisors. In 1982 he liked the zero option. The people he listened to told him to stay with it. Their feeling was that the United

States had given too much away in SALT, that in the past the art of compromise had degenerated into the pornography of appeasement. They didn't want to repeat those mistakes in the 1980s. A year after it was formulated, the zero option remained as rigid as ever.

The president's firmness on this point was a tremendous asset for Perle. He knew it was only a matter of time before the arms controllers began to bridle under the inflexibility of the zero option. He knew, also, that when they did begin to rebel, they could make a strong case for more flexibility, a case grounded both in the exigency of the European crisis and in the traditions of arms control. Yet Perle was confident that with the backing of Weinberger and the president, he could crush an effort to undermine the zero option before it gained momentum.

Paul Nitze knew all of this, too. If he went to the bureaucracy to appeal for more flexibility, who would listen? Already Nitze was viewed with uneasiness by conservatives within the administration. What would they say if this Democrat and former SALT negotiator began pushing for an abandonment of President Reagan's chosen negotiating position? And how long would such a proposal last in the delicate interagency channels that had proven so vulnerable to sabotage and disruption? After the cruise missile episode, the answer was disturbingly obvious. Some day the bureaucracy would move away from the zero option, but that move would come slowly and was far in the future— farther than the people of western Europe would wait.

So Nitze looked for another way. In talks with Eugene Rostow, one of the few people in the government he could trust, Nitze emphasized the need to open up a back-channel negotiation in the INF talks. Rostow supported the idea. During the early SALT years it was Henry Kissinger who had cultivated a back channel. At that time Nitze had been alarmed by the secret talks because he felt that Kissinger had moved hastily and sloppily and because Kissinger had left the SALT delegation uninformed about what was happening. In principle, however, Nitze accepted that back-channel negotiations could achieve results. He himself had engaged in secret, informal exchanges with Aleksandr Shchukin during SALT I in an effort to push forward the ABM negotiations. The great advantage of such an exchange was that the search for solutions could be purely substantive, detached from the sluggish pace and stultifying formality of the plenary sessions. Back-channel negotiation was among the few ways to break a deadlock. And if ever there was a time when it was imperative to break a negotiating deadlock, the summer of 1982 was that time.

To many in Washington and Geneva, the stalemate at INF seemed permanent. To Nitze, any negotiating deadlock could be broken if sufficient creativity were marshaled. With zero-zero an unacceptable proposal, Nitze began sculpting an alternative. As always, he began with the numbers. In long meetings with the delegation, in talks with individual members, and by himself, Nitze manipulated the data on missile deployment in Europe, breaking down the numbers, changing them around, playing out the moves and countermoves that a new proposal would produce, studying various hypothetical agreements. After nearly six months of negotiations, he had developed a keen sense of where the Soviets might make concessions. What remained now was to find the magic combination of numbers that could be the basis for an agreement.

Watching Nitze search for a solution, the delegates were impressed by his optimism. "He felt that there existed out there—in contrast to a lot of people—the potential for an agreement," recalled Woodworth, "that mutual interest between the two sides could exist that would lead to an agreement." The challenge was to test the Soviets to see where that mutual interest lay.

But who was going to do this? Secretary of State Haig had recently resigned and there was no other senior administration official who knew enough about arms control to open up a back channel. George Shultz, Haig's successor, was still new to his job. William Clark, the national security advisor, was largely unversed in arms control matters. Eugene Rostow and Richard Burt did not have enough regular contacts with the Soviets.

There was only one person who could open up the desperately needed back channel: Nitze himself.

In Geneva Nitze quietly discussed such a move with Norm Clyne, his chief sounding board on the delegation. A powerfully built man who spoke with the hint of a Texan twang and smoked Marlboro cigarettes, Clyne seemed an unlikely confidante to the refined and frail Nitze. But he had a blunt and hard-charging style that Nitze valued, and as the delegation's executive secretary, Clyne occupied a pivotal position in Geneva.

Finally, Nitze made a veiled overture to Yuli Kvitsinsky, asking him whether the Soviet government was genuinely interested in a Reagan-Brezhnev summit in the fall of 1982. Kvitsinsky replied that his superiors were very interested in such a summit. When Nitze asked what subject matter was far enough along to serve as the centerpiece for such a meeting, Kvitsinsky gave the obvious answer that only the INF negotiations could yield something in time for a summit. "If that's so," continued Nitze, "shouldn't we put our heads together and explore ways to contribute to that possibility?"

Kvitsinsky agreed that they should.

In the days that followed, Nitze made his meaning more explicit. He related the story of how he and Shchukin had had a private lunch and taken a long walk in the woods in an effort to make a breakthrough on the radar issue during the ABM negotiations. The message to Kvitsinsky was clear: Back-channel talks between senior negotiators was not a new phenomenon.[18]

On July 11 Rostow visited the INF delegation in Geneva for several days. He was told by Nitze that the foundation had been laid for back-channel exchanges with Kvitsinsky. Rostow approved. He looked over a draft of the proposal that Nitze intended to put forward and also tried to encourage Kvitsinsky, telling the Russian that "I've always had a special regard for ambassadors who have the acuity and foresight to propose changes in their own instructions from time to time."[19]

The stage was now set for Nitze to make a compromise offer. For some time he had been thinking about what an equitable INF deal might look like. The hours of hypothesizing and playing with numbers had yielded the general contours of a possible agreement. Now, with some help from Norm Clyne, Nitze went a step further and developed a detailed proposal.

The solution he selected was relatively simple. To remain credible, the United States would have to follow through with some kind of deployment if the Soviets didn't agree to the zero option. The component of that deployment that caused Moscow the most anxiety was the Pershing II missile. With its short flight time and great accuracy, the Pershing II was ideal for destroying hardened targets in the Soviet Union. Nitze believed that if the United States offered to not deploy the missile, the Soviets might be willing to make major cuts in its SS-20 force. The agreement Nitze had in mind was that the U.S. would cancel the Pershing II and only deploy 300 Tomahawk missiles; in return, the Soviets would reduce their SS-20 arsenal to 75 missiles, each carrying three warheads for a total of 225 warheads. The slight numerical advantage in warheads for the United States would be compensation for the faster flight time of the SS-20. The monopoly of ballistic missiles for the Soviets, in turn, would be compensation for the French and British forces that caused them so much concern.

After feeling Kvitsinksy out in numerous private talks, Nitze put forward his proposal on July 16. The setting was the Swiss Jura Mountains near the French border. Driving out in Kvitsinsky's chauffeured car, Nitze and the Russian embarked on a long walk down a mountain. They began their talk by rehashing old points.

Kvitsinsky said that any agreement would have to compensate the Soviets for French and British forces. He reiterated that his government could not accept the zero option as it now stood.

Nitze responded with his basic points. The United States could not accept limitations on NATO fighter planes capable of carrying nuclear weapons. Nor would it allow the Soviets simply to shift their SS-20 force into Asia as a result of an agreement.

Both men had been making these points for a long time. Now Nitze urged that they explore a deal that could exist within those limits. Kvitsinsky was open to suggestions.

Settling down on a log, the two men started talking specifics. Nitze had brought with him four short papers. The first three outlined the areas where they agreed and disagreed. The fourth, Paper D, was an outline of the proposal Nitze had developed, which he began reading aloud. Kvitsinsky soon interrupted to offer modifications. Slowly, they went through the paper paragraph by paragraph. A light drizzle began to fall and the men took refuge in Kvitsinsky's car, where they continued to work. After some tinkering and a few concessions on both negotiators' parts, Kvitsinsky expressed his satisfaction with the deal. But he was nervous about what they were doing. The Russian was far younger than Nitze. He had a long career before him. He did not want to jeopardize his ambitions. "You can blame this on me with your people," Nitze said, trying to put him at ease. "I'll tell them it's your scheme, and you tell them it's mine," said Kvitsinsky.[20]

Following the outing, Nitze wrote two memorandums of the conversation. The first was a general defense of his actions. He explained that the private negotiations with Kvitsinsky were designed to break the INF stalemate. He stated further that it was an effort with a precedent, citing his talks with Shchukin during SALT I. What Nitze didn't say in the first memorandum was what he and Kvitsinsky had achieved. Those details were included in the far more secret second memorandum. Both were to be presented to his superiors when Nitze returned to Washington in late July. In the delegation (with the exception of Norm Clyne), Nitze did not brief his colleagues before the walk with Kvitsinsky, and later gave them only a vague sense of what had transpired.

Back in Washington Eugene Rostow was trying to communicate to Shultz about Nitze's actions. At one of the secretary's regular morning staff meetings, Rostow recalled, "I passed a note to him that I had to see him at once."[21] Shultz took the news well. As a matter of principle he was annoyed, but he expressed admiration for the lengths to which Nitze would go in search of a breakthrough.

When Nitze returned, he cautiously spread the word of his informal talks with Kvitsinsky. He gave a vague account of the venture to Richard Perle and told the full story to Richard Burt. Burt's reaction was mixed. He saw some merits in the proposed agreement, but worried that Nitze had embarked on a risky course of action. "Watch your step as you proceed with this thing," Burt warned.

After some preparation, Nitze and Rostow revealed the walk in the woods to William Clark. The first reaction of the national security advisor was to tell both men not to breathe a word about the development to anyone. President Reagan would want to call an NSC meeting to discuss the idea, and in the meantime Clark didn't want to see a major interagency debate on the question. Clark's next move was to turn to his deputy, Robert McFarlane, for an analysis of the Nitze deal. McFarlane said he was impressed by what he saw as new Soviet concessions, but he was also disturbed by the episode. In his private talks with Kvitsinsky, Nitze had overstepped his authority and violated the chain of command, McFarlane believed. What was more, Nitze had taken the dubious step of offering to bargain away the highly valued Pershing II missile system.

In briefing President Reagan, McFarlane emphasized the fact that the United States would be relinquishing the Pershing II while the Soviets kept some SS-20s. And in his blurry conception of arms control, Reagan perceived this as a bad deal. It would leave the United States with only cruise missiles, or "slow flyers" as the President called them, to counter a far more lethal arsenal of ballistic missiles, or "fast flyers."

Others in the government were more positive about the Nitze-Kvitsinsky package. In a special early August session of the National Security Council that included most top administration officials with the exception of President Reagan and Vice-president Bush, Nitze's proposal received guarded support from Defense Secretary Weinberger and the Joint Chiefs of Staff. Influenced by Fred Ikle, who saw merits in the Nitze plan, Weinberger was favorably inclined toward the development because of the new concessions from the Soviets. That Weinberger didn't move to kill the plan immediately was a major boost to Nitze's position. Things seemed to be moving in his direction. It seemed possible that his attempt to lead the government out of its paralysis might actually succeed. And then Richard Perle returned from Colorado in mid August.

Perle had been in Aspen when the initial NSC meeting was held. All he knew about the walk in the woods was the little that Nitze had told him. Finally informed about what Nitze had actually done in Switzerland, Perle was ready for a fight. "This is a totally outrageous way of doing business," he told a colleague. If the West Germans found out that the U.S. was ready to abandon the Pershing II, Perle speculated, they would be furious. Organizing his allies, Perle was determined to crush Nitze's proposal before it got any further.[22]

Meanwhile, at the White House Clark and McFarlane were giving more thought to what Nitze had done. The more they thought, the angrier they became. For having "wandered off the reservation," they concluded the INF chief negotiator merited a reprimand. It took the form of a memorandum in the president's name to Secretary of State Shultz in which Nitze and Rostow were not named specifically, but Shultz was reminded that the interagency system had to approve all arms control initiatives. During his nearly thirty years in government, the memorandum to Shultz constituted one of the sharpest reprimands Nitze had ever received.

But it wasn't the reprimand that worried Nitze as he tried to relax in late August at his summer home in Maine; it was the counteroffensive that was being plotted at the Pentagon. Before Nitze left for vacation, he provided Rostow with all the memorandums from the secret negotiations. Taking advantage of the government's August lull, ACDA officials began devising a strategy to sell the proposed agreement. "Our main point was that we'd be better off taking this deal than not," recalled a Rostow aide. "This was better than anything, no matter what you projected for NATO INF deployments. . . . In every case you're better off with the walk-in-the-woods equal formula than you'd be without an agreement."

Nitze's allies devoted special attention to buttressing the case for trading away the Pershing II. A highly accurate missile with a range of 1,500 miles and a flight time from West Germany to Moscow of only 12 minutes, the Pershing II was considered a great asset by the government's more hawkish officials. Yet because the missile hadn't become operational and was fraught with problems, arms controllers thought they could make a good case for giving it up. "We didn't know where we were going with the Pershing II program," commented one Nitze aide. "We had money problems, we had a great deal of testing problems, we didn't know whether the damn thing was going to work. So, now, why not give away the goddamn thing?" In arguing for the walk-in-the-woods formula, ACDA officials found that most of the government was receptive to this logic. But it was a receptivity that proved emphemeral. "We were doing pretty well while Perle was in Aspen," the Rostow aide recalled. "We did a lot worse when Perle got back."

Perle's strategy for killing the proposed deal was simple. In meetings with Weinberger, he argued that the Pershing II was the flagship of the INF deployment and that, in any case, it was far too early for the U.S. to abandon its opening position. Weinberger agreed, and by early September the Pentagon's obstructionist machinery was operating at full throttle.

The decisive showdown occurred at an NSC meeting on September 13. Speaking on behalf of his proposal, Nitze concentrated on attacking the arguments in favor of preserving the Pershing II. He pointed out that there was no compelling military need for the missile. The United States would gain far more by trading the Pershing II for reductions in SS-20s than it would by deploying it. At first, Reagan seemed to be following Nitze. Then Weinberger joined the conversation and repeated all of Richard Perle's arguments in favor of the Pershing II. As usual, the president agreed with Weinberger, and returning to the zero option, he asked Nitze why the Soviet Union couldn't get rid of all its missiles in Europe if the United States was willing to do the same. Nitze answered that it was unrealistic to expect the Soviets to dismantle a fleet of modern missiles in exchange for an American promise to cancel deployment of missiles that it hadn't even built.

The president remained unswayed. "Well, Paul," he said, "you just tell the Soviets that you're working for one tough son of a bitch." Two days later the president signed a document reaffirming the administration's commitment to zero-zero. It emphasized that any moderation from this formula would work only if it allowed the United States to deploy Pershing IIs. Nitze had been rebuffed.[23]

Rebuff hardened into defeat on his return to Geneva, where Yuli Kvitsinsky informed Nitze that Moscow had also rejected the plan they had worked out in the woods. The negotiations were back to stalemate.

The fall of 1982 was a frustrating time for Paul Nitze. His bid to introduce new flexibility into the talks had not only failed, it had made him a marked man in an administration that rewarded extremists and penalized moderates. Worse still, the deadline for progress in Geneva which Helmut Schmidt had set almost a year before was fast approaching.

As the leaves along the Rhône river changed color and dropped to the ground and the limousines of the delegations shuttled between the U.S. and Soviet missions in the chilly autumn air, there was still no progress. The third round of the talks came to an end on November 30.

It was a strained and tense Nitze who returned to Washington. If the talks didn't move soon, the tide of public opinion in Europe could turn solidly against the deployment. And if that happened, Nitze argued, the costs of trying to push through with deployment could be destructively high. For nearly forty years Nitze had worked for a unified west. Now, as the streets of European cities were convulsed with demonstrations against missile deployment and jittery allies charged the United States with not negotiating seriously and the Soviets mounted a frighteningly effective propaganda effort aimed at western public opinion, it seemed to Nitze that NATO unity would be the first casualty of the failed INF talks.

With all the persuasiveness he could muster, Nitze took this message to the bureaucracy. The effort proved in vain. Richard Burt told him that he "fundamentally disagreed" with his pessimistic assessment. At the Pentagon Nitze's panic was viewed with contempt. "I think there's a danger in getting too close to these things and I think Paul has done that," commented Perle's deputy, Frank Gaffney. The shrill intensity with which Nitze prophesied doom in Europe caused even his allies to conclude that their old friend had finally blown a fuse. "Paul's lost his mind," Robert Grey said sadly.[24] People at the State Department felt the mounting crisis in Europe had temporarily transformed Paul Nitze into a fanatic who made no sense.

But there were some in Washington to whom Nitze's behavior would have seemed perfectly normal. Like him, they were old. Unlike him, they had left government long ago to live out their final years in quiet sections of Georgetown or Northwest Washington. The Paul Nitze they remembered from the days of the Marshall Plan and the Policy Planning Staff was a systematic pessimist, a man who worried whether the states of western Europe would survive at all as independent entities. And had they gone to the State Department one day in late 1982 or early 1983, taken the elevator up five flights to the floor where Dean Acheson used to have his office, and sat in on a meeting with Nitze and his colleagues, they would not have seen an overwrought fanatic. They would have seen the Paul Nitze they had worked with three decades earlier.

But times had changed. The younger officials now in power took NATO for granted. They didn't remember how hard it had been to build that alliance and they didn't see the growing cracks in western unity that caused Nitze such alarm. They simply didn't share his sense of urgency about the talks.

December dragged into January, and still there was no movement from the zero option. With deployment now only eleven months away, Nitze's instructions were as maddeningly inflexible as when he had first gone to Geneva. Unless something dramatic happened, there would be no agreement.

On Paul Nitze's seventy-sixth birthday something dramatic did happen. On the morning of January 16, 1983, the *New York Times* ran a front-page story with the headline "U.S. Aide Reached Arms Agreement Later Ruled Out."[25] In considerable detail the paper revealed what had been one of the administration's most closely held secrets, the tale of Nitze's back-channel negotiations with Yuli Kvitsinsky.

Nitze was furious when he saw the story. And his fury was directed at the man he knew had leaked it, Eugene V. Rostow. Four days earlier Rostow's rocky relations with the administration had come to a head and he had been fired by Secretary Shultz. President Reagan, Rostow was told, no longer had confidence in him.

The loss of his principal backer was a major setback to Nitze. His friend from the Committee on the Present Danger had been one of the few people Nitze could trust in the administration. The search for flexibility would now be lonelier than ever, that is, if Nitze could even keep his job. Rostow's leak of the story of the walk in the woods appeared to be a major blow to Nitze's credibility, both in Washington and in Geneva. The administration's tight leash on him became clear for all to see. Rostow's dismissal—however unrelated to the walk in the woods—put Nitze on public notice that unless he fell into line, he might be next.

But in his rage Paul Nitze failed to find consolation in a hopeful quotation contained in the *Times* article. "A mythology may be created in Europe about all this," a senior State Department official was quoted as saying, "that somehow Rostow and Nitze negotiated a breakthrough that Neanderthals in Washington blocked."[26] Perhaps that was true. Perhaps a mythology would someday be created. But how much good would it do if the reality in Geneva continued to be total inflexibility?

A lot of good, it turned out. While most myths take years to be formed, the walk in the woods became myth almost overnight. Finally able to speak freely, Rostow called for more flexibility in the arms talks. He also stressed that the informal accord proposed by Nitze had been a good one, meeting the basic American goals of "a sharp limit on destabilizing weapons, that the agreement achieve equality and that there be a limit in the Far East on the number of Soviet missiles." Rostow said further that without "firmness and intelligent flexibility" there would be no arms control. And without arms control, he said, the western alliance would be in "grave peril."[27]

The timing was perfect. In Europe and on Capitol Hill there was a deep sense that the rigidity of the Reagan administration had led the superpowers into a confrontation of mounting danger. There was a feeling that relations were so bad that a major crisis might propel the world toward nuclear war. And now this man with impeccable hard-liner credentials—who had fought against SALT II only three years before—was putting his career on the line to break the stalemate in Europe. Since 1981 critics of the Reagan administration had looked for someone in whom they could place their hopes for a more reasonable foreign policy. Among the frightening conglomeration of zealots in government, they had searched for someone who would fight for moderation, someone who made sense.

Picking up the *New York Times* on that chilly January morning, they found him. During the following three days the *Times* ran front-page stories about the agreement that Paul Nitze had tried to work out. For those who didn't know what to think about this extraordinary development, the *Times* told them. "The deal that America's negotiator, Paul Nitze, explored in July was along the lines now being urged by the Europeans," an editorial read. "He was far from concluding a verifiable treaty, but he was negotiating in the real world."[28]

Sensing that Rostow's firing was a prelude to his own dismissal, Nitze saw that he had little to lose and a lot to gain by capitalizing on the situation. If a momentum in favor of flexibility could be generated, the administration might feel compelled to back away from the zero option. And if Nitze himself became a symbol of flexibility, it might prove politically impossible for the president to fire him.

Two days after the walk-in-the-woods story broke, Nitze gave an interview to NBC news. Speaking wishfully, he said that he was "confident that if it becomes wise for the United States government to change its position . . . it will in fact do so." Nitze also portrayed his position as a strong one, saying that he was "completely satisfied" with the backing he had received from the administration. In an interview with reporters on the same day, Nitze said, "I have had and will continue to have the necessary flexibility." As for what had happened last summer, Nitze said, "I was not reprimanded and indeed did not at any time exceed my instructions as negotiator."[29]

It was a defiant tone. Nitze might go down, but not without a fight. On Friday he met with Reagan to receive instructions for the next round of negotiations due to start on January 26. A briefing for reporters afterward underscored the delicacy of Nitze's position.

Will there be any "give" in the American position? a reporter asked.

"There will be if the Soviets come forward," Nitze said quickly. He then caught himself. "Wait a minute. Let me change that. The President's directive to me is to negotiate seriously, and he made that clear 14 months ago at the beginning of these negotiations. But in order to negotiate seriously it requires some give on the Soviet side. And if the Soviet side gives, then I'm sure we will give serious consideration to any serious proposal of theirs."

"So we're not absolutely locked in on zero-zero?" pressed another reporter.

"I won't answer that," Nitze said.[30]

After the maelstrom of the preceding week, Nitze was relieved when he finally boarded the plane for Europe. But if he could escape Washington, he could not escape the controversy he had sparked. Almost as soon as he arrived in Bonn to confer with Helmut Kohl, a dispute broke out in the West German government over the INF negotiations. Franz Joseph Strauss, the Bavarian Conservative, charged that the U.S. zero option proposal was unattainable and "utopian." When word of Strauss's comments reached Washington, Larry Speakes, the White House spokesman, reiterated President Reagan's commitment to the U.S. position.

It was a minor incident, but a telling one. The revelation of Nitze's walk in the woods and Rostow's calls for flexibility had served to embolden critics of the zero option who had kept their silence for over a year. A flood of newspaper columns and speeches, in Europe and the United States, by liberals and conservatives alike, called for negotiating flexibility. Nitze's secret talks with Kvitsinsky had failed to move the administration in July, but the furor generated by the revelation of those talks in January might have that effect. Even British Prime Minister Margaret Thatcher, Reagan's most steadfast European ally, joined the chorus of voices calling for flexibility. "One hopes to achieve the zero option," she said on January 18, "but in the absence of that, we must achieve balanced numbers."[31]

As Nitze sat down in Geneva for another round of negotiations with Kvitsinsky, he felt sufficiently confident about his position to answer the question that he had turned aside at the White House. The United States, he said, was "certainly not locked into" the zero option proposal.[32]

Coming on the heels of one White House reaffirmation of zero-zero after another, Nitze's remark was an extraordinary act of insubordination. "How is it," one newspaper writer asked, "that an American arms control negotiator can take a walk in the woods near Geneva with his Soviet counterpart, work out an understanding that violates his instructions, be rebuked by the White House and then lobby half the world to change the administration's strategy—all without being dismissed . . . ?"[33]

To Nitze's enemies in the bureaucracy—men like Perle who had watched him battle Kissinger a decade earlier—the answer to this question was self-evident. Alexander Haig had foreseen something like this a year and a half ago. He knew how Nitze could amass influence by forging alliances with the JCS, the western Europeans, or whomever. He had tried to keep Nitze out of the administration, but the White House—with its Californians new to the ways of Washington— had ignored Haig. And now Paul Nitze, a Democrat and an arms controller, had this very conservative administration right where he wanted it.

On February 22 President Reagan finally swung around to reality. In a speech before the American Legion, Reagan backed away from the zero option, saying that "ours is not a take-it-or-leave-it proposal" and announcing that he was giving Nitze wider latitude to search for an agreement.[34]

A month later the president went even further. After an intense round of squabbling between State and Defense, Reagan formally accepted the idea of what Nitze had tried to achieve ten months earlier: an interim agreement that would reduce INF arsenals down to equal, but not zero, levels. "When it comes to intermediate nuclear missiles in Europe, it would be better to have none than to have some. But if there must be some, it is better to have few than to have many," Reagan said.[35]

The Washington bureaucracy is like a massive supertanker on the high seas. It can move with great power and efficiency in one direction, but should a decision suddenly be made to change course, it can be a most unwieldy vehicle. For almost twenty months the United States government had striven for an agreement based on zero-zero. Now, with deployment set for November, officials had five months to refine a set of new positions and fall-back positions that might be acceptable to the Soviets. To do so was certainly difficult, but not impossible. However, if the American ship of state lacked agility, it was no worse than the Soviet bureaucracy. As the two delegations haggled in Geneva through late May, all of June, and into July, it became apparent that the Soviet leadership had no intention of helping to move the arms control process along.

Late on the night of August 31, 1983, the prospects for an INF agreement were dealt a further blow when a Soviet fighter plane shot down a Korean 747 in the northern Pacific. The already chilly relations between the superpowers grew even colder. In Europe the street demonstrations against missile deployment became larger. Hundreds of thousands of people jammed public squares in Britain, Holland, Denmark, and West Germany. The missile issue was giving the European left tremendous new power. All of Nitze's fears about the deployment seemed to be coming true. Kenneth Adelman, Rostow's successor at ACDA, was shocked by Nitze's panic. "He thought that NATO was falling apart and that we should do almost anything to not deploy the missiles because the alliance would just disintegrate."

Nitze could think of only one possible solution: to revive the walk-in-the-woods formula. Both the west Europeans and the Soviets had expressed an interest in the idea. Even Richard Perle told Nitze that he was prepared to support an effort to trade away Pershing II. President Reagan, however, still held his "fast flyers" dear. When Nitze made a final appeal to William Clark for permission to put the walk-in-the-woods formula to Kvitsinsky one last time, Clark refused.

As the sixth round of the negotiations sputtered into October, President Reagan and Soviet leader Yuri Andropov competed in the arena of public opinion to demonstrate their flexibility, both putting forward last-minute offers. But none of the new proposals amounted to much. In Geneva the Americans on the INF delegation talked more of when the Soviets would walk out than they did of when a breakthrough would come.

In mid November the first shipment of sixteen U.S. cruise missiles arrived in Great Britain, and the talks hovered on the verge of collapse. The Soviets, however, indicated that they would not walk out until the Pershing II missiles had been formally approved for deployment by the West German government later in the month. During the little time remaining Nitze made a final push to end the stalemate. It failed.

On November 22 the West German Parliament approved deployment of the Pershing IIs. The following day, the U.S. and Soviet

delegations met for a twenty-five-minute plenary session. There, Kvitsinsky announced that the Soviets were discontinuing the present
round of talks. He offered no date for their resumption.

Somber but not shocked, Nitze called the move "unjustified" and
"unfortunate." But he was not without hope. Looking forward to better
days, Nitze said, "These negotiations should continue until an agreement is reached."[36]

Heretic at State

WITH THE BREAKDOWN of the INF negotiations came the collapse of Paul Nitze's hopes for an agreement that would save NATO and crown his long career. Three years of toil in Geneva had produced a spectacular failure, Nitze's greatest since entering government in 1940. The collapse of the talks also left Nitze looking foolish. For months he had been warning that the western alliance might crumble if the United States tried to deploy missiles in Europe. Now, as weeks and then months passed following the Soviet walk-out and as missile deployment proceeded smoothly, Nitze's panicked predictions appeared ludicrous in retrospect. Europe was convulsed by large antinuclear demonstrations, but NATO did not crumble.

Returning to Washington, Nitze faced smug comments from colleagues he had anxiously berated a few months earlier. And he faced something worse: the absence of a job. With the INF talks over, what was the chief negotiator to those talks supposed to do? Nobody was intent on forcing Nitze to resign since the Reagan administration fervently hoped the Soviets would return to Geneva, but if ever there was a dead-end job, this was it. For four months—during one of the coldest winters in U.S.-Soviet relations since the early 1960s—Nitze dressed in his finely tailored suits every morning and went to his fifth floor office in the State Department to carry on his duties as chief negotiator, duties that consisted mainly of preparing for a resumption of the talks that everybody agreed would not happen soon. In March 1984 Nitze was given a wider mandate when he was made Special Representative for Arms Control and Disarmament Negotiations. But since there were still no talks, this post was meaningless as well. By fall Nitze was ready to leave the government.

Ironically, it was Robert McFarlane, the man who had engineered Nitze's reprimand in 1982, who changed his mind about leaving. Succeeding William Clark as national security advisor, McFarlane had moderate political instincts and a deep interest in strategic matters. His greatest hope was to put arms control back on track, to keep it on track, and to be the architect of new agreements with the Soviets. To do this, McFarlane had to end the bitter infighting over arms control that had crippled the INF effort and bring State and Defense together. Had his days been less cluttered by crises throughout the world, he might have dealt with this task himself. Instead, McFarlane felt he needed an arms control "czar" who could give all his time to bringing unity to the government and push the stalled negotiations ahead. He asked Nitze to take the job.

Nitze liked the idea, but told McFarlane that he would accept only if Shultz approved. An arms control czar was needed, desperately needed, but Nitze didn't want to usurp the secretary of state's authority in this area. The proper palace of a diplomatic czar was the State Department, not the White House. Shultz agreed, telling McFarlane that Nitze was "too valuable for me to lose."[1] The secretary also made Nitze's life at Foggy Bottom more pleasant by giving him a new title—Special Advisor to the President and Secretary of State on Arms Control—and new offices, a suite on the seventh floor close to his own. With these perks came a new mandate: to work the problems of arms control on a policy level in Washington. The appointment was sweetened by a trip to the White House with Shultz, after which President Reagan issued the statement naming Nitze.[2]

Since 1981 Richard Perle and the other opponents of arms control had held a critical advantage over Paul Nitze. They operated from a bureaucratic power base, while he did not. Now, as George Shultz's point man on arms control, Nitze no longer suffered from that handicap. Although the realities of the Reagan administration had changed little—it remained an environment that nourished extremism—Nitze was at least in a position to fight the hard-liners on an equal footing.

And fight he did.

Norm Clyne, Nitze's confidante from Geneva, took an office in his suite. Another arms control expert, Steve Pifer, was brought in also. In comparison to the Pentagon's vast reservoir of expertise, this two-man staff was tiny. Yet over the years Paul Nitze had become a master at maximizing the output of his staff. He did this by making them feel important, by listening to them, by giving them a sense that the work they did would have an impact and that if they toiled late into the night or through the weekend on a paper, their overtime would make a difference. Nitze had become especially good at working with younger officials, the foot soldiers of bureaucratic warfare. He inspired them with his status and achievement, but also built their confidence by respecting their expertise and deferring to their judgment. "He's constantly bringing new people in, learning from them and teaching them," remarked one younger expert. Nitze's staff on the seventh floor may have been small, but it was extremely dedicated.

And Clyne and Pifer were not Nitze's only resources in the government. Since the days of the Marshall Plan, when he had drawn on the expertise of half a dozen agencies to write his brown books, Nitze had been adept at cultivating intragovernmental ties. As a special assistant to both the secretary of state and the president, Nitze's mandate gave him entrée throughout the administration, and he used it to circulate as much as possible, collecting insights and information and refining new ideas through continuing dialogue. Nitze also compensated for his small staff through his own expertise. Unlike some top officials who could direct staff work but not do it themselves, Nitze was a staff man by nature. He enjoyed delving into the substance of a problem, studying the data, working with the numbers, and crafting complex lines of argument. Unlike many top officials, also, Nitze had the technical knowledge to do this. "It's not a great deal," commented one of the State Department's top arms control experts, "but it puts him in a different league than almost everybody he deals with."

For over forty years Paul Nitze had been honing his skills as a master bureaucrat and strategic thinker. Now, in the twilight of his career, with the odds stacked heavily against him, he would need all the savvy and creativity he could muster.

Downstairs, Kenneth Adelman, the new head of ACDA, was fuming at Nitze's promotion. A neoconservative who had little arms control experience when he was picked as an antidote to Rostow's moderation,

Adelman had developed his political philosophy during the 1970s as a prolific writer and member of the Committee on the Present Danger. Unlike Nitze and Rostow, Adelman had not dropped his hard-line rhetoric and views once he was on the inside. He took seriously the anti-arms control gospel that the committee had preached so energetically in its crusade against SALT. Occupying Dean Acheson's grand old wood-paneled office, Adelman rapidly aligned himself with the Pentagon on many arms control issues. If the Arms Control and Disarmament Agency had once been a place where Nitze could find allies and sustenance, it wasn't any more. During his final year at the INF talks and in the empty months that followed, Nitze bristled at interference from Adelman's office. He couldn't help sniping at Adelman himself, quipping caustically that the ACDA head undermined the U.S. arms control effort by "the reality of his own frivolity."

Adelman, in turn, was put off by his ancient colleague. He had found Nitze's panicked prophecies of the doom that would follow the INF deployment to be absurd and naive. Adelman also thought that Nitze's independent streak was far too wide. "Paul tends to do things, and likes to do things, by himself," he said. After "fifty years" in government that was not surprising. But, Adelman added, sucking on his pipe, "That's generally not the best way to get things done because there's a lot of resentment of that."

There had been resentment when Nitze was in the office across the hall from Adelman's working on INF issues. With Nitze's move to the seventh floor to be closer to Shultz, there was anger. "We worked better before he went upstairs," Adelman remarked coolly. Nitze dismissed the awkward protocol change. "The problems are difficult, but the relationships are not," he said two days after being appointed.[3]

To official Washington, obsessed by who is up and who is down, who is in and who is out, the message of Nitze's promotion was clear. Rather than relying principally on the director of ACDA for arms control guidance, the secretary of state would be relying on Paul Nitze.

That Shultz would devise such an arrangement came as no surprise. Adelman had not been his choice to head ACDA. Philosophically and socially there was little to tie Shultz to this thirty-seven-year-old neoconservative. Paul Nitze, in contrast, was living history—a man who had worked on the Marshall Plan, had been a top official in the State Department thirty five years earlier, and was the last survivor of a generation of public servants who had entered government during World War II. George Shultz could appreciate that background. "Wise men come and wise men go," he would say later, "but decade after decade there is Paul Nitze."[4]

More immediately, the secretary of state valued Nitze for the strengths that he brought to his job. Even if Ken Adelman had wanted to push U.S. arms control efforts to their furthest extreme, he would have lacked the standing to do so. If the moderates were going to win the battle over arms control, they needed to build a coalition that could force the president's hand—a coalition that not only included State, Defense, and the NSC, but stretched even further to encompass the Joint Chiefs of Staff, congressional leaders, and European allies. To build this coalition, Shultz needed someone who was respected by these various players. And while Nitze had his share of critics, he had just as many admirers, especially on Capitol Hill and in Europe.

George Shultz needed Nitze at his side for another reason, too. For the first three years of the Reagan presidency, the focus in arms control had been the INF negotiations. But proceeding simultaneously in Geneva, and receiving far less attention, were negotiations between the superpowers on long-range nuclear weapons known as the Strategic Arms Reduction Talks, or START. And in the grand scheme of things, these talks were of far greater importance. The number of nuclear warheads on intermediate-range nuclear forces was counted in the hundreds; on strategic weapons the United States and Soviet Union had a combined total of nearly 20,000. If the fears generated by the arms race were ever to be allayed, and the costs of maintaining nuclear stability were ever to be reduced, these weapons had to be controlled. INF had dominated the arms control agenda during Reagan's first term; START would dominate it during his second.

The new debate was far more complex. Ronald Reagan made sure of that. To the already puzzling question of how to slow the strategic nuclear arms race, he added an additional consideration. Near the end of a televised speech on defense spending on March 23, 1983, the president had pronounced the strategy of mutual assured destruction to be "a sad commentary on the human condition." Wouldn't it be better, he asked, "to save lives than to avenge them?"

It would be, Reagan answered. He then dropped a bomb of his own. "After careful consultation with my advisors, including the Joint Chiefs of Staff, I believe there is a way. Let me share with you a vision of the future which offers hope. It is that we embark on a program to counter the awesome Soviet missile threat with measures that are defensive."[5]

Eleven years after Brezhnev and Nixon signed the ABM Treaty, President Reagan was reopening the debate over defensive technology. Eleven years after the national security establishments of both superpowers had painfully come to a mutual consensus that defenses were destabilizing, Ronald Reagan—in consultation with only a few people, among them Edward Teller—had decided to challenge this consensus.

Like everything else the president put his energies behind, this attack on the status quo blossomed rapidly. Dubbed "Star Wars" by the press and "strategic defense initiative" (SDI) by the administration, the effort to develop defensive technologies that could shoot down ballistic missiles soon became a top priority. By 1985 the United States was spending several billion dollars a year on SDI. Few other programs were dearer to the president's heart. Among his loyalists, support for SDI became a litmus test of fidelity to Ronald Reagan. For hard-liners, it was the ultimate weapon in the war on arms control. To the Soviets, Star Wars posed an ominous new threat.

And for the arms controllers in the State Department, the revival of defensive technologies was a nightmare. It inserted a bewildering set of new calculations into the strategic arms control equation. If George Shultz was ever going to sort out this mess, he would need the aid of someone who had sorted it out once before. As a veteran of the Johnson and Nixon administrations, Paul Nitze was such a person.

The education of the secretary of state began late in 1984 after it was announced that he and Soviet Foreign Minister Andrei Gromyko would meet in Geneva in January 1985. Eager to hold his own with this famed Soviet diplomat, Shultz immersed himself as never before in the arcane details of strategic arms control. Almost every day Nitze took the short walk to Shultz's spacious office for long private sessions on the ins and outs of negotiating with the Russians. When Shultz went out to California for the Christmas holiday, Nitze was on the phone with him constantly. The relationship between the two men ripened quickly. Not since Dean Acheson's tenure at State had Nitze enjoyed such a close, mutually respectful relationship with one of his superiors. Beneath the bland exterior that caused many in Washington to underestimate George Shultz was a quick mind honed by years of teaching economics and mastering new government posts, a mind adept at synthesizing reams of information. Nitze appreciated this facility, and he appreciated something else that lurked beneath the blandness: Shultz's value system. Rare in Ronald Reagan's Washington, it was the system that Nitze had learned from Dillon and Forrestal and Acheson. Its principal component was loyalty: loyalty to subordinates and superiors, to the system and its rules, to substance and integrity.

In the dreariness of modern Washington, with its status-obsessed bureaucrats and unremitting infighting, George Shultz was the only top official who Nitze respected. He was also the only one who listened to Nitze's ideas on strategic arms control. In this Paul Nitze was fortunate, because his views constituted heresy.

To President Reagan and his most devout followers, Star Wars held out the promise of a world free of nuclear arms. Its aim was not to achieve American nuclear superiority nor to protect American missile silos from a first strike. "Protecting weapons represents no change in current policy," said George Keyworth II, Reagan's science advisor and one of SDI's most ardent proponents. "It simply strengthens—entrenches—the doctrine of mutual assured destruction."[6] Only a defensive system that protected people would end the doctrine of MAD. The aim of Star Wars was to achieve this kind of system. To talk of any other kind of system was to defy White House policy. And to talk about getting rid of Star Wars altogether was to go beyond mere defiance. It was heresy.

Nitze's weakness was that he found it impossible to think of strategic defenses without calculating their value as a bargaining chip. He remembered the rhetoric that had surrounded ABMs when they were first being researched in the early 1960s. A nationwide ABM system could protect American cities from nuclear attack, its advocates had argued; real security was within grasp.

But the rhetoric rapidly changed. By 1967 the ABM system was being justified as a defense against a future threat from Chinese nuclear forces. Two years later officials talked instead of defending missile silos from a Soviet first strike and of developing ABMs so that they could be bargained away in SALT. The bargaining argument was the one that Nitze had embraced most fervently. His fight to keep the U.S. ABM program alive in the spring and summer of 1969 had been, in his mind, a fight to keep alive hopes for an ABM treaty.

During the mid 1980s, Nitze's thinking ran along the same lines. But there was a key difference. Under Nixon the ABM system was to be a bargaining chip used to get an ABM treaty, nothing more. Star Wars could get a lot more than that, Nitze felt. The allure of using SDI as a bargaining chip was that it was so valuable. A defensive space shield may have been a high tech fantasy whose complexities and expenses made it unattainable, but it was a fantasy that played on the Soviet Union's worst insecurities. Quite possibly, they would do nearly anything to kill SDI. They might even be willing to scrap a good portion of their heavy land-based missiles in exchange for a U.S. promise to cancel SDI.

It was this idea that so intrigued Paul Nitze. For over a decade and a half, Nitze had sought a way to force the Soviet Union to dismantle its arsenal of massive land-based missiles. All his efforts had failed. Now, in a burgeoning effort by the United States to develop a space shield, Nitze saw a new form of leverage. If SDI could be harnessed for negotiating purposes, if the United States offered the Soviets a trade—defensive technologies for offensive missiles—it might be possible finally to shatter the Soviet lead in heavy missiles and ensure American security into the twenty-first century.

Earlier in 1984 Nitze had laid out the broad contours of this idea in a paper for Shultz. He emphasized the lessons of SALT I and urged that the administration begin to sort out the relationship between defensive technologies and strategic arms talks. During the preparation for Shultz's meeting with Gromyko, Nitze worked to refine these thoughts and to package them in way that would both appeal to the president and place SDI on the bargaining table.

What he came up with was a complicated policy statement, which became known as the "strategic concept": "During the next ten years, the U.S. objective is a radical reduction in the power of existing and planned offensive nuclear arms, as well as the stabilization of the relationship between offensive and defensive nuclear arms, whether on earth or space. We are even now looking forward to a period of transition to a more stable world, with greatly reduced levels of nuclear arms and an enhanced ability to deter war based upon an increasing contribution to non-nuclear defenses against offensive nuclear arms. This period of transition could lead to the eventual elimination of all nuclear arms, both offensive and defensive."[7]

On its surface the statement warmly embraced Ronald Reagan's dream of a world free of nuclear weapons. Read more carefully, though, it implied a need to bring SDI into the arms control fold. If work on space shields could proceed uninhibited and at any pace, what were the chances of stabilizing the "relationship between offensive and defensive" weapons? Not high. Stabilization, decoded, was a synonym for predictability. And in the fast-paced world of military competition, only arms control could impose that element.

Still, while the subliminal message of the strategic concept may have been pro-arms control, Nitze's statement helped perpetuate much of the deluded thinking surrounding SDI. Again and again administration critics argued that the superpowers could never move safely from deterrence based on MAD to peace based on SDI. They pointed out that the Soviets would never agree to a mutual transition to defenses—a realm in which U.S. technology was superior. Therefore, any move to deploy such defenses by the United States would trigger a hostile Soviet reaction and accelerate the strategic competition. By laying out the steps for a transition away from offenses without rebutting the argument that such a process would be impossible, Nitze was not overcoming the illogic of SDI. He was simply refining it.

This behavior was typical of Paul Nitze. Whether he liked it or not, the SDI program had been started. "Nitze's logical, scientific mind then went to work and created a rationale for it which he was comfortable with," explained Max Kampleman. "He had a capacity for then believing it, accepting it, embracing it in every way." The premise of the strategic concept may have been logically flawed, but given the chaotic state of administration thinking on SDI, it represented a great step forward. And herein lay the problem.

In January 1985 President Reagan formally approved the strategic concept when he signed National Security Decision Directive 153. For almost two years the administration had lacked a cogent rationale for SDI. Besides the president's dream and some scattered talk of defending missile silos, SDI had been a program without a policy. Now, thanks to Nitze's cleverness, there was a policy. But instead of sparking interest in trading away SDI, the strategic concept was hailed as a visionary declaration of a new strategic policy in which SDI would be integral. "Adoption of the position that deterrence is dependent on defenses," wrote one observer, "represents the most radical shift in nuclear strategy since mutual assured destruction (MAD) was recognized during Robert McNamara's years as Secretary of Defense."[8] By accepting and refining the president's flawed logic, Nitze risked undermining the superior logic that dictated that SDI should be used as a bargaining chip.

Amid these ominous signs that Nitze's efforts might ultimately backfire, the short-term goal of placing SDI in an arms control context appeared within reach. When Shultz, McFarlane, and Nitze met with Gromyko in January, the secretary of state outlined the strategic concept. The Soviet foreign minister responded with interest, but the two sides remained light years apart on the question of defensive technologies. The Geneva meeting led to the resumption of talks on strategic and intermediate-range nuclear forces, but achieved little else.

*   *   *

Nitze's effort to deal with the problem of SDI did not stop at the strategic concept. Placing the pursuit of a space shield within a broader context was only the first step toward formulating a coherent national policy. The question of feasibility had to be addressed as well. Ever since the president's 1983 speech his dream had been under fire from those who said that Star Wars would not work, that the technology for building an impenetrable defense against ballistic missiles did not exist. Administration officials were repeatedly asked under what circumstances SDI would be deployed; they had no answer. Since SDI remained more a costly fantasy than a policy, it was difficult to be specific about deployment. Aside from several Pentagon statements, the administration's position on the question remained hopelessly muddled.

On a sunny and mild February day in 1985 Paul Nitze again moved to fill a conceptual vacuum with a policy of his own. In a speech before the Philadelphia World Affairs Council, Nitze said: "The feasibility of such technologies will be demanding. The technologies must produce defensive systems that are survivable; if not, the defenses would themselves be tempting targets for a first strike. This would decrease rather than enhance stability.

"New defenses must also be cost effective at the margin—that is, it must be cheap enough to add additional defensive capability so that the other side has no incentive to add additional offensive capability to overcome the defense. If this criterion is not met, the defensive systems could encourage a proliferation of countermeasures and additional offensive weapons to overcome deployed defenses. . . .

"As I said, these criterion are demanding. If the new technologies cannot meet these standards, we are not about to deploy them."[9]

Hailed almost immediately by the press as the "Nitze criteria," these conditions for deployment were quickly adopted as administration policy. Their effect was opposite to that of the strategic concept. By imagining a transition away from MAD, the concept had energized SDI proponents. In contrast, the Nitze criteria brought the Star Wars debate back to earth by focusing attention on the weaknesses of strategic defenses: their susceptibility to countermeasures and their relative expense. During the 1960s Nitze had argued that a nationwide ABM system would never work because the Soviet Union could always build more missiles and warheads to overcome any defensive shield and American cities would never be safe from attack.

In promulgating his criteria in 1985, Nitze was not repeating this argument. Rather he was saying that if future schemes to shoot down missiles turned out to be akin to previous efforts, they would be unacceptable. This was a demanding precondition indeed. Already, critics of SDI were pointing out the myriad ways in which the Soviets could bypass a space shield. In the years that it took the United States to build SDI, the Soviet Union would be working on countermeasures, and these countermeasures would be far less expensive. Vast fleets of bombers and cruise missiles could be built to fly under a shield. Enough missiles and warheads—thousands or even tens of thousands—could be built to overwhelm it. Dummy missiles and dummy warheads could be designed to confuse it. Special antisatellite weapons could be built to destroy the space platforms on which much of SDI would be based. And if these countermeasures were not enough, the Soviets could smuggle hundreds of nuclear bombs into the United States on boats and planes in much the same way that drug lords smuggled cocaine.[10] Render nuclear weapons impotent and obsolete? Most scientists thought it was impossible. In all likelihood, Nitze's criteria could never be met.

Although Robert McFarlane managed to get the criteria through the bureaucracy, they were viewed with intense uneasiness by SDI supporters. "The Nitze criteria were put in to kill—not to enhance— the prospects for SDI," charged Daniel Graham, now heading the pro-SDI lobby High Frontier.[11] At the Pentagon there was grumbling that the criteria were too rigid and that Nitze had thrust them on the government without warning. Perle's deputy Frank Gaffney was given the task of unraveling the criteria's policy implications. He found the job exasperating. "Nobody knows what the hell that is," said Gaffney. "Nobody knows how to define it. Nobody knows how to calculate it." After endless hours of toil, Gaffney came to share Graham's feeling that the criteria were nothing more than a ruse aimed at crippling SDI. "What it essentially amounted to was a basis upon which one would always say 'it isn't good enough.'"

Nitze's allies defended the criteria. William Burns, now heading policy making at State, scoffed at the notion that Paul Nitze sought to extinguish hopes for a strategic defense system. Instead, said Burns, the criteria "was a formula for killing an early, imprudent deployment of SDI when we didn't know what we were deploying or whether it would work."

Still, to hard-liners in the Reagan administration, it appeared that Paul Nitze was up to his old tricks. None of them had forgotten Nitze's walk in the woods or his subsequent attempts to manipulate the administration. If there was any doubt by the end of the INF talks about whose side Nitze was on, it was dispelled the following year when *Time* magazine editor Strobe Talbott published his inside account of the talks, *Deadly Gambits*. In intricate detail the book portrayed the bitter infighting that had divided the administration during the early 1980s. It also provided a blow-by-blow account of the wrangling in Geneva, going so far as to recount the dialogue between Nitze and Kvitsinsky during their walk in the woods.

With the 1984 presidential election fast approaching, *Deadly Gambits* was seized on by the Democrats as evidence that the Reagan administration had no commitment to arms control. Walter Mondale cited the book in a debate with President Reagan, saying that all Americans should read *Deadly Gambits* to understand what was wrong in Washington. For those who did read it the message of the book was clear: Villains such as Richard Perle and Caspar Weinberger were systematically sabotaging the arms control talks. Assisting them in this effort was a lazy and ignorant President.

Just as clear was the message that not everyone in the administration was evil. In fact, *Deadly Gambits* had a distinct hero, a tenacious and inventive man who had tried to break the arms control stalemate—Paul Nitze. In chapter after chapter the book showed Nitze fighting almost singlehandedly against the narrow-minded hawks in the Pentagon. The climax of the book was Nitze's secret negotiation with Yuli Kvitsinsky.

To the better informed readers, Paul Nitze was not just the hero of *Deadly Gambits,* but obviously one of Talbott's main sources. After years of poring over articles based on interviews with unnamed "senior officials," insiders in Washington had little trouble seeing that several of the key episodes in the book, especially the colorful account of the walk in the woods, could only have come from Nitze. A decade earlier Nitze had railed against Henry Kissinger for leaking material to John Newhouse. Now Nitze had done much the same thing for Talbott, and conservatives were fuming. Nitze had provided powerful ammunition for a damaging attack on the Reagan administration during an election year.

When Shultz promoted Nitze in December to the position of special advisor on arms control, there was more evidence of whose side he was on. On Capitol Hill Democrats and moderate Republicans praised the appointment. Even some of Nitze's more bitter foes, now residing in Washington's liberal think tanks, had good words to say. Echoing this applause was the *New York Times.* "Making Mr. Nitze a chief advisor to Secretary Shultz instead of just Euromissile negotiator was a good way for the President to point a new direction," it editorialized.[12] Five years earlier Paul Nitze had been the archenemy of SALT II and a traitor in the good fight for arms control. Now he was hailed by former detractors as the "great white hope," a voice of reason in an administration of extremists.

After the bruising and somewhat embarrassing battles of the Carter years, Nitze was pleased to resuscitate his reputation among long-time friends and former colleagues. Unfortunately, these people were not in the government. And while support from liberals and moderates in Congress was helpful—one of Nitze's assignments now was to keep the Senate informed about superpower negotiations—it was the Senators who harbored suspicions about arms control who needed the most stroking. "I think he's done a superb job consulting the Senate," remarked Adelman. "The trouble is that the Senators who feel consoled and warm about it tend to be center-left, more liberal, who are going to vote for anything that has to do with arms control. They are not our target group. Those that we need for ratification tend to think that Paul really left his convictions when he went into government."

The daunting task of building the coalition needed to move arms control forward required that Nitze be trusted throughout the government. But in the months following the reopening of talks in Geneva, Nitze's position remained weak. Little in the Reagan administration had changed since the early 1980s. As before, Pentagon hard-liners like Richard Perle wielded enormous power in interagency meetings. As before, the president remained largely uninterested and uninformed about arms control. Consequently, the talks in Geneva went nowhere; the arms control process remained moribund.

It would take the imagination and power of Mikhail Sergeyevich Gorbachev to break the stalemate.

A peasant's son from southern Russia, Gorbachev succeeded Konstantin U. Chernenko as Soviet leader on March 12, 1985. At 54 he was part of a new generation of Soviet officials, one that had come of age after Stalin's purges and Nazi Germany's surprise attack. To his post in the Kremlin, Gorbachev brought a fervent desire to lift the Soviet Union from its economic and political stagnation. He believed that without dramatic action his country would become irrelevant on a world stage increasingly dominated by economic rather than military might. "We will have to carry out profound transformations in the economy and in the entire system of social relations," Gorbachev said shortly before taking power.[13]

One of the changes he pressed for was a scaling back of the Soviet arms effort. On the day he took power, Gorbachev called for a "real and major reduction in arms stockpiles." In the following months he repeated that call many times. This kind of talk had been a staple of Kremlin propaganda for decades. Gorbachev's statements were nothing new to the west. And western experts were not impressed when the Soviets proposed a 25 percent cut in strategic missiles in June 1985. Nitze promptly labeled the plan "counterproductive."[14] But when Gorbachev visited Paris in late September, he carried with him an arms control proposal that finally attracted attention. For the first time the Soviet leader announced that the Soviets were willing to accept a 50 percent cut in strategic missiles.

From the Pentagon came predictable skepticism. To Richard Perle, the Soviet offer was nothing more than a public relations ploy aimed at derailing the Strategic Defense Initiative. "Let's not kid ourselves," he said. "What the Soviets have in mind is halting the American program." At the State Department, however, Shultz and Nitze were encouraged by the proposal. "They're addressing the subject matter," Shultz said, "and if they're addressing the subject matter, presumably that means that you can talk about it."[15] What intrigued Nitze most was that in the clarifications that followed the initial proposal, the Soviet Union expressed a willingness for the first time ever to make "drastic reductions" in their heavy land-based missiles.[16]

Since the late 1960s Nitze had sought a way to force the Soviets to give up their counterforce behemoths. Finally the idea was being discussed. Equally encouraging was the new air of cordiality in superpower relations. By 1985 the tense cold war climate that had marked most of Reagan's presidency was beginning to warm. Gone from the president's speeches were references to "the evil empire." With a young and dynamic leader heading the Soviet Union, there seemed to be a rare, perhaps even a historic opportunity to end the hostilities of the past four decades.

Several months before Gorbachev's ascendancy to power, Nitze had written, "A host of internal and external factors could combine to effect changes in Soviet policies and now make possible a genuine peaceful coexistence between the United States and the Soviet Union." Nitze predicted that these changes would be pushed by a new generation of Soviet leaders.[17] With Chernenko dead and Mikhail Gorbachev talking of sweeping reforms in the Soviet system, this process was already underway. And it was already improving U.S.-Soviet relations. During his four years at the White House Ronald Reagan had never met a Soviet leader. In fall 1985 it was announced that he would meet Gorbachev in Geneva in November.

* * *

If the rise of Gorbachev presaged an end to the Cold War, there was still no lack of issues to divide the superpowers. One issue was the future of the ABM Treaty.

The president's dream of a missile defense shield and continued adherence to the ABM Treaty were fundamentally incompatible. Some day in the future it would be necessary to choose between pushing ahead with SDI or staying within the terms of the treaty. At the latest, that day would come when the Pentagon began testing components of SDI. At the earliest, it could come if the administration chose to repudiate the treaty. Unlike some in the administration, Paul Nitze was in no hurry to kill the ABM Treaty. He had fought for Safeguard in 1969 to make a treaty possible. He had spent three years constructing the agreement. He believed that in most respects it was an excellent treaty, probably the best ever negotiated. In his public statements on SDI, Nitze had always stressed that the program would be pursued "in full compliance with the ABM Treaty."[18]

In May 1985 Nitze delivered the keynote speech at the commencement of the Johns Hopkins School of Advanced International Studies. The focus of the speech was SDI and the ABM Treaty. For the first time Nitze laid out what he meant by "full compliance." During the long months of negotiating the ABM Treaty, he argued, neither the United States nor the Soviet Union had perceived the treaty as one which would be "locked in concrete." Rather, "When we and the Soviets were crafting the agreement, we envisaged a living accord—that is, one that would make allowance for and adapt to future circumstances."

And now that SDI was changing the world, Nitze said, it was time to think anew about the 1972 agreement. This reexamination necessarily began with a look at the provisions of the ABM Treaty that allowed for modifying the treaty, primarily Articles XIII and XIV. The latter gave each party the right to propose amendments to the treaty. It also provided for a joint review of the treaty every five years. Article XIII created a forum known as the Standing Consultative Committee (SCC) in which amendments would be considered and disagreements about the treaty could be ironed out. If there was to be a major change in the ABM Treaty, it would first have to be approved by the SCC. In the meantime, Nitze said, the research on SDI was compatible with the treaty since it included no ban on research. The president's dream of a space shield posed no immediate or long-term threat to the ABM Treaty, Nitze concluded.[19]

As Nitze was reassuring his audience in Washington, Ken Adelman had a more ominous message for a group in Boston. Foreseeing testing of antimissile technology in the near future, the ACDA head said that "modifications" of the treaty might be needed to "permit more definitive demonstrations" of space-based technologies.[20] Adelman's speech, however, contained no specifics about how or when such "modifications" might be proposed. The message seemed to be that the Reagan administration didn't like the ABM Treaty, but harbored no intentions of abrogating it anytime soon.

Following these two statements, the issue of SDI and the ABM Treaty appeared to be settled. Among most top administration officials, there was little enthusiasm for modifying the treaty. Such a move would be certain to attract concentrated fire from Congress, the media, and even that largely uninformed and infrequently aroused political force known as "the public." Gutting the ABM Treaty would dramatically confirm the charge that the Reagan administration was opposed to arms control. It could cause big trouble for SDI funding on Capitol Hill, and in all likelihood it would throw the already jittery Allies into a panic. And since the Soviet Union had no intention of sanctioning an arms race in space during a polite SCC meeting, any modification of the treaty would have to be a unilateral step, a move that would be tantamount to a repudiation. With SDI still years away from the testing phase, there was no reason to fight this battle now.

No reason, that is, unless the actual goal was to deal a death blow to the legacy of SALT and thereby advance the crusade against arms control.

At the Pentagon Richard Perle had been giving some thought to how SDI was affected by the ABM Treaty. For years one of his main lines of attack on arms control was that even the best agreements tended to have dangerously large loopholes. In the past Perle had charged that it was the Soviets who always took advantage of those loopholes. But perhaps this pattern could be reversed.

In mid 1985 Perle asked Pentagon lawyer Philip Kunsberg to "take a fresh look at the treaty and tell us what it actually said." A 35-year-old former assistant district attorney from New York, Kunsberg had built his reputation fighting pornographers and Mafia kingpins. He had little experience in international law. Going through the voluminous negotiating record of the ABM Treaty in less than a week, Kunsberg did take a fresh look, and his conclusions were unusual. Kunsberg told Perle that the limitations on the development of exotic antimissile technologies were not as ironclad as many thought. In a nineteen-page report

Kunsberg argued that the United States had never formally agreed to restrict the testing and deployment of such technologies. Therefore, there was no legal reason why SDI could not go forward at whatever pace the United States chose.

Perle recalled that he "almost fell off the chair" when he heard Kunsberg's conclusions. Still, this was only one lawyer and one view— no match for thirteen years of precedent and the powerful forces that stood behind the ABM Treaty. Only a stronger legal foundation and then a decision by the president could provide the ammunition for a successful insurrection. In September 1985 the former was provided by an unlikely ally, the State Department's legal advisor, Abraham Sofaer. Like Kunsberg, Sofaer had come to Washington from the rough-and-tumble world of New York City where he had been a judge on the U.S. District Court. To assess the validity of Kunsberg's conclusions, he began his own study of the ABM Treaty. Poring over the negotiating record for long hours, Sofaer began to believe that Kunsberg's interpretation was right. He then went to Nitze with his conclusions.[21]

Paul Nitze may have known a great deal about a great many things, he may have been the government's leading expert on arms control, but he did not know law. And as Sofaer dissected the treaty article by article, hammering away at its weak spots and ambiguities, Nitze became convinced that he was correct. By making the first thorough review of the negotiating record in thirteen years, Nitze would say later, Sofaer had found convincing evidence that "the Soviets resisted U.S. efforts to negotiate more restrictive limitations on future systems. Consequently, no agreement was reached on such limitations."[22] Given this new interpretation, there was nothing in the ABM Treaty that restrained SDI.

Although Nitze agreed with Sofaer, there was a fundamental difference between embracing the new interpretation in private and promulgating it. In preparation for a White House meeting on October 4 to discuss the interpretation question, Nitze wrote up a short memorandum that outlined the many pitfalls of going public with a new stance on the ABM Treaty.

Once at the meeting, however, Nitze was confronted with the nearly unanimous view that the administration should go forward with the new interpretation. Pentagon officials argued forcefully for the new interpretation, saying that the ABM Treaty not only allowed developing and testing of SDI, but deployment as well. Nitze agreed that the broad interpretation was justified, but argued that it allowed only development and testing, not deployment. McFarlane, who was chairing the meeting, agreed with Nitze's position.

On the critical question of whether to go public, however, Nitze was silent. Only ACDA's lawyer, Thomas Graham, was fighting the idea. For Nitze to circulate his memorandum would place him in the same unpalatable position he had so often occupied over the past four years, that of the lonely arms controller. It would mean identifying himself once again as a confused dove whose flight pattern ignored the prevailing winds. Nitze decided to keep his memo under wraps.

After the meeting Nitze returned to his office and told Norm Clyne to write a paper for McFarlane which elaborated on the nondeployment argument. Nitze worried that he had blundered in not arguing against going public, so on Saturday morning he wrote a memo for McFarlane in which he expressed the view that the administration "should not implement a decision adopting the broad interpretation without full prior discussion with its allies and with the Congress." Nitze planned to have the memo delivered to the NSC director by Tuesday.[23]

McFarlane did not see the memo in time. On Sunday morning he went public with the new interpretation on "Meet the Press," saying that research, testing, and development of new defensive weapons was "approved and authorized by the treaty. Only deployment is foreclosed." Nitze was aghast. In a frantic effort to limit the damage, he persuaded Shultz that the United States had to back away from McFarlane's statement. The best way to do this without losing face, Nitze suggested, was to contend that the new interpretation was legally correct but to reassure the world that the administration would abide by the traditional interpretation. Shultz agreed. In a White House meeting on October 11 with the president, McFarlane, Weinberger, and Adelman, Shultz insisted that the administration take this position. After a draining and emotionally charged meeting, the president consented.[24]

Still, the damage had been done. As Nitze had expected, there was an instant uproar. Powerful congressional officials condemned the decision and major newspapers editorialized against it. From Europe came diplomatic notes expressing alarm. Writing in *Pravda,* a leading Soviet military official accused the United States of having "distorted the essence of the treaty."[25] At the Geneva arms talks Max Kampleman, now the chief START negotiator, bore the brunt of the Soviet backlash. "I thought that was one of these totally unnecessary steps," he said later. "We were really not at the point of doing research that required us to abandon the narrow definition. So why inject the issue at that time? It soured the atmosphere terribly."

The most damaging attack on the new interpretation was made by the men who had negotiated the treaty. Gerard Smith ridiculed the move, saying "that it was not our intention that any type of technology for space-based ABM systems could be developed or tested under the treaty."[26] A month earlier John Rhinelander, the SALT I team's lawyer, had dismissed a possible reinterpretation, saying "this is too ridiculous to take seriously."[27] Now he could hardly believe what the administration was doing. Royal Allison added his voice to the clamor, saying "Nowhere did I understand that we retained the right to development and full-scale testing of new systems."[28] Almost every member of the SALT I delegation—except Paul Nitze—agreed that the new interpretation was dead wrong.

Following the walk in the woods and the publication of *Deadly Gambits,* Nitze's reputation in Washington's arms control community had been dramatically revived. Now it again lay shattered. Like his savage attack on Paul Warnke and his implacable opposition to SALT II, Nitze's role in the reinterpretation scandal left his old colleagues confused and angry. "I'm puzzled," said Gerard Smith, a sad edge in his voice. "Nobody knows more about the ABM Treaty than Paul Nitze," remarked John Rhinelander. "Nobody has more respect for rigorous logic. How could a couple of lawyers who don't know the first thing about arms control come along and turn him around on a dime?" It was almost inconceivable.[29]

Being publicly named as a coconspirator in the reinterpretation of the ABM Treaty was one of the most humiliating episodes in Nitze's career. But it got worse. As the administration's point man on arms control, Nitze had no choice but to defend the new interpretation. Two weeks after McFarlane's announcement, Nitze and Sofaer made an unpleasant appearance before a House committee. Arrayed against the two men were Gerard Smith, Ralph Earle, and John Rhinelander. Usually among the cleverest of witnesses, Nitze was argued to a standstill by Congressman Norman Dicks. For months Nitze had said that any changes in the ABM Treaty would have to be worked out by both superpowers within the Standing Consultative Committee. Dicks asked about this condition. "Why can't we do that?" he pressed. "Why doesn't that make more sense than having a broad interpretation and a restrictive policy? Why not go to the SCC and negotiate it with the Russians and get an answer?"

"Let me take it under advisement," Nitze replied lamely.[30]

* * *

In the context of U.S.-Soviet relations, the new interpretation could hardly have come at a worse time. For months the administration had been sprucing up its image and trying to score points in the critical public relations war surrounding arms control. With McFarlane's statement it had lost points, a whole lot of them. Moreover, the Geneva summit was only weeks away. By getting tangled up in the ABM controversy, the administration drained attention and energy from the job of making progress when Reagan met with Gorbachev.

High-level officials at the White House and Defense Department were working furiously to lower expectations of the summit. The Reagan administration was publicly calling it only a chance for the superpower leaders to "get acquainted." Only Nitze was prepared to say that progress could be made. "There is a big gap between our proposal and their proposal," he said in early November, but hopefully "we can work something out."[31]

What Nitze had in mind was an agreement in principle between the United States and the Soviet Union on the rough outlines of a strategic arms control deal. For months Nitze had been quietly pushing an ambitious plan of his own. Known cryptically as the Monday Package, Nitze's proposal envisioned deep cuts in strategic arms coupled with an agreement to abide by the strict interpretation of the ABM Treaty. The Monday Package was essentially the trade-off between SDI and heavy Soviet missiles that Nitze had long pondered. Heresy though it was, Shultz and McFarlane were firmly behind the idea.

In preparing for Geneva, Nitze's greatest challenge was to make the Monday Package the centerpiece of the summit. His maneuvering received a boost when Weinberger and Perle were excluded from the American entourage that would go to Geneva. Nitze was further encouraged when he was given a major role in drafting the proposal for new arms control guidelines that President Reagan would present to Gorbachev. As finally accepted by the bureaucracy, this document echoed the Monday Package's call for a 50 percent cut in strategic missiles. It stated further that "the sides should provide assurance that their strategic defense programs shall be conducted as permitted by, and in full compliance with, the ABM Treaty." Lest this point was lost on the Soviets, both Shultz and Nitze made sure to repeat it many times in the weeks leading up to the summit. "SDI is not a deployment program," Nitze said in October, "it is a research program only." Moreover, it was a research program, Shultz emphasized, that "will continue to be conducted in accordance with a restrictive interpretation of the treaty's obligations."[32]

If the Soviets became genuinely convinced on this point, if they felt they were not in any way sanctioning SDI, there was a chance they would accept the U.S. proposal at the Geneva summit. This would constitute a dramatic step toward the big trade-off or grand compromise that Nitze sought. But as always in this administration, there was a snag. In its journey through the bureaucracy, the guidelines document had been laden with language that extolled SDI and called for a transition to defensive forces, the sort of language that always triggered a Soviet reflexive *nyet*. And when Ronald Reagan presented the document to Gorbachev as the two men sat by a fire in the poolhouse of a villa on Lake Geneva, tthat was precisely the response he got. Instead of breaking the deadlock in the strategic arms talks, the meeting produced only a weak joint statement that contained little that was new.

Through 1985 Gorbachev had moved with caution in the realm of foreign affairs. An official who had focused on domestic issues for most of his career, it was not his strong point. Still, the moves Gorbachev did take had thrown the United States onto the defensive. For the first time it was the Soviet Union that was the more dynamic and conciliatory power. Stagnating amidst bitter infighting and shackled to a vociferous anticommunist ideology, the Reagan administration was unprepared for movement on the arms control front. Years of mock negotiations had lent an unreal air and sense of futility to U.S.-Soviet relations. Even optimists had a difficult time imagining the Soviet Union—diplomatically hidebound for so long—making any dramatic concessions. Many thought that the new Soviet leader was making the customary propaganda flourishes that precede more serious negotiations. It was assumed that these statements would soon trail off.

But Mikhail Gorbachev had only begun.

In January 1986 the Soviet leader issued a sweeping proposal for the elimination of all nuclear weapons by the year 2000. Stage one of this process would be the reduction of superpower nuclear arsenals by 50 percent over the next five to eight years, the removal of all U.S. and Soviet intermediate-range missiles from Europe, and an end to nuclear testing. Stage two would be the elimination of all tactical nuclear weapons and a ban on what the Soviets referred to as "space strike weapons." Stage three would be the dismantling by the superpowers of their remaining weapons.[33]

To make this all possible and insure that neither side could cheat,

Gorbachev expressed a new willingness to allow U.S. inspectors onto Soviet soil to verify compliance with the agreements. For decades the issue of on-site inspections had hobbled arms control efforts. Soviet opposition to on-site inspection and U.S. insistence on it had helped to kill the prospects for both a comprehensive test ban treaty and a MIRV ban. Now, if the Soviet leader were true to his word, this would no longer be a stumbling block.

Like Ronald Reagan's dream of an impenetrable space shield, Gorbachev's vision of a world free of nuclear arms was too fantastical to take seriously. Even if such a goal were achievable Nitze had long been of the view that it would not be desirable. During his days under Truman he had toyed with the idea of complete disarmament only to conclude that "it was not feasible and really not realistic." By the 1980s his views had changed little. "I do not see how it could be done with any great security," he said in 1982. "I think you would leave yourself open to great instability. It is too easy for people to make nuclear weapons. I do not think that you can put that genie completely back into the bottle. I wish one could, but I do not think one can."[34]

Yet if Gorbachev's ultimate goal was undesirable, his suggested process was not. In talking boldly and insistently about deep reductions, the Soviet leader was speaking to Nitze's most cherished dream. During SALT I Nitze had failed in his push for deep reductions. During SALT II nobody in either superpower took the idea of reductions seriously. And in Reagan's first term many arms control experts dismissed the deep missile cuts proposed under START as chimerical. By early 1986, however, Gorbachev had placed deep cuts at the top of the Soviet arms control agenda. What remained was for the United States to match his imagination and to test his sincerity. It was a task Paul Nitze relished.

Meeting Gorbachev's challenge required unity and discipline. To reach an agreement on strategic weapons before Reagan's second term came to an end, the administration would have to focus its energies and mend its rifts. It would need to make bold moves and quick decisions. It would need a president who was engaged in the process of arms control, who could resolve disputes in the bureaucracy and push the government forward.

What the administration needed, in other words, was sweeping changes in the way it worked. That these changes would be slow in coming—if they ever came at all—was evidenced by the debate over SALT II.

When the Soviet Union invaded Afghanistan in December 1979,

Jimmy Carter had withdrawn the SALT II treaty from consideration by the Senate. Under President Reagan the treaty was not resubmitted, but it remained in effect in its unratified state. Throughout the 1980s Reagan administration officials regularly inveighed against SALT and the "decade of disarmament." At times it seemed as if the campaign of 1980 had never ended. At times, also, the Administration gave the impression that SALT II had been discarded long ago. This impression was bolstered by common sense. After all, why would President Reagan abide by a "fatally flawed" treaty that he had so bitterly criticized? Especially if that treaty were not legally binding?

The answer could be found in the nature of SALT II. For all of its alleged weaknesses, SALT II did constrain the buildup of Soviet nuclear forces. Under the terms of the treaty neither superpower could deploy more than 820 ICBMs which carried multiple warheads. In the early 1980s the Soviet Union deployed almost 1,400 ICBMs. To abandon SALT II would allow them to put multiple warheads on some 500 more missiles. And because SALT II limited the number of warheads that each missile could carry, the Soviets would also be free to pile yet more warheads onto the missiles that were already MIRVed. The overall result of abrogating the treaty could be to increase the Soviet nuclear arsenal by thousands of warheads. One estimate by the CIA was that the Soviets could have 21,000 warheads by the mid 1990s.[35]

SALT II might have been the whipping boy of choice when Reagan's forces were camped outside the gates of Washington, but now that they had power, the more pragmatic among them could see that the hated treaty was needed to stave off an unrestrained race in strategic arms—a race the Soviets would win.

Of course, it was not the pragmatists who held sway under the new order; it was the ideologues. And for them, some of whom had defined their political personalities in the fight against SALT, the chance to finally do away with SALT II was the chance of a lifetime.

The assault began once President Reagan had secured the White House for a second term. In late 1985 a new Trident submarine was scheduled for deployment. It would carry twenty-four missiles. Unless the United States took an older Poseidon submarine out of service when it deployed the new sub, it would violate the limits of SALT II. Through much of 1985 Caspar Weinberger and Richard Perle lobbied for the deployment of both ships. "There were three reasons" for abandoning SALT II, recalled Frank Gaffney, who along with Perle had helped torpedo the treaty as a junior member of Scoop Jackson's staff. "The first was that it had been violated repeatedly by the Soviets.

The second was that it had never been ratified by the United States Senate. And the third was that even if it had been ratified, it had expired. . . . For reasons that Paul Nitze among others articulated powerfully, it wasn't a good deal from our point of view back in 1979, it certainly wasn't a good deal by 1985."

Nitze disagreed. In 1979 he had felt that ratifying SALT II would have furthered a dangerous complacency in the realm of national security. In 1985 abrogating SALT II would feed the perception that the United States government was against arms control. Times had changed and so had the rationale for abiding by SALT II. In an awkward twist Nitze found himself as the treaty's most vociferous defender in the administration. Pointing to the military and political repercussions of abandoning SALT II and dismissing the cheating charges as not serious, Nitze called for the United States to stay within the treaty's limits. "We thought that continued constraints on the Soviets were useful," recalled a State Department expert who aided Nitze's effort. "They were still stuck with the same number of ICBM launchers that they had back in the seventies." What was the point of abolishing useful constraints? Backing Nitze up were Congress and the Joint Chiefs of Staff. In mid 1985, the administration agreed to retire the Poseidon. "I learned that the Soviet Union had the capacity to increase weaponry much faster than the treaty permitted, and we didn't," Reagan said, explaining why he backed off.[36] Nitze's side had won, but only for the moment.

In early 1986, as Gorbachev wooed the western world with his peace campaign and extended his unilateral moratorium on nuclear testing, administration hard-liners opened a spring offensive against SALT II. Another Trident submarine was slated for deployment in May, and later in the year an air force program to put cruise missiles on B-52s could also push the United States over the SALT II limits. In this second round of battle Paul Nitze again had several powerful allies. Prime Minister Margaret Thatcher of Britain wrote President Reagan in February and said that she hoped the United States would abide by SALT II. Fifty-two senators signed a letter to Reagan urging compliance. In the administration Secretary Shultz joined the fight to keep the treaty in force.

The weight of these allies, however, proved to be no match against administration hard-liners. Of particular disgust to Nitze was Ken Adelman's defection. Officially, ACDA was the institutional voice of the pro-arms control position, the only agency in the government concerned solely with the promotion of arms control. To many in Washington, Adelman had long made a mockery of that mandate by consistently siding with Pentagon hard-liners. Now, in the second round of the SALT II debate, the ACDA director was in the unseemly position of trying to kill one of the few arms control accords that restrained the growth of U.S. and Soviet arsenals. Like Perle, Gaffney, and others, Adelman and his aides believed that sticking to SALT II made no sense. "The Soviets were violating the hell out of the treaty," said Patrick Glynn, a confirmed anti-arms controller who worked as Adelman's special assistant. "It's damaging to our credibility that we don't do anything when the Soviets violate treaties." The argument that discarding SALT II would hurt the United States was nonsense. "Basically the Soviets had their accelerator to the floor," said Glynn. "They were already building as much as they could." In contrast, "our forces were beginning to bump up against the limits of the treaty."

More powerful than the particulars of the case against SALT II was Ronald Reagan's lingering gut-level distaste for the treaty. After another acrimonious round of administration infighting, the White House announced on May 27 that it would no longer abide by SALT II. Five months later, with the deployment of the 131st B-52 bomber, the United States officially abrogated the treaty.

Several years had passed since the INF talks stalled amid bureaucratic chaos. But in the time since nothing had changed in the Reagan administration.

Nothing at all.

Reykjavik and Beyond

By MID-1986 Mikhail Gorbachev's crusade to reform the Soviet Union was well under way. The new Soviet leader was determined to overhaul all aspects of Soviet society. There would be more freedom of expression and less intolerance of dissent. Gorbachev pushed a bold agenda of economic decentralization. His goal was greater fluidity in the marketplace and reduced power in the hands of party bureaucrats. Around the globe Soviet diplomats shed their stale dogmatism, seeking to diversify Moscow's ties and soften its image. Negotiations began on the withdrawal of Soviet troops from Afghanistan.

As he entered his ninth decade of life, Paul Nitze was finally seeing real changes in the Soviet Union, the kind of changes that could make a lasting peace possible. But the revolution underway in Russia was not translating into progress in Geneva, where the two sides remained far apart on how to limit SDI and implement the 50 percent missile reductions agreed upon at the 1985 summit. A main sticking point was the issue of subceilings, that is, what particular categories of missiles would have to be reduced under a START agreement.

As usual, the United States pressed for deep cuts in the Soviet's large land-based missiles, while Moscow wanted to hold onto those missiles. In 1986 the Soviet Union had over six thousand warheads on its ICBMs. American negotiators sought to cut that number in half; the Soviets wanted a slightly higher number.

In August negotiations inched forward when Nitze led a high-level arms control mission to the Soviet Union. The talks were held in Meshcherino, a rustic village of several dozen houses on the southern outskirts of Moscow. In an airy conference room of a dacha owned by the Foreign Ministry, Nitze and the U.S. team met with Soviet officials to explore possible areas of agreement.[1] This meeting was followed by a trip to the United States by Eduard Shevardnadze, the energetic and open-minded foreign minister who had replaced Gromyko. Over two days he and Shultz spent fourteen hours in meetings. "There are quite a few items that seemed to be insoluble a year ago that are working themselves out," Shultz said afterward. Lubricating the diplomatic exchanges was a growing rapport between Shultz and Shevardnadze. "I might say that we have, on a personal level, I think, a very good capacity to communicate," the secretary of state said. "I don't have any doubt in my mind that Mr. Shevardnadze has approached our discussions in a good faith way."

Before he returned to the Soviet Union, Shevardnadze delivered a personal letter from Gorbachev to President Reagan suggesting that the two leaders meet in Reykjavik, Iceland, to break the diplomatic stalemate. It would not be a full-fledged summit. Instead, the aim would be to achieve breakthroughs and lay the groundwork for a Washington summit later in the year. Reagan accepted the offer.

In the scramble to prepare for Iceland, Washington's arms control bureaucracy expected that the issue of European missiles would dominate the meeting. In his bold disarmament proposals Gorbachev had expressed a willingness finally to accept the zero option and ban all intermediate-range missiles from Europe. If Reykjavik produced an agreement that could be signed in 1986, many assumed it would be an INF treaty.

Beyond that few had high hopes for the Iceland meeting. In the State Department the rumor circulated that Gorbachev had something big planned for the summit, but there was no concrete evidence of this. "We went into Reykjavik with the thought that it would simply be an updating meeting," recalled Edward Rowny. With such short notice the United States didn't have time to put together any new positions. It was assumed the Soviets hadn't either.

The American delegation arrived in Reykjavik on a drizzly Thursday evening in early October. A city of eighty thousand people, Iceland's capital was surrounded by bleak windswept hills. Its skyline was dominated by four twelve-story buildings, the tallest in the entire country. The cod-fishing industry had helped build Reykjavik, and from the docks came the smell of fish and the sound of squawking seagulls. Downtown, there was a statue of Leif Ericsson, the intrepid Norse explorer who had been born in Iceland.

Watching the Soviets arrive, Nitze sensed that this summit would be unusual. The tip-off was Gorbachev's entourage. In addition to the usual arms control officials and security personnel, Nitze noticed that "the delegation was flooded with people ordinarily associated with the media, propaganda, and psychological warfare, and political dirty tricks." Most prominent was Valentin Falin, head of the Novosti Press Agency and a top Soviet ideologue. Also in Reykjavik was Georgi Arbatov, the cheerful director of Moscow's Institute of U.S. and Canadian Studies, whose impeccable English and keen understanding of American thinking made him a regular guest on U.S. television. Clearly, the Soviets expected an important event to take place, one they would want to portray in a favorable light.

Something else was different, too. Instead of a veteran arms control official to lead the Soviet negotiators, Gorbachev had brought along the chief of staff of the Soviet armed forces, Marshal Sergei Akhromeyev, to play this role. As planes from both sides of the Atlantic kept landing and the small city of Reykjavik filled up on Friday night with several thousand American, Russian, and international observers, the mood of mystery deepened.

The site chosen for the talks was Hofdi House, a two-story turn-of-the century building that legend said was haunted. While the rest of the American delegation killed time reading or watching television, Reagan and Gorbachev met in a small conference room for their first session on Saturday morning. There, the president discovered that the Soviet leader wanted to talk about much more than the missiles in Europe. In his hands was a thick folder. In the folder was a set of proposals that covered the entire arms control spectrum.

On strategic arms Gorbachev said that he was ready to go forward with 50 percent cuts and announced that he would accept deep cuts in heavy land-based missiles.

On intermediate-range missiles the Soviet leader embraced the zero option and said that Moscow would dismantle all their SS-20s in Europe in exchange for a removal of America's cruise missiles and Pershing IIs.

On strategic defenses Gorbachev made yet another concession. The long-standing Soviet position had been that both superpowers must abide by the ABM Treaty for fifteen years. Now Gorbachev said he would settle for a ten-year period.

It was a stunning set of proposals. For Paul Nitze, a man who had spent years in negotiations that crept forward at an excruciatingly slow pace, the breadth and boldness of the Soviet offers was almost unbelievable. Gathering in a cramped, bug-proof room in the American embassy, President Reagan and the American team debated Gorbachev's opening bid. "He's brought a whole lot of proposals," Reagan said, "but I'm afraid he's going after SDI." Nitze was more upbeat. He told the group that the Soviet proposals were the best he had ever seen. "I'm excited by it," Nitze said. Kenneth Adelman, Richard Perle, and Ed Rowny were predictably more skeptical. They argued that when it came time to hash out the specifics, the Soviets would seek to keep their big lead in heavy land-based missiles.[2]

During Reagan's second session with Gorbachev later in the day, the two leaders agreed to set up a working group to explore the Soviet offer. Nitze was chosen to chair the American team, an unwieldy group that included Perle, Kampleman, Rowny, Adelman, and several other U.S. arms control officials. Marshal Akhromeyev would lead Moscow's team, which was similarly large and varied.

A wiry and compact man in his sixties, Akhromeyev had joined the Red Army in his teens and fought against the Germans through two bitter winters during the nine-hundred-day siege of Leningrad. After forty years in the army, Akhromeyev occupied his country's top military post and was the last World War II veteran in the Soviet high command. Of all the elements of the Reykjavik summit, he was most unfamiliar. Walking up the circular wooden stairway for the working group meeting that evening, U.S. officials didn't know what to expect from the Soviet marshal. Some, like Ken Adelman, feared the session would be like most other "experts" meetings—"repetitious, unproductive, and excruciatingly boring."[3] Still, to U.S. experts anxious to see what lay behind Gorbachev's startling offers, the meeting promised to be instant gratification. Normally arms proposals were debated in a slow-motion ritual of stilted bargaining in Geneva and bureaucratic bickering in Washington. Too often that ritual was destructive, smoth-

ering real dialogue in a blizzard of qualifiers. Now, with the top leaders
of both superpowers present to approve negotiating changes immediately, the talks at Hofdi House could be flexible and substantive. It was
summitry of the highest order.

At eight in the evening, the two teams assembled across a long table
in a small but comfortable conference room. Off to the side were
beverages and buffet foods. Akhromeyev began on a positive note. "I'm
no diplomat like all of you," he said in essence. "And I'm no negotiator.
I'm a military man. So let's not repeat all the familiar arguments. Let's
see how much progress we can make tonight. That's what I want, and
that's what Gorbachev wants."[4] Through the night Akhromeyev impressed the Americans by allowing none of the usual diatribes from
Soviet START negotiator Victor Karpov or the other Russians.

Nitze and Akhromeyev agreed to go through the Soviet proposals
one by one and to move on when they encountered a deadlock. At the
start of the meeting the Soviets presented the U.S. team with a chart
laying out the strategic balance. It contained a surprising concession.
Throughout START the Soviets had always insisted on counting U.S.
aircraft in western Europe that could deliver nuclear weapons onto
Soviet soil. They reasoned that any weapon that would reach Russia
must be considered strategic and must be included in the tally of
weapons to be limited under START. It was a view the United States
rejected, and its irresolution had hampered progress in the talks.

Looking over the chart, the American team saw that the Soviets had
removed forward-based systems from their tally. "It became clear at
that point," recalled Richard Perle, "that one critical obstacle to a
START agreement had been, or would be, removed in the course of
the discussions that evening."

But if the chart conveyed some good news, said Perle, it also had a
"fundamental defect that made it difficult for us to reach an agreement." The Soviet proposal for a 50 percent cut was presented as an
across-the-board cut of all systems. In some areas, such as land-based
missiles, it left the Soviets with a numerical advantage. In Nitze's view
the proposal would produce an inequitable agreement, and in a reference to the 1972 Jackson amendment that prohibited unequal arms
levels, Nitze reminded the Soviets that this type of deal was unacceptable. "If Scoop Jackson was observing those proceedings he was smiling
at that point," Perle remarked later.[5] What the Americans proposed
was to reduce the forces of both sides in a manner that would insure
equal ceilings of nuclear warheads on land-based missiles.

The Soviets found this logic tiresome. As they saw it, the United

States had more warheads, more bombers, and better submarines. Even if the Soviet Union kept an advantage in land-based missiles, it would all balance out in the end.

But to the Americans, and especially to Paul Nitze, the whole point of START was to bring down the number of Soviet heavy land-based missiles and thus mitigate long-standing fears of a Soviet first strike. A treaty that failed to do this would be a treaty that failed to serve U.S. interests. Nitze insisted that the Soviets agree to strict subceilings on their ICBMs, telling Akhromeyev that the United States would not accept more than three thousand warheads on those missiles.

For over three hours the two sides haggled over the question of subceilings without result. Finally, Akhromeyev said that he thought the group was wasting their time. "We have instructions to discuss this document and come to an agreement, then report to our principals by morning," he said. "We seem to be getting nowhere. It looks as though we can't come to agreement on any points, so I guess we should report to our principals that we've failed."[6]

Nitze decided it was time for the U.S. side to make a concession. He indicated to his colleagues that he was going to give in to the Soviet demand for more warheads on their ICBMs and raise the proposed subceiling from three thousand to thirty-six hundred. Ed Rowny immediately scribbled a note and passed it to Nitze demanding a break. Huddling upstairs in another room, Rowny insisted to Nitze that the United States must not modify its position. "I always thought the sublimit was important and that there was no reason to allow a higher sublimit on ICBMs," he recalled. "If we were going to get the most destabilizing forces under control—and those forces were Soviet heavy ICBMs—I attached a great deal of importance to sublimits." Impervious to the spirit of Reykjavik and the lure of an agreement, Rowny was preaching Nitze's own gospel.

Anxious for some progress, Nitze replied that Akhromeyev was trying to push the talks forward and that the United States had to move as well. It had to make concessions.

"But ICBMs are the Soviet specialty," Rowny said.

"I know that, Ed," Nitze said, beginning to lose his temper.

Adelman and Perle backed Rowny up. Nitze was outnumbered.

"You're forcing me to be as rigid as the Russians are at their worst," Nitze fumed. "I'm absolutely furious."

Returning to the negotiating table, Nitze repeated the American position. He felt immensely uncomfortable about stonewalling in the presence of such an opportunity for compromise. Akhromeyev's reply made Nitze feel worse. "We have explained already why these proposals of yours are not acceptable. Now it is clear that you are not ready to negotiate on the basis of our proposal. In that case we have to report to our superiors. I see no other way out." As the two sides adjourned for a break at two in the morning, the talks seemed near collapse.[7]

During the break Nitze went to wake Shultz, who sat in his suite in a robe and pajamas and listened intently to the update on the talks. After hearing about the actions of Rowny, Perle, and Adelman, Shultz told Nitze that he had the authority to change the proposed subceilings.

At three o'clock the two sides reconvened at the negotiating table. Akhromeyev had been talking to his superiors also. When the session resumed, he made no concessions on subceilings, but did announce that the Soviet would agree to equal ceilings in strategic forces. It was a major breakthrough. "And from that point on," Nitze recalled, "it was possible to get agreement on some important points which were consistent with the preprepared U.S. positions."[8] As the session stretched into its eighth and then ninth hour, the two sides worked to hammer out a statement outlining their points of agreement. Officials on both sides of the table had now been up for nearly twenty-four hours, but Nitze for one hardly felt even a hint of fatigue. Indeed, he had seldom felt more awake in his entire life. Akhromeyev was just as alert, and as night wore on, Nitze came to have great respect for his negotiating partner. "He was tough, determined, but he was trying to get an agreement," Nitze recalled.[9]

By six in the morning the two sides had completed a draft of a statement which agreed to limit strategic launchers to sixteen hundred on each side. Warheads would be limited to six thousand. Still, with time running out, the issue of how deeply to cut ICBM-based warheads remained unresolved. Failure to limit strictly the number of warheads on Soviet heavy missiles could doom the entire accord. But Akhromeyev wouldn't budge on the matter. The best he could do was assure Nitze that the United States could raise the matter of subceilings in future negotiations.

By the time the morning light began streaming through the windows of Hofdi House, American and Soviet negotiators had made more progress in ten hours of negotiation than they had during months of talks in Geneva. For Nitze it was the breakthrough he had sought since first floating a proposal for 50 percent missile reductions in the spring of 1970. When Nitze briefed Shultz in the morning, the secretary was elated. "My own judgment," he said later, "is that in a few years we will look back at the meeting in Hofdi House as something of a watershed, a potential turning point in our strategy for deterring war and encouraging peace." Even Richard Perle, master cynic, echoed this sentiment, saying that "the recent summit meeting at Reykjavik . . . has changed, perhaps permanently, the spectrum of arms control along which the positions of the United States and the Soviet Union are arrayed. No longer will treaties like SALT I and SALT II, which allowed for enormous increases in nuclear forces, be regarded as meaningful and effective."[10]

The all-night session in Hofdi House was a pivotal moment in U.S.-Soviet relations. However, the Reykjavik summit as a whole was destined to founder on the question of strategic defenses.

Jamming into the bug-proof chamber on Sunday morning, the American team briefed President Reagan on the progress made over the night. Reagan was elated by the news. He was further encouraged when he and Shultz sat down for another meeting with Gorbachev and Shevardnadze. At that meeting the two leaders made a dramatic breakthrough on INF. In addition to scrapping all SS-20s in Europe, Gorbachev offered to reduce the number of warheads on Asian SS-20s to one hundred. In return, the U.S. could keep one hundred intermediate-range missiles in the United States. Before they parted, Gorbachev and Reagan agreed to hold another meeting of experts headed by Shultz and Shevardnadze which would recapitulate the progress made at the summit and deal with the last stumbling block to total success, SDI.

When this session got under way, the Americans found that the Soviets would not agree to anything unless there was agreement on strategic defense. And for there to be an agreement on this matter, the Soviets insisted that the United States agree to abide by the ABM Treaty for ten years. "That's got to be settled," said Shevardnadze. "If it's not, nothing else is agreed. We're prepared to come down to ten years, but no lower. If not, let's go home."[11]

To break the impasse, Richard Perle and Colonel Robert Linhard, an arms control expert on the NSC, quickly put together a proposal which called for abiding by the ABM Treaty for five years while the 50 percent missile cut was implemented. After that there would be another five-year period during which both sides abided by the ABM Treaty while striving to eliminate all ballistic missiles. At the end of ten years, when all ballistic missiles were gone, both sides would be free to deploy strategic defenses.

It was a fantasy proposal. And when Reagan and Gorbachev came together for one last meeting, the Soviet leader countered the U.S. offer with something even more far out. He suggested that by the end of ten years, both sides eliminate all nuclear weapons.

"Suits me fine," said Reagan.[12]

But there was a catch. Before he would embark on the ten-year plan, Gorbachev wanted the Americans to agree that SDI research be confined to the "laboratory." He felt that only a fool would begin destroying expensive ballistic missiles while his enemy was developing a system that could shoot down the missiles left over. To Ronald Reagan, however, Gorbachev's talk of limiting research to the "laboratory" was a ploy to kill SDI. It was an unacceptable proposal. "The President was prepared to go very far," recalled Richard Perle. "What he was not prepared to do was agree to an arrangement that would have made it virtually impossible to carry out the strategic defense initiative. To suggest that one can develop and test strategic defense in the laboratory . . . is a bit like suggesting that submarines must be tested on land. You simply can't do it."[13]

Reagan suggested putting the issue aside and dealing with it at Geneva or the next summit. Gorbachev refused. There would be no summit and no agreement unless the Soviet offer on SDI was accepted. Reagan stood firm. Despite the great distance that the two sides had come at Reykjavik, despite the historic agreement that now lay within reach, there would be no agreement that weekend.

Nitze had slept only four hours since arriving in Iceland. "We tried," he told reporters, looking haggard and strained. "We tried, we tried. By God, we tried. And we almost did it."[14]

From a public relations viewpoint, Reykjavik was a stunning debacle. The most widely circulated photograph from the encounter was of Ronald Reagan and Mikhail Gorbachev, looking exhausted and grim, standing face to face in the night chill and engaging in a final unpleasant exchange. To many observers, it appeared that the president had passed up an opportunity to reduce the world's bloated nuclear stockpiles in order to pursue the chimera of SDI. It seemed like another example of American rigidity in the face of Soviet conciliation.

But while an agreement may have slipped away during the summit, it was not lost altogether. The limits on strategic weapons agreed to at Hofdi House became the foundation of START. The breakthroughs on INF were also embraced. "For the first time in the long history of arms control talks, a genuine possibility of substantial reductions in Soviet and American arms appeared," Shultz said afterward.

*   *   *

In arms control momentum can be a strange thing. When the spirit of goodwill is running high and when an agreement, with all of its political rewards, seems within reach, almost no obstacle is insurmountable. Both sides begin making more compromises; neither wants to take the blame for holding up progress.

But momentum can dissipate nearly as quickly as it gathers. Much as the tide of opinion can shift suddenly against a presidential candidate or a cabinet nominee, the optimism surrounding arms talks can be washed away nearly overnight.

In arms control momentum may seem to be a series of breakthroughs on highly arcane matters, but in reality, it is a more delicate matter of mood. And as a man who had studied the mood swings of arms control for over two decades, Paul Nitze knew that the months following Reykjavik were the critical time to push hard for a finished START treaty. The meeting in Iceland had given both sides the feeling that nearly anything was possible. With the adrenaline pumping in Moscow and Washington, there would never be a better moment to make a dash for the finish line. "We must both nail down the details of the agreements we have achieved in principle," Nitze said shortly after Reykjavik.[15]

In early November Shultz reassembled the Americans who had labored through the night at Hofdi House and flew to Vienna for what he and Nitze hoped would be a productive follow-up session with the Soviets. "Our two nations now have a historic opportunity to move quickly to formal agreement on these reductions in offensive nuclear weapons." Shultz said in Vienna. It was assumed that the Soviets shared this optimism.

But there was something wrong in Vienna. Nitze had wanted a rematch with Marshal Akhromeyev. After years of dealing with traditional Soviet diplomats, Akhromeyev's blunt and nonpolemical manner was a relief. Nitze was therefore disappointed when he arrived in Vienna and found that Akhromeyev was not part of the Soviet entourage. In fact, Shevardnadze hadn't brought much of a team at all. The only senior Soviet arms control official in Vienna was Victor Karpov, the monotonously polemical START negotiator.

Nitze and the other Americans had hoped that the spirit of conciliation that marked the negotiations in Hofdi House would be alive in Vienna. They were wrong. Weeks of mutual recrimination about who botched the Reykjavik summit had angered the Soviets. One casualty of that anger was Nitze's oral agreement with Akhromeyev that the United States could raise the critical issue of subceilings in future negotiations. "It was clear," Karpov said at the negotiating table, "that we agreed in Reykjavik there would be no subceilings."

Nitze was stunned and angry. "You're a damn liar," he said pointing his finger at Karpov.[16]

Karpov was unmoved. Truth can be a cheap commodity in the game of arms control, and for the moment the Soviets didn't want to hear anything more about subceilings. They would remain inflexible on this point for many long and frustrating months to come. The Soviets also hardened their insistence on linking all progress in the realm of START and INF to an agreement on space weapons.

Nitze returned from Vienna disappointed about the dearth of progress amid so much promise. "The Soviets seemed more interested in attempting to make propaganda points by misstating what had happened at Reykjavik than in advancing the negotiations," he complained.[17]

At the end of 1986 the arms control process suffered a setback when the Iran-contra scandal erupted. With the president besieged and the NSC in chaos, decisive action on any foreign policy problem was impossible. The long-term effect of the affair, however, was to strengthen Shultz's hand in the bureaucracy. National Security Advisor John Poindexter was replaced by Frank Carlucci, and Howard Baker took over Donald Regan's job as chief of staff. Both men were moderates and pragmatists. Carlucci's appointment was particularly important. Unlike Poindexter, the new national security advisor was knowledgeable about arms control issues and determined to work on the problem. He leaned toward the view of Shultz and Nitze that concessions on SDI would probably be necessary to move arms control forward. By early 1987 a new alliance between the State Department and NSC was beginning to take shape. Pro-arms control forces got a further boost when Richard Perle announced in March that he would be leaving the government.

At the same time that the hard-liners were losing power, Nitze's own position was improving. The main reason was George Shultz. During the first days they had worked closely together in late 1984, Nitze and Shultz had established an immediate bond. Over the years that bond had become stronger as the two men discovered that they had much in common. Shultz's first love was economics. As a university professor he had taught economics and in the Nixon Administration he had been secretary of the treasury. Shultz could appreciate Nitze's financial prowess and his experience in foreign economic policy. Often conversations between the two men would turn to economics, and as Shultz discovered that his arms control advisor knew quite a bit about the subject, he came to solicit Nitze's advice on international finance problems. "It was not unusual for Shultz to get a position paper from his senior advisor on economics and pass it on to Paul for comment," said one aide familiar with the relationship. Shultz asked for advice on other matters as well, freely tapping Nitze's vast reservoir of expertise on almost every component of American foreign and military policy. Some in the State Department joked that the secretary wouldn't go to the bathroom without asking Nitze what color toilet paper he should use.

Nitze's growing rapport with Shultz did not mean that he neglected his other allies in the government. As always, Nitze was talking to many people throughout the government, taking them out to lunch at the Metropolitan Club, pumping them with questions, and intently scribbling notes on the yellow legal pads he was never without. In the Pentagon he worked to establish ties with the JCS chairman Admiral William Crowe, talking frequently to his deputy Robert Herres. At the Office of the Secretary of Defense—enemy territory—Nitze cultivated Weinberger's military assistant Bruce Jackson, whose father he had known on Wall Street. In the White House Nitze opened up lines of communications with Chief of Staff Baker, a man he found to be well meaning and easygoing. And as ever Nitze paid a lot of attention to the younger experts at State and ACDA who dealt daily with the esoteric details of the arms control process.

What made these contacts so valuable was not only that Nitze had people who would hear out his ideas, but that he had varied sources of information and insights. As always, those who spoke with Nitze found that he paid attention. "You can change Nitze's mind on a question by exposing him to analysis," said one mid-level arms control expert. "Everybody finds that he listens; he listens to people. If you have a good point or if you have an analysis that leads to some conclusion, he will look at the logic chain and if he finds that the starting point is beyond question and each point of logic is beyond question, he will accept the conclusion even if it's uncomfortable."

In a town where officials often determined their position first and then developed the reasoning to support it, Nitze's approach was unusual to say the least. "Nitze follows the logic wherever it goes," said the expert. "And it's led him to some pretty strange places."

After the meetings at Reykjavik and Vienna one place the logic led Nitze was toward the development of new ideas for placing SDI on the bargaining table. By early 1987 it was clearer than ever that Reagan's dream of a space-based missile defense was not compatible with arms control. To move START forward, a creative initiative was needed to break the deadlock over Star Wars. It would have to be a plan that assuaged Soviet fears about strategic defenses, but did not hamper the U.S. program. The initiative would only work, moreover, if it were negotiable and verifiable. Nitze had an idea.

During the final tense hours of the Reykjavik summit, much of the disagreement had been over a single word: laboratory. Gorbachev wanted to confine SDI development to the laboratory. Reagan was sure that such a move would kill his dream. The problem was that both sides had different ideas about what the restriction to the laboratory would mean. To the Soviets, keeping SDI in the laboratory meant stopping the U.S. from abandoning the ABM Treaty. To the Americans, however, laboratory research was perfectly compatible with the treaty. What Gorbachev was asking for, as they saw it, was to rewrite the ABM Treaty. "The Soviets intended to impose constraints on our research program more severe than those imposed by the ABM Treaty," Nitze charged after Reykjavik.[18]

In a vague discussion about a vague issue, compromise was impossible. Nitze believed that if this complicated matter could be unraveled and resolved, if both superpowers could agree to an interpretation of the ABM Treaty that allayed their mutual concerns, then START could go forward.

What Nitze had in mind was something the Soviets had suggested at the failed meeting in Vienna: to open negotiations on what kind of testing and development of strategic defenses was permitted and prohibited under the terms of the ABM Treaty. These talks would seek to bring the ABM Treaty into the era of new technologies and eliminate its ambiguities. In signing onto the broad interpretation of the ABM Treaty in 1985, Nitze had helped undermine the agreement. Now he wanted to fix it. Motivating this desire, in great part, was the unending flap over the reinterpretation scandal. Since October 1985 nearly every independent arms control expert in Washington, including a bipartisan group of influential senators led by Sam Nunn, had condemned the administration's move.

For Nitze, the situation had become embarrassing and untenable. Even Judge Sofaer had backed away from the broad interpretation, blaming the debacle on other officials. Ever prideful, Nitze refused to acknowledge any errors, but he did hope that the administration could finesse the broad versus narrow debate by negotiating on what was permitted and prohibited under the ABM Treaty.

Among those both in and out of government who desired progress on START, Nitze's suggestion was warmly embraced. Jeremy Stone and John Pike, two scientists with the Federation of American Scientists, a pro-arms control group, supported Nitze's effort, having pushed a similar idea for several years. But in their enthusiasm arms control advocates failed to see that while it would speed START, Nitze's proposals might also help to push SDI forward in the long run. "Nitze wanted a threshold below which you could test with impunity, above which you couldn't do anything at all," said one close aide. "Nitze hoped that the thresholds would finesse the idea of a broad versus a narrow interpretation and would permit or even facilitate the testing that we needed to do on the SDI program without transgressing on the ABM Treaty."

Nitze's plan might restrain American efforts to chip away at the treaty, but it would also leave the SDI program largely unrestrained and undermine the spirit of Article V of the treaty: "Each side undertakes not to develop, test, or deploy ABM systems or components which are sea-based, air-based, space-based, or mobile land-based." In this sense, the proposal would have the same impact as adopting the broad interpretation.

Despite the freedom that it would give to test strategic defense, Nitze's plan was adamantly opposed by administration hard-liners. "We shouldn't debate with the Soviet what can and can't be prohibited," Weinberger said at a White House meeting in February.[19] To Pentagon officials who had labored so hard to entomb the ABM Treaty, Nitze's plan was anathema. It would nullify all their efforts. "As a practical matter what it was going to do was aid and abet an effort to shore up, reinforce, improve, augment, whatever you want to call it, a treaty which was not ultimately in our interests," said Frank Gaffney. Downstairs at ACDA came a predictable echoing of the Pentagon's position. "I think it's a waste of time to get into that," scoffed one of Adelman's aides. "All it does is kick the football down the field." To those who had long distrusted Nitze, his latest proposal seemed like yet another ploy for trading away SDI.

Indeed, Nitze got more support for his plan from the Soviets, who proposed something very similar in Geneva. They suggested that the two sides agree to ban from space a list of SDI-related devices. These would include some of the emerging mainstays of strategic defenses such as large mirrors, particle beams, and lasers. The decision to place an item on the prohibited list would be based on how powerful it was and whether it could be part of a strategic defense system.

Nitze was enthusiastic about the Soviet idea. "The ABM Treaty has a hole in it as to what are components of ABM systems based on other physical principles," he said. "The list approach would give us a way to fill that hole with the right definition. Whenever we've left holes in treaties in the past, we're the ones who have ended up falling into them."[20] Nitze strongly pressed the idea of taking up the Soviet offer to Max Kampleman, the chief START negotiator in Geneva and Nitze's old friend from the Committee on the Present Danger.

Kampleman had tremendous respect for Nitze, but he wasn't interested in the list approach. He thought such negotiations would turn into a messy and protracted struggle. "There was no way we were going to come up with an agreed upon answer," he said later. "I didn't want to get into that quagmire—to me that was a swamp." Kampleman's response to Nitze underlined a difference of thinking that had existed between the two men for some time. "I didn't want any movement on SDI," said Kampleman. "Unlike Paul, I believed that the treaty could not be ratified if we hurt SDI." Right-wing senators, Kampleman believed, would withold their votes if they felt that START inhibited the pursuit of strategic defenses.

Kampleman understood Nitze's rationale for pushing the list approach, but didn't think he appreciated the political considerations involved. "Paul is a master logician," Kampleman explained. "He was correct logically and he was a man who, when he sees a position is correct logically, he pursues it." The problem as Kampleman saw it was that "politics is not logical or rational, and if you try to develop a political position based on logic you're frequently wrong."

In making his list approach pitch to other officials, Nitze encountered the same sentiment. The idea hadn't gotten past the first hurdle and already it seemed doomed. Nitze's opponents hurried to amplify the impression that their white-haired colleague had isolated himself once again. "I don't know anybody else in the government except perhaps Norm Clyne who likes the idea," said Ken Adelman dismissively. "He hasn't found one supporter."

In much the same way that Nitze's position had been damaged by his dogged efforts to chip away at the zero option, his persistence on the list approach made him vulnerable. When Adelman announced in July 1987 that he would be resigning as head of ACDA, Shultz recommended that Nitze take his place. The promotion would have given Nitze a more powerful position from which to push his proposals. But with right-wing suspicions of Nitze running high, the president named

Major General William Burns to the post instead.

Compounding the setbacks that Nitze suffered in the first half of 1987 was the failing health of his wife Phyllis. For years Phyllis had been wracked by a severe case of emphysema. It was clear that the illness would continue until it took her life, and by the spring of 1987 her time was limited. She was in a wheelchair and losing weight quickly. Oxygen was given to her by the nurses who now stayed in the house twenty-four hours a day. On Easter weekend Phyllis presided over a final family gathering with the four children and eleven grandchildren at her favorite place in the world, Causein Manor Farms. In June she died at the age of 75 and was buried at the farm. She and Nitze had been married for nearly fifty-five years.

In fall 1987 the pro-arms control forces in the Reagan administration were strengthened when Caspar Weinberger announced he would soon retire. Over the years Nitze had come to loathe Weinberger's stubborn dogmatism and aggressive manner. The defense secretary reminded him of another presidential confidante who had once dominated national policy, John Foster Dulles. Nitze was happy to see Weinberger on the way out. And he was also encouraged by President Reagan's decision to put Frank Carlucci in the Defense post.

Like the resignation of Richard Perle and the pending exit of Ken Adelman, Weinberger's retirement was ironic. While Nitze hung on day after day at the age of 80 and slowly put the pieces of the START puzzle in place, his younger opponents were becoming exhausted and dropping out of the game. Since the 1940s Nitze had believed that bureaucratic warfare was an endurance contest. Those who did their homework and cultivated the most allies and reworked the best ideas would prevail in the end. However, during the extended slugging match over arms control in the 1980s, the president's stubborness often prevented the force of logic from triumphing. This added a new dimension to the endurance contest: frustration toleration. Because he could tolerate frustration, enduring one rebuff after another, and could bear up under long hours without obvious rewards, Nitze was able to outlast bureaucrats less than half his age.

And in the twilight of the Reagan era, there were signs that Nitze's persistence was finally paying off. By the end of 1987 the dividends of the long struggle for arms control were accumulating. In October Shultz led a team to Moscow to speed up negotiations on an INF treaty. Following the breakthroughs at Reykjavik both sides had agreed to remove intermediate-range missiles from the face of the earth. All that remained was to work out the details and eliminate some outstanding points of contention. Shultz's trip made major strides toward a final pact. "In the field of intermediate-range missiles we have made progress through some of the stickiest issues," he told reporters afterward. "We are—I think both sides agree—virtually there."

In late November the secretary of state led another high level team to Geneva to put the final touches on the INF Treaty and pave the way for a Washington summit in December. After two days of intensive talks he called a news conference at the American embassy. "We have now completed agreement on all of the outstanding INF issues," Shultz announced. "This treaty, which is now basically complete, will for the first time, by agreement, result in major reductions in nuclear arms."

Two weeks later Gorbachev arrived in Washington to sign the historic accord. Amid an enthusiastic celebration of the new detente, progress was also made toward a START treaty. As had been the case at Reykjavik, Nitze and Marshal Akhromeyev headed U.S. and Soviet working groups. Meeting at the State Department, the two groups again haggled over the questions of subceilings and strategic defenses.

At Reykjavik Nitze had pushed without success for strict controls on the number of warheads that could be placed on Soviet land-based missiles. In Washington this goal again slipped out of reach. But the two superpowers did narrow their differences by agreeing that no more than forty-nine hundred of the six thousand warheads allowable under START could be kept on ballistic missiles.

Resolving the differences over strategic defenses proved a trickier matter. In drafting a joint statement for release at the end of the summit, the Americans wanted language that would affirm the U.S. right to push ahead with its strategic defense program and carry out SDI testing in space.

The Soviets balked. They wanted language that would oblige both sides to observe the ABM Treaty as "signed and ratified." The clear hope was that this wording would lock the United States into observing the traditional interpretation of the ABM Treaty, which set strict limits on Star Wars testing. Earlier in the year Senator Sam Nunn had reviewed the SALT I negotiating record and delivered a stinging rebuke of the administration's new interpretation on the Senate floor. He warned that any effort to implement this interpretation would trigger a constitutional crisis. Nunn's attack came at a time of mounting doubts in Washington that a missile shield was either possible or affordable. In proposing that both sides abide by the ABM Treaty as "signed and ratified," the Soviets hoped to further hobble SDI.

When Nitze and Akhromeyev were unable to reach agreement on this point, the matter was turned over to higher authorities. Following some back and forth between Shultz, Nitze, and Foreign Minister Shevardnadze, the final communiqué was deliberately vague on the question of SDI. It gave both superpowers much of what they wanted, stating that they would pursue "an agreement that would commit the sides to observe the ABM Treaty, as signed in 1972, while conducting their research, development, and testing as required, which are permitted by the ABM Treaty." After implementing START and conducting intensive discussion on strategic stability, "each side will be free to decide its course of action."[21]

In agreeing for the moment to cordially disagree on Star Wars, Reagan and Gorbachev were warming up for the final dash to finish START. The great hope of both sides was that the treaty could be completed in time for a spring summit in Moscow. The great fear was that this magical moment in U.S.-Soviet relations would suddenly end, and that an election year and the takeover by a new president would push START far into the future, if not kill the treaty altogether. "I believe that the time framework in which it is possible to get a START agreement is not that long," Nitze said after the Washington summit, a tone of urgency in his voice. "I think if we don't get it . . . worked out during the first six months of '88, it will be difficult for a new administration, of either party, to come in and really get cracking on this thing in less than a year or two. And that will be three years from today. And I think that time gap is too long."[22] There was no time to waste.

In late February Nitze flew to Moscow with Shultz and other top arms control officials to speed up work on START. While none of the lingering obstacles to a treaty was removed, the mood was mutually optimistic during the twenty hours of talks. Shultz was upbeat about the prospect that an agreement could be clinched in time for the next summit in May or June. "It's more probable than I thought it would be," he said. Shevardnadze echoed this view: "After a sober, sensible, and realistic assessment of the state of affairs we have come to the conclusion that there are no unresolvable problems. Although there are major difficulties, they can be resolved."[23]

Back in Washington, however, there was a creeping sense that a treaty by June was too ambitious and that the administration was deluded to think it could bulldoze through the pile of complex issues that remained unresolved. Also, conservative opposition to START was growing, and there was a mounting fear in some quarters that deep cuts in strategic arms would leave the United States even more vulnerable than before.

During the 1970s Paul Nitze had guarded the right flank of the political spectrum and snapped at the heels of arms controllers. In his crusade against SALT II he had preached a sober gospel of skepticism. Now, in the late 1980s, as Nitze labored furiously to put together one of the greatest diplomatic agreements in postwar history, conservatives were giving him a powerful dose of his own logic. And in much the same way that Nitze had been tongue-tied in arguing against a Vietnam war fueled by the axioms of NSC 68, he had difficulty refuting anti-START arguments based on an updated version of those axioms, a version that Nitze had refined during his years with the Committee on the Present Danger.

In March *Commentary* published "Reagan's Rush to Disarm," a lengthy attack on START by Patrick Glynn, Kenneth Adelman's former special assistant at ACDA. The article succinctly stated the conservative case against the emerging treaty. Nitze wrote a letter to the editor in response. "The President is not 'rushing' toward a START agreement," Nitze said. Rather, the treaty was the culmination of a twenty-year effort to achieve strategic arms control. The goal was "not reductions for reduction's sake or agreement for agreement's sake." Instead, START would achieve "stabilizing and verifiable reductions on both sides." It would go far "toward reducing the Soviets' advantage in the aggregate power of their ballistic missiles." For these reasons, START was a good thing. Nitze also reminded the readers that "arms control has long been a necessary component of our national security policy." The United States will not be secure if people tried to fight that fact, he said.

Glynn's rebuttal to Nitze's letter was scathing. And it was particularly so because in tone and logic the letter had an eerily familiar ring. If one substituted the term SALT II for the term START and changed a few facts, Glynn's broadside could easily have been authored by another hard-liner ten years earlier.

Point for point, the letter could have been written by Paul Nitze.

In attacking SALT II Nitze had raised the specter of a Soviet first strike. Glynn revived this notion, writing that "under START, U.S. strategic vulnerability would not improve; it would worsen." Glynn also made use of Nitze's old boogeyman, Soviet throw-weight. "True, the Soviets would have less throw-weight under START," he wrote. "But because of steep reductions in U.S. land-based missiles they would also need less throw-weight to accomplish the same mission—i.e., destroying U.S. ICBMs preemptively."

During the 1970s Nitze had attacked agreements that limited offensive weapons but left untouched other measures like civil defense and air defenses which affected the strategic balance. Glynn made the same point. He noted that START would cut U.S. missile-carrying submarines without reducing the number of Soviet attack subs designed to seek out and destroy America's sea-based deterrent. Glynn observed also that U.S. bombers would be cut, but not Soviet air defenses.

When SALT II was in front of the Senate, Nitze had opposed the treaty in part because it was vague on the critical question of mobile missiles. Glynn echoed this concern, saying that the failure to deal with this issue was symptomatic of the confusion surrounding START.

Finally, Glynn rehabilitated one of Nitze's central reservations about SALT II: START would sap America's resolve to deal with the Soviet threat by creating a false sense of euphoria. There was no basis whatsoever, Glynn wrote, "to believe that conclusion of the treaty would reinforce congressional support for defense. Indeed, historical evidence suggests just the opposite." That Paul Nitze could imagine otherwise, jabbed Glynn, was "Alice-in-Wonderland political logic, unworthy of the principal author of NSC 68."[24]

Underlying Glynn's attack on START was the same queasy, gut-level distrust of the Soviet Union that had motivated Nitze's crusade against SALT II. To truly rebut the arguments made by the critics that Glynn represented—some of whom were members of the Committee on the Present Danger—Nitze would have had to use the arguments that his detractors had made during the 1970s. To the claim of strategic vulnerability, people like Sidney Drell and Paul Warnke had answered that the Soviets would never gamble on a first strike because the risks were astronomical. They had argued that Soviet civil defense and air defenses weren't important because enough American bombs would always get through to destroy the Soviet Union as a functioning society. And they had dismissed the threat of euphoria, saying that the overall effect of SALT II would be to improve U.S.-Soviet relations and reduce the risk of nuclear war.

These were the sort of fundamental arguments that bolstered the case for START. But Paul Nitze didn't make these arguments. He didn't make them because they contradicted the beliefs he had held for forty years. They contradicted the axioms of NSC 68, axioms Nitze had never abandoned.

In 1965 Nitze had watched in horror as Robert McNamara applied the logic of NSC 68 to the situation in Vietnam. In 1988 he again found his own ideas arrayed against him. As the START negotiations stumbled toward paralysis, it became obvious that Nitze's brand of anti-Soviet skepticism and strategic pessimism had taken on a life of its own. If Paul Nitze alone controlled the Washington bureaucracy, it might be easy to flit between the hard line and the soft line. But as Nitze had learned during the INF talks, many of his hard-line colleagues from the 1970s did not abandon the canon preached by the Committee on the Present Danger when they were on the inside in the 1980s. Instead, they stuck to their principles, arguing, as their hero Paul Nitze once had, that arms control accords with Moscow should be viewed with grave doubts.

In the final and most ambitious crusade of his life, Paul Nitze had to contend with a monster partly of his own making. He had to cope with the fact that, in a country where the ideas of NSC 68 had a strong constituency, arms control efforts could easily be derailed by a skeptical minority. The Soviet Union could change, it could cut troops around the world and make massive concessions at the bargaining table, but there would still be those who questioned Moscow's good faith.

By championing the ideas of NSC 68 so vigorously and for so long, by executing his crusade for greater vigilance so effectively, Paul Nitze had helped to delay a stable and lasting peace between the superpowers.

When Ronald Reagan arrived in Moscow in the last days of May 1988, it was clear that no START treaty would be signed by the two leaders. During the spring any lingering hopes for finishing the accord had faded amid a debate in the U.S. government over the tricky issue of nuclear-armed sea-launched cruise missiles (SLCMs). For the Soviets the issue was of critical importance. As they saw it, American naval vessels carrying SLCMs were deadly strategic delivery vehicles which could fire nuclear weapons at targets inside the Soviet Union. The Soviets insisted that SLCMs be included in START. At the State Department officials were ready to move in the Soviets' direction. Nitze was ready to go even further. Since his days as secretary of the navy, he had pondered the idea of trying to ban nuclear weapons at sea with the exception of submarine-launched ballistic missiles.

Now he revived the idea. "If you stack our navy up against the Soviet's navy and say only conventional weapons can be used, our navy is going to do awfully well," explained one analyst who worked with Nitze on the idea. Predictably, the Pentagon balked. "Controls on sea-launched cruise missiles make a mockery of arms control because there is absolutely no way to verify that they are being fulfilled," said Frank Gaffney, who fought SLCM controls shortly before leaving the Pentagon in late 1987. In any case Defense officials were inclined to keep the weapons. "Having the ability to attack targets on land with nuclear-armed sea-launched cruise missiles is a very nice force multiplier," explained Gaffney. "It's very cheap, and it does, unquestionably, augment deterrence." With the Pentagon throwing up the usual roadblocks—roadblocks not unlike those Nitze had helped erect when arms controllers had tried to put MIRVs on the negotiating table nearly two decades earlier—the issue remained unresolved.

While substantively sterile, the summit in Moscow was of great symbolic importance. For much of his political career Ronald Reagan had blasted the communist system as the embodiment of evil in the modern world. Since Gorbachev's ascendancy, Reagan's rhetoric had dramatically softened. Now, amid the euphoria of Glasnost, Perestroika, and the Moscow Spring, Reagan strolled arm in arm with the new Soviet leader through Red Square. Lingering mutual distrust may have blocked START, but on a broader level that distrust—the foundation of much of world politics for forty years—was fading fast and the Cold War was losing its icy edge.

For Paul Nitze the summer of 1988 was a time of frustration and sickness. Publicly Nitze tried to remain optimistic. "Given a positive effort by the Soviets," he wrote after the summit, "I believe it is possible to complete a worthwhile START agreement before President Reagan leaves office in January 1989."[25] Yet to a man who knew well the cycles of American politics, it was clear that START would now be delayed for at least a year and probably longer as a presidential election consumed the nation's attention and a new administration settled into office.

At the same time that the momentum of arms control was breaking down, Nitze himself was hit with a case of Bornholm disease, or "devil's grip," a type of rheumatism that causes periods of intense exhaustion. Combined with the strain of the last year, the "devil's grip" made Nitze frail and haggard. "He looked a lot older than I remember him," said one friend who saw Nitze over the summer.

Nitze recovered and kept working at his usual pace through the fall. Even as the START negotiations virtually stopped moving during the

1988 presidential contest and many in the administration slackened work and abandoned hope, Nitze labored away day after day on the thorny outstanding issues related to START. The big picture may have been clear, but it was the details that ultimately made the difference. Clarence Dillon would have understood.

EPILOGUE

Dusk

MORE THAN any president in the postwar era, George Herbert Walker Bush was Paul Nitze's kind of president. As it was in Nitze's, social status and wealth were taken for granted in the Bush family. The son of Connecticut Senator Prescott Sheldon Bush, George was educated at Phillips Academy and Yale. After a detour through Texas and a stint in Congress, Bush settled in Washington where he became an establishment insider and master resumé builder. Like Nitze, he had a sprawling family and a house on the Maine coast where he would escape the sweltering Washington summers.

Bush was a moderate Republican. He believed in working within the system and making policy through compromise and consensus. Although twice Ronald Reagan's running mate, he didn't share the Californian's ideological temperament and disdain for government bureaucrats. Nor did Bush have an innate distrust of negotiated agreements with the Soviet Union. He had been an emissary to China after President Nixon normalized relations, and the U.S. ambassador to the United Nations. True to his eastern establishment roots, George Bush, like Paul Nitze, was an internationalist, a person who believed that the world could be made safer and more stable through sagacious American diplomacy.

But Bush was no dove. As director of the CIA, he had appointed Team B and accepted their conclusions. During the late 1970s he had voiced many of the same criticisms of President Carter as the Committee on the Present Danger. Unlike Reagan, Bush was fluent in the language of the strategic nuclear debate. When asked once how it was possible to win a nuclear war, he responded as Nitze might have, "You have a survivability of command and control, survivability of industrial potential, protection of a percentage of your citizens, and you have a capability that inflicts more damage on the opposition than it can inflict on you."[1] Bush's idea of security paralleled Nitze's. He believed that the United States should have a large and stable defense budget coupled with a sustained but prudent effort to negotiate arms control accords.

In appointing his foreign policy team, George Bush looked to people like himself. James Baker, a moderate Republican problem solver, was made secretary of state. Brent Scowcroft, a strategic expert and consummate Washington insider, was picked to head the NSC. Richard Cheney, a Wyoming congressman and former White House chief of staff under Ford, was named defense secretary. Never in living memory had a president assembled a more homogeneous foreign policy team than this. All three men were long-time friends. All were well versed in Washington's byzantine rituals. All were committed to avoiding the bloody interagency feuding that had crippled the Reagan administration. This was the type of administration, it seemed, that could really get things done.

From his seventh floor office in the State Department, Nitze watched as Shultz packed his things and prepared to return to academic life at Stanford University in California. Over the years their relationship had been remarkably close and fruitful, the best that Nitze had had with a superior since Dean Acheson. Shultz's respect for Nitze never faltered. "Paul Nitze has played all the positions in the game and done so with great skill, grace, and accomplishment," Shultz said. "In the Situation Room at the White House, in committee rooms on Capitol Hill, and at the negotiating table, Paul brings a firm sense of the national interest, the keenest of analysis, and integrity to follow the logic wherever it may lead. All of the achievements of the past eight years bear the imprint of Paul Nitze."[2]

During a touching farewell ceremony for Shultz at the State Department, Nitze rose to commend his boss, praising him for his persistence and integrity. Then, with a band playing, Shultz left Foggy Bottom for the last time.

Nitze was now very much alone in Washington. George Shultz was not part of the generation of bankers and lawyers who had helped shape the postwar world, but he possessed many of the same values. With Shultz gone, Paul Nitze stood as the last of his breed, something of a relic in the new Washington. Many of Nitze's colleagues from the days of the Marshall Plan and the Korean War had risen higher than he, but none had lasted on the inside for so long.

Robert Lovett and John McCloy, two of the Truman administration's brightest stars, had left government by the 1960s and both had died by early 1989. Chip Bohlen had gone on to become ambassador to the Soviet Union and France. Over the years Nitze and Bohlen never did agree on Soviet intentions, but their friendship remained strong and the Bohlens were frequent residents of the guest house at Causein Manor. Bohlen died in 1974, a year after publishing his memoirs.

Clark Clifford stayed out of government after leaving the Pentagon, the "snake pit" as he called it. Merging his practice with Paul Warnke's, he returned to the law. Still smooth and impeccably dressed, still speaking in the same deliberate and eloquent way, Clifford ran his practice from a large antique desk in a stately office. For him, once the keenest of hawks, the pain of Vietnam with its fifty-eight thousand dead would linger, and the lesson of that war would be forever clear: America could not and should not determine the fate of other nations through military force.

George Kennan, of course, had faded from the government long ago. Following a stint as ambassador to Yugoslavia under Kennedy, Kennan returned to his books in the quiet town of Princeton. His pen as elegant as ever, the diplomat continued to battle the distrust and illogic which he saw as fueling the Cold War. With the rise of Gorbachev, Kennan's views became more fashionable than at any time since the 1940s. And in a flurry of interviews and articles, a kind of cold war postmortem, he sought to vindicate the positions he had taken over the years, arguing that the Soviets never had any plans for invading western Europe or launching a first strike. Looking back on the Cold War, Kennan saw it almost as a great mistake. If the words of Mr. X hadn't been so distorted, and if the obsession with capabilities hadn't triumphed over the appreciation of intentions, the postwar era might have been less perilous and wasteful. Instead of embracing the axiom of total theoretical hostility and preparing endlessly for the bold Soviet attacks which would never come, America could have defused the Cold War at an earlier date, Kennan felt.

Dean Acheson, Nitze's most important mentor, had died in 1972. In the last years Nitze's Pentagon jobs and work on SALT had cut into their lunches at the Metropolitan Club, but the pleasure that the two men took in each other never faded. Washington had become a very different place from the days when Acheson ruled the State Department. The growth of a vast national security bureaucracy ended the clubby atmosphere in which foreign policy had been made, replacing it with a cold politicization that catered to the basest instincts of bureaucratic opportunists. Yet even as Paul Nitze mastered the rules of this changed world and took on the new breed of policy experts in bitter infighting, he remained dignified and loyal, a man of style and principle—an Achesonian to the end.

In his persistence Paul Nitze had even survived the second generation of postwar foreign policy officials, "the best and the brightest." Never again were the architects of the Vietnam war trusted in positions of power. Men like Robert McNamara, Dean Rusk, McGeorge Bundy, William Bundy, and Walt Rostow retired from government permanently. McNamara was so traumatized by his role in the war that he refused to speak publicly about it or explain his actions. However, he was willing to talk about the mistakes he had made in the realm of strategic weaponry. Over the years McNamara's black, slicked-back hair had thinned and turned silvery, and his demeanor had softened and become less robotic. Still, he remained intense, his speaking style alternately factual and passionate. In articles, books, and lectures, McNamara lambasted the notion that nuclear weapons were usable components of military power. Like Nitze, McNamara had sat with President Kennedy during the great crises in Berlin and Cuba. But to him, the lesson of these episodes was that nuclear weapons were worthless for bolstering the position of either superpower. The advent of strategic parity in the late 1960s served to strengthen this conviction, and although the two men maintained a friendly and respectful relationship over the years, McNamara condemned Nitze's fixation with nuclear superiority as dangerous and archaic.

McGeorge Bundy felt the same way. In a cluttered, book-lined office near Washington Square Park, New York City, Bundy spent years trying to sort out the history of nuclear weapons. The product of these labors was an eight-hundred-page account of the nuclear age that attacked many of the assumptions at the foundation of Nitze's strategic philosophy. From the hydrogen bomb decision to the Star Wars debate, Bundy saw the nuclear age as a melancholy drama of missed opportunity and shortsighted judgment, a drama in which pessimists like Paul Nitze had too often dominated the stage.

Graying and repentant, McNamara and Bundy felt that they had learned from their errors, that they had come to see the insanity of preparing to use nuclear weapons in a limited or selective manner. They had escaped from Dr. Strangelove's temple, while, as they saw it, Paul Nitze continued to worship at his altar.

But Nitze, esconced high above the streets of Washington in an office near that of the secretary of state, believed it was he who remained relevant. As he began working in his eighth administration, Paul Nitze still felt, as always, that the best place to be was on the inside. In the Bush administration especially, life on the inside had the potential for immense rewards. Not since the Kennedy years had Nitze been in a government that functioned normally. Under Johnson, the Vietnam war tore the administration apart, creating an atmosphere of bitterness and distrust. A similar sickness had infected the Nixon team, exacerbated by the secret maneuverings of Henry Kissinger. The Reagan years, of course, had been the most trying of all.

And now, after decades of waiting for an administration that functioned smoothly and with integrity and that balanced a vigorous defense effort with a commitment to arms control, Nitze had lasted long enough to see what appeared to be the creation of such a government by George Bush. This development was promising indeed. In an atmosphere of declining tensions with the Soviets and with an administration that operated harmoniously, the potential for pursuing START and other arms control measures was greater than ever before. With Ronald Reagan gone, the stubborn attachment to SDI also promised to fade. Unlike Reagan, who often reasoned in cinematic metaphors, George Bush entertained no real hope of erecting a missile shield in space. Although he was vague on the question of strategic defenses during his first few months in office, it appeared that if a choice had to be made between finishing START and pursuing SDI, Bush and his pragmatic lieutenants would choose START. Following eight years on the defensive, arms controllers were preeminent once again.

Since the days of SALT I, Nitze had pressed for deep cuts in strategic missiles. Inch by inch, against tremendous odds, he had helped push START forward during Reagan's second term. With Bush's ascendancy, Nitze was poised to join the final push for a completed treaty. After so many setbacks and so much frustration, he would be able to cap his career with the greatest arms control agreement in history. Or so it seemed.

For weeks following Bush's inaugural claim that "a new breeze was blowing," there was dead calm in the realm of foreign policy. Instead of getting on with the job of finishing START, the new administration decided to undertake a lengthy review of America's policy toward the Soviet Union. If it had been a fundamental reassessment of U.S.-Soviet relations in the age of Gorbachev, such a review might have warranted the many months spent on it. But Bush bluntly admitted that the review would not propose any radical changes in America's Soviet policy. "I don't expect this review to invent a new strategy for a new world," he wrote in March.[3] Almost as soon as it began, there were complaints that the review was moving too slowly. In arms control especially, the administration was having difficulty determining its policies.

These delays were a source of mounting frustration to Nitze. There was no need to reassess START, he felt. It was a logical continuation of an arms control process that had been going forward for two decades. The premises of that process had been debated over and over again. The time for more analysis had passed. Instead, it was time to get on with the job of finishing the treaty.

Nitze was frustrated also by the sluggishness and uncertainty that pervaded the State Department. Never in memory had a secretary of state moved so slowly to fill key positions. By the beginning of March only five top officials had been confirmed. The nomination of Richard Burt, Baker's choice to be the top START negotiator, had not even been sent to the Senate. Other critical posts related to arms control were also unfilled. Baker had not nominated anybody to take the job of assistant secretary of state for European and Canadian affairs. The Bureau of Politico-Military Affairs did not yet have a director. Indeed, the whole State Department seemed to have ground to a halt. Regular staff meetings had been discontinued, and except for a small group of Baker intimates, nobody was dealing with policy. People who tried found that their efforts were useless. "Most people had the experience that nobody read their papers or even called them back," Nitze said. "It was an eerie kind of world."

Like most Reagan holdovers, Nitze's future remained uncertain. Around the time of the inauguration, Baker had asked to see Nitze in his office. Nitze talked with the secretary and a few assistants about arms control for forty-five minutes, and the discussion went well. But Nitze heard nothing from Baker for nearly a month afterward.

Finally, in late February Baker called Nitze and said he had been thinking about what to do with him. The idea he had settled on was to leave Nitze with the same office, the same job, and the same pay, but to add "emeritus" to his title.

When Nitze asked who he would work with and what he would do, Baker was vague. After a month of receiving the cold shoulder from the secretary's inner circle, however, Nitze assumed the worst. "It became perfectly clear that I wasn't going to see anybody," Nitze said later. "I was going to have all kinds of honors and good pay and be free to do whatever I goddamn wanted, but it wasn't clear that I was going to see any documents or see anybody in the department who was authorized to talk to me."

Rather than be shunted to the sidelines and treated as a wise man of marginal relevance, Nitze decided to quit. He wrote up a letter of resignation and sent it to Baker. The secretary of state accepted it, and Nitze was given until May 1 to close up his office and leave the department.

The first thing Nitze did after resigning was to go skiing with some friends in Aspen. After a wonderful trip, he spent some time at Causein Manor Farms. One day he went riding with the woman who took care of the stables, who suggested they go see a mare that had just given birth to a foal. At the corral Nitze saw a beautiful young horse prancing about. His riding partner whistled to the foal and it came over to the fence.

Suddenly the mare began to show anger, making terrible noises and rearing up on its hind legs. Nitze's horse reacted by rearing up as well. Seeing that his horse was losing its balance, Nitze slipped out of the saddle. As he did so, the horse fell and the saddle hit Nitze's knee, throwing it out of joint. Nitze ended up on the ground in tremendous pain. Next to him the horse thrashed about, trying to get on its feet. Because there was a feeding trough on one side of the horse, it could move in only one direction—toward Nitze. In what seemed like slow motion, the huge animal rolled onto Nitze and crushed his pelvis.

It took three hours for a helicopter to fly out to the farm and airlift Nitze to a hospital. Doctors were surprised that a man of 82 had even survived the accident, and it was predicted that Nitze would be in the hospital for eight weeks. Nitze confounded the doctors and surprised his friends and family by recovering far more quickly. By the second week in April he was ready to go home. His recovery proceeded at a stunning pace, and in a short time he was able to walk without crutches.

When he had recovered, Nitze took an office at his old haunt on Massachusetts Avenue, the Johns Hopkins School of Advanced International Studies. In an unexpected honor, the Johns Hopkins University board of trustees had recently voted to rename SAIS the Paul H. Nitze School of Advanced International Studies. What began as an animated conversation with Christian Herter in the 1940s had evolved into a small shrine to Nitze's career. Sitting in his airy eighth-floor office a few blocks down from Dupont Circle, Nitze shrugged off the renaming of SAIS. Many schools were named after forgotten people, he said. Why would the Nitze School be different?

Besides visiting with friends and family and managing his fortune, Nitze had much to occupy his time. His memoirs, eight years in the making, were finally nearing completion. The project had been unusually tortuous. Initially, Nitze had hoped to publish his collected writing in a book, *Getting from Here to There*. But after hiring an assistant to edit the project and devoting considerable time to it, Nitze was disappointed when no publisher would take on the book. There was interest in his memoirs, however. Hiring another assistant Nitze began the long job of assembling his recollections. Even though his assistants were to ghostwrite nearly the entire book, progress was slow. With work in the Reagan administration keeping Nitze frantically busy, his assistants found it difficult to get hold of him. And when the book did begin to come together, there were problems. Publishers found the writing bland and lifeless. Absent were the great clashes with Dulles, Kissinger, Warnke, and Perle. Forever respectful, even of the dead, Nitze avoided passing judgment on men he had fought and sometimes loathed. What his memoirs amounted to, complained one publisher, was a "public document." When the book came out in October 1989, reviewers echoed this sentiment, expressing regret that such an exciting life should be recounted so dryly.

Of course, the failure of Nitze's memoirs was predictable; he had always been a man of political action not literary reflection. And in the early months of 1989, when he might have been consumed with last-minute work on his book, Nitze was instead immersing himself in yet another policy problem—acid rain. It was an odd diversion for someone who had devoted forty years to foreign policy. But while Nitze had never been an active environmentalist, he had always loved the outdoors. From the mountains of Aspen to the quiet meadows of Causein Manor, Nitze had spent many days skiing, hiking, riding, and fishing. Acid rain caught his attention because its effects were so visible and devastating. Caused by smokestack emissions in the Great Lakes industrial belt which were carried east, acid rain was killing the forests and lakes of New England and Canada. Nitze believed that by energizing government and the business community, the problem could be solved. He hoped to play a role in that process during the last years of his life.

Nitze looked his age now, stooped and frail, his chiseled face more wrinkled. The blue eyes were still clear and the days next to the pool at Causein Manor kept him tan, but he moved slowly and friends could see that the accident had taken its toll. It was hard to imagine such an old man getting back on the inside and waging bureaucratic warfare with officials in their forties. Yet Nitze had been treated to more than one premature farewell party. And if, at 82, his career in government had finally come to end, Nitze had no plans to fade away. He still had the same drive, the same desire to get in on the action. For decades his life had followed a predictable cycle: work as a team player on the inside, operate as a relentless critic on the outside. In case anybody had forgotten about this cycle, they were soon reminded.

Through April and May, the Bush administration grappled with the issue of short-range nuclear forces in Europe (SNF). The Soviet Union wanted to open up negotiations on the matter, as did the western Europeans. But the administration balked, believing that such negotiations would be a slippery slope toward eliminating all NATO short-range nuclear weapons. Instead of negotiating limits, Bush's team wanted to modernize existing U.S. missiles. In West Germany, however, Chancellor Helmut Kohl was under intense domestic pressure to stop modernization and promote negotiation. With the United States and a key NATO ally at loggerheads, the Bush administration faced its first foreign policy crisis.

Nitze had seen the crisis coming months earlier. Before leaving government, he had suggested that the United States negotiate on short-range missiles, pointing out that Moscow had a big lead in these weapons and that such talks could only benefit the west. The administration rejected this advice.

In May, with the administration under fire from both European and American critics, Nitze added his voice to the bombardment. With perfect timing, he attacked the administration's inflexibility, saying the approach was "politically impossible for much of Europe."[4] The attack, which made the front page of the *New York Times*, crystallized the emerging consensus that Bush was wrong. Over the next two weeks Nitze repeated his criticism on television talk shows and in newspaper opinion pieces.[5]

Nearly a decade had passed since Nitze last played the role of outside critic, but his attack on the administration proved that he hadn't lost his touch. What had changed, however, was the tone of Nitze's criticism. With the changing times, Nitze's traditional occupation of doomsayer was no longer relevant. For over thirty years he had been content with the basic analysis of NSC 68. But now, finally, Nitze was ready to abandon that analysis.

Almost every month there came new evidence that the Cold War was ending.

In December 1988 Gorbachev addressed the United Nations and announced that the Soviet Union was unilaterally cutting its armed forces by half a million. Some of these cuts, the Soviet leader promised, would be of offensive oriented troops in eastern Europe.

In February 1989 the Soviet Union pulled out the last of its troops from Afghanistan. After a bloody ten-year effort to pacify a nation of fifteen million, the Soviets had acknowledged defeat and withdrawn almost unconditionally.

In March Gorbachev's promise to bring more democracy to the Soviet Union produced the first election in seventy years in which Soviet citizens could choose among competing candidates.

In early April the Polish government signed an accord with the labor union Solidarity that would eventually result in a free parliament and noncommunist prime minister in Warsaw. So long the symbol of an eastern Europe subordinate to the Soviet Union and isolated by an iron curtain, Poland suddenly exemplified the liberalization that was sweeping the area.

Most dramatic of all were the events in Berlin. After several years of resisting the wave of reform, East Germany underwent a sudden transformation in early November 1989. Throwing open the gates of the Berlin Wall, it announced a new policy of free travel and two million East Germans visited West Berlin in a single joyous weekend.

"The Cold War is over," editorialized the *New York Times*. George Kennan hurried to echo this sentiment, writing that "whatever reasons there may once have been for regarding the Soviet Union primarily as a possible, if not probable, military opponent, the time for that sort of thinking has clearly passed."[6] Even the Joint Chiefs of Staff believed the great superpower struggle had run its course, issuing a lengthy report called "1989 Joint Military Net Assessment," in which it repeated the arguments made by Kennan and Bohlen four decades earlier. "Since the 1940s, the Soviets have demonstrated hesitancy to use military power as a means to achieve their foreign policy goals," the report said. "The primary Soviet concern . . . is the security and integrity of the Soviet homeland." As for the first strike threat that so worried Nitze in the 1970s, the chiefs stated that the Soviets had amassed their menacing nuclear arsenal "as a more comprehensive form of deterrence, rather than as an expression that they could 'win' a nuclear war."[7]

With Gorbachev's admission that the Soviet system was a failure, there was gloating in some quarters. The United States had won the Cold War, many argued. It had contained Soviet power and thwarted the spread of communism. One academic hastened to point out that the goals of NSC 68—the goals of rolling back Soviet influence and forcing fundamental changes in the Soviet system—had been achieved. If NSC 68 constituted a declaration of Cold War, Gorbachev's new policies were a white flag. Nitze himself felt a sense of vindication. Over the past forty years the American government had largely followed Nitze's prescription: It had spent trillions of dollars on building the kind of defenses called for in the Pacific Summary Report, in NSC 68, in the Gaither report, and in the papers of the Committee on the Present Danger. In doing so, it had won the Cold War.

But what had the United States really won?

In 1953 Paul Nitze had helped write Eisenhower's famous "Chance for Peace" speech. Its most striking passage said, "Every gun that is fired, every warship launched, every rocket fired signifies, in the final sense, a theft from those who hunger and are not fed, those who are cold and are not clothed. The world in arms is not spending money alone. It is spending the sweat of its laborers, the genius of its scientists, the hopes of its children."[8] The speech reflected concern that there was a price to pay for lavishing vast quantities of national treasure on the military.

Now, in 1989, after decades of a giving up to a third of every year's federal budget to the Pentagon, after keeping more than two million people under arms for nearly three generations, and after a particularly excessive eight-year military spending spree under Reagan, that price was all too clear.

And it was far too high.

At the time that NSC 68 was written, the United States was the world's unchallenged economic power. Forty years later it was the world's largest debtor nation. It was a nation that was rapidly losing its capacity to compete in numerous areas of industry and high technology. It was a nation where thirty million people lived in poverty and millions more hovered on the brink. In the great cities adequate housing was scarce, infrastructures were crumbling, and infant mortality rates in some areas rivaled those of the third world. Around the country toxic waste dumps and nuclear weapons plants were contaminating soil and water supplies. America's educational system, once the envy of the world and the ultimate foundation of its prosperity, lay in shambles.

In following the blueprint of NSC 68, in spending trillions of dollars on the military, the United States may have won the Cold War, but it had lost the fight to create more equity and opportunity. In the twilight of the twentieth century, the United States was going the way of other great powers that had faltered. At home it was lowering its expectations and standard of living. Abroad it was losing its markets and its credibility. Once the most prosperous and hopeful nation on earth, the United States was fast becoming a second-rate power polarized along class and racial lines.

For Paul Nitze, victory in the Cold War was something he experienced personally. It was pushing through the Marshall Plan; it was getting the hydrogen bomb first; it was winning the battle for higher defense expenditures and a more flexible nuclear strategy, it was facing down Khrushchev in Berlin and Cuba; it was regaining resolve in the 1980s and compelling Gorbachev to quit the arms race. And if the Cold War had taken a toll on America's economy, it hadn't touched Nitze's own finances. By the late 1980s Nitze was wealthier than ever, a millionaire many times over.

In the high-powered, rarefied world in which Paul Nitze traveled, the victories had been real indeed. But to younger Americans—the first generation in U.S. history that had less opportunity than their parents—there was no victory.

Only a lost dream.

A C K N O W L E D G M E N T S

Writing a book, as nearly every author will attest, is an education. For me, this is especially true. I began this book as a college junior at Hampshire College with only the most general notion of how biography and critical history are researched and written. I had read widely in the field of national security, but was unfamiliar with the details of many key episodes in American postwar history. The longest paper I had ever written was forty-six pages.

My success in getting from there to here is due in part to the guidance and inspiration I have received from others—both personally and through the great political books of our time. My largest debt is to the authors—almost none of whom I actually met—who by their example taught me how to research and write. Fred Kaplan, John Lewis Gaddis, and Daniel Yergin showed me the remarkable dividends that primary research in history could yield. Seymour Hersh, Strobe Talbott, and Bob Woodward provided inspiring examples of how to write about the Washington bureaucracy. And Robert Caro defined for me what it meant to chronicle the pursuit and use of political power.

I have been educated and helped by many people. My parents, Sidney and Daniel Callahan, taught me to value ideas and scholarship, setting an example in their own lives of the rewards that can come from the pursuit of knowledge. They also provided unending help and encouragement during the four years it took to write this book. My brother Stephen imbued me early on with a love and respect of the English language. Edward Burlingame, my editor at Harper & Row, expertly pinpointed the chief weaknesses in an earlier draft of this book and made all the right suggestions for dealing with them. He is a superb editor. Gregg Herken, whose work has long inspired me, undertook a careful last-minute read of the manuscript. Michael Klare, a military affairs specialist and Five College professor, assisted and encouraged me in numerous ways during some of the darkest days of this project. Allan Krass, an arms control expert and Hampshire professor, taught me at a critical juncture in my education that no point is persuasive unless it is proved. Allan also devoted many hours to helping me shape this book's argument. Dan Mahoney helped me conceptualize this book from the beginning and then brought his remarkable intelligence and uncanny editorial skills to bear on the entire manuscript. Nearly every page incorporates one of his revisions. Raphael Sagalyn, my literary agent, demonstrated great patience, persistence, and professionalism at every point in this project. Arthur Samuelson, my first editor at Harper & Row, impressed me with his confidence in my book and his courage as an editor. Adele Simmons gave me much encouragement and considerable help in pushing this book forward. Strobe Talbott proved a great ally, not just for his knowledge and scholarship when it came to arms control and Paul Nitze, but for his kindness and interest in helping a newcomer to the field learn the ropes. Christa Weil, assistant editor at Burlingame Books, was unfailingly helpful. Four of my earlier teachers, Charles Aschmann, Robert Tucker, Karen Ural, and particularly Robert Rittner, planted the seeds of critical thought and literary interest that led to this project.

In the realm of research, I'm indebted first to the dozens of friends and former colleagues of Paul Nitze who shared their thoughts with me; to Paul Nitze himself, who made his time and some of his papers available to me; to Stephen Rearden and Ann Smith, his assistants, who helped me on a number of occasions; to Laurence Chang, who assisted me at the National Security Archive; to the staff of the Hastings library, who dutifully processed hundreds of interlibrary loan requests; to archivists at the Kennedy Library and National Archives, who helped me locate the files I wanted.

For moral support I'm indebted to my friends who politely feigned interest for month after month and then year after year in a book that some thought was about Paul "Nietzsche." Those particularly adept at humoring me included John Clancy, Michael Csenger, Eric D'Amato, William Driscoll, Shcheryar Hassan, Solomon and Philip Karmel, Jessie Klein, Mark Koplik, Hal Reinstein, Laura Ring, Eric Schaper, Mark Schor, Mario Spanguolo, Ted Van der Clute, and John Weiss.

Finally, I owe a tremendous debt to Suzanne M. Guerzon, who is surely unique in her ability to remain interested in a four-year conversation about Paul H. Nitze. Whenever the momentum behind this project began to dissipate or its value seemed temporarily obscured, Sue would be there to push me along and assure me that it would all be worth it. And she was right.

DAVID CALLAHAN
Princeton, N.J.
November 1989

S O U R C E S

Researching the life of Paul Nitze was daunting. As he had never been a cabinet secretary or national security advisor, details of his activities were virtually nonexistent in books on the Roosevelt, Truman, Kennedy, Johnson, and Nixon administrations. A search of standard memoirs and secondary historical sources revealed few details about Nitze's career. Newspaper and magazine indexes proved to be a similar dead end. Not until the Reagan years was Nitze's name mentioned in the major newspapers more than several times a year.

Investigations into the archives at the Kennedy and Johnson libraries also turned up little on Paul Nitze. Nearly all his papers from his Pentagon and SALT years remain classified. The picture was brighter at the National Archives, but still disappointing. Many of Nitze's papers from the Policy Planning Staff had been opened. To my surprise, however, the working papers of the State-Defense Review Group which produced NSC 68 remained closed and declassification review was still pending at the time of publication. Fortunately, there was no problem seeing the papers of the Strategic Bombing Survey which have been well indexed by the National Archives.

The continued classification of material from the Policy Planning Staff years proved only a minor setback, thanks in great part to the Foreign Relations of the United States series (FRUS). In these books, dozens of Nitze's memorandums have been reproduced, and from them it was possible to document in detail Nitze's thinking on nearly every major national security issue from 1949 through early 1953. FRUS also provided a fascinating glimpse into the bureaucratic infighting of the Truman administration, reproducing not just papers from the State Department, but from the Defense Department, CIA, Atomic Energy Commission, and National Security Council. And while not all of the working papers from the hydrogen bomb debate and NSC 68 are found in FRUS, most of the key documents are included.

Researching Nitze's role in the Kennedy administration was done with mixed success. ISA's work on Berlin contingency planning remains classified, as are the many papers Nitze and his staff produced during the Cuban missile crisis. However, the torrent of documentation from the Cuban crisis—declassified in great part by the National Security Archive—proved of much help in reconstructing Nitze's positions at Excomm meetings and in revealing the workings of Nitze's Subcommittee of the Executive Committee on Berlin. The documentation on the Berlin crisis is far less voluminous and proved less helpful. As with the Cuban material, the documents related to Berlin that are emerging are, for the most part, coming from NSC and State Department files. Pentagon documents remain far less accessible.

The documentation relating to the test ban negotiations was the least available. Not only are ISA's papers on this subject classified, but there is also little material from State, the NSC, and the AEC. Moreover, Nitze's top aide during that episode, John McNaughton, died in the 1960s. What made my account of the test ban negotiations possible was Glenn Seaborg's illuminating memoir. By quoting extensively from his diary and the minutes of Committee of Principals meetings, Seaborg provided crucial information on the positions taken by Paul Nitze and the Department of Defense in general.

From the end of the Kennedy period through the Reagan era, my research in government documents encountered an impenetrable wall of classification, broken only by the Pentagon Papers, which contained less than half a dozen references to Paul H. Nitze.

Mitigating this primary source deficit were two factors: Nitze's writing, recollections, and congressional testimony and the recollections of his colleagues.

After some fifty years in public life, Nitze's public papers are voluminous, including at least two dozen articles, uncounted speeches, over forty appearances before congressional committees, a lengthy memoir, and a massive oral history. Critical though this material was, however, its vastness proved deceiving. As a loyal public official, Nitze's speeches while he was inside government were often bland recitations of administration policy that provided few clues to his real policy positions. Much of his congressional testimony was similarly disappointing.

Of great value, however, were Nitze's writings and his public statements and testimony while outside of government. In these, particularly during the 1950s and 1970s, Nitze lays out his ideological positions in a frank and polemical style. It is in his congressional testimony of the 1970s, for example, that I found the most detailed exposition of Nitze's hard-line views of that time.

Nitze's memoirs and oral history were invaluable sources for this book, but using them was not without risk. As other observers of Paul Nitze have found, he has a tendency to repeat the same stories again and again complete with verbatim dialogue. Many of these stories were nearly impossible to confirm, and in any case, even with his remarkable memory, it seems unlikely that Nitze could recall the exact words of a conversation many years later. Thus, while I have used the Nitze stories that seem plausible, I have dropped much of the verbatim dialogue.

To reconstruct Nitze's bureaucratic maneuvering over four decades, the recollections of his closest aides and colleagues proved indispensable. They include Nitze's principal aide from the Strategic Bombing Survey; five key members of the Policy Planning Staff, including two of Nitze's closest colleagues from the staff, Robert Tufts and Charles Burton Marshall; nearly every top staff member at ISA; two aides from Nitze's navy years; two of Nitze's three military assistants from OSD; several key members of Nitze's SALT staff and nearly every member of the SALT I delegation; six members of the Executive Committee of the Committee on the Present Danger; three members of the INF delegation; and six top Reagan arms control officials, several of whom did not want to be identified. Through these interviews I was able to compensate in large part for the lack of declassified information, especially in tracing Nitze's activities at ISA and the evolution of his positions during SALT I.

INTERVIEWS
BY THE AUTHOR

KENNETH ADELMAN. Washington. D.C., November 4, 1987

ROYAL ALLISON, Telephone, July 15, 1988

DEWITT ARMSTRONG. Alexandria, Va., October 4, 1988; October 26, 1988

GORDON ARNESON, Alexandria, Va., July 25, 1989

GEORGE BALL, Princeton, N.J., January 30, 1989

LUCIUS BATTLE, Washington, D.C., May 23, 1989

MCGEORGE BUNDY, New York, N.Y., February 8, 1986

WILLIAM BUNDY, Princeton, N.J., January 30, 1989

WILLIAM BURNS, Telephone, November 15, 1989

JOHN CHASE, Telephone, November 30, 1988

CLARK CLIFFORD, Washington, D.C. May 26, 1988

LLOYD CUTLER, Washington, D.C., May 25, 1988

JOHN PATON DAVIES, Telephone, November 30, 1988

RALPH EARLE, Washington, D.C., May 23, 1988

RON EASLEY, Telephone, December 1, 1988

PHILIP FARLEY, Telephone, September 20, 1988; November 11, 1989

DOROTHY FOSDICK, Washington, D.C., October 27, 1988
RAY FURLONG, Telephone, September 20, 1988
FRANK GAFFNEY, Washington, D.C., May 23, 1989
RAYMOND GARTHOFF, Washington, D.C., November 2, 1987
RICHARD GARWIN, Yorktown, N.Y., April 9, 1986
ROSWELL GILPATRIC, New York, N.Y., November 14, 1985
PATRICK GLYNN, Telephone, April 12, 1989
NAJEEB HALABY, Telephone, November 10, 1989
MORTON HALPERIN, Washington, D.C., May 23, 1988
TOWNSEND HOOPES, Washington, D.C., December 11, 1985
U. ALEXIS JOHNSON, Washington, D.C., November 5, 1987
T. K. JONES, Telephone, March 10, 1989
MAX KAMPLEMAN, Washington, D.C., July 25, 1989
JOHN MARSHALL LEE, Telephone, September 21, 1988: November 30, 1988
ANDREW MARSHALL, Telephone, December 7, 1988
CHARLES BURTON MARSHALL, Washington, D.C., December 10, 1985; October 26, 1988
LAWRENCE McQUADE, New York, N.Y., January 28, 1989
PAUL H. NITZE, Northeast Harbor, Me., August 11, 1988; Washington, D.C., July 26, 1989
EUGENE V. ROSTOW. Washington, D.C., December 11, 1985
HENRY ROWEN, Telephone, September 15, 1988; February 28, 1989
EDWARD ROWNY, Washington, D.C., July 25, 1989
CARLTON SAVAGE, Telephone, August 3, 1988
WILLIAM F. SCHAUB, Telephone, August 3, 1988
IVAN SELIN, Arlington, Va., October 26, 1988
WALTER SLOCOMBE, Washington, D.C., November 6, 1987
GERARD SMITH, Washington, D.C., November 4, 1987
TIMOTHY STANLEY, Washington, D.C., October 25, 1988
ROBERT TUFTS, Telephone, July 26, 1988; December 6, 1988
CHARLES TYROLER II, Washington, D.C., May 27, 1988
WILLIAM VAN CLEAVE, Telephone, December 7, 1988
JAMES WADE, Alexandria, Va., July 25, 1989
CHARLES WALKER, Washington, D.C., May 24, 1988
JAMES B. WILSON, Telephone, September 22, 1988
THOMAS WOLFE, Telephone, September 16, 1988
JOHN WOODWORTH, Telephone, December 7, 1988
JAMES WOOLSEY, Washington, D.C., October 28, 1988
ELMO ZUMWALT, Washington, D.C., December 10, 1985; October 27, 1988

N O T E S

CHAPTER 1

1. Unless otherwise noted, recollections by Paul Nitze are taken from interviews by the author and an extensive oral history interview conducted with Nitze by John N. Hicks and James C. Hasdorff, October 2–28, 1977; May 19–20, 1981; and July 14–16, 1981, U.S. Air Force Oral History Collection, Maxwell Air Force Base, Alabama. The literature on Nitze's life has been expanding rapidly in recent years. See Nitze's memoirs (with Steven L. Rearden and Ann M. Smith), *From Hiroshima to Glasnost: At the Center of Decision* (New York: Weidenfeld & Nicolson, 1989); and Strobe Talbott, *The Master of the Game: Paul Nitze and the Nuclear Peace* (New York: Knopf, 1988). A useful monograph on Nitze appeared in 1984. See Steven L. Rearden, *The Evolution of American Strategic Doctrine: Paul H. Nitze and the Soviet Challenge* (Boulder, Colo.: Westview Press, 1984).

2. Paul H. Nitze, Address at Atlantik-Brueck, Hamburg, Germany, April 11, 1962, Public Statements of Paul H. Nitze, Assistant Secretary of State for International Security Affairs (Washington, D.C.: Department of Defense, n.d.), p. 96.

3. Walter Isaacson and Evan Thomas, *The Wisemen: Six Friends and the World They Made* (New York: Simon & Schuster, 1986), p. 95.
4. *New York Times,* December 4, 1932.
5. Isaacson and Thomas, p. 483.
6. Nitze, p. 7.

CHAPTER 2

Interviews: George Ball, Lucius Battle, Clark Clifford, Phillip Farley

1. Zachary Criton, "The Conversion of Paul." *The New Republic,* January 30, 1989.
2. For an in-depth account of the Black Tom episode and Hilken's role in it, see Jules Whitcover, *Sabotage at Black Tom: Imperial Germany's Secret War in America,* 1914–1917 (New York: Algonquin Books, 1989).
3. Paul H. Nitze, p. 23.
4. David MacIsaac, *Strategic Bombing in World War Two: The Story of the United States Strategic Bombing Survey* (New York: Garland, 1976), p. 14. Based largely on the archives of the survey, this book is the most authoritative account of the survey.
5. MacIsaac, p. 51.
6. Ibid., p. 65.
7. John Kenneth Galbraith, *A Life in Our Times* (Boston: Houghton Mifflin, 1981), p. 201.
8. Ibid., pp. 206–215.
9. For Ball's exposition on enemy morale, see "Report of the USSBS and JTG Conferences," Meetings Folder, USSBS Office of the Chairman, General Correspondence, 1944–1947, Box 2, R.G. 243, National Archives.
10. Galbraith, p. 211. For the complete figures, see U.S. Strategic Bombing Survey, *The Effects of Strategic Bombing on the German War Economy* (Washington, D.C.: GPO, 1945).
11. Nitze, p. 33.
12. Speer quoted in Galbraith, p. 213. For the complete account of Speer's interrogation, see United States Strategic Bombing Survey Special Document, *Speer on the Last Days of the Third Reich* (Washington, D.C.: GPO, 1945).
13. MacIsaac, p. 95.
14. This account of the meetings between survey members and the JTG is based on "Report on the USSBS and JTF Conferences."
15. MacIsaac, p. 101.
16. Ibid., p. 106.
17. The most in-depth account of what happened to Hiroshima can be found in The Committee for the Compilation of Materials on Damage Caused by the Atomic Bombs in Hiroshima and Nagasaki, *Hiroshima and*

Nagasaki: The Physical, Medical and Social Effects of the Atomic Bombings (New York: Basic Books, 1981).

18.   U.S. Strategic Bombing Survey, *Summary Report (Pacific War)* (Washington, D.C.: GPO, 1946), p. 24.

19.   Ibid. The survey did an extensive report on the bombings of Hiroshima and Nagasaki that was compiled by Nitze's assistant Philip Farley. See U.S. Strategic Bombing Survey, *The Effects of Atomic Bombs on Hiroshima and Nagasaki* (Washington, D.C.: GPO, 1946).

20.   U.S. Strategic Bombing Survey, *Summary Report (Pacific War)*, p. 26. For a more in-depth account of Japan's thinking on the war, see U.S. Strategic Bombing Survey, *Japan's Struggle to End the War* (Washington, D.C.: GPO, 1946).

21.   Gregg Herken, "The Great Foreign Policy Fight," *American Heritage*, May 1986, p. 66.

22.   U.S. Strategic Bombing Survey, *Summary Report (Pacific War)*, pp. 30–32.

23.   Harvard College, *Class of 1928: Fiftieth Annual Report* (Cambridge, Mass.: 1978), p. 484.

24.   Clayton quoted in Walter Isaacson and Evan Thomas, *The Wisemen: Six Friends and the World They Made* (New York: Simon & Schuster, 1986), p. 410.

25.   Interview with Paul Nitze, Marshall Plan Project, OHR, Columbia University, p. 5.

26.   "Memorandum by the Under Secretary of State for Economic Affairs: The European Crisis," United States Department of State, Foreign Relations of the United States (hereafter FRUS), 1947, vol. III, pp. 230–232.

27.   Ibid., p. 230.

28.   "Policy with Respect to American Aid to Western Europe: Views of the Policy Planning Staff." FRUS. 1947, vol. III, p. 233.

29.   "Press Release Issued by the Department of State, June 4, 1947." FRUS, 1947, vol. III, pp. 237–238.

30.   "The Assistant Chief of the Division of Commercial Policy to the Directory of the Office of International Trade Policy at Geneva." FRUS, 1947, vol. III, p. 239.

31.   "Memorandum by Mr. Wesley C. Haraldson of the Office of the United States Political Advisor for Germany," FRUS, 1947, vol. III, pp. 345–350.

32.   *New York Times,* June 4, 1987.

33.   Isaacson and Thomas, p. 434.

34.   Nitze, p. 65.

35.   George Kennan, *Memoirs: 1925–1950* (Boston: Little, Brown, 1967), p. 326.

CHAPTER 3

Interviews: Gordon Arneson, Lucius Battle, William Bundy, John Paton Davies, Dorothy Fosdick, Carlton Savage, Robert Tufts

1. Robert J. Donovan, *Tumultuous Years: The Presidency of Harry S Truman, 1949–1953* (New York: Norton, 1982), p. 99. For a detailed description of how the Soviet explosion was detected and assessed, see Richard G. Hewlett and Francis Duncan, *Atomic Shield, 1947–1952,* vol. II of *History of the United States Atomic Energy Commission* (University Park: Pennsylvania State University Press, 1969), pp. 362–366.
2. "Memorandum by the Executive Secretary of the Policy Planning Staff," FRUS, 1949, vol. I (Washington, D.C.: GPO, 1976), p. 536.
3. "Statement by the President," Department of State Bulletin, October 6, 1949, p. 487.
4. "Statement by Secretary Acheson," Department of State Bulletin, October 6, 1949, p. 487.
5. Galbraith quoted in Walter Isaacson and Evan Thomas, *The Wisemen: Six Friends and the World They Made* (New York: Simon & Schuster, 1986), p. 410.
6. "The Soviet Atomic Explosion: An Intelligence Estimate prepared by the Estimates Group, Office of Intelligence Research," R.G. 59, Paul Nitze Folder, Papers of the Policy Planning Staff, Diplomatic Branch, National Archives.
7. "Report to the President by the Special Committee of the National Security Council on the Proposed Acceleration of the Atomic Energy Program," FRUS, 1949, vol. I, p. 562.
8. John Lewis Gaddis and Paul Nitze, "NSC 68 and the Soviet Threat Reconsidered." *International Security,* Spring 1980, p. 171. The opinion of U.S. intelligence on the military situation in Europe can be found in Report of a Joint Ad Hoc Committee, "Possibility of Direct Soviet Military Action During 1949," R.G. 330, Records of the Office of the Secretary of Defense, CD 103-7-40, Modern Military Records Branch, National Archives.
9. Dean Acheson, *Present at the Creation: My Years in the State Department* (New York: Norton, 1969), p. 308.
10. "Minutes of the 148th Meeting of the Policy Planning Staff," FRUS, 1949, vol. I., p. 402.
11. Ibid.
12. George F. Kennan, *Memoirs: 1925–1950* (Boston: Little, Brown, 1967), pp. 9–10.
13. Ibid., p. 49.
14. Isaacson and Thomas, p. 149.
15. The Long Telegram is reprinted in Kennan, pp. 545–559.
16. Ibid., p. 295.

17. Ibid., p. 326.

18. Ibid., p. 364.

19. Ibid., pp. 426–427.

20. Ibid., p. 466.

21. Ibid., p. 472.

22. "Minutes of the First Meeting of the Policy Planning Staff on the International Control of Atomic Energy," FRUS, 1949, vol. I, p. 191.

23. Ibid., p. 192.

24. "Minutes of the Second Meeting of the Policy Planning Staff on the International Control of Atomic Energy," FRUS, 1949, vol. I, p. 193.

25. "Minutes of the Eighth Meeting of the Policy Planning Staff on the International Control of Atomic Energy," FRUS, 1949, vol. I, p. 205.

26. "Statement Appended to the Report of the General Advisory Committee," FRUS, 1949, vol. I, p. 571.

27. Ibid. On November 9, 1949, the AEC released its own report on the hydrogen bomb. The commissioners were sharply divided on the matter. See "Memorandum for the President by the United States Atomic Energy Commission," FRUS, 1949, vol. I, pp. 576–585.

28. Gordon Arneson, "The H-bomb Decision," The Foreign Service Journal, May-June, 1969, p. 29. For further discussion of the H-bomb decision see Henry Borowski, A Hollow Threat: Strategic Air Power and Containment Before Korea (Westport, Conn.: Greenwood Press, 1982); McGeorge Bundy, "The Missed Chance to Stop the H-bomb," The New York Review of Books, May 13, 1982; Gregg Herken, The Winning Weapon: The Atomic Bomb in the Cold War, 1945–50 (New York: Knopf, 1980), pp. 307–320; Steven Rearden, The Formative Years: History of the Office of the Secretary of Defense, 1947–50 (Washington, D.C.: GPO, 1984), pp. 450–460; David Alan Rosenberg, "American Atomic Strategy and the Hydrogen Bomb Decision," Journal of American History, June 1979, pp. 62–87; Warner Schilling, "The H-bomb Decision: How to Decide Without Actually Choosing," Political Science Quarterly, March 1961, pp. 24–46.

29. David McLellan, Dean Acheson: The State Department Years (New York: Dodd, Mead, 1976), p. 179.

30. Acheson, p. 346.

31. "Minutes of the Policy Planning Staff," FRUS, 1949, vol. I, p. 576.

32. Ibid., p. 575.

33. Acheson, p. 346.

34. Gaddis and Nitze, p. 176.

35. Arneson, p. 25.

36. Arneson, p. 25; Nitze, From Hiroshima to Glasnost, pp. 86–91.

37. Nitze quoted in Gregg Herken, Counsels of War (New York: Knopf, 1985), p. 48.

38. Acheson, p. 347.

39. "Draft Memorandum from the Director of the Policy Planning Staff

to the Secretary of State," FRUS, 1949, vol. I, p. 586.

40. Acheson, p. 346.

41. "President Truman to the Executive Secretary of the National Security Council," FRUS, 1949, vol. I, p. 587.

42. Ibid. The Department of Defense representatives of the group were Robert LeBaron, Lieutenant General Lauris Norstad, Major General Kenneth D. Nichols, and Rear Admiral T. B. Hill. The AEC members were Henry D. Smyth, Gordon Dean, and Paul C. Fine.

43. "Memorandum by the Under Secretary of State," FRUS, 1949, vol I, pp. 599–600.

44. "Memorandum Circulated by the Defense Members of the Working Group of the Special Committee of the National Security Council: The Military Implications of Thermonuclear Weapons," FRUS, 1949, vol. I, pp. 604–610.

45. "Memorandum by the Deputy Director of the Policy Planning Staff," FRUS, 1949, vol. I, pp. 610–611.

46. "Memorandum by the Secretary of State," FRUS, 1949, vol. I, pp. 612–617.

47. David Lilienthal, The Journals of David Lilienthal: The Atomic Energy Years, vol. II (New York: Harper & Row, 1964), pp. 613–614.

48. Acheson p. 348.

49. Hewlett and Duncan, pp. 400–401.

50. Letter from Senator Brian McMahon to President Truman, R.G., 330, Records of the Office of the Secretary of Defense, CD 16-1-17, Modern Military Branch, National Archives.

51. "Memorandum by the Joint Chiefs of Staff to the Secretary of Defense," FRUS, 1950, vol. I, p. 511.

52. Donovan, p. 155.

53. "Memorandum of Telephone Conversation, by the Secretary of State," FRUS, 1950, vol. I, p. 512.

54. Acheson, p. 349.

55. Kennan, p. 475.

56. Ibid., pp. 474–475.

57. Ibid., p. 473.

58. Ibid., p. 474.

59. "Memorandum by Mr. R. Gordon Arneson, Special Assistant to the Under Secretary of State," FRUS, 1950, vol. I, p. 2.

60. "Memorandum by the Assistant Secretary of State for United Nations Affairs," FRUS, 1950, vol. I, p. 10.

61. "Memorandum by the Director of the Policy Planning Staff to the Secretary of State," FRUS, 1950, vol. I, pp. 13–17.

62. "Memorandum by the Counselor: International Control of Atomic Energy," FRUS, 1950, vol. I, p. 22.

63. Kennan quoted in Strobe Talbott, The Master of the Game: Paul

Nitze and the Nuclear Peace (New York: Knopf, 1988), p. 57.

64. Letter to author, December 13, 1988; Talbott, p. 53.

65. Nitze quoted in Gregg Herken, "The Great Foreign Policy Fight," *American Heritage,* May, 1986, p. 80.

66. Lilienthal, p. 620.

67. Arneson, p. 27.

68. Lilienthal, p. 633.

CHAPTER 4

Interviews: Gordon Arneson, Lucius Battle, John Paton Davies, Dorothy Fosdick, Najeeb Halaby, Townsend Hoopes, Carlton Savage, Robert Tufts, William Schaub

1. "Draft Memorandum by the Counselor to the Secretary of State," FRUS, 1950, vol. I, pp. 160–167.

2. Walter Isaacson and Evan Thomas, *The Wisemen: Six Friends and the World They Made* (New York: Simon & Schuster, 1986), p. 491.

3. Dean Acheson, *Present at the Creation: My Years in the State Department* (New York: Norton, 1969), p. 360.

4. Ibid., p. 373.

5. "Record of the Eighth Meeting of the Policy Planning Staff," FRUS, 1950, vol. I, p. 143.

6. "Study Prepared by the Director of the Policy Planning Staff: Recent Soviet Moves," FRUS, 1950, vol. I, p. 145.

7. Emily Morison Beck, ed., *Familiar Quotations* (Boston: Little, Brown, 1968), p. 920.

8. "Recent Soviet Moves," FRUS, 1950, vol. I, p. 147.

9. Central Intelligence Agency Report, ORE 91-49, "Estimate of the Effects of the Soviet Possession of Atomic Bomb upon the Security of the United States and upon the Probabilities of Direct Soviet Military Action," CD 11-1-2, R.G. 330, Records of the Office of the Secretary of Defense, Modern Military Records Branch, National Archives, p. B-2.

10. "Recent Soviet Moves," p. 147.

11. "Draft Report by the National Security Council Staff: Measures Required to Achieve U.S. Objectives with Respect to the U.S.S.R.," FRUS, 1949, vol. I, pp. 271–277.

12. "Memorandum by the Director of the Policy Planning Staff to the Deputy Under Secretary of State for Political Affairs," FRUS, 1949, vol. I, p. 381.

13. "Memorandum by the Executive Secretary of the National Security Council to the Council," FRUS, 1949, vol. I, pp. 417–418.

14. "Memorandum by the Director of the Policy Planning Staff to the Deputy Under Secretary of State for Political Affairs," p. 381.

15. "Report by the Special Committee of the National Security Council to the President," FRUS, 1950, vol. I, p. 517.

16. Paul H. Nitze, "The Operations of the Policy Planning Staff," Address Before the National War College, May 4, 1951, Paul Nitze Folder, Papers of the Policy Planning Staff, R.G. 59, Diplomatic Branch, National Archives, p. 12.

17. "Memorandum by the Director of the Policy Planning Staff to the Secretary of State," FRUS, 1950, vol. I, p. 14.

18. Paul H. Nitze, "The Development of NSC 68," *International Security*, Spring 1980, p. 172.

19. Walter Poole, "History of the Joint Chiefs of Staff: Volume IV, 1950–1952," R.G. 218, Records of the United States Joint Chiefs of Staff, Modern Military Branch, National Archives, p. 6.

20. Robert J. Donovan, *Tumultuous Years: The Presidency of Harry S Truman, 1949–1953* (New York: Norton, 1982), p. 62. For more on Louis Johnson at the Pentagon, see Stephen L. Rearden, *History of the Office of the Secretary of Defense: The Formative Years, 1947–50* (Washington, D.C.: GPO, 1984), p. 44.

21. "Memorandum by the Secretary of Defense," FRUS, 1949, vol. I, p. 366.

22. Landon's conversion is documented in Paul Y. Hammond, "NSC 68: Prologue to Rearmament," in Warner R. Schilling, Paul Y. Hammond, and Glenn H. Snyder, *Strategy, Politics, and Defense Budgets* (New York: Columbia University Press, 1962), p. 229. Despite the fact that Hammond's account was written before any documents from the State-Defense Policy Review Group were declassified, it remains one of the best accounts of NSC 68 available because Hammond interviewed many of the participants in the review.

23. Hammond, p. 303.

24. Nitze quoted in Stephen L. Rearden, *The Evolution of American Strategic Doctrine: Paul H. Nitze and the Soviet Challenge* (Boulder, Colo.: Westview Press, 1984), p. 19.

25. Nitze, "The Operations of the Policy Planning Staff," p. 13.

26. "Record of the Meeting of the State-Defense Policy Review Group," FRUS, 1950, vol. I, pp. 168–175.

27. "Memorandum by the Deputy Chief of the Division of Estimates, Bureau of the Budget to the Executive Secretary of the National Security Council," FRUS, 1950, vol. I, pp. 298–306.

28. Nitze, "The Development of NSC 68," p. 170.

29. "Record of the Meeting of the State-Defense Policy Review Group," pp. 176–82.

30. "A Report to the President Pursuant to the President's Directive of January 31, 1950," FRUS, 1950, vol. I, p. 284.

31. "Record of the Meeting of the State-Defense Policy Review Group," pp. 190–195.

32. "Record of the Meeting of the State-Defense Policy Review Group." pp. 196–200.

33. "A Report to the President," pp. 239–240.

34. Central Intelligence Agency Report, ORE 91–49, p. B-12.

35. Isaacson and Thomas, p. 498.

36. "Memorandum by Mr. Charles E. Bohlen to the Director of the Policy Planning Staff," FRUS, 1950, vol. I, pp. 221–225.

37. "A Report to the President," p. 238.

38. Acheson, p. 373.

39. Ibid., 375.

40. Paul H. Nitze Oral History Interview, U.S. Air Force Oral History Collection, p. 241.

41. "Memorandum from General Burns to Secretary Johnson, March 13, 1950," CD 16-1-17, R.G. 330, Records of the Office of the Secretary of Defense, Modern Military Records Branch, National Archives, p. 2.

42. "Memorandum by the Director of the Policy Planning Staff to the Secretary of State," FRUS, 1950, Vol. I, p. 202.

43. "Memorandum of Conversation at the Department of State," Ibid., pp. 203–6.

44. Acheson, p. 373.

45. "Memorandum of Conversation," p. 206.

46. Acheson, p. 373.

47. Ibid., p. 374.

48. "A Report to the President," pp. 235–292.

49. Acheson, p. 374.

50. "Memorandum by the Under Secretary," FRUS, 1950, vol. I, p. 210.

51. Rearden, History of the Office of the Secretary of Defense, p. 526.

52. "Memorandum by the Deputy Assistant Secretary of State for European Affairs to the Secretary of State," FRUS, 1950, vol. I, pp. 213–214.

53. "Memorandum by Mr. Charles E. Bohlen to the Director of the Policy Planning Staff," pp. 221–225.

54. "Memorandum by the Assistant Secretary of State for Public Affairs to the Secretary of State," FRUS, 1950, vol. I, pp. 225–226.

55. "The President to the Executive Secretary of the National Security Council," FRUS, 1950, vol. I, p. 235.

56. Acheson, p. 374.

57. "Memorandum by the Deputy Chief of the Division of Estimates, Bureau of the Budget to the Executive Secretary of the National Security Council: Comments of the Bureau of the Budget on NSC 68." FRUS, 1950, vol. I, pp. 298–306. Thirty-eight years after his work on the the Ad Hoc Committee, at the age of 89, Schaub felt vindicated. "We wrecked our

economy," he said. "We don't produce anything anymore. Military spending is not productive."

58. Nitze, "The Development of NSC 68," p. 173.

59. "Memorandum by Mr. Hamilton Dearborn of the Council of Economic Advisors to the Executive Secretary of the National Security Council," FRUS, 1950, vol. I, p. 311.

60. "Memorandum by the National Security Resources Board," FRUS, 1950, vol. I, pp. 316–321.

61. "Memorandum of Conversation by the Director of the Executive Secretariat of the Department of State: Meeting of the Advisory Committee, June 6," FRUS, 1950, vol. I, pp. 323–324.

CHAPTER 5

Interviews: Lucius Battle, John Paton Davies, Dorothy Fosdick, Najeeb Halaby, Charles Burton Marshall, Carlton Savage, Robert Tufts

1. "The Ambassador in Korea to the Secretary of State," FRUS, 1951, vol. VII, pp. 125–126.

2. Paul H. Nitze, "The Development of NSC 68," *International Security,* Spring 1980, p. 174.

3. "Memorandum by the Acting Director of the Mutual Defense Assistance Program to the Assistant Secretary of State for Far Eastern Affairs," FRUS, 1951, vol. VII, p. 82.

4. Paul H. Nitze, "Estimate of the International Situation," Address at the National Political Orientation Conference, November 30, 1950, p. 10.

5. Paul H. Nitze, *United States Foreign Policy, 1945–1955* (New York: Foreign Policy Association, 1956), p. 31.

6. "Memorandum of Conversation by the Ambassador at Large," FRUS, 1951, vol. VII, pp. 178–183.

7. "Memorandum of a Meeting in the Office of the Under Secretary of State," FRUS, 1951, vol. VII, p. 212.

8. "The Commander in Chief, Far East to the Secretary of State," FRUS, 1951, vol. VII, p. 249.

9. Nitze, "Estimate of the International Situation," p. 10.

10. "United States Objectives and Programs for National Security," NSC 68, FRUS, 1950, vol. I, p. 240.

11. George F. Kennan, *Memoirs: 1925–1950* (Boston: Little, Brown, 1967), p. 486.

12. Gregg Herken, "The Great Foreign Policy Fight," *American Heritage,* May 1986, p. 74.

13. Kennan, p. 488.

14. "Memorandum by Mr. John Foster Dulles, Consultant to the Secre-

tary of State, to the Director of the Policy Planning Staff," FRUS, 1950, vol. VII, p. 386–387.

15. "Memorandum by the Director of the Office of Northeast Asian Affairs to the Assistant Secretary of State for Far Eastern Affairs," FRUS, 1950, vol. VII, pp. 393–395.

16. "Draft Memorandum Prepared by the Policy Planning Staff," FRUS, 1950, vol. VII, pp. 469–473.

17. Donovan, p. 286.

18. "Memorandum of Conversation, by the Ambassador at Large," FRUS, 1950, vol. VII, p. 159.

19. "Memorandum by the Director of the Policy Planning Staff," FRUS, 1950, vol. VII, pp. 1041–1042.

20. Robert J. Donovan, *The Tumultuous Years: The Presidency of Harry S Truman, 1949–1953* (New York: Norton, 1982), p. 303.

21. "The Commander in Chief, Far East to the Joint Chiefs of Staff," FRUS, 1950, vol. VII, pp. 1237–1238.

22. Nitze, "Estimate of the International Situation," p. 11.

23. "Memorandum of Conversation by the Ambassador at Large," FRUS, 1950, vol. VII, p. 1246.

24. "Memorandum by the Central Intelligence Agency: Soviet Intentions in the Current Situation," FRUS, 1950, vol. VII, pp. 1308–1310.

25. "The Commander in Chief, United Nations Command to the Joint Chiefs of Staff," FRUS, 1950, vol. VII, p. 1321.

26. "Memorandum of Conversation by the Ambassador at Large," pp. 1323–1334.

27. Nitze, "Estimate of the International Situation," p. 12.

28. "Memorandum of Conversation by the Director of the Executive Secretariat," FRUS, 1950, vol. VII, p. 1384.

29. Donovan, p. 319.

30. "A Report to the National Security Council by the Executive Secretary on United States Objectives and Programs for National Security," December 8, 1950, NSC Policy File, R.G. 273, Records of the National Security Council, Judicial, Fiscal, Social Branch, National Archives, p. 1.

31. "Report to the President by the National Security Council: Status and Timing of Current U.S. Programs for National Security," FRUS, 1951, vol. I, pp. 127–157.

32. "The Counselor to the Director of the Policy Planning Staff," FRUS, 1951, vol. I, pp. 106–109.

33. "Memorandum by the Counselor," FRUS, 1951, vol. I, pp. 163–166.

34. "Memorandum by the Counselor," pp. 170–172.

35. "Policy Planning Staff Memorandum," FRUS, 1951, vol. I, pp. 172–175.

36. "Memorandum by the Counselor to the Secretary of State," FRUS, 1951, vol. I, pp. 177–178.

37. "The Counselor to the Secretary of State," FRUS, 1951, vol. I, pp. 180–181.

38. *New York Times,* December 8, 1984.

39. "Memorandum for the Record of State–Joint Chiefs of Staff Meeting Held in the Pentagon Building, January 24, 1951, 11 A.M.," FRUS, 1951, vol. I, pp. 33–37.

40. Paul H. Nitze, "The Operations of the Policy Planning Staff," Address Before the National War College, May 4, 1951, Paul Nitze Folder, Papers of the Policy Planning Staff, R.G. 59, Diplomatic Branch, National Archives, p. 10.

41. "Notes of the Meeting of the Under Secretary's Advisory Committee," FRUS, 1951, vol. I, pp. 445–448.

42. Ibid.

43. "Notes of the Meeting of the Under Secretary's Advisory Committee," Ibid., pp. 453–455.

44. "Report to the National Security Council by the Secretaries of State and Defense: Formulation of a United States Position with Respect to the Regulation, Limitation and Balanced Reduction of Armed Forces and Armaments," FRUS, 1951, vol. I, pp. 477–496.

45. "Memorandum by the Director of the Policy Planning Staff to the Secretary of State," FRUS, 1952–1954, vol. II, part 2, pp. 958–963.

46. "Memorandum by the Panel of Consultants on Disarmament: The Timing of the Thermonuclear Test," FRUS, 1952–1954, vol. II, part 2, pp. 994–1008.

47. "Memorandum for the Files by R. Gordon Arneson, Special Assistant to the Secretary of State for Atomic Energy Affairs: Meeting of the Special Committee of the National Security Council," FRUS, 1952–1954, vol. II, part 2, pp. 1033–1036.

48. See also Leonard Mosley, *Dulles* (New York: Dial Press, 1978), pp. 307–309.

49. This story was related in an interview with Charles Burton Marshall and is told in greater detail in Mosley, pp. 327–380.

50. Mosley, pp. 330–335.

51. *Washington Times-Herald,* June 13, 1953.

52. "Paul Nitze to Charles Wilson," June 22, 1953. Paul Nitze Folder. Papers of the Policy Planning Staff, R.G. 59, Diplomatic Branch, National Archives.

CHAPTER 6

Interviews: John Kenneth Galbraith, Charles Tyroler II, Robert Tufts

1. *New York Times,* June 24, 1953.
2. Joseph and Stewart Alsop, "Another Surrender," *Washington Post,* June 25, 1953.
3. Walter Isaacson and Evan Thomas, *The Wisemen: Six Friends and the World They Made* (New York: Simon & Schuster, 1986), p. 582.
4. David C. Acheson and David S. McLellan, eds., *Among Friends: Personal Letters of Dean Acheson* (New York: Dodd, Mead, 1980), p. 83.
5. Ibid., p. 89.
6. "Report to the National Security Council by the National Security Council Planning Board," FRUS, 1952–1954, vol. II, part I, pp. 489–514.
7. John Foster Dulles quoted in John Lewis Gaddis, *Strategies of Containment: A Critical Appraisal of Postwar American National Security Policy* (New York: Oxford University Press, 1982), p. 137.
8. Dulles Speech to Council on Foreign Relations, January 12, 1954. Department of State Bulletin, no. 30 (January 25, 1954), p. 108.
9. "Analysis of Dulles Speech January 13, 1954 (sic) on Security Policy," by Paul Nitze for Robert Bowie, Policy Planning Staff, Fred Kaplan Papers, National Security Archive.
10. Stevenson quoted in John Bartlow Martin, *Adlai Stevenson and the World: The Life of Adlai E. Stevenson* (Garden City, N.Y.: Doubleday, 1977), p. 97, and *The Papers of Adlai Stevenson,* vol. IV, ed. Walter Johnson (New York: 1974), p. 327.
11. "Joint Civilian Orientation Conference Number Sixteen: Estimate of the International Political Situation," March 26, 1953, p. 15, Paul Nitze Folder, Papers of the Policy Planning Staff, R.G. 59, Diplomatic Branch, National Archives.
12. Paul H. Nitze, "The Word and the Woods," Address at Johns Hopkins University, February 22, 1984. Reprinted in *Wall Street Journal,* March 23, 1984.
13. Paul H. Nitze, "Atoms, Strategy and Policy," *Foreign Affairs,* January 1956.
14. *The Papers of Adlai Stevenson,* vol. VI, p. 118.
15. *The Papers of Adlai Stevenson,* vol. IV, p. 441.
16. *New York Times,* August 15, 1956.
17. Paul H. Nitze, *United States Foreign Policy, 1945–1955,* (New York: Foreign Policy Association, 1956), p. 39.
18. *New York Times,* August 15, 1956.
19. Nitze, *From Hiroshima to Glasnost,* p. 148.
20. John Kenneth Galbraith, *A Life in Our Times* (Boston: Houghton Mifflin, 1981), p. 358.

21. Harriman quoted in Galbraith, p. 359.

22. Ibid., p. 359.

23. *Robert F. Kennedy: In His Own Words*, ed. Edwin O. Guthman and Jeffrey Shulman (Boston: Houghton Mifflin, 1988), p. 36.

24. Paul H. Nitze, "Outlook for the Continuing Conflict," Address Before the U.S. Air War College, Maxwell Air Force Base. Quoted in U.S. Congress, Senate Armed Services Committee, Hearings: Nominations of Paul H. Nitze and William P. Bundy (Washington, D.C.: GPO, 1963), p. 34.

25. Council on Foreign Relations, Study Group on Nuclear Weapons and Foreign Policy, First Meeting, November 8, 1954.

26. Strobe Talbott, *The Master of the Game: Paul Nitze and the Nuclear Peace* (New York: Knopf, 1988), p. 65.

27. Paul H. Nitze, "Limited Wars or Massive Retaliation," *The Reporter*, vol. 17, no. 3 (September 5, 1957), p. 40.

28. Nitze to Acheson, September 4, 1957, Acheson Papers, Sterling Library, Yale University.

29. Fred Kaplan, Wizards of Armageddon (New York: Simon & Schuster, 1983), p. 124.

30. Public Statements of Deputy Secretary of Defense Paul H. Nitze, 1967 (Washington, D.C.: Department of Defense, n.d.), p. 306.

31. U.S. Congress, Senate Foreign Relations Committee, Subcommittee on Disarmament, Hearings: Control and Reduction of Armaments (Washington, D.C.: GPO, 1957), p. 1050.

32. U.S. Congress, 94/2, Joint Committee on Defense Production, Report: Deterrence and Survival in the Nuclear Age (The "Gaither Report" of 1957). (Washington, D.C.: GPO, 1976).

33. "Memorandum of Discussion, Wednesday, November 6, 1957, at the State Department," and Nitze to Dulles, November 16, 1957, John Foster Dulles Correspondence, National Security Archive.

34. Eisenhower quoted in Gaddis, p. 186.

35. Nitze to Dulles, November 16, 1957.

36. Dwight D. Eisenhower, *The White House Years: Waging Peace, 1956–1960* (Garden City, N.Y.: Doubleday, 1963), p. 223.

37. Morton Halperin, "The Gaither Committee and the Policy Process," *World Politics*, no. 13 (1961).

38. Kaplan, pp. 298–299.

39. U.S. Congress, 95/1, Senate Foreign Relations Committee. Subcommittee on Arms Control, Oceans and International Environment, Hearings: United States/Soviet Options (Washington, D.C.: GPO, 1977), p. 107.

40. U.S. Congress, 95/1, Joint Committee on Defense Production. Hearings: Civil Defense (Washington, D.C.: GPO, 1977), p. 71.

41. William M. Arkin, Thomas Cochran, and Milton M. Hoening, *U.S. Nuclear Forces and Capabilities*, vol. I of *Nuclear Weapons Databook* (Cambridge, Mass.: Ballinger, 1984), p. 15; Tom Gervasi, *Arsenal of Democracy:*

America's War Machine (New York: Grove Press, 1984), p. 90.

42. Eisenhower, p. 390.

43. George F. Kennan, *Russia, the Atom and the West* (New York: Harper and Brothers, 1957), pp. 51–53.

CHAPTER 7

Interviews: McGeorge Bundy, William Bundy, Clark Clifford, Roswell Gilpatric, Townsend Hoopes, Charles Burton Marshall, Lawrence McQuade, Timothy Stanley, Thomas Wolfe

1. U.S. Congress, 86/1, Executive Sessions of the Senate Foreign Relations Committee (Historical Series) (Washington, D.C.: GPO, 1982), pp. 569–592.

2. Arthur M. Schlesinger, Jr., *A Thousand Days: John F. Kennedy in the White House* (Boston: Houghton Mifflin, 1965), p. 508.

3. Ibid., p. 554.

4. Ibid., p. 104.

5. Ibid., p. 553.

6. Walter Isaacson and Evan Thomas, *The Wisemen: Six Friends and the World They Made* (New York: Simon & Schuster, 1986), p. 590.

7. Schlesinger, p. 310.

8. Ibid., p. 311.

9. Ibid., p. 60.

10. *New York Times,* August 31, 1960.

11. "Report of Senator Kennedy's Committee on National Security," attached to Paul H. Nitze Oral History Interview, John F. Kennedy Library (hereafter JFKL).

12. Schlesinger, p. 127.

13. Isaacson and Thomas, p. 592.

14. Dean Acheson Oral History Interview, JFKL, p. 7.

15. Isaacson and Thomas, p. 592.

16. Schlesinger, p. 126.

17. Herbert S. Parmet, *JFK: The Presidency of John F. Kennedy* (New York: Penguin Books, 1983), p. 73.

18. *Robert F. Kennedy: In His Own Words,* ed. Edwin O. Guthman and Jeffrey Shulman (Boston: Houghton-Mifflin, 1988), p. 37.

19. Schlesinger, pp. 129–130.

20. Nitze, *From Hiroshima to Glasnost,* p. 179.

21. Memorandum by Adam Yarmolinksy, Yarmolinsky Papers, Box 42, Talent Hunt, 1960–1962, JFKL.

22. *New York Times,* December 25, 1960.

23. John F. Kennedy, Inaugural Address, January 20, 1961, Department of State Bulletin, February 6, 1961, pp. 175–176.

24.   Richard Barnet, *The Roots of War: The Men and Institutions Behind U.S. Foreign Policy* (New York: Simon & Schuster, 1972), p. 119.

25.   Lee Iacocca, *Iacocca: An Autobiography* (New York: Bantam Books, 1984), p. 42.

26.   Phil Goulding, *Confirm or Deny: Informing the People on National Security* (New York: Harper & Row, 1970), p. 171.

27.   Iacocca, p. 42.

28.   Gregg Herken, *Counsels of War* (New York: Knopf, 1985), p. 46.

29.   McNamara interviewed in James G. Blight and David A. Welch, *On the Brink: Americans and Soviets Reexamine the Cuban Missile Crisis* (New York: Farrar, Straus & Giroux, 1989).

30.   For details on the history and working of ISA, see Thomas J. Bigley, "The Office of International Security Affairs," *The United States Naval Institute Proceedings*, 92 (1966), and Geoffrey Piller, "DoD's Office of International Security Affairs: The Brief Ascendancy of an Advisory System," *Political Science Quarterly*, vol. 98, no. 1 (Spring 1983), pp. 59–78.

31.   Piller, pp. 63–64.

32.   Bigley, p. 66.

33.   Williston Palmer Oral History Interview, JFKL, p. 8.

34.   Lucius Heinz Oral History Interview, JFKL, p. 12.

35.   Thomas Wolfe Oral History Interview, JFKL, p. 16.

36.   Lucius Heinz Oral History Interview, JFKL.

37.   "How Kennedy Plans to Run Defense and Foreign Policy," *U.S. News and World Report*, January 9, 1961, p. 38.

38.   Paul H. Nitze Oral History Interview, JFKL.

39.   Paul H. Nitze, *Political Aspects of a National Strategy* (Washington, D.C.: Washington Center of Foreign Policy Research, 1960), p. 8.

40.   Schlesinger, p. 300.

41.   Ibid., p. 435.

42.   Morton Halperin, *Bureaucratic Politics and Foreign Policy* (Washington, D.C.: Brookings Institution, 1974), p. 229.

43.   Nitze quoted in Piller, pp. 63, 65.

44.   Thomas Wolfe Oral History Interview, JFKL, p. 17.

45.   U. Alexis Johnson, *The Right Hand of Power: The Memoirs of an American Diplomat* (Englewood Cliffs, N.J.: Prentice-Hall, 1984), p. 318.

46.   Ibid.

CHAPTER 8

Interviews: DeWitt Armstrong, John Marshall Lee, Lawrence McQuade, Henry Rowen, Timothy Stanley, Thomas Wolfe

1.   Arthur M. Schlesinger, Jr., *A Thousand Days: John F. Kennedy in the White House* (Boston: Houghton Mifflin, 1965), p. 289.

2. Ralph Martin, *A Hero for Our Time* (New York: Macmillan, 1983), p. 333.

3. Peter Wyden, *Bay of Pigs: The Untold Story* (New York: Simon & Schuster, 1979), p. 124.

4. U.S. Congress, 87/1, Senate Foreign Relations Committee, Hearings: Executive Sessions of the Senate Foreign Relations Committee (Historical Series) (Washington, D.C., GPO, 1984), p. 65.

5. Ibid.

6. Schlesinger, p. 248.

7. Ibid., p. 252.

8. Nitze, *From Hiroshima to Glasnost,* p. 182.

9. Wyden, pp. 148–149.

10. Martin, p. 331.

11. Schlesinger, pp. 358–374.

12. Paul H. Nitze, "The World Situation: Strengthening of the United States Armed Forces," Address to the Annual Meeting of the Association of the United States Army, Washington, D.C., September 7, 1961. Reprinted in *New York Times,* September 8, 1961.

13. Ibid.

14. Schlesinger, p. 382. While still classified, Acheson's paper is summarized at great length in Honoré M. Catudel, *Kennedy and the Berlin Wall Crisis: A Case Study in U.S. Decision Making* (Berlin: Berlin Verlag, 1980).

15. Paul Nitze Oral History Interview, U.S. Air Force Oral History Collection, p. 289.

16. Paul H. Nitze, Address to the Cleveland Council on World Affairs Luncheon, March 2, 1963, Department of Defense Folder, Box 273, National Security Files, JFKL.

17. Walter Isaacson and Evan Thomas, *The Wisemen: Six Friends and the World They Made* (New York: Simon & Schuster, 1986), p. 610.

18. Address by the President to the Nation, July 25, 1961, Department of State Bulletin, July 31, 1961, pp. 175–178.

19. Catudel, p. 210.

20. Isaacson and Thomas, p. 614.

21. Schelling paper quoted in Catudel, p. 224.

22. Herken, p. 159.

23. Memorandum from Nitze to Bundy, August 22, 1961, Germany-Berlin Folder. General 8/23/61–8/24/61, Box 82, National Security Files, JFKL.

24. Nitze, "The World Situation."

25. Paul H. Nitze, "Security and Strategy in the Nuclear Age," Remarks Before the U.S. Army War College, August 31, 1962, Public Statements of Paul H. Nitze, Assistant Secretary of Defense for International Security Affairs, 1961–1963 (Washington, D.C.: Department of Defense, n.d.), p. 228. Rowen's plan is described in Fred Kaplan, *Wizards of Armageddon* (New

York: Simon & Schuster, 1983), pp. 294–301.

26.   Paul H. Nitze, Remarks to the Radio-TV Directors Association, Washington, D.C., September 27, 1961. Excertps reprinted in U.S. Congress, 88/1, Senate Armed Services Committee, Hearings: Nominations of Paul H. Nitze and William P. Bundy, November 7 and 14, 1963 (Washington, D.C.: GPO, 1963), pp. 42–43.

27.   Paul Nitze to John Ausland, April 24, 1984.

28.   Khrushchev quoted in Schlesinger, p. 400.

CHAPTER 9

Interviews: DeWitt Armstrong, George Ball, McGeorge Bundy, Roswell Gilpatric, Alexis Johnson, Lawrence McQuade, Henry Rowen, Timothy Stanley, Thomas Wolfe, Elmo Zumwalt

1.   The most extensive interview of Paul Nitze on the Cuban missile crisis can be found in James G. Blight and David A. Welch, *On the Brink: Americans and Soviets Reexamine the Cuban Missile Crisis* (New York: Farrar, Straus & Giroux, 1989). The book also contains interviews with several other key members of Excomm. Unless otherwise noted, all of the Nitze quotations are taken from this interview. For the general history of the crisis, this chapter relies largely on the "History of the Cuban Crisis," Box 49, National Security Files, JFKL. This 250-page analysis of the Cuban missile crisis was ordered done by President Kennedy immediately after the crisis to assess how the administration performed. It was written by Frank Sieverts, special assistant to Assistant Secretary of State Robert Manning. It was declassified with deletions in June 1985. This chapter also relies heavily on McGeorge Bundy's daily official minutes of the Excomm meetings, Executive Committee Summary Record of Action, Executive Committee Meetings Folders, Box 316, National Security Files, JFKL.

2.   Walter Isaacson and Evan Thomas, *The Wisemen: Six Friends and the World They Made* (New York: Simon & Schuster, 1986), p. 619.

3.   U.S. Congress, 96/2, Senate Intelligence Committee, Hearings: National Intelligence Act (Washington, D.C.: GPO), p. 368.

4.   Paul H. Nitze, "Political Responsibility and the Use of Power: The Problem of Limited Options," Remarks to the Seminar on Religion and International Responsibility, March 14, 1962, Public Statements of Paul H. Nitze (Washington, D.C.: GPO), p. 395.

5.   Isaacson and Thomas, p. 620.

6.   Robert McNamara interview in Blight and Welch.

7.   Nitze, *From Hiroshima to Glasnost,* p. 219.

8.   Douglas Dillon interview in Blight and Welch.

9.   Robert F. Kennedy, *Thirteen Days: A Memoir of the Cuban Missile Crisis* (New York: Norton, 1969), p. 15.

10. Nitze, "Political Responsibility and the Use of Power," p. 398.

11. Robert McNamara interview in Blight and Welch.

12. "History of the Cuban Crisis," p. 53.

13. Dean Rusk interview in Blight and Welch.

14. Thomas Wolfe Oral History Interview, JFKL, p. 20.

15. Alexis Johnson, *The Right Hand of Power: The Memoirs of an American Diplomat* (Englewood Cliffs, N.J.: Prentice-Hall, 1984), pp. 383–388.

16. Isaacson and Thomas, p. 625.

17. Nitze's note was never handed to the President. It was reprinted in Elie Abel, *The Missile Crisis* (New York: Bantam, 1966), p. 104.

18. Dean Rusk interview in Blight and Welch.

19. Address by the President to the Nation, October 22, 1963. Department of State Bulletin, November 12, 1962, pp. 715–720.

20. "CIA Memo: Current Intelligence Memorandum: Readiness Status of Soviet Missiles in Cuba, October 23, 1962," Executive Committee Meetings Folder, 10/23/62–10/25/62, Box 315, National Security Files, JFKL.

21. "Executive Committee Minutes, October 23, 1962, 10:00 A.M.," Executive Committee Meetings Folder, 10/23/62–10/25/62, Box 315, National Security Files, JFKL.

22. Paul Nitze interview in Blight and Welch.

23. Kennedy, p. 46.

24. Ibid., p. 48.

25. Ibid., p. 49.

26. "Executive Committee Summary Record of Action, October 26, 1962, 10:00 A.M.," Executive Committee Meetings Folder, 10/26/62–10/28/62, Box 316, National Security Files, JFKL.

27. Ibid.

28. Ibid.

29. Ibid.

30. "CIA Memo: The Crisis, Information as of 0600, 26 October, 1962." Executive Committee Meetings Folder, 10/26/62–10/28/62, Box 316, National Security Files, JFKL.

31. Kennedy, p. 67.

32. "History of the Cuban Crisis," p. 69.

33. Dean Rusk interview in Blight and Welch.

34. Abel, p. 191.

35. Robert McNamara interview in Blight and Welch.

36. "Executive Committee Summary Record of Action, October 27, 1962, 10:00 A.M.," Executive Committee Meetings Folder, 10/26/62–10/28/62, Box 316, National Security Files, JFKL.

37. "Executive Committee Summary Record of Action, October 27, 1962, 4:00 P.M.," Executive Committee Meetings Folder, 10/26/62–10/28/62, Box 316, National Security Files, JFKL.

38. Ibid., p. 76.

39. "Executive Committee Summary Record of Action, October 27, 1962, 9:00 P.M.," Executive Committee Meetings Folder, 10/26/62–10/28/62, Box 316, National Security Files, JFKL.

40. "Executive Committee Summary Record of Action, October 28, 1962, 11:00 A.M.," Executive Committee Meetings Folder, 10/26/62–10/28/62, Box 316, National Security Files, JFKL.

41. "Executive Committee Summary Record of Action, November 9, 1962," Executive Committee Meetings Folder, 11/62, Box 316, National Security Files, JFKL.

CHAPTER 10

1. U.S. Congress, 95/1, Senate Foreign Relations Committee, Hearings: Consideration of Mr. Paul C. Warnke to be Director of the U.S. Arms Control and Disarmament Agency and Ambassador (Washington, D.C.: GPO, 1977), p. 138.

2. Paul H. Nitze, *Political Aspects of a National Strategy* (Washington, D.C.: Washington Center of Foreign Policy Research, 1960), p. 243.

3. Ibid.

4. Paul H. Nitze, "Security and Strategy in the Nuclear Age," Remarks Before the U.S. Army War College, August 31, 1962. Public Statements of Paul H. Nitze, Assistant Secretary of Defense for International Security Affairs, 1961–1963 (Washington, D.C.: Department of Defense, n.d.), p. 232.

5. McNamara quoted in Fred Kaplan, *Wizards of Armaggedon* (New York: Simon & Schuster, 1983), p. 284.

6. Tom Gervasi, *Arsenal of Democracy: America's War Machine* (New York: Grove Press, 1984), p. 92.

7. *Time*, September 27, 1982, p. 85.

8. Maxwell Taylor, "The Legitimate Claims of National Security," *Foreign Affairs*, April 1974, p. 582.

9. Paul H. Nitze, Address at U.S. Air War College, May 14, 1963. Public Statements of Paul H. Nitze, Assistant Secretary of Defense for International Security Affairs, 1961–1963 (Washington, D.C.: Department of Defense, n.d.), p. 427.

10. Kaplan, pp. 315–327.

11. Nitze, *Political Aspects of a National Strategy*, p. 246.

12. U.S. Congress, 87/2 Senate Armed Services Committee, Preparedness Investigating Subcommittee, Hearings: Arms Control and Disarmament (Washington, D.C.: GPO, 1963), p. 15.

13. Ibid., p. 13.

14. Glenn Seaborg, *Kennedy, Khrushchev and the Test Ban* (Berkeley: University of California Press, 1981), p. 45. As director of the Atomic Energy Commission during the early 1960s, Seaborg was a key player in the test ban

deliberations. His book is based largely on his extensive diaries and is the chief source for this chapter.

15. Arthur M. Schlesinger, Jr., *A Thousand Days: John F. Kennedy in the White House* (Boston: Houghton Mifflin, 1965), pp. 368–370.

16. Seaborg, p. 104.

17. Ibid., p. 122.

18. U.S. Congress, Consideration of Mr. Paul C. Warnke, pp. 152, 177.

19. Nitze, *From Hiroshima to Glasnost*, p. 190.

20. Seaborg, p. 165.

21. Schlesinger, p. 897.

22. Ibid., p. 912.

23. Ibid., p. 913.

24. Ibid.

25. U.S. Congress, 88/1, Senate Armed Services Committee, Hearings: Nominations of Paul H. Nitze and William P. Bundy, November 7 and 14, 1963 (Washington, D.C.: GPO, 1963), p. 49.

26. Raymond Garthoff, *Intelligence Assessment and Policymaking: A Decision Point in the Kennedy Administration* (Washington, D.C.: Brookings Institution, 1984). Garthoff describes the drafting of an interagency report in mid 1962 which was commissioned by the president to assess the implications of a revised intelligence estimate of Soviet military capabilities. (The report is reprinted in his monograph.) Alexis Johnson chaired the group and Nitze headed a working group that reviewed American defense programs. In the section on defense policy, the report stated: "The broad conclusion to be drawn for our defense policy is to reaffirm the importance of shaping our military posture so as to provide credible military options over a wide spectrum of contingencies." Despite the substantially reduced estimate of future Soviet missile deployments, the report advocated no cutback in planned American strategic programs.

27. Nitze describes the drafting of the SFSDA paper in the interview in the U.S. Air Force Oral History Collection, p. 430. The SFSDA paper is also discussed in Elmo Zumwalt, Jr., *On Watch: A Memoir* (New York: Quadrangle, 1976), p. 31.

28. Memorandum to the Secretary of Defense by Paul H. Nitze, Considerations Involved in a Separable First Stage Disarmament Agreement, October 1, 1963. Copy provided to author.

CHAPTER 11

Interviews: John Rhinelander, Elmo Zumwalt

1. *New York Herald Tribune,* May 22, 1963.

2. *Robert F. Kennedy: In His Own Words,* ed. Edwin O. Guthman and Jeffrey Shulman (Boston: Houghton Mifflin, 1988), p. 27.

3. The Waggoner newsletter can be found in Central File, Name File, Nitze Folder, Box 2039, JFKL.

4. Jerry Wulf to John F. Kennedy, Central File, Name File, Nitze Folder, Box 2039, JFKL.

5. See Joseph J. Lombardo, Commander in Chief, Veterans of Foreign Wars of the United States, to Honorable Harry Flood Byrd, reprinted in U.S. Congress, 88/1, Senate Armed Services Committee, Hearings: Nominations of Paul H. Nitze and William P. Bundy (Washington, D.C.: GPO, 1963), p. 64.

6. Paul H. Nitze, Director, Foreign Service Educational Foundation, "Power and Policy Problems in the Defense of the West," Speech, reprinted in U.S. Congress, 88/1, Senate Armed Services Committee, Hearings: Nominations of Paul H. Nitze and William P. Bundy (Washington, D.C.: GPO, 1963), pp. 53–58.

7. Elmo Zumwalt, Jr., *On Watch: A Memoir* (New York: Quadrangle, 1976), pp. 32–33.

8. U.S. Congress, Nominations of Paul H. Nitze and William P. Bundy, pp. 1–87.

9. Editorial, *Navy* magazine, August 1967, p. 7.

10. Paul H. Nitze, Personal Letter to Flag and General Officers, November 29, 1963. Provided by U.S. Naval Institute, Operational Archives Branch.

11. Paul H. Nitze, "The Future of the Navy," Address, January 9, 1964. Reprinted in Vital Speeches of the Day, February 1, 1964.

12. U.S. Congress, 88/2, House Appropriations Committee. Hearings: Defense Appropriations for Fiscal Year 1965 (Washington, D.C.: GPO, 1964), p. 674.

13. Ibid., p. 649.

14. U.S. Congress, 89/1, House Committee on Armed Services. Hearings: Defense Appropriations for Fiscal Year 1966 (Washington, D.C.: GPO, 1965), p. 664.

15. Ibid., p. 658.

16. Nitze, "The Future of the Navy."

17. U.S. Congress, Defense Appropriations for Fiscal Year 1966, p. 662.

18. Paul H. Nitze, Address at the Forty-sixth Annual Dinner of the American Ordnance Association, Chicago, Ill., May 19, 1964. Public Statements of Paul H. Nitze, Secretary of the Navy, vol. 1 (Washington, D.C.: Department of Defense, n.d.), p. 156.

19. Paolo E. Coletta, ed., American Secretaries of the Navy, vol. II, 1913–1972 (Annapolis, Md.: Naval Institute Press, 1980), pp. 941–961. Unless otherwise noted, most of the material on Nitze's tenure at the Navy is taken from this study. For further material on this period of Nitze's career, see U.S. Congress, 89/2, House Committee on Appropriations. Hearings: Department of Defense Appropriations for FY. 1967, part I (Washington, D.C.: GPO, 1966), and U.S. Congress, 90/1, House Committee on Appro-

priations, Hearings: Department of Defense Appropriations for 1968, part 2 (Washington, D.C.: GPO, 1967).

20. Coletta, p. 945.

21. Paul H. Nitze, Address, Navy War College Review, September 1964, pp. 1–9.

22. U.S. Congress, Defense Appropriations for Fiscal Year 1965, p. 643.

23. U.S. Congress, Defense Appropriations for Fiscal Year 1966, p. 661.

24. U.S. Congress, Defense Appropriations for Fiscal Year, 1965, p. 654.

25. U.S. Congress, Defense Appropriations for Fiscal Year 1966, p. 660.

26. Editorial, *Navy* magazine, June 1966, p. 7.

27. Thomas B. Allen and Norman Polmar, *Rickover* (New York: Simon & Schuster, 1982), pp. 17–18.

28. Ibid.

29. "Memorandum for Flag Officers and General Officers of the Navy and Marine Corps," June 30, 1967. Provided by U.S. Naval Institute, Operational Archives Branch.

CHAPTER 12

Interviews: William Bundy, Clark Clifford, Roswell Gilpatric, James B. Wilson, Elmo Zumwalt

1. William P. Bundy Oral History Interview, Lyndon B. Johnson Library, p. 10.

2. Paul H. Nitze, *United States Foreign Policy, 1945–1955* (New York: Foreign Policy Association, 1956), p. 37.

3. Elmo Zumwalt, Jr., *On Watch: A Memoir* (New York: Quadrangle, 1976), p. 35.

4. William C. Westmoreland, *A Soldier Reports* (Garden City, N.Y.: Doubleday, 1976), p. 194. Some two decades later Westmoreland mounted a libel suit against CBS News when the network ran a documentary accusing the general of inflating enemy troop strength. Westmoreland won the case.

5. Elie Abel and Marvin Kalb, *Roots of Involvement: The United States in Asia, 1784–1971* (New York: Norton, 1971), pp. 89–90.

6. U.S. Congress, 89/2, Senate Committee on Armed Services. Hearings: Military Procurement Authorizations for Fiscal Year 1967 (Washington, D.C.: GPO, 1966), p. 636.

7. Dialogue between Nitze and Johnson is from McGeorge Bundy's minutes of the meeting quoted in Larry Berman, *Planning a Tragedy: The Americanization of the War in Vietnam* (New York: W. W. Norton, 1982), p. 113.

8. Paul H. Nitze, Talking Paper for ICA Conference, March 16, 1961, Public Statements of Paul H. Nitze, Assistant Secretary of Defense for Inter-

national Security Affairs, 1961–1963 (Washington, D.C.: Department of Defense, n.d.), p. 54.

9. Paul H. Nitze, Remarks at Foreign Service Institute Seminar, Washington, D.C., June 7, 1966, Public Statements of Paul H. Nitze, Secretary of the Navy (Washington, D.C.: Department of Defense, n.d.), p. 735.

10. Paolo E. Coletta, ed., *American Secretaries of the Navy*, vol. II, *1913–1972* (Annapolis, Md.: Naval Institute Press, 1980), p. 955.

11. U.S. Congress, 90/1, House Committee on Armed Services. Hearings: Defense Department Vietnam Conflict Military Operations, Fiscal Year 1968 (Washington, D.C.: GPO, 1967), p. 833.

12. Paul H. Nitze, Remarks at Navy Day, Long Beach, Calif., October 27, 1965. Public Statements of Paul H. Nitze, Secretary of the Navy (Washington, D.C.: Department of Defense, n.d.), p. 592.

13. Paul H. Nitze, Remarks Before the 1968 Share in Freedom Conference, Washington, D.C., January 10, 1968, Public Statements of Paul H. Nitze, Deputy Secretary of Defense, 1967–1969 (Washington, D.C.: Department of Defense, n.d.), vol. 3, p. 833.

14. U.S. Congress, Military Procurement Authorization for Fiscal Year 1967, p. 638.

15. Paul H. Nitze, Remarks at the Change of Command Ceremony, Chief of Naval Operations, U.S. Naval Academy, Annapolis, Md., August 1, 1967, Public Statements of Paul H. Nitze, Deputy Secretary of Defense (Washington, D.C.: Department of Defense, n.d.), p. 218.

16. Nitze, Remarks at Navy Day, p. 592.

17. *Navy* magazine, August 1966, p. 3.

18. Abel and Kalb, p. 219.

19. U.S. Congress, 90/1, Senate Committee on Armed Services, Hearings: Nominations of Charles F. Baird et al. (Washington, D.C.: GPO, 1967), p. 11.

20. *The Pentagon Papers: The Defense Department History of United States Decisionmaking on Vietnam*, Senator Gravel Edition (Boston: Beacon Press, 1971), vol. IV, pp. 186–187.

21. Nitze quoted in Herbert Y. Schandler, *The Unmaking of a President: Lyndon Johnson and Vietnam* (Princeton, N.J.: Princeton University Press, 1977), pp. 125–126.

22. Ibid., p. 220.

23. An excellent inside account of the Department of Defense's handling of the Vietnam war from 1967 to 1968 can be found in Philip Goulding, *Confirm or Deny: Informing the People on National Security* (New York: Harper & Row, 1970). The events of early 1968 are also described in detail in Townsend Hoopes, *The Limits of Intervention: An Inside Account of How the Johnson Policy of Escalation Was Reversed* (New York: MacKay, 1969).

24. John B. Henry II, "February 1968," *Foreign Policy*, no. 4 (1971), p. 15.

25. U.S. Congress, 90/1, Committee on Armed Services. Hearings: Air War Against North Vietnam, part 4 (Washington, D.C.: GPO, 1967), p. 280.

26. Abel and Kalb, p. 223.

27. Westmoreland quoted in Karnow, p. 514.

28. *Wall Street Journal,* February 23, 1968.

29. Hoopes, pp. 145–146.

30. Walter Isaacson and Evan Thomas, *The Wisemen: Six Friends and the World They Made* (New York: Simon & Schuster, 1986), p. 376.

31. "Clifford/Nitze: We're Sure There Are Better Ways," *Armed Forces Management,* October 1968, p. 771.

32. Goulding, p. 311.

33. Abel and Kalb, p. 281.

34. Ibid., p. 220.

35. Nitze quoted in Henry, p. 28.

36. Goulding, p. 320.

37. Clifford quoted in Schandler, p. 129.

38. *Pentagon Papers,* vol. IV, p. 261.

39. Clark Clifford Oral History Interview, Lyndon B. Johnson Library, p. 15.

40. *Pentagon Papers,* vol. IV, p. 549.

41. Clark Clifford, "A Vietnam Reappraisal: The Personal Account of One Man's View and How It Evolved," *Foreign Affairs,* vol. 47, no. 4 (July 1969), pp. 609–610.

42. Ibid., pp. 611–112.

43. Nitze quoted in Schandler, p. 214.

44. Clifford Oral History Interview, p. 3, tape 4.

45. Paul Nitze quoted in Jerry Sanders, *Peddlers of Crisis: The Committee on the Present Danger and the Politics of Containment* (Boston: South End Press, 1983), p. 142.

46. Ibid.

47. Paul Warnke Oral History Interview, Lyndon B. Johnson Library.

CHAPTER 13

Interviews: Royal Allison, Clark Clifford, Ron Easley, Philip Farley, Dorothy Fosdick, Ray Furlong, Raymond Garthoff, Morton Halperin, T. K. Jones, John Rhinelander, Ivan Selin, Walter Slocombe, Gerard Smith, William Van Cleave, James Wade, James B. Wilson, James Woolsey

1. "Clifford/Nitze: We're Sure There Are Better Ways," *Armed Forces Management,* October 1968, p. 771.

2. U.S. Congress, 90/1, Joint Committee on Atomic Energy, Subcommittee on Military Applications. Hearings: Scope, Magnitude, and Implica-

tions of the United States Antiballistic Missile Program (Washington, D.C.: GPO, 1968), p. 29.

3. Ibid., pp. 6–8.

4. U.S. Congress, 91/1, Senate Committee on Armed Services. Hearings: Authorization for Military Procurement, Research and Development, Fiscal Year 1970 (Washington, D.C.: GPO, 1969), p. 1111.

5. *New York Times*, May 27, 1969.

6. U.S. Congress, Authorization for Military Procurement, Research and Development, Fiscal Year 1970, p. 1204.

7. Paul H. Nitze, "Between Hope and Skepticism," *Foreign Policy*, Winter 1974/75, p. 141.

8. U.S. Congress, 95/1, Senate Select Committee on Intelligence. Hearings: National Intelligence Act of 1980 (Washington, D.C.: GPO, 1980), p. 369.

9. Seymour Hersh, *The Price of Power: Kissinger in the Nixon White House* (New York: Summit Books, 1983), p. 41. See also Strobe Talbott, *The Master of the Game: Paul Nitze and the Nuclear Peace* (New York: Knopf, 1988), p. 116.

10. *New York Times*, November 18, 1969.

11. Raymond Garthoff, "Negotiating SALT," *Wilson Quarterly*, Autumn 1977, p. 78.

12. U.S. Congress, 95/1, Senate Committee on Armed Services. Hearings: Consideration of Mr. Paul C. Warnke to be Director of the Arms Control and Disarmament Agency and Ambassador (Washington, D.C.: GPO, 1977), p. 221.

13. Garthoff, p. 78.

14. Gerard Smith, *Doubletalk: The Story of SALT I* (Garden City, N.Y.: Doubleday, 1980), p. 52.

15. Smith, p. 45.

16. Garthoff, p. 82.

17. Smith, p. 166.

18. Ibid.

19. Melvin Laird quoted in Smith, p. 161.

20. Memorandum by the Secretary of Defense by Paul H. Nitze, "Considerations Involved in a Separable First Stage Disarmament Agreement, October 1, 1963, p. 14. Copy provided to author.

21. U.S. Congress, Consideration of Paul C. Warnke, p. 138.

22. Nitze, *Between Hope and Skepticism*, p. 142.

23. John Rhinelander and James P. Rubin, "Mission Accomplished: An Insider's Account of the ABM Treaty Negotiating Record," *Arms Control Today*, September 1987, p. 4.

24. Ibid., p. 11.

25. John Newhouse, *Cold Dawn: The Story of SALT* (New York: Holt, Rinehart and Winston, 1973), p. 242.

26. Smith, p. 435.
27. Ibid., p. 417.
28. Ibid.

CHAPTER 14

Interviews: Ralph Earle, Philip Farley, Alexis Johnson, T. K. Jones, Walter Slocombe, James Wade, Elmo Zumwalt

1. U. Alexis Johnson, *The Right Hand of Power* (Englewood Cliffs, N.J.: Prentice-Hall, 1984), p. 573.
2. Ibid.
3. Ibid.
4. Rowny quoted in Strobe Talbott, *Deadly Gambits* (New York: Knopf, 1984), p. 318.
5. *Wall Street Journal,* June 29, 1979.
6. U.S. Congress, 93/1, House Committee on Armed Services, Special Subcommittee on Arms Control and Disarmament (Washington, D.C.: GPO, 1974).
7. Johnson, p. 591.
8. Seymour Hersh, *The Price of Power: Kissinger in the Nixon White House* (New York: Summit Books, 1983), p. 342.
9. Ibid.
10. Johnson, p. 623.
11. Elmo Zumwalt, Jr., *On Watch: A Memoir* (New York: Quadrangle, 1976), p. 490.
12. Ibid.
13. "Peace With Freedom: A Discussion by the Committee on the Present Danger Before the Foreign Policy Association." Reprinted in Charles Tyroler, II, ed., *Alerting America: The Papers of the Committee on the Present Danger* (New York: Pergamon-Brassey, 1984), p. 27.
14. Roger P. Labrie, ed., *SALT Handbook: Key Documents and Issues, 1972–1979* (Washington, D.C.: American Enterprise Institute, 1979), p. 146. A more complete version of Nitze's comments on the SALT I treaty can be found in U.S. Congress, 92/2, Senate Armed Services Committee, Hearings: Military Implications of the Treaty on the Limitation of ABM Systems and the Interim Agreement on Limitation on Strategic Arms (Washington, D.C.: GPO, 1972), and U.S. Congress, 92/2. House Committee on Armed Services, Hearings: Military Implications of the Strategic Arms Limitation Talks Agreements (Washington D.C.: GPO, 1972).
15. Paul H. Nitze, "The Vladivostok Accord and SALT II," *Review of Politics,* vol. 37, no. 2 (April 1975).
16. Paul H. Nitze, "The Strategic Balance: Between Hope and Skepticism," *Foreign Policy,* No. 17 (Winter 1974/75), p. 146.

17. *New York Times,* February 9, 1974.
18. *New York Times,* March 22, 1974.
19. Ibid.
20. Zumwalt, p. 491.
21. Ibid.
22. Nitze's resignation statement is reprinted in his July 2 testimony, p. 70.
23. Johnson, p. 601.
24. *New York Times,* June 23, 1974.
25. Nitze Testimony.
26. Ibid.
27. Nitze, "The Vladivostok Accord and SALT II," p. 154.
28. Ibid., p. 154.

CHAPTER 15

Interviews: McGeorge Bundy, William Bundy, Ralph Earle, Max Kampleman, Charles Burton Marshall, Eugene V. Rostow, Walter Slocombe, Charles Tyroler II, Charles Walker, James Woolsey, Elmo Zumwalt.

1. Jerry Sanders, *Peddlers of Crisis: The Committee on the Present Danger and the Politics of Containment* (Boston: South End Press, 1983), p. 150.
2. Rostow quoted in Sanders, p. 152.
3. Tyroler quoted in Sanders, p. 153.
4. Kampleman quoted in Sanders, p. 153.
5. Charles Tyroler II, ed. *Alerting America: The Papers of the Committee on the Present Danger* (New York: Pergamon-Brassey, 1984), p. xvi.
6. Ibid., pp. 3–5.
7. Ibid., p. xviii.
8. Kirkpatrick quoted in Sanders, p. 162.
9. U.S. Congress, 94/2, Senate Armed Services Committee. Hearings: 1976, First Concurrent Resolutions on the Budget, part 2 (Washington, D.C.: GPO, 1976), p. 184.
10. Graham quoted in Sanders, p. 198.
11. Nitze, *From Hiroshima to Glasnost,* p. 349.
12. The most detailed account of Team B yet available is Richard Pipes, "Team B: The Myth Behind the Reality," *Commentary,* October 1986, pp. 25–40.
13. U.S. Congress, 98/2, Senate Intelligence Committee. Hearings: National Intelligence Act (Washington, D.C.: GPO, 1980), p. 366.
14. Pipes, p. 36.
15. *New York Times,* January 11, 1977.
16. Hart quoted in Pipes, p. 38.

17.　For a detailed exposition of Nitze's first strike scenario, see his articles "Deterring Our Deterrent," *Foreign Policy*, vol. 25 (Winter 1976/77), and "Assuring Strategic Stability in an Era of Detente," *Foreign Affairs*, vol. 54, (January 1976). The latter article was prepared with help from T. K. Jones and military experts at Boeing. A classic exposition of this scenario is made also by Richard Pipes, "Why the Soviet Union Thinks It Can Fight and Win a Nuclear War," *Commentary*, July 1977.

18.　Raymond Garthoff, "Mutual Deterrence and Strategic Arms Limitation in Soviet Policy," *International Security*, vol. 3 (Summer 1978), p. 139.

19.　Ibid., p. 117. Analysts of the Soviet strategic arsenal have cast doubt on the supposition that the Soviet strategic buildup of the 1970s represented a conscious bid for nuclear superiority. They point out the third generation of Soviet ICBMs—the SS-9, SS-11, and SS-13—deployed during the mid and late 1960s suffered from considerable operational difficulties. As a consequence, the Soviet missile design bureaus stepped up development of a fourth generation of ICBMs—the SS-17, SS-18, and SS-19. Each of these new missiles had been under development since 1965. Their deployment, it has been argued, represented the normal and necessary modernization of inadequate equipment, not a bold bid for a first strike capability. The menacing size and weight of the missiles also had an explanation. When the heavy SS-18 was begun in 1965, Soviet missile accuracy technology was still poor and an ABM race was beginning. The chief way to compensate for inaccurate missiles was large warheads: the best hope for fooling ABM radars was decoy devices that would look like warheads on a radar screen. The heavy booster on the SS-18 was designed to have enough power to carry both a large warhead and the necessary decoys. For an excellent account of Soviet strategic force modernization, see John C. Baker and Robert P. Berman, *Soviet Strategic Forces: Requirements and Responses* (Washington, D.C.: Brookings Institution, 1982).

20.　George Kennan, *The Cloud of Danger* (Boston: Little, Brown, 1977), p. 200.

21.　Fred Kaplan, *Wizards of Armaggedon* (New York: Simon & Schuster, 1983), p. 370.

22.　U.S. Congress, 95/1, Senate Foreign Relations Committee, Subcommittee on Arms Control, Oceans and International Environment, Hearings: United States/Soviet Options (Washington, D.C.: GPO, 1977), p. 83.

23.　Ibid.

24.　Matthew Bunn and Kosta Tsipis, "The Uncertainties of a Preemptive Nuclear Attack," *Scientific American*, vol. 249 (November 1983), pp. 38–47. The authors conclude that "although the current Russian ICBM force could present a severe threat to a small number of particularly valuable targets, it could not provide a planner with reasonable confidence of destroying significantly more than half of the current U.S. ICBM force." They note also that "Because of the immense destructive power of modern nuclear arsenals, any nuclear first strike would represent a gamble on a scale absolutely unprecedented in human history."

25. U.S. Congress, United States/Soviet Options, p. 66.

26. Paul Warnke, "Apes on a Treadmill," *Foreign Policy*, Fall 1975, p. 15.

27. Strobe Talbott, *The Master of the Game: Paul Nitze and the Nuclear Peace* (New York: Knopf, 1988), p. 148.

28. Ibid., pp. 148–149.

29. Zbigniew Brzezinski, *Power and Principle: Memoirs of the National Security Advisor, 1977–1981* (New York: Farrar, Straus & Giroux, 1983), p. 13.

30. Talbott, p. 149.

31. The MacNeil/Lehrer Report, "Carter Appointments," Transcript: Library no. 310 (December 3, 1976), p. 4.

32. Talbott, p. 149.

33. Nitze's letter to Sparkman is reprinted in U.S. Congress, 95/1, Senate Armed Services Committee, Hearings: Consideration of Mr. Paul C. Warnke to be Director of the U.S. Arms Control and Disarmament Agency and Ambassador (Washington, D.C.: GPO, 1977), pp. 165–66.

34. Sanders, pp. 204–206.

35. Anthony Lewis, "The Brooding Hawks," *New York Times*, February 20, 1977.

36. Acheson's son-in-law Bill Bundy defended Nitze's attack on Warnke. Acheson, he said, "would have felt appalled by Warnke's waffling on statements he had made."

37. U.S. Congress, 95/2, Senate Foreign Relations Committee, Hearings: Nomination of Mr. Paul C. Warnke (Washington, D.C.: GPO, 1977).

38. The rebuttal of Nitze's testimony is reprinted in U.S. Congress, Senate Armed Services Committee, Consideration of Mr. Paul C. Warnke, pp. 205–215.

39. Carter quoted in U.S. Congress, Senate Foreign Relations Committee, Nomination of Mr. Paul C. Warnke, p. 156.

40. Jackson quoted in Sanders, p. 209.

41. U.S. Congress, Senate Armed Services Committee, Consideration of Mr. Paul C. Warnke, pp. 163–228.

42. Ronald Brownstein and Nina Easton, *Reagan's Ruling Class* (Washington, D.C.: Presidential Accountability Group, 1982), p. 519.

43. Nitze quoted in ibid.

CHAPTER 16

Interviews: Lloyd Cutler, Ralph Earle, Ray Furlong, Richard Garwin, Alexis Johnson, Max Kampleman, Eugene V. Rostow, Walter Slocombe, Charles Walker, James Woolsey, Elmo Zumwalt

1. Paul Nitze, "What to Do About SALT," unpublished paper, p. 2.

2. Strobe Talbott, *Endgame: The Inside Story of SALT II* (New York: Harper & Row, 1979), p. 53.

3. Ibid., p. 60.

4. *New York Times*, April 3, 1977.

5. Paul H. Nitze, "Where We Stand on SALT," in Charles Tyroler, ed., *Alerting America: The Papers of the Committee on the Present Danger* (New York: Pergamon-Brassey, 1984), p. 19.

6. *New York Times*, May 15, 1977.

7. Strobe Talbott, *The Master of the Game: Paul Nitze and the Nuclear Peace* (New York: Knopf, 1988), p. 155.

8. Nitze quoted in Jerry Sanders, *Peddlers of Crisis: The Committee on the Present Danger and the Politics of Containment* (Boston: South End Press, 1983), p. 191.

9. *New York Times*, November 3, 1977.

10. Ibid.

11. Richard Garwin to Paul Nitze, August 20, 1979.

12. Roger Molander quoted in Robert Scheer, *With Enough Shovels: Reagan, Bush, and Nuclear War* (New York: Random House, Vintage Books, 1983), p. 174. Nitze had no doubt that civil defense could translate into strategic superiority. As he said in congressional testimony, "The absence of a U.S. capability to protect its own population gives the Soviet Union an asymmetrical possibility of holding the U.S. population as hostage to deter retaliation following a Soviet attack on U.S. forces. . . . if we forgo a civil defense program and the Soviets do not, you could then end up in a situation where one side has a clearly dominant position in the event of a crisis." See U.S. Congress, 95/1, Joint Defense Production Committee. Hearings: Civil Defense (Washington, D.C.: GPO, 1977), p. 59.

More than most of Nitze's pessimistic arguments of the 1970s, this one was dismissed by mainstream experts who pointed out that Soviet civil defense measures would take several days to implement and thus would increase the alert status of U.S. strategic forces. As the Congressional Budget Office stated, "Since efforts by the Soviet Union to harden industrial machinery and evacuate population would likely be detected by the U.S. in enough time to place U.S. nuclear forces on an alert status, the number of U.S. weapons that should survive a Soviet first strike would likely be sufficient to achieve at least as much industrial and military destruction as would occur with no civil defense program." Specifically, the CBO estimated that "some 1,200 additional Poseidon warheads and 1,300 more bomber warheads could be expected to survive a Soviet attack, in addition to the 5,000 weapons surviving under peacetime alert conditions." Congressional Budget Office, Retaliatory Issues (Washington, D.C.: GPO, 1978), pp. 21, 23.

13. U.S. Congress, 95/1, House Committee on Armed Services. Hear-

ings: Review of the State of U S Strategic Forces (Washington, D.C.: GPO, 1977), p. 361.

14.   Jimmy Carter, *Keeping Faith* (New York: Bantam, 1982), p. 251.

15.   U.S. Congress, 96/1, Senate Foreign Relations Committee. Report: The SALT II Treaty (Washington, D.C.: GPO, 1979), p. 156.

16.   U.S. Congress, 96/1, Senate Foreign Relations Committee. Hearings: The SALT II Treaty, part I (Washington, D.C.: GPO, 1979), p. 483.

17.   Talbott, *Master of the Game*, p. 156.

18.   *Wall Street Journal,* June 29, 1979.

19.   Harvard College, *Secretary's Fiftieth Annual Report, Class of 1928* (Cambridge, Mass.: 1978), p. 484.

20.   Carter, p. 262.

21.   Carter quoted in Kenneth Adelman, "Rafshooing the Armageddon: The Selling of SALT," *Policy Review* (Summer 1979), p. 88.

22.   The SALT II Treaty, p. 143. Rebutting Nitze's frequent claim that after a Soviet first strike Soviet missiles would be safe in their silos, Brown adds: "In the aftermath of an attack on U.S. ICBM's, the remaining Soviet ICBM's would not be in sanctuary. Our air-launched cruise missiles and surviving bombers would have the accuracy, the numbers, and the ability to penetrate defenses sufficiently well to allow the United States very significantly to reduce the residual Soviet ICBM force."

23.   Ibid., p. 162.

24.   Zbigniew Brzezinski, *Power and Principle: Memoirs of the National Security Advisor, 1977–1981* (New York: Farrar, Straus, & Giroux, 1983), p. 344.

25.   *Wall Street Journal,* June 29, 1979.

26.   Warnke Nomination, p. 150.

27.   Paul H. Nitze, "Is SALT II a Fair Deal for the United States?" in Charles Tyroler, ed., *Alerting America: The Papers of the Committee on the Present Danger* (New York: Pergamon-Brassey, 1984), p. 162.

28.   U.S. Congress, Hearings: The SALT II Treaty, p. 523.

29.   Ibid., p. 506.

30.   U.S. Congress, 96/2, Senate Armed Services Committee, Hearings: Military Implications of the Treaty on the Limitations of Strategic Offensive Arms and Protocol Thereto (Washington, D.C.: GPO, 1979), p. 923.

31.   Ibid.

32.   Paul H. Nitze, "Strategy in the Decade of the 1980s," *Foreign Affairs,* vol. 59 (Fall 1980), p. 90.

CHAPTER 17

Interviews: Kenneth Adelman, William Burns, Eugene V. Rostow, Timothy Stanley, Charles Tyroler II, John Woodworth

1. Charles Tyroler quoted in Robert Scheer, *With Enough Shovels: Reagan, Bush, and Nuclear War* (New York: Random House, Vintage Books, 1983), p. 41.

2. Reagan quoted in Scheer, p. 41.

3. Paul H. Nitze, "Strategy in the Decade of the 1980s," *Foreign Affairs,* vol. 59 (Fall 1980), p. 90.

4. Strobe Talbott, *The Master of the Game: Paul Nitze and the Nuclear Peace* (New York: Knopf, 1988), p. 167.

5. Alexander Haig, *Caveat: Reagan, Realism and Foreign Policy* (New York: 1983), p. 231.

6. Strobe Talbott, *Deadly Gambits* (New York: Knopf, 1984), p. 54.

7. Haig, p. 231.

8. Talbott, *Deadly Gambits,* p. 82. Talbott's inside account of the INF and START negotiations during Reagan's first term is the most authoritative account of these events available. It is based on extensive, mostly off-the-record interviews with the officials involved in the negotiations.

9. *Washington Post,* December 5, 1981.

10. U.S. Congress, 97/2, House Committee on Appropriations. Subcommittee on the Department of Defense. Hearings: Department of Defense Appropriations for Fiscal Year 1983 (Washington, D.C.: GPO, 1982), p. 841.

11. Talbott, *Deadly Gambits,* pp. 101–102.

12. See Richard Burt, "The Relevance of Arms Control in the 1980s," *Daedalus,* Winter 1981.

13. Talbot, p. 104.

14. U.S. Congress, 97/2, Senate Foreign Relations Committee. Hearings: The Nomination of Paul H. Nitze (Washington, D.C.: GPO, 1981), p. 6.

15. U.S. Congress, Department of Defense Appropriations for Fiscal Year 1983, p. 821.

16. Nitze gives a detailed account of the first round of the talks in ibid., pp. 812–821.

17. Talbott, *Deadly Gambits,* p. 92.

18. Ibid., p. 119.

19. Rostow recounted his participation in the walk in the woods scheme in a press conference on January 16, 1983, reported in *New York Times,* January 17, 1983.

20. Talbott, *Deadly Gambits,* pp. 127–130.

21. *New York Times,* January 17, 1983.

22. Talbott, *Deadly Gambits,* pp. 135–136.

23. Ibid., pp. 141–144.

24. Ibid., p. 164.

25. *New York Times,* January 16, 1983.

26. Ibid.

27. *New York Times,* January 17, 1983.

28. *New York Times,* January 19, 1983.
29. Ibid.
30. *New York Times,* January 22, 1983.
31. *New York Times,* January 25, 1983.
32. *New York Times,* January 26, 1983.
33. *New York Times,* February 2, 1983.
34. *New York Times,* February 23, 1983.
35. *New York Times,* March 31, 1983.
36. *New York Times,* November 24, 1983.

CHAPTER 18

Interviews: Kenneth Adelman, William Burns, Max Kampleman, Edward Rowny, John Rhinelander, Gerard Smith

1. Strobe Talbott, *The Master of the Game: Paul Nitze and the Nuclear Peace* (New York: Knopf, 1988), p. 210.
2. *New York Times,* December 5, 1984.
3. *New York Times,* December 8, 1984.
4. Shultz quoted in Talbott, p. 9.
5. Ronald Reagan, "Defense Spending and Defensive Technology," Speech, March 23, 1983. Reprinted in Office of Technology Assessment, Strategic Defenses (Princeton, N.J.: Princeton University Press, 1986), pp. 297–298.
6. George A. Keyworth, II, "The President's Strategic Defense Initiative," Speech to the SDIO University Review Forum, March 29, 1985.
7. Paul H. Nitze, "On the Road to a More Stable Peace," Speech to the Philadelphia World Affairs Council, February 20, 1985.
8. William Arkin, "The New Mix of Defense and Deterrence," *Bulletin of Atomic Scientists,* June/July, 1986, pp. 4–6.
9. Nitze, "On the Road to a More Stable Peace," p. 3.
10. See, for example, Sidney Drell and Panofsky Wolfgang, "The Case Against Strategic Defenses: Technical and Strategic Realities," *Issues in Science and Technology,* Fall 1984, and Richard Garwin, "Countermeasures: Defeating Space-Based Defenses," *Arms Control Today,* May 1985.
11. Daniel Graham quoted in Talbott, p. 219.
12. *New York Times,* December 9, 1984.
13. *New York Times,* March 12, 1985.
14. *New York Times,* June 25, 1985.
15. *New York Times,* October 5, 1985.
16. *New York Times,* October 18, 1988.
17. Paul H. Nitze, "Living with the Soviets," *Foreign Affairs,* Winter, 1984/85, p. 371.
18. Paul H. Nitze, "SDI and the ABM Treaty," Speech Before the Johns

Hopkins School of Advanced International Studies, Washington, D.C., May 30, 1985, p. 2.

19. Ibid.

20. *New York Times,* May 31, 1985.

21. *Washington Post,* October 22, 1985.

22. U.S. Congress, 99/1, House Committee on Foreign Affairs, Subcommittee on Arms Control, International Security and Science. Hearings: ABM Treaty Interpretation Dispute (Washington, D.C.: 1986), p. 342.

23. Talbott, pp. 245–246.

24. *Washington Post,* October 27, 1985.

25. *New York Times,* October 19, 1985.

26. *New York Times,* October 23, 1985.

27. *Washington Post,* October 22, 1985.

28. Ibid.

29. Rhinelander quoted in Talbott, p. 248. Rhinelander and James P. Rubin later wrote an authoritative rebuttal, based on the ABM Treaty negotiating record, of the administration's new interpretation: "Mission Accomplished: An Insider's Account of the ABM Negotiating Record," *Arms Control Today,* vol. 17 (September 1987), pp. 3–14. Raymond Garthoff, the SALT I delegation's executive secretary, mounts a more elaborate attack on the new interpretation in his book *Policy vs. Law: The Reinterpretation of the ABM Treaty* (Washington, D.C.: Brookings Institution, 1987).

30. U.S. Congress, ABM Treaty Interpretation Dispute, p. 40.

31. *New York Times,* November 11, 1985.

32. *New York Times,* November 17, 1985.

33. *New York Times,* January 7, 1986.

34. U.S. Congress, Hearings: Nomination of Paul H. Nitze, p. 7.

35. *New York Times,* April 16, 1986.

36. Leslie Gelb, "The Mind of the President," *New York Times Magazine,* October 6, 1985, p. 21.

CHAPTER 19

Interviews: Kenneth Adelman, William Burns, Max Kampleman, Edward Rowny

1. *New York Times,* August 13, 1986.

2. Strobe Talbott, *The Master of the Game: Paul Nitze and the Nuclear Peace* (New York: Knopf, 1988), pp. 316–317. In addition to Talbott, this account draws on Nitze's recollection of Reykjavik in his memoirs, *From Hiroshima to Glasnost: At the Center of Decision* (New York: Weidenfeld & Nicolson, 1989), pp. 424–434, and Kenneth Adelman's more detailed account in *The Great Universal Embrace: Arms Summitry—A Skeptic's Account* (New York: Simon & Schuster, 1989), pp. 19–88.

3. Adelman, p. 49.

4. Ibid.

5. U.S. Congress, 99/1, House Committee on Armed Services, Defense Policy Panel. Hearings: Process and Implications of the Iceland Summit (Washington, D.C.: GPO, 1987), p. 9.

6. Talbott, p. 319.

7. Talbott, pp. 319–320.

8. U.S. Congress, Process and Implications of the Iceland Summit, p. 261.

9. Nitze, p. 149.

10. U.S. Congress, Process and Implications of the Iceland Summit, p. 3.

11. Talbott, p. 323.

12. Ibid., p. 325.

13. U.S. Congress, Process and Implications of the Iceland Summit, p. 15.

14. Talbott, p. 325.

15. U.S. Congress, Process and Implications of the Iceland Summit, p. 226.

16. Nitze, p. 433.

17. U.S. Congress, Process and Implications of the Iceland Summit, p. 323.

18. Paul H. Nitze, "Arms Control After Reykjavik," *Washington Post,* November 9, 1986.

19. Talbott, p. 333.

20. Ibid., p. 348.

21. The text of the joint U.S.-Soviet statement is reprinted in *New York Times,* December 11, 1987.

22. Nitze on "MacNeil/Lehrer Report," December 11, 1987.

23. *New York Times,* February 23, 1988.

24. The exchange between Glynn and Nitze is printed in *Commentary,* May 1988, pp. 2–6.

25. Paul H. Nitze, "The Case for Cutting Strategic Arms," *Washington Post,* June 21, 1988.

EPILOGUE

1. Bush quoted in Robert Scheer, *With Enough Shovels: Reagan, Bush, and Nuclear War* (New York: Random House, Vintage Books, 1983), p. 261.

2. Shultz quoted in Strobe Talbott, *The Master of the Game: Paul Nitze and the Nuclear Peace* (New York: Knopf, 1988), p. 313.

3. *New York Times,* April 2, 1989.

4. *New York Times,* May 3, 1989.

5. See, for example, Paul H. Nitze, "What Bush Should Do to Solve the

NATO Flap," *Washington Post,* May 14, 1989.

6. George F. Kennan, "Just Another Great Power," *New York Times,* April 9, 1989.

7. JCS report quoted in *New Yorker,* August 14, 1989, p. 24.

8. Leonard Mosley, *Dulles* (New York: Dial Press, 1978), p. 335.

INDEX

ABMs (anti-ballistic missiles), 321, 449, 451
Congress and, 326–28, 342
SALT and, 336, 341–48
ABM Treaty, 336, 337, 342–49, 350, 354, 391
broad vs. narrow interpretation of, 461–65, 482–84
future technology provisions of, 344–46
initialing and signing of, 347–48
radars and, 343–44, 347
SDI and, 459–65, 482–84, 486–87
ten-year extension of, 473, 477
A-bomb. *See* Atomic bomb
ACDA. *See* Arms Control and Disarmament Agency
Acheson, Dean, 52, 60–61, 63, 67, 186, 241, 316, 391, 496
ABM systems and, 327

assistant secretaries and, 139–40
Berlin crisis of 1961 and, 218
in Democratic Advisory Council (DAC), 162–64
H-bomb development and, 74–75, 79, 83, 85–87, 89, 90, 143–45
Hiss case and, 93–94
Louis Johnson and, 102
Kennan and, 70–71
Kennedy and, 190–91
Korean war and, 126, 129, 131, 133
1950 review of national security policy and, 111–15
Nitze's relationship with, 95–96, 141, 154–55
NSC 114 and, 136, 137
on NSC 68, 111–12, 120–21
Policy Planning Staff and, 138–40
Webb and, 139
Acid rain, 500–501

Adelman, Kenneth, 443, 447–48, 457, 460, 468–69, 473, 475, 484
Adenauer, Konrad, 150, 231
Africa, 1959 trip by Nitze to, 181–83
Aircraft carriers, 277, 278, 279
Akhromeyev, Marshal Sergei, 472–76, 479, 486
Alexander, Henry C., 38, 45, 48
Algeria, 186
Allen, Richard V., 375, 418
Allison, John, 130
Allison, Royal, 324, 329, 332, 334, 339, 340, 343, 348, 351, 463
Alsop, Joseph, 154, 205
Alsop, Stewart, 154
Anderson, Robert, 191
Andropov, Yuri, 443
Anti-ballistic missiles. *See* ABMs
Anticommunism, in the U.S., 93
Antisubmarine warfare (ASW), 278, 281–83
Arbatov, Georgi, 472
Arms control (or reduction), 141–42, 189, 320–21. *See also specific weapons systems, negotiations, agreements, and other topics*
    commitment of Nitze to, 322
    goal of, Nitze on, 266, 267
    intelligence report on Soviet objectives, 330
    under Kennedy, 199, 256–69
        Nitze's views, 256–57
        nuclear proliferation, 257–58
        test ban. *See* Nuclear test ban
    1951 plan proposed by Nitze, 142–43
    1951 views of Nitze on, 142–45
    Nitze's paper on bilateral (1963), 266–68
    NSC 112 proposals, 142–43
    survivability of strategic arsenals and, 267, 268
Arms Control and Disarmament Agency (ACDA), 266, 340, 344, 448, 468–69, 483
    intermediate nuclear forces (INF) talks and, 436–37
    "massacre" at, 351
    Rostow appointed to head, 418

Warnke's nomination as head of, 389–95
Arms race
    Kennan on, 176–77
    1951 views of Nitze on, 144, 145
Armstrong, DeWitt, 219–20, 222–24, 227–28, 243–44
Arneson, Gordon, 63, 77, 80, 81, 86, 145
Aspen Skiing Corporation, 372–73
Assured destruction, doctrine of, 255. *See also* Mutual assured destruction (MAD)
Atomic bomb (A-bomb)
    H-bomb development and, 78–79
    Hiroshima and Nagasaki, bombing of, 48–51
    1952 U.S. stockpile, 78
    Soviet Union's development of, 62–67, 71–72
Atomic Energy Commission (AEC), 72, 83
    General Advisory Committee of (GAC), 73, 79
Atomic weapons policy. *See* Nuclear weapons policy
Austin, Adm. Robert, 426

Bacon, Whipple & Company, 17
Baker, Howard, 480, 481
Baker, James, 494, 498–99
Balance of terror, 160
Balance of trade, post–World War II, 54–55
Ball, George, 37, 38, 40, 43, 44, 48, 235, 247, 255
Barnard, Chester, 108
Barnes, Tracy, 210
Barnet, Richard, 195–96
Barret, Edward, on NSC 68, 119–20
Battle, Lucius, 57, 58, 70, 93
Baxter, James Phinney, 167, 169
Bay of Pigs invasion (1961), 209–14
Berlin
    Cuban missile crisis (1962) and, 243
    1961 crisis over, 215–31, 251
        abatement of, 231
        brinkmanship, policy of, 220, 224–25

first-strike option, 254
game-type analysis, 224
interdepartmental group formed,
    217
International Security Affairs
    Office (ISA) and, 219–20,
    222–24, 226, 230
military contingency plans and
    scenarios, 219, 226–30, 278
nuclear weapons use, possibility of,
    218–21, 223–30
Soviet goals, 217–18
summit meeting and, 215–16
Washington Ambassadors' Group,
    221–22
sealing of border (Berlin Wall), 222,
    223
Bilateral arms control (or reduction).
    See Arms control (or reduction)
Bissell, Richard, 121, 212
Black Tom munitions terminal,
    explosion at, 11, 34–35
Board of Economic Warfare (BEW),
    36–37
Bohlen, Charles ("Chip"), 15, 56,
    109–11, 151, 158, 215, 233, 495
    1950 review of national security
        policy and, 110–11
    NSC 114 and, 135, 138
    on NSC 68, 119
    on Soviet intentions, 135–38
Bombers, 176
    Gaither report on, 170
    Soviet first-strike scenario and, 382
B-1 bomber, 382
Bowie, Robert, 150, 156, 188
Bowles, Chester, 161
Bradley, Gen. Omar, 84, 142
    1950 review of national security
        policy and, 113, 114
Brandt, Willy, 231
Brezhnev, Leonid, 346–47, 368, 403
Brinkmanship, Berlin crisis of 1961
    and, 220, 224–25
Brodie, Bernardie, 159
Brown, Harold, 300, 310–11, 332, 334,
    389, 397–99, 402
    SALT II and, 406–8
Bruce, David, 187, 191

Brzezinksi, Zbigniew, 388, 398, 399,
    407
Bulganin, Nikolai, 157, 158
Bullitt, William, 24–25, 69
Bundy, McGeorge, 193, 202–3, 214,
    224, 233, 240, 242, 247, 255,
    391, 496–97
Bundy, William (Bill), 95, 205, 246,
    289
    at International Security Affairs
        Office (ISA), 199, 200, 202,
        203, 210, 213, 221
    Vietnam War and, 302
Bureau of the Budget, NSC 68 and,
    121–22
Burke, Adm. Arleigh, 214
Burns, Maj. Gen. James, 103, 104,
    112–15
Burns, Maj. Gen. William, 429, 455,
    485
Burt, Richard, 421, 422, 425–27, 435,
    438
Bush, George
    as president, 493–94, 497–98
    review of Soviet intentions ordered
        by (1976), 378, 380
Bush, Vannevar, 72
Butler, George, 102
Butler, Paul, 162
Byrd, Harry, 272, 274

Cambodia, 302
Canada, 54, 148
Carlucci, Frank, 480, 485
Carter, Jimmy (Carter administration),
    387–89, 415
    Nitze not asked to join, 388–89
    Nitze's support for candidacy of, 387
    SALT II and, 396–411. See also
        SALT II treaty
        March 1977 proposal, 397–99
    seminar on defense policy held by
        (1976), 387
Castro, Fidel, 212
Causein Manor, 153–54, 325, 371
Center for Foreign Policy Research,
    188
Central Intelligence Agency (CIA),
    133, 139, 233, 243, 246, 336

Central Intelligence Agency *(cont.)*
  Bay of Pigs invasion (1961) and,
    210–13
  1950 report on Soviet intentions, 98,
    110
  1976 review of Soviet threat, 378–81
Chase, John, 15
Chemical and biological weapons, 142
Cheney, Richard, 494
China, 92, 94, 300, 326
  Korean war and, 131, 134
Chu Lai (South Vietnam), 292, 297
Churchill, Winston, 98
Civil defense, 67, 72, 135, 166–67, 170
  Soviet, 381, 401–2
Clark, William, 432, 435
Clayton, Will, 36, 37, 53, 55–56, 58,
    60
Clifford, Clark, 58, 190, 392, 495
  MIRV testing and, 324
  as secretary of defense, 306–10,
    312–16, 319
Clyne, Norm, 432, 433, 447, 462, 484
Coalition for a Democratic Majority,
    371, 390, 397–98
Cold War, 105
  end of, 502
  Kennan on, 92
  Nitze as personifying American
    approach to, 6–7
  psychology of, in NSC 68, 118
Committee of Principals, 258, 261
Committee on National Security Policy,
    187–89
Committee on the Present Danger,
    374–77, 390, 409
  March 1977 SALT proposal and,
    397–99
  Reagan and, 416
Committee to Maintain a Prudent
    Defense Policy, 327–28
"Common Sense and the Common
    Danger" (Committee on the
    Present Danger), 376
Communism, 29–30
  Kennan on, 93
Conant, James, 107, 188, 375
Connally, John B., 374

"Considerations Involved in a Separable
    First Stage Disarmament
    Agreement" (Nitze), 266–68
Container Corporation of America,
    16–17
Containment, policy of, 69, 70, 92–93,
    100
Conventional wars, limited, 170–71
Conventional weapons, 1950 review of
    national security policy and, 106
Council on Foreign Relations, 165,
    166, 182
Counterforce targeting (no-cities)
    strategy, 254, 255
Crowe, Adm. William, 481
Crowley, Leo, 37
Cruise missiles, 428, 429, 435
  sea-launched (SLCMs), 490–91
Cuba, Bay of Pigs invasion of (1961),
    209–14
Cuban missile crisis (1962), 232–50,
    271
  air strike option, 236–38, 240, 248,
    249
  Berlin and, 243–44
  blockade (quarantine), 238, 240–42,
    244–45, 248
  Executive Committee (Excomm)
    and, 235, 238–40, 243
  invasion of Cuba contemplated, 245,
    248
  Kennedy's speech of October 22,
    241, 242
  Khrushchev and, 235, 236, 243, 249
    letter of October 26, 246
    missiles from Turkey, 246–48
  nuclear superiority and, 254–55
  Turkey, removal of U.S. missiles
    from, 246–48
Cutler, Lloyd, 403, 406–8
Czechoslovakia, 118, 182
  1968 invasion of, 324

Da Nang (South Vietnam), U.S. air
    base, 292, 297
Darmstadt, 46
Davies, John Paton, 64, 97, 129
Davis, Lynn, 387
Davis, T. J., 128

Deadly Gambits (Talbott), 456
Dean, Arthur, 259–61
Dearborn, Hamilton, 121, 122
Deaver, Michael, 416
Decline of the West, The (Spengler), 29
Decter, Midge, 374
Defense Department, U.S. *See also* Defense spending; International Security Affairs (ISA), Office of
H-bomb development and, 81–82
Kissinger and, 362
1950 review of national security policy and, 100–102. *See also* State-Defense Policy Review Group
1953 offer of assistant secretary of defense for ISA job to Nitze, 150–52
Nitze as deputy secretary, 287, 288, 301–16
management of department turned over to Nitze, 319–20, 323
offer and withdrawal of offer of post, 192–93
resignation threat, 313, 314
Defense policy. *See* National security policy; Nuclear weapons policy
Defense spending, 157
Carter administration and, 397, 398
Committee on the Present Danger on, 376
Gaither report on, 171
1950 review of national security policy and, 101, 104
NSC 68 and, 118, 120–23, 134–35
Soviet, in 1970s, 370–71
Defensive technologies. *See* ABMs (anti-ballistic missiles); Strategic defense initiative (SDI; Star Wars)
Democratic Advisory Council (DAC), 162–64
Democratic party, 164, 192, 374
Detente, 373, 383
Deterrence, 167
Gaither report on, 170
Kennan on, 177
minimum, 252–53, 255

"Deterrence and Survival in the Nuclear Age" (Gaither report) (Nitze), 169–75
Dicks, Norman, 463
Diem, Ngo Dinh, 288–89
Dillon, Clarence, 17–23, 27, 29, 33, 325
Dillon, Dorothy ("Dot"), 25
Dillon, Douglas, 236, 316
Dillon, Read and Company, 17, 21–22, 26, 27, 29, 31, 34, 36
Disarmament. *See also* Arms control (or reduction); Nuclear disarmament
1959 Geneva conference on, 256
Truman and, 141–42
Dobrynin, Anatoly, 242, 357
D'Olier, Franklin, 38–40, 45, 48, 49
Donovan, Robert, 84–85
Draper, Bill, 36
Drell, Sidney, 384–85
Dresden, 43
Dulles, Allen, 214
Dulles, John Foster, 152, 155–58, 391
alternative defense strategy proposed by, 156–57
Gaither report and, 172–73
Korean war and, 130
Nitze and, 146–50
nuclear weapons policy, 173
Stalin's death and, 149
Truman's defense policy attacked by (1954), 156–57

Earle, Ralph, 330–31, 355, 356, 364, 386, 389, 390, 395, 408, 411, 463
SALT II treaty and, 403–5
Early warning radar system, 170
Easley, Ron, 328, 329, 337, 339, 343
East Berlin. *See also* Berlin
sealing of the border (Berlin Wall), 222, 223
East Germany. *See also* Berlin
1961 summit meeting and, 215–16
refugee problem, 222, 223
Economic aid to Europe, after World War II, 54–57. *See also* Marshall Plan

Eighteen Nation Disarmament
    Conference (1962), 261
Eisenhower, Dwight D. (Eisenhower
    administration), 5, 146, 154–58,
    167, 176, 503
  Gaither report and, 172–74
  at 1955 summit meeting, 157–58
  nuclear weapons policy, 156, 158–59
  Stalin's death and, 149
Ellsworth, Robert, 330
Elsey, George, 309
Emergency Coalition Against Unilateral
    Disarmament, 392–93
Europe
  economic aid to, after World War
    II, 54–57. See also Marshall
    Plan
  post–World War II economic crisis
    in, 53–56
Evans, Rowland, 270
Executive Committee (Excomm), 235,
    238–40, 243, 245, 246, 249

Falin, Valentin, 472
Farley, Philip, 40–42, 324, 336, 339,
    340, 351
Federal Civilian Defense
    Administration, 166
Fermi, Enrico, 73
First-strike capability (surprise attack),
    Soviet, 488, 489
  Berlin crisis of 1961 and, 226
  Nitze's scenario of, 381–82
First-use policy, 86. See also
    No-first-use policy
Fisher, Adrian, 80, 81, 267
Flexible response policy, 229, 253–54,
    255. See also Limited nuclear war
Ford, Gerald, 368
Ford Foundation, 167
Foreign Affairs (magazine), 377
  Nitze's 1956 article in, 159
Foreign aid. See Economic aid to
    Europe; Military aid
Foreign Economic Administration
    (FEA), 37
Foreign Policy (magazine), 377
Foreign Service Educational
    Foundation, 154

Forrestal, James, 23, 31–36, 52, 69,
    102, 335
Fosdick, Dorothy, 70–71, 95, 96, 129,
    139, 328
Foster, William, 167, 174, 188, 204
Fowler, Henry, 375, 398
France, 54, 148, 182, 186, 428, 433
  Vietnam and, 290, 292
Freedom, Soviet fear of, 109–10
"Free-fire zones," in Vietnam War,
    296–97
Fuchs, Klaus, 94
Fulbright, J. William, 190, 212, 213,
    312
Furlong, Ray, 320, 322, 323, 328, 410

Gaffney, Frank, 438, 455, 467, 483,
    491
Gaither, Rowan, 166
Gaither committee (Security Resources
    Panel), 166–73
  report of, 169–75, 377
Galbraith, John Kenneth, 40, 42, 44,
    64, 162–64
"Game Warden" program, 296–97
Garthoff, Raymond, 267, 332, 334,
    335, 339, 344, 345, 383
Garwin, Richard, 401, 410
Gelb, Leslie, 303, 367
Geneva Conference on the
    Discontinuance of Nuclear
    Weapons Tests, 258–61
Germany, 15. See also West Germany
  in 1920s, 17–21
  in 1930s, 27–29
  after World War II, 2
  in World War II, 31, 34, 38–46
Gilpatric, Roswell, 174, 185, 187,
    193–94, 196–97, 204, 235, 255,
    270, 289
Glynn, Patrick, 469, 488–89
Goldwater, Barry, 5, 272, 362–63
Gorbachev, Mikhail, 457–58, 470–74,
    482, 486, 487, 502, 503
  elimination of all nuclear weapons
    proposed by, 465–66
  Reykjavik summit (1986) and,
    471–74, 477–78
  summit meeting of 1985, 464, 465

Goulding, Phil, 196, 307, 309
Graham, Daniel, 330, 378, 392, 455
Graham, Thomas, 462
Great Britain, 66, 133, 148, 428, 433
Greece, 56
Grey, Robert, 438
Gromyko, Andrei, 348, 450
Ground-launched cruise missiles
        (GLCMs), 424
Guinea, 182–83

Haig, Alexander, 418–19, 425, 442
Halaby, Najeeb, 102–4, 113
Haldeman, Bob, 351
Halle, Louis, 99
Halperin, David, 357
Halperin, Morton, 320–24
Hamburg, World War II bombing of,
        41–42
Hammarskjöld, Dag, 54
Hammond, Paul, 104
Harriman, Averell, 265, 388, 392
Hart, Gary, 380
Harvard University, Nitze at, 15–16,
        29–30
Heinz, Adm. Luther, 199–201
Henderson, Deirdre, 185
Herres, Robert, 481
Herter, Christian, 154
Herter, Mary Caroline, 325
Hickerson, John, 86, 128
High Frontier, 455
Hilken, Paul, 34, 35
Hilsman, Roger, 232
Hiroshima, 1–3
   atomic bombing of, 48, 51
Hiss, Alger, 36, 93–94
Hitch, Charles, 275
Hitler, Adolf, 27–29, 34, 44–45
Ho Chi Minh, 289
Hoffman, Paul, 58
Holmes, Oliver Wendell, Jr., 116
Hoopes, Townsend, 101, 107
Hoover, Herbert, 25, 26
Horse Blanket, 228
Hughes, Emmett, 149
Humphrey, Hubert, 185
Hungary, 164
Hydrogen bomb (H-bomb), 176
   development of, 73–90
      Acheson and, 74–75, 79, 83,
         85–87, 89, 90, 143–45
      Defense Department and, 81–82
      feasibility issue, 75–77
      Kennan and, 74, 85–89
      Lilienthal and, 79, 80, 82–84,
         89–90
      memorandum written by Nitze,
         82–83
      national security policy and, 89–91
      Nitze and, 75–84, 86–90, 141,
         143–45
      by Soviet Union, 76–79
      Teller and, 76–77
      testing, 1951 debate on, 143–46
      Truman and, 80, 84–85, 90–91,
         143
      Z Committee (Special Committee
         of the National Security
         Council), 80–84, 143, 145

ICBMs (intercontinental ballistic
        missiles), 170, 175, 321, 355,
        381
   50 percent cuts in, 472, 474, 477
   Interim Agreement and, 359
   mobile, 402–3, 489
   SALT and, 338–39
   SALT II and, 467
   subceilings on, 470–71, 475–76,
        479–80, 486
Ikle, Fred, 351, 418, 435
Incendiary bombing, in World War II,
        43, 46, 48
Institute for Defense Analysis, 188
Intercontinental ballistic missiles. See
        ICBMs
Interim Agreement, 347, 349, 351,
        353, 355, 359–60, 367
   SALT II and, 367
Intermediate nuclear forces (INF) talks,
        423, 485–86
   climate of, 428
   collapse of, 443–45
   conventional cruise missiles, 424–25,
        427
   draft treaties presented by both sides,
        427–28

Intermediate nuclear forces (INF) talks
    (cont.)
  duration of treaty, 425
  informal accord between Nitze and
      Kvitsinsky (walk-in-the-woods
      formula), 434–37, 439–40, 443
  news blackout, 423
  Nitze as chief negotiator in, 418–45
    back-channel negotiations, 431–36,
      439
    Haig's opposition to choice of
      Nitze, 418–19
    opening phase of, 422–23
    proposal made by Nitze in
      informal talks with Kvitsinsky,
      433–36
    relationship with the delegation,
      429
    reprimand for back-channel talks,
      436
  Perle's view of, 421–22
  Reykjavik summit (1986) and, 477,
      478
  zero-option proposal, 421–22, 424,
      430–31, 433, 434, 437, 473
    calls for flexibility on, 441–42
Intermediate-range missiles, 170. See
    also Intermediate nuclear forces
    (INF) talks
International Security Affairs (ISA),
    Office of, 233, 238
  arms control and, 262
  Berlin crisis of 1961 and, 219–20,
      222–24, 226, 230
  Cuban missile crisis (1962) and,
      239
  history of, 198
  under Kennedy, 198–99
    foreign policy role, 206–7
  Nitze as head of, 193–94, 198–202
    access to the president, 201–2
    Schlesinger's offer of post to Nitze
      (1974), 362
    staff, relationship with, 199–202
    work style and pace, 200–201
Iran-contra scandal, 480
Irwin, John, 200
Italy, 54, 148

Jackson, Bruce, 481
Jackson, Henry, 187, 274–75, 286, 328,
    351–53, 360, 393
  SALT II and, 396–97
Jackson amendment, 351
Japan, in World War II, 46–51
Johns Hopkins University
  Paul H. Nitze School of Advanced
      International Studies, 500
  School for Advanced International
      Studies (SAIS) at, 154
Johnson, Alexis, 207, 240–41, 351,
    351–56, 358, 365, 409–10
Johnson, Louis, 80, 84, 125
  1950 review of national security
      policy and, 101–4, 112–15
Johnson, Lyndon B. (Johnson
    administration), 286
  arms control (or reduction) and,
      320–21
  Vietnam War and, 294–95, 303–4,
      306, 308, 310, 312–13, 316
Joint Chiefs of Staff (JCS), 206, 248,
    502–3
  intermediate nuclear forces (INF)
      talks and, 425–26
  MIRV ban and, 336–37
  MIRV testing and, 324
  Nitze's relationship with, 138
  nuclear test ban and, 265
  SALT II and, 353, 354, 356
Joint Target Group (JTG), 46–48
Jones, Gen. David, 426
Jones, T. K., 340, 353, 401, 402

Kampleman, Max, 374, 375, 453, 462,
    484
Karaberis, Rear Adm., 281
Karpov, Victor, 479, 480
Katzenbach, Nicholas, 302, 303
Kaufmann, William, 159, 226, 253
Kaysen, Carl, 224
Kennan, George F., 51, 56, 60, 62,
    67–72, 120, 161, 383, 495–96,
    502
  Acheson and, 70–71
  on arms race, 176–77
  background of, 68–69
  containment policy and, 69, 70, 92

departure from Policy Planning Staff,
71, 87
on deterrence, 177
H-bomb development and, 74,
79–80, 85–89
Korean war and, 128–30
Long Telegram, 69
Nitze compared to, 96–97
nuclear weapons policy and, 67, 71,
85–87
reviews of national security policy
and (1949–50), 100
Kennedy, John F. (Kennedy
administration)
appointments made by, 189–92
arms control (or reduction) and, 199,
256–69
Nitze's views, 256–57
nuclear proliferation, 257–58
test ban. See Nuclear test ban
Bay of Pigs invasion (1961) and,
210–14
Berlin crisis of 1961 and. See Berlin,
1961 crisis over
choice of jobs offered to Nitze, 192
Committee on National Security
Policy formed by, 187–89
Cuban missile crisis (1962) and. See
also Cuban missile crisis
blockade (quarantine), 238, 241–42
removal of U.S. missiles from
Turkey, 246–48
speech of October 22, 241, 242
Cuban policy, 214
International Security Affairs Office
(ISA) under, 198–99
national security policy, 194–95
Nitze as advisor to, 185, 187, 191
Nitze compared to, 184–85
Nitze offered deputy secretary of
defense post, 270–71
Nitze's relationship with, 203
nuclear weapons policy, 253–56
personal characteristics of, 184–85
as presidential candidate, 185–88
Soviet Union, policy toward, 204
at summit meeting (1961), 214–16
third world and, 194, 198–99

third world policy, 183–84
Vietnam War and, 289
Kennedy, Joseph P., 25
Kennedy, Robert, 164, 191, 214, 241,
249, 271
Keyserling, Leon, 122
Keyworth, George, II, 451
Khrushchev, Nikita, 204
arms control (or reduction) and,
260–61
Berlin crisis of 1961 and, 215–19, 231
Cuban missile crisis (1962) and, 235,
236, 243, 249
letter of October 26, 246
missiles from Turkey, 246–48
1955 summit meeting and, 157, 158
1961 summit meeting and, 214–16
Kirkland, Lane, 375, 376
Kirkpatrick, Jeane, 377
Kissinger, Henry, 224, 371, 373–74
on limited nuclear war, 165–66
Nitze's campaign against, 358–59
Nuclear Weapons and Foreign
Policy, 165–66
SALT and, 330, 340–41, 348, 349
leaks of classified information,
357–58
SALT II and, 356–57, 358–59, 365
Schlesinger and, 361–62
Team B report and, 378, 380
Knocke, Otto, 15
Knowland, William, 151
Kohl, Helmut, 501
Kohler, Foy, 214, 217, 222, 378
Korean war, 124–36, 290
atomic weapons and, 131–32
China and, 131–34
counterinvasion in, 131
Policy Planning Staff paper on,
129–31
Soviet Union and, 125–27, 130–31,
132–34, 136
Korth, Fred, 271
Kosygin, Aleksei, 321
Kvitsinksy, Yoli, 423, 432–35

Laird, Melvin, 328, 337, 392
Landon, Maj. Gen. Truman ("Ted"),
103–5, 112, 113

Lansdale, Gen. Edward, 210, 213
Laos, 214, 302
Latin America, 35–37
Lawrence, Ernest, 77–78, 109
Lay, James, 99, 113, 120, 121
LeBaron, Robert, 76, 103, 104
Lee, John Marshall ("Squidge"), 224, 226–29
Lehman, John, 351
LeMay, Gen. Curtis, 48, 230
Lemnitzer, Lyman, 259
Lilienthal, David, 75–76
  H-bomb development and, 79, 80, 82–84, 89–90
Limited nuclear war. *See also* Flexible response policy
Limited Test Ban Treaty (1963), 265
Lincoln, Col. George A., 188
Linhard, Col. Robert, 477
Long Telegram, 69
Loper, Gen. Herbert, 132
Lovett, Robert, 39, 43, 58, 59, 108–9, 167, 188, 190
  H-bomb testing and, 145–46
Luftwaffe, 43–44

MacArthur, Gen. Douglas, 49
  Korean war and, 126–28, 131–34
McCarthy, Joseph, 94, 162
McCarthyism, 162
McCloy, John, 167, 316
McCone, John, 238, 245
McDonald, Adm. David L., 280
McFarlane, Robert, 435, 446, 455
  ABM Treaty and, 462, 464
McGovern, George, 390, 398
McIntyre, Thomas, 393–94
McMahon, Brien, 84
McNamara, Robert S., 228, 271, 273, 275, 287, 321, 392, 496
  ABM systems and, 326
  appointed secretary of defense, 192
  arms control (or reduction) and, 261
    test ban debate, 263–65
  Berlin crisis of 1961 and, 216, 220
  Cuban missile crisis (1962) and, 233, 235, 238, 243–45, 247–49, 255
  International Security Affairs (ISA) job offered to Nitze, 193–94
  navy and, 277
  Nitze's relationship with, 197–98, 203–4
  nuclear weapons policy and, 253–54
  personal characteristics of, 195–98
  as secretary of defense
    first month, 196–97
    foreign policy role, 206
    as primary defense advisor and policy maker, 202–3
    Soviet Union as viewed by, 204
    Vietnam War and, 289–91, 293–94, 299–301, 306, 307
    negotiating plan of 1967, 303–4
McNaughton, John, 262, 301, 320
McQuade, Larry, 199–200, 202, 231
MAD. *See* Mutual assured destruction
Mao Tse-tung, 94
Marcy, Carl, 400
Marine Corps, U.S., in Vietnam War, 292, 297
Marshall, Burt, 139, 148
Marshall, Charles Burton, 128–30, 138–39, 184, 374, 375
Marshall, George C., 36, 46, 56–57, 60, 69
Marshall Plan, 57–60
Martell, Vice Adm., 281–82
Maryland, Nitze's farm in. *See* Causein Manor
Massive retaliation, policy of, 156, 159, 169, 172, 173
  abandonment of, 253–54
Matthews, H. Freeman, 140
Meese, Edwin, 416, 425
Mekong delta, 296
Menshikov, Mikhail, 223
Merton, Robert, 30
Military aid, 200
Military spending. *See* Defense spending
Military Thought (magazine), 383
Minimum deterrence, 252–53, 255
Minnow, Newt, 163
Minuteman missiles, 338
  SALT II and, 406–7, 410
MIRVs (multiple independently targetable reentry vehicles), 321
  banning of, 336–38

SALT II and, 355–56, 368, 397
  testing of, 323–24, 337
Missile gap, 226
  Gaither report and, 175
Missiles. *See also specific types of missiles*
  throw-weight of, 338–41
Mitchell, John, 358
Molander, Roger, 402
Monday Package, 464
Moral issues, in NSC 68, 115–17
Morgenthau, Hans, 140
Moses, Robert, 30–31
MPS (multiple point system), 403–4
Muccio, John J., 124, 125
Multiple independently targetable
  reentry vehicles. *See* MIRVs
Multiple point system (MPS), 403–4
Mutual assured destruction (MAD)
  Nitze as secretary of, 271–87
  Nitze's criticism of, 381–82
  SDI and, 451
  Soviet policy toward, 378, 379, 383, 384
Mutual Defense Assistance Program, 198
MX missiles, 361, 402–3

Nagasaki, 2–3
  atomic bombing of, 48, 51
Nash, Frank, 150, 151
National Liberation Front (NLF)
  (Vietcong), 289, 296, 299–301, 303
National Security Council (NSC), 83
  1949 reviews of national security policy, 99
  1950 review of national security policy and, 100
  Nitze offered job as national security advisor, 192, 193
National Security Council
  memorandum 68 (NSC 68), 115–23, 128, 142, 145, 155, 156, 177, 256, 377, 386, 490, 502–4
    Acheson on, 111–12, 120–21
    Ad Hoc Committee on, 121, 122
    Berlin crisis of 1961 and, 217
    on defense spending, 118, 120–23, 134–35
    economic issues in, 117–18, 120–23
    fight over implementation of, 121–22
    final draft of (NSC 68/3), 134–37
    freedom vs. slavery approach of, 106, 109–10
    mid-1950s events and, 164–65
    moral righteousness of, 115–17
    psychology of the Cold War in, 118–19
    Reagan and, 417
    responses of government officials to, 119–20
    rollback theme of, 107, 109
    on Soviet Union's fundamental objectives, 109–11, 116, 136, 137
    Truman and, 120, 121, 134, 135
    Vietnam War and, 294
National Security Council
  memorandum 109 (NSC 109), 229
National Security Council
  memorandum 112 (NSC 112), 142–43
National Security Council
  memorandum 114 (NSC 114), 135–37
National Security Council
  memorandum 162/2 (NSC 162/2), 155
National Security Council
  memorandum 242, 384
National Security Decision Directive 153, 453
National security policy. *See also* Nuclear weapons policy
  Dulles's, 156–57
  H-bomb development and, 89–91
  under Kennedy, 194–95
  1950 review of, 90–91, 99–123. *See also* National Security Council memorandum 68 (NSC 68); State-Defense Policy Review Group
    Bohlen and, 110–11
    Landon and, 103, 105, 112, 113
    Louis Johnson and, 101–4, 112–15
    Warnke on, 385–86

National Security Resources Board, 122
NATO (North Atlantic Treaty
    Organization), 133, 135, 169,
    171, 172, 214, 215, 253–54,
    273, 418, 438–39
  Berlin crisis of 1961 and, 219, 220,
    222, 228, 230
  debate over overall defense doctrine,
    229
  intermediate nuclear forces (INF)
    talks and, 429
  naval warfare and, 283
  SALT and, 330
Navy, Department of the
  independence of, 276
  Nitze as secretary of
    antisubmarine warfare (ASW),
      278, 281–83
    confirmation hearings and vote,
      272–75
    inaugural speech, 277–78
    intellectual and managerial
      challenge, 276–77
    limited-war strategy, 282–83
    management and personnel issues,
      283–85
    McDonald and, 280
    politically usable seapower, concept
      of, 278–80
    Rickover and, 285–86
    Vietnam War, 290–301
    "War at Sea" project, 282–83
Navy (magazine), 275
Navy, U.S.
  limited-war capabilities of, 282–83
  in Vietnam War, 295–98
Newhouse, John, 347, 456
New York Times, 84, 154, 194, 362,
    439, 456
Nguyen Cao Ky, 292
Nigeria, 183
Nitze, Anina (mother), 12–13
Nitze, Elizabeth. See Paepcke,
    Elizabeth
Nitze, Heidi (daughter), 27
Nitze, Paul. See also specific topics
  business interests in 1970s, 371–73
  childhood and adolescence of, 12–15

consensus decision-making approach
    of, 197
  critics of, 4–5, 384–86
  as deputy secretary of defense, 287,
    288, 301–16
    management of the department
      turned over to, 319–20, 323
    offer and withdrawal of offer of
      post, 192–93
    resignation threat, 313, 314
  as director of Policy Planning Staff,
    94–97
    asked by Dulles to leave post,
      146–47
    relationship with State
      Department, 207
    staff, relationship with, 140–41
  at Harvard, 15–16, 29–30
  as head of Office of International
    Security Affairs (ISA), 198–202
    access to the president, 201–2
    Schlesinger's offer of post to Nitze
      (1974), 362
    staff, relationship with, 199–202
    work style and pace, 200–201
  health of, 491
    accident involving horse, 499–500
  as independent consultant, 371
  influence in 1951, 138–41
  marriage, 26
  memoirs of, 500
  in 1920s, 16–23
  1955 visit to Soviet Union, 158
  overview of career of, 3–7, 365
  personal characteristics and style of,
    98, 205
    Carter on, 388
    good listener, 322–23, 481
    pessimism, 99
  physical appearance, 5, 64, 205
  real estate holdings, 371–72
  resignation from Bush administration,
    499
  as secretary of the navy, 271–87
    antisubmarine warfare (ASW),
      278, 281–83
    confirmation hearings and vote,
      272–75
    inaugural speech, 277–78

intellectual and managerial
challenge, 276–77
limited-war strategy, 282–83
management and personnel issues,
283–85
McDonald and, 280
politically usable seapower, concept
of, 278–80
Rickover and, 285–86
Vietnam War, 290–301
"War at Sea" project, 282–83
as Special Advisor to the President
and Secretary of State on Arms
Control, 446–57
Adelman and, 447–48
SDI, 449–55
strategic concept, 452–53
as Special Representative for Arms
Control and Disarmament
Negotiations, 446
Nitze, Peter (son), 27
Nitze, Phyllis (wife), 36, 47, 205, 287,
307, 325, 334, 422
at Causein Manor, 153–54
death of, 485
Nitze, William (father), 12–14, 16
Nitze, William (son), 52
Nixon, Richard M., 174, 325, 358
ABM systems and, 326
Nitze's letter to (1974), 363–64
nuclear weapons policy (nuclear
strategy), 384
resignation of Nitze from SALT II
delegation and, 364–65
SALT and, 330–31, 338, 341,
344–45, 346–48
Watergate scandal and, 356, 363–64
No-first-use policy, 67, 72, 86, 105
Non-group, 302, 304
Norstad, Gen. Lauris, 220
North Vietnam, bombing of, 299–301,
303–4, 308, 310–11
Novak, Robert, 270
NSC 68. See National Security Council
memorandum 68 (NSC 68)
Nuclear arms control. See Arms control
Nuclear arms race, 67
Nuclear disarmament, 72. See also
Arms control

total, Gorbachev's proposal for,
465–66, 478
Nuclear energy (atomic energy),
international control of, 71, 72
Nuclear proliferation, 257–58, 264
Nuclear strategy. See Nuclear weapons
policy
Nuclear superiority
Soviet drive for, 377, 379, 381–83
U.S., 251–52, 254–55, 265, 266,
273–74
Nuclear test ban, 79
Kennedy administration and, 256–66
control system, 258–60, 262–64
factual issues concerning, 263
Geneva talks, 258–61
Limited Test Ban Treaty (1963),
265
Nitze's views, 261–62
on-site inspections, issue of, 259,
260
resumption of atmospheric testing
by the Soviet Union, 260–61
resumption of atmospheric testing
by the U.S., debate over, 261
nuclear proliferation and, 264, 265
Nuclear war. See also Nuclear weapons
policy
limited
Kissinger on, 165–66
Nitze on, 165, 166
surprise attack, assumption that
Soviets might launch, 175–77
victory in, Nitze's 1956 views on,
159–60
Nuclear weapons. See also Atomic
bomb; Hydrogen bomb; Nuclear
weapons policy
Berlin crisis of 1961 and possibility
of using, 218–21, 223–30
as deterrent. See Deterrence
Korean war and, 131–32
proliferation of, 257–58, 264
tactical, 165
U.S. stockpile of (1957), 176–77
Nuclear Weapons and Foreign Policy
(Kissinger), 165–66
Nuclear weapons policy (nuclear
strategy), 141. See also National

Nuclear weapons policy *(cont.)*
    security policy; Nuclear arms
    control; Nuclear superiority; *and*
    specific policies, doctrines, and
    weapons systems
  Dulles's, 173
  under Eisenhower, 156, 158–59
  Kennan and, 85–87
  Kennan on, 67, 71
  under Kennedy, 194–95, 253–56
  1949 reassessment of, 71–72
  1950 review of national security
    policy and, 100–101, 105–6
  Soviet, 383–84
    Team B assessment of (1976), 379
  strategic buildup proposed by Nitze,
    382
  "win" capability, 188–89
Nunn, Sam, 486

O'Connor, Rod, 147
Office of Estimates, 65
Office of Inter-American Affairs, 35–36
Office of International Security Affairs.
    See International Security
    Affairs (ISA), Office of
Office of International Trade Policy,
    53, 57
Office of the Secretary of Defense
    (OSD), 301
On-site inspection
  arms control (or reduction) and, 339
  Gorbachev's willingness to allow, 466
Oppenheimer, Robert, 73, 74, 76, 79
  1950 review of national security
    policy and, 105–6
Option D, 341
Option E, 341

Pace, Gen., 127
Pacific Summary Report, 51–52
Packard, David, 328–29, 375, 376
Paepcke, Elizabeth ("Pussy"), 12–14,
    373
Paepcke, Walter, 372, 373
Palmer, Gen. Williston, 200
Panel of Consultants on Disarmament,
    144–45
Pastore, John O., 286
Paul H. Nitze and Company, 31

Peace through strength, notion of,
    51–52
Pearson, Drew, 84
Pell, Claiborne, 409
Percy, Charles, 391
Perkins, James A., 187
Perle, Richard, 327, 351, 397, 458,
    467, 473, 474, 480
  ABM Treaty and, 460–61
  arms control opposed by, 420
  intermediate nuclear forces (INF)
    talks and, 424–27, 435, 435–37,
    443
    cruise missiles, 424–25
    zero-option proposal, 421, 430–31
  Reykjavik summit (1986) and, 475,
    477, 478
Pershing II missiles, 428, 429, 433,
    434, 435–37, 473
Personnel Policy Board (U.S. Navy),
    284–85
Persons, Maj. Gen. Wilton, 151
Pettee, George Sawyer, 30
Pifer, Steve, 447
Pike, John, 483
Pipes, Richard, 378–80
Plank, John, 210–11
Pleiku (South Vietnam), 292, 297
Podhoretz, Norman, 374
Point defenses, 341
Policy Planning Staff, State
    Department, 60–64, 71–72
  Acheson and, 138–40
  Joint Chiefs of Staff (JCS) and, 138
  Korean war and, 129–31
  Nitze as director of, 94–97
    asked by Dulles to leave post,
      146–47
    staff, relationship with, 140–41
    State Department, relationship
      with, 207
Pony Blanket, 228–29
Poodle Blanket, 228, 229
Poseidon submarines, 381
Pratt, Ruth, 25–26
President's Foreign Intelligence
    Advisory Board (PFIAB), 378,
    380
Pursely, Col. Robert E., 309

Rabi, Isador, 73
Radars, ABM Treaty and, 343–44, 347
RAND Corporation, 167, 188, 224, 275
Reagan, Ronald (Reagan administration), 411, 417
ABM Treaty and, 460
conflicts within administration, 419–20
intermediate nuclear forces (INF) talks and. *See also* Intermediate nuclear forces (INF) talks
conventional cruise missiles, 427
zero-option proposal, 421, 430–31
Reykjavik summit (1986) and, 471–74, 477–78
SALT II and, 467–69
Strategic Arms Reduction Talks (START) and, 449
strategic defense initiative (SDI; Star Wars) and, 449–55
summit meeting of 1985, 458, 464, 465
Talbott's book on arms control and, 456
Reinkemeyer, Hans-Albert, 232
Reporter, The (magazine), 166
Rhee, Syngman, 126
Rhinelander, John, 284, 285, 345, 346, 463
Ricketts, Adm. Claude V., 278
Rickover, Adm. Hyman G., 285–86
Right, the (conservatives), 5, 162
START and, 488–89
Rockefeller, Laurence, 174
Rockefeller, Nelson, 36
Rockridge (Maine) house, 371–72
Rogers, William, 330
Rollback, concept of, 130, 144, 165
in NSC 68, 107, 109
Rolling Thunder, 291
Roosevelt, Franklin D., 24, 35, 37
Roper, Elmo, 174
Rostow, Eugene V., 371, 373–76, 387, 398, 400, 418–20, 422, 425
dismissed by Shultz, 439
intermediate nuclear forces (INF) talks and, 431, 433, 434–36, 439
zero-option proposal, 441, 442
Rostow, Walt, 195, 224, 289, 304

Rowen, Henry (Harry), 199, 201, 219, 221, 222, 224, 225, 243, 247, 253
Cuban missile crisis (1962) and, 233, 234, 237, 238
Rowny, Gen. Edward, 351, 354–55, 418, 471, 475
Royal Air Force (RAF), 39, 46
Rusk, Dean, 113, 125, 190, 222, 232, 238, 242, 246, 249, 255, 324
nuclear test ban and, 263–64
personal characteristics of, 205–6
as secretary of defense, 214
as secretary of state, 205–6
Vietnam War and, 304
Russell, Richard, 274
Russia. *See* Soviet Union

Sachs, Alexander, 125
Safeguard program, 326, 342. *See also* ABMs (anti-ballistic missiles)
SALT (Strategic Arms Limitation Talks), 328–52
ABM systems and, 341–48
ABM Treaty. *See* ABM Treaty
antimissile technology (future technology) and, 344–46
back-channel talks, 356
deep reductions (Option D) and, 341
Interim Agreement, 347, 349, 351, 353, 355, 359–60, 367
leaks of classified information, 357–58
MIRV ban and, 336–38
MIRV testing and, 323–24
negotiations
first round of, 332–33
Nitze's bitterness about final days of talks, 348–49
Nitze-Shchukin relationship and, 344
second round, 342–49
secret (back-channel) talks, 330–31
ratification of, 350–51
throw-weight issue and, 338–41
SALT Guidance Committee, 329, 341
SALT II (Strategic Arms Limitation Talks II), 350–61, 396–411, 466–69. *See also* SALT II treaty

SALT II *(cont.)*
  back-channel talks, 356–57
    revealed by Nitze, 366–67
  Carter administration and, 396–411.
    See also SALT II treaty
    March 1977 proposal, 397–99
  deep reductions proposal, 353–54
  Interim Agreement and, 359–60, 367
  Jackson amendment and, 351
  location of the talks, 352
  MIRVs and, 355–56
  Nitze's criticisms of, 365–69
  Nitze's sources of information on,
    400–402
  nuclear supremacy as Soviet goal, 361
  Reagan administration and, 467–69
  resignation of Nitze from SALT II
    delegation, 364–65
  SLBMs and, 357
  strategic parity and, 351–53
  Vladivostok Accord and, 368–69
  Warnke's nomination as chief SALT
    negotiator, 389–95
SALT II treaty, 403–11
  Minuteman vulnerability and, 406–7,
    410
  multiple point system (MPS) and,
    403–4
  ratification of, 405–7
  Reagan and, 416
  real reasons for Nitze's opposition to,
    409–10
Saltonstall (senator), 274
Savage, Carlton, 95, 97, 102, 140
Schaub, William, 121–22
Schelling, Thomas, 223, 224, 262
Schlesinger, Arthur, Jr., 161, 162, 184,
  206, 210, 212
Schlesinger, James, 361–63, 370–71,
  374
Schmidt, Helmut, 430
School for Advanced International
  Studies (SAIS), 154
Schroeder, Gerhard, 232
Schwartz, Harry, 102
Scowcroft, Brent, 494
SDI. *See* Strategic defense initiative
Seaborg, Glenn, 263
Sea-launched cruise missiles (SLCMs),
  490–91

Security Resources Panel. *See* Gaither
  committee
Selin, Ivan, 322–24
Semenov, Vladimir, 332, 335, 352
Separable First Stage Disarmament
  Agreement (SFSDA), 266, 267
Shchukin, Aleksandr N., 344–47, 404
Sherman, Adm., 133
Shevardnadze, Eduard, 471, 477, 479,
  487
Short-range nuclear forces (SNF), 501
Shultz, George, 432, 434–36, 439, 446,
  448–53, 456, 458, 464, 468,
  487, 494–95
  intermediate nuclear forces (INF)
    talks and, 485–86
  Nitze's relationship with, 480–81
  Reykjavik summit (1986) and,
    476–78
Single Integrated Operational Plan
  (SIOP-62), 253
Slocombe, Walter, 387–89, 402, 404,
  421
Smith, Adm. Page, 281
Smith, Bedell, 147
Smith, Gerard, 173, 330, 331, 333–35,
  338–40, 342, 344, 346–49, 351,
  356, 357, 392, 463
Smyth, Henry, 108
Sofaer, Abraham, 461, 463
Sorensen, Theodore, 214, 241, 249
Sorokin, Pitirim, 29–30
Souers, Adm. Sidney, 85, 99–100, 113
South America, 148
South Korea. *See* Korean war
Soviet Union, 24, 25, 56, 57. *See also*
  specific topics
  atomic bomb, development of,
    62–67, 71–72
  Bay of Pigs invasion (1961) and, 213
  Berlin crisis of 1961 and. *See* Berlin,
    1961 crisis over
  Central Intelligence Agency (CIA)
    review of intentions of (1976),
    378–81
  civil defense, 381, 401–2
  Committee on the Present Danger's
    views on, 376, 377
  Cuban missile crisis (1962) and. *See*
    Cuban missile crisis

expansionism of, NSC 68 on, 110
Gaither report on, 169–70
Kennedy administration and, 204
Korean war and, 125–27, 130–31,
    132–34, 136
1950 assessment of intentions of,
    97–99. *See also* National
    Security Council memorandum
    68 (NSC 68); National security
    policy, 1950 review of
Nitze's 1955 visit to, 158
NSC 114 on intentions of, 135,
    136
NSC 68 on intentions of, 109–11,
    116, 136, 137
post–World War II threat posed by,
    51, 54
Sputnik launched by (1957), 168–69
Spaak, Paul-Henry, 191
Sparkman (senator), 389–90
Speakes, Larry, 441
Special Committee. *See* Z Committee
Speer, Albert, 44, 47
Spengler, Oswald, 29
Spivak, Sidney ("Spiv"), 24
Sprague, Robert, 167, 169
Sputnik, 169
SS-20 missiles, 428, 433, 434, 473,
    477
Stalin, Joseph, 51, 52, 125
death of, 149
Standing Consultative Commission
    (SCC), 346, 459, 463
Stanley, Timothy, 197, 199–200, 205,
    222, 223, 416–17
START. *See* Strategic Arms Reduction
    Talks
Star Wars. *See* Strategic defense
    initiative
State-Defense Policy Review Group,
    112–15
March 22 briefing of Johnson and
    Gen. Bradley, 113–15
outside consultants and, 105–9
selection of members of, 102–3
State Department, U.S. *See also*
    individual secretaries of state and
    other officials
assistant secretaries in, 139–40

Defense Department relationship
    with, during Kennedy years, 207
Kennedy and, 206
search for a secretary of defense,
    191–92
Korean war and, 128–29
1950 review of national security
    policy and, 100–102. *See also*
    State-Defense Policy Review
    Group
Nitze's relationship with, during
    Kennedy years, 207
Office of Estimates, 65
Office of International Trade Policy,
    53, 57
Policy Planning Staff. *See* Policy
    Planning Staff
Stevenson, Adlai, 40, 157, 161–63
Stimson, Henry, 102
Stoertz, Howard, 380
Stone, Jeremy, 483
Strategic Air Command (SAC), 168,
    170, 172, 175, 242, 273
Strategic Arms Reduction Talks
    (START), 449, 486–92
Bush and, 497–98
conservative opposition to, 488–89
Reykjavik summit (1986) and, 474,
    475, 478, 479
SDI and, 482–84
sea-launched cruise missiles (SLCMs)
    and, 490–91
Strategic bombing, 38
Strategic Bombing Survey, 1, 38–52
Strategic concept, Nitze's, 452–53
Strategic defense initiative (SDI; Star
    Wars), 449–55, 473, 480–84
ABM Treaty and, 459–65, 482–84,
    486–87
as bargaining chip, 451–52
feasibility of, 454
list approach to, 483–84
mutual assured destruction (MAD)
    and, 451
Nitze criteria and, 454–55
Reykjavik summit (1986) and, 477,
    478
START and, 482–84
Strauss, Franz Joseph, 441
Strout, Richard, 404–5

Suave plan, 169
Subceilings, 470–71, 475–76, 479–80, 486
Submarine-launched ballistic missiles (SLBMs), 321, 382
  Interim Agreement and, 353, 357, 367
Submarines, START and, 489
Summit meetings
  1955, 157–58
  1961, 214–15
  1972, 346–47
  1982, 432–33
  1985, 458, 464, 465
  1986, 471–78
Surface-to-air missiles (SAMs), 336
Surprise attack. See First-strike capability
Sweden, 54
Symington, Stuart, 186

Taber, John, 59
Tactical nuclear forces, 258
Talbott, Strobe, 456
Taylor, Gen. Maxwell, 214, 248, 255, 265, 289
Team B, 378
Teller, Edward, 450
  H-bomb development and, 76–77
Test ban. See Nuclear test ban
Tet offensive, 305–6, 308
Thatcher, Margaret, 441, 468
Thermonuclear weapon. See Hydrogen bomb
Third world, 162, 170–71, 181–84, 194, 198, 295
  decolonization of, 181
Thompson, Llewellyn, 119, 215
Throw-weight, 338–41, 351
  Drell on, 384
  SALT II and, 360
  START and, 488–89
Thurmond, Strom, 272, 275
Tokyo, firebombing of, 48, 49
Tomahawk missiles, 433
Torpedoes, 282
Total theoretical hostility, 377–78
Toure, Sekou, 182
Treasury Department, U.S., 54–55
Trident submarines, 467, 468

Trident II missiles, 382
Truman, Harry S (Truman administration), 56, 62, 63
  Acheson's relationship with, 139
  disarmament and, 141–42
  H-bomb development and, 80, 84–85, 90–91, 143
  Korean war and, 126, 131, 134
  1950 review of national security policy and, 115
    directive issued, 90–91
  NSC 68 and, 120, 121, 134, 135
  NSC 112 and, 143
  NSC 114 and, 135, 138
Tsarapkin, Semyon K., 259
Tufts, Robert, 96, 102, 104, 115, 138–40, 148–49
Turkey, 56
  Cuban missile crisis (1962) and, 246–48
Twentieth Century-Fox, 373
Tyroler, Charles, II, 162–64, 416

Ulbricht, Walter, 222
United Nations, 72, 273
  Korean war and, 126–27
U.S. News & World Report, 202
USSR. See Soviet Union
U.S. Vitamin Corporation, 31

Vance, Cyrus, 286–87, 301, 387–89, 403
  SALT II and, 397
Van Cleave, William, 328, 329, 340, 341, 378
Vandenberg, Gen., 132
VELA, 263
Vietnam War, 288–316
  bombing of North Vietnam, 299–301, 303–4, 308, 310–11
  Clark Clifford's change of position on, 314–15
  estimates of enemy strength in, 292–93
  "free-fire zones," 296–97
  incrementalism, policy of, 310, 312
  Johnson and, 294–95, 303–4, 306, 308, 310, 312–13, 316
  lessons of, 385–86

navy operations in, 295
"Game Warden" program, 296–97
negotiating plan of 1967, 303–4
negotiations to end, 308
Nitze's early views on, 289–91
Non-group and, 302, 304
rift in foreign policy community and, 390
Taylor-Rostow recommendation (1961), 289
Tet offensive, 305–6, 308
ugly side of, 298
Wheeler-Westmoreland troop request (1968), 306, 308, 310–12
withdrawal of U.S. troops recommended by Nitze, 293–94, 315–16
Vladivostock Accord (1974), 368–69, 397
Voorhees, Tracy, 121

Wade, James, 345
Waggoner, Joe D., Jr., 272
Walker, Charls, 374–76, 407
Wallace, Henry, 37
Wall Street Journal, 305
"War at Sea" project, 282–83
Warnke, Paul, 301, 309, 321, 385–95, 403, 421
on lessons of Vietnam War, 385–86
Nitze's relationship with, 315–16, 386–87
nominated as head of ACDA and chief SALT negotiator, 389–95
Nitze's letter to Senator Sparkman, 389–90
rebuttal of Nitze's testimony, 392
Senate Armed Services Committee hearings, 393–94
Senate Foreign Relations Committee hearings, 391–92
Vietnam War and, 303, 305, 315–16
Washington Ambassadors' Group, 221–22
Watergate scandal, 356, 363–64
Webb, James, 71, 81, 119
Acheson's relationship with, 139

Weinberger, Caspar, 420, 421, 425, 435, 437, 467, 483, 485
Weiss, Seymour, 237
West Berlin, 215
Western Europe, Soviet A-bomb capability and defense of, 65–67
West Germany, 423
deployment of Pershing II missiles approved by, 443
intermediate nuclear forces (INF) talks and, 441
Westmoreland, Gen. William, 293, 302, 305, 308
Wheeler, Gen. Earle, 302, 306
Wilcox, Clair, 53
Wilson, Charles, 150, 151
Wilson, James, 303, 315, 316, 320, 322–23, 327
Wilson, Peter, 327
Wilson, Woodrow, 24
Wohlstetter, Albert, 159, 160, 167, 168, 327
Wolfe, Thomas, 199, 201, 207, 219, 227, 237, 239, 243, 378
Wolfowitz, Paul, 327
Woodring, Harry, 102
Woodworth, John, 421, 424, 430, 432
Woolsey, James, 337, 338, 387, 388
World War I, 11–12
World War II, 31–52
Germany in, 31, 34, 38–46
Japan in, 46–51

Yarmolinsky, Adam, 193

Z Committee (Special Committee of the National Security Council), 80–84, 90, 143, 145
Working Group of, 80–81
Zero-option proposal, 421–22, 424, 430–31, 433, 434, 437, 473
calls for flexibility on, 441–42
Zumwalt, Elmo (Bud), 233–34, 237–38, 262, 270, 272, 276, 280, 281, 286–87, 290, 357–59, 363, 374, 399

PICTURE CREDITS

INSERT

Page 1: *top*, National Archives; *bottom*, Wide World Photos.
Pages 2–5: *all*, Wide World Photos.
Page 6: *top and bottom*, UPI/Bettmann Newsphotos.
Page 7: *top*, UPI/Bettmann Newsphotos; *bottom*, Wide World Photos.
Page 8: *top*, Wide World Photos; *bottom*, Committee on the Present Danger.
Page 9: *top and middle*, Wide World Photos; *bottom*, UPI/Bettmann Newsphotos.
Pages 10–11: *all*, Wide World Photos.
Page 12: *top and bottom*, UPI/Bettmann Newsphotos.
Page 13: *top*, UPI/Bettmann Newsphotos; *bottom*, Wide World Photos.
Page 14: *top and bottom*, Wide World Photos.
Page 15: *top*, UPI/Bettmann Newsphotos; *bottom*, Wide World Photos.
Page 16: Wide World Photos.

	DATE DUE		